The League of Nations in retrospect
La Société des Nations: rétrospective

United Nations Library, Geneva
Serial publications
Series E: Guides and Studies
3

Walter de Gruyter · Berlin · New York 1983

The League of Nations in retrospect

Proceedings of the Symposium

organized by
The United Nations Library
and
The Graduate Institute of International Studies
Geneva, 6–9 November 1980

La Société des Nations: rétrospective

Actes du Colloque

organisé par la
Bibliothèque des Nations Unies
et
l'Institut universitaire de hautes études internationales
Genève, 6–9 novembre 1980

W DE G
Walter de Gruyter · Berlin · New York 1983

The views expressed in this publication are those of the authors and do not necessarily reflect the views of the Secretariat of the United Nations.

Library of Congress Cataloging in Publication Data

Main entry under Title:
The League of Nations in retrospect : proceedings of the symposium.
(Serial publications / United Nations Library, Geneva. Series E, Guides and studies ; 3)
Includes index.
1. League of Nations-History-Congresses.
I. United Nations Library (Geneva, Switzerland)
II. Graduate Institute of International Studies (Geneva, Switzerland) III. Title: Société des Nations, rétrospective. IV. Series: Serial publications (United Nations Library, Geneva, Switzerland). Series E, Guides and studies ; 3.
JX1975.L363 1983 341.22'09 83-1421

ISBN 3-11-008733-2

CIP-Kurztitelaufnahme der Deutschen Bibliothek

The **League of Nations in retrospect** : proceedings of the symposium, Geneva 6–9 November 1980 = La Société des Nations: rétrospective / organized by the United Nations Library and the Graduate Inst. of Internat. Studies. – Berlin ; New York : de Gruyter, 1983.
(Serial publications / United Nations Library Geneva : Ser. E, Guides and studies ; 3)
ISBN 3-11-008733-2
NE: United Nations / Library <Genève>: Serial publications / E; PT

Dust Cover Design: Rudolf Hübler, Berlin. – Printing: Georg Wagner, Nördlingen. – Binding: Verlagsbuchbinderei Dieter Mikolai, Berlin.
Printed in Germany

Table of Contents
Table des Matières

Chapter/Chapitre III
Security problems
Les problèmes de la sécurité

Chapter/Chapitre IV
The League of Nations: aspects of financial, economic, social and humanitarian cooperation
La coopération financière, économique, sociale et humanitaire de la Société des Nations

Abbreviations
Abréviations

AD	*Archives Diplomatiques* (Paris)
ADAP	*Akten zur deutschen auswärtigen Politik* (Göttingen)
AE	Archives du Ministère des Affaires Etrangères (Paris)
AF	Archives fédérales (Berne)
ASdN	Archives de la Société des Nations – Bibliothèque des Nations Unies (Genève)
BIT	Bureau International du Travail (Genève)
BM	Bundesministerium für Finanzen, Archiv (Wien)
BSI	Bureau socialiste international (Bruxelles)
CIJ	Cour internationale de justice (La Haye)
CL	Comité de liquidation, SdN
CPC	Commission permanente consultative pour les questions militaires, navales et aériennes, SdN
CPD	Commission préparatoire pour la Conférence du Désarmement, SdN
CPM	Commission permanente des mandats, SdN
CPNU	Commission préparatoire des Nations Unies
DBFP	*Documents on British Foreign Policy* (London)
DDF	*Documents diplomatiques français* (Paris)
DDS	*Documents diplomatiques suisses* (Berne)
DGFP	*Documents on German Foreign Policy* (London/Washington D.C.)
DPF	Département politique fédéral (Berne)
DVP	*Dokumenty Vnešnej Politiki SSSR* (Moskva)
ECOSOC	Economic and Social Council of the United Nations
FA	Federal Archives (Bern)
FRUS	*Papers Relating to the Foreign Relations of the Unites States* (Washington, D.C.)
ICRC	International Committee of the Red Cross (Geneva)
IGCR	Intergovernmental Committee on Refugees (Geneva)
ILO	International Labour Organization (Geneva)
IRO	International Refugee Organization (Geneva)
JO	*Journal Officiel*, SdN
JOSS	*Journal Officiel, Supplément Spécial*, SdN
LNA	League of Nations Archives – United Nations Library (Geneva)
LNU	League of Nations Union (London)
LoN	League of Nations (Geneva)
MF	Archives du Ministère des finances (Paris)

OIT	Organisation internationale du travail (Genève)
OJ	*Official Journal*, LoN
OJSS	*Official Journal, Special Supplement*, LoN
OMS	Organisation mondiale de la santé (Genève)
ONU	Organisation des Nations Unies (New York)
PMC	Permanent Mandates Commission, LoN
PRO	Public Record Office (London)
RCADI	*Recueils des cours* de l'Académie de droit international (La Haye)
SD	Department of State Archives – National Archives (Washington, D.C.)
SDFP	*Soviet Documents on Foreign Policy* (London)
SdN	Sociéte des Nations (Genève)
TSF	Télégraphie Sans Fil
UNCIO	United Nations Conference on International Organization (San Francisco)
UNESCO	United Nations Educational, Scientific and Cultural Organization (Paris)
UNRRA	United Nations Relief and Rehabilitation Administration (Washington, D.C.)

Preface

HEINZ WALDNER
Chief Librarian
United Nations Library at Geneva

It is with great pleasure and satisfaction that I see the Proceedings of this first international Symposium on the League of Nations made publicly available in such a convenient form. This once more gives me the opportunity to express my deep appreciation to all those who helped to organise and who participated in the Symposium, in particular Professor Christian Dominicé, Director of the Graduate Institute of International Studies, and his collaborators Professor Marlis Steinert, Jean-Claude Frachebourg, Victor Ghebali, as well as my own colleagues at the Library, Elizabeth Beyerly, Sven Welander, Werner Simon, and all the scholars who contributed the essays published here. I am also most grateful to His Excellency Vladimir Socoline, former Under-Secretary-General of the League of Nations whose charming personality and vivid reminiscences lent an unforgettable touch of oral history to our gathering.

If we look at the League of Nations, what it was and what it might have been in the difficult context of the inter-war situation, it seems to me that the picture has considerably changed compared with the time when the League was regarded as a failure and dissolved. The overall balance of the League's achievements now, after 37 years' experience of the United Nations, appears to me much more favourable than one was led to expect. While fully aware of the reservations which still exist among many contemporaries, I do not hesitate to state that more than respect is due for what the League accomplished.

The League was a great beginning of a global venture which was not only necessary at its time but still continues on a much larger scale. Especially if we approach our subject from the viewpoint of the problems the League had to face, the continuity of so many of them – such as international security, conflict settlement, disarmament and economic co-operation, but also refugees, drug abuse, international organisation of science and education – is striking, and if we compare them with what the United Nations has been able to do up to now, the League clearly can be considered as the first major step towards a goal which will still take a long time to reach. The impressive variety of themes dealt with in the Symposium have revealed not only many interesting new aspects of the League but have certainly also thrown new ligtht on the continuity of problems from the League to the United Nations. Seen from this perspective the United Nations appear much more a revised form of the League than a real new beginning.

The UN Library at Geneva, itself a precious heritage of the League of Nations and the keeper of its archives, came to organise this Symposium with a particular motivation. Independent of spectacular anniversaries, we felt for some time the need for a League of Nations' bibliography*. As this project progressed, the idea evolved for bringing together experts on the League who would not only evaluate past and current research, but would also suggest avenues for improving further work in this field. Access to many archives is now being extended, thus permitting researchers to examine source materials from the period between the two World Wars. It is in this sense that we at the United Nations Library in Geneva helped to bring about the Symposium and the editing of its papers. We are proud that these valuable contributions to the research on the League now appear in one of our Library series.

* A provisional edition in three volumes of the *Bibliographical Handbook on the League of Nations/Manuel bibliographique sur la Societé des Nations*, Prepared by/Etabli par Victor-Yves Ghebali (Geneva, UN Library, 1980) was distributed to the participants of the Symposium. The revised final version of this Handbook is in preparation.

Avant-propos

Christian Dominicé
Directeur de l'Institut universitaire de hautes études internationales, Genève

L'exposition qui, comme le colloque dont les travaux sont publiés dans le présent ouvrage, a été organisée pour commémorer le soixantième anniversaire de la première assemblée de la Société des Nations, à Genève, a permis de faire réapparaître des documents émouvants. Je pense particulièrement aux vieilles photographies montrant la foule enthousiaste, heureuse à l'idée que la Société d'Etats qui venait d'être créée allait marquer le début d'une ère résolument nouvelle.

Le Pacte, on le sait, porta les espoirs de peuples entiers, las de la guerre et des conflits, aspirant à une vie meilleure.

Ces témoignages des espoirs de 1920, vus avec le recul du temps et la connaissance de ce qui allait se passer moins de vingt ans plus tard, ne sont-ils pas cruels? Ne viennent-ils pas souligner avec d'autant plus de vigueur l'ampleur de l'échec?

Convient-il, en définitive, de faire revivre un passé douloureux?

La science a pour mission et pour devoir de ne rien négliger de ce qui peut contribuer à une meilleure connaissance de l'homme et des sociétés. L'époque de la Société des Nations, avec ses lumières et ses ombres, mérite aujourd'hui l'attention. Elle marque l'avènement d'une dimension nouvelle des relations internationales, celle de l'organisation internationale. Elle préfigure de nombreux développements contemporains. Elle appelle aussi à la sagesse, à la mesure, à la raison, si l'on veut bien se rappeler que la folie des hommes a conduit les foules joyeuses de 1920 sur les chemins douloureux de l'exil, des ruines et des cimetières.

Les historiens, parmi lesquels je remercie tous ceux qui ont apporté leur contribution au symposium de 1980 et à cet ouvrage, assument une lourde et belle responsabilité. Il leur appartient d'identifier et mettre à nu les émotions et les passions, sans y céder. De comprendre avant de juger. De distinguer le permanent du contingent, et de permettre en définitive de mieux saisir, dans sa complexité, un présent si largement façonné par le passé.

L'organisation internationale, lieu de convergence des pulsions du monde, des intérêts contradictoires, mais aussi de grandes espérances, offre à l'historien un champ d'investigation prodigieusement riche, complété qu'il est désormais, les années passant, par l'ouverture des archives nationales.

J'exprime la gratitude de l'Institut universitaire de hautes études internationales à tous ceux qui ont permis l'organisation du colloque de 1980, et la publication de ce volume – la Bibliothèque de l'Office des Nations Unies à Genève et son chef, M. Heinz Waldner, méritent une mention toute particulière – ainsi qu'aux auteurs des études ici réunies.

Je remercie également l'Etat de Genève, plus particulièrement son chef du Protocole, M. Robert Vieux, ainsi que la Ville de Genève, de leur précieux soutien. Je forme le voeu que ces travaux contribuent à une meilleure connaissance d'une époque de l'histoire des peuples qui est importante pour qui veut comprendre le présent et construire l'avenir.

Introductory essay

ZARA STEINER
New Hall, Cambridge University

"The League of Nations is dead; long live the United Nations." Lord Robert Cecil's words, despite their unfortunate historical parentage, might be taken as one of the coordinating themes of our conference. Historians have looked back on the workings of the League to draw conclusions about the nature of the nation state and the international state system both in the inter-war period and today. They look for the lessons which might be learnt and applied in the realm of crisis management, conflict resolution and war termination to use the current verbiage of the political scientist. We also look at the institutions and organizations of the League to see how they functioned in the past, and for the ways in which they were adopted for use by the United Nations and its off-shoots. The latter, and various other multinational organizations – as many of our authors have insisted – owe much to these earlier experiments in international co-operation. Historians and statesmen alike have studied the League not just to learn from the past, but to learn the right lessons from the past so that current efforts at cooperation could benefit from the League's successes without repeating its mistakes. As the model-builders abandoned their theoretical constructions – popular in the 1950's and 1960's: those mathematical analyses of state behaviour which proved so deceptively clear and inaccurate – subsequent analysts reverted to the historical example as a basis for both the study of today's problems and the forecast of tomorrow's events. Moreover, for the historian the urge is always present for exploiting the newest treasure trove of documents. Many of the archives pertaining to the inter-war period have been recently opened or are in the process of being organized for scholarly scrutiny. Recent bibliographic research[1] indicates just how fresh and exciting some of this new material can be. The story of the League of Nations – its organization and its functions – is currently being re-written in a different form and manner than we have inherited from a previous generation of statesmen and commentators.

The process of re-writing has revealed central paradoxes which one cannot ignore. Almost all the authors concerned with the functioning of the League, particularly those focusing on collective security and disarmament, have insisted that we must separate myth from reality, illusion from practice. Obviously, when an historian looks back, he attempts to understand yet needs to divorce himself from the vocabulary of the era he is studying. But the problem with regard to the League goes much deeper. The Covenant emerging from the deliberations in Paris in 1919 was not the document either the British or the French governments had in mind when they came to the Peace Conference. The Wilsonian League, embodying the ideology of 'liberal internationalism' as Professor Egerton[2] has defined it, was a very different structure from that which the British and the French thought appropriate to the international system they believed existed in 1919. Rather than a peace-keeping mechanism based on obligatory international coercion – a concept which had been rejected by the majority of the Phillimore Commission, that war-time body appointed to study the question – the British had in mind an enlarged concert of powers, a voluntary arbitration system and a measure of functional co-operation between states. The French, never very enthusiastic about the whole Anglo-Saxon view of this form of international co-operation, accepted the League grudgingly. They hoped it could become a peacetime alliance system with automatic sanctions; even when convinced of the wisdom of accepting Wilson's offspring, Clemenceau reserved his doubts. It was an ironic beginning for the League for reasons fully understood, and generally accepted, by the leading statesmen in London and Paris. What had been viewed as a means by which the Americans could join a European settlement became one of the reasons why the United States refused to enter the League.

From the beginning the League was an organization dressed in Wilsonian clothes. This idealized structure appealed to large sections of the European public, above all in Britain which, after the American desertion, shared with France the main burden of making the Versailles settlement work. Whatever their doubts – and there were many – about articles X through XVI, the Allied statesmen were forced to accept the core of these articles and they were forced in part, especially in Britain, by the democratic nature of their states and because the Wilsonian image appealed to their electorates which had just emerged from the shock of an unbelievable war. In the eyes of contemporaries, peace-keeping was the League's chief function. The League became synonimous with the idea of collective security well before this term emerged in the 1930's as a description of what could hardly be termed a 'system' in any real sense of that word. After all, the problem of how to resolve conflicts without resorting to war had preoccupied statesmen since the eighteenth century when war began to become too expensive and too destructive to be used as a tool of statecraft. Given a war of unprecedented scope involving all classes of society and producing casualty lists of an entirely new dimension, it was not at all surprising that the prevention of war had become a popular cause, and that statesmen were forced to respond to the expectations of their supporters.

It was natural though tragic that in the long series of crises which punctuated the post-war settlements of the 1920's and 30's, the League should have been called upon to exercise these peace-keeping functions and that the belief in a collective security system, meant to check the actions of any aggressor, should have been exposed to the test of reality. By failing first with regard to Japan and then Italy, the League disappointed not only its articulate defenders but a wider section of the population which looked to it for an alternative to war. By the 1930's, even before Hitler's first attacks on the European *status quo*, the expectations raised by the founders of the League had led to deep disillisionment. At the height of its popular appeal, the myth of collective security was brutally exposed, and the prestige of the League – despite success in other ways – was irremediably diminished. Statesmen soon resumed traditional ways of resolving inter-state conflicts without more than a glance towards Geneva.

Looking back at the problems of collective security, of peace keeping and of conflict resolution, one can now see what the League might have been expected to accomplish, and why it succeeded or failed within these relatively narrow limits. In the Corfu incident[3], or in the Manchurian crisis, in the Leticia[4] dispute and in the Italian-Ethiopian war, our contributors have exposed the gap between statemen's words and their deeds. We know, for instance, that Corfu was not settled through the League, despite the lip service given to its role, but by a conference of ambassadors. We know with regard to Manchuria that the Japanese could not have been checked by the Council of the League unless the British – and even more important, the Americans, for they had the power – had decided to impose sanctions. And as M. Baer has argued, even when the League was successful, as in the Peru-Columbia crisis in 1934, it did not impose a settlement but held the ring, and by a judicious policy of carrot and stick got the disputants to work out a solution without resorting to war.

The Ethiopian crisis represented the most brutal divorce between expectation and performance. In earlier cases, this gap had been somewhat disguised. But in the case of Italy, both the British and French governments pursued double policies: working with the League to maintain a public image while negotiating with Italy to bring about a resolution of the crisis which would leave the Stresa front intact. The League was brought into action on false pretenses, in the British case as a result of public pressure and the need to find a paper solution when no real solution could be found. But using the League, the two governments increasingly returned to traditional forms of nineteenth century diplomacy. This dual policy not only exposed the differences between Britain and France but very much undermined the authority of the League. The results satisfied none; Italy was left in control of Ethiopia but also alienated from her Stresa front partners. Yet it was the League, rather than the governments of Britain and France that bore the brunt of public disappointment. And the League itself was discarded as a means of keeping the peace and checking aggression.

It has become a commonplace to maintain that the League could only reflect the existing state of international realities. The League had to rely on sovereign states, some of which were more sovereign than others. Any form of collective action could work only if the powerful states – and this meant Britain and France throughout most of this period – would act together and in unison. But the League was seen in public as something more than the sum of its parts. This was the Wilsonian image. The League was expected to enlist the support of all for finding solutions to disputes, as well as to enforce these solutions without involving the nations in a new world war. It must be added that few statesmen attempted to explain to their constituents the dangers of this approach to international politics. On the contrary, they often masked their own actions by using the acceptable vocabulary and thereby encouraged false hopes. When the League failed, or was seen to fail because so much more had been expected from it, the

League itself was discredited and then by-passed not just by the statesmen but by the public as well.

Myth and reality also dogged the history of disarmament. The British believed, rightly or wrongly, that the arms race had, in part, created the conditions for war in 1914. Written into the Covenant was the assumption that after Germany would be disarmed, the rest of the world would follow suit. As M. Vaïsse[5] insists, reality intruded even at this early stage for nations were not to be disarmed but only to reduce their armaments to a level compatible with national security. What this meant was to become the major point of a continuous dispute between Britain and France. The French never accepted the abolition of the distinction between victors and vanquished. Their whole behaviour was patterned on the assumption that Germany would once again be able to make a bid for the hegemony of Europe. With the American withdrawal from Europe – impeding one way of achieving French security – it was only the British who could provide the moral and the military support so deeply craved by the French. But the British, or at least important sections of a large number of British Governments, believed that their continental commitment in 1914 had been a very expensive mistake. They looked to a return to their pre-1914 position, some even to the imperial orientation at the turn of the century. By insisting on disarmament without fully facing the French demand for compensation, repeated British cabinets avoided an unpopular choice.

There is little doubt that in Britain the demand for disarmament was widespread and the need for economic retrenchment encouraged Governments to cut back on both the army and navy. Military men were not in high favour in the twenties; only in Germany had their reputations been refurbished. The myths of the 'merchants of death' balanced the public response to the rising number of unemployed which followed from the closing of shipyards and foundries. The public not only wanted to disarm; they did not want to have to come to the aid of France on the continent. Even the limited British pledge to the French under the Locarno treaties was not translated into military terms. There was no army available for European responsibilities. It was the public assumption that the League could be the wolrd's policeman and that collective security was an alternative to national rearment. The Governments knew that the League could not assume this role unless it was ready to use force which only the Member States could supply. But neither the British nor the French intended to supply it, and the British were exceedingly reluctant to offer even in more traditional ways the underwriting which the French demanded.

It was in this sense that the Disarmament Conference came far too late. The British and French had not really come to acceptable terms despite appearances and Hitler could easily exploit their differences. Unable to keep Germany at the Conference or force Hitler to return, the two Powers turned to settlements outside the competence of the League. M. Vaïsse's[6] conclusion that the collapse of the Disarmament Conference cannot be imputed to the League of Nations is perfectly just. The League could not do more than what its members agreed to do. It could provide the vantage point, it could establish the conditions of discourse, it could bring together the experts, but it could not act independently of the Member States. It was the shock of depression that caused the States to restrict defense spending but gradually all, slowly but inevitably, began to rearm. The atmosphere was changed by Hitler, however pacific he might have wanted to appear. What was true for the case of collective security was also true in the matter of disarmament. The failure of the Disarmament Conference dealt yet another, and an almost final blow to the core of the League mechanism.

Looking back, it is not surprising that present-day historians condemn the high hopes engendered by the Geneva spokesmen. Illusions that the League could or would do more than what the States willed produced negative results. The States had retained their full sovereign powers; the international structure had not evolved beyond the stage of independent States. Myth operated at many levels, all dangerous. Statesman used the terminology of liberal internationalism and practiced old-fashioned bi-lateral diplomacy. People were encouraged to believe that if only the League had been permitted to act, aggressors would have been checked and war averted. Until recently, most histories were written by the actors; but what now appears to be their realistic or necessary policies were at the time presented as Machievellian plots and the deeds of evil men. Analysing these crises, concentrating on what States and statesmen did now helps us not only to identify the reality of inter-war diplomacy, but also to understand the conditions that determined the outcome of League action in this reality.

The search for security in the inter-war period took many forms. The one with which our own generation has become most familiar was the form still in its infant stage during the 1920's. The League played only a partial and secondary role in the economic reconstruction of Europe. Curiously enough, though economic aims were discussed, reparations had not been extensively examined before the Powers met in Paris. There, the technical questions tended to be left to so-called 'experts' while those excluded felt powerless and increasingly alarmed. Warned by Keynes, the men in the Foreign Office delegation to Paris were distressed by the roles of Cunliffe and Sumner, viewing the sums demanded from Germany by the British and the French representatives as unrealistic and dangerous. But neither then nor later were the diplomats sufficiently informed, nor had they the necessary understanding about the international economy to intervene in matters left to central banks and national Governments at one level and to the financiers and industrialists at the other.

Those drawing up the peace treaties with Austria and Hungary condemned particularly the financial and economic settlements for which they were not responsible. Mme Pietri's[7] paper on the Comité financier illustrates one case of the League actually assuming a role in the economic reconstruction of a European nation; Hungary and a failed attempt in Poland were other cases. It is interesting to note the key role played by Montagu Norman, head of the Bank of England, and the role of civil servants trained in economic and financial rather than in diplomatic matters. Of course their actions spilled over into the political arena. The blurring of political and economic affairs, the entrance of new figures into this semi-diplomatic world heralded the extension of the diplomatic canvas and the shrinkage of traditional controls and hierarchies.

Both M. Dubin[8] and M. Halperin[9] indicate how a new form of multinational diplomacy was being expanded; one which depended less on States, though States were involved, than on bankers, investors and economic specialists, and one far more concerned with the economic health of the international community than its defense and security aspects. In a sense, both with regard to the Economic Conference of 1927 and to the forms of economic and technical assistance described by M. Menzies,[10] the League was extending the dimensions of traditional diplomacy and opening up areas of international co-operation which had only been barely explored in the pre-1914 period. M. Meienberger describes the efforts made by the League to assist in the economic and social reconstruction of China. Successful collaboration in such fields as hygiene, education, transportation and agriculture owed far more to a few officials within the Secretariat than to the political organs of the League. It is important to stress how marginal and tentative much of this work was; the emphasis was on the collection of information and the writing of opinions rather than on the actual interference with the operations of the international economy. The discussion of technical and economic issues defined an area for international co-operation and promoted links between League and non-League agents. But even in China, the League representatives had no executive powers and their roles were necessarily circumscribed by the political realities of the day.

Much was done outside the League. All States were far more sensitive to the pressures from the central banks, bankers, industrialists and even unions than they were in the pre-1914 world. As the war debt-reparations controversy continued, and as the United States began to capitalize on its newly won creditor position, not only were such negotiations carried on outside the League, but by firms which enjoyed a semi-autonomous position. Thus the partners of J. P. Morgan in their role as the main lenders to France could obtain in 1924 French acceptance of the Dawes Plan, and were playing a similar role in 1930. Bankers, like industrialists, crossed national lines, creating conditions which we now associate with the ever-expanding domain of semi-private and even private diplomacy. The resolution of problems relative to the gold standard and the stabilizations of currencies, which also fell outside the jurisdiction of the League, crossed traditional lines between domestic and foreign affairs and eroded traditional distinctions.

M. Halperin[11] has concluded that the Economic Conference of 1927 'marquait l'entrée du facteur économique dans l'orbite des décisions politiques.' He has illustrated the increasing attention specialists focused on economic and commercial problems on an international scale. It was, of course, only the beginning of a new form of international co-operation. M. Dubin[12] goes further and suggests that in 1935 just as the whole political role of the League had been discredited, a decisive change in the character of the League's economic and social programs set in. The nature of the depression and the expanding role of almost all States in the economic and social lives of their citizens, led delegates to place increasing emphasis on the social, economic and technological factors in society and on the need to solve such problems through the collaboration of League and non-League international agencies. The experience of the ILO and Health Organization with extensive and broadly based activities contributed to the revival of the

Economic and Financial Committees of the League. Thus, on the eve of the war, Assembly delegates – in part looking for a way to ensure the League's continued existence – affirmed the League's commitment to social and economic activities and appealed for recommendations from non-League members. It is paradoxical that at a time when most States opted for national solutions to many such problems, the League looked forward to a new international role.

There was yet another way in which the League attempted to re-shape the international environment. Mention should be made of a subject not covered in the contributions to this Symposium, namely the role of the Permanent Court of Justice, the model for the present International Court of Justice. The Court delivered 31 judgments and gave 27 advisory opinions, with 54 States accepting some degree of compulsory arbitration. Although Americans never joined the League, an American jurist sat on the Court throughout this period. The cases heard were of considerable importance and decisions rendered prevented disputes between States from escalating into major crises. Court action (advisory opinion, 1931) with regard to the Austrian attempt to join a customs union with Germany, the resolution in 1932 of the Franco-Swiss dispute over Upper Savoy and, in 1933, the settlement of the conflict between Denmark and Norway over Eastern Greenland, illustrate the ways the Court extended the scope of international law. Interestingly enough, American and British writers of the pre-1919 period saw in an extended arbitration system a practical approach of settling disputes peacefully. Leon Bourgeois brought great pressure on an extremely reluctant Woodrow Wilson in this direction. A student of the Hague Peace Conference has recently argued that a Permanent Court and a periodic conference system would have proved acceptable to the American Senate and that the Wilsonian determination to break with the Hague tradition was a costly error. Convinced though he was of the necessity for including the Court in the Covennant, Wilson never conceded to it a central role; by its very nature the Court could move only slowly in building up an international structure of law with no ultimate sanction except the self-interest of the States.

This brief review of the League's role in international relations illustrates an expansion of the methods for dealing with inter-State problems. But ist must be remembered that the League mechanism was only one such path open to the sovereign States. Even at the height of the so-called Geneva system, States resorted both to the old and the new forms of diplomacy. They entered into bi-lateral agreements, joined regional groupings – e.g. Pan-American Union, Locarno Pact, the Balkan Entente, Baltic Union, etc. – and became Members of the League. As M. Svolopoulos[13] reminds us, contradictions did exist, sometimes in the spirit but more often in the practice, resulting from membership in a regional group and/or in the League. Behind the fights between universalists and regionalists were often conflicting political aims of Governments intent on protecting their security by more limited agreements as well as by League membership. Though the League encompassed more States than any other contemporary multi-national organization, there existed also great Powers outside the League. Within the League structure there were States dissatisfied with the *status quo* the institution had been designed to support. Thus the Powers turned to a variety of means to protect or advance their interests. The French made their pacts with Poland, the Little Entente and the Soviet Union. They joined the Locarno Pact which though linked with the League can also be seen as an alternative to it, and helped create the Briand-Kellogg Pact, a statement of moral intent; and they used their investments in Germany and in Central Europe to provide an alternative to political forms of diplomatic leverage. A similar list can be made for the British. Britain's interests in the Far East brought her to the Washington Conference settlements, while the concern for her imperial position made her particularly vulnerable to the American absence from the League. One must be careful not to think of the League 'system' as an all embracing one; it was only one form, albeit a new form, of multinational diplomacy. Moreover, it bears stressing that in the thirties when the League had lost much of its political *raison d'être* and States reverted to non-aggression treaties and bi-laterial pacts, old methods did not work any better than new ones. If the presence of the League with its false hopes complicated the tasks of traditional diplomacy, there is little evidence that the latter enjoyed any greater measure of success when unencumbered by League obligations.

What did States think they would achieve by joining the League? Like the Nuremberg trials, the fact that the League was shaped by the victors gave it one meaning to those inside and another to those excluded. In a sense, each Government created its own League not necessarily corresponding either to the structure in 1919, or to that which evolved during the 1920's. The French hoped to use the League to enforce the *status quo*. In Germany, the opposite hope, namely that the League would provide an instrument for change, obtained. As M. Kimmich[14] has shown, the German people expected that League membership would allow them to press for the revision of an unjust treaty. Thus, even under Stresemann, when the Germans behaved as good members of the international community, difficulties arose when disarmament or the minorities issue came to be discussed. Germany was in an ambiguous position from the very time of her joining the League. Not only was she a revisionist Power but her position between the great and small Powers was a difficult one. She sat on the League Council and was a full Member of the Locarno Pact, yet she was not a real equal with regard to Britain and France. After 1929, finding that she was making little progress in revising the Versailles Treaty, her diplomats began to act more aggressively, alienating the small nations without achieving the equality of status Germany sought. In the eyes of successive German Governments, the League had proved far too inflexible an instrument to respond to the shifting power relations on the continent of Europe. For in fact, the League could not go beyond the area of Anglo-French agreement. The Germans were disappointed in their expectations even before Hitler came to power. From their point of view it was a failed form of diplomacy.

The Soviet Union joined the League because of its identification with a collective security system. Faced with a resurgent Japan and Germany, the Soviet Union had everything to gain from any collective effort to check aggression. It is curious that it was articles X and XVI, those very provisions which had alienated the Americans and so worried the British, that most attracted the Soviet Union.

She was far less interested in the technical aspects of the League's works or in the use of the Assembly as a public forum. Soviet policy, as Mme Plettenberg[15] underlines, was thoroughly consistent, whether in terms of paying the next to highest financial contribution to the League, or with regard to Soviet support for collective action against Germany, Italy, and, more debatably, Spain. Like most other statesmen, Litvinov was hardly blind to the reality of the weaknesses inherent in the League structure. The Soviet Union would not act alone but she would associate herself with any collective action that might be taken against a disturber of the peace. Though different theoretical arguments were presented, it was clear that in her own self-interest, the Soviet Union had joined the Powers supporting the *status quo*. Even before it became apparent to the Soviets that the League was a paper tiger, neither Britain nor France (despite a treaty with the Soviet Union) was prepared to treat her as a full partner. Although she remained a League Member until her expulsion over the Russo-Finish war, the Soviet Union had already deserted the League in all but name before Munich. Her diplomatic isolation acted as a catalyst in the re-orientation of Soviet policy away from Britain and France, and towards Berlin and the Soviet-German Pact. The Soviet Union did try to strengthen the League in its role as a bloc against aggression, only to find that the bloc did not exist and that her own intentions roused great suspicion among both great and small Powers. For the Soviets, too, the League failed.

In 1919 for their part, the Americans felt that they could provide for their own security by using economic rather than political means to underwrite their Great Power status. Thus, although the USA shunned a political connection with the League, American investors moved into Germany, France and Central Europe while the American Government insisted on the re-payment of war debts owed it. In sharp contrast to the Soviets, while Americans disassociated themselves from the collective security aspect of the Leagues activities, they were soon drawn into its technical and humanitarian efforts. Nonetheless, when faced with challenges which demanded more active responses than those shaped at the Washington Conference, a more complex relationship with the League began to evolve. The Manchurian crisis presented the first real test. The vacillations about the proper response to Japanese aggression stemmed not only from domestic pressures but from fears that any association with the League would result in the latter's 'passing the buck' to the United States. M. Ostrower[16] illustrates the vacillating role Secretary of State Stimson played in his relations with the League during the mounting crisis. At some point Stimson must have realised that collective security would become meaningful only if the United States and the British supplied the muscle power. Under such conditions, co-operation with the League was far less attractive. Because the United States was not a Member of the League, she could not hide behind it when forced to decide whether to impose sanctions or let the Japanese action go unchecked. Stimson had never really accepted sanctions and at a given moment retreated; the non-recognition doctrine was but a moral and legalistic statement of the American position with a long and honourable past history in American diplomatic non-action. Under Roosevelt, it was again only when faced with the realities of aggression that the President looked to Geneva – three thousand miles of sea gave the Americans more protection than that enjoyed by the Soviet Union. Mr. Ostrower argues that Roosevelt and Hull were genuinely worried in 1935 and in subsequent years tried to see how the Neutrality Acts could be used to complement League action. It was the weakness of the League response over Ethiopia which led Roosevelt to shift American policy towards London and Paris rather than towards Geneva. The League was no longer of primary interest; it could not perform any function for the United States which would relieve her of the necessity for acting on her own.

It was obvious that nations join an international organization because they hope to be strengthened by that association. Given the League's accomplishment in the realm of peace keeping, neither the Soviets nor the United States could have taken a very sanguine stand. Still, this preoccupation with the collective security aspects of the League should not obscure the fact that many States within the League structure saw other positive features in the various Geneva institutions, making them a center of world diplomacy. An international institutional framework was developing where none had previously existed and this structure, or its off-shoots, was becoming operational in domains not previously subject to any international body or any expression of international public opinion. Most of the daily work of the League did not revolve about either collective security or disarmament or the revision of the Covenant- a subject little discussed by the contributors to our Symposium though of central concern to a first generation of writers. Geneva was becoming a place where statesmen from different countries, large and small, could congregate and talk; where problems of all kinds – political, social, economic, technical – could be discussed and where, through daily contact, numerous ways of adjusting the international scene could be evolved. M. Siotis[17] looks at the institutions of the League from a vantage point to which I hope to return at the end of this paper. He underlines the important difference between the Executive Council and the Assembly tracing the latter's evolution from a Conference or Board of Delegates to a new form of national representation. From the start, even Wilsonian internationalists wavered on the subject of using public opinion rather than sanctions as a means of checking aggression. It was through the Assembly that the former was being mobilised and given a world arena. It was neither desired nor expected that the Assembly should assume executive powers. However, as the Council became paralysed by quarrels among its members, the Assembly did try to expand its own jurisdiction under Artile XI to XVII. The same experiment was later tried under Dag Hammarskjöld; both attempts proved unsuccessful and in each case the Assembly was forced to return to its primary purpose of public discussion. It may well be that this Assembly function is better performed by today's Third World powers than it used to be by the small nations at Geneva.

M. Siotis[18] and M. Barros[19] focus on the powers of the Secretary General; discussions about his role have reflected different views about the state system and the stage at which the international community had arrived. Cecil's politically powerful chancellor with extensive executive powers emanated from the British statesman's hope that the League would become something more than a reinforced Concert of Powers. Once this image was rejected a far weaker secretarial type was sought. Obviously, administrative power can mask political influence; the study of Hankey's role in the British government is a case in point and parallel examples can be found in France and Germany. But political power must be adroitly handled in an international context where one must balance the claims of one's country against those of the international organization, and where one is asked to preserve political neutrality in disputes between States. Sir Eric Drummond's reputation is a very mixed one; for many he was Britain's agent though his battles with the Foreign Office suggest that the flow was not all one way. But there seems little doubt that under his rule the Secretariat of the League served the interests of the great powers dominating it. We also have a study of Avenol whose papers are now available for public scrutiny at the Quai d'Orsay.[20] Whatever the roles of these two Secretaries-General, M. Siotis is surely right when he stresses the attempt of this first generation of international civil servants to create something more than a purely national civil service and in trying to develop an international ideology going beyond narrow national interests. These problems still exist though we have moved from Great Power Secretaries-General to men recruited from the small, non-committed, or neutral States.

Apart from the Council, Assembly and Secretariat, the Symposium papers make only passing references to a wide range of functional institutions. It would have been useful to have examined the work of one of these (e. g. the Health Organisation, ILO, etc.) under the highly centralised League system. The kind of technical institutions, now so numerous and often completely autonomous, have become a permanent part of the multinational scene. The problems are no longer those of development but of co-ordination, duplication and even competition in a constantly proliferating series of private, state and multinational organizations. But the contributors to the Symposium have looked at three areas of League activities, i. e. mandates (M. Collart[21]), refugees (M. Grahl-Madsen[22]) and minorities (M. Veatch[23]) not previously subject to any form of international scrutiny.

The functioning of the Permanent Mandates Commission provided an interesting lesson in the use of expert and international pressure to monitor the behaviour of even Great Powers. Though the Commission was dominated by the Mandate Powers and certain questions, e. g. progress to self-government were carefully avoided, reports were demanded and made, forthright questions were asked about the economic state of the territories under supervision, and both Britain and France were prodded when the experts felt all was not well. William Rappard played the critical key role on the Commission making it a considerable force in colonial matters. M. Veatch suggests that in minority matters the use of private pressure and careful negotiation carried out behind the scenes enabled the Minorities Committee of the Council and the Minorities Section of the Secretariat to influence the behaviour of some of the offending States. Here, too, the threat of publication – also used with regard to colonial questions – and the possibility of public criticism could be mobilized if States proved recalcitrant. The vitality of this system was also sapped as the League lost its political prestige. In the past the Germans had brought many cases before the Committee; but they refused to include the protection of the Jews within the minority clauses; this along with the Polish rejection of League jurisdiction brought the system to a practical halt.

Neither of these spheres of action were of major concern in the post-1945 world. Though the trusteeship system owed a great deal to the mandate structure, the dependent territories soon gained their independence and became full Members of the United Nations. Moreover, today, the focus is rather more on human than on national rights, international organizations reflecting the special needs – necessarily changing – of their own time. On the other hand, the refugee problem reflects the continuities of our age. Neither in the inter-war period nor at present has either the League or the United Nations provided the funds or support needed to deal with a problem the magnitude of which was not anticipated in 1919. The early work of the League regarding the repatriation of prisoners of war as well the problems of Russian, Greek, Armenian and Bulgarian refugees was primarily due to the energy and devotion of one man, Fritjof Nansen. But the unwillingness of the League of Nations to face the political questions raised by Nazi persecutions almost entirely impeded the effectiveness of already limited efforts. The onset of the war found the League in no position to respond. What little had been done depended on outside financing and activity; individuals rather than institutions carried the brunt of the burden. Political and humanitarian considerations did not necessarily coincide.

Where the goals were modest and the political limits fully understood, some measure of success was achieved. Individuals and even groups of specialists did look after the interests of those who found it difficult, if not impossible, to speak for themselves. Often the efforts were far greater than the results – and that there were results must be attributed to such men as Rappard and Nansen rather than to the Member States represented in the League. Still, it might be argued that the League's intervening at all in such questions was a mark of progress in the internationalist approach to humanitarian questions.

With the time at our disposal no Symposium on the League of Nations could possibly handle all the issues raised by recent research and writing. Yet there are certain lacunae worth underlining if only to stimulate further discussion and investigation. In the absence of published material, it is not surprising though disconcerting that we lack a contribution on the French conception of the League and its functions, on the French efforts made to strengthen the League, or France's virtual abandonment of the League for political purposes. This should not be construed as a criticism of our Swiss hosts but a commentary on the present state of publication, if not research, in France today. Though there are scattered throughout contributions to our Symposium many references to the French role, particularly in the Franco-British antagonism so central to the collapse of collective efforts, far more needs to be understood about French attitudes and behaviour. Resulting in part from the secondary role played by the French government, the current tendency is to concentrate on London. But it should not be forgotten that in the twenties and well into the thirties France was a Great Power, strong enough to have ambitions outside Europe and prosperous enough to extend her financial interests into Germany and Central Europe. France stood at the very centre of European politics and her central role affected the strengths and weaknesses of the League structure. To study the League without analysing the role of France is like playing Hamlet without the Prince.

Also essential to our understanding of the Geneva experiment is another missing link, namely the absence of a paper on the contribution of the Small Powers within the League. The three discussions of Switzerland reveal the complex attitudes of a neutral power – drawn into the League's orbit by her very neutrality and by the internationalism of some of her leading citizens. Without scrutinizing the attitudes and actions of the Small Powers in the League it is impossible to understand the attraction of Geneva for the statesmen of so many nations. The concentration on the realities of power politics has obscured the reason why the Small Powers looked often with hope and always with interest to the meetings of the Assembly. The Assembly was a public arena making it possible to hear the voice of the weaker States. Individuals counted; there was not only Beneš but Joseph Beck of Luxembourg. Interestingly, almost every Foreign Ministry of Europe created whithin its Ministry a League of Nations department/section; these departments/sections, instead of being mere backwaters were often staffed by the most daring and amibitious of civil servants. Jostled out of traditional attitudes by World War I, countries like Belgium, Holland and those of Scandinavia, were forced to re-think their former aloofness from Great Power politics, gradually abandoning inherited views on neutrality and isolation. Moreover, the economic realities of the post-war world created economic and social problems for all States drawing them to Geneva to listen and to be heard.

This ist not to claim too important a role for the smaller States. The differences between Great and Small Powers were writ large in the heart of the Covenant and later even more prominently in the Charter of the United Nations. But the Small Powers were not heard at all at the Congress of Vienna and their influence in post-Bismarkian Europe was exceedingly limited. The break-down of the Hapsburg Empire not only led to the creation of a number of new States, but increased the room for manoeuvre in the corridors of power. Clearly, the influence of the smaller States was limited but individuals and Governments could make their mark at Geneva and derive benefits from their membership in the League. It is not without significance that today's new prestige of the UN General Assembly is derived from the ability of the smaller Powers to present their case to world opinion. The small countries have learnt to use both the UN and other international organizations to further their own interests, often against the very Powers which had been instrumental in the creation of the United Nations.

A third ommission for this Symposium deserves a final comment. Placing the League in its historical framework, the League represents one of those significant turning points in the history of the international state system. The ability of international organizations to achieve lasting peace is as doubtful today as it was in any earlier period of our history. But this should not lead one to minimize the steps taken, or to dismiss the theories – the myths, if you wish – which created such organizations. Today it is fashionable to stress the key changes which occurred in the international system in 1815 – i. e. when the Great Powers found in the balance of power a method by which joint consultation could be substituted for war. "The settlement marked the first recognition of it by governments, not merely by theorists and critics of government, and by all the European governments not merely by one or another of them. States had duties as well as rights; and this was especially true of the great states".[24]

For Professor F. H. Hinsley the creation of the concert system helped consolidate new views about the functioning of the European state system which had emerged during the previous century. The new system worked because the States were prepared to make it work. It was successful because it was in the interest of each of the participating States to make it successful. The system corresponded to the realities of State power.

In 1919 a stable international order required far greater changes in the behaviour and attitudes of States than the concert system had ever demanded, in fact, a change for which the States were not ready.

The League was launched at a difficult moment, and its expectations were naïve. The participants never could accept the fact that there was a contradiction between their own reluctance to go to war, and the need to rely on force to uphold both their own interests and the stability of the new international order they had created. In a very fundamental way and for very basic reasons the League failed and was doomed to fail. Yet the ideals of the liberal internationalists, muddled, unclear, even dangerous as some of our contributors have insisted, have an importance of their own.

These ideals have become part both of our intellectual and institutional inheritance. The Charter of the United Nations reflects a good ideal of the League experience; other institutions have taken up, refined and adopted principles and procedures developed at Geneva. Given their many offspring, one cannot dismiss these conceptions at the origin of the League; ideas which men like William Rappard continued to believe in even when the superstructure itself had been destroyed. Such ideas cannot be confined to the international scrap-heap. The break with the past in 1919 was far more radical than what happened in 1815. Ideas always outrun institutions. Metternich and Alexander I were far removed indeed from the theories of Kant and Rousseau. But the ideas, however limited their practical results, have become part of our thinking about the international environment and continue to shape that environment. They cannot be eradicated.

I would go further. The ideas of collective security are not dead. There are still people – not confined to Western Europe – who believe in the corrective power of international public opinion. There are still those who believe that arms lead to war and that even in questions of nuclear weapons, Small Powers can affect the behaviour of the Great. There are idealists today who would go beyond the Wilsonian internationalists. Some of the paths followed by the League proved to be dead ends, and dangerous dead ends at that. Even the study of dead ends has its utility. The failures of history often are the most instructive. But it is not popular among historians to argue in favour of the study of lost causes. "History is not merely what happened; it is what happened in the context of what might have happened. Therefore it must incorporate the alternatives, the might-have-beens. They may, as a necessary element be in the dustbin now, but so, after all, are those who put them there and who is to say with assurance, which is the 'dead-end'?«[25]

It is often said that the Palais des Nations is the home of lost causes; fortunately there are always new tenants.

Notes

1 Cf. Heinz Waldner, p. IX/note* in the *Proceedings.*
2 Cf. George Egerton, p. 95 in the *Proceedings.*
3 Cf. James Barros, p. 31 in the *Proceedings.*
4 Cf. George Baer, p. 282 in the *Proceedings.*
5 Cf. M. Maurice Vaïsse, p. 245 in the *Proceedings.*
6 Cf. Maurice Vaïsse, p. 245 in the *Proceedings.*
7 Cf. Nicole Pietri, p. 319 in the *Proceedings.*
8 Cf. Martin Dubin, p. 42 in the *Proceedings.*
9 Cf. Jean Halperin, p. 343 in the *Proceedings.*
10 Cf. Alexander Menzies, p. 295 in the *Proceedings.*
11 Cf. Halperin, p. 343 in the *Proceedings.*
12 Cf. Martin Dubin, p. 42.
13 Cf. Constantin Svolopoulos, p. 266 in the *Proceedings;* cf. C. A. Davis, *The United States and the Second Hague Peace Conference.* Durham, N. C., Duke University Press, 1975.
14 Cf. Christoph Kimmich, p. 118 in the *Proceedings.*
15 Cf. Ingeborg Plettenberg, p. 144 in the *Proceedings.*
16 Cf. Gary Ostrower, p. 128 *in the Proceedings.*
17 Cf. Siotis, p. 19 in the *Proceedings.*
18 Cf. M. Jean Siotis, p. 19 in the *Proceedings.*
19 M. James Barros, p. 31 in the *Proceedings;*
20 M. James Barros, *Betrayal From Within. Joseph Avenol, Secretary-General of the League of Nations, 1933–1940.* New Haven, Yale University Press, 1969.
21 Cf. M. Yves Collart, p. 384 in the *Proceedings.*
22 Cf. M. Atle Grahl-Madsen, p. 358 in the *Proceedings.*
23 Cf. M. Richard Veatch, p. 369 in the *Proceedings.*
24 F. H. Hinsley, *Nationalism and the International System* (London Hodder and Stoughton 1973) p. 84.
25 H. Trevor-Roper (Lord Dacre of Glanton) "History and Imagination" reprinted in the *Times Literary Supplement* 25 July 1980.

Chapter/Chapitre I

The League of Nations: Institutional aspects

Les institutions de la Société des Nations

The institutions of the League of Nations

JEAN SIOTIS
The Graduate Institute of International Studies, Geneva

I. Introduction

The League of Nations was the first institutionalized sub-system, born as a result of the explicit expression of the political will of a group of States. The League's composition was intended to be universal and its functional orientation global. In the course of this paper, I shall analyse the League experience in terms of a critical transition from the early institutionalized forms of multilateral organization in the 19th century to the global world institution established after the Second World War.

With few exceptions, scholarly works on the inter-war period in general and on the League of Nations in particular have tended to minimize or to misjudge the League's contribution towards building up the contemporary system of international organization. The false and exaggerated expectations placed in the League and its 'inability' to change the course of events leading to the Second World War to a large extent explain the distorted views found in the literature. At the same time, the belief that an institutionalized system for the maintenance of peace can have a decisive effect on a given environment – itself marked by the growing hostility among its actors of whom many followed aggressive policies – has led many authors to attribute the outbreak of World War II to a 'failure' of League institutions. Such views, however, reflect a basic fallacy about the nature of international institutions, for their characteristics as superstructures of a given international system are not properly taken into account. Institutions facilitate the conduct of multilateral relations and they provide the necessary framework, for the elaboration and implementation of co-operative programmes; but, left to themselves, in an environment characterized by growing heterogeneity, hostility and polarisation, they are of little avail as effective instruments for the maintenance of peace.

The League institutions – and their effectiveness – must therefore be judged in their systemic context. The institutions were established in the wake of the First World War which differed qualitatively from all previous international conflicts, and these institutions whithered away on the eve of the Second World War which was the first global armed conflict.

In the interval, i.e. during the 'twenty years crisis', the very systemic foundation an which the League institutions had originally rested was gradually eroded. The international system which gave birth to the League was dominated by the French cabinet, was submitted on 3 February 1919 to the Commission of the was dominated by two opposed coalitions: the Axis Powers united in their aggressive designs and, the loose – and for much too long – ineffective and heterogeneous alignment of States opposed to German, Italian or Japanese expansionism. Given the collapse of the international system which had given birth to the League it is, therefore, not surprising that the institutions became but the shadow of what the Covenant had set out to establish.

These opening remarks should allow us to place the discusison of the League institutions in a proper perspective. Moreover, the historical perspective should extend beyond the twenty-odd years of the League's active life, and should include references to its antecedents, as well as to the United Nations system. In an attempt to evaluate the League's contribution to the development of contemporary international organization, I propose to examine some of the League's institutional characteristics, relating them to those of the Concert of Europe, on the one hand, and to those of the United Nations, on the other. In particular, I shall touch upon the following aspects of the League's institutional structure: its instruments of multilateral diplomacy, its Secretariat and its functional agencies. While placing the structural and practical changes of the institutions in their sytemic setting, it should be constantly kept in mind that the behavioural autonomy of the institutional sub-systems is determinded and limited by the institutional environment.

II. League Institutions as Conduits for Multilateral Diplomacy

Diplomatic historians have exhaustively studied the Congress of Vienna, but only few – notably Golo Mann, Charles Webster and Maurice Bourquin – have paid any attention to its significance as the first major manifestation of 'modern' multilateral diplomacy. The Congress itself, particularly during its second phase, was organized, along proposals submitted by its President, Prince Metternich. Functionally, specific committees and working groups were established and, in preparing and presiding over its sessions, Metternich was assisted by his private secretary Friedrich von Gentz, who rapidly acquired the status of Secretary of the Congress. The plenipotenitaries representing the Powers, subsequently forming the *Directoire*, served as members of a *de facto* Bureau or Steering Committee – with extensive prerogatives – compared to the delegates representing more than a hundred sovereign States. In short, the Congress of Vienna set a number of precedents, which later served as models for the organization of 19th century multilateral diplomatic meetings.

The structure of the Congress reflected both the hierarchy among participating States, and the concern of the leading actors to exert a firm control over its proceedings. Given the number of delegations and the complexities of the issues facing Europe at the end of the Napoleonic wars, the leaders of the victorious alliance organized the proceedings according to an agenda, set, and periodically revised, by the President in consultation with selected plenipotentiaries. What above all enabled the Congress to proceed rapidly towards the objectives set by the leading Powers was the establishment of bodies with a limited composition.

The lessons as to the most effective ways to organize and conduct multilateral diplomatic meetings learnt in Vienna subsequently served as guidelines for the organization of intergovernmental meetings held within the framework of the Concert of Europe. Although the Concert did not have a formal constitutional foundation, the Final Act of 1815, as well as many other multilateral treaties and declarations laid the cornerstones for the first multi-functional system of international organization. Its structure was flexible and it was continuously adapted to the changing needs and to changes in the systemic context.

The next stages in this direction were the Congress of Paris (1857), the Berlin Congress (1878), and the two Hague Conferences (1899 and 1907). We should note, however, that during the lifetime of the Concert of Europe (1815–1914) more than 60 multilateral meetings were held. They were entitled Congresses, Conferences, or Conferences of Ambassadors; and although there was no fixed periodicity, meetings of limited, or all-European composition were held at an average of every two years. The Conferences of Ambassadors were always of a limited composition and they were convened normally to deal with issues relating to the Ottoman Empire or other extra-European problems. Finally, the Hague Conferences were the first meetings with participating States outside of Europe. The presence of the United States, several Latin American countries, China and Japan were evidence of the expansion in the direction of universalism of the Concert's structure and functions.

The basic rules for the conduct of multilateral diplomatic relations were progressively codified in the course of the nineteenth century; at least in this respect the League of Nations once in existence did little to innovate. As examples of the continuity between the Concert and the League the rules of procedure of the Hague Conferences and those of the League Assembly may be cited. The only major change was the publicity of debates in implementing Wilson's principles of 'open diplomacy'. Despite the rule of confidentiality prevailing before the First World War, the latter part of the Concert's existence was also to some extent influenced by public opinion, which along with the media directly influenced the multilateral diplomacy of the League.

The early plans for a League of Nations – the later Phillimore Plan, the Draft of Colonel House and Wilson's First Draft – referred to the 'Conference', the 'Delegates' or still to the 'Body of Delegates' in order to designate the sole multilateral organ entrusted with various functions relative to the settlement of disputes among Member States. In all three cases, this organ was no more than the periodic meeting of plenipotentiaries, with its own rules of procedure and presided over by the Minister of Foreign Affairs of the host country. In all respects, this was the continuation of the Concert of Europe practice of periodic conferences and congresses. Moreover, most private individuals and various peace groups writing during the war proposed an organization using the classical methods of 19th century multilateral diplomacy for the settlement of disputes and, ultimately, with recourse to a judicial body.

The earliest form of institutionalized multilateral machinery may be found in the report (dated 18 June 1918) of the Committee appointed by the French Government and presided over by Léon Bourgeois. This report, adopted by the French cabinet, was submitted on 3 February 1919 to the Commission of the

League of Nations of the Peace Conference. Specifically, the report contained provisions for the establishment of an 'International Council', composed of the Heads of Government of all Member States or by their duly authorized representatives. The Council was to meet at least once a year and it was empowered to take binding decisions. In the intervals, a 'Permanent Delegation', composed of fifteen Member States designated by the Council was to prepare sessions, receive communications addressed to the Council and, if need arose, propose a meeting of the Council. The proposed 'Delegation' was certainly more than a Secretariat, but it certainly did not have any powers of its own. No headquarters were assigned to the two bodies and the Council remained master of its procedures.

The Smuts Plan – dated 18 December 1918 – went a step further, suggesting the establishment of a "general conference or congress of all the constitent states, which will partake of the character of a Parliament, in which public debates of general international interest will take place." General Smuts also spelled out the functions of the general conference as follows: the adoption of "general resolutions," the adoption of "general measures or codes of an international character dealing with questions like disarmament or world peace or rules of international law," as well as the "discussion of the reports of the various administrative committees or commissions." In addition to the conference, however, Smuts proposed the creation of "a small body called the Council of the League which will have to be the executive and carry on the ordinary administration of the League." Contrary to the French plan, Smuts proposed a functional differentiation between the two organs, the conference being "viewed largely from the point of view of favorably influencing and educating public opinion in all constituent countries," while "the real work . . . will be done by its Council, whose constitution and powers ought therefore to be very carefully considered." The permanent members of the Council were to have been the Great Powers – the British Empire, France, Italy, the United States and Japan – and four additional members to have had rotating membership. Two of these members were to be designated from a panel comprising the "important intermediate Powers below the rank of Great Powers and the other two from a panel comprising the 'minor states'." The Smuts Plan also made detailed provision for the operations of the Council, in relation to the Conference, the Secretariat and the international administrative bodies.

At least in terms of the institutional arrangements President Wilson's Second Draft (or First Paris Draft), dated 10 January 1919, was largely inspired by the Smuts Plan. Wilson's draft provided for a plenary 'Body of Delegates' and for an 'Executive Council', the latter comprising five permanent and four rotating members. The draft also contained detailed provisions for the functional differentiation between the Delegates and the Council. Wilson's Third Draft repeated the same proposals while the British Draft Convention of 20 January 1919 referred not only to a General Conference and to a Council but to a 'capital' of the League as well. The Cecil-Miller Draft of 23 January 1919 confirmed the tenor of the previous plans, also true for Wilson's Fourth Draft.

The Draft Covenant submitted to the League Commission on 26 March 1919 and the Hurst-Miller Draft of 31 March 1919 still referred to the 'Body of Delegates' and to the 'Executive Council'. The first mention of the term 'Assembly' was to be found in the British proposals of 1 April 1919. All subsequent drafts followed the same line; the only change concerned membership in the Council, to the extent that the Assembly was empowered to approve, by a simple majority, the addition of new members to the Council. Moreover, the Assembly was granted the power to elect non-permanent members of the Council, without any reference to the 'panels' provided for in the previous drafts. We should note, however, that the Drafting Committee's text of 5 april 1919, is practically the same as that of the Covenant and does not functionally differentiate between the two organs. Both texts contain the same provision concerning their powers, i.e. "the Assembly (the Council) may deal at its meetings with any matter within the sphere of action of the League or affecting the peace of the world." The former hierarchic relation between the Council and the Body of Delegates was thus abandoned and the Council was no longer the organ *preparing* the work of the plenary body but assuming administrative responsibilities.

The parallel autority granted to the Assembly and the Council to deal with any subject within the field of competence of the League, as well as the change from 'Conference' or 'Body of Delegates' to 'Assembly' reflected a change in the overall conception of League institutions. First, the term 'Assembly' contained a symbolic element of popular representation which was absent from the earlier proposals about a 'Body of Delegates'. It is interesting to note that the terminological change took place, at least chronologically, following the meeting in Bern of the International Labor and Socialist Conference which asked that "representation in the central organ of the League shall be not by delegates of the executive branches of the Governments . . ., but by delegates from the Parliaments representing all parties therein, ensuring thus, not an alliance of cabinets or Governments, but an union of peoples." The term designating the body proposed by the Bern Conference was 'Representative Assembly.' This proposal was supported by General Smuts, acting in his personal capacity, while the delegations of the Great Powers rejected it outright, with David Hunter Miller qualifying it a "wildly impossible proposal." Nonetheless, 'Assembly' became part of the Conference vocabulary and, although nothing was changed in substance, the term finally replaced that of 'Body of Delegates', with its narrower diplomatic connotation. Secondly, the elimination of the hierarchically structured relations between the two multilateral bodies may also be explained by the introduction of provisions for the Secretariat, designated to prepare the work of the multilateral bodies. In the last analysis, the only explanation for the establishment of two multilateral bodies with practically identical functions, may be traced partly to the recognition of the need for public debate on issues of general concern, and partly to the need for greater efficiency in settling specific disputes and other matters requiring action via a body of limited composition – in which the Great Powers would have had a more decisive voice. Although articles 11–17 of the Covenant referred specifically to the Council, matters related to the maintenance of peace and the settlement of given disputes could, at any time, be referred to the Assembly; and this was done on all occasions of major import to the League.

Both the final text of the Covenant and the League practice, set aside the distinction which originally entrusted the Council with the role of a preparatory organ for the Assembly (or the Conference, in earlier drafts); thus the two organs acquired concurrent functions and, more importantly, they acted accordingly. The fact that the Convenant did set forth the principle of concurrent responsibility was the result of a compromise between the Great Powers, the medium and small States, but articles 11–17 clearly gave the Council the key role relative to the settlement of disputes and the collective security matter. However, from the very beginning of the League the failure of the Council to act in many critical situations led the small States to refer to the Assembly disputes or matters threatening the peace. During the League's early years, the Assembly was viewed as an organ which could act when the Council was paralysed owing to the policies of one or more Great Powers; but as the years went by and the sky of world peace increasingly clouded over, recourse to the Assembly simply meant drawing the attention of public opinion to the issue.

One of the practical consequences of this situation was that politically sensitive issues, as well as other matters of the League were debated in the same fora. Progress in the direction of functional co-operation was slowed down, because of political stalemates on questions related to collective security, and because cooperation with non-Member States was particularly difficult. In 1939, the Bruce Committee was entrusted with the task of proposing reforms of the League's institutional structure in the field of economic and social co-operation; as the Committee submitted its report an the eve of the Second World War it was too late to take any action. The Bruce Report did, however, represent a valuable input in the preparatory work towards the Charter of the United Nations.

The principal recommendation of the Bruce Report [1] focused, both in the interest of economic and social co-operation and in that of collective security, on the need for institutionally separating the various functions performed by the Organization. The separation of functions was meant to improve the Organization's effectiveness but, it was aimed above all at facilitating the participation of non-Member States – in particular of the United States – in some of the League's activities. The lessons drawn by the Bruce Committee guided the authors in their proposals for a United Nations Charter. In this respect, the League experience served as yardstick by which various subsequent proposals could be evaluated.

Although the United Nations Charter established six principal organs, the General Assembly was clearly the *primus inter pares* – except for matters relative to the maintenance of peace and the settlement of disputes. The recognition of the need in this field to concentrate responsibility in the Security Council stemmed from the determination of the Great Powers to keep firm control over such matters; but it was also argued that vesting concurrent responsibilities in the League Assembly and Council was one of the reasons for stalemates on collective security matters. Notwithstanding the Charter provisions when, as a result of the Korean War and the frequent recourse by the Soviet Union to its veto powers, the Security Council became paralised, the United Nations like previously the League, faced the same problems of institutional overlapping.

In all other fields, the functional decentralization of the United Nations has led the system far beyond the expectations of those who drafted the Charter. I shall discuss some questions relative to the institutions for socio-economic co-operation at the end of this paper; but, at this point, I should simply state that the institutionalized multilateralism in the UN system was largely influenced by the lessons drawn from the League experience. In particular, the central role of the Security Council drawn up in Chapters VI and VII of the Charter represents an attempt to set the limits between public debate and effective action in the field of collective security. In spite of the departures from the Charter provisions after 1950, the principle of functional differentiation was never seriously questioned. Moreover, the expansion of membership no longer allowed for any illusions about the possibilities for using the General Assembly as an action-oriented body.

III. The League Secretariat

In my earlier reference to the Congress of Vienna, I mentioned the name of Friedrick von Gentz. No doubt his activities established some precedents later used in the conduct of multilateral meetings. For more than six decades the tasks of the Congress or Conference Secretariat were carried out by members of the diplomatic service of the host country, which also provided the president of such meetings. The Congress of Berlin, in 1878 marked an important step in the development of international Secretariats for two reasons: a) for the first time, the German Secretary appointed by Bismarck was assisted by a non-host country diplomat, and b) the long-standing practice for delegations to keep their own minutes was abandoned in favour of a single record produced by the Congress Secretariat under the President's responsibility. The Hague Conference progresses still further, their Secretariats, with wide-ranging responsibilities for the preparation of Conference documents, comprised officials from most participating States and whenever necessary assisted the delegations.

Beyond these essentially technical Secretariats, the Concert of Europe gave rise to international administrations carrying out executive functions. The Secretariats of the river commissions – particularly the European Danube Commission; the civilian components of certain territorial operations such as the international administration of Crete, etc. – and the international Bureaux established in the framework of various administrative unions were forerunners of the League Secretariat. The practice of entrusting a group of internationally appointed officials with the responsibility of administering small international bodies established by international treaties, and assuming certain public functions within a given territory, served as precedents for the League Secretariat.

At about the same time, 10 January and 20 January 1919 respectively, Wilson's Second Draft and the British Draft Convention contained references to a League Secretariat. The former simply stated that the "Executive Council shall appoint a permanent secretariat and staff," while the latter proposed specifically that the Secretariat be placed "under the general control and direction of the Chancellor of the League, who shall hold office during the pleasure of the Council." The term 'Chancellor' used in the British Draft implied that its authors envisaged extensive powers for the Head of the Secretariat, powers well beyond the administrative functions of Secretariats during the period of the Concert of Europe. The British representatives in Paris, to some extent supported by the French, initiated steps first with Eleftherios Venizelos and, later, with Thomas Masaryk for having one of the leading statesmen from the smaller powers accept the responsibility of becoming the first League Chancellor. Clearly, such approach implied that the authors of the draft intended to have at the helm of the League a political figure rather than simply a chief administrator.

The two subsequent drafts, prepared by Cecil and Miller and revised by Hurst, also referred to the appointment of a Chancellor, but in Wilson's Fourth Draft, of 2 February 1919, the term was replaced by that of Secretary-General. In the interval, both Venizelos and Masaryk had indicated that they were not prepared to accept such an appointment. These refusals, along with second thoughts on the part of the British and the French about the wisdom of granting the Secretariat extensive powers, led the members of the Council of Four to conclude that the administration of the League should be in a more 'traditional' vein. As a result, the title of Chancellor was changed and a senior British civil servant, Sir Eric Drummond was apponted first Secretary-General of the League. If during late January 1919 the appointment of a statesman from a small or medium country and wielding some measure of political power was envisaged, subsequently a national of a Great Power was selected and his functions were to be essentially administrative.

The League Secretariat was the first international administration with a wide range of functions and serving a quasi-universal organization. Although the Concert of Europe precedents were undoubtedly useful during the League's early days, the small group which formed the nucleus of the Secretariat in London faced indeed formidable challenges. First of all, it was essential to recruit and organize an international staff whose loyalty to the League could not be questioned, and secondly these men and women had to gain and keep the confidence of the Governments they were serving.

The first of these challenges was met with usccess, at least for the first ten years. Not only were the senior League officials men of great talents and competence, but they were also guided in their work by their conviction of being pioneers in the realm of a new international system. Among those who formed the nucleus of the Secretariat, Jean Monnet, Dionisio Anzilotti, Raymond Fosdick, Arthur Salter, Thanassis Aghnides and Paul Mantoux should be mentioned in particular; soon thereafter they were joined or replaced by Salvador de Madariaga, Pablo de Azcarate and Frank Walters. It was indeed a unique list not only of distinguished individuals but also of men representing the hightest form of internationalist ideology. Even though some left the Secretariat after a short period, they all left their mark on the institution.

A distinction should be made between those Powers representing the political mainstays of the organization, e.g. France and the United Kingdom with their European friends and allies, and other Member States, outside the 'inner circle' of League decision-makers. Although the Secretariat was dominated by nationals from the first group of countries, there was no contradiction in its commitment to defend the general interests of the League. The new international system established by the Peace Treaties and their institutional expression, the League, coincided with the interests of the group of victorious Powers. In the minds of those responsible for the Secretariat, the confidence of the Governments meant essentially the confidence of the British and French Governments and also of some of their closest European associates. Given this perception of League interests, it was inevitable for the Secretariat to lose confidence of those Member States beginning to challenge the 'Versailles order'. The tension between Mussolini's Government and the Secretariat was the first example of such a crisis involving a major Power, but during the ensuing years many more involved smaller States. Notwithstanding these crisis of confidence, I would conclude that given the League's power structure, as well as its political function of institutionally guaranteeing the 'Verseiilles order', the Secretariat did act in accordance with the principal actors' expectations.

During the Second World War, the experience gained by the League Secretariat was taken into account when plans for the United Nations Charter were elaborated. Not only did a number of private groups and individual authors study the League's experience and publish significant works on the subject, but the British and US governments sought the advice of former League officials when it came to drafting the relevant Charter provisions. The Royal Institute of International Affairs, the Carnegie Endowment for International Peace and former League officials – Egon Ranshofen-Wertheimer, Alexander Loveday and Pablo de Azcarate – analysed the experience of the League Secretariat and their views influenced the authors of the Charter. The basic principles on which an international civil service should be founded were codified in the Charter, whose article 99 embodied the right of initiative by the Secretary-General. There is no doubt that the formulation of article 99 was primarily influenced by the experience gained in the inter-war period, and by the firm belief expressed by many former League officials that the Secretary-General be given greater powers both to act as a third party and as the spokesman for United Nations interests.

IV. Functional Cooperation in the League

By the end of the nineteenth century, as a result of the industrial revolution and at least in Europe following the spectacular development of technology and communications the States participating in the Concert of Europe established a vast network of functionally specific international agencies. Organizations such as the Universal Postal Union, the International Telegraphic Union, the International Bureau of Standards, the Bureaux established by the Bern and Paris Conventions on Intellectual and Industrial Property were functionally specific; others, such as the River Commissions also had a territorial sphere of action. This experience in international co-operation was studied during the wartime by Leonard Woolf, whose work *International Government* (New York, 1916) was known to the delegates in Paris. The provisions of the Covenant's article 24 represented an attempt to promote functional co-operation, by placing under the League auspices "all international bureaux already established by general treaties if the parties to such treaties consent." But, above all, the establishment as a distinct institution of the International Labour Organisation was a further indication of the importance accorded by the Peace Conference to the promotion of socio-economic activities, under the authority or relative to the League.

In practice, the League activities in this field followed a different course from that envisaged by the authors of the Covenant. On the one hand, the provisions of article 24 were never implemented, and practically all existing international agencies remained independent-essentially, because the United States was a Member in most of these agencies and Washington did not consent to have them placed under League auspices. On the other hand, the League went far beyond what had originally been planned. The League established specialized bodies with responsibilities in matters related to education, health, housing, taxation, emigration, nutrition, cultural and scientific activities and, naturally, related to the whole range of economic and financial aspects of international co-operation. In this respect mention should be made of the *Economic and Social Organisation*, with its two Committees, the *Communications and Transit Organisation*, the *Health Organisation*, the *Advisory Committee on the Traffic of Women and Children*, the *Advisory Committee on Traffic in Opium and Dangerous Drugs*, the *Refugee Organisation*, the *Committee on Intellectual Co-operation* (which closely cooperated with the International Institute of Intellectual Co-operation in Paris, the International Institute of Cinematography in Rome and the International Bureau of Education in Geneva) and other temporary or permanent institutions active in various sub-fields of socio-economic co-operation. The League also engaged in Technical Assistance activities – particularly in China – of a type very similar to the United Naitons programmes.

This multiplicity of functionally specific bodies, all placed under the authority of the League Council and Assembly was bound to lead to serious difficulties, since it was materially impossible for the two organs to guide and coordinate activities of such different nature. Appointed in May 1939, the task of the Bruce Committee was to study and draw institutionally-weighted conclusions from the League's experience of almost twenty years.

The Report of the Bruce Committee was submitted to the Assembly at the end of August 1939 but, obviously, could never really be examined within the League's framework. The Report did, however, have a great influence on the elaboration of the U.N. Charter.

The Bruce Committee Report principally recommended the establishment of a Central Committee for Economic and Social Questions, which would have exercised effective power over all League bodies engaged in socio-economic activities. Although the Committee's composition was to have been determined by the Assembly, the Committee, once established, would have been granted the same authority in its field as the Council had in the field of political and collective security. Beyond any consideration of organizational efficiency, the creation of such an organ would have facilitated – at least according to the authors of the Report – the participation of non-Member States, particularly the United States, in the League's non-political activities.

The overall structure of the United Nations system and the UN Economic and Social Council, have largely been inspired by the recommendations of the Bruce

Committee Report and, more generally, by the lessons drawn from the League experience. The functional differentiation among the principal organs of the Organization has clearly been established in the Charter, but the UN system remains much more decentralized than the one envisaged in the Bruce Committee Report. If the original model for the UN system was 'confederal' or loosely 'federal', the U.N. now rather tends to resemble a feudal system in that the UN Organisation itself is unable to exercise any real authority over its constituent parts.

V. Conclusion

In the course of this paper, I tried to highlight the principal institutional characteristics of the League of Nations. I viewed the League as the successor to the Concert of Europe and as the predecessor of the United Nations. In some respects, the League's institutional structure differed qualitatively from those both of its predecessor and of its successor; on the whole, however, the first conclusion one may draw is that the changes were of a quantitative nature. When, in 1938, William Rappard wrote that the "League of Nations is as different from the ententes, alliances and confederations of which history tells us, as an aeroplane, for example, is from a litter, a sedan-chair, a coach, a train or a motor car",[2] he undoubtedly neglected – unwittingly or not – the experience of the Concert. Similiarly when during the Second World War North-American – and a few other – statesmen and scholars heralded the coming of a world organization which owed nothing to its prececessors, they, too – unwittingly or not – neglected to take into account the impact of the League experience on the United Nations. Both attitudes may be explained in terms of the need for impressing the novelty of a given institution upon public opinion in order to enlist its support. However, scholars who now know much more about the League than did their colleagues of a generation ago, should shy away from such evaluations and should attempt to place this remarkable institutional experiment in its proper historical setting.

A second conclusion to be drawn points to the need for viewing the functional differentiation among the various organs and institutions, and written into the United Nations Charter, as a principal lesson derived from the League experience. In more than one respect, the Bruce Committee Report represented not only a thorough analysis of the League practice but also served as a blueprint for the structure of the intrnational organization in the post-war period. At least on paper, the UN Charter conforms to the prescriptions – implicit or explicit – of the Bruce Committee Report. However, in practice the centrifugal forces inherent in any large functional decentralization have transformed the UN system into a loosely bound union of institutions – institutions, moreover, without the kind of leadership which could have been provided by the Central Committee proposed by the Bruce Committee, or by the ECOSOC. In discussing the overall institutional structure of the League or of the United Nations, structural dislocation, frequently the consequence of functional decentralization, must always be kept in mind.

Finally, this cursory view of League institutions should show that a careful study of the League's history could yield valuable lessons which in turn could improve our understanding of present-day international organization. The various institutional crises which have shaken the United Nations since it's inception should remind us that, given certain changes in the systemic setting of the Organization, a crisis becomes inevitable if the institution fails do adapt. Students of the history of the League can draw the same conclusion from the first quasi-universal experiment in multi-functional international organization. Globalism in the composition and the functions of the Organization were not attained by the League; the United Nations have come much closer to this objective. However, had it not been for the League and for those dedicated to its ideals, the United Nations would again have been – at best – a short-lived alliance of the victorious Great Powers.

Notes

1 cf. Martin Dubin p. 42–72 in the *Proceedings.*

2 RAPPARD, William, "What is the League of Nations" *In:* The World Crisis, by the Professors of the Graduate Institute of International Studies. – London, Longmans Green & Co., 1938. – p. 58.

The role of Sir Eric Drummond

JAMES BARROS
Department of Political Economy
University of Toronto, Toronto

I. The Political Chancellor

In order better to understand the role Sir Eric Drummond played during his fourteen years as Secretary-General of the League of Nations it might be useful to stop for a moment and examine the political role that was initially envisaged for the holder of this high international office.

Though the conventional wisdom is that the League's Covenant was largely a product of Woodrow Wilson's imagination, it would not be unfair to say that much of the detailed work of molding and shaping the Covenant owed more to British than American endeavors.[1] This was especially true on the question of the powers and responsibilities to be given to the administrative director of the world organization. Thoughts on this matter appear to have been largely British and restricted to Lord Robert Cecil, head of the League of Nations section of the British delegation to the Paris Peace Conference, and Philip Noël-Baker, Cecil's young assistant.

Indeed, as early as Christmas Eve of 1918 Cecil explained to the Imperial War Cabinet that the future world organization would be headed by a person of the highest ability.[2] He was to be called the 'Chancellor' and would direct the League's multinational secretariat. In addition, he was to be the League's representative to the world community, the "mouthpiece – and the suggester, if not the director" of the League's policy. The person appointed was to be an eminent political figure, influential politically, and thus more than a permanent civil servant.[3] In fact, one of the powers that would have been given to the Chancellor under the Covenant would habe been the right unilaterally to summon meetings of the League Council, and maybe even meetings of the League Assembly.[4] It was hoped that the Chancellor's "relations to the members of the Council should be that of an equal among equals and that his international authority would be a factor of great importance in establishing the practical utility and the moral authority of the League."[5]

Cecil, however, had to offer some explanation to justify the extensive powers that would be bestowed upon the Chancellor. Not only would this have represented a sharp break with prior tradition – keeping in mind that the powers of heads of pre-World War I international organizations were largely administrative in nature – but even more important, neither Prime Minister Clemenceau nor Prime Minister Orlando were "particularly enthusiastic" about Cecil's notion of a Chancellor possessing tangible executive powers.[6]

Cecil defended the proposal of a politically powerful Chancellor on the grounds that one of the League's great dangers would be that Member States of the world organization, especially the small States, would be wary of assuming political initiatives and would lack political courage. This void would be filled, Cecil hoped, by the Chancellor who would not only take the necessary political steps, but would be a person unafraid to expose himself to international criticism.[7]

The explanation left unanswered what would occur should the Chancellor publicly use his powers against a Member State of the world organization. The obvious answer was that he would be at odds with that State. It would not be unfair to say that his subsequent relations with that State would be less than cordial and that his ability to tender advice or restrain the actions of this State in world affairs would be undercut. In addition, there was no guarantee under the powers proposed for the Chancellor that the Council or Assembly of the League would either respond to his summons or act on his complaint should they convene.

On the surface Cecil's proposal of a politically powerful Chancellor appears idealistic. It appears to be founded on the assumption that an international official acting on his own initiative and without control over any armed forces could, merely through the force of his personality and the influence and prestige of his office, affect the course of inter-state relations.

In contrast to Clemenceau and Orlando, Lloyd George appears to have been favorably disposed to Cecil's notion of the Chancellor.[8] In view of the fact that Lloyd George was, like his French and Italien counterparts, less than altruistic when it came to sharing political power, whether in domestic politics or in international politics, suspicions were naturally raised whether Cecil's explananation of the intended political role of the Chancellor in world politics was the truth, the whole truth, and nothing but the truth. In actual fact, it was not.

What Cecil never admitted in public and indeed what can only be discerned between the lines of the available documentation was that the notion of the Chancellor was inextricably tied to the idea that anyone appointed as Chancellor would have to be someone whose attributes, orientation, and activities would dovetail with or complement British foreign policy desires.

This becomes obvious in an examination of what occurred just prior to Cecil's comments to the Imperial War Cabinet on Christmas Eve of 1918. On December 18 Captain Gerald Talbot, the naval attaché in Athens, wrote to the Director of Naval Intelligence, Admiral Sir Reginald Hall. Talbot had been assigned as aide-de-camp to the Greek Prime Minister, Eleftherios Venizelos, during his stay in London. In his letter to Hall, Talbot raised the possibility of using Venizelos as a conduit to inspire some of Britain's allies to assume a stance – where there might be disagreement – more in line with London's desires. Specifically, Talbot had the United States and President Wilson in mind. Opportunities, he thought, might often occur where unofficially Venizelos could be made to follow a particular approach or expound a particular idea or theory. Few men, he noted, were endowed with Venizelos' talent for argument and persuasion. Indeed, he exercised an amazing influence on any discussant. Talbot thought that this talent would apply especially in dealing with Americans, who were not, he imagined, particularly familiar with Europe's complex conditions.

In conveying the letter on 23 December, Sir William Tyrrell, the Foreign Office's Assistant Under-Secretary assured Cecil that Talbot was an able naval officer both tactful and discreet. Talbot's suggestion had to be "kept in mind" Cecil scribbled in red ink, and London should "work closely with Venizelos."[9]

What better way was there for the British to placate the United States and control President Wilson in view of the forthcoming Paris Peace Conference, than to attempt to do so through the pro-British and dynamic Venizelos? Obviously, the best way to work closely with Venizelos, to use Cecil's expression, was to appoint him as Chancellor. Accordingly, Cecil proposed his appointment to the Imperial War Cabinet during the Christmas Eve session of 1918.[10] The fact that Venizelos was interested in the concept of a postwar world organization, and preferred England to France, were additional incentives to press his appointment.[11]

When offered the Chancellorship by Cecil about mid-January 1919 Venizelos turned it down on the grounds that Greece needed him.[12] Despite Venizelos' rejection the idea was kept alive and others were considered as possible substitutes for Venizelos. They included Thomas Masaryk of Czechoslovakia and General Smuts of South Africa. Indeed, Cecil himself was considered. For various reasons all of these candidatures fell through. President Wilson himself toyed with the idea of assuming the Chancellorship. His aspiration was probably unknown to the British authorities, but if they had known, it would have given Whitehall many a sleepless night.[13] With no acceptable candidate on the horizon to assume the political role tailored for Venizelos, Cecil was forced to modify the powers of the office as well as its title.

II. Drummond's Perceptions

Because the office was to be downgraded in power and in importance Cecil now sought someone who was more a trained civil servant than a well-known political figure. His first choice fell upon Sir Maurice Hankey the Secretary to the Cabinet, the Committee of Imperial Defense, and the Imperial War Cabinet. After extended delay Hankey rejected the offer based on the advice he had received and because of his own inclinations. Cecil, however, along with Colonel Edward M. House, President Wilson's chief political adviser, had developed a contingency plan to substitute Sir Eric Drummond of the Foreign Office should Hankey reject the offer. The possible appointment of Drummond, like Hankey's possible appointment made sense. He was known to House, and of course to Cecil. He was readily available and attached to the British delegation to the Peace Conference. Furthermore, he was a well-trained and experienced Foreign Office official who had acted as the liaison officer with the Cabinet during the war. He had expressed himself about postwar international organization and the reduction of armaments as early as 1915, had established contact in early 1916 with Lord Bryce who was dealing with postwar international organization, and had been involved in

Cabinet considerations about the League in 1917 when Colonel House had visited London.[14] Most important, especially from Cecil's perspective, Drummond was a British national. No matter how de-politicized the Secretary-Generalship appeared to be, the office was still intrinsically political. It was desirable, in fact one could say necessary in London's view, that it be held by a British national. It was a viewpoint that was not lost sight of years later when time came to pick Drummond's successor.[15]

Drummond was of course not unaware of the rôle initially envisaged for the office under Cecil's concept of the Chancellor.[16] His own powers under the Covenant, at least on surface, appeared to be largely administrative in nature. In addition, his own value system, personality, as well as his prior training and experience in the Foreign Office, did not lend themselves to an interpretation or execution of the Secretary-General's office that leaned heavily on public action or public exposure. "I was neither a Parliamentarian nor a politician," he told one student of the Office in the early 1950's. Indeed, Drummond was absolutely certain that if Albert Thomas, the publicly acitve and dynamic Director of the International Labour Organisation had been Secretary-General Thomas would have been "forced to resign." Thomas' attempt to be a "Chancellor" would have been doomed to failure.[17]

Thus Drummond's approach to his rôle was conservative and in step with his prior training and experience which clearly marked him a product of the secret diplomacy of the pre-World War I period. This training and experience had its value, however, for it educated him to the Hobbesian world of international politics and to the paramount importance of the Great Powers in that world. It instilled in him a wariness of panaceas for the world's ills no matter how well packaged or convincingly offered. In fact, during this period there was no diminution in the position of the Great Powers whose imperiousness was little affected by the war and the establishment of the League. One could argue that their permanent seats on the League Council publicly acknowledged their paramount rôle in world affairs. Respect for state sovereignty was still the order of the day, compounded by the establishment of a host of new States as jealous of defending their newly won sovereignty as were other established States in the world community. In this new postwar world any international official no matter how well-meaning or discreet would have to move with the furtiveness of a hare.

Some of Drummond's attitude can probably be traced to his cautious Scots nature, but most of it was based on a sound practicality which questioned whether men's possessive nature and the anarchic international state system had evolved because of the war's impact. The League in such a setting had a rôle to play and so did its Secretary-General, but not a rôle that was divorced from the inescapable fact that unbridled competition moved the world community. Drummond, therefore, unlike well-meaning people everywhere was more restrained in what he expected the League could accomplish in regulating international relations, and what he, in particular, could accomplish as Secretary-General in accomodating and moderating the conflicting desires of States.[18]

Drummond also faced acute problems that seriously affected his rôle as

Secretary-General. Because the United States had rejected the League, a blow from which the world organization never recovered, Drummond was faced from the beginning with the added difficulty that for the League to succeed support from Britain, from France and Japan, as well as from the smaller States would be absolutely necessary. The League could be destroyed by London's hostility. At the minimum, London's toleration would allow the League to survive. Accordingly, during his tenure as Secretary-General Drummond attempted to maintain the closest contacts with the Foreign Office and make the acquaintance of new Governments as they ensconced themselves at 10 Downing Street. For Drummond to have done otherwise, to have avoided using his excellent contacts in London, and especially at the Foreign Office, to ensure Britain's support of the League would have been foolish in the extreme.

This position in turn was complicated by the fact that though England and France were comitted to the *status quo* established by the Peace Treaties of 1919, both of these States disagreed on how this *status quo* was to be maintained. As to the League's rôle in the maintenance of this *status quo*, London unlike Paris, did not view the world organization as an organ whose primary purpose was to keep Germany in her place. On this issue London's was a more flexible stance, based on historical as well as on political factors. France, intrinsically weaker than Germany, and with two recent German invasions still in mind, could ill afford such liberality. Caught between these two Great Powers Drummond had to show the greatest care.

Far greater caution had to be exercised in dealing with an anti-*status quo* power like Mussolini's Italy. Here, the problem was multiplied by Rome's creditable and omnipresent threat to leave the League. An active public stance by Drummond against the aggressive policies that Mussolini pursued whether in the Balkans, East Africa, or Europe in general, would have probably led, at the least, to a lack of Italien cooperation with the League unless Drummond were replaced as Secretary-General. And where would Drummond have acquired political support in any anti-Mussoloni stance? Certainly not from the Anglo-French who would have viewed his action as irresponsible since both States wanted only the smoothest relations with the Duce.

At the least, any public stance by Drummond would have destroyed the trust in his advice and judgement of the Foreign Office and the Quai d'Orsay and thus undermined his influence. Drummond was boxed in and his possibilities for action even behind the scenes was limited. Drummond never over-estimated the powers of his office or the influence that he could wield in world politics, to believe that any initiatives he took could be anything more than marginal in handling the Duce.

As for Germany, likewise an anti-*status quo* power, Drummond faced a problem which was different in form but similar in substance. Different in form, for Germany had been the loser in 1919. French suspicions of Germany, one might even say fears, were strong, and an appeal to Paris by Drummond might have given him the kind of political support that he could never have mustered against Italy. Drummond's position against Germany was far stronger than against Italy as was reflected in his comment to the Germans in 1929 "You are in the League, but not of the League." Though caught in a less rigid situation than with Italy, he was never foolish enough to lose sight of the fact that Germany as a Great Power had to be shown the kind of deference that she was entitled to. Germany could not be handled in the same manner as a Ruritania.

Though Drummond's relationship with the Foreign Office was intimate, he did not necessarily always agree with it, and on certain issues was diametrically opposed. Italy's policies in Albania, for example, are a case in point. In time, however, the Foreign Office realized that in some matters there was a mutuality of interests. For instance, it was to Britain's advantage to give Drummond access to Foreign Office information in order to assist the Secretariat in dealing with questions submitted to the Council. This led to an *ad hoc* arrangement whereby Drummond was allowed to examine confidential and secret Foreign Office documents, especially about questions of interest to the League.[19] This relationship was in many respects a symbiotic one, therefore, subsequent comments by former Secretariat associates during World War II that Drummond "was known or believed to be, to some extent" a British Government representative within the Secretariat and that he was "accustomed to consider" the British Foreign Secretary his only master were both unfair and a sad misreading, as well as an oversimplification of his complicated relationship with Whitehall.[20]

Aside from the Foreign Office, Drummond's contacts on a regular basis but in a more circuitous manner with the Quai d'Orsay, the Palazzo Chigi, the Gaimusho, and subsequently the Wilhelmstraße, were conducted through senior members of the Secretariat. They were the conduit between Drummond and the more important Members of the League. Of these Secretariat officials Drummond was probably closest to his French associates. Initially he was blessed with Jean Monnet. When Monnet resigned from the Secretariat – Drummond held Monnet's successor Joseph Avenol in low regard – his main contact with the Quai d'Orsay was Pierre Comert, the Director of the Press and Information Section of the Secretariat.

Next in importance, certainly initially, were Drummond's American associates like Arthur Sweetser in the Press and Information Section through whom he attempted to establish and maintain contact with the American Government. At first it was in order to influence the Senate's consent to the Versailles Treaty and with it the League Covenant. Subsequently, he used his American associates to maintain contact with pro-League or sympathetic elements in the United States. It was a kind of holding action which allowed American passions toward the League to cool. Who knew what the future might bring? This was an important consideration for as each year passed America's hostility toward the League diminished. Slowly Washington began to involve itself in the League's so-called non-political work or technical work; on rare occasions it involved itself in matters more political in nature, especially when it thought the League could be used to protect what it construed to be America's national interests: Liberia, Latin America, or the Far East, reaching its high point with the Manchurian crisis. Engaging America in the League, was a slow process, but by the time Drummond departed from Geneva and a new and friendlier administration under President

Roosevelt and Secretary of State Cordell Hull assumed the direction of American foreign policy, there was hope for optimism.

As for Japanese Secretariat officials, aside from being Drummond's conduit with Tokyo about Far Eastern matters and especially during the Manchurian crisis, he could use them to play a special role, namely, to investigate questions and engage in tasks that, if assigned to European members of the Secretariat, could have contributed to resentment and tension.

The Italian and German members of the Secretariat fell into a special category for Drummon in that during his tenure as Secretary-General both countries were basically anti-*status quo* powers. Both countries as well as their nationals in the Secretariat had to be handled with the greatest care and circumspection. This is not to say that Rome and Berlin were not consulted, as others were consulted on various political matters, or on who should be appointed to the Secretariat. However, the problem of split loyalty between the world organization they worked for, and their national States that all Secretariat officials grapples with was more a problem for the Italian and German members of the Secretariat than it was for other Secretariat officials.[21] To turn a phrase by French Foreign Minister Louis Barthou, though devoted to their own countries Italian and German members of the Secretariat did not know how to conciliate this devotion with international interests.[22]

The Secretariat, therefore, was one of Drummond's most important political tools, albeit behind the scenes; it was necessary for Drummond in his public role to disguise this fact and to propagate the myth of the non-political, impartial international civil service. To have done otherwise would have been impolitic in the extreme. With this in mind his selection of personnel for the upper echelons of the Secretariat was weighted toward nationals of the Great Powers keeping in mind the paramount rôle that they played in world affairs then - as now. The more powerful the State the greater would be Drummond's deference in accepting its nominations for possible Secretariat appointments, in consulting the State about the proposed candidates, and in accepting and acting upon the adivice and recommendations of the State concerned.

It was only years after his retirement that Drummond publicly admitted the political nature of the Secretariat,[23] an admission late in coming, but one that erases any idealistic notions that international civil servants are immune from the vagaries of world politics.

III. Conflict Resolution

Because of his limited powers under the Covenant and the nature of the international state system as it existed during his tenure as Secretary-General, Drummond's involvement in political issues was restricted to what he could do behind the scenes. He used the Secretariat, as we have seen, to assist him in this task. On the other hand, because of his aversion to public exposure he never addressed the Assembly in plenary session even though the rules of procedure allowed him to do so, nor did he use the annual report to the Assembly to discuss and focus international public opinion on major world problems - a procedure successfully used by the Secretaries-General of the United Nations. His annual report to the

Assembly was merely an enumeration of the world organization's activites for the previous year. Likewise, in the Council where he was entitled to sit, his comments were in substance those of a committee secretary.[24] Yet as guarded and discreet as Drummond was, in his political activites behind the scenes he was suspected in Geneva of playing „too active a rôle."[25] This suspicion of him required that he move with caution and was clearly reflected in the Assembly's early warnings to the Secretariat to curb its activities.[26]

How did Drummond actually operate behind the scenes in view of the fact that his political arsenal was virtually empty? Since the Council met periodically and the Assembly once a year, exept when there was a special session, Drummond was relatively free from the constant supervision that a national civil servant is generally subjected to. Accordingly, for the better part of any year Drummond had great room for manoeuvre, and for the inception and direction of any political initiatives and actions he desired. He was assisted by the fact that under the Covenant he was, legally speaking, the hub of the League's administrative wheel. As the director of a large multinational staff whose most important responsibility was the continual surveillance of world events, Drummond was either willingly or unwillingly involved in discussions with Member States of the world organization concerning the use of the League's political procedures, its facilities or its staff. His reaction to these requests, the attitude he assumed, and what League resources or its organs he made available, quickly drew Drummond, like it or not, into a political whirlpool where his choices furthered the political drives and desires of one State against another. Though Drummond might rationalize his actions and moves on legal or administrative grounds, he was nevertheless involved in what were essentially political decisions. The Secretary-General's office was by its very nature unavoidably political.

Unlike his United Nations successors, Drummond never faced a cold war disguised in ideological garb, in a bipolar world. Neither did he experience the emergence of the so-called Third World which led the constituent organs of the Organization to delegate power and authority to the Secretary-General. Drummond was forced to act within narrower confines. Despite this he proved to be a master of invention. He was second to none as a ceaseless source of ideas, advice, recommendations, proposals, schemes and formulas. There were tendered not merely to the delegations assigned to Geneva, but to the involved Governments, or to those Governments not involved but intent on peacefully solving a particular question. Drummond's initiatives, as noted, were behind the scenes and to remove himself further as the originatior of a proposal he sometimes transmitted it through third parties, using among others, as already mentioned, the Secretariat.

There was of course an advantage to this secretive non-public approach and that was that if Drummond's proposal was unacceptable to either side, it did not exclude subsequent amendments or proposals. Since his endeavors did not drag Drummond into the public arena where public failure and public comments, especially by the concerned parties, might have led to an erosion of his position and the thwarting of additional probes he was allowed to continue his work. An added value to this behind-the-scenes approach was that it shielded Drummond if he committed mistakes of omission or commission. These mistakes, if exposed to public view, would habe damaged Drummond's own image and underminded the prestige of his office. The longer Drummond remained in office, the greater was the trust he inspired. The more experience he had, the greater was the consideration given to his initiatives. Certainly during the latter part of his Secretary-Generalship he could assume initiatives that would have been far more difficult to undertake in his earlier years.

One can of course criticize Drummond's approach as too timid. A greater public stance by a Secretary-General assumes that public political activity is more effective political activity in that it can influence, affect, or have an impact on other entities in world affairs. It also assumes that Drummond had a constituency which would support him. Drummond denied any such constituency. Even if he perceived such a constituency he would have had to weigh the advantages that might accrue from a public stance, against the disadvatages that might develop not only in the question he was grappling with, but also in his long term relationships with the State involved.

One may ask the question whether Drummond could convince someone by public acts if he could not convince him by private advice and discussions. This would be particularly true when he dealt with a permanent member of the Council. Indeed, lacking any control over armed forces he had little to lean on except the weak reed of world public opinion, the appeal to world morality, the norms of international law or the political support that might be forthcoming from some, but not all, the Member States of the Organization.

The public stances and actions of the United Nations Secretaries-General have of course been more dramatic than those of Drummond, but one may question whether in the long run or in the short run, they proved useful and practical. Their actions exposed them to public view, appeared to show favor, led to second guessing, and destroyed their usefulness as an impartial bridge between the contending States.

The real difficulty in appreciating Drummond's method of operations is that it is tedious, one might say undramatic. Executing the Secretary-General's office demands considerable self-control, the greatest discretion, endless imagination and energy, and a knowledge of international relations, as well as a knowledge – second to none of the Secretariat's technical experts – of the subject discussed. This mode of operation requires that you gain and hold the confidence of the other parties.

It is a method of operations that does not appeal to many investigators of the Secretary-General's office more swayed as they may be by dramatic public acts. For exactly these reasons Drummond is often compared less favorably to Hammarskjöld. Yet the postwar world of 1919, and one can even argue today's world, needs not Secretaries-General who claim the public's eye, but Secretaries-General who like Drummond are discreet, active behind the scenes, but still maintain the trust and confidence of the vast majority of the world' organizations's Member States, and especially the Great Powers. This approach might help heighten their influence and increase the possibilities for their admonitions and advice to be heeded, and conceivably, even to be followed. Like the British monarch the real value of the Secretary-General is his power, in private, to warn, advise and recommend. These were the qualities that made Drummond so effective a Secretary-General.

Though Drummond had no equivalent to Article 99 of the Charter which allows the United Nations Secretary-General to bring to the Security Council's attention any matter which may threaten the maintenance of international peace and security, in practice Drummond enjoyed just such a power. The discretion he exercised, and the trust placed in him by the League's membership made an Article 99 unnecessary, for he enjoyed the confidence of the Council's president. Drummond, therefore, quietly and effectively could influence the Council's president to have important political questions examined by the Council.

Drummond was too much of a realist to fall prey to the illusion that public political activities on his part could have a lasting impact on an imperfect world governed by imperfect men. His success as Secretary-General is mirrored in the fact that thought he was politically active behind the scenes, and though this was known and acquiesced to by the political world at Geneva and in the capital cities of Europe and Asia, when Drummond resigned as Secretary-General it was written that he was still greatly trusted and respected by the League's Member States. One would be hard pressed to make a similar statement of any of Drummond's successors.[27]

Notes

1 George W. Egerton, *Great Britain and the Creation of the League of Nations.* Chapel Hill, University of North Carolina, 1978. - *passim.*

2 PRO, CAB/23/42. See also David Lloyd George, *The Truth about the Peace Treaties.* London, Gollancz, 1938. - v. 1, p. 629.

3 Lord Robert Cecil, *All the Way.* London, Hodder and Stoughton, 1949. - p 150. See also Philip [Noël-] Baker, "The making of the Covenant from the British point of view", in: *Les origines et l'œuvre de la Société des Nations,* publié sous la direction de P. Munch par Rask-Ørstedfonden. Copenhague, Gyldendalske Boghandel, 1924. - v. 2, p. 41.

4 Philip [Noël-] Baker, *op. cit.* p. 41. See also Stephen M. Schwebel, *The Secretary-General of the United Nations.* Cambridge, Harvard University Press, 1952. - p. 4.

5 Philip [Noël-] Baker, *op. cit.* p. 41.

6 Jean Siotis, *Essai sur le Secrétariat international.* Genéve, Droz, 1963. - p. 61, 64. See also Minutes of a Meeting held in the Secretary-General's Room, 3 December 1919. LNA 1919-1927/40/2278/854 (R1569).

7 Interview with Philip Noël-Baker, 24 July 1971.

8 David Lloyd George, *op. cit.* v. l, p. 629.

9 [Talbot] to Hall, 18 December 1918 and the attached note by W[illiam] T[yrrell] to Cecil, 23 December [1918], as well as a minute by R[obert] C[ecil], 23 December 1918, Philip Noël-Baker Papers, PRO, FO 800/249, PRO, CAB/23/42, Cecil, *All the Way, op. cit.* p. 150.

10 PRO, CAB/23/42, Cecil, *All the Way, op. cit.* p. 150.

11 Cecil Diary, 10 January 1918, p. 7. Add. MS. 51131, Robert Cecil Papers, British Library, London. (Hereafter cited as BL).

12 Cecil Diary, 12 January 1919. p. ll, *ibid.* and Cecil, *All the Way, op. cit.* p. 150-151. Lord Robert Cecil, *A Great Experiment.* London, Jonathan Cape, 1941. - p. 89.

13 Lord Salter, *Memoirs of a Public Servant.* London, Faber and Faber, 1961. - p. 146. Lord Salter, "James Eric Drummond," *Dictionary of National Biography 1951-1960.* London, Oxford University Press, 1971. - p. 314. Raymond B. Fosdick, *The League and the United Nations after Fifty Years. The Six Secretaries-General.* Newtown, Conn. [privately printed] 1972. - p. 13 footnote; Arthur W. Rovine, *The First Fifty Years. The Secretary-General in World Politics 1929-1970.* Leyden, Sijthoff, 1970. - p. 24; Siotis, *op. cit.* p. 61.; F. Yeats-Brown, "The League of Nations. The Character of Sir Eric Drummond," *The Spectator,* 5 January 1929. p. 14.

14 James Barros, *Office without Power: Secretary-General Sir Eric Drummond 1919-1933.* Oxford, The Clarendon Press, 1979. - p. 7-19.

15 James Barros, *Betrayal from Within: Joseph Avenol, Secretary-General of the League of Nations, 1933-1940.* New Haven, Yale University Press, 1969. - p. 1-14.

16 Schwebel, *op. cit.* p. 4 (see note 4).

17 *Ibid.*, p. 3.

18 James Barros, *Office without Power op. cit.* p. 20-23.

19 *Ibid.*, p. 51-55, 310, 387, 392-394.

20 *Proceedings of the Exploratory Conference on the Experience of the League of Nations Secretariat, held in New York City on 30 August 1942 under the auspices of the Carnegie Endowment for International Peace.* [mimeographed] Washington, 1942. p. 48-50.

21 Barros, *Office without Power, op. cit.* p. 60-74.

22 Barros, *Betrayal from Within, op. cit.* p. 179.

23 Schwebel, *op. cit.*, p. 10.

24 *Ibid.*, p. 6. *Proceedings of the Conference on Experience in International Administration, held in Washington on 30 Janurary 1943 under the auspices of the Carnegie Endowment for Intermational Peace,* [mimeographed] Washington, 1943. p. 11. See also Egon F. Ranshofen-Wertheimer *The International Secretariat: A Great Experiment in International Administration.* Washington, Carnegie Endowment for International Peace, 1945. - p. 38-39.

25 Hugh R. Wilson, *Diplomat Between Wars.* New York, Longmans, Green 1941. - p. 213.

26 Felix Morley, *The Society of Nations.* Washington, The Brookings Institution, 1932. - p. 322-323. Howard-Ellis, *The Origin, Structure and Working of the League of Nations.* London, Allen and Unwin, 1929. - p. 197-198.

27 The wartime Acting Secretary-General, Sean Lester, was *sui generis.* Barros, *Office without Power, op. cit.* p. 383-402.

Toward the Bruce Report: the economic and social programs of the League of Nations in the Avenol era

Martin D. Dubin
Northern Illinois University

The report of the Special Committee on the Development of International Co-operation in Economic and Social Affairs was issued on August 22, 1939, and came to be known as the Bruce Report. The Report has attracted considerable attention as a document encapsulating the finest achievements and highest ideals of the League of Nations.[1] The report distilled the League's experience in the growing global interdependence of the late 1930's and described new international machinery for the development and expansion of the League's social, economic, and humanitarian activities. While the proposed reforms came on the eve of the Second World War, too late be implemented, ideas contained in the Bruce Report were adapted by those drafting the United Nations Charter. These ideas were reflected in the provision for an Economic and Social Council.[2]

Joseph Avenol, the second Secretary-General of the League of Nations, properly is regarded as the father of the Bruce Report.[3] His career has been seen retrospectively through a haze of antagonisms and resentments associated with his last years in office.[4] Some critics have suggested that the Bruce Report represented an about-face by Avenol who previously had subordinated, constrained, and discouraged the development of the League's so-called "non-political" programs. It has been claimed that the Bruce reforms might have worked had they been introduced before the League's collapse in 1936 and that, when introduced in 1939, they were designed to transform the League into an ethically neutral organization to which the totalitarians might return.[5] Avenol, in any event, has been accused of sponsoring the Bruce Report geared to abandoning the League's main responsibility as an instrument for international political adjustment.

Avenol was indeed a conservative French nationalist who moved in the wake of British, and to a lesser degree, because of shifting orientations in Paris, French policies to minimize antagonisms with Tokyo, Berlin, and Rome. Nonetheless, to interpret his initiative in developing the Bruce Report as an act of appeasement, or as a device to accomodate the totalitarians, would be wrong.

The Bruce Report stemmed from three major developments of the 1930's after the failure of the July 1933 London Monetary and Economic Conference: efforts by senior officials in the League of Nations Secretariat to improve the League's machinery for economic diplomacy;[6] a growing global interdependence fueled by the recognition in national governments that certain socio-economic problems could not be overcome solely by national action; and the promotion of a social welfare ethic in the programs of the League by the former Australian prime minister, Stanley M. Bruce.[7]

Discussion of the Bruce Report has been colored by the League's jargon which described economic, social, and humanitarian programs, not immediately associated with the peaceful settlement of disputes, coercive sanctions, or disarmament, as "technical" and "non-political" activities. These programs, however, were recognized as having a distinctly political character within domestic contexts, and were treated by government representatives in League advisory committees as having important dimensions of political sensitivity.

In the early postwar years the League of Nations sponsored a myriad of programs concerned with relief and resettlement of refugees, commerce, health, transit and communications, finance, the opium trade, prostitution, child welfare, and intellectual cooperation. William E. Rappard, the Swiss internationalist, in 1927 described the League "as the great administrative agency for the promotion of voluntary international cooperation . . . . The technical advisory committees, which multiply in number and specialize in function year to year are the structural expression of a world need."[8]

A major shortcoming existed, however, in the League's programs in economics and finance. The Americans and British instrumental in drafting the League of Nations Covenant in 1919 rejected French and Italian proposals bestowing on the new organization substantial responsibilities of an economic nature. As a result, Article 23 (e) of the Covenant simply stipulated that League members agree "to make provisions to secure . . . . equitable treatment for the commerce of all Members of the League."[9]

During the complicated and acrimonious negotiations on reparations, war debts, trade restrictions, tariffs, and currency exchange in the 1920's, economic nationalists, rejecting a liberal international economic order, excluded the League from a central role.[10] The League's Financial Committee, composed of treasury and central bank officials and private bankers, helped reconstruct Austrian and Hungarian finances, and finance the resettlement of Greek and Bulgarian refugees. It provided technical assistance to Albania, Danzig, Estonia, Portugal, and the Saar; helped float various loans; developed an international convention to suppress counterfeiting of currencies; studied the fluctuation in the value of gold and problems of double taxation; and advised the Council on financial assistance to states victims of aggression. In 1928 its activities led to the creation of a Fiscal Committee and a Committee of Statistical Experts. The League's Economic Committee concluded commercial conventions dealing with customs formalities, the protecion of industrial property, bills of exchange, arbitration and whaling. It studied the problem of access to raw materials, methods of competition, and equitable treatment of foreign firms.

Behind these advisory committees was the Secretariat's Economic and Financial Section (divided in 1931 into separate Economic Relations and Financial Sections) which provided information, analysis, drafting and liaison services. A special unit was the Economic Intelligence Service, created to continue statistical reporting and analysis provided at the Paris Conference by the Supreme Economic Council. Together these committees and the corresponding Secretariat section(s) were known as the Economic and Financial Organization.

The League's record in economics and finance, however, was limited. Following the Wall Street crash in October 1929, Secretary-General Sir Eric Drummond concluded that there had been over-optimism about the possibility of international commercial agreements.[11] He thought that the League's very limited results "inevitably compel the conclusion that the League is endeavouring, in economic matters, to go faster and further than the great majority of countries either desire or find possible." Subsequently, as economic nationalism intensified the League's Commission of Enquiry for European Union and a variety of intergovernmental conferences failed.

The failure of the economic and financial advisory bodies was blamed by some League partisans on their lack of connection with the centers of national power. They believed that if the League's agencies were tied more directly into national economic decision-making centers their advice would be more palatable to governments. To rectify the perceived defect, Giuseppe Bottai, the Italian Minister of Corporations, proposed to the Twelfth Assembly in September 1931 that national economic councils be associated closely with the League.[12] Sir Arthur Salter, a distinguished British economist who recently had retired as director of the Economic and Financial Section, endorsed this idea which proved unworkable.

Another victim of economic nationalism was the League's Communications and Transit Organization.[13] International conferences at Barcelona in 1920 and Geneva in 1923 had produced general conventions to facilitate land and water transit and to promote the arbitration of disputes. A third conference in 1927, however, yielded only modest results, and a fourth in 1931 ground to a halt with little accord. When in mid-1933 the London Monetary and Economic Conference also failed, most immediately because the United States would not collaborate on currency stabilization, Avenol and his associates concluded that major international conferences are clumsy instruments for complex negotiations and that League advisory bodies, linking responsible and technically competent national government ministers in functional committees, might work better.

In January 1934 the League of Nations was in deep trouble. The depression was taking its toll; the World Disarmament Conference in 1932-33 and the London Monetary and Economic Conference in July 1933 had failed; the League had not invoked sanctions against Japan for aggression in Manchuria; Japan and Germany had renounced League membership; and Mussolini had demanded radical change in the Covenant.

The League was reeling from these setbacks. The new Secretary-General, Joseph Avenol, an expert in international finance, who served from 1923 to mid-1933 as deputy Secretary-General, had recently reorganized the League's Secretariat. Now he sought to reform the League's committees. With authorization from the Council, Avenol in the summer of 1934 prepared a lengthy report describing and comparing the membership, terms of office, and operating rules of the committees.[14]

The Assembly on September 26, 1934 recommended that the Council submit Avenol's report to Member Governments for comment and to "a suitable body" for study.[15] In December-January 1934/35 a Secretariat committee chaired by Deputy Secretary-General Massimo Pilotti, suggested that reforms be limited to the League's advisory committees in communications and transit, economics, finance, health, intellectual cooperation, narcotics, and social questions.[16] Pilotti's committee focused on the advisory committees in economics, finance, and transit which for historical reasons had fragmented or overlapping jurisdiction, but no authority to innovate, and no way to coordinate their efforts. Members of Pilotti's committee realized that the main defect actually existed in the system for guiding and coordinating the advisory committee members and approved their reports, but also determined their agendas and controlled their communications with governments. In fact, the Council was composed of foreign ministers and diplomats disinterested in economics. The Assembly supervised these bodies through its Second Committee, an organ overshadowed by political forums, and whose participants often lacked instructions, knowledge, and time.

Pilotti's committee offered various remedies. It proposed that each advisory committee appoint an executive committee composed of government officials to function between its sessions and to develop ideas which might be adopted, subject to Council approval. Alternatively, the League might hold triennial conferences to develop "a plan of study" to guide the committees and Secretariat and to instruct the Council as to the make-up of the advisory committees.

Alexander Loveday, director of the Financial Section, doubted the advisability of creating multiple executive committees with no function other than emitting ideas.[17] He preferred that the Assembly should appoint "certain of their members or substitute experts . . . to consider and co-ordinate reports" and "to consider and report upon the organisation and functioning of committees." Such a body, with expertise and time for reflection, should be joined by representatives of each advisory committee. Avenol's response to Loveday is unknown, but he commented that triennial conferences, while superficially attractive, left much to be desired.[18]

The Secretariat committee did not produce an accepted formula for directing and coordinating the advisory committees, but it did highlight the problem. The Council on January 19, 1935 appointed a committee to study Avenol's report.[19] This committee with former Under Secretary-General Bernardo Attolico, the Italian ambassador to the USSR, as chairman, and Sir Arthur Salter, as rapporteur, met in Geneva from 12-18 June 1935.[20] According to Vladimir D. Pastuhov, of the Central Section - Avenol's secretariat within the Secretariat - who had aided the Secretary-General in preparing his 1934 report and who drafted Pilotti's committee-report, the remarks of Secretariat directors "were not recorded even in the confidential minutes of the committee" so as to promote "the frankest and most detailed information possible."[21] Not surprisingly, they aimed their sharpest blows at the Council and Assembly. Pastuhov, who was present, notes that members of the committee were "struck by these observations," which many of them shared.

Avenol, like members of his staff, blamed the Council and Assembly. His prescription, like theirs, was to create new planning mechanisms separate from those agencies exercising ultimate authority. He feared, however, that if they were composed of national officials, they would become stalemated.

Salter denied that the basic problem was structural. He believed the absence of results, in the main, reflected the limits of the willingness of governments to cooperate. he favored, nonetheless, reform aimed at bringing government ministries into more effective collaboration with League committees. This might be accomplished through special Council sessions attended by economics and finance ministers, or by a Council committee of ministers, including even those of non-Council and non-Member States.

In a draft report on June 21 Salter called for improved government representation and "more adequate discussion" in the Second Committee.[22] After Second Committee meetings, the Council each year should arrange for a Council committee to develop a program in economics, finance, and transit and to allocate specific tasks to existing advisory committees or *ad hoc* ones. The Council committee should not be limited to representatives of governments in the Council, but should include those of countries of special importance. The United States, in particular, should be invited to participate. The members of this committee would be functional ministers, for example, in finance, commerce, and agriculture, depending each year upon the committee's agenda. Since public opinion was important, provision also should be made for soliciting the views of non-governmental associations and highly qualified persons outside of governments.

Attolico, however, argued that proposals to change the Council exceeded the committee's competence. He conceived instead a new body intermediate between the Council and the advisory committees. The Secretary-General's concern about committees composed of officials could be obviated by giving the organ such broad responsiblities that governments would appoint ministers with authority rather than civil servants to engage in the tasks of planning, coordination, and control. Beneath such an intermediate body, instead of the existing advisory committees in economics, finance, and transit, should be *ad hoc* expert committees with specific tasks.

A compromise was embodied in the committee's report of 5 August 1935.[23] It recommended that reform of the advisory bodies rest upon the premise that the Council and Assembly should "remain constitutionally in supreme control." The report distinguished between "general plans, co-ordination, direction and control," which it labelled "governmental functions" and "executive work" - implementation - the task of the advisory committees. It noted that while the governmental functions could be accomplished at sessions of the Council composed of economics and finance, rather than foreign, ministers such a recommendation exceeded its frame of reference. However, "suitable arrangements" would have to be devised to develop a program of work, and to coordinate and supervise its execution.

The Second Committee in September 1935 recognized a need for general regulations governing League committees, but rejected a new coordinating body alluded to obliquely in the committee's report.[24] The rapporteur for the Second

Committee declared that it "would be premature to lay down the principles of a reorganization" in the League's methods for considering economic issues, but that the League already possessed within existing organs means for ensuring "the necessary initiatives and coordination." The Council might hold sessions attended by economics and finance ministers, organize a Council committee for coordination, or appoint a committee of experts to discuss particular problems. The Second Committee might also be strengthened "by a methodical preparation of its discussions" on the part of participating governments. The question of new machinery would "remain open" for future consideration.

Pastuhov, rather surprisingly, reports that while many people in the Secretariat "were somewhat reluctant" to accept the views of the Second Committee they "reflected the personal attitude of the Secretary-General, who succeeded in convincing some important members of the Second Committee . . . that the opinions in question were sound."[25] By his account, it was Avenol, despite having recognized the need for new machinery, who rather strangely sabotaged the reform. In any event, Avenol not only worked avidly in September 1937 to implement the reform submitted to the Second Committee in 1935, but he sponsored an even broader reform in 1939. In 1934/35 the reform was conceived as a means for improving the League's efficiency. In 1937 it was designed to compensate for the League's political collapse. When in 1939 the reform, covering all the League's social as well as economic activities was finally approved, the Second World War not only threatened the foundering League, but the very existence of the whole international order.

The Assembly routinely approved the actions of the Second Committee, and in January 1936 in Council, following suit, adopted detailed regulations.[26] The Council thereby set in motion a process for restructuring the League's advisory committees that would occupy the remainder of the interwar period.

The initial phase of committtee reform in the Avenol era coincided with a growing challenge to the *status quo* by Hilter and Mussolini. In June 1936 the Assembly began a long and painful assessment of the League's future.[27] Governments were asked to communicate their views on what euphemistically was called "the application of the principles of the Covenant." This extended and futile exercise achieved only an Assembly agreement in September 1938 proposing to remove from the Covenant references to the peace treaties ending the First World War.[28]

In October 1936, after the start of the Spanish Civil War had further complicated international politics, the American consul in Geneva, Prentiss B. Gilbert, reported to Washington that "[o]utstanding League proponents," including "rather important Britishers and Americans," had told him that the League as it existed "is absolutely finished."[29] They proposed totally divorcing "all its technical and humanitarian activities . . . from its political status." The political League would continue, but "there would be three separate Leagues, the third being, in addition . . . the International Labor Organization." They felt that "a movement in this direction must begin quickly," although "[a]t the present time, they are completely at sea as to how these ideas may be advanced."

Gilbert did not identify the sources of these ideas, but on 25 July 1940, in a telegram announcing his resignation as Secretary-General, Avenol would assert "[u]ntil September 1936, I believed that certain inevitable reforms would enable [the] League [of] Nations, in order that its task might be successful, [to] regroup forces which were moving away from it. Since that time amendment of [the] Covenant has formed part of [the] agenda of [the] League of Nations, but [the] situation has constantly deteriorated."[30]

This telegram, written under great stress, perhaps should not be taken literally. In September 1936 a Committee on the Applications of the Principles of the Covenant was indeed considering Covenant amendments. The role of Avenol on these efforts remains unknown, but it is not unlikely that he and his associates, among them Alexander Loveday and Arthur Sweetser, the American enthusiast who had been since the League's day its chief liaison agent in the United States, entertained the thought of transforming the League along the lines reported to Washington. The trail is obscure, but in September 1937 proposals by Avenol and his staff, similar to those made in 1934/35, were espoused freely in London and Paris and at the Eighteenth Ordinary Session of the League Assembly.

Widespread human misery caused by the economic depression altered domestic politics in many States, leading to new and unprecedented measures to promote domestic social welfare. Designed to ameliorate unemployment, hunger, poor housing, and a host of associated social ills, these measures soon found expression on the social and economic agendas of the League of Nations. Many of the League's social programs of the 1920's dealing with narcotics, prostitution, slavery, and aspects of its concern for child welfare were essentially technical, regulatory, and negative. They functioned independently of each other. The new programs of the 1930's had a positive cast and required an integrative approach which led to new organizational forms, including clearing houses and technical assistance programs.

The development of a welfare ethic in the League of Nations in large measure can be traced to the ideas of Stanley M. Bruce. As Australia's Resident Minister and then High Commissioner in London, Bruce represented one of the world's major agricultaral economies. At the London Monetary and Economic Conference in 1933, he rejected the orthodox suggestion that producer prices should be increased through agreements restricting production.[31] Bruce preferred, instead, to reduce trade barriers, arguing that lower barriers would increase the markets for agricultural products in industrial countries, reduce the poverty of the agrarian countries, enhance their demand for industrial goods, and thereby provide the basis for breaking the back of the depression.

The London Conference did not embrace Bruce's approach, but he persisted, stating in mid-1935 that Europe should not restore her pre-1914 agricultural self-sufficiency.[32] Such a parochial policy would ignore overseas states, encourage inefficient European agriculture, and keep European living standards low. Rather, Bruce proposed, with wide support at the Assembly in September 1935, that the League recognize the simultaneous existence of millions of hungry people and huge agricultural surplusses.[33] Citing a study of nutrition by the League's Health Organization, he asserted that League technical organizations should collect data on national efforts to improve nutrition, and that a committee of agricultural, economic, and health experts should be appointed to report their findings on "the agricultural and economic effects of improved nutrition." The Assembly approved this program, and the Council appointed a Mixed Committee on the Problem of Nutrition which produced an extremely influential series of publications in 1936 and 1937 linking poverty, poor eating habits, bad health, and early death.[34] It sponsored studies establishing standards of "good nutrition," inspired the formation of many national nutrition committees, and stimulated international meetings of these national committees.

The League's welfare orientation was manifested in other ways. The British Government observed to the Attolico-Salter committee in June 1935 that the League's Advisory Commission for the Protection and Welfare of Children and Young People was both too negative and too limited in scope. A redefined and reorganized committee should "give more time to the constructive side of its work and less to the negative side."[35]

Shortly thereafter, a new Advisory Committee on Social Questions emerged.[36] It changed the previous focus on child welfare to one of family welfare and developed new programs for the training of social workers and social work administration as well as for the rehabilitation of prostitutes and released prisoners, penal reform, and assistance to indigent foreigners. In 1938 the Committee was mandated by the Assembly to develop programs jointly with the Health Organization and the International Labor Organization.

In 1931 the Health Organization sponsored a European Conference on Rural Hygiene at which a staggering array of topics was examined,[37] thus illustrating the League's new role as a clearing house and coordinator for social programs. The success of this conference led to similar conferences, e. g. a Pan-African Health Conference in 1935 and an Inter-Governmental Conference of Eastern Countries on Rural Hygiene in 1937. By 1937, moreover, plans were well-developed for a conference conceived on the vastly broader theme of European rural life. With this redefinition, sponsorship passed from the Health Organization to a widely-based *ad hoc* Secretariat committee.

In 1936 the League Assembly recognized human housing as a global problem requiring international attention.[38] Responding to Bruce, the Assembly in 1937 agreed to study ways for improving the living standards of the world's impoverished people and averting future economic depressions, and in 1938 expanded its inquiries into the socio-economic aspects of agriculture.

The League's failure to overcome economic nationalism became an increasingly serious problem as the international political climate deteriorated. Paul von Zeeland, prominent economist, banker, and Belgian Prime Minister, in his capacity as president of the League Assembly, on 4 July 1936 called attention to the danger in dealing with the political crisis by "relying entirely upon political methods and neglecting economic considerations."[39] Van Zeeland pointed to "an increased danger" of Hitler and Mussolini's elaborate currency exchange controls which were enmeshing the dependent economies of Central and Southern Europe.

Pietro Stoppani, director of the League's Economic Relations Section, shared van Zeeland's concern.[40] Stoppani feared that the continued drift inevitably would lead to war, expecially since Germany's autarchy rested on rearmament. His program for currency stabilization and trade liberalization, bridging the prevailing views in Paris, London, and Washington, was discussed in the Economic and Financial Committees, setting the stage for a radical devaluation of the French franc on 26 September 1936.[41] With the Seventeenth Assembly in session, the French action was announced as part of a tripartite alignment of American, British, and French currencies. It was hailed as a major breakthrough. British Foreign Secretary Anthony Eden, readily acknowledging the influence of economic factors on peace, and as a gesture to the Germans, called for an impartial inquiry regarding equal commercial access to raw materials.[42]

The Assembly called on all States to promote the elimination to trade barriers and exchange controls, in turn making possible durable and stable economic relations, expanded trade, prosperity, and improved living standards. Bruce proposed, as a possible negotiating forum, a committee composed of members of the Economic and Financial Committees and of representatives of non-Member States. Discussions in the corridors, however, led to another tactic.[43] To assuage Hitler, it was agreed that Great Britain and France should invite van Zeeland to undertake a private diplomatic mission outside the League. He was to consult the major powers and others with a view to restoring international economic health.

The Assembly also called for an inquiry into the question of "equal commercial access for all nations to certain raw materials."[44] This study was to be undertaken with "the collaboration of the principal States, whether Members or non-Members of the League, having a special interest in the matter." It was to be accomplished through a committee "composed in suitable proportion" of members of the Economic and Financial Committee and of "other qualified persons, irrespective of nationality." On 26 January 1937 the Council formed such a committee, but Germany and Italy would not cooperate. Indeed, Hitler in November 1936 entered into an "anti-Comintern pact" with Japan.[45] During the next months, Hitler and Mussolini condemned the "haves," criticized the territorial *status quo*, and defended their economic policies. Eden, backed by French Premier Leon Blum, deplored this polarization and made repeated overtures for political and economic reconciliation. Some German spokesmen professed a readiness to discuss abandoning autarchy, reaching an agreement on arms, and providing for Germany's return to a reformed League. A precondition, however, was colonial realignment, which at the time the British were unprepared to concede.

By way of contrast, U. S. Secretary of State Cordell Hull on 10 February 1937 asserted that an economic settlement would pave the way for a political settlement.[46] On 24 February 1937 Bruce sounded the same note at Birmingham, and on 1 March 1937 he wrote to Avenol, stating that it would be impossible to solve Europe's political problems without economic solutions.[47]

Bruce also offered a memorandum, drafted by his economic adviser Frank L. McDougall, which was different "from the usual proposals for a frontal attack" upon trade barriers. This memorandum contained suggestions for expanded technical assistance and socio-economic programs. Too vague for implementation, a revised version of it was discussed subsequently in the Economic Committee which endorsed the objective of improved living standards.[48]

In July 1937 Bruce furnished U. S. officials with notes which would "guide his attitude" at the next League Assembly.[49] Bruce's general position was that political problems would run into difficulties of solution and that delegations should "give special prominence to economic issues" in their Assembly speeches. In presenting a picture of the League "actively concerned to secure a general improvement in human welfare through practical economic measures," there "might well be . . . a greater spirit of cooperation than has existed for several years." In short, if universality of membership was "an essential to progress toward peace" an active interest in economic reconstruction was the best way by which this could be furthered. "Economic appeasement" would, in fact, lead to "economic disarmament," which, in turn, should ease political tensions, thereby rendering major political tasks feasible.

For months van Zeeland's mission remained on a back-burner. He was preoccupied by internal Belgian politics and by Anglo-Belgian negotiations to revise the 1925 Locarno guarantees. During van Zeeland's mission exploring the possibility of economic settlement, King Leopold of Belgium, on 21 Juli 1937, proposed that the major states form a new international organization for direct negotiations outside the League. Given Japan's renewed attack upon China in the late summer of 1937, van Zeeland's lack of success, and Leopold's initiative, Avenol proposed that the Economic and Financial Organization be reorganized along the lines suggested by the Attolico-Salter committee in 1935 – i. e., creating an "autonomous," sometimes labelled "independent," mechanism amenable to the cooperation of non-Member States.[50] Avenol's overture coincided with a report by Eden's assistant, Viscount Cranborne, that there were "evidently very great" possibilities of collaboration with respect to a wide range of matters with non-Member States.[51]

In describing the proposed reforms, Loveday and others spoke of an Economic and Financial Organization whose structure would be similar to those of the League's Communications and Transit Organization and the International Labor Organization.[52] The idea was to replace the Council and Assembly's Second Committee as directing organs in economics and finance, and to substitute an intermediate body in which Member and non-Member States would participate as equals in triennial conferences.

The British and French were sceptical, and their doubts were reinforced after inquiries were made in the United States and Brazil.[53] Finally, however, London and Paris reluctantly acceded to Avenol's view that the Assembly should invite the Council to create a study committee "with a view to extending the basis of international cooperation in economic and financial spheres."[54] The Assembly also recommended that a coordinator of the Economic and Financial Committees be appointed. Meanwhile, the League's feebleness was further demonstrated when in November 1937 a Nine Power Conference on the Far East was held in Brussels rather than Geneva.

In January 1938 Avenol clashed with the British and French Governments.[55] The Secretary-General was eager to appoint an "economic superman" and believed that Bruce's proposals to conduct the League principally as an economic organization provided the only hope of saving it. Avenol asked Bruce to accept the position of coordinator.[56] Bruce, "somewhat sceptical," felt that since he had been responsible for many items on the League's economic agenda, he "could not escape responsibility for their execution." The British were displeased that Avenol enlisted Bruce without first consulting them, and taking great care not to offend a senior Dominion statesman, they obtained Bruce's withdrawal.

The League's Council on 29 January 1938 created the study committee with Bruce as chairman.[57] Before Hitler's move into Austria forced a postponement of its meeting scheduled for 15 March, Bruce called again for "economic appeasement" and described a limited reform of the League's machinery. On or before 1 March 1938 he wrote to British Prime Minister Neville Chamberlain warning that a new economic depression would preclude the restoration of trade and increase the danger of a swing within the democracies toward communism or fascism.[58] Early economic action was necessary. To be successful, it would have to "appeal to the idealism and self-interest of the average man." Aspects of his program were before the Economic and Financial Committees, and he hoped that Chamberlain would place Great Britain in support of them.

Shortly thereafter, McDougall furnished the British Foreign Office with a brief Bruce would employ in discussing reform of the Economic and Finanical Organization.[59] It rested upon the idea that "owing to the present lack of prestige of the League in the political fields, it has become essential, if the League is to continue to function as an effective organization, that its work on the social, economic, and financial side should be recognized as being of great importance." Reforms should provide "a solid foundation" upon which after three or four years the League's political prestige "might gradually be re-established." Reform was needed to permit the League to function more effectively in the economic realm, and not as a means of enticing into the League non-Member States. Bruce doubted that the totalitarians would be interested and believed that the United States would be embarrassed by any "large alterations" designed to bring her into formal collaboration.

Bruce had in mind improving the Assembly as a forum and strengthening the Secretariat. He did not go so far as Avenol, for, as he would later indicate, he feared that an autonomous Economic and Financial Organization would weaken the League. To upgrade the Assembly, he proposed a new committee devoted exclusively to economic and social questions. Moreover, the Secretariat should develop, and the Economic and Financial Organization should approve, in advance of each Assembly, an annotated agenda to be used by governments in preparing their Assembly representatives.

The Australian also sought to strengthen the Secretariat by reuniting the Economic Relations and Financial Sections that had been given separate status upon Salter's retirement in 1931 and by adding to its competence in agricultural and social policy. He thought that the Secretariat should create a unit on agricultural policy and compensate for the absence in the Secretariat of persons knowledgeable about "the social effects of economic and financial policy . . . [or] the economic effects of social policy."

Even before Bruce's brief, the Secretariat was in retreat.[60] Loveday told American consul Howard Bucknell after the January Council meeting that reform proposals had stemmed from dissatisfaction with the Second Committee. He, however, was strongly opposed to the creation of an autonomous Economic and Financial Organization. In early March, the French noted that Rene Charron, Loveday's assistant, and one of Avenol's main liaison agents with Paris, had left the impression that the Secretary-General would not push his views; and Stoppani told an American diplomat that the Secretariat's views had "more or less crystallized" in favor of two proposals: an annual joint meeting of the Economic and Financial Committees directed by a "superchairman", and the creation of a separate Assembly committee devoted solely to economic and financial questions.[61]

These views represented a step back, one Avenol took with little grace and much impatience. Late in March, two weeks after Hitler destroyed Austria, the Secretary-General complained that it had been six months since the Assembly had authorized a study of the Economic and Financial Organization, and nothing had yet happened.[62] The small Central and Southern European states were confronted by an enormous German state economy and would be further reduced to satellites. The only "mechanism for collective organization" that might help them resided in the League's technical programs.

Late in April Avenol visited London where he discussed League reform with Sir Frederick W. Leith-Ross, the chief economic adviser to the British Government.[63] Recognizing there was no change of engaging Germany, Italy, or Japan, and claiming that he would not propose to reorganize for that purpose, the Secretary-General spoke of promoting greater interest in the League's work. Otherwise, the League would soon be dead, "and he, for his part, did not want to go on living with a corpse." It was the Council that presented a problem. In its place as directing organ the Secretary-General now proposed an Economic Council, or perhaps an economics subcommittee of the Council. These alternatives had been discussed in 1935.

Leith-Ross was discouraging. When the Secretary-General shortly thereafter met Eden's successor as British Foreign Secretary, Viscount Halifax, neither man raised the subject of League reorganization.[64]

The Committee on the Structure and Functions of the Economic and Financial Organization finally met in Geneva from 5–7 May 1938 with Bruce as chairman.[65] It consisted of Leith-Ross; Georges Brunet of France; Maurice Frere of Belgium, an assistant to van Zeeland; C. Parra-Perez, Venezuelan minister to Switzerland; and three permanent delegates to the League of Nations, Tytus Komarnicki of Poland, Karl I. Westman of Sweden, and H. Hume Wrong of Canada. Present, but unacknowledged in its minutes, was an American observer arranged for by the Secretariat.

Having little hope of expanding economic cooperation and fearing that the creation of an autonomous economic agency might seriously undermine the "political League," the committee embraced what were essentially Bruce's ideas in a report Loveday had drafted even before the committee met.[66] In that report, it was noted that while a major reform "at this moment . . . would . . . not promote . . . the object the Assembly had in mind," in recent times the work of the Economic and Financial Committees had changed. International conditions now were "less favourable to collective commercial agreements" than previously, but "the growing complexity of economic life" and "the application of science to economic activity" made an international center for information exchange and joint study increasingly important. The changing focus of the League's work warranted adaptation of its machinery. A single "guiding body" – a Coordination Committee – was desirable to initiate proposals, to allocate tasks among committees, and to coordinate work generally.

The committee also considered modifying the Secretariat, but Avenol deflected a proposal to merge its Economic Relations and Financial Sections.[67] The Committee settled instead for the Secretariat to be authorized to hire experts to serve in technical assistance programs and to keep in touch with Member and non-Member States, particularly overseas.

Describing the Assembly as "the mainspring of all the work of the Economic and Financial Organization," the panel recommended that an annotated agenda be distributed to governments prior to Assembly meetings, and that the Second Committee's jurisdiction be limited to questions of economics, finance, and transit and its meetings scheduled so as not to conflict with those of the Sixth (Political) Committee.

Avenol was not pleased by the stunted reform, despite Leith-Ross's claim that the Secretary- General, "who was at first very discontented," became "more or less satisfied."[68] Rumors of Avenol's unrest reached the press, and he was forced to deny that he intended to resign.[69] Loveday thought the report did not amount to much.[70] Arthur Sweetser also had other ideas. In April 1938 while visiting America to help arrange a League of Nations exhibit at the 1939 World's Fair in New York City, Sweetser spoke with Secretary of State Cordell Hull and President Franklin Roosevelt.[71] Roosevelt, welcoming a visit by the Secretary-General, advised Sweetser that the League should abandon its political activities, disband its Council, and concentrate on non-political questions. It may be doubted from the record Sweetser made of his talk with Roosevelt, that the American President had given the matter serious thought. However, by the end of May 1938 Sweetser clearly had concluded that the United States might join an "independent Economic and Financial Organization."[72] When Dr. James T. Shotwell of the Carnegie Endowment for International Peace, president of the American League of Nations Association, visited Geneva, Sweetser "doped" him on the subject. Loveday, believing that Shotwell was "inclined to agree" with Sweetser, concurred.

In any event, Avenol in May 1938 was eager to acquire Bruce's services as chairman of the Co-ordination Committee, but the Australian showed "a good deal of reluctance," and "was anxious to see what developed at the next Assembly before he took a decision."[73] Avenol persisted.[74] As a result, the Council on 13 May 1938 not only approved the Committee's recommendations but appointed Bruce.

As the Nineteenth Assembly approached, German pressure was mounting on Czechoslovakia. Resigned to the political disutility of the League, on 3 September Avenol expressed the view that it "must maintain its present vitality and prepare for the future in the study of technical problems."[75] The Assembly, meeting as Hitler was about to triumph at Munich, was an irrelevant sideshow. Political issues, such as the Spanish Civil War, were divisive, and Czechoslovakia was barely discussed. Much time was devoted to League reform but the representatives could agree only to remove from the Covenant references to the Treaties ending the First World War. The Second Committee was reorganized, but Bruce, who had been invited to lead its discussion was absent.[76]

Austria's destruction, the dismemberment of Czechoslovakia, and desertion of an increasing number of States portended severe financial trouble for the League. Soon there would be wholesale reductions in the Secretariat, charges that Avenol was using financial stringency as an excuse to purge liberal officials, and a streamlining of the League's organization. During this period the Economic Relations, Financial, and Communications and Transit Sections were merged under Loveday. Recognizing that political conditions were changing rapidly, Loveday considered keeping alive the Committee on the Structure and Functions of the Economic and Financial Organization.[77] The British, for their part, wanted to follow up Cranborne's 1937 report on collaboration with non-Member States.

On a "chance visit" to the Assembly, Claude D. Pepper, a member of the U. S. Senate Committee on Foreign Relations, observed that in Washington it was not widely recognized that non-Member States were able to participate in the League's non-political activities.[78] Subsequently a resolution unofficially drafted by an American group, including Leo S. Pasvolsky, of the Department of State, was introduced into the Assembly by the British and adopted without debate on 30 September 1938.[79] The resolution citing the League's collaboration with non-Members and Cranborne's report, invited "any comment or suggestion" non-Member governments would care to make on expanding collaboration. The Council concurred, and on 17 October 1938 Avenol sent copies of the resolution to an approved list of states.[80] Sweetser then headed for the United States where he lobbied vigorously for a positive reply.[81]

The post-Munich winter of 1938–39 was turbulent. At the Assembly, during the Munich crisis, the French, speaking of "economic appeasement," had proposed new economic programs.[82] In mid-January 1939, Avenol and the British emphasized the League's "non-political" activities. To Carlos A. Pardo, an Argentine on the League's Supervisory Commission, Avenol characterized the international situation as being one of a "demi-guerre", a half-war, in which the "ordinary principles of order and international law were suspended." Avenol thought, however, that the League should promote model social programs and emphasize the work of its new Economics, Finance, and Transit Section.[83] Almost simultaneously, Halifax no doubt partially for domestic political reasons, was assuring Lord Robert Cecil "that with the restriction of the political activities of the League, it is precisely these educational, social and humanitarian activities of the League that must be maintained and developed."[84]

Avenol's American campaign took a quantum leap forward when, on 2 February 1939, Cordell Hull, in an effusive public statement, responded to the

League's invitation.[85] The Secretary of State, in what Sweetser called "the first general opinion on the League expressed by the United States since 1920,"[86] noted the League's reaffirmation of its policy of collaboration with non-Members, praised the League's accomplishments, and pledged to "consider with a sympathetic spirit means of making its collaboration more effective."

Avenol received Hull's remarks with great satisfaction. They came, however, as Hitler and Mussolini were preparing new measures of aggression. Speaking with American consul Howard Bucknell on 10 March 1939, Avenol indicated that until "some sort of international conference" settled basic problems, "no long-range or final settlement was possible in Europe." The "present situation of relative calm," however, might change drastically. This was no time for the League to "make political pronouncements or to undertake political maneuvers."[87]

Hardly were these words recorded when "the relative calm" ended abruptly. On 14–15 March 1939 Hitler managed the secession of Slovakia from Czechoslovakia; on 26 March 1939 Mussolini threatened France; on 31 March 1939 Great Britain guaranteed Polish independence; and on 7 April 1939 Mussolini invaded Albania, which led to British guarantees to Greece and Rumania. On 28 April 1939 Hitler renounced the 1934 German-Polish Non-Aggression Treaty and the 1935 Anglo-German Naval Agreement. The period was marked by rumor, rancor, confusion, fear, and above all, maneuvering. After overtures by the Soviet Union for an anti-Nazi front, Stalin on 3 May 1939 dismissed Litvinov as foreign minister and veered in the direction of the August 1939 Nazi-Soviet pact.

Faced with increasing disorder, Avenol in mid-April 1939 cancelled a trip to the United States. Instead, on 2 May 1939 at the World's Fair in New York City, Adrianus Pelt, director of the Secretariat's Information Section and League commissioner at the Fair, read a prepared text in which Avenol observed that if the League had not been powerful enough to avert the existing world crisis, it had at least promoted international cooperation for orderly processes of change.[88] He described the League's varied contributions and cited Hull's pledge of continued collaboration. Washington_s support was reflected in speeches by various officials who praised the League's contribution to human welfare.

Late in May 1939 Europe was in a turmoil and war was in the air. Avenol used the occasion to strike for a reorganization of the League. At a private meeting of the Council on 23 May 1939 he regretted that "a period of serious tension" in Europe had prevented him from going to the United States, and reminded the Council about the September 30, 1938 Assembly resolution and Hull's response.[89] He was sure that Council "would not want the dialogue so happily inaugurated to be discontinued." Appropriate organizational measures were needed to make the proposed collaboration more effective, to develop and expand machinery for dealing with technical problems, and to promote active participation by all nations. To achieve speedy and effective action, he proposed that the Council set up "a very small committee of persons qualified by their experience" to report in September 1939.

Avenol was applauded by Lord Halifax, Wellington Koo of China, and Dr. Francisco Tudela, Peru's former foreign minister, who indicated that while Peru had given notice of her intention to leave the League, she was a "sincere and enthusiastic supporter" of its technical work. In a public session Halifax and French foreign minister Georges Bonnet recognized that their Governments had contributed to the League's political weakness. Halifax was glad that many non-Member States "are still fully alive to the great value" of the League's work "through the labour, health, social or technical organizations of the League." Perhaps hinting at what Avenol intended, he observed that the great end for which the League had been formed transcended "any organisation or outward form."

Subsequently, Avenol said that no precedent should bind the proposed committee, and that it should be entirely free to explore new ground and to suggest new solutions or procedures.[90] Avenol hoped that "in an entirely private and unofficial way" the committee would be able to sound out Washington so as to avoid conflict. If the next Assembly approved the committee's report, Avenol would visit the United States to confer with appropriate authorities.

On 27 May 1939, following Avenol's request, the Council authorized a committee of five to seven persons to be chaired by Bruce, who, in consultation with the Secretary-General, was to select the other members.[91] The whole procedure was extraordinary. The committee was created without a specific mandate or fixed composition solely on Avenol's initiative. It is not clear how much of what took place at the Council had been cleared in advance with Bruce who, through June 1939 feared that the Secretary-General's scheme "might kill the political side of the League without giving birth to anything new."[92]

Following the Council's action, Avenol wrote to Bruce indicating that the task was "urgent" and Bruce's services were "especially important."[93] Avenol hoped the committee would prepare a report "of a very wide nature" allowing the League to "escape the 'impasse'" confronting it. The committee's work might lead "to still more important developments in the whole field of international organization." Avenol was sure "[s]uch ideas are . . . moving in other minds as well as in mine." Bruce might consider Cranborne for the committee, and together they might consult Salter and Harold Butler, former director of the International Labor Organization.

Although Deputy Secretary-General Sean Lester would say that it was the Secretary-General's policy "to take only a slight initiative in making suggestions or otherwise guiding the Committee's deliberation," and Avenol himself would declare that he did not intend to urge his views on the committee, from the very start the Bruce Committee was Avenol's show.[94] Bruce's role remains obscure. Avenol had distinct ideas concerning the committee's membership and mission; but despite certain steps undertaken by the Secretariat, no Brazilian was appointed and Washington indicated that no American should be appointed to the Committee.[95] By July 5 the select committee consisted of Bruce; Butler; Tudela; Charles Rist, a preeminent French economist and president of the Scientific Institute for Economic and Social Research in Paris; Maurice Bourquin, a Belgian diplomat and professor at the University of Geneva; Kyriakos Varvaressos, one-time minister of finance, and deputy governor of the Bank of Greece; and "possibly a Scandianavian."[96] By July 20, Carl J. Hambro, president of the Norwegian Storting and chairman of the League's Supervisory Commission had been added.

In a briefing paper on 6 July 1939 Avenol suggested that the time had come to consider taking League reform "a stage further with good practical results."[97] Avenol only hinted at the specifics of reform. He thought two principles, both embodied in the International Labor Organization, appropiate: the directing bodies should be composed on "a non-political basis", and representation should be "functional." By the former, he meant that the directing bodies should contain in addition to government representatives, individuals appointed in their own right due to their expertise or special standing. By the latter, he was proposing the appointment of individuals who represented distinct economic, social or cultural interests for whom they could speak. Loveday and Salter had proposed just such representation in 1935. Loveday, in fact, argued that for the new organization to be effective, functional representation was essential "at the top of the whole structure as well as in the lower storeys.[98] Butler concurred in the need for functional representation.

The Secretary-General hoped the Assembly would approve a new organ which would inherit the function of overseeing the technical agencies, but retain constitutional links to the Council and Assembly, thus preserving their authority under the Covenant.[99] In subsequent negotiations the precise terms of contract between the League and non-Member States would be established.

Late in July, Avenol received a cautionary note from Royall Tyler, an American Secretariat member, warning that any desire to recruit the United States had better remain hidden.[100] Even at the next Assembly, "speakers had better keep buried in their bosoms any hopes they may entertain of the U.S.A., and in any case avoid using the words 'American membership.' There is still dynamite in them." A similar message had come earlier from Sweetser. Perhaps it was this sensitivity that motivated Sean Lester to indicate on July 19 that he did not think the Bruce Committee would take action that might embarrass the United States.[101]

Amidst growing European alarm, weeks before the start of the Second World War, the Bruce Committee met in Paris from 7 to 12 August 1939.[102] According to Pastuhov, Paris was selected as a way of insulating the committee from unwanted influences in the Secretariat and permanent government missions stationed in Geneva.

The committee's report issued on 22 August 1939, ten days after it adjourned, reflected Bruce's views on international processes and Avenol's proposals for reorganization of the League. It embodied a sophisticated discussion of global interdependence linked to the dynamics of domestic politics and major international tensions.

The Committee had four main objectives: a) to unite all social and economic activities under a single effective and representative agency; b) to recognize a growing interconnection among activities, and provide for "co-ordinating direction," c) to increase the "efficiency and vigour" of these activities through greater publicity, and d) to give non-Member States an opportunity to participate as equals in the direction and supervision of these activities.

Accordingly, Bruce and his associates proposed establishing a Central Committee for Economic and Social Questions to direct and supervise all relevant committees. Its initial membership would consist of twenty-four States chosen by the Assembly on the recommendation of its bureau; the committee itself would have the right to coopt no more than eight persons of special competence appointed in their own capacity. Subsequently, the Central Committee would select its own members and include non-Member States under terms to be negotiated with them.

The Central Committee for Economic and Social Questions would meet at least once a year, consider a budget presented by the Secretary-General, and draft an annual report which would lay out a program for budgetary credits. Since Assembly approval would be needed, non-Member States, in fact, would have remained on less than a fully equal footing.

The Bruce Report marked the culmination of Secretariat efforts during the Avenol era to reform the methods for directing and coordinating the technical advisory committees of the League of Nations, begun shortly after Avenol had assumed office as Secretary-General. Over the years, as the League's political fortunes declined, the proposed reforms acquired a changing significance. Originally, they were intended to improve the League's effectiveness in economic diplomacy; subsequently, they were intended also to help the League remain productive in the absence of political success; and ultimately, in the summer of 1939, they furnished the League with a means for survival as Europe was headed into a general war. The early reorganization proposals were designed to improve the League's ability to foster trade and to help stabilize financial relations. As the depression unfolded, the League's activities increasingly acquired a socio-economic cast reflected in the growth of its social and humanitarian programs. The Bruce Report, therefore, provides a benchmark by which may be measured the changes in conception and program of international economic and social cooperation through the League of Nations during the 1930's.

The Bruce Report was printed in English, French, Spanish, Portuguese, and Norwegian with the intention of obtaining wide publicity, but its timing could hardly have been worse.[103] McDougall, in sending copies to the U.S Department of State on August 30, admitted that it was by no means easy to think about matters other than "war or no war."[104] For Sweetser, however, while the world was "trembling on the verge of war," the report met "every possible American difficulty," and furnished the United States with a practical way of showing "our real faith and goodwill vis-a-vis peace and international co-operation."[105]

Hitler's invasion of Poland on 1 September 1939 caused scheduled meetings of the League's Council and Assembly to be postponed, yet Avenol was determined to keep the League alive and to implement the Bruce reforms.[106] The Assembly was to meet on 4 December 1939, but it was decided instead to reconvene the Fourth (Budgetary and Administrative) Committee of the Nineteenth Assembly, which in October 1938 had not formally adjourned. While legally tenuous, Avenol saw this arrangement – the Fourth Committee reconstituting itself as the Second Committee – as a means for enacting the Bruce reforms. Without the proposed Central Committee, he believed, "the League might as well close down."[107]

On 30 November 1939 the USSR invaded Finland, and on 3 December the latter called on the League's Council and Assembly to condemn Soviet aggression. The Fourth Committee, meeting between 4–12 December 1939, gingerly worked through its agenda avoiding political controversy, but decided it could approve portions of the Bruce Report on financial controls, if the Assembly approved the report as a whole.[108] On 11 December the Assembly convened to hear the Finnish appeal and, named a special committee to review the Bruce Report.[109]

Since its appearance the Bruce Report had attracted sympathetic interest in the U.S Department of State.[110] The approach of the 1940 presidential election, however, rendered it unlikely that the United States would become more closely associated with the League. In Great Britain, where attention was riveted on the war, Bruce's recommendations were not actively considered until Philip Noel-Baker, a Labour M.P. and former Secretariat member, proposed in the House of Commons on 21 November that they be enacted so that the League might be in a position to help solve problems at the war's end.[111] British Under-Secretary of State for Foreign Affairs, R.A. Butler, acknowledged Noel-Baker's idea as constructive and "worthy of our earnest consideration." On 28 November Prime Minister Neville Chamberlain also praised the Bruce Report. He wanted to see the League's work in economic and social collaboration "extended very considerably."[112]

The Bruce Report also had come to the attention of the Emergency Committee of the Governing Body of the International Labor Organization which was dismayed by the proposal to create a new League organ intruding into its "sphere of action.'[113] John G. Winant, Director of the Organization, sought and obtained from Avenol prior to the Assembly assurances that the autonomy and competence of the labor body would be respected.[114]

The Assembly's special committee chaired by Bourquin met on 12–13 December 1939. The idea of a Central Committee for Economic and Social Questions was supported warmly and opposed by none, but four concerns were manifested: that the Bruce reforms cover humanitarian, health, and social questions as well as cooperation in economics and finance; that respect be shown for the autonomy and competence of the International Labor Organization; that adequate provision be made for functional representation; and that the proposed Central Committee, in supervising the League's work in narcotics control, not undermine the existing system. The last issue was the subject of critical observations after the Assembly by the United States and Canada and subsequently by Canada, China, and Switzerland at a meeting of the Advisory Committee on Traffic in Opium and Other Dangerous Drugs in May 1940.[115]

After extensive discussion, the British introduced a resolution approving the Bruce reforms as "experimental" and observing that the League's economic, financial, and social activities should, despite current conditions, continue in as "efficacious a way and on as broad a basis as possible." The Committee accepted an Australian amendment, eliminating the word "experimental" and proposing other slight changes, and the resolution was approved.[116]

In the evening of 13 December, the Assembly's General Committee proposed creating an "Organizing Committee of representatives from Australia, Belgium, the United Kingdom, France, the Netherlands, Norway, Portugal, Switzerland, Turkey", and "a Latin American country to be designated as soon as possible."[117] This committee was to establish the principles governing the choice of the eight persons to sit on the Central Committee and to establish contacts with non-Member States. On December 14, the Assembly approved the resolution of Bourquin's committee and the slightly divergent report of the General Committee. Loveday noted that the Bruce reforms passed the Assembly "with the greatest ease" and with "a support which, in view of . . . Finland, was surprisingly enthusiastic."[118]

The actions of the Assembly in expelling the USSR and approving the Bruce Report raised spirits in the Secretariat. Speculating about the future, Avenol, at the end of December 1939, thought the Central Committee would acquire broad support and that the new structure would strengthen the roles of the Secretariat and of the Secretary-General.[119]

Meanwhile, there were more immediate concerns. The Latin American seat on the Organizing Committee originally had been offered to Argentina which had declined for political reasons.[120] By mid-January, when these reasons had disappeared, Argentina became a member of the Organizing Committee. However, the biggest catch remained the United States, whose officials had been privately and unofficially encouraging. Shortly after the Assembly adjourned, Sweetser wrote to Henry Grady, chairman of the League's Economic Committee, who recently had been named a U.S. Assistant Secretary of State, describing the reform as by "far and away the greatest change in the history of the League."[121] It provided for participation of non-Members "on complete equality with all other States and without any political implications whatsoever."

On 28 December 1939, Sweetser reported the "gratifying news" that Grady had "spoken highly of the Report and had said that the Government was anxious to support it."[122] As it turned out, this sentiment, shared by Hull and the President himself, represented a preference rather than a policy. On 19 February 1940 Hull explained that the United States had followed the Bruce proposals "with great interest" and was in "complete sympathy" with the League's efforts to improve and continue its technical and non-political activities.[123] It appeared, however, that membership in the Central Committee would incur automatic financial obligations which could not be undertaken by the U.S. without prior authorization from Congress. It was inexpedient to bring the matter before Congress, and a refusal by Congress might even prejudice the more limited collaboration that had been maintained in the past. Avenol, Lester, and Charron denied that any automatic financial obligations existed.[124] Lester, moreover, suggested that U.S. membership would "be distinctly advantageous in bringing about reconstruction in Europe along lines consonant with what he felt were American principles." The issue of U.S. membership, however, had been settled.

Internationalists in the United States were eager to support the Geneva reforms. The Rockefeller Foundation seemed prepared to donate $ 100,000 to the Central Committee, and a citizens' committee organized by the American League of Nations Association was considering a public subscription to raise a like amount.[125] Ironically, as prospects for the Central Committee were fading in April 1940, President Roosevelt publicly endorsed the efforts of the citizens' committee, saying that the League's technical and humanitarian programs were "not only worthy, but definitely essential."[126]

Developing the Central Committee was no easy task. States did not flock to the cause. Among those which declined invitations, or which volunteered that political difficulties prevented them from joining, were Brazil, which previously had shown significant interest, Chile, China, Finland, Hungary, Italy, Peru, and Sweden in addition to the U.S.[127] Great Britain and France, moreover, wanting to preserve future options, were wary.

The Organizing Committee met at the Permanent Court of International Justice at the Hague on 7–8 February 1940, but accomplished little.[128] Former Dutch Prime Minister Hendrikus Colijn was co-opted in his personal capacity and then appointed chairman. The committee agreed to select only eight of the possible fourteen States and only four or five of the possible eight individuals. Ideas concerning the Central Committee's program ranged widely, but the British and French refused to agree that it should study possible terms of peace. Guidelines also were required to govern the relationships between the Central Committee and the Supervisory Commission, the advisory committees, and other international organizations, including the International Labor Organization. Avenol late in February would describe the latter as "seeing ghosts",[129] but at The Hague the relationship of the two bodies was a bone of contention and subsequent efforts to achieve accord were unsuccessful.

Pelt, one of Avenol's most trusted aides, in reflecting upon the meeting, noted that "when it came to defining the composition, functioning and programme of work there was a general feeling that it would be premature after only six months of war and with the future completely obscured before us to do anything definite."[130] Lester, commenting similarly, thought "the spade work" for the Central Committee was being done "with more persistence than enthusiasm, but not without some faith and hope provided the British and French Governments become more charitable in their attitude."[131]

Early in March, Colijn and Avenol conferred in Geneva concerning the nomination of additional Governments for membership in the Central Committee.[132] The list they issued on 19 March contained only seven states: Canada, Denmark, Egypt, India, Iran, Mexico, and the Union of South Africa. It corresponded to a list furnished by London, but differed significantly from one offered by Paris. Contemporary references to the Bruce reforms producing the basis for a "neutral" League had no foundation in fact. The Central Committee would have functioned within the limits set by the British and French.

Subsequently, Colijn and Pelt visited Paris and London to discuss aspects of the proposed organization. Colijn was received in Paris "with sympathy but without enthusiasm and with some reserve."[133] The reception in London was more cordial, but perhaps out of respect for Colijn rather than as a sign of support for his mission.

The period of relative calm on the Western Front ended on 9 April 1940 with Hitler's invasion of Denmark and Norway. Necessarily, a meeting of the Central Committee scheduled for mid-June was abandoned.[134] The extension of Germany's offensive into Holland, Belgium, Luxemburg, and France finally ended prospects for implementing the Bruce reforms.

*

The Bruce Report was a long-deferred product of discussions initiated by senior officials of the League of Nations Secretariat desiring to improve the organization's role in economic diplomacy after the failure of the London Monetary and Economic Conference in July 1933. It reflected a growing global interdependence which had transformed the League into a center for the study of great national socio-economic concerns, a clearing house for national experiences, and a sponsor of programs of technical assistance. Encouraging these developments and promoting the idea that international economic policies should be directed toward improving the well-being of the masses, was the Australian Stanley M. Bruce, who, like members of the Secretariat, wanted to strenghten the League's ability to facilitate international economic cooperation.

Only in the severe crisis atmosphere of the spring and summer of 1939, when European peace and the League's very existence were endangered, did Governments, led by the British and French, finally agree to restructure the League's Economic and Financial Organization. Any suggestion that the resulting Bruce Report was intended to put aside the League's central political responsibilities overlooks the fact that the League already had been rendered impotent, if not irrelevant, in dealing with German, Italian, and Japanese aggression.[135]

The Bruce Report was not an instrument for appeasement. It contained a proposal for a Central Committee for Economic and Social Questions which would have been dominated by the British and French, as was the League's Assembly which was to retain control over the Central Committee's budget. Moreover, a prime purpose of this new agency was to promote the very kind of open international economic system the Germans and Italians had rejected. Even "economic appeasement" as proposed by Bruce had as its purpose expanding international trade and inducing Hitler and Mussolini to abandon autarchic policies. Finally, in preparing for the Bruce reforms, neither Loveday nor Avenol thought that the aggressors would cooperate, although Colijn with British and French approval unsuccessfully approached the Italians in January 1940.[136] Sweetser, commenting upon aspirations in the Secretariat, referred to the possible cooperation particularly of States which had left the League "for less fundamental reasons."[137] Clearly, he had in mind some of the Latin Americans.

On the other hand, the hope of those favoring League reform, that the creation of an "autonomous" and "non-political" organ for economic and social collaboration would result in closer cooperation by the United States and certain Latin American countries, particularly Brazil, failed to materialize. Americans serving in League bodies and some U.S. officials had encouraged Secretariat members to believe that the U.S. might take a more active part if an autonomous organization existed. When the chips were down the U.S. would not join the Central Committee. This has led one commentator to label the U.S. policy a "defection."[138]

During the war Avenol was criticized by former colleagues, for supporting reforms only when it was "too late."[139] These observations were part of a larger attack by disappointed and embittered Secretariat members who detested Avenol's support of the Munich settlement, his firing of liberal officials during the winter of 1938/39, and his reportedly pro-Nazi utterances in the late spring of 1940. They saw the Bruce Report as an "about-face" by Avenol on the League's "non-political" programs for which, they charged, he previously had shown little sympathy. It was a matter of great suspicion that he would sponsor the Bruce reforms on the very eve of the Second World War.[140]

Such antagonism to Avenol no doubt was rooted in a clash of values. There is no denying that the Secretary-General favored a policy of appeasement, and in this respect had followed closely London and Paris. Moreover, from existing evidence, it is clear that after the fall of France in the spring of 1940, Avenol became unnerved and said and did foolish things. Still, supporting the Bruce Report – embodying a sophisticated expression of humane idealism and liberal internationalism – seems to have been motivated not by Avenol's desire to appease the totalitarians, but by a desire to save and improve that portion of the international apparatus not yet paralyzed by big power conflicts in the 1930's.

Finally, with regard to the idea that the Central Committee for Economic and Social Questions was to be a "technical" rather than a "political" organ, one must penetrate the League's jargon. Loveday and others had argued that an "autonomous" Economic and Financial Organization would enable States to avoid political entanglements while participating in international economic and social programs. This did not mean, however, that the issues coming before the "autonomous" League body would be "non-political." Rather they meant that many League Members, particularly the United States and many Latin American States, could participate in economic and social programs while remaining aloof from those Euro – or Asian – centered conflicts they wished to avoid. Indeed, when Bruce urged the League to expand its socio-economic programs he had in mind serving important domestic political needs through the instrumentalities of the League of Nations. The best evidence for this can be found in the Bruce Report itself.[141] The report discounted the League's terminology and stressed the distinctly political character of the concerns which would fall within the jurisdiction of the proposed Central Committee for Economic and Social Questions. An interpretation of the Bruce reforms as separating social and economic issues from politics justifies the "functionalist" theory of David Mitrany.[142] However, what actually was occurring in the 1930's, and what senior international officials were advocating, was the development of sectoral political linkages across state boundaries, a development today described as the processes of "transgovernmentalism."[143] These transgovernmental links provide this basis for issue-oriented coalitions of national government ministries sharing a professional perspective or a functional interest. Today, these dynamics of the 1930's would be recognized as an early stage in the development of "complex interdependence."

Although the Bruce Report was not implemented, it provided a model for an integrated approach to international economic social, and humanitarian problems. It influenced those drafting the United Nations Charter to provide for an Economic and Social Council which, however, has lacked the autonomy of the League's proposed Central Committee as well as the direct participation of non-governmental experts.

Notes

1 "The Development of International Co-operation in Economic and Social Affairs, Report on the Special Committee," Special Supplement to the *Monthly Summary of the League of Nations* (August 1940). The standard article on "functionalism" in the League of Nations is Victor-Yves Ghebali, "Functionalism in the League of Nations." *In:* A. J. R. Groom and Paul Taylor, editors, *Functionalism: Theory and Practice in International Relations.* New York, Crane, Russak, 1975. – p. 141–189. M. Ghebali also has written the standard study of the Bruce Committee proposals. Victor-Yves Ghebali, *La Société des Nations et la réforme Bruce 1939–1940.* Genève, Centre européen de la Dotation Carnegie pour la paix internationale, 1970. – 113 p.

2 Martin Hill, *The United Nations System: Coordinating its Economic and Social Work,* Cambridge, Cambridge University Press, 1978. – p. 11.

3 There are two studies of Avenol's career as Secretary General. James Barros, *Betrayal from Within, Joseph Avenol, Secretary-General of the League of Nations, 1933–1940,* New Haven, Yale University Press, 1969. – 289 p.; and Arthur W. Rovine, *The First Fifty years, The Secretary-General in World Politics, 1920–1970,* Leyden, A. W. Sijhoff, 1970. – p. 105–172. Avenol's resignation is discussed in Stephen M. Schwebel, *The Secretary-General of the United Nations. His Political Powers and Practice,* Cambridge, Harvard University Press, 1952. – p. 8–10 and 215–224.

4 His contemporaries treated Avenol harshly. See, for example, F. P. Walters, *A History of the League of Nations,* London, Oxford University Press, 1952, p. 809–810; Carnegie Endowment for International Peace, *Proceedings of the Exploratory Conference on the Experience of the League of Nations Secretariat.* Washington, D. C., Carnegie Endowment for International Peace, 1942, and *Proceedings of the Conference on Experience in International Administration,* Washington, D. C., Carnegie Endowment for International Peace, March 1943; and Barros, *op. cit.,* especially p. 206 ff. One can not read the proceedings of the Carnegie Endowment conferences without sensing the frustrated idealism, indeed utopianism, of many of Avenol's staff who were critical of him.

5 Some contemporary accounts suggest that a group in the Secretariat wanted an ideologically neutral League to which Germany might return. See, for example, Verax, "En pleine guerre transformera-t-on la SdN?, Un Projet de l'idéologie neutre," *L'Europe nouvelle,* 23ème année, no. 151 (2 mars 1940), p. 245–246. James Barros, *op. cit.,* p. 261 sees Avenol's interest in "depoliticizing the League's activities" as running contrary to the "very purpose of the world organization as an organ for political action."

6 A strongly anti-Avenol account of the movement to reform the League's technical advisory committee in the 1930's was written by a member of the Secretariat who had been deeply engaged in aspects of the process. Vladimir D. Pastuhov, *Memorandum on the Composition, Procedures and Functions of Committees of the League of Nations.* Washington, D. C., Carnegie Endowment for International Peace, 1943. – 96 p.

7 There are two biographies of Bruce. Cecil Edwards, *Bruce of Melbourne, Man of Two Worlds*. London, Heineman, 1965. – 475 p.; and Alfred Thorpe Stirling, *Lord Bruce: The London Years*, Melbourne, The Hawthorne Presse, 1974. – 509 p.
8 William E. Rappard, "Evolution of the League of Nations," *American Political Science Review*, XXI, No. 4 (November 1927), p. 796.
9 Martin Hill, *The Economic and Financial Organization of the League of Nations*, Washington, D. C., Carnegie Endowment for International Peace, 1946. – p. 18–20; and H. R. G. Greaves, *The League Committees and World Order*, London, Oxford University Press, 1931. – p. 33–34.
10 See also Michael A. Heilperin, "Economic and Financial Issues," *World Organization, A Balance Sheet of the First Great Experiment, A Symposium of the Institute on World Organization*, Washington, D. C., American Council on Public Affairs, 1942. – p. 50–82.
11 Eric Drummond, untitled memorandum, 11 December 1929, LNA, P. 33.
12 LoN, Records of the Twelfth Ordinary Session of the Assembly, Minutes of the Second Committee, 18 September 1931, *OJSS* no. 95, p. 30–31; see also LoN doc. C.74.M.39.1932. II.B., p. 3–4; and LoN, Records of the Thirteenth Ordinary Session of the Assembly, Minutes of the Second Committee, September/October 1932, Annex 6, *OJSS* no. 106, p. 53.
13 On the Communications and Transit Organization, see Jan Hostie, Communications and Transit, World Organization, *op. cit.*, [see note 10], p. 158–188.
14 LoN, Minutes of the Seventy-eighth Session of the Council, 17 January 1934, *OJ*, p. 116; and LoN, doc. C. 287.M.125. 1934.
15 LoN, Records of the Fifteenth Ordinary Session of the Assembly, Plenary Meetings, 27 September 1934, *OJSS* no. 125, p. 78.
16 Minutes and correspondence of this committee are in LNA, 1933–1946/50/15773/956 (R.5678). Some correspondence and drafts bearing on this committee's work are in the Vladimir Pastuhov Papers at the Hoover Institution on War, Revolution and Peace, Stanford University.
17 A. Loveday to Secretary-General, 16 Januar 1935, LNA, 1933–1946/50/15773/956 (R.5678).
18 J. A., untitled memorandum, 8 janvier 1935, *ibid.*
19 LoN, Minutes of the Eighty-fourth Session of the Council, 19 January 1935, *OJ*, p. 161–162.
20 Correspondence and drafts of the committee's report are in LNA, 1933–1946/50/13801 (R.5739). Minutes and papers of the committee are LoN docs. C.C.F.C./p.v. 1–7, and C.C.F.C. 1–5, Parts I and II, and 5(2). Handwritten notes taken during the meetings are in the Pastuhov Papers.
21 Pastuhov, *op. cit.*, [see note 6], p. 18.
22 League of Nations, Committee Appointed to Study the Constitution, Procedure and Practice of Committees of the League of Nations, *Draft Report of the Committee*, 21 June 1935, LoN doc. C.C.F.C.5(Part II).
23 LoN doc. A.16.1935.
24 LoN, Records of the Sixteenth Ordinary Session of the Assembly, Minutes of the Second Committee, 25 September 1935 (& Annex), *OJSS* no. 140. p. 58 ff. & p. 83 f.
25 Pastuhov, *op. cit.*, [see note 6], p. 25.
26 LoN, Minutes of the Ninetieth Session of the Council, 24 January 1936, *OJ*, p. 129–136.
27 For the start of the debate, see, LoN, Records of the Sixteenth Ordinary Session of the Assembly, Plenary Meetings, June/July 1936 *OJSS* no. 151.

28 LoN, Records of the Nineteenth Ordinary Session of the Assembly, Plenary Meetings, 29 September 1938 (& Annex), *OJSS* no. 183, p. 99 and p. 143–152.
29 P. B. Gilbert to H. S. Cumming, 20 October 1936, SD, Decimal File 1930–1939, RG 59, 500. C 111/1006 1/2.
30 LoN doc. C. 121.M.111. 1940.G.
31 *The Times,* (London), 21 June 1933; Lord Boyd Orr, *As I Recall,* Garden City, N. Y., Doubleday and Company Inc., 1967. – p. 118–119; and John Boyd Orr, *The White Man's Dilemma,* London, George Allen and Unwin, Ltd., 1953. – p. 83–86.
32 LoN, Minutes of the Eighty-sixth Session of the Council, 24 May 1935, *OJ,* p. 631–632.
33 LoN, Records of the Sixteenth Ordinary Session of the Assembly, Plenary Meetings, 11 September 1935, *OJSS,* no. 138, p. 51–53; and *ibid.,* Minutes of the Second Committee 19 September 1935, *OJSS* no. 140, p. 15–18.
34 LoN, Minutes of the Eighty-ninth Session of the Council, 28 September 1935, *OJ,* p. 1208. See Dame Janet M. Campbell, "The Nutrition Report," *International Affairs* 17, No. 2 (March–April 1938), p. 251–253.
35 "Reply from the Government of the United Kingdom to Circular Letter 170.1934". LoN doc. C.C.F.C.2.
36 Key documents reporting the activities of the League's Advisory Committee on Social Questions during the years 1937–1939 are LoN docs. C.235.M.169.1937.IV., C.147.M.68.1938.IV., C.214.M.142.1939.IV., and C.203.M.132.1939.IV.
37 "Report of the Health Organization for the period January 1931 to September 1932," 12 September 1932. LoN doc. A.28.1932.III. For a general review of the League's health activities see Frank G. Boudreau, Nutrition and Housing. *In: World Organization. op. cit.,* [see note 10], p. 83–98.
38 LoN, Records of the Seventeenth Ordinary Session of the Assembly, Minutes of the Second Committee, 25 September 1936, *OJSS* no. 140, p. 9–10.
39 LoN, Records of the Sixteenth Ordinary Session of the Assembly, Plenary Meetings, 4 July 1936, *OJSS* no. 151, p. 69–71. See also W. C. Bullitt, "Memorandum for Secretary of State," 20 May 1936, FRUS, 1936, v. I, p. 306–308.
40 P. B. Gilbert to Secretary of State, 14 July 1936, *ibid.,* p. 454–456. P. B. Gilbert to Secretary of State, 18 September 1936, SD, Decimal File 1930–39, RG 59, 500. C 1199/230; and L. Thompson to M. Feis, 6 August 1936, *ibid.,* 500. C 1199/217.
41 P. B. Gilbert to Secretary of State, 17 and 22 September 1936, *ibid.,* 500. C 1199/227, and 231; and LoN, Records of the Seventeenth Ordinary Session of the Assembly, Minutes of the Second Committee, September/October 1936, *OJSS* no. 157, and H. V. Hodson, World Economic Affairs, A. J. Toynbee, *Survey of International Affairs 1936,* Oxford, Oxford University Press, 1937. – p. 161–204.
42 LoN, Records of the Seventeenth Ordinary Session of the Assembly, Plenary Meetings, 25 September 1936, *OJSS* no. 155, p. 44–47.
43 *ibid.,* p. 141 (Annex); *ibid.,* Minutes of the Second Committee, 6 October 1936, *OJSS* no. 157, p. 62: and A. Loveday to Dr. D. Crena de Iongh, 28 Dec. 1937, LNA, P. 17.
44 LoN, Records of the Seventeenth Ordinary Session of the Assembly, Plenary Meetings, September/October 1936, *OJSS* no. 155, p. 141–142; LoN, Minutes of the Ninety-sixth Session of the Council, 26 January 1937, *OJ,* p. 106–108; and Karl W. Kapp, The League of Nations and Raw Materials, *Geneva Special Studies,* 12, no. 3 (September 1941) p. 51 ff.
45 A. J. Toynbee, *Survey of International Affairs 1937,* 2 v., Oxford, Oxford University Press, 1938, I, p. 1 ff., and p. 30–31. See also, for example, J. Davies to the President and Secretary Hull or Judge Moore, 20 January 1937, SD, Decimal File 1930–39, RG 59, 740.00/100.

46 Quoted in Allan G. B. Fisher, "World Economic Affairs," *ibid.*, p. 56.
47 *The Times* (London), 28 February 1937; and S. M. Bruce to J. A. Avenol, 1 March 1937, LNA, 1933–1946/10A/28167 (R.4440).
48 Various versions of the memorandum are in LNA, 1933–1946/10A/28167/28167 (R.4440). One version appears as an annex to "Remarks on the Present Phase of International Economic Relations," 1 September 1937, LoN, Minutes of the Ninety-ninth Session of the Council, September 1937, Annex no. 1681, p. 1222–1229. For comments on Mc Dougall see *The Memoires of Lord Gladwyn*, London, Weidenfeld and Nicolson, 1972. – p. 63–65.
49 J. P. Moffat to Secretary of State, 21 September 1937, SD, Decimal File 1930–39, RG 59, 500. C 111/1039.
50 There is a lengthy file of Foreign Office minutes and correspondence in PRO, FO 371/21237.
51 Committee on the Application of the Principles of the Covenant, "Participation of All States in the League of Nations, Report Submitted . . . by Viscount Cranborne," and "Collaboration Between the League of Nations and Non-Member States, Report Submitted . . . by Viscount Cranborne," both 7 September 1937. LoN docs. C.S.P. nos. 20 and 21.
52 Minute by F.T.A. Ashton-Gwatkin, 15 September 1937; F. W. Leith-Ross to H. M. G. Jebb, 17 September 1937; and draft telegram to Sir F. Phillips, 21 September 1937, PRO, FO 371/21237.
53 H. M. G. Jebb to F. W. Leith-Ross, 16 September 1937, PRO FO 371/21237.
54 "Review of the Economic and Financial Work of the Second Committee of the League of Nations Assembly, September-October 1937", 26 October 1937, PRO, FO 371/21237; and LoN, Records of the Eighteenth Ordinary Session of the Assembly, Plenary Meetings, September/October 1937, *OJSS* no. 169, p. 144.
55 F. W. Leith-Ross to F. T. A. Ashton-Gwatkin, 3 January 1938, and attached minutes, PRO, FO 371/22516. Apparently Leith-Ross had been approached earlier to serve as coordinator. He had declined and also had discouraged the suggestion of van Zeeland as coordinator.
56 "Note of a Telephonic Conversation with Mr. McDougall – 25 January 1938," LNA, P. 18; F.T.A. Ashton-Gwatkin Note for January 1938 League of Nations Council meeting, 6 January 1938, and Minute by R. C., 14 January 1938, and attached minutes, PRO, FO 371/22516; G. H. F. Abraham to F. Walters, 8 January 1938 and attached R. Makins to A. Loveday, 5 January 1938, LNA,1933–1946, 10A/32252/1778 (R.4384).
57 LoN, Minutes of the Hundredth Session of the Council, 29 January 1938, *OJ*, p. 109–110.
58 S. M. Bruce to N. Chamberlain attached to O. Cleverly to C. C. Harvey, 1 March 1938, PRO, FO 371/22517.
59 F. L. McDougall to R. C. S. Stevenson, 9 March 1938, *ibid.*
60 H. Bucknell, Jr. to Secretary of State, 2 February 1938, SD, Decimal File 1930–39, RG 59, 500. C 1/110.
61 Sir E. Phipps to the Rt.Hon. The Viscount Halifax, 5 March 1938, PRO, FO 371/22517; and H. Bucknell, Jr. to Secretary of State, 11 March 1938, SD, Decimal File 1930–39, RG 59, 500. C 1/115.
62 J. A. Avenol to A. Loveday, le 26 mars 1938, LNA, P. 17.
63 F. W. Leith-Ross to C. C. Harvey, 25 April 1938, PRO, FO 371/22517.
64 C. C. Harvey to F. W. Leith-Ross, 30 April 1938, *ibid.*
65 The committee's report is printed in LoN, Minutes of the Hundred-and-first Session of the Council, May 1938, Annex no. 1712, p. 551–555. Provisional minutes and a

draft report can be found in LNA, 1933–1946/10A/32252/1778(R.4384). An original member of the committee, Stephen Osusky, the Czech minister to France, was absent. Georges Bonnet, originally named as the French member was replaced by Georges Brunet. Maurice Frere was added to the committee after the initial appointments. See also H. Bucknell, Jr. to Secretary of State, 2 February 1938, SD, Decimal File 1930–39, RG 59, 500. C 1/110.

66 Committee of Experts of Consider the Structure and Functions of the Economic and Financial Organization. "Conclusions. Proposal sumitted by Sir Frederick Leith-Ross (United Kingdom)," Org. E.F./3 in LNA, 1933–1946/10A/32252/1778 (R.4384); and A. Loveday to Rene Charron, 9 May 1938, LNA, P. 18. "There are one or two interpolations I don't much like, but probably they don't much matter – as indeed the whole report doesn't. We all felt that it was *pariunt montes* – excepting possibly the father." H. Bucknell, Jr. to Secretary of State, 16 October 1938, SD, Decimal File 1930–39, RG 59, 500. C/949.

67 H. Bucknell, Jr. to Secretary of State, 18 May and 15 July 1938, *ibid.*, 500. C 1/121, and 500. C 1199/354. Avenol wanted to defer the merger of the sections while some experimental coordination was tried. By July, "reliable sources" were saying that when Stoppani reached the mandatory retirement age within the year, the sections would be merged under Loveday. Stoppani then would be hired as a special liaison agent to facilitate cooperation with certain countries.

68 F. W. Leith-Ross to R.C.S. Stevenson, 7 May 1938, PRO, FO 371/22517. Leith-Ross thought the recommendations "may not be of much use but they are, at any rate, harmless."

69 H. Bucknell, Jr. to Secretary of State, 6 May 1938, SD, Decimal File 1930–39, RG 59, 852.00/7863.

70 A. Loveday to R. Charron, 9 May 1938, LNA, P. 18.

71 "Interview with President Roosevelt," 4 April 1938; A. Sweetser to N. Davis, 7 April 1938; and A. Sweetser to Dear Mr. President, 9 April 1938, Arthur Sweetser Papers, Library of Congress. A Sweetser to the Secretary-General, 21 April 1938, LNA, 1933–1946/50/33702/26744 (R.5766).

72 A. Loveday to R. Tyler, 25 May 1938, LNA, P. 18.

73 A. Loveday to Mr. Wilson, 10 May 1938, LNA, 1933–1946/13/30989/1265 (R.5167). Bruce, apparently, often used the tactic of playing "hard to get." Edwards, *op. cit.*, p. 5–6.

74 J. A. Avenol to S. M. Bruce, 10 May 1938, LNA, P. 18, S. M. Bruce to J. A. Avenol, 11 May 1938, LNA, 1933–1946/10A/33968/33968 (R.4461); LoN, Minutes of the Hundred-and-first Session of the Council, 13 May 1938, *OJ*, p. 350–351.

75 Barros, *op. cit.*, [see note 3], p. 173.

76 LoN, Records of the Nineteenth Ordinary Session of the Assembly, Minutes of the Second Committee, 22 September 1938, *OJSS* no. 185, p. 21–26.

77 H. Bucknell, Jr. to Secretary of State, 18 October 1938, SD, Decimal File 1930–39, RG 59, 500 C/949.

78 Pepper's role is described in *ibid.;* A Sweetser to J. A. Avenol, 22 February 1939, LNA, 1933–1946/50/37221/8871 (R.5732); A. Sweetser to C. Pepper, 31 August and 18 December 1939, Sweetser Papers; and C. Pepper to author, 9 July and 11 August 1981.

79 LoN, Records of the Nineteenth Ordinary Session of the Assembly, Plenary Meetings, 30 September 1938 (& Annex), *OJSS* no. 183, p. 99 and p. 142.

80 The Council approved dispatch of the Assembly's invitation to the United States, Saudi Arabia, Brazil, Costa Rica, Iceland, Germany, Guatemala, Honduras, Japan, Liechtenstein, and Nicaragua. Italy technically still belonged to the League, for its

notice of withdrawal had not yet taken effect. Japan, however, on 2 November 1938, shortly after the dispatch of the invitation for cooperation, ceased all cooperation, as a consequence of a Council resolution of 3 September condemning Japanese aggression in China and declaring that members were entitled to take such steps as they might wish under Article 16 of the Covenant. LoN, Minutes of Hundred-and-Third Session of the Council, 30 September 1938, *OJ*, p. 878–880, and LoN doc. C 415. M.260.1938.

81 A. Sweetser to J. A. Avenol, 22 February 1939, LNA, 1933–1946/50/37221/8871(R.5732).

82 LoN, Records of the Nineteenth Ordinary Session of the Assembly, Plenary Meetings, 21 September 1938, *OJSS* no. 183, p. 70–74; and *ibid.*, Minutes of the Second Committee, 22 September 1938, *OJSS* no. 185, p. 26–27.

83 H. Bucknell, Jr. to Secretary of State, 16 January 1939, SD, Decimal File 1930–39, RG 59, 500.C/960.

84 Quoted in Barros, *op. cit.*, [see note 3], p. 187.

85 Avenol's letter and Hull's reply are printed in LoN doc. C.77.M.37.1939.VII.

86 A. Sweetser to J. A. Avenol, 22 February 1939, LNA, 1933–1946/50/37221/8871(R.5732).

87 H. Bucknell, Jr. to Secretary of State, 10 March 1939, SD, Decimal File 1930–39, RG 59, 740.00./654, partly printed in *FRUS, 1939*, I, p. 31–32.

88 The texts of the speeches are in LoN doc. C.160.M.95.1939.

89 LoN, Minutes of the Hundred-and-fifth Session of the Council, 23 May 1939, *OJ*, p. 263–264.

90 H. Bucknell, Jr. to Secretary of State, 24 May 1939, SD, Decimal File 1930–39, RG 59, 500.C/974.

91 LoN, Minutes of the Hundred-and-fifth Session of the Council, 27 May 1939, *OJ*, p. 272–273.

92 A. Loveday to R. Tyler, 5 July 1939, LNA, P. 19.

93 J. A. Avenol to S. M. Bruce, 27 May 1939, LNA, 1933–1946/50/38247/38247 (R.5805).

94 C. T. Everett to Secretary of State, 20 and 28 July 1939, SD, Decimal File 1930–39, RG 59, 500, C/980 and 982.

95 H. Bucknell, Jr. to Secretary of State, 24 May 1939, *ibid.*, 500. C/974; and R. Tyler to A. Loveday, 14 June 1939, LNA, P. 19.

96 Much of the preparatory work can be traced in LNA, 1933–1946/50/38247 (R.5805) and 50/38332 (R.5805). For a discussion of these preparations see Ghebali, *La Société des Nations et la réforme Bruce, op. cit.*, [see note 1], p. 32–37.

97 Committee on the Development of International Co-operation in Technical, Social and Humanitarian Fields, "Memorandum by the Secretary-General," 6 July 1939, LoN doc. C.D.C.I./1.

98 A. Loveday to S. Lester, 11 July 1939, LNA, 1933–1946/50/38743/38332 (R.5805). Butler's views are in a memorandum dated 4 August 1939, LoN doc. C.D.C.I./2.

99 Pardo, in speaking with Avenol, reported him as wanting to separate the "non-political" activities from the political activities and organs "as far as possible." C. T. Everett to Secretary of State, 28 July 1939, SD, Decimal File 1930–39, RG 59, 500. C/982.

100 R. Tyler, "Notes on Visit to U.S.A.," 20 July 1939, LNA, 1933–1946/10C/33667/9854 (R.4605); and A. Sweetser to A. Loveday, 3 July 1939, LNA, P. 19.

101 C. T. Everett to Secretary of State, 20 July 1939, SD, Decimal File 1930–39, RG 59, 500. C/980.

102 LoN doc. A. 23.1939. Only Varvaressos was absent. For partial minutes of the meetings of the Bruce Committee see LNA, P. 101. For a critique of the Bruce Committee's report see Pastuhov, *op. cit.*, [see note 6], p. 71 ff.
103 For information on the printing of the report see LNA, 1933–1946/50/39259/38332 (R.5805). The League's treasurer, Seymour Jacklin, objected to a German edition.
104 F. L. McDougall to J. P. Moffat, 30 August 1939, SD, Decimal File 1930–39, RG 59, 500. C/991.
105 A. Sweetser to C. Pepper, 31 August 1939, Sweetser Papers.
106 H. H. Tittmann to Secretary of State, 31 October 1939, SD, Decimal File 1930–39, RG 59, 500. C/995.
107 H. H. Tittmann to Secretary of State, 17 and 28 November 1939, *ibid.*, 500. C111/1116 and 1120.
108 LoN, "Summary of the Meetings of the Fourth Committee of the Nineteenth Session of the Assembly" (Geneva, 1940), p. 62.
109 LoN, "Twentieth Ordinary Session of the Assembly. Revised Minutes of the Special Committee for the Study of the Bruce Report." A/C.S.R.B./1939 p.v. 1 à 3 revisés. See also H. H. Tittmann to Secretary of State, 28 December 1939, SD, Decimal File 1930–39, RG 59, 500. C/1001.
110 J. A. Avenol to F. P. Walters, 17 November 1939, LNA, P. 34.
111 Great Britain, Parliamentary Debates, 5th Series, Volume 353, columns 1179–80.
112 *Ibid.*, Volume 355, column 29.
113 International Labour Office, Emergency Committee, Third Session, "Draft Minutes of the Fourth Sitting, September 21, 1939," p. 21; and "Draft Minutes of the Fourth Session, Sixth Sitting, October 12, 1939," p. 16–17. Copies in Registry File, International Labor Organization, Geneva. See also Ghebali's *La Société des Nations et la réforme Bruce; op. cit.*, [see note 1], p. 67–74.
114 LoN doc. A./C.S.R.B./1/1939.
115 The views of the United States and Canada are reported in U.S. Department of State, *FRUS, 1940*, II, p. 307 ff. See also Advisory Committee on Traffic in Opium and Other Dangerous Drugs, "Minutes of the Twenty-Fifth Session Held at Geneva from 13 to 17 May 1940," LoN doc. C. 162.M.147.1940. The discussion of the Bruce Report is on p. 13–19.
116 LoN, doc. A./C.S.R.B./3/1939.
117 LoN, Records of the Twentieth Ordinary Session of the Assembly (December 11th-14th, 1939), p. 22–23.
118 A. Loveday to L. Rasminsky, 16 December 1939, LNA, P. 19.
119 Untitled memorandum, 31 December 1939, LNA, P. 34.
120 R. Charron to S. Lester, 16 January 1940, and S. Lester to C. Hambro, 17 January 1940, LNA, 1933–1946/50/39746/39557 (R.5806).
121 A. Sweetser to H. Grady, 18 December 1939, Sweetser Papers.
122 A. Sweetser to Secretary-General, 28 December 1939, Sweetser Papers.
123 Secretary of State to H. H. Tittmann, 19 February 1940, U.S. Department of State, *FRUS, 1940*, v. II, p. 313–314.
124 C. T. Everett to Secretary of State, 27 February 1940, *ibid.*, p. 315–316; L. E. Thompson, "Participation of the United States in the Technical Work of the League of Nations," February 1940, SD, Decimal File 1940–44, RG 59, 500.C 1/137. See also, H. Bucknell, Jr. to Secretary of State, 25 November 1939, SD, Decimal File 1930–39, RG 59, 500. C 1/129, and H. H. Tittmann to Secretary of State, 10 November 1939, *ibid.*, 500 C/994.
125 A. Sweetser to H. Grady, 10 April 1940, Sweetser Papers.
126 F. D. Roosevelt to M. Woolley, n.d., in S. Shepard and D. P. Myers, eds., *Docu-*

ments on American Foreign Relations, July 1939–June 1940, Boston, World Peace Foundation, 1940. – p. 607–608.

127 See LNA, 1933–1946/50/39705 (R.5806).

128 Committee for Organising the Central Committee for Economic and Social Questions. Session held on 7 and 8 February 1940, at the Permanent Court of International Justice. The Hague, "Summary of Decisions," LNA, 1933–1946/50/39930/39557 (R.5806); C. T. Everett to Secretary of State, 24 February 1940, U.S. Department of State, *FRUS, 1940,* v. II, p. 314–315; and C. T. Everett to Secretary of State, 28 February 1940, and enclosure, SD, Decimal File 1940–44, RG 59, 500.C1/143.

129 C. T. Everett to Secretary of State, 28 February 1940, *ibid.*

130 A Pelt to C. Eichelberger, 6 March 1940, Sweetser Papers; G. A. Gordon to Secretary of State, 9 February 1940, SD, Decimal File 1940–44, RG 59, 500. Cl/136; and C. T. Everett to Secretary of State, 28 February 1940, ibid., 500.C1/143.

131 C. T. Everett to Secretary of State, 28 February 1940, *ibid.*

132 LNA, 1933–1946/50/39715/39705(R.5806). The French list consisted of Finland, Poland, Canada, Egypt, China, Rumania, Columbia, and Mexico. Poland, of course, was by this time no longer independent. For the Avenol-Colijn nominees, see J. A. Avenol to Minister for External Affairs (Canberra) Australia, 19 March 1940. LNA, P. 24. See also Ghebali, *Organisation internationale et guerre mondiale. Le cas de la Société des Nations et de l'organisation internationale du travail pendant la seconde guerre mondiale.* Grenoble, Université des Sciences Sociales de Grenoble, 1975. – p. 168 ff.

133 H. H. Tittmann to Secretary of State, 10 April 1940, SD, Decimal File 1940–44, RG 59, 500. C1/144.

134 Barros, *op. cit.*, [see note 3], p. 261. In August 1951, Avenol denied that he wished to sabotage the League. "The documents M. Avenol sent you, show that up to the moment, knowing that the political machinery of the League was dead, he did what he could in the hope of saving its technical machinery." V. Lever to S. Schwebel, 9 August 1939, LNA, P. 34.

135 LNA, 1933–1946/50/40360/39705(R.5806); and "Memorandum of Conversation," 1 May 1940, attached to H. H. Tittmann to Secretary of State, 3 May 1940, SD, Decimal File 1940–44, RG 59, 500. C1/145.

136 *The Times* (London), January 16, and 17, 1940; Verax, *op. cit.;* and Ghebali, *Organisation internationale et guerre mondiale, op. cit.*, [see note 132], p. 170.

137 A. Sweetser to H. Grady, 18 December 1939, Sweetser Papers.

138 Ghebali, *La Société des Nations et la réforme Bruce, op. cit.*, [see note 1], p. 55–56.

139 Pastuhov, *op. cit.*, [see note 6], p. 72, and 78; and Egon F. Ranshofen-Wertheimer, *Victory is not enough*, New York, Norton & Co., Inc., 1942, p. 268, and *The International Secretariat, A Great Experiment in International Administration*, Washington, D. C., Carnegie Endowment for International Peace, 1945, p. 5–6, and p. 162 ff.

140 Ranshofen-Wertheimer, *The International Secretariat, op. cit.*, p. 379–380.

141 LoN, The Development of International Co-operation in Economic and Social Affairs, *op. cit.*, [see note 1], p. 5–6.

142 Cf. in particular D. Mitrany's essays, *A Working Peace System* (1943), and, The Problem of Equality in Historical Perspective (1955), in D. Mitrany, *A Working Peace System*, Chicago, Quadrangle Press, 1966, p. 25–99 and p. 103–120, respectively. For a critique of Mitrany, see E. B. Haas, *Beyond the Nation-State, Functionalism and International Organization*, Stanford, Stanford University Press, 1964, 595 p.

143 R. O. Keohane and J. S. Nye, "Transgovernmental Relations and International Organizations", *World Politics*, XXVII, No. 1, October 1974, p. 39–62.

La transition de la Société des Nations à l'Organisation des Nations Unies

Victor-Yves Ghebali
Institut universitaire de hautes études internationales, Genève

Le problème de la substitution de l'Organisation des Nations Unies à la Société des Nations soulève trois séries de questions principales dont on se propose ici d'esquisser l'analyse: quels furent les facteurs qui incitèrent les grandes puissances alliées à condamner la SdN au point de décider la création de toutes pièces d'une autre institution internationale? Quelles furent les circonstances, les conditions et les étapes de la disparition de la Société? Quelle est la nature et l'étendue de l'héritage sociétaire assumé par les Nations Unies?

I. Le principe de la disparition de la SdN: une décision implicite

La condamnation de la SdN fut essentiellement le fait des deux grandes puissances alliées qui, à la veille de la défaite de l'Axe, ne faisaient pas ou ne faisaient plus partie de l'institution genevoise: les Etats-Unis et l'URSS. Pour des raisons bien différentes, mais néanmoins décisives, les gouvernants américains et les gouvernants soviétiques ne pouvaient sérieusement envisager l'éventualité du voyage à Canossa qu'aurait constitué une adhésion à la Société.

Depuis l'entrée en guerre des Etats-Unis, en décembre 1941, les sentiments isolationnistes du peuple américain avaient eu tendance à s'estomper. La grande majorité du pays prenait graduellement conscience de certaines réalités – à savoir qu'une organisation internationale dotée de pouvoirs forts aurait pu contribuer à éviter le déclenchement de la guerre et que la participation américaine était l'une des conditions *sine qua non* du succès de toute entreprise future de ce genre. Alors qu'en janvier 1936 57,4% des personnes interrogées exprimaient leur opposition à l'idée d'une adhésion à la SdN, ce chiffre allait baisser constamment jusqu'à atteindre 20% en juin 1944[1]. Les résultats s'avéraient davantage éloquents lorsque la question se ramenait à savoir si, à la fin de la guerre, les Etats-Unis devaient ou non faire partie d'une nouvelle institution internationale: quelques mois seulement avant Pearl Harbor, les réponses positives et négatives s'équilibraient à peu près; mais à partir de 1942, la tendance favorable l'emporta sans cesse de facon croissante – 62% en novembre 1942, 68% en novembre 1943, 71% en novembre 1944 et 90% en mars 1945[2]. Ce revirement de l'opinion n'était pas sectoriel; il touchait sans distinction l'ensemble des couches sociales et des milieux politiques, y compirs le Parti Républicain où se recrutaient les plus farouches isolationnistes et ennemis de la SdN[3]. Cette évolution vers l'»internationalisme« ne tournait donc guère à l'avantage de celle-ci. Il y avait à ce paradoxe apparent deux raisons principales.

D'une part, il y avait le fait que le Congrès se composait essentiellement d'isolationnistes reconvertis de fraîche date en internationalistes et qui ne pouvaient favoriser l'entrée du pays à la SdN sans s'infliger un désaveu de taille. La création d'une institution nouvelle supprimait cet obstacle psychologique et politique: sénateurs et représentants trouvaient là un moyen de sauver la face en arguant que l'organisation nouvelle ne présentait pas les »tares« de la Société. L'Exécutif prêtait une attention toute particulière à cette dimension du problème. Il n'oubliait pas la bataille livrée et perdue par Woodrow Wilson devant le Sénat en 1919–1920: le concours du Législatif étant indispensable, la SdN se devait d'être sacrifiée. D'autre part, le président Roosevelt lui-même estimait que l'aura de faillite entourant le seul nom de la SdN entamait par avance la crédibilité de cette dernière auprès d'un peuple américain appelant de ses voeux un monde nouveau[4]. En fait, ce fut dès 1943 que le *Special Sub-Committee on International Organization* (constitué au sein du Département d'Etat en 1941 dans la perspective de la reconstruction du monde d'après-guerre) recommanda le remplacement de la SdN par une organisation à créer de toutes pièces[5]. Ce rejet de la Société par les Etats-Unis intervenait 23 ans après une première répudiation autrement plus lourde de conséquence.

Mais si à Washington l'évocation de la SdN suscitait surtout de la gêne, à Moscou elle provoquait plutôt de l'hostilité. Les Soviétiques avaient, en effet, des motifs beaucoup plus concrets de s' opposer au maintien et à la revitalisation de la Société.

Admise à la SdN en 1934 (sur l'initiative des démocraties alors soucieuses de trouver un contrepoids à la force montante du nazisme), l'URSS n'avait jamais eu à se féliciter de sa présence à Genève. D'une part, elle demeura à l'écart de la coopération fonctionnelle qui ne l'intéressait pas véritablement. D'autre part, sa volonté de jouer le jeu de la sécurité collective ne fut guère prise au sérieux: les Soviétiques restèrent politiquement isolés et ne cessèrent de susciter la méfiance des autres membres. En un mot, l'URSS pouvait à juste titre estimer avoir été traitée avec bien moins d'égards que l'Allemagne hitlérienne ou l'Italie fasciste. Staline gardait un souvenir vivace de cet événement humiliant qu'avait été l'exclusion de son pays[6]. Pour cette seule raison déjà, il paraissait peu concevable qu'une grande puissance s'infligeât de son propre fait une humiliation plus grande en sollicitant une réintégration au sein de la SdN – institution ayant de surcroît son siège en Suisse, pays avec lequel l'URSS n'entretenait plus de relations diplomatiques.

Par ailleurs, les dispositions du Pacte étaient conçues de façon telle qu'elles rendaient possible une action coercitive de la SdN contre tout Etat membre, y compris une grande puissance. L'affaire italo-éthiopienne et l'affaire russo-finlandaise l'avaient on ne peut mieux démontré. Par conséquent, adhérer à la Société c'était courir à nouveau le risque de voir les Etats bourgeois organiser une coalition anti-bolchévique contre celle qui représentait alors la seule puissance communiste du monde. Seule une institution dont la charte exclurait l'hypothèse de la condamnation d'une grande puissance dans tous les cas pouvait, à la rigueur, trouver grâce auprès de Staline. Cette exigence fondamentale sera à l'origine de la procédure dite du »veto« retenue par la Charte des Nations Unies.[7]

Face à ce double obstacle, les trois grandes puissances qui appartenaient encore à la SdN s'accomodèrent sans trop de difficulté de la nécessité de créer une nouvelle organisation internationale:

– La *France* ne se trouvait pas véritablement confrontée à l'alternative du maintien ou de la suppression de la SdN. Du fait du statut international restreint des instances de la Résistance extérieure, elle fut constamment tenue à l'écart des sommets interalliés qui donnèrent naissance aux grandes institutions internationales du système des Nations Unies[8]. Placé devant le fait accompli de la disparition future de la SdN, le général de Gaulle exprimera néanmoins à Staline, lors de son voyage à Moscou à la fin de 1944, sa satisfaction de voir les mécanismes sociétaires céder la place à des procédures plus réalistes basées sur le consensus des grandes puissances[9].

– Promue au rang de grande puissance par Roosevelt, la *Chine* occupait au sein de la coalition alliée une place visiblement disproportionnée par rapport à son poids réel. Dans un débat aussi capital que celui de la nature de la future organisation internationale d'après-guerre, les Chinois ne pouvaient que soutenir la position des Etats-Unis. La création des Nations Unies leur apportait la certitude d'un siège permanent au conseil exécutif – éventualité beaucoup moins certaine dans l'hypothèse d'un aménagement des structures de la SdN[10].

– La *Grande-Bretagne* était la seule grande puissance dont les intérêts pouvaient, au moins en apparence, se trouver affectés par le non-maintien de la SdN: les Britanniques avaient toujours exercé sur l'institution genevoise une influence considérable, qui était devenue totale à partir de la défaite française, en juin 1940. La liquidation de la Société ne leur paraissait cependant pas un prix trop cher pour obtenir la participation des Etats-Unis aux affaires du monde et la »neutralisation« des ambitions soviétiques – ou, autrement dit, la réalisation du principe de l'universalité et celui de l'unanimité des grandes puissances[11]. Le gouvernement britannique était en outre trop réaliste pour ne pas comprendre que le discrédit entourant le nom de la SdN s'opposait à toute tentative efficace de résurrection de celle-ci; l'essentiel demeurait pour lui que fut prise en considération aussi pleinement que possible l'expérience de Genève, lors des travaux préparatoires de la nouvelle organisation internationale.

La suppression de la SdN ne fit à aucun moment l'objet d'une décision *formelle* des Alliés: elle découla indirectement du processus d'élaboration des Nations Unies entamé au lendemain de la Déclaration quadripartite de Moscou du 30 octobre 1943. Par le point 4 de cette Déclaration, les signataires reconnaissaient en effet »la nécessité d'établir à la date la plus proche possible, une organisation internationale générale pour le maintien de la paix et de la sécurité, basée sur le principe de l'égalité souveraine de tous les Etats épris de paix et ouverte sans discrimination à tous les Etats grands ou petits«[12].

Sous l'effet de la Déclaration de Moscou, le travail de réflexion et recherche entrepris par les Anglo-Américains s'accéléra considérablement. A Washington comme à Londres, l'expérience de la SdN occupa une place centrale dans cette préparation intensive. Le recours aux enseignements du passé fut, comme en

1918–1919, une sorte de réflexe naturel[13]. De fait, il ne s'agissait pas tant d'innover que de reformuler les principes du Pacte sous une nouvelle étiquette politique: comme l' a souligné l'un des artisans britanniques de ce processus »the makers of the Charter had far less choice than the makers of the Covenant once the decision to set up an universal international organisation had been taken«[14]. L'organisation prévue dans les Propositions de Dumbarton Oaks du 7 octobre 1944 ainsi que par la Charte élaborée à la conférence de San Francisco suivait sensiblement, sur le plan des principes comme sur le plan des institutions, le modèle de la SdN[15].

Mais si les fondateurs de l'ONU ne pouvaient bâtir qu'à partir des acquis de la SdN, ils refusèrent en revanche de témoigner au grand jour leur considération vis-à-vis d'un cadavre embarrassant et qu'ils souhaitaient voir oublié au plus vite. La Charte ne comporta ainsi aucune disposition ou indication indirecte sur sa filiation avec le Pacte ou sur celle de l'ONU avec la SdN. La conférence de San Francisco se caractérisa d'ailleurs par un certain courant anti-sociétaire assez fort. Outre l'hostilité naturelle de l'URSS, il y eut le fait que l'ensemble des délégations succombèrent à la tentation, un peu facile, de prendre la SdN comme bouc émissaire des échecs de la sécurité collective pendant l'entre-deux-guerres[16]. La Société ne trouva de défenseur que dans le maréchal Smuts qui développa en ces termes l'idée selon laquelle le Pacte avait représenté une étape dans l'histoire de l'organisation des rapports mondiaux: »C'était là un grand et noble effort qui allait bien au-delà de ce qui avait été fait ou même tenté auparavant. Aujourd'hui il est de bon ton de déprécier la Société des Nations ou même de se moquer d'elle. Il faut bien dire cependant qu'au moment de sa naissance elle constituait un immense et réel progrès et ceux qui dans ce pays ou ailleurs ont travaillé en faveur de cette noble cause n'ont ni regrets ni excuses à exprimer«[17].

Représenté à San Francisco par une délégation d'observateurs composée du Secrétaire général par interim Sean Lester, du Trésorier Seymour Jacklin et d'Alexander Loveday (Directeur des Services économiques et financiers), le Secrétariat de la SdN put mesurer l'étendue et la profondeur du discrédit de la Société. La délégation sociétaire, comme il est vrai celle des autres institutions internationales invitées, ne comportait que des »représentants officieux«, formule on ne peut plus restrictive[18]. Ces »représentants officieux« reçurent en outre un traitement très peu favorable (par rapport, par exemple, aux nombreux organismes privés américains présents à la conférence) et même particulièrement désobligeant: à la suite du mécontentement des Soviétiques devant l'admission d'observateurs ressortissants de pays non membres de la coalition des Nations Unies, le Département d'Etat fit savoir un moment à Sean Lester que sa présence à San Francisco était jugée indésirable[19]. Sean Lester – celui que la presse americaine appelait »l'homme oublié de San Francisco« – quittera plus tard la conférence sans attendre la clôture des débats et sans avoir eu la possiblité de prendre une fois la parole sur les problèmes en discussion.

Néanmoins, le fiasco de la SdN ne fut pas total à San Francisco. D'une part, les observateurs sociétaires semblent avoir malgré tout déployé une certaine activité dans les coulisses, conseillant ici certaines délégations ou faisant circuler là des memoranda sur l'expérience de Genève[20]. D'autre part, soucieux d'éviter une dispersion prématurée des effectifs du Secrétariat – qui se serait notamment traduite par l'arrêt des activités de coopération fonctionelle plus indispensables que jamais dans une période de transition – les Britanniques firent adopter une décision de principe au sujet de la succession de Genève. Les »Arrangements provisoires« adoptés par la conférence le 26 juin 1945 instituaient une Commission préparatoire des Nations Unies (CPNU) chargée de multiples tâches dont celle de »formuler des recommandations sur le transfert éventuel des fonctions, activités et avoirs de la Société des Nations qu'il pourra sembler utile de confier à la nouvelle Organisation dans des conditions à fixer«[21].

La déconvenue à laquelle la SdN s'était heurtée à San Francisco faillit se renouveler lors des travaux de la CPNU: l'URSS obtint d'entrée de jeu la suppression de toute mention expresse à l'institution genevoise dans le règlement du Comité exécutif de la Commission. Mais à la suite de l'opposition de certains pays (dont la Grande-Bretagne), il fut convenu que les organes subsidiaires du Comité exécutif devraient »utiliser les connaissances et l'expérience spéciales des institutions internationales (. . .) qualifiées et consulter ces institutions«[22]. Les organes en question prirent en fait comme base de travail ou de réflexion un grand nombre de textes d'origine sociétaire: règlements internes des organes de la SdN, rapports »historiques« (par exemple: rapport Noblemaire, rapport Bruce . . .), memoranda rédigés par le Secrétariat de la Société à l'intention spécifique du Comité exécutif, etc. Seymour Jacklin et Alexander Loveday furent sollicités de contribuer aux travaux, le premier au sujet des questions budgétaires et le second pour la mise sur pied de l'ECOSOC[23]. Pour sa part, Sean Lester sut maintenir – à partir d'un quartier général improvisé, à Londres – une liaison directe et pragmatique avec le secrétariat de la CPNU. Le dernier Secrétaire général de la SdN et le premier Secrétaire général de l'ONU (Trygve Lie) purent, en définitive, entretenir des relations de travail assez satisfaisantes; Lester se verra même appelé à assister en observateur à la première session de l'Assemblée générale des Nations Unies. En 1945–1946, la SdN et l'ONU coexistaient encore: la suppression formelle de la première devait mettre fin à cette situation pour le moins singulière et paradoxale.

II. Les étapes de la disparition de la SdN

A partir de l'entrée en vigueur de la Charte des Nations Unies, il y eut coexistence de deux institutions internationales visant les mêmes fins. Nul n'avait intérêt à maintenir longtemps un tel état de fait générateur de confusion juridique et de double emploi pratique. La SdN représentait pour les 32 de ses membres qui appartenaient en même temps à l'ONU une charge financière improductive; sa survie devenait même à la longue nuisible, car il était clair que l'ONU ne pouvait commencer à exercer certains services fonctionnels d'intérêt primordial (contrôle du trafic de l'opium, etc.) qu'en prenant la relève directe de l'institution genevoise.

La procédure qui mit fin à l'existence de la SdN fut arrêtée par le gouvernement britannique. L'opération se déroula alors en deux phases: *dissolution* et *liquidation.*

La Grande-Bretagne admettait que l'intérêt de l'ONU exigeait une disparition rapide de la SdN. Mais il lui semblait en même temps indispensable que cet effacement s'effectuât dans des conditions compatibles avec la dignité de la Société et le respect dû à une grande institution qui avait symbolisé pendant près de deux décennies l'espoir du monde. Il fallait également veiller à ce que fussent sauvegardés les intérêts de tous les Etats membres de la SdN, membres ou non membres des Nations Unies. Mais ces conditions étaient difficiles à satisfaire simultanément en raison de la nature complexe des données juridiques et politiques du problème.

En effet, le problème de la suppression pure et simple d'une organisation intergouvernementale se posait en 1945 pour la première fois semble-t-il – jusqu'alors l'on n'avait connu que des cas de refontes, parfois totales, des actes constitutifs des Unions publiques internationales[24]. Juridiquement, trois procédures étaient en théorie concevables: notification au Secrétariat d'une série de dénonciations unilatérales du Pacte, abrogation du Pacte par la voie constitutionnelle de l'amendement et conclusion d'un instrument conventionnel spécial abrogeant le Pacte. Aucune de ces solutions ne parut praticable aux Britanniques. L'idée d'une cascade de dénonciations du Pacte avait un caractère plutôt ridicule; à supposer qu'elle ne le fût point, il fallait songer que les notifications ne seraient effectives (aux termes de l'article l er § 3 du Pacte) qu'au bout d'un délai de 2 ans. Quant à la procédure d'amendement et celle d'un traité abrogatif, elles avaient l'inconvénient majeur d'être extrêmement lentes – sans compter qu'il eût fallu (en vertu du principe de l'unanimité) obtenir l'accord de certains Etats (comme les pays Baltes ou l'Albanie) dont le statut politique demeurait encore incertain.

Le comité interministériel britannique chargé d'étudier, sous la présidence de Sir William Malkin (Conseiller juridique du Foreign Office), la question de la disparition de la SdN recommanda finalement que l'on confiât à l'Assemblée – et à elle seule – la tâche de prononcer la dissolution de la Société[25]. Mais dans l'optique britannique, la SdN ne devait disparaître que pour mieux préparer le terrain à l'ONU, c'est-à-dire pour léguer à celle-ci la somme de son expérience pratique et de ses biens matériels[26]. Arrêter une procédure de dissolution n'était donc pas tout: il fallait déterminer aussi le moment de sa mise en application de façon à ce que la disparition de la Société coïncidât avec la mise sur pied des Nations Unies. Le Rapport Malkin développa cette idée en détail, en partant de l'hypothèse que les Nations Unies prendraient l'initiative de proposer à la SdN d'assumer sa succession. Il proposa ainsi la réunion de deux Assemblées sociétaires. La première se serait contentée d'approuver le principe de la succession et de nommer un comité chargé de négocier une formule de transfert avec l'ONU. Quant à la seconde, elle aurait approuvé les arrangements conclus et prononcé la dissolution de la Société[27]. Mais ce scénario s'avéra impraticable pour deux séries de raisons.

D'une part, le Foreign Office estima qu'il n'était pas très indiqué de convoquer deux sessions de l'Assemblée de la SdN. Pour la plupart, les délégués nationaux compétents se trouvaient retenus à Londres par les travaux de la CPNU; l'envoi à Genève de délégués de moindre envergure n'aurait pas donné à la disparition de la SdN ce cachet nécessaire de solennité et de sérieux. Pourquoi alors ne pas se passer d'une première session censée esentiellement désigner un organe chargé d'entrer en négociation avec l'ONU, rôle que la Commission de contrôle – seul organe de la SdN en exercice pendant la tourmente de la guerre – pourrait remplir convenablement? Le 20 septembre 1945, Lester s'adressa officiellement aux Etats membres de la SdN pour leur proposer cette procédure qui fut aussitôt acceptée[28]. Il fut ainsi acquis qu'une seule Assembleé serait tenue, en 1946, à Genève.

D'autre part, l'une des hypothèses fondamentales du rapport Malkin se trouva vite infirmée par les faits. Rédigé avant l'ouverture de la conférence de San Francisco, le rapport avait tablé sur l'éventualité d'une reprise »en bloc« par les Nations Unies du passif aussi bien que de l'actif sociétaire. Or, comme l'on verra plus loin, tel ne fut finalement pas le cas par suite des objections de l'URSS. Par conséquent, la SdN se devait avant de disparaître de prendre elle-même diverses mesures tendant au recouvrement de ses créances, au règlement de ses dettes et à la disposition des éléments résiduels (ou non transmissibles) de son héritage.

La XXIème et ultime Assemblée de la SdN siégea du 8 au 18 avril 1946. Elle réunit 35 pays membres sur 44[29]. Deux ex-membres devaient, en revanche, se manifester à cette occasion et rendre un hommage inattendu à l'institution genevoise. Dans une lettre adressée le ler avril 1946 à Sean Lester, le gouvernement autrichien annonça son intention de se faire représenter de plein droit à l'Assemblée en invoquant l'argument selon lequel depuis sa libération – et l'annulation rétroactive de l'Anschluss – l'Autriche devait être considérée comme membre de la SdN [30]. Le Bureau de l'Assemblé décida, tout en éludant l'aspect juridique du problème, d'inviter officiellement le gouvernement autrichien à envoyer des observateurs à Genève[31]. De son côté, le gouvernement italien rappela, dans une communication destinée au président de l'Assemblée, que son pays avait été l'un des créateurs principaux de la SdN et l'un de ceux qui coopérèrent avec celle-ci pendant de longues années, notamment par l'intermédiaire de personnalités éminentes telles Vittorio Scialoja[32].

Sans avoir une composition aussi prestigieuse que lors des grandes sessions des années vingt ou trente, les délégations à la XXIème Assemblée présentaient cependant certains traits remarquables. On pouvait y relever la présence de personnalités ayant représenté leur pays à la première Assemblée en 1920, comme Lord Cecil ou certains délégues de la Suisse et des Pays-Bas. En outre, ne manquaient à l'appel ni certains »ténors« comme Paul-Boncour ou Carl Hambro, ni d'autres personnalités éminentes telles Georges Scelle, Maurice Bourquin ou José Caeiro da Matta. La continuité se manifestait aussi d' autres façons: plusieurs délégués nationaux n'étaient que d'anciens fonctionnaires de la SdN (G. Kaeckenbeeck, H. McKinnon Wood, F.T.B. Friis, T. Aghnidès, R. I. B. Skylstad, D. Secrétan, J. Nogueira) – et la même remarque valait pour A. Pelt, observateur à la session au nom des Nations Unies.

Trois fausses notes se manifestèrent dans les débats. En premier lieu, l'Argentine fut sur le point de se retirer de l'Assemblée devant l'échec de sa candidature à la vice-présidence[33]. En deuxième lieu, le délégué tchécoslovaque accusa presque ouvertement l'ancien Secrétaire général Joseph Avenol d'avoir encouragé les »forces réactionnaires« qui freinèrent l'activité démocratique de la SdN[34]. En troisième lieu, ayant refusé une proposition soumise par certaines délégations tendant à inclure l'URSS au nombre des pays bénéficiaires de la liquidation des avoirs sociétaires, l'Assemblée dut en contrepartie adopter une résolution – fort humiliante pour la SdN vu l'attitude prise par celle-ci dans le conflit russo-finlandais – rendant hommage aux Soviétiques[35].

A l'exception de ces fausses notes sans véritable portée, la sérénité la plus parfaite caractérisa la réunion de bout en bout. Paul-Boncour, Lord Cecil et Hambro – ce dernier en qualité de président – dominèrent les débats qui se situèrent constamment à un niveau élevé. A l'occasion de la discussion générale sur le rapport de Sean Lester consacré à l'activité de la SdN pendant la guerre, quelque 22 délégués prirent la parole. Avec une émotion qui transparait parfois derrière le moule classique de leurs discours, les orateurs dressèreut à tour de rôle un bilan lucide de l'expérience genevoise. Nul d'entre eux ne songea à nier, voire à minimiser, ce qui avait été l'échec d'une génération entière à maintenir la paix[36]. Les multiples facteurs de cet échec furent relevés sans fard et l'on conclut à la culpabilité non de la SdN mais de toutes les puissances – grandes ou petites: »Nous n'ignorons pas que nous avons souvent manqué de courage moral, que souvent nous avons hésité quand il eût fallu agir, que nous avons parfois agi quand il eût été sage d'hésiter. Nous savons que nous n'avons assumé qu'à contre-coeur la responsabilité de grandes décisions quand la grandeur s'imposait, et que nous ne pourrons échapper au jugement de l'histoire« osa reconnaître courageusement Carl Hambro[37].

Le caractère non totalement déficitaire de l'expérience genevoise et l'avènement tout récent de l'ONU – faits qui démontraient que l'idée des fondateurs de la SdN restait plus vivante que jamais – permirent à l'Assemblée d'être en définitive animée moins par des sentiments de découragement que d'espoir. En ouvrant les débats, Hambro avait lui-même déclaré: »Nous nous sommes assemblés, non pas afin de mettre un terme aux activités qui ont encore ici leur centre, mais afin, pour ainsi dire, de transfuser à un nouvel organisme toutes nos valeurs durables – tant morales que matérielles . . .«[38]. Aucun des orateurs suivants ne manqua de reprendre cette idée selon laquelle la création de l'ONU représentait le meilleur hommage que l'on pouvait rendre à la SdN[39]. Si la XXIème Assemblée fut une cérémonie de funérailles, celles-ci n'étaient à tout prendre, selon la formule du délégué bolivien Costa du Rels, que celles d'un phénix[40].

Sur le plan concret, l'Assemblée après avoir tranché un grand nombre de questions budgétaires et administratives prononça la dissolution de la SdN en ces termes:

»L'Assemblée de la Sociéte des Nations,

Considérant que, à des fins analogues à celles qui motivèrent la création de la Sociéte des Nations, la Charte des Nations Unies a établi une organisation internationale – les Nations Unies – dans laquelle tous les Etats peuvent être admis en qualité de membres, aux conditions prescrites par la Charte, et dont la grande majorité des Membres de la Société font déjà partie;

Désirant favoriser, autant qu'il est en son pouvoir, la poursuite, le développement et le succès de la coopération internationale sous la forme nouvelle adoptée par les Nations Unies;

Considérant que, la nouvelle organisation ayant assumé ses fonctions, la Société des Nations peut être dissoute, et

Considérant qu'aux termes de l'article 3, paragraphe 3, du Pacte, l'Assemblée connaît de toute question qui rentre dans la sphère d'activité de la Société des Nations:

Adopte la résolution suivante:

Dissolution de la Société des Nations.

. . . Dès le lendemain de la clôture de la présente session de l'Assemblée, la Société des Nations cessera d'exister, sous réserve des mesures de liquidation prévues par la présente résolution.

. . .«[41].

Mais cet acte de dissolution ne mettait un terme à l'existence de la SdN qu'en tant qu'association d'Etats poursuivant des fins spécifiques à l'aide d'un mécanisme institutionnel. Il laissait subsister la personnalité juridique de la Sociéte pour une période strictement limitée à la durée des opérations pratiques de liquidation confiées par l'Assemblée à un organe créé à cet effet: le Comité de liquidation (CL).

Composé de 9 membres, le CL tint, sous la présidence de Carl Hambro, 42 séances de travail – du 23 avril 1946 au 23 juillet 1947 – et soumit 4 rapports intérimaires avant de déposer son bilan final, le 31 juillet 1947[42]. Sa tâche consista en premier lieu à éteindre les obligations contractuelles pesant sur la SdN: celle-ci avait en effet des obligations à l'égard de ses propres fonctionnaires, devait faire face à un certain nombre de réclamations formulées contre elle et fixer le sort de divers Fonds spéciaux dont elle était dépositaire ou fidéicommissaire. En deuxième lieu, le CL s'attacha à obtenir le recouvrement des créances de la SdN dont la quasi-totalité se composait des contributions arriérées des Etats membres; au terme de cette entreprise particulièrement ardue, il parvint à faire rentrer une somme de plus de 28 millions de francs suisses – le montant des arriérés annulés ne s'élevant finalement qu'à 5,6 millions de francs-or[43].

Après avoir mené à chef ces deux premières tâches, le CL parvint au stade décisif de son action: le partage des avoirs matériels (bâtiments et mobilier, propriétés diverses, etc.) et des avoirs liquides (c'est-à-dire les soldes en caisse résultant de la liquidation des dettes et créances) entre les gouvernements des Etats membres. Le système de répartition arrêté par la XXIème Assemblée prévoyait que la part de chaque ayant droit serait déterminée par la proportion existant entre les contributions versées par celui-ci et le total des contributions reçues par la Sociéte depuis sa création. Deux conditions étaient toutefois requises des intéressés: être quittes de toute obligation financière vis-à-vis de la SdN avant le 31 décembre 1946 et posséder la qualité de membre au moment de la liquidation. La seconde condition avait pour effet d'éliminer de nombreux pays ennemis ou pays membres des Nations Unies. L'Autriche, l'Italie et le Chili tentèrent en vain d'être associés au partage[44] et malgré une offensive lancée par la France en faveur des Soviétiques, la XXIème Assemblée refusa de faire entorse à sa décision[45].

La distribution des avoirs liquides disponibles à la fin des opérations de liquidation (plus de 15 millions de francs suisses) ne posa pas de difficulté. En revanche, celle des avoirs matériels (évalués à plus de 46 millions de francs suisses) fit l'objet d'une procédure plus complexe. La part des membres sociétaires appartenant aux Nations Unies fut notifiée à cette organisation afin d'être imputée, dans sa comptabilité, au crédit des ayant droit. Quant à ceux qui n'étaient pas membres des Nations Unies, ils reçurent des sommes en avoirs liquides. Ne furent finalement exclus du partage que les pays membres défaillants (Albanie, Bulgarie, Ethiopie, Liberia), ceux qui avaient préféré céder la totalité de leur part à la SdN pour régler leurs dettes (Colombie) ou ceux qui n'existaient plus juridiquement (les trois Baltes). Les résultats montrèrent sur ce point la valeur et l'habileté de la gestion financière de la Société.

La tâche ultime des liquidateurs consista à tranférer à l'ONU ainsi qu'à certaines autres institutions internationales (OIT, OMS, UNESCO, CIJ) divers éléments du patrimoine sociétaire. Dans son rapport final, le CL estima d'ailleurs que sa propre oeuvre avait été »moins une oeuvre de liquidation qu'une oeuvre d'organisation et de transmission des services«[46].

III. La transmission de l'héritage sociétaire aux Nations Unies

La succession d'une organisation internationale par une autre était, en 1946, un événement qui n'avait pas de réel précédent[47]. Comme la Charte des Nations Unies avait été conçue sans liaison aucune avec l'abrogation du Pacte ou la dissolution de la SdN, un transfert ne pouvait être juridiquement opéré que sur la base d'accords organisationnels *inter se*. Au départ, deux formules seulement paraîssaient possibles: un transfert en bloc(préconisé par les Britanniques et par le Secrétariat de la Société) ou un tranfert sélectif, »à la carte« – ce dernier soutenu par les Soviétiques. L'idée directrice du Rapport Malkin, établi le 19 février 1945 au sein du Foreign Office avec la collaboration officieuse du Secrétariat de la SdN, était que la dissolution et la succession de la Société devaient se dérouler dans des conditions d'extrême dignité et en même temps montrer que »that what is done constitutes not only the end of a chapter, but the beginning of a new one«[48]. Pour réaliser cette continuité, il convenait que l'ONU poursuivit les *activités* fonctionnelles de la SdN au stade où celle-ci les avait laissées, assumât les *fonctions* particulières attribuées à l'institution genevoise par une multitude de traités internationaux et, enfin, héritât des *avoirs* matériels sociétaires. En somme, si le Rapport Malkin ne recommandait pas la reprise intégrale de l'héritage sociétaire, il ne se prononçait pas moins d'une façon nette en faveur du transfert en bloc du plus grand nombre possible d'éléments. Cette solution était sans doute profitable à l'institution genevoise. Elle lui permettait d'éviter l'opération, inévitablement longue et mortifiante, de l'auto-liquidation, tout en lui laissant l'impression qu'elle disparaissait en faveur d'un successeur moral et politique.

Le problème ainsi posé des fonctions, activités et avoirs de la SdN fut confié par le Comité exécutif de la CPNU à l'un de ses organes subsidiaires – le Comité 9 – lequel se prononça formellement en faveur d'un transfert en bloc moyennant toutefois quelques »exceptions«: ce transfert ne devait couvrir que les seules activités d'ordre technique et non politique ainsi que les seules fonctions portant sur les activités expressément continuées par l'ONU et ne pas impliquer l'obligation pour cette dernière de reprendre le personnel sociétaire[49]. Mais au sein du Comité exécutif, cette formule se heurta au veto catégorique de l'URSS. Schématiquement, la thèse soviétique consistait à revendiquer pour l'ONU le droit de faire un tri mûrement réfléchi de l'héritage sociétaire, c'est-à-dire en clair à subordonner la liquidation de la SdN au bon vouloir exclusif de la nouvelle organisation[50]. La perspective d'une prolongation de l'agonie sociétaire laissait l'URSS indifférente. Celle-ci croyait, ou feignait de croire, que les Nations Unies feraient leur choix assez rapidement – en fait, laisser la Societé dans une situation humiliante ne lui déplaisait guère. En outre, n'appartenant plus à la SdN, elle se se trouvait nullement lésée par le coût financier d'une liquidation prolongée.

L'hostilité de l'URSS vis-à-vis de la SdN ne devait plus désarmer[51]. Le souvenir de l'exclusion de décembre 1939 demeurait toujours sous-jacent[52] et il faut voir là l'une des causes principales de l'opposition à toute recommandation pouvant impliquer la reconnaissance d'une continuité juridique entre la SdN et l'ONU[53]. Un transfert en bloc était impensable pour l'URSS car, d'un point de vue pratique, il risquait de marquer un retour subreptice à Genève: l'acquisition rapide des bâtiments et propriétés sociétaires pouvait, par exemple, influencer les décisions sur le choix du siège permanent des Nations Unies. En outre, les Soviétiques concevaient les Nations Unies comme une institution de sécurité ne devant pas, à l'instar de la SdN, s'engager dans une multiplicité d'activités susceptibles de la détourner de ce but.

Le rapport du Comité 9 fut finalement adopté par le Comité exécutif par 10 voix contre 2 (URSS et Australie) et avec 2 abstentions (Tchécoslovaquie et Yougoslavie). Mais cela ne résolvait rien car la CPNU ne pouvait être liée par les recommandations majoritaires de son Comité exécutif. La CPNU (à travers son Comité 7) réexamina donc l'ensemble du problème. Bien que le débat prît parfois un ton assez vif, les parties finirent par composer. Le compromis intervenu le 18 décembre 1945 consista à faire une *séparation* complète entre le transfert des avoirs et la prise en charge d'un certain nombre de fonctions, pouvoirs et activités de la SdN. En fin de compte, la dévolution de l'héritage sociétaire aux Nations Unies entraîna trois processus distincts concernant respectivement les *avoirs*, les *fonctions basées sur des dispositions conventionelles et les fonctions non basées sur des dispositions conventionnelles.*

Le *transfert des avoirs* s'opéra sur la base d'un certain nombre de principes élaborés conjointement par un Comité spécial restreint de la CPNU et la Commission de contrôle de la SdN[54]. Il donna lieu, le ler août 1946, à la conclusion d'un Accord et d'un Protocole entre le Secrétaire général de la Société et un représentant du Secrétaire général des Nations Unies – W. Moderow[55]. Ces deux instruments furent ultérieurement complétés par un autre Protocole en date du 6 mars 1947 relatif à l'évaluation définitive des avoirs. Le total de l'inventaire final s'élevait alors à plus de 46 millions de francs suisses, soit à prés de 11 millions de dollars de l'époque. Pour plus de détails, nous renvoyons à l'Annexe 1.

A la clôture des travaux du Comité de liquidation, le Secrétaire général de la SdN notifia aux Nations Unies la liste des 32 Etats membres en droit de participer à la répartition des avoirs, matériels sociétaires, ainsi que les parts respectives de ces Etats. L'affaire du transfert des avoirs semblait devoir être vite classée à partir du moment où l'Assemblée générale des Nations Unies aurait décidé de l'affectation à donner aux crédits. Il n'en fut rien. Lors de la discussion à la Cinquième Commission, le délégué soviétique dénonça l'injustice du plan de répartition décidé originellement par la XXIème Assemblée de la SdN et réclama en conséquence que l'URSS fût associée au partage. La proposition fut mal accueillie dans l'ensemble. Mais le délégué soviétique repoussa tous les arguments qu'on lui opposait et déclara que s'il n'était pas fait droit à la demande de son gouvernement, ce dernier se verrait obligé »de décliner toute obligation résultant de la liquidation des avoirs«, ce qui – devait-il ajouter – risquait de provoquer »des difficultés financières autrement plus grandes que les difficultés juridiques auxquelles il a été fait allusion«[56]. Par esprit de conciliation, la Grande-Bretagne se déclara alors prête à réexaminer le problème en vue de donner satisfaction à l'URSS, mais à elle seule, car »les pays qui ont renoncé volontairement à leurs droits et obligations en tant que membres de la Société des nations se trouvent, évidemment, dans une situation quelque peu différente de celle d'une nation dont la participation à la Société des Nations a cessé par suite de circonstances échappant à son contrôle«[57]. Mais les autres Etats qui avaient dans le sillage de l'URSS soumis une demande de compensation protestèrent tant et si bien que la discussion fut arrêtée sous réserve que des consultations directes seraient entreprises entre tous les intéressés. Au terme de ces consultations, la Grande-Bretagne et la France – les deux pays dont les parts aux avoirs étaient les plus importantes – soumirent à l'Assemblée générale de 1948 un projet de résolution destiné à associer au partage des avoirs certains anciens membres de la SdN qui avaient émis des revendications[58]. La résolution fut adoptée par 33 voix et 3 abstentions le 8 décembre 1948[59]. Comme le montre l'Annexe 2, l'URSS ainsi que les Latino-Américains furent les principaux bénéficiaires de cette décision[60].

La *»prise en charge«* (et non le »transfert« – terme repoussé par l'URSS comme impliquant une continuité juridique qui ne devait pas exister) *des fonctions et pouvoirs appartenant à la SdN en vertu d'instruments internationaux* fut limitée et conditionnelle. Elle se fit sur la double base de la résolution 24(I) adoptée le 12 février 1946 par l'Assemblée générale des Nations Unies et de la résolution du 18 avril 1946 prise par la dernière Assemblée de la SdN. A partir de là, l'Assemblée générale des Nations Unies adoptera, entre 1946 et 1953, 5 protocoles qui amendaient une dizaine d'instruments multilatéraux en vue d'attribuer aux organes appropriés de l'ONU les fonctions et pouvoirs jusqu'alors du ressort de la Société. Il y eut ainsi prise en charge de 4 secteurs de l'héritage sociétaire: *contrôle des stupéfiants, questions sociales* (répression de la traite des femmes et des enfants, répression de la traite des femmes majeures, répression de la circulation et du trafic des publications obscènes), *statistiques économiques* et *esclavage*[61]. La question des traités conclus sous les auspices de la SdN devait revenir à l'ordre du jour dans les années soixante à l'occasion des travaux effectués par la Commission du droit international sur le droit des traités: au terme d'une procédure assez complexe, 11 de ces traités furent déclarés ouverts à l'adhésion spécifique des Etats en voie de développement qui avaient acquis leur indépedance bien après la dissolution de la SdN[62].

La *»prise en charge« des fonctions et activités non politiques exercées par la SdN* *autrement qu'en vertu de traités internationaux* fut tout aussi complexe mais plus ample. Conformément aux recommandations de la CPNU, la première Assemblée générale des Nations Unies confia à l'ECOSOC une double tâche importante. D'une part, elle le chargea de »procéder à un examen des fonctions et activités de caractère non politique précédemment exercées par la Société des Nations, en vue de déterminer celles qui devraient, sous réserve des modifications désirables, être assumées par les organes des Nations Unies, ou confiées à des institutions spécialisées reliées à l'Organisation«. D'autre part, elle le pria, en attendant les résultats de cet examen, d'»assumer et de poursuivre, à titre provisoire, la tâche accomplie précédemnt par les sections suivantes de la Societé des Nations: les sections économique, financière et du transit (. . .), la section d'hygiène (. . .), la section de l'opium et la section du Comité central permanent de l'opium et de l'Organe de contrôle«[63]. Cette même résolution recommandait au Secrétaire général de »procéder aux arrangements nécessaires pour reprendre et maintenir en activité, les services de la Bibliothèque et les Archives ainsi que pour compléter le Recueil des Traités de la Société des Nations«, et laissait entendre qu'il serait également souhaitable que l'Organisation engageât à cette occasion »tels membres du personnel expérimenté actuellement chargé de ce travail, que le Secrétaire général estimera bon de choisir«[64]. L'ECOSOC demanda au Secrétaire général de s'occuper lui-même de l'examen d'ensemble de la question attendu par l'Assemblée générale. Le rapport qui lui fut alors soumis le 26 septembre 1946 annonça que le Secrétariat des Nations Unies assurait déjà, à titre provisoire, les fonctions autrefois exercées par les diverses sections du Secrétariat de la SdN dans les domaines non politique et recommandait que les autres commissions techniques de l'ECOSOC devraient examiner à leur tour la mesure dans laquelle elles auraient intérêt à poursuivre certaines autres activités ou fonctions sociétaires[65].

L'URSS combattit farouchement cette proposition derrière laquelle se profilait à nouveau l'idée, inacceptable à ses yeux, d'une prise en charge *globale* de l'héritage sociétaire. Mais ce fut en vain: l'Assemblée se rangea à cette solution le 14 décembre 1946[66] qui marquait un indubitable revirement par rapport aux recommandations originelles de la CPNU. La décision de l'Assemblée générale annonçait, en effet, la poursuite de l'*ensemble* des fonctions et activités non politiques de la Société. Il était par conséquent clair qu'allait ainsi s'instituer entre les deux organisations internationales une continuité pratique davantage significative peut-être que la continuité juridique à laquelle l'URSS avait réussi à faire jusque ici obstacle.

Nonobstant presque toujours l'hostilité de l'URSS, les Nations Unies purent ainsi développer l'œuvre de la SdN dans pratiquement tous les domaines techniques. L'ONU proprement dite reprit et poursuivit les activités sociétaires en matière de transports et communications, de problèmes économiques et financiers, de stupéfiants, d'enregistrement des traités, de problèmes sociaux, d'esclavage et – dans une certaine mesure – de protection des minorités[68]. En revanche, trois autres grands domaines d'activité autrefois de la compétence de simples organes subsidiaires de la SdN, furent confiés à des institutions spécialisées à part entière: la protection des réfugiés (Organisation internationale pour les réfugiés), l'hygiène (Organisation mondiale de la santé) et la coopération intellectuelle (UNESCO).[68].

Enfin, malgré une position de principe apparemment intransigeante, l'ONU engagea plus de 200 anciens fonctionnaires à l'occasion de la prise en charge des diverses sections techniques du Secrétariat de la SDN[69]. D'anciens »Genevois« chevronnés comme T. Aghnidès, E. Colban, A. Sweetser, P. de Azcarate, A. Pelt, B. Lukac, H. Vigier, etc., furent appelés à jouer un rôle important dès les débuts des Nations Unies. Certains d'entre eux pourront même se targuer d'avoir connu le privilège de servir les trois Secrétaires généraux de la SdN ainsi que les trois premiers Secrétaires généraux de l'ONU!

En conclusion, dès sa naissance l'ONU ne put que suivre assez fidèlement la voie royale tracée par un quart de siècle d'expérience sociétaire. Quoiqu'elle s'en défendît, l'Organisation commença à fonctionner comme une version nouvelle de la SdN – version simplement révisée sur le plan de la sécurité collective et version développée en matière de coopération fonctionnelle.

ANNEXE 1
Inventaire final

Approuvé par le Comité de Liquidation au nom de la Société des Nations et par le Comité consultatif des questions administratives et budgétaires et le Secrétaire général de l'Organisation des Nations Unies au nom de cette organisation.

		Francs suisses
1) Secrétariat et Salle des Assemblées[1] . .		38 742 999,43
2) Bâtiment de la Bibliothèque[2]		Néant
3) Propriétés de la Société des Nations, d'une superficie de 203 446 m², comprenant quatre villas et d'autres constructions		2 889 453,45
4) Mobilier, installations diverses, machines à écrire, etc., pour l'usage du Secrétariat, y compris les bureaux auxiliaires[3], et les autres bâtiments à Genève:		
Total selon les inventaires	3 332 922,61	

A déduire:

	Francs suisses
a) Montants inclus sous Secrétariat . .	1 454 080,45
b) Montants relatifs à des comptes extra-	

budgétaires (Don Rockefeller)	25 782,99		
c) Montants relatifs au Fonds de Dotation de la Bibliothèque .	4 514,15		
		1 484 377,59	
			1 848 545,02
5) Mobilier, installations diverses, machines à écrire, etc., pour l'usage de la Cour permanente de Justice internationale à La Haye			199 810,55
6) a) Stocks de papeterie, papier d'impression, fournitures de bureau et matériel à Genève et auprès des bureaux auxiliaires			132 625,54
b) Publications à Genève et auprès des bureaux auxiliaires			400 000.–
7) Livres, stocks de papeterie, papier d'impression et publications, fournitures de bureau et matériel de la Cour permanente de Justice internationale à La Haye . .			55 562,35
8) Dons[4]			Néant
9) Bibliothèque: Livres, etc., à Genève[5] .			1 925 572,95
10) Archives de la Société des Nations et de la Cour permanente de Justice internationale			Néant
Total			46 194 569,29

1 Coût du bâtiment et du matériel du Secrétariat et de la Salle des Assemblées. La Société des Nations avait un droit cessible à l'usage des terrains sur lesquels s'élèvent les bâtiments, d'une bande de terrain de 100 mètres de largeur à l'entour et des deux routes conduisant aux bâtiments. En outre, la Société des Nations avait un droit incessible à l'usage des autres parcelles de terrain du parc de l'Ariana dans lequel s'élèvent les bâtiments. Ces droits ont été portés au bilan pour mémoire.

2 Le coût de ce bâtiment, don de M. Rockefeller, a été de francs suisses 5 564 206,22.

3 *Y compris* les bureaux de Londres, Princeton, Washington, New-Delhi et de Singapour, mais à l'*exclusion* de celui de Paris.

4 Les dons comprennent des tableaux, des sculptures et autres oeuvres d'art, pour lesquels on ne peut fixer de valeur monétaire. Y est également compris du mobilier évalué à francs suisses 1 234 640.

5 Sans tenir compte des volumes provenant de dons ou d'échanges et dont la valeur est estimée à francs suisses 1 592 516,05.

SOURCE: SdN, doc. C.5.M.5.1947, p. 60.

ANNEXE 2

Liste indiquant les crédits fixés par la Société des Nations et les ajustements nécessaires en vue de mettre des crédits à la disposition de neuf participants supplémentaires

(En dollars des Etats-Unis)

États Membres ayant droit à des crédits conformément à la liste établie par la Société des Nations	*Montant des crédits fixés par la Société des Nations*	*Part qu'il est recommandé de mettre à la disposition des participants supplémentaires*	*Montants auxquels les premiers participants devront renoncer en vue de mettre des crédits à la disposition des participants supplémentaires*	*Montants ajustés des crédits*
1. Afghanistan . . .	8 229,97	–	394,35	7 835,62
2. Argentine	417 665,43	–	20 012,84	397 652,59
3. Australie	553 285,85	–	26 511,22	526 774,63
4. Belgique	307 743,09	–	14 745,80	292 997,29
5. Bolivie	32 150,60	–	1 540,53	30 610,07
6. Canada	729 261,83	–	34 943,28	694 318,55
7. Chine	464 359,57	–	22 250,23	442 109,34
8. Cuba	103 300,17	–	4 949,73	98 350,44
9. Danemark	213 336,20	–	10 222,21	203 113,99
10. Égypte	73 477,12	–	3 520,73	69 956,39
11. Equateur	3 737,31	–	179,08	3 558,23
12. France	1 363 713,33	–	65 343,63	1 298 369,70
13. Grèce	117 988,73	–	5 680,42	112 308,31
14. Inde	1 084 228,32	–	51 951,84	1 032 276,48
15. Irak	30 673,10	–	1 469,73	29 203,37
16. Iran	67 060,44	–	4 446,96	62 613,48
17. Luxembourg . .	22 230,04	–	1 065,17	21 164,87
18. Mexique	74 259,54	–	5 642,04	68 617,50
19. Norvège	173 666,11	–	8 321,38	165 344,73
20. Nouvelle-Zélande	182 239,24	–	8 732,17	173 507,07
21. Panama	24.107,24	–	1 155,12	22 952,12
22. Pays-Bas	399 538,23	–	19 144,26	380 393,97
23. Pologne	507 049,04	–	24 295,74	482 753,30
24. République Dominicaine	12 669,58	–	607,08	12 062,50
25. Royaume-Uni . .	2 012 725,83	–	96 441,69	1 916 284,14
26. Siam	143 240,75	–	6 863,52	136 377,23
27. Suède	388 340,50	–	18 607,70	369 732,80
28. Tchécoslovaquie .	447 092,27	–	21 422,85	425 669,42
29. Turquie	102 243,66	–	4 899,10	97 344,56
30. Union Sud-Africaine	344 443,02	–	16 504,33	327 938,69
31. Uruguay	85 879,24	–	4 114,98	81 764,26
32. Yougoslavie . . .	319 593,86	–	15 386,45	304 207,41
. . . .	10 809 529,21	–	521 366,16	10 288 163,05

États Membres supplémentaires devant être admis à recevoir une part des crédits en vertu d'un accord conclu entre les premiers participants	*Montant des crédits fixés par la Société des Nations*	*Part qu'il est recommandé de mettre à la disposition des participants supplémentaires*	*Montants auxquels les premiers participants devront renoncer en vue de mettre des crédits à la disposition des participants supplémentaires*	*Montants ajustés des crédits*
. . . .	10 809 529,21	–	521 366,16	10 288 163,05
1. Chili	–	120 537,57	–	120 537,57
2. Guatemala	–	7 567,24	–	7 567,24
3. Haïti	–	20 085,51	–	20 085,51
4. Honduras	–	4 793,08	–	4 793,08
5. Nicaragua	–	2 671,20	–	2 671,20
6. Pérou	–	38 180,60	–	38 180,60
7. Salvador	–	11 789,47	–	11 789,47
8. Union des Républiques socialistes soviétiques .	–	256 392,68	–	256 392,68
9. Venezuela	–	59 348,81	–	59 348,81
Totaux	10 809 529,21	521 366,16	521 366,16	10 009 529,21

SOURCE: ONU, Assemblée générale, Résolution 250 (III), Annexe B.

Notes

1 Cf. *Public Opinion, 1935-1946*. Hadley Cantril, ed. Princeton, Princeton University Press, 1951. - p. 373, 403 et 903-915.

2 *Ibid.*, p. 908.

3 Parmi les facteurs qui expliquent le revirement du Parti Républicain, il y eut sans doute les prises de position publiques de Wendell Wilkie (l'un de ses leaders et adversaire malheureux de Roosevelt à la présidence des Etats-Unis en 1940) qui, par exemple le 11 mai 1942, déclara qu'au terme de la guerre les Américains n'auraient le choix qu'entre trois politiques: l'isolationnisme (qui constituerait à la longue un danger pour la sécurité nationale), l'impérialisme (instrument d'asservissement des autres pays) et l'internationalisme - ce dernier synonyme de toutes les libertés (cf. *The New York Times* du 12 mai 1942). Rappelons aussi la déclaration Mackinac par laquelle le Parti Républicain annonça en 1943 qu'il approuvait l'entrée des Etats-Unis dans l'organisation internationale future.

4 Cf. Ruth B. Russell, *A History of the United Nations Charter. The Role of the United States*, 1940-1945. Washington, Brookings Institution, 1958. - p. 101.

5 Cf. *Postwar Foreign Policy Preparation, 1939-1945*. Washington, Government Printing Office, 1949. - (Department of State Publication 3580, General Foreign Policy Series 15), p. 112.

6 Dans ses mémoires, Churchill rapporte les paroles suivantes prononcées par Staline à Yalta en 1945: "My colleagues in Moscow cannot forget what happened in December 1939, during the Russo-Finnish War, when the British and the French used the League

of Nations against us and succeeded in isolating and expelling the Soviet Union from the League (. . .). - Winston S. Churchill, *The Second World War*, v. 6: *Triumph and Tragedy*. London, Cassell, 1954. - p. 311." Voir aussi la version assez proche du Secrétaire d'Etat américain James F. Byrnes, *Cartes sur table*. Paris, Morgan, 1947. - p- 86 ainsi que *FRUS, The Conference at Malte and Yalta*, 1945. Washington, Government Printing Office, 1955. - p. 666-667.

7 *Ibid.*

8 Pour plus de détails, voir notre ouvrage *La France en guerre et les organisations internationales, 1939-1945*. Paris. Mouton, 1969. - p. 142 ff.

9 Cf. Charles de Gaulle: *Mémoires de guerre. Le salut, 1944-1946*. Paris, Plon, 1959. - p. 374.

10 L'élection ou la réélection de la Chine comme membre non permanent au Conseil de la SdN n'alla jamais sans difficulté.

11 Cf. Geoffrey L. Goodwin: *Britain and the United States*. New York, Manhattan Publishing Company, 1959. - p. 3 et 5.

12 Cf. Russell, *op. cit.*, p. 133-137 et *FRUS*, 1943/I, p. 756.

13 La SdN à sa naissance ne fut elle-même rien d'autre qu'une version améliorée à la fois du Concert européen, du système des conférences de la Haye, des Unions internationales et la coopération fonctionnelle interalliée cf. Alfred Zimmern, *The League of Nations and the Rule of Law, 1918-1935*. London, MacMillan, 1936. - p. 264 ff.

14 Charles K. Webster: "The Making of the Charter of the United Nations" *History*, v. cg., March 1947. - p. 17.

15 Voir sur ce point Leland M. Goodrich: "From League of Nations to United Nations" *International Organization*, v. l, février 1947. - p. 3-21 et Gerhart Niemeyer, "The Balance Sheet of the League Experiment" *International Organization*, v. 6, novembre 1952. - p. 537-558. Les différences fondamentales entre la SdN et l'ONU sont magistralement analysées dans Stanley Hoffman, *Organisations internationales et pouvoirs politiques des Etats*. Paris, Colin, 1954. - p. 265-283.

16 Cf. *United Nations Conference on International Organization* (ci-après UNCIO). New York, United Nations Information Organization, 1945-1955, v. l: p. 149-150, 154, 215, 256, 261, 314, 388, 395, 399, 463, 467, 490, 494, 526, 536, 542, 581-582, 591-592, 593, 597, 600, 608, 667; v. 12, p. 309-310 et 322-323.

17 *Ibid.*, v. l, p. 461.

18 *Ibid.*,v. l, p. 3.

19 Cf. Raymond B. Fosdick, *The League and the United nations after Fifty Years: the Six Secretaries-General*. Newtown, s.e., 1972. - p. 74 et la version plus brutale de Arthur W. Rovine: *The First Fifty Years: The Secretary-General in World Politics, 1920-1970*. Leyden, Sijthoff, 1970.- p. 193.

20 Cf. le discours du délégué canadien à la 2ième Assemblée: SdN, Actes de la Vingt et unième Session Ordinaire de l'Assemblée, Compte rendu des Sessions plénières, 10 avril 1946, *JOSS* no. 194, p. 39.

21 *UNCIO*, v. 15, p. 517.

22 Cf. ONU, doc. PC/EX/20, p. 8.

23 *Ibid.*, docs. PC/9, p. 13; PC/EX/ES/24; PC/EX/ES/26(1); PC/EX/ES/29; p. 1-4.

24 Ou d'institutions à durée prédéterminée comme, par exemple, l'Office international Nansen pour les réfugiés (1930-1938).

25 Report of the Committee on the Liquidation of the League of Nations *PRO* 371, v. 50636, p. 18-56. cf. aussi ONU, doc. PC/EX/LN/2 et *FRUS* 1945/I, p. 176-178.

26 Paragraphe 124 du Rapport Malkin, *loc. cit.*

27 *Ibid.*, paragraphes 124-131.

28 Cf. doc. SdN. C.103.M103.1945.

29 Six des 9 absents n'avaient pas été invités pour des raisons d'opportunité politique - l'Albanie, les trois Baltes, le Siam et la Bulgarie; quant aux 3 autres (Ethiopie, Irak, Liberia), la question ne semblait probablement pas les intéresser considérablement.
30 Cf. doc. SdN, A.22.1946.
31 Cf. SdN, Actes de la Vingt et unième Session ordinaire de l'Assemblée, Compte rendu des Séances plénières; (Annexe 27) *JOSS* no. 194, p. 277. Voir aussi doc. SdN, A.29.1946, et les Archives de la SdN, 1933-1946/15/43788/43781(R5258).
32 Cf. doc. SdN. A.27.1946.
33 L'incident n'est pas mentionné dans les procès-verbaux officiels de l'Assemblée. Voir *The New York Times*, 9 avril 1946, p. 3, col. 3; du 10 avril 1946, p. 4 col. 4 et p. 5 col. 2.
34 Cf. SdN, Actes de la Vingt et unième Session Ordinaire de l'Assemblée, Compte rendu des Séances plénières, 21 avril 1946; *JOSS* no. 194, p. 42, et *Le Monde* du 13 avril 1946, p. l, col. 4.
35 Cf. SdN, Actes de la Vingt et unième Session Ordinaire de l'Assemblee, Procès-verbaux de la Deuxième Commission, et Annexes nos. 26 & 27; *JOSS* no. 194, p. 129, 133, 135-136, 137, 268, 380. Voir aussi *The New York Times,* 14 avril 1946, p. l col. 6; 16 avril 1946, p. 16, col. 6; 17 avril 1946, p. 4, col. 5.
36 Pour une classification thématique des interventions faites à la XXIème Assemblée, voir *L'héritage de la Société des Nations* (doc. SdN, 1946.l, p. 27-63).
37 SdN, Actes de la Vingtième (fin) Session Ordinaire de l'Assemblée, Compte rendu des Séances plénières, 8 avril 1946; *JOSS* no. 194, p. 19.
38 *Ibid.*
39 *Ibid.*, (note 36.
40 SdN, Actes de la Vingt et unième Session Ordinaire de l'Assemblée, Compte rendu des Séances plénières, 9 avril 1946; *JOSS* no. 194, p. 28.
41 SdN, Actes de la Vingt et unième Session ordinaire de l'Assemblée, Compte rendu des Séances plénières; Annexe no. 27; *JOSS* no. 194, p. 281.
42 Cf. SdN, doc. C.83.M.83.1946; C.89.M.89.1946; C.3.M.3.1947; C.4.M.4.1947 et C.5.M.5.1947.
43 Pour plus de détails, voir notre ouvrage *Organisation internationale et guerre mondiale. Le cas de la Sociéte des nations et de l'Organisation internationale du travail pendant la seconde guerre mondiale.* Grenoble, Université des Science sociales de Grenoble, 1975. - p. 766 ff.
44 Cf. doc. SdN, B.L/P.V.l, p. 2, 9-10 et doc. CC/1511.
45 SdN, Actes de la Vingt et unième Session Ordinaire de l'Assemblée, Procés verbaux de la Deuxième Commission; *JOSS* no. 194, p. 128, 129, 133, 135, 136.
46 Doc. SdN, C.5.M.5.1947, p. 19-20.
47 Cf. Henry Reiff, *Transition from League of Nations to United Nations.* Washington, D. C. - United Information Series (Department of State Publications 2542), 1946. - p. 3.
48 Paragraphe 124 du Rapport Malkin, *loc. cit.*
49 ONU, doc. PC/EX/113/Rev. l, p. 108.
50 *Ibid.*, docs. PC/EX/LN/28. paragraphe 3; PC/EX/LN/29, paragraphes 2 et 4; PC/EX/ON/96, p. 5; PC/EX/LN/5.
51 A l'occasion de la dissolution de la SdN, on pouvait lire ces phrases révélatrices dans une revue soviétique publiée à Londres: "So the League of Nations has been buried in Geneva. The funeral ceremony was of the proverbial "pauper" type - where nobody follows the coffin and the hearse is pulled by one melancholy hack . . . It was quite a good example of what an international organization should not do . . . It was as talkative as a magpie and as cowardly as a hare. The League was permeated with duplicity. Its

language was democratic but its soul reactionary. It deceived the nations . . ." (D. Zaslavaski, "An Obituary. The League of Nations", *Soviet News*, 29 avril 1946, p. 2.)

52 Cf. *supra* note 6.

53 Au sein du Comité exécutif de la CPNU, le délégué soviétique (A. Gromyko) fit valoir que "there was no juridical or political connection between the two organizations . . ." (ONU, doc. PC/EX/96, p. 2). Le délegué australien, qui partageait ce point de vue, dit au cours de la même séance: "The United Nations was not a direct continuation of the League of Nations, although certain functions and assets of the League should obviously be taken over by it . . . Functions could not be attributed to the United Nations Organisation just because they were functions of the League" (*ibid.*, p. 2-39

54 ONU, docs. A.18 et A.18 Add.1 et 2; SdN, doc A.81.1946.X (Annexe).

55 SdN, doc. C.83.M.83.1946, p. 14-16.

56 Assemblée générale des Nations Unies (lère session, 2ème partie), Cinquième Commission, p. 123.

57 *Ibid.*, p. 159.

58 ONU, doc. A/C.5/285.

59 Résolution 250 (III).

60 Sur les dix autres pays qui avaient été membres de la SdN, 7 ne faisaient pas encore partie des Nations Unies: Japon, Allemagne, Autriche, Italie, Hongrie, Espagne, Roumanie. Les autres pays restants étaient le Costa Rica, le Brésil (les 2 premiers Etats a s'être retirés de la SdN et dont, par conséquent, la part aux avoirs était faible) ainsi que le Paraguay (pays en défaut). Quelle que fût l'opportunité - ou l'équité - de cette nouvelle répartition, il nous semble qu'un pays méritait peut-être plus que tout autre d'y participer: l'Autriche qui avait perdu sa qualité de membre contre son gré en raison de l'Anschluss.

61 Pour plus de détails, voir/Ghebali, *Organisation internationale et guerre mondiale, op. cit.* p. 80 ff.

62 Cf. ONU, docs. A/5209, A/5287, A/CNU/162, A/C.6L.498, A/5759. Voir aussi Michael Hardy, "The United Nations and General Multilateral Treaties concluded under the Auspices of the League of Nations" *British Year-Book of International Law*, 1963. - p. 425-438.

63 Assemblée générale des Nations Unies, résolution 24 (I) du 12 février 1946.

64 *Ibid.*

65 ONU, doc. E/177/Rev. 1.

66 Assemblée générale des Nations Unies, résolution 51 (I).

67 Pour plus détails voir/Ghebali *Organisation internationale et guerre mondiale, op. cit.*, p. 831 ff. Le cas de la protection des minorités présente un intérêt particulier car s'il y eut solution de continuité entre l'œuvre de alle SdN et cel de l'ONU, ce fut dans ce domaine préçis (*ibid*)., p. 848 ff).

68 *Organisation internationale et guerre mondiale, op. cit.*, p. 855 ff

69 Cf. docs. SdN, C.5.M.5.1947, p. 21; C.83.M.83.1946, p. 4; C.89.M.89.1946, p. 2; C.3.M.3.1947, p. 3, C.4.M.4.1947, p. 4. et Internal Circular 21, 1946.

Chapter / Chapitre II

States and the League of Nations: case studies

Les Etats et la Sociéte des Nations: études de cas

Great Britain and the League of Nations: collective security as myth and history

George W. Egerton
University of British Columbia, Vancouver, B.C.

"The policy of UN sanctions is infinitely precious: it is the alternative to war.

Diplomatic sanctions (withdrawal of ambassadors from Tokyo) as proposed by Cecil in 1931, could have ended the Japanese militarist rebels' aggression in Manchuria in 1931; the rebels had to murder *three* civilian prime ministers who opposed them. Oil sanctions could have prevented Mussolini's conquest of Abyssinia in 1936. A general trade embargo would have rendered Hitler helpless in 1937–8 . . . .

If [the principle of sanctions] had been observed faithfully, all the wars since 1920 would have stopped as soon as they began."

Taken from recent pages of the *Guardian*,[1] these are the words of Lord Philip Noel-Baker, a patriarch of the League of Nations and of the twentieth century peace movement. Noel-Baker of course is defending one of the most alluring and important themes in twentieth century international politics – the concept of collective security. From its birth in the crucible of the Great War, through its incorporation in the League of Nations Covenant, its testing and failure in the thirties, its rebirth after the Second World War in the United Nations Charter, to its transformation and demise in the Cold War and the age of nuclear strategy, the concept of collective security has served as one of the most potent ideals in attempts to structure a peaceful international order. Indeed, Inis Claude has argued perceptively: "If the movement for international organization in the twentieth century can be said to have a preoccupation, a dominant purpose, a supreme ideal, it is clear that the achievement of collective security answers that description."[2] And for Michael Howard the consistent aim of liberal statesmen throughout this century has been to transcend the balance of power by the creation of a "genuine world system of collective security."[3]

Much ink has been spilt on defining and refining the concept of collective security. Although the term was not used widely until 1932–33, its integral ideas were all systematized during the wartime league of nations movement under such terms as enforced peace and mutual defence.[4] The core ideas were as simple as they were appealing to peoples caught in the tragedy of total war. What was needed was a new international organization which would base itself on agreed principles and procedures for resolving international disputes peacefully. To ensure respect for these principles and procedures the peace-loving States would pool their preponderant collective power in a system of mutual guarantees and sanctions to deter or punish any aggressors. The most hopeful result of such a system would be the abolition of war itself. At the least, peaceful States would enjoy a security which they could not achieve alone, and which could not be provided by the old system of alliances, armaments, and the balance of power. It was a system of "each for all and all for each," or, for its many Christian advocates, the principle of being one's brother's keeper applied internationally.

The appeal of such ideas, as heralded by Wilson and leaders of the wartime league of nations movement in Britain, America, and the Allied countries, would be of massive significance. Wilson elevated the league idea to the summit of the Allies' liberal war aims programme after 1917. And with the drafting of the League of Nations Covenant at the Peace Conference of 1919, the collective security ideal was incorporated into the structure of postwar international relations.

The concept of collective security as a possible approach to peace has attracted enormous attention, both from proponents and critics, as well as from practitioners and theorists of international politics. Using sociological and historical methodologies this paper proposes to analyze collective security the thesis being that it can best be comprehended as a myth – indeed the central myth of the twentieth century liberal internationalist ideology.

The use of myth as an analytical tool requires, of course, both clarity and caution. Of major heuristic value to anthropologists, sociologists, theologians, and literary critics, the concept of myth must for our purposes be differentiated immediately from its pejorative common usage as connoting falsehood or illusion. Myth, modern as well as ancient, functions as a major vehicle (perhaps the medium, par excellence) for the definition, communication, maintenance and socialization of values and belief, political values in the case of political myth. The particulars believed may be true or false, or more likely a mixture of both; but to be effective the myth must be perceived socially as truth.

This paper analyzes the myth of collective security, using the concept of myth in two distinct but related ways: first as a central, emotive image or ideal which focuses or symbolizes a more generalized, abstract ideology – in this case the ideology of liberal internationalism; second, as a dramatic, didactic narrative – for our purposes the rise and fall of the League of Nations. Both usages of the concept of myth involve the element of narration or story. In the first usage, the focus is largely on the future where the myth depicts an eschatological political transformation. The second usage has its focus primarily on the past, the myth appropriating the form of history. The first usage of myth may, after attempted realization and perhaps failure, shift to the second, as continued legitimation and consolation are sought for in history. In both cases, whether eschatological or historical, the myth is functional to present needs and purposes; political myth is designed to serve needs and further the goals of a socio-political group.[5]

Sir Leslie Stephen, the Victorian critic and author, once wrote that "the doctrines which men hold do not become operative upon their conduct until they have generated an imaginative symbolism."[6] The Europe of Stephen's time, the seed-bed of mass politics, was not lacking in imaginative symbolisms – the myths of nation, race, class, and empire to name but a few. It was Sorel, in his *Reflections on Violence,* who first made the potent political functions of myth explicit in propounding the myth of the general strike. For Sorel, experience showed that "the *framing of a future, in some indeterminate time,* may, when it is done in a certain way, be very effective . . ; this happens when the anticipations of the future take the form of those myths, which enclose with them all the strongest inclinations of a people, of a party or of a class, inclinations which recur to the mind with the insistence of instincts in all the circumstances of life; and which give an aspect of complete reality to the hopes of immediate action by which, more easily than by any other method, men can reform their desires, passions, and mental activity".[7]

Such "motor images,", according to Sorel, distilled in propaganda, constantly rejuvenated by the feelings aroused by participation in violence, would produce "an entirely epic state of mind," bending all the energies of mind and group to the realization of the goal. If the myth of the general strike was focused on the future (eschatological), Sorel was nevertheless clear that "the myth must be judged as a means of acting on the present."[8]

For Sorel it was "to violence that Socialism owes those high ethical values by means of which it brings salvation to the modern world."[9] Violence there would surely be with the advent of general war in 1914, soon violence beyond anything imagined by Sorel. But where would the modern world find salvation? Writing in the wake of the war, the Oxford classicist Gilbert Murray surmized: "The League has got to redeem the world and naturally it starts with a world badly in need of redemption."[10] Murray's liberal internationalism was but one of the world-redeeming ideologies struggling for pre-eminence in the post-war period. The war, with its mass destruction and dislocation of the old order, evoked a new surge of ideological consciousness and conflict – especially after the Bolshevik revolution of 1917. As of 1919 the principal ideological competitors were the forces of reformist liberal capitalism led by Wilson and the parties of revolutionary socialism who looked to Lenin, with the ideologies of the Right biding their time.

Differing radically of course in content, and steeped in mutual hostility, the competing ideologies each served similar socio-political functions. They refracted the inchoate perceptions of reality of a social group into an ordered consciousness; they explained the origins and causes of present evils while prescribing the appropriate remedial programme; they projected a utopian future; they furthered social integration of a group and legitimated the leadership of a political elite. Just as Sorel depicted the general strike as the central myth of syndicalism, so also each of the major ideologies had their integral myth: revolution in the case of bolshevism, evolutionary progress for liberalism, race for fascism and nazism, and civilization for conservatives. Though the myths like the ideologies varied radically in substance, functionally they were equivalents. In each instance they served as an image with tremendous emotive appeal to a social group or class, giving its experience moral coherence, reinforcing its identity and cohesion, deliniating appropriate roles and above all inspiring and motivating its collective behavior. The myth, a construct largely of faith rather than rational analysis, might well contain ambiguities or inner contradictions. This did not matter and could even enhance its potency – so long as the process of translating the myth into political reality remained remote or impossible.

The myth of collective security, as it evolved in the wartime league of nations movement, at the Peace Conference, and during the inter-war period, integrated and extended the fundamental themes and internationalist aspects of ninteenth century and pre-war liberalism –, i. e. the belief in the essential harmony of interests and desire for cooperation underlying the relations of nation states and peoples (rightly organized and properly educated); the hopes for peace through the progressive extension of world political and legal structures; and the critique of the balance of power, the arms race, secrecy, and imperialism attributed to the old diplomacy.[11] The myth was sometimes structured as an international analogue to the classic liberal myth of the social contract, with the League of Nations Covenant and its system of collective security ending the pre-war Hobbesean state of latent war or "international anarchy."[12]

Collective security had tremendous appeal to those individuals and social groups whose progressive and irenic world-view had been shaken if not shattered by the carnage of the war. To conservatives or socialists war was, if not natural, at least ideologically comprehensible. For the liberal conscience, modern Europe's reversion to barbarism was bearable and meaningful only if it could be translated into a struggle for liberal goals. Hence, the psychological and sociological dynamics generating the war to end war, the war to make the world safe for democracy, the Fourteen Points, and the league of nations movement.

In both Britain and America the ideas of enforced peace and mutual defence were integral to the pro-league movement from its inception.[13] It was in this theme that pro-leaguers consciously advanced beyond the pre-war peace movement. For liberal internationalists the collectivist theme presented a solution to the endemic problem of putting force behind justice. Despite the critics and the skeptics, Wilson and leaders of the struggle for a league saw the collective enforcement principle as the key to the establishment of a peace organization. Lawrence Lowell, president of Harvard and a leader of the League to Enforce Peace, gave perhaps the most dramatic and concise rationale for collective force: "We feel that the only thing that will prevent war is the certainty that the country going to war will have to meet the world in arms, and we believe that any country which is fully convinced that if it commits acts of hostility towards another before submitting the question in dispute to arbitration it will have to fight all the world, will never commit such acts of hostility, and hence that such a universal war will never be needed . . . It seems to me that the repressive or preventive action provided for by any league must be automatic if it is to be effective and that the only automatic action that would really be effective is an agreement for universal war; and such an agreement, if genuine, would never need to be carried into execution?."[14]

In Britain the programme of the League of Nations Union, which united the principal British pro-league groups at the end of the war, had at its centre the obligation of league members "to suppress jointly, by the use of all the means at their disposal, any attempt by any State to disturb the peace of the world by acts of war."[15]

Plans for enforced peace inspired extremely successful propaganda. On the surface the schemes appeared simple, plausible, and above all, necessary to a world experiencing the social cataclysm of modern warfare. And if the war provided the social bases for the pro-league movement, Wilson served as an effective ideologue and rhetorician of the liberal internationalist programme. Although the American President never used the term, he has rightly been recognized as the father of the collective security concept. Wilson's earliest reflections on the league ideal in August 1914, projected "an association of the nations, all bound together for the protection of the integrity of each, so that any one nation breaking from this bond will bring upon herself war; that is to say, punishment, automatically."[16] From this date, through the war and the Fourteen Points, the struggle for Article Ten in the drafting of the Covenant, and the tragic campaign in America for ratification of the treaty without Senate reservations, Wilson never deviated from his commitment to the security guarantees which he considered the heart of the Covenant. Indeed, by 1919 Wilson was a man seemingly possessed by the collective security myth.

With the defeat of Wilson's programme by the Senate and the consequent failure of the United States to ratify the Treaty of Versailles and join the League of Nations, the myth of collective security passed primarily to British hands for safekeeping and cultivation. Whatever reservations the British government had on the Covenant (and they were many)[17], the League of Nations Union devoted itself to massing public opinion behind the League cause and ensuring that British foreign policy did not deviate from the letter and spirit of the new order.

The history of the League of Nations Union (LNU) has yet to be published,[18] but it is widely acknowledged to have been "the single most important and influential pressure group" concerned with inter-war British foreign policy.[19] Under the brilliant leadership of Lord Robert Cecil and Gilbert Murray, the LNU, surmounting its early organizational and financial difficulties, met from the beginning an extremely receptive British public. Membership rolls grew from approximately 100,000 in 1921 to 500,000 in 1925, reaching over a million in 1933. Figures on those actually paying annual fees were lower, but still impressive, peaking at 406,000 in 1931.[20] Local branches were recognized as the life of the Union and they quickly spread throughout the cities and towns of the United Kingdom, over 3000 being active in 1931.

The tactics of the Union showed real genius in the mission of converting and nurturing British public opinion on behalf of the League cause. Literature was a major vehicle, with the monthly journal *Headway* being supplemented by a battery of publications designed to serve specific groups. LNU speakers were provided for public meetings, over 3,000 such addresses being arranged in 1927. Newspapers were fed a steady diet of information and publicity, and the new media of radio and film were also exploited. Most important, however, the LNU was extremely successful in penetrating the traditional socializing institutions of British society – schools and churches. Teachers were widely cooperative in disseminating the LNU message, aided by the *League News*, a publication specifically designed for teachers and school children. The Union's Christian Organizations Committee brought representatives from all major British denominations together to further religious support for the League. Church and chapel leaders and their clergy provided major support in preaching a League of Nations gospel of practical Christianity. The bi-yearly *Church and Home* (later *Church and World*) presented the faithful with appropriate League material. The rituals of church and school, picnics and holidays, scouts and guides activities, were often wedded to the League cause, the most significant perhaps being the infusion of Armistice Day commemorations with pro-League sentiment.

The League of Nations Union remained solidly middle-class, drawing its political supporters primarily from the displaced ranks of the Liberal Party, and to a much lesser degree from the liberal wings of the Labour and Conservative Parties. For LNU leaders like Cecil, Murray, and Norman Angell, whose party links were tenuous at best, the Union provided something of a surrogate party of the centre. Claiming non-partisan status, the Union was always viewed with suspicion or hostility by the Labour Left and the Conservative hierarchy. The Executive Committee, the LNU's most important organ, was predominantly Liberal in numbers, willing Conservatives of any standing being difficult to find. Cecil, nominally a Conservative, had no qualms about giving his political blessing to Liberals or Labourites whose first loyalty was to the League.

The principal concerns of the LNU in its early years were to build up its numbers and to act as the watchdog or conscience of British foreign policy on the League of Nations. Writing to Prime Minister Stanley Baldwin in November 1923, the LNU General Secretary, Maxwell Garnett, asked pointedly for a statement on Government foreign policy and the League, in order that he might "circulate it to our 1,500 Branches for their information and also distribute it, as far as possible, among our 320,000 members."[21] Cecil and other leaders were anxious to capture as wide a section of the British public as possible within the structure of the LNU. This required a programme that was generalized enough to appeal to most sections of the British peace movement and moderate enough not to alienate Government leaders. Membership build-up and pro-League propaganda, then, were accompanied by constant pressure on the Government to respect and use the facilities of the fledgling League of Nations. The ideal of collective security remained central to the outlook of the LNU leadership and proved admirably servicable to the needs and interests of the organization. While talk about military sanctions or international police forces was muted and sidetracked so as not to cause trouble with absolute pacifists, the obligations and guarantees of the Covenant were presented as the most promising way forward in the post-war diplomatic reconstruction.[22]

With Britain enjoying an obvious security and anxious to promote the pacification of Europe and arms reduction, the formula of collective security seemed to LNU leaders the most propitious means to meet the insistent, if understandable, French concern for increased security as a precondition to disarmament and rapprochement with Germany. Accordingly, in the debates leading from the famous Resolution XIV of the 1922 League Assembly, through the 1923 Draft Treaty of Mutual Assistance to the Geneva Protocol of 1924, the ideas of mutual defence and "pooled security" were revived within the trilogy of arbitration, security, and disarmament. The LNU lobbied steadily and vigorously on behalf of these projects, Cecil himself being a major architect of the Draft Treaty while serving in Baldwin's first Government.[23] At the same time the LNU voiced its disappointment and concern at the Government's failure to support a tougher League of Nations policy of resistance to Italian actions against Greece in the Corfu crisis.[24]

With the defeat of the Draft Treaty and the Geneva Protocol – both Labour and Conservative Governments being equally resistant to building on the security function of the League – and with the successful completion of the Locarno Agreements, the question of security temporarily retreated. After German admission to the League, and with the League Council functioning pretty much after the favoured British pattern of an institutionalized European Concert, the difficult questions of security were submerged in the brief wave of prosperity and pacification which washed the West in the later twenties. The optimism of the period culminated in the sanguine renunciation of war enshrined in the Kellogg-Briand Pact of 1928, while preparations for the long-awaited disarmament conference were spurred on. The LNU joined in the general acclaim which greeted the formal renunciation of war, but its concurrent efforts to integrate the Kellogg Pact with the Covenant, and to further efforts at enhancing the League's security functions through support for the draft General Convention to Improve the Means of Preventing War and the draft Convention on Finance Assistance (for Victims of Aggression), met with frustration and disappointment.[25]

The LNU had purposefully downplayed its commitment to the coercive features of collective security in the late twenties in order to build the broadest possible coalition behind the most urgent concern of the peace movement – disarmament.[26] The Disarmament Conference would finally meet in 1932; but by this time the shadows of war and the dilemmas of security had returned in the wake of the economic collapse and the attendant political turbulence. With the challenge to post-war international order, first by Japan in Asia, and then by Italy and Germany in Africa and Europe, the time of testing for the League and liberal internationalism had come. This period would witness the greatest attempt to translate the myth of collective security into actual policy and action as the threatened States, the potential "consumers" of security, engaged in a desperate attempt to obtain the justice and protection proffered by the Covenant. Concurrently the pro-League forces in the European democracies, joined after 1934 by the Soviet Union and loyal Communist parties, pointed to the League and its system of collective security, as the path to continuing peace.

In Britain, a major "producer" of security, the process of attempting to translate the myth of collective security into reality brought major challenges and problems for the LNU. Sections of the Union had always been fascinated with the questions of sanctions and the possibilities of developing an international police force to serve the League. On the analogy made with the extension of law and order within states, such ideas possessed a certain logic and appeal. By the beginning of the thirties, several factors combined to bring the question of guarantees, sanctions, and international forces once more to the forefront.[27] The position of France and her allies in the disarmament discussions remained focused on security as a precondition to any arms reduction. The rapid development of international aviation and the widespread attendant fears of the bomber inspired plans for the international control of aviation and the creation of an international air force to serve as the policing arm of the League.

David Davies, the immensely wealthy Welsh coal and railway magnate, had always been attracted to the idea of an international police force, since his role in founding the League of Free Nations Association in 1918. His efforts to convert the LNU to this cause, however, had been repeatedly frustrated. In 1930 Davies set forth in great detail the case for an international police force in *The Problem of the Twentieth Century.*[28] The Welsh LNU would come to support Davies' cause, and in 1932 he would found the New Commonwealth Society, a well-endowed elitist study group with branches in several countries but centred in Britain.[29] Davies and the New Commonwealth Society would provide a principal focus for debate and propaganda on the international police force idea, pressing at the same time to convert the LNU to their position.

With the return of Labour in 1929, and with Henderson strongly favouring the security function of the League as the path to disarmament, LNU leaders were quite willing to renew debate and support of collective security. Writing in the February 1931 edition of *Headway* Gilbert Murray presented the principle of "common action" embodied in Articles 10, 11, and 16 of the Covenant as "the root principle of the League." Disarmament would come only on the basis of "Pooled Security." A LNU seminar on security the next month drew closer to supporting French demands for enhanced security.[30] The LNU, however, would find detailed debate on the international air force and police questions extremely divisive and problematic, as both pacifist and Conservative members of the Union, for very different reasons, found such schemes unacceptable. Many LNU leaders including Cecil, Murray, Noel-Baker, and Norman Angell would come to support the principle of an international police force, but despite all of Angell's best efforts to convince his socialist and pacifist friends of the legitimacy of force exercised by an international police, most remained unconvinced, some being alienated completely from the Union.[31] Murray would caution Davies in early 1932 that the LNU was "violently divided" on his proposals for an international police force.[32]

By this time the question of sanctions had become more than theoretical for the LNU. Japan's forceful extension of imperial control over Manchuria presented Members of the League of Nations with the dilemma of imposing sanctions to protect China and expel Japanese forces, if all attempts at peaceful settlement were to fail. Under Cecil's directing hand, the LNU initially muted its concern for the principles of the Covenant and acquiesced in the National Government's slow and cautious response to the challenge, culminating in the Lytton mission.[33] As the Japanese operation spread, however, and after Chapei was bombed, the LNU placed the dispute in the crucial context of defending "the collective system and the sanctity of treaties." Cecil and LNU leaders now called for the imposition of diplomatic and economic sanctions under Article 16 of the Covenant, in concert with the United States.[34] The cabinet's clear and considered aversion to any coercion of Japan would frustrate LNU leaders and alienate them from Simon, the Foreign Secretary, and the Government. By early 1933, after publication of the Lytton Report, the LNU pressed for firm action to uphold collective security: "The first and most important point to be remembered is that the doctrine of collective security is in jeopardy." If the Covenant were ignored, "the disturbances in the Far East will be repeated ever nearer and nearer home . . ."[35] The British government, however, remained unmoved, as the Japanese consolidated their hold on "Manchukuo" and left the League.

For the LNU the outcome of the Manchurian test could only be seen as a real failure. This failure had "reduced to a very low ebb the faith of the nations in one another's readiness to apply the League's principle of 'pooled security'." The only hope for both security and disarmament was to return to the principle of "collective action."[36] Following the Manchurian defeat the LNU experienced growing difficulties. Memberships and financing fell off discouragingly after 1932. Bureaucratic infighting also distracted leaders. There were serious policy divisions on the questions of international police and air forces, with Murray claiming in November 1932 that quarrels on this issue and pacifism now tended "to occupy the whole horizon."[37] Furthermore, the Disarmament Conference was by now becoming stalemated.

The appeal of collective security to LNU leaders, nevertheless, remained undiminished. There was encouragement from the fact that the Labour Party, preferring the policies of Henderson, Bevin, Atlee, Dalton, and Noel-Baker over those of Cripps and the Left, had endorsed the principle of collective security as the path to disarmament at its 1934 conference. By 1934 the term collective security was in wide popular usage and attracting the attention of British circles beyond the confines of the LNU.

The International Studies Conference[38] in the spring of 1933, had initiated a wide-ranging debate on collective security within its participating national organizations which culminated in the Eighth International Studies Conference held in London 3–7 June, 1935.[39] This Conference inspired voluminous submissions and discussions on many aspects of the collective security topic.[40] As the rapporteur later explained, the submissions largely focused on the means necessary to employ a collective security system, assuming explicitly or implicitly "as a sort of postulate, the necessity of working towards this goal."[41]

There were, nevertheless, some heretics at the Conference, namely several Italian fascist professors. An exchange between Francesco Coppola, Professor of International Law at the University of Rome, and Gilbert Murray provides rich insight into competing European ideologies and mythologies as they related to the League and collective security. Professor Coppola presented a fascist critique of collective security which he concluded was "absurd," "anti-historical," and "impossible." States would invariably and rightly seek national security through armaments and alliances. What was needed to preserve peace was that elasticity and flexibility be given to the legal equilibrium established by the post-war treaties, to accomodate changes in "the real balance of forces and needs." The doctrine of collective security was depicted as "a new mythology" deriving from Wilson's attempt to sanctify the victors' peace of 1919. The Covenant, embodying the "statutes and doctrines of the new religion," and ensuring the victors their gains in the war, "was cleverly disguised as a decalogue of international redemption." Rather than follow the "myth of security" Coppola recommended vigilance in defending the primacy of the white race and European civilization against the "forces of eternal barbarism" within Europe and outside.[42]

Gilbert Murray, speaking to the closing session of the Conference in his capacity as President of the International Committee on Intellectual Co-operation, drew attention to the competing "mystiques" which underlay the "beliefs of various nations and statesmen in the matter of public policy." Professor Coppola, to Murray, had "defied us all and put forward ideals which were totally different from the ideals most of us were pursuing." Murray proceeded to deliver an ideological rebuttal of Coppola's case, point by point. Was collective security unhistorical for Professor Coppola? "We reply: has he not noticed that the whole of history has led up to the League of Nations?" Was it against human nature? Human nature can change and learn certain lessons. Was it true that nations would fight only for their own interests? The resort to League sanctions, if necessary, would be in nations' "real" interests: "We want to make every sacrifice and every effort for collective security, because we believe that collective security is the most peaceful and far-reaching interest of civilization." Murray then turned to Coppola's dismissal of collective security as illusory myth. Coppola had argued nations must fight for their national honour: "Is not the national honour of a nation almost *par excellence* the typical myth, the typical unreality, for which people have fought?" Murray concluded his defence by locating and legitimating collective security in the context of classical liberal ideology. The League of Nations was portrayed as rectifying internationally the "social contract" of Rousseau, Hobbes, and Plato, ending the anarchy of sovereign states and forming a society with attendant duties. The past war was damned by Murray, not just for the mass suffering it produced, but for the resultant moral anarchy – "the utter reversal of all right and wrong; the way that for those interminable four years we were turning evil into good, and good into evil." As a liberal Murray saw future war as leading not to the defence of Western civilization but rather its destruction.[43]

If the International Studies Conference concerned itself principally with doctrinal clarification, evangelization on behalf of collective security remained largely the province of the LNU. Given the uncertain response of the League in the Manchurian test, the National Government's own mixed League record, and the flagging morale of the LNU itself, in November 1934, mainly on Cecil's impetus, the Union launched a mass campaign to rally British support for the League and specifically for collective security. The result was the famous Peace Ballot, or in its formal title, the National Declaration on the League of Nations and Disarmament. The Peace Ballot campaign, mounted by the LNU in cooperation with thirty-eight other organizations, would see more than a half million workers systematically canvass British households, soliciting support for the cause of the League, disarmament and collective security. The results, surpassing even Cecil's most sanguine expectations, were announced to a dramatic meeting in the Albert Hall, 27 June 1935. Over 11 million British adults had responded, demonstrating overwhelming support for British membership in the League, for all-round disarmament, the abolition of military aircraft, and the end to private trade in armaments. On the crucial collective security question, 86.8% of respondants favoured the application of economic and non-military sanctions to halt aggression, while 58.6% supported military measures if necessary.[44]

The response to the Peace Ballot was impressive on any scale, with over half of the numbers voting in the 1935 elections participating. LNU leaders understandably hailed the figures as demonstrating that "the people of Great Britain [were] facing up to the need for collective security."[45] The statistics certainly illustrated the wide-ranging peace sentiment in Britain; they also validly could be claimed as showing broad support for collective security. But the linkage of collective security with disarmament and the significant differentiation between those supporting non-military and military sanctions, indicated that the myth of collective security retained its broad social appeal and potency only in its generalized form. The plans for military sanctions and other details involved in implementing the myth were fraught with problems.

The LNU showed no hesitation in portraying the Ballot as "a mandate no Government could neglect to fulfil."[46] The results were brought to the attention of politicians in each constituency and in July the new Prime Minister, Baldwin, together with Hoare, the Foreign Secretary, and Eden, Minister for League Affairs, received a deputation from Peace Ballot organizers. Baldwin, having recently attacked "a collective peace system" as "perfectly impracticable" now solemnly embraced the League as "the sheet-anchor of British policy."[47]

The Peace Ballot had been conceived and planned before the rise of the Abyssinian question, which by the summer of 1935 was very much in the news. With a general election pending, the timing of the Peace Ballot was as awkward for the Government as it seemed fortuitous for the LNU. All the major parties declared their support for the League and most candidates gave unreserved positive responses to queries on their League position submitted by the LNU. The National Government's election manifesto declared the League would "remain the keystone of British foreign policy."[48]

By the summer of 1935, given Italian policy declarations and military preparations, the Abyssinian question was being presented in Britain as "a test case" for the League and collective security. For the LNU the League was being challenged with "the gravest crisis it has ever faced" and, should aggression occur, "inaction would be a self-betrayal from whose disastrous effects recovery by the League would be neither merited nor possible."[49] The Government was petitioned by the LNU Executive Committee in August to make its commitment to Covenant obligations clear.[50]

The Government's response to the crisis was contained in Hoare's dramatic speech before the League Assembly, 11 September. Here the Foreign Secretary, in the passage seized upon by LNU enthusiasts and most often cited subsequently by historians, pledged: "In conformity with its precise and explicit obligations the League stands, and my country stands with it, for the collective maintenance of the Covenant in its entirety and particularly for steady and collective resistance to all acts of unprovoked aggression."[51] Throughout Hoare's speech, and in subsequent government policy, emphasis was placed on the *collective* nature of Covenant obligations. The Foreign Secretary portrayed collective security as "an inspiring conception, . . . one of the most inspiring of the history of mankind." It was, however "not a simple but a complex conception." A careful reading of the conditions, mainly unfulfilled, considered by Hoare necessary to its successful operation indicated that his leading advisers and Cabinet colleagues viewed collective security as much more complex than inspiring.[52] The dictates of electioneering, however, meant that the government's qualifications of its League commitments and hopes for appeasement of Italy were generally muted.

With the invasion of Abyssinia by Italian forces on 3 October, the principle of collective security faced its crucial challenge. From the condemnation of Italy as an aggressor and the application of selective economic sanctions, through the infamous Hoare-Laval débacle and the subsequent frustrated efforts at organizing effective sanctions, to the ultimate victories of Italian forces in the spring of 1936 and the forlorn appeals of Haile Selassie, the drama played out in Geneva marked both the apotheosis of collective security and its nemesis. The LNU at each stage in the crisis lobbied vigorously for a firm British lead at Geneva, ultimately pressing for the application of oil sanctions and the closing of Italy's lifeline through the Suez Canal.[53] But the Government, unwilling to go beyond France and strategically having no desire to make Italy into a Mediterranean enemy, proved unresponsive. After the German reoccupation of the Rhineland and irreversible Italian victories in Abyssinia, the sanctionist effort would be terminated despite all the objections of the LNU.

The greatest attempt to reify the collective security myth, then, had failed disastrously. This failure meant the end of the League of Nations as a potential security organization; it also meant the end for the LNU as a powerful lobby in British politics. Pacifists and Conservatives would now abandon the Union in droves. The mass of British public opinion mobilized by the Peace Ballot would be cast adrift as the government attempted to cover the tracks of its duplicity and confusion, following the path of appeasement and gradual rearmament. Cecil would pour his energies into the International Peace Campaign.[54] Churchill and the Focus group would attempt to bend the vestigal appeal of collective security to the cause of rearmament in his "Arms and the Covenant" campaign.[55] All of this made little difference in the drift to war which marked the period from 1936 to 1939.

The forces of the LNU, like the League itself, might now be in rapid and permanent decline, but its core membership and its leadership remained unshaken in the faith. Rededicating themselves to the League and the cause of collective security, they fought all efforts to "reform" the Covenant by excising its coercive features. LNU leaders were also anxious that the correct lessons be drawn from the events of 1935–36. The idea suggested by sceptics and several governmental leaders that collective security had been tried and shown to be a failure was utterly rejected.[56] Rather, as Cecil pointed out in his 1937 New Year's message to the Union: "Failure was due to the fact that the Governments of the leading Powers in the Council were not prepared to take the necessary practical steps to act on the condemnation of the aggressor." The invasion of Abyssinia could have been "stopped easily", if France and England had shown "courageous action" through the League.[57] This was the lesson communicated consistently in the literature of the LNU. It was also the message regularly communicated in the *Survey of International Affairs* published by the Royal Institute of International Affairs.

It is at this point that we encounter myth in the second sense proposed at the outset of this paper – myth as dramatic, didactic, narrative, presented in historical form. The lessons drawn by liberal internationalists from the progressive breakdown of European and world order through the thirties were now translated into a comprehensive historical account. The LNU certainly suffered from no lack of historical talent in this exercise. At hand was not only Gilbert Murray, Britain's most famous classicist, but also his son-in-law, Arnold Toynbee, whose annual *Survey of International Affairs* offered instalments of current international history to a wide and influential readership.[58]

Toynbee quite consciously located the detailed narration of international events in an interpretive framework based firmly on the fortunes of collective security, which he depicted as "the supreme political challenge of the age."[59] The challenge was placed in the broadest "Toynbeean" context. During the four centuries of Western history since the break-up of Western Christendom, "the international anarchy had been almost complete," as the struggle of sovereign States for primacy resulted in general wars. Such wars, in light of their social costs, had usually been followed by attempts at establishing "an oecumenical system of law and order embodied in some international institution and maintained by some international authority." The League of Nations represented the fourth and "most serious" of such endeavours. The demonstration of modern industrialized warfare's barbarism and costs put an "unprecedentedly powerful spiritual driving-force" into the League after the war. But it faced concurrently a new and more sinister version of the doctrine of sovereignty in the latter's fusion with the nationalism of the masses. The great test for the "Law of the Covenant" came first in Manchuria, and more effectively in Abyssinia.[60]

Toynbee devoted a whole volume of the *Survey* to the Abyssinian test, arguing passionately that the preservation of the British Commonwealth and "the honour and vital interests of the United Kingdom" demanded the loyal fulfilment of Covenant obligations, "completely, whatever the consequences."[61] The record demonstrated that this standard of conduct had not been observed by the Government, which Toynbee charged with a "lack of courage and sincerity." The result was the "collapse" of the League and a return to the international anarchy, unmitigated now "by any vestige of any system at all."[62] The new arms race and the desperate grouping of alliances led inexorably to another war.[63]

With the coming of the war in 1939, leaders of the LNU were anxious to establish clearly the fundamental causes for the tragedy. These were not complex. Indeed, Gilbert Murray suggested one could write "a sort of Sunday School story" showing how the increasing "neglect of international obligations" led to disaster.[64] The Sunday school lesson, as delivered to an Oxford audience in the fall of 1939, presented in classic form the myth of collective security. If British leaders and policies had been loyal to the League system through the twenties and thirties, "the whole course of history would have been different." Disarmament would have been realized, probably with the backing of an international air force; the Manchurian crisis would have been settled by negotiation; the Abyssinian aggression would have been "nipped in the bud." Instead the aggressor was left "free to do his worst against smaller victims." There followed in gradual ascending scale: "the re-militarization of the Rhineland, the overrunning of Austria, the hideous persecution of the Jews . . ., the preposterous hypocrisies of non-intervention in Spain, the invasion and persecution of Czechoslovakia . . ., till at last, with the League broken and the collective security that had once existed thrown away, England and France found themselves alone clinging together for mutual protection and ready for almost any sacrifice if only they might be left in peace. It was not to be. At last they [were] forced in mere self-preservation to face alone a peculiarly dangerous war on behalf of the vital interests of the whole civilized world: the very war which the League was intended to prevent, and would have prevented if it had not been betrayed!"[65]

The war of course brought evil days upon the League of Nations and believers in collective security. The flame of truth and hope was kept alive among the faithful by the conviction and sonsolation that history would vindicate their cause. The greatest of the believers – Cecil – sought vindication in his memoir-history of the League, *A Great Experiment*, published in 1941.[66] Cecil's political apologia was structured around his personal struggle, in London and Geneva, to see the system he had helped design in 1919 fully realized. For Cecil this was often a "heart breaking" struggle against the suspicion and semi-hostility of "reactionary" British officials and "halfhearted" leaders.[67]

As with Toynbee, Murray and other liberal internationalists, the collective security question was pivotal to Cecil's narrative – it was the "central doctrine of the Covenant."[68] Realizing this, doctrine provided a constant animus for Cecil's interwar political activity. He portrays in detail his leading role in shaping the Draft Treaty of Mutual Assistance, the principles of which he was convinced, still in 1941, were vital to solving the interlocking problems of security, disarmament, and peace. Had the British government not killed the Draft Treaty, resorting to arguments which were "a fantastic perversion of the proposal," and had the Treaty been implemented, for Cecil it was "morally certain that the Italian invasion of Abyssinia and the German invasion of Czechoslovakia and Poland would never have taken place."[69]

Cecil's analysis of the Manchurian and Abyssinian episodes and the subsequent crises culminating in the war conforms to the logic of the collective security myth. Aggression in each case was manifest. Peace was indivisible. Moral exhortation without the backing of collective coercion was futile. Sanctions would have restored justice and deterred subsequent aggression. Appeasement was shortsighted, and, on the Abyssinian betrayal, Cecil accused his government of sacrificing the interests of other nations and its own reputation for courage and good faith.[70]

Cecil's memoirs made a signal and enduring contribution to liberal internationalist tradition on the League. Although too old to participate in the next peace making, Cecil was concerned with the allies taking his lessons to heart when time came to shape the peace settlement. The same lessons were presented in almost liturgical form in 1946, when Cecil, Noel-Baker and the principal surviving luminaries of the League gathered in Geneva for a requiem Assembly to mark the formal death of the League.[71] By this time, of course, the spirit of collective security had been reincarnated in the United Nations Charter, with the United States now the most recent and powerful convert. Indeed collective security would experience a tremendous revival in the immediate post-war period as the North American and European democracies tried to expiate the sins of pre-war isolation and appeasement. The popular hopes once again reposed in collective security would soon prove valuable in legitimating Western positions in the Cold War. All of this understandably influenced historical perceptions of the League of Nations. And it was just at this time that F. P. Walters was researching his major *History of the League of Nations* which would be published early in 1952.[72]

By far the most detailed, dramatic and influential of all the general treatments of the League, Walters' work stands unrivalled as the classic presentation of the collective security myth in historical form. Walters was associated with the League right from the beginning, serving on Cecil's personal staff at the Peace Conference. From 1919 to 1940 he was a member of the League Secretariat, rising ultimately to become the senior British official and Deputy Secretary-General, 1939–40. When Walters undertook to write the League's history he was in a highly advantaged position. From his work in the Secretariat he knew the personalities and politics of the League from the inside; he was familiar with the system of documentation and was given full access; the Rockefeller Foundation gave generous funding; and the Royal Institute of International Affairs offered its facilities and professional assistance. Walters proved he was worthy of the task entrusted to him. Under his hand the story of the League is told with narrative mastery, the vastly detailed and complex intersection of international activity at Geneva being organized into a coherent and absorbing drama.

Walters' *History*, from first to last, is informed by his passionate devotion to the institutions of the League, the spirit which animated its leading supporters, and the system of collective security – "the whole conception on which the League was based."[73] Indeed, it is Walters' liberal internationalist commitment to collective security which functions as the central organizing and interpretive device in his narrative, shaping the dramatic agenda of most chapters. It is a tale of villains and heroes where, in what one might call the "Whig internationalist interpretation of history," the agents of progress who fought for collective security are lined up against the forces of reaction – the old diplomacy, the sceptics, militarists, opportunists, and traitors. On the one hand there is Wilson, "by far the most commanding figure in the world" after the war; Cecil, "the most clear-sighted statesman of the time;" Briand, "whose name stood for European reconciliation, for essential humanity, and for all that the world admired in France"; Litvinov, with whose views on international questions "no future historian will lightly disagree"; and a pantheon of lesser luminaries – Nansen, Noel-Baker, Henderson, Bevin, Salter, Eden, Smuts, Paul-Boncour, and de

Madariaga.[74] In juxtaposition are not so much the obvious villains – Mussolini, Hitler, and the Japanese militarists – but the nameless professional diplomats and military advisers, cold, hostile, and jealous, and the opportunistic politicians – Lloyd George, Austen Chamberlain, MacDonald, Baldwin, Simon, and Hoare, who, together ruined the League and collective security.

The myth-narrative moves through the conventional stages: the creation story, the American desertion, the attempts to strengthen the collective system 1923–25, the illusory irenic interlude from the Locarno agreements to the Kellogg-Briand pact (both of which Walters treats as regressive to collective security), and then the time of testing in Manchuria and Abyssinia.

For Walters the Manchurian crisis marked "a turning point in the history of the League and of the world."[75] While there was "no possible doubt" of Japan's violation of the Covenant, the great powers were unwilling to risk war with Japan by undertaking coercive measures.[76] Simon, the British Foreign Secretary, "stupidly wasted" the chance to establish an effective common front with America.[77] Indeed Western leadership through this period "seemed painfully unequal to their immense responsibilities."[78] Given the vacillations of the Great Powers on the Council, although the Lytton Report would present a "substantial vindication of the Chinese case on all fundamental issues,", the failure of the League to resort to sanctions resulted in "men's faith in the Covenant as an effective barrier against war [being] shaken."[79]

From Manchuria and the Disarmament Conference, sabotaged in Walters' view by the influence of the European General Staffs, the narrative is brought to its culmination in the Abyssinian crisis, "the most decisive chapter in the history of the League."[80] Walters is concerned from the outset to place the dispute in "its true setting," a setting well understood by the supporters of the Peace Ballot if not by Foreign Office advisers and political leaders: "Defence of peaceful States against war, defence of small States against injustice, defence of the coloured races against foreign oppression, were seen as depending upon a single issue. The maintenance of the Covenant would ensure each of these great purposes. Its failure would mean their abandonment so far as international action was concerned . . . It was a struggle between Fascist Italy and the League; and everywhere the forces of isolationism and reaction set themselves to encourage Mussolini."[81]

Walters' disgust at British government policy through the crisis comes through clearly. While Liberals and Labour supported collective security as a long-held conviction and "all liberty-loving and generous men" backed the League, the Government 'hoisted the League flag and would betray it as soon as they . . . secured a fresh lease of power."[82] The Hoare-Laval betrayal and the subsequent demoralization of the sanctions effort destroyed the collective system and the League itself. For Walters it is a story not just of shortsighted or incompetent leadership, nor even a vain policy of sacrificing Abyssinia and the League to buy Italy's support against Germany; rather the professionals of the Foreign Office and the Quai d'Orsay and government leaders had no desire to be "bound by the fetters of the Covenant," and, "for their own reasons, deliberately saved Mussolini from defeat."[83]

Walters provides a radically positive projection of what would have followed had Britain and France loyally applied sanctions: the fascist regime would most probably have collapsed; a democratic or socialist Italy would have returned to the League; the Covenant would subsequently have functioned as "the effective guarantee of world peace"; America would likely have joined the League; and the Germans would have been deterred from their aggressive path. Instead the betrayal of the Covenant opened the gates once again to 'isolation, nationalism, rearmament, and war." The international anarchy returned with a vengeance.[84]

Given the comprehensive nature of Walters' treatment of League affairs and its superb dramatic and narrative quality, his work understandably has served as the standard history of the League. As such, it has had more influence than any other study, directly and indirectly through derivative literature, in shaping and reinforcing the dominant liberal internationalist mythology of the League. Others, writing from realist or Marxian perspectives, at an early point provided challenges to the liberal internationalist version – notably Zimmern's *The League of Nations and the Rule of Law* and E. H. Carr's brilliant *The Twenty Years' Crisis.*[85] But Walters' study retained its primacy in Western historiography through the fifties and most of the sixties.

It would not be until the late sixties, following upon the opening of major archives, that the dominance of liberal internationalist historiography on the League would be widely challenged. In Britain the "thirty year rule" governing access to government records laid down in 1966 inspired a whole new historical literature on British foreign policy, not least on Britain's relationship with the League. With scores of scholars having by now produced theses, articles and books, many of the crucial aspects of Britain's role in the League, together with its domestic underpinnings, have been addressed. We now have or shortly will have available, new studies of the British wartime league of nations movement, the role of the British government in the creation of the League, the career of Cecil, the making of the Draft Treaty of Mutual Assistance, the Geneva Protocol, and the Locarno agreements. The crises in the Far East and Abyssinia have attracted an ample and sophisticated scholarship. And, supplementing studies of the larger political and diplomatic topics, scholars have addressed themselves to both the socio-economic and technical functions of the League, and the social and intellectual history of the British peace movement in the twentieth century.

In the new understanding now available on the history of Britain and the League, several common features worth noting run through most of the recent studies. Perhaps most significant is the near-universal liberation from the collective security myth. While Cecil, Murray and the ranks of the LNU may well have been on the side of the angels, (and one cannot help but admire both their cause and their zeal), for the historian the making of British foreign policy did not take place in heaven. Indeed, the strategic dilemmas faced by Britain and the European democracies in the thirties ressembled more the images of the abyss. It is new information on the strategic debates of the twenties and thirties which has, perhaps more than anything else, injected clearer historical perspective into British League of Nations studies. Detailed knowledge, then, of the perception of external and domestic realities held by British leaders and advisers, and the constraints on British policy, has elicited much more historical empathy and a consequent retreat from the trenchant moralizing of collective security mythology.

The author can perhaps claim some of these features for his own study of *Great Britain and the Creation of the League of Nations.* The dominant historiography on this topic prior to the opening of the archives was liberal internationalist and permeated by the collective security myth. Ray Stannard Baker grouped Lloyd George with Clemenceau in the alleged conspiracy of the old order against Wilson, the League, and the "new diplomacy."[86] Walters argued that there were those in Britain's military and diplomatic circles who strongly opposed the league project and that "Lloyd George as Prime Minister cared nothing about the idea of a League."[87] Cecil's version was that while the Prime Minister officially supported the League, his approval was always "chilly" and he regarded it "as of secondary importance."[88] Henry Winkler; from the evidence available in 1952, emphasized the conservatism of British policy on the league question and concluded that the Covenant, projecting a limited League, could "safely be said to have reflected the official British position in many of its most important aspects."[89] There was, however, precious little historical documentation showing the real attitudes of professional advisers and political leaders, especially those of Lloyd George.

From the abundance of material available to researchers of British policymaking since the late sixties, the following conclusions seem warranted. The League idea came to enjoy major public support in wartime Britain as the principal theme in the response of Anglo-American liberalism to the world crisis. The idea was thoroughly studied by officials in the light of British traditions and interests. By late in the war most government leaders were positively attracted to the idea of international organization and, following largely the visionary thinking of Smuts, placed the League project at the centre of Britain's approach to the peacemaking. The League was viewed by Lloyd George and his colleagues as a means of fusing creatively several distinct but overlapping strands in British post-war strategy: the liberal internationalism favoured by the powerful league of nations movement and championed by Wilson; the atlanticism of those who wished to bring the new world into an Anglo-American entente; the continentalism of the Foreign Office and the War Office, whose eyes remained fixed on the balance of power; and the liberal imperialism whose proponents envisioned an increasingly cooperative British-led Commonwealth with a paternal and modernizing mission in "backward" areas of the world. At its best the League could be made to function as a new, institutionalized world concert, bringing America into an expanded balance of power focused on the Rhine, enhancing international peace and cooperation while promoting the long-range interests of the British Empire.

British officials and leaders, however, held deep reservations as to the viability of a system of enforced peace, of territorial guarantees, and obligatory sanctions against aggression. Unfortunately, it was just these features – the collective security myth in embryo – which had captured the public mind and also lay at the heart of Wilson's peace programme. At the Peace Conference the Covenant was drafted largely on the terms laid down by Cecil and Wilson. The League was given an alluring if ambiguous security function, despite the admonitions of Lloyd George and British advisers like Philip Kerr and Maurice Hankey that Articles 10 and 16 would cause serious problems in the American Senate, would alienate major Powers from the League, and, in the end, either remain 'nugatory' or result in the destruction of the League itself.[90] These were all accurate predictions. The type of League favoured by most British government leaders and professional advisers in 1919, while promoting the maximum of conference diplomacy and 'functional' cooperation, would have eschewed any independent executive powers or a security role based on obligatory international coercion. These attitudes would be held with remarkable consistency by British officials right through the history of the League, despite rhetorical support for collective security and the obligations of the Covenant.[91] Given a modern perspective on international organization there is much to be said in favour of the more limited conception of the League favoured by the British political elite. The Government's greatest and enduring dilemma, however, was that it could offer the public no viable counter-myth as an alternative to collective security.

The myth of collective security would undergo many twists and turns after its resurrection in the U.N. Charter. Not only would it be used to legitimate N.A.T.O. and the Korean War, but also such enterprises as S.E.A.T.O., the Warsaw Pact, and the Suez intervention. The ghost of Wilson must have groaned when, in 1974, Dean Rusk instructed American television viewers that "we were very much concerned about the structure of collective security with respect to Vietnam. It wasn't just Vietnam or even Southeast Asia; it was the structure of collective security.[92] By this time, indeed, the myth of collective security had been mutated or mutilated beyond any semblance of its original version.

In conclusion it might be said that myth and history make unhappy if not uncommon bedfellows. The resurgence of the League of Nations historiography now underway has, in large measure, been a process of demythologization. To rephrase, somewhat irreverently, Cecil's dictum at the 1946 Assembly: "The myth of collective security is dead; Long live the history of the League of Nations."[93]

Notes

1 *Manchester Guardian Weekly*, 23 March, 29 June 1980. p. 4,2.

2 *Swords Into Plowshares: The Problems and Progress of International Organization.* 3rd. ed. London, University of London Press, 1964.-p. 223.

3 Michael Howard, *War and the Liberal Conscience.* London, Temple Smith, 1978.-p. 132.

4 The *Supplement to the Oxford English Dictionary* dates the term at 1934 in popular usage. But Benes was using the term in 1932 and in early 1933 the International Studies Conference selected "collective security" as its next topic for analysis. A.J.P. Taylor, *English History: 1914–1945.* London, Penguin Books, 1970.-p. 376.

5 For theoretical treatments of myth, the author is indebted to Henry Tudor, *Political Myth*. London, Pall Mall, 1972.-157 p. and Raphael Patai, *Myth and Modern Man*, Englewood Cliffs, Prentice-Hall, 1972. –

6 Cited by Mark Schorer, "The Necessity of Myth" *in: Myth and Mythmaking*. Henry A. Murray, editor, New York, George Braziller, 1960.-p. 355.

7 Georges Sorel, *Reflections on Violence*. Trans. by T.E. Hulme. London, Collier-Macmillan, 1961.-p. 124-25. Sorel's *Reflections* were published orginally 1906-8. The emphasis is in the original.

8 *Ibid.* p. 126, 149–50, 248.

9 *Ibid.* p. 249.

10 Cited in James Avery Joyce, *Broken Star: The Story of the League of Nations, 1919–1939*. Swansea, Christopher Davies, 1978.-p. 57.

11 For analyses of nineteenth century liberalism and dissent see E.H. Carr, *The Twenty Years' Crisis, 1919–1939*. London, Macmillan, 1939. 313 p., and A.J.P. Taylor, *The Trouble Makers*. London, Hamish Hamilton, 1957. 207 p.

12 G. Lowes Dickinson, *The European Anarchy*. London, George Allen and Unwin, 1916.-p. 9–10, 151–52; see also Gilbert Murray's use of the social contract analogue.

13 For details see George W. Egerton, *Great Britain and the Creation of the League of Nations: Strategy, Politics, and International Organization, 1914–1919*. Chapel Hill, University of North Carolina Press, 1978.-p. 3–23.

14 Lowell to G. Lowes Dickinson, 7 August 1915, W. H. Dickinson Papers, v. 402, Bodleian Library, Oxford.

15 *The Westminster Gazette*, 18 November 1918; reprinted in Henry R. Winkler, *The League of Nations Movement in Great Britain: 1914–1918*. New Brunswick, Rutgers University Press, 1952.-p. 77.

16 Wilson to Stockton Axson,mid-August 1914, R.S. Baker Papers, Library of Congress, Washington.

17 See the author's "The Lloyd George Government and the Creation of the League of nations," *American Historical Review* 79: 419–444, April 1974.

18 Information on the LNU an be found in Donald S. Birn, "The League of Nations Union and Collective Security," *Journal of Contemporary History* 9: 131–59, July 1974. Ernest Bramstead, "Apostles of Collective Security: The LNU and its Functions," *Australian Journal of Politics and History* 13: 347–64, December 1962. David Waley, *British Public Opinion and the Abyssinian War, 1935-6*. London, Maurice Temple Smith, 1975.-chap. 4. P.F. Bartz, "The League of Nations Union Between the Wars." (unpublished Ph. D. dissertation), University of Kentucky, 1972. – M. Pugh, "British Public Opinion and Collective Security, 1926–1936," (unpublished Ph. D. dissertation), East Anglia University, 1975, and Barry Buzan, "The British Peace Movement from 1919 to 1939," (unpublished Ph.D. dissertation), University of London, 1973. – Donald Birn will publish a major study of the LNU shortly with Oxford University Press.

19 D.C. Watt, *Personalities and Policies*. Notre Dame, Notre Dame University Press, 1965.-p. 33; Howard, *op. cit.* [see note No 3] p. 86.

20 Figures on LNU memberships can be found in the *Annual Reports and Yearbooks*. They are listed in Buzan, *op. cit.* [see footnote No 18] p. 37.

21 Garnett to Stanley Baldwin, 16 November 1923. LNU Papers, British Library of Political and Economic Science, London.

22 *Headway*, August 1926.

23 LNU Pamphlet No. 142, "Draft Treaty of Mutual Assistance". London, March 1924. *Headway*, November/December 1924. Bartz, *op. cit.* [see note No. 18] p. 29–33.

24 Minutes of the Executive Committee, 25 October 1923, LNU papers.

25 LNU Revision of Covenant Commitee, June-July 1927, LNU papers; *Headway*, June 1928.
26 J.A. Thompson, "Lord Cecil and the Pacifists in the League of Nations Union," *The Historical Journal* 20: 953, no. 4, 1977.
27 The pressures for an international force are analyzed in Pugh, *op. cit.*, [see note No. 18] chap. IV.
28 David Davies, *The Problem of the Twentieth Century*. London, Ernest Benn, 1930. – 795 p.
29 Davies' career is analyzed in Goronwy J. Jones, *Wales and the Quest for Peace. From the Close of Napoleonic Wars to the Outbreak of the Second World War*. Cardiff, University of Wales Press, 1969. – 187 p. Davies' most famous supporter was Einstein. *Einstein on Peace*. Otto Nathan and Heinz Norden, editors, New York, Simon and Schuster, 1960. – p. 225–26, 255, 258.
30 *Headway*, March 1931.
31 See Louis R. Bisceglia, "Norman Angell and the 'Pacifist' Muddle," *Bulletin of the Institute of Historical Research* 45: 104–121, May 1972.
32 Pugh, *op. cit.* [see note No 18] p. 109.
33 See Christopher Thorne, "Viscount Cecil, the Government and the Far Eastern Crisis of 1931," *The Historical Journal* 4: 805–826, 1971.
34 *Headway*, March 1932.
35 *Headway*, March 1933.
36 *Headway*, December 1933.
37 Gilbert Murray to Kathleen Courtney, 17 November 1934. Murray Papers, Bodleian Library, Oxford.
38 The International Studies Conference was established by the International Institute of Intellectual Co-operation in 1928 to be a permanent organ of cooperation, liaison and co-ordination for national institutions engaged in the scientific study of international affairs. Its principal objects were to develop a system of technical collaboration among its affiliated institutions and to organise collective research on specific problems in international relations.
39 Arrangements for the conference were undertaken by a British Co-ordinating Commitee, whose members came mainly from the Royal Institute of International Affairs. The R.I.I.A. itself provided the principal forum for British analysis and debate on collective security in preparation for the conference.
40 Seventh Session of the Permanent Conference on International Studies: A short record of a Preliminary Study Conference on "Collective Security" held in Paris on 24–26 May 1934. Paris, International Institute of Intellectual Co-operation, June 1934. 320 p. (document code: C.93.1934), also in French. Eighth International Studies Conference on "Collective Security" held in London from 3–7 June 1935. Paris, International Institute of Intellectual Co-operation, July 1935. 273 p. (document code: K.24.1935), also in French. The memoranda submitted to the 1935 Conference were circulated in mimeographed form to participants. Copies of the minutes and memoranda are available in the Chatham House Library, London. They are also available for consultation, along with the correspondence files of the Institute concerning the International Studies Conference, in the UNESCO Archives, Paris.
41 See Maurice Bourquin, Ed., *Collective Security: A record of the Seventh and Eighth International Studies Conference*. Paris, International Institute of Intellectual Co-operation, 1936. p. 6.
42 *Ibid.*, p. 144–148, 182–184.
43 *Ibid.* p. 458–462.
44 Dame Adelaide Livingstone, *The Peace Ballot: The Official History*. London, Victor

Gollancz, 1935. 64 p. When all the votes were in more than $11^1/_2$ million citizens would have participated.
45 *Headway*, March 1933.
46 *Ibid.*
47 *D. Waley, op. cit.* [see note 18] p. 20.
48 *Ibid.* p. 38.
49 *Headway*, Juli 1935.
50 *Headway*, September 1935.
51 Hoare's speech is reprinted in *Headway*, October 1935.
52 The making of government policy is analyzed in R. A. C. Parker, "Great Britain, France and the Ethiopean Crisis, 1935–1936," *English Historical Review* 89: 293–332, April 1974, and George W. Baer, *Test Case: Italy, Ethiopia, and the League of Nations.* Stanford, Hoover Institution Press, 1976, 367 p.
53 *Headway*, November 1935–February 1936.
54 Birn, *op. cit.* [see note 18] p. 148–51.
55 *Ibid.* p. 145–47.
56 Neville Chamberlain to the 1900 Club, 10 June, and Baldwin in the Commons, 18 June 1936, cited in *Headway*, July 1936.
57 *Headway*, January 1937.
58 The publication of Toynbee's multi-volume *Study of History* after 1935 made him something of a household name.
59 Arnold J. Toynbee, *Survey of International Affairs, 1938.* London, Oxford University Press, v. 1, 1939 – p. 52.
60 *Survey, 1937*, v. 1, London, Oxford University Press, 1938. – p. 1–5.
61 *Survey, 1935*, v. 2, London, Oxford University Press, 1936. – p. viii.
62 *Survey, 1937*, v. 1, London, Oxford University Press, 1938. – p. 6.
63 *Survey, 1938*, v. 1, London, Oxford University Press, 1939. – p. 53.
64 Gilbert Murray, *From the League to U. N.* London, Oxford University Press, 1948. – p. 75.
65 *Ibid.*, p. 71, 75–76.
66 Viscount Cecil, *A Great Experiment – An Autobiography.* New York, Oxford University Press, 1941. –
67 *Ibid.*, p. 108, 109, 146–47, 163, 188–89.
68 *Ibid.*, p. 152.
69 *Ibid.*, p. 158.
70 *Ibid.*, p. 279, 344.
71 The "lessons" of the final Assembly are excerpted *In: The League Hands Over.* Geneva, League of Nations Publications, General 1, 1946.
72 F. P. Walters, *History of the League of Nations.* 2 vs. London, Oxford University Press, 1952. Citations are from the one volume reprint of 1960.
73 *Ibid.*, p. 769.
74 *Ibid.*, p. 33, 228, 482, 712.
75 *Ibid.*, p. 465.
76 *Ibid.*, p. 466.
77 *Ibid.*, p. 484.
78 *Ibid.*, p. 485.
79 *Ibid.*, p. 499.
80 *Ibid.*, p. 623.
81 *Ibid.*, p. 635–36.
82 *Ibid.*, p. 660.
83 *Ibid.*, p. 673, 686.

84 *Ibid.*, p. 811.
85 Sir Alfred E. Zimmern, *The League of Nations and the Rule of Law 1918–1935*. London, Macmillan, 1936. – 527 p. (2nd ed., 1939), and Carr, [see note 11] *op. cit.* Although Zimmern was active in the LNU, he chose the path of "objectivity" in his study. *Headway* gave it a frosty review, while Norman Angell later savaged *The Twenty Years Crisis*. *Headway*, March 1936; January 1940.
86 Ray Stannard Baker, *Woodrow Wilson and World Settlement*. 3 vs. New York, Doubleday, Page, 1923. – v. 1, p. 240.
87 Walters, *op. cit.* [see note 72], p. 19, 73.
88 Cecil, *All the Way*. London, Hodder and Stoughton, 1949. – p. 155–56.
89 Winkler, *op. cit.* [see note 15] p. 254.
90 P. H. Kerr, "The League of Nations," Lothian Papers, Scottish Record Office, G.D. 40/17/54, cited *In:* G. W. Egerton, *op. cit.* p. 122.
91 There is a striking similarity between the type of league favoured by Lloyd George and his closest advisers in 1918–19 and the circumscribed definition of League functions endorsed by Britain at the 1938 Assembly. See Walters, *op. cit.* [see note 72] p. 716–17, 778–80.
92 Transcript of "Firing Line," telecast on Public Broadcasting System, 27 January 1974. Columbia, S.C., Southern Educational Communications Association, 1974. – p. 6.
93 Cecil's words were "The League is dead: long live the United Nations!"

Germany and the League of Nations

CHRISTOPH M. KIMMICH
The City University of New York

In Germany, the League of Nations never enjoyed much sympathy or support. Since the Covenant was part of the Versailles Peace Treaty, the League was linked inseparably with the Treaty and the Germans regarded it with much the same hostility and suspicion as they regarded the Treaty itself. In the early postwar years, when the League was involved in the execution of the Treaty, it became known among the Germans as a "league of enemies," intent on keeping Germany weak and divided. Its failure to act on such matters as the occupation of German territory or the quarrels over reparations payments led the Germans to conclude that its commitment to international peace and conciliation was hollow. Its treatment of such responsibilities as the protection of German minorities, the administration of the Saar, and the guarantee of Danzig's integrity and independence caused the Germans to doubt its impartiality. In the minds of the Germans therefore the League had a history to live down. They proposed to judge the League by what it would do to make good the wrongs of the past.[1]

Germany joined the League because she believed that, as a member, she could promote the revision of the Peace Treaty and hasten her return to prewar status. At Geneva, the Germans thought, they would appear as representatives of one of the Great Powers, prominent in the affairs of the Council and the Assembly. They would be in close contact with the representatives of the other Great Powers, who, as defenders of the treaty, held the key to revision. Meeting with them regularly, the Germans would press for the resolution of their various grievances (the occupation of the Rhineland, the burdensome reparations, unilateral disarmament) and lay the groundwork for the revision of Germany's borders in the East. The Germans could also directly affect the determination of the issues that the Treaty had entrusted to the League, and it was this possibility which, especially to its own sceptical public, the Government had adduced as a major reason for joining the League. The Germans proposed to take the offensive, shaping discussions and decisions to their advantage. Over time, they would also seek to extend their influence, for they knew that as long as the League was dominated by the Versailles Powers, it could not be used in the revisionist cause. They would have to work with the smaller Powers, who wanted to democratize the League and strengthen its principles, in order to eliminate what they deemed "anti-German" tendencies and to "neutralize" or "refound" the League.[2]

Germany's interest in revision limited her interest in the concerns of the League and compromised her position at Geneva. Thus she could not give her full support to the League's efforts to enhance international security, for she feared that further security treaties would freeze the *status quo* and that stronger sanctions would undercut her case for equal rights in armaments. She could not seize on opportunities to ease the lot of German minorities or to improve the situation in Danzig, for high levels of tension in eastern Europe were needed to justify broad-scale territorial revision. And she could not push for greater democratization and equality in the League, rallying the smaller powers to her standard, simultaneously expecting to treat in confidence with the Great Powers, using the sessions of the Council merely as a convenient setting.[3]

There is no clear evidence that the Germans ever understood the full implications of their policy. In Stresemann's day, to be sure, German diplomacy at Geneva rarely provoked open conflict. It remained cool and conciliatory even on such contentious issues as general disarmament. It was flexible, conceding a point here, compromising an issue there, and it never took on the aggressive cast that German rhetoric had led many to expect. But even such forethought and forbearance could not deliver Germany from the contradictions and inconsistencies of her policy toward, and in the League.

These did not emerge right away. In the euphoria of September 1926, when Germany was admitted to the League, it seemed that the Germans were on the right track. Meeting at Thoiry, Stresemann and Briand explored the dimensions of a "comprehensive solution" that would lead to the evacuation of the Rhineland and the Saar, the possible return of Eupen-Malmédy, and a generous cash settlement through the commercialization of German reparations bonds. In the Council and the Assembly, the Germans took the occasion to speak on matters clearly of importance to Germany, and to intervene on behalf of Danzig and Memel. In December 1926, Stresemann persuaded the members of the Council to accept an arrangement that removed Allied military controls from Germany, and at the same time limited the League's powers to investigate infractions of the terms of disarmament. He also took a hand in resolving various minority complaints that reached the Council, stressing his concern and objectivity (and remaining alert to the possibility of setting favorable precedents). In March 1927 Stresemann scored a triumph when the Council insisted on the withdrawal of French troops from the Saar, where they had been garrisoned since the war, as well as when the Council retained the services of the head of the Saar Government Commission, an agreeable Canadian, but required that the Belgian member of the Commission be replaced by someone from a neutral State. In September 1927 Stresemann succeeded in orchestrating the Great Powers' rejection of a Polish proposal for a general non-aggression pact that the Germans considered a thinly-veiled attempt to create an Eastern Locarno. He was also able to secure a seat for Germany on the Mandate Commission, redeeming a pledge he had made to Germany's colonial lobby. All the while, he and his delegation took an active part in League affairs, conducting themselves in a manner befitting a Great Power. The Germans took their responsibilities seriously and discharged their duties conscientiously. They came up with proposals, solutions, or mediation, acted as rapporteurs on economic questions, and, when the chance arose, took the floor as outspoken champions of Covenant principles. On the whole, they kept within the boundaries of established convention. They accepted necessary compromises, acceded to the League's procedures on minorities, and acquiesced in the delays of the Preparatory Commission for the Disarmament Conference. In fact, it would seem that the Germans were not discontent with the Commission's uncertain progress (as long as they could escape the blame), for it postponed unavoidable conflicts until Germany stood on firmer ground.[4]

In an assessment of their accomplishments after the first year of membership, the Germans expressed satisfaction, even optimism. Stresemann reported that he had developed a close personal relationship with Chamberlain and Briand, his Locarno partners, a relationship which had proved solid even under stress. His experiences at Geneva "justified the expectation" that the Western Powers would show a "loyal spirit of accommodation" in settling such issues as the evacuation of the Rhineland and the restoration of the Saar. The smaller States, originally rather vexed by Germany's conclaves with the Great Powers, had been won over by Germany's espousal of League principles and by her adherence to the so-called optional clause of the Statute of the Hague Court requiring adherents to lay their disputes before the Court for arbitration, but being in fact legally meaningless. Bernhard von Bülow, who was responsible for League affairs in the German foreign ministry, remarked that the League had already begun to change: it had lost much of its character as an "instrument of the victorious Powers," accustomed to having its will with the other Members. He cited some recent elections and resolutions in the Assembly, where the smaller Powers had shown considerable independence. This augured well for the future, for greater democratization would benefit the growth of German influence in the League. To Bülow's colleague Walter Poensgen everything seemed to be going Germany's way. Germany had warded off possible investigations of her military disarmament, had helped to "strengthen and improve" the position of Germans living in formerly German territories, and had "successfully opposed" France's argument that general disarmament could be discussed only after security had been firmly established. Germany's election to the Mandate Commission was proof that she was being considered a Great Power with equal rights. Her activities at Geneva, Poensgen predicted, would give her a strong and influential position, "of great significance when Germany returned to world status."[5]

As the Locarno spirit waned, however, and as German policy at the League began to yield returns more slowly than expected, the ambiguities in Germany's position emerged more clearly. This is best illustrated by Germany's frustrations in the League in 1928–29, first in what became known as the "minorities offensive" and later in the negotiations over security and disarmament.

When Germany entered the League, the German public expected that she would improve the protection the League extended to German minorities abroad. Privately, German diplomats were sceptical about making improvements, for the League had devised procedures that curtailed Germany's freedom to intervene in disputes affecting German minorities. Furthermore, since the issue of minorities was 'linked inextricably' with the issue of territorial revision, the diplomats believed that they would have to practice restraint in order not to raise the issue of revision prematurely. In consequence, the German delegations at Geneva moved cautiously, searched the treaty texts for solutions, accepted suitable compromises, and refrained from raising minority grievances in the Assembly. Such restraint, however, put the Government under pressure at home, and when confronted with a Polish initiative certain to land him in political difficulties in Berlin, Stresemann at the Council session in December 1928 launched a campaign for a general review of the League's procedures. The campaign, pursued with much oratory and posturing at the Council sessions in March and June 1929, produced few results. Since Great-Power negotiations on reparations had reached a critical juncture, the German foreign ministry rejected the radical measures urged by the German members of the League's Secretariat in favor of a proposal to implement a few formal, but highly visible, changes in procedure. But the overt resistance of the minority States and especially the reluctance of the Great Powers proved too obdurate. The outcome, a barely disguised defeat of Germany's proposal, served neither to allay rising doubts about German intentions abroad, nor to still the clamor of Germany's restive public and the German minorities.[6]

The Germans assumed from the start that genuine progress in limiting or abolishing armaments would come only at a general disarmament conference. They therefore sought to have such a conference convened at an early date and to prepare the ground for successful prosecution of the German case. In the Preparatory Commission, the German delegation argued the urgency of general disarmament. Not only had Germany been assured at Versailles that her disarmament was the prelude to a limitation of armaments all around, but as long as Germany was the only country to be disarmed, she was unprotected and at the mercy of her highly-armed neighbours. These arguments made little impact, for the Commission could not decide whether, as the French argued, further security was required before disarmament was possible, or, as the British held, that further security would follow automatically upon disarmament. A special Committee on Arbitration and Security met in 1927–28 to find a way out of this impasse. Nothing came of it, not least because the Germans, who considered new security arrangements inimical to their revisionist objectives, bent their efforts to formulating proposals that would safeguard their objectives, and to sidetracking those that would not. When the Preparatory Commission resumed its discussions, it was still deeply divided. For Germany, the situation was awkward: the delegation found itself outvoted on issues it considered crucial, and the conference, originally projected for 1927, was postponed from one year to the next. At the same time, the Germans' continued presence in the Commission made it appear that they approved its lack of progress. Though they toyed with the notion of expressing their displeasure by going into opposition or even by resigning from the Commission, they did not force the issue during Stresemann's lifetime. They did no more than disassociate themselves from the Commission's draft disarmament scheme when it came up for its second reading in May 1929, though the scheme clearly undermined their position at the future conference.[7]

Meanwhile, Germany's position in the Council began to deteriorate. From the outset, Germany had been at pains to exploit her status as a permanent Member of the Council in order to strengthen her prestige as a Great Power. She had hoped that the permanent Members would gradually become a kind of inner cabinet in the Council and had encouraged regular rotation of non-permanent Members in order to enhance the power of the permanent Members. The Locarno statesmen also made a practice of meeting behind closed doors, however, and it soon became apparent that they discussed matters affecting not only their respective countries but Europe in general – matters that should have been put on the agenda of the Council. Thus their conclaves began to rival the sessions of the Council and even appeared to supersede them. The authority of the Council, never really well established and respected, now declined further. The balance among the institutions of the League began to tilt, and power shifted toward the Secretariat and the commissions of the Assembly, in neither of which Germany enjoyed a privileged position. As a latecomer to the League, she had been unable to secure influential posts in the Secretariat. She had to content herself with a post of Under Secretary General and with appointments of ranking members in various sections and commissions. The German officials in the Secretariat soon complained that they lacked power and influence, but since the Germans could not try to "neutralize" the Secretariat while they were courting the British and the French, the foreign ministry disregarded these complaints. By virtue of their sheer number, the smaller States dominated the commissions of the Assembly. The net result was that, as the Council slipped in standing among the institutions of the League, Germany's standing slipped in the League itself.[8]

Stresemann condoned these developments in order not to jeopardize his revisionist strategy. Time and again he chose to protect his diplomatic options at the risk of losing his domestic support. In the "minorities offensive," he pressed for results favorable to the minorities but settled for a weak compromise in order to keep on good terms with the Great Powers. In the disarmament debates, he urged the League to make good on its commitment to reduce armaments but acquiesced in digressions and delays. The German public expressed growing impatience at the failure of Germany's membership in the League to produce tangible results. But could the Government produce results which would justify its presence in the League if producing results jeopardized its strategy of revision?

In 1929, after three years of membership, Germany's diplomats made some critical assessments. Bülow found that nothing had changed. The Peace Treaty still shaped Europe, and the Allies still dominated the League, which they had created for their own purposes. Ernst von Weizsäcker, who had succeeded Bülow as the foreign ministry's expert on the League, reached similar conclusions: in these three years nothing had been accomplished that truly impressed the German public. Germany's attempts to change the League's character and orientation had miscarried, and the League was as conservative as ever. Germany's permanent seat on the Council was token equality, not true parity with the Great Powers. The following year, after Germany had negotiated a reparations settlement that opened the way to the evacuation of the Rhineland, Weizsäcker took the time to review Germany's position at Geneva. It was still too early to extract revisionist concessions. The League remained hostile and hidebound, and Germany could do no more than state her case, make her claims, and win moral victories. He suggested that the Germans make better use of the League's machinery, especially on such issues as equality of armaments, mandates and minorities, Danzig and the Saar, and that they consider becoming more aggressive, pressing for results with greater urgency, and resorting to firmer and more open language. Unless her revisionist strategy impelled her to exercise restraint, Germany should improve her status in the League, so that she would be stronger for the time when she would turn once again to issues outside the League. In sum, Weizsäcker recommended a change in style not in substance.[9]

Germany's strategy between 1930 and 1933 reflected Weizsäcker's recommendations. In conversation with Secretary General Drummond, Curtius, who had become Foreign Minister after Stresemann's death, made clear that, unlike his predecessor, he wanted to "bring Germany more completely into the regular domain of League work." In the Assembly he spoke with unwonted bluntness. The League, he said, had disappointed Germany. Its members were bound to a "system of obligations and engagements," but most of these still remained to be fulfilled – an obvious allusion to Germany's claims to equality. And he rebuked those who, he said, equivocated on their legal and moral duty and refused to disarm. It was a new tone in Germany's rhetoric at Geneva. The Germans were no longer willing to moderate their demands for the sake of appearances. They became strident and uncompromising, without any qualms about the damage they might thereby inflict on the League.[10]

A spectacular example of this new approach came in 1931, when Germany took Poland to task for "terrorizing" its German minority population during the parliamentary elections in the fall of 1930. Though the German Government was as disinclined as ever to open the question of territorial revision prematurely, it clearly was prepared to exploit minority grievances. With public indignation in Germany running high, the government disregarded custom and protested directly to the League, lodging three separate letters of complaint before the minority had submitted any complaint at all. At the Council meeting in January 1931, Curtius minced no words. He accused the Polish authorities of complicity and worse, and he repeatedly asserted Germany's long-standing commitment to the eventual revision of her borders with Poland. The Council reprimanded the Polish government and obviously wanted to close the case, but Curtius refused to drop the matter. At the Council meeting in May and again in September, he reverted to it, using the Council as a forum from which to address the public at home. When he desisted at last, he pointedly reserved the right to raise the "terrorism issue" again at any time. His agitated defense of minority rights proved popular in Germany, as Stresemann's initiative had proved popular in 1929. But the popularity was fleeting, and the cost was high. It led Adolf Müller, Germany's minister in Berne and a sceptical friend of the League, to remark that Members of the League had come to believe that Germany thought that gratification of the public was more important than "the League, our position in the League, our foreign policy, and even the minorities problem.«[11]

These remarks, perhaps somewhat exaggerated for effect, were not entirely off the mark. Germany was beginning to lose the good will she had accumulated at

Geneva over the years. The other Members began to close ranks to prevent Germany's using the League for her own purposes. Consequently, when Germany tried to use the deliberations on reform of the Secretariat to "neutralize" it, she could find no allies. The smaller Powers, whose interest in reform the Germans had tried to tap, withheld their support; they found Germany's attempt to expand her influence in the Secretariat in the name of "equality for all" too transparent.

The Secretariat had long been a prime symbol of what the Germans held to be Anglo-French predominance in the League. During Stresemann's lifetime, the Germans had taken no steps to correct this predominance, and they had ignored the complaints of German nationals in the Secretariat. In the deliberations on reform which occupied the League between 1929 and 1932, however, the Germans saw an opportunity to act. The most significant issues of reform were the length of service for Secretariat officials and the organization of the *haute direction.* These apparently technical issues were in fact highly political. If the top echelons of the staff were given life-time contracts, then the current staff, which was heavily British and French, would remain in office for years. If, as proposed, the *haute direction* were enlarged by turning the various directors into Under-Secretaries-General, then Germany's Under-Secretary-General, one of three such officials, would lose importance. Such changes were all the more intolerable if Avenol, the Deputy-Secretary-General, should become Drummond's successor. The German delegation voted against life-time tenure for senior officials, against the increase in the number of Under-Secretaries-General, against a French Secretary-General, and they found themselves in the minority on every vote. When it became apparent that Avenol was the favored candidate, the Germans proposed, again unsuccessfully, that the Under-Secretaries-General be made into a kind of cabinet to assist the Secretary-General. Ultimately, the reform discussions ended inconclusively. The Germans acquiesced in Avenol's appointment, settled for minor changes in organization, and, in compensation, took over the Secretariat's economic and financial section, long promised them. The foreign ministry called this "considerable progress" – but it could express no more than "hope" that these changes would "assure Germany's views a better hearing in Geneva."[12]

In the negotiations over disarmament in 1932 Germany's attitudes emerged most plainly. The Disarmament Conference was to be the German Government's test of the League's effectiveness. The German Government would make a case for the legal and moral validity of Treaty provisions and Covenant principles and rest the case on the juridical equality implicit in membership in the League. If this case was rejected, Germany would have reason to leave the League.

Germany's position at the Conference was simple. She demanded *Gleichberechtigung* – equal treatment with the other Powers in military matters. She argued that such equality could readily be achieved if the other Powers disarmed to Germany's level, or if they approved a scheme that applied equally to all and thereby released Germany from the discriminatory stipulations of Versailles. If the Powers could not agree on any such scheme, Germany claimed the right to acquire those armaments that the others refused to relinquish. In either case, she would have equality. In practice she was prepared to adhere to certain limits if given equality in rearmament. Not surprisingly, the negotiations did not meet Germany's demands. After six months of fruitless discussion, the Germans threatened to leave the Conference; a month later, they made good their threat. This open rebellion against the conventions of the League, this resort to blackmail, did not fail of an effect. Apprehensive that Germany would rearm freely unless she were locked into a disarmament scheme, the other Powers accepted a formula that assured German equality and allowed her to return to the conference in 1933. Vindicated, the Germans announced that if the Conference failed, they might be obliged to withdraw from membership in the League. The success of its resort to intransigence and extortion was not lost on the German Government.[13]

By 1933, it was only a matter of time before Germany left the League. Her interest was waning patently. Her Foreign Minister no longer made a habit of attending the sessions of the Council; her delegations to the annual Assemblies appeared unprepared and indifferent. At the end of 1932 Germany Appointed a "permanent representative on the Council," following the practice of States that found the expense of regular delegations prohibitive. Disenchantment with the League became a theme in the foreign ministry's annual appraisals. In March 1932, after yet another long debate on the Manchurian crisis, the Germans observed that the growing scepticism about the League had turned into a "dangerous crisis of confidence"; some months later they alluded to the Leagus's "internal weakness," its lack of authority, its failure to come to grips with the major issues of the day. Leading articles in the German press took up the question of whether Germany should leave the League.[14]

The German Government was looking for the proper moment. Foreign Minister Neurath, representing the traditionalists in his ministry, was fully prepared to break up the Disarmament Conference, using the same tactics that had succeeded the year before. He thought that Germany might withdraw from membership in the League if continued membership was "incompatible with German dignity." Hitler, who had no use for the League and its international ties and commitments, differed with Neurath only over timing. He wanted no action until he had consolidated his power at home, and for much of 1933 he was obliged to patch up the damage done by his foreign minister's intransigence. When the time came in October 1933, they were both agreed: the Disarmament Conference had not corrected the discrimination against Germany; debate at the League was futile, and the League's criticism of Germany's new regime offensive. To the public they justified Germany's withdrawal in familiar phrases: the League had not given Germany the equality that was hers by law and right; it had perpetuated the status quo of 1919, violating its own avowed principles of conciliation and justice. The reasons that Germany had adduced for joining the League she now adduced for leaving it.[15]

Throughout the years of their membership, the Germans thought of the League not in terms of what they could contribute by supporting the Covenant and limiting German's sovereignty, but in terms of the use they might make of it. This instrumentalist approach encompassed contradictions which made German policy ineffective at Geneva and difficult to defend at home. The consequences were obvious by 1929. They troubled German diplomats, who looked for ways to reshape the League's orientation, to "refound" it, but who never considered reshaping their own policy. They were convinced that attempts to increase the League's powers would diminish chances for revision. In fact these chances of revising the Treaty would probably have been improved if the Germans had supported attempts to enlarge the powers of the League. In doing so, Germany would have been obliged to adjust her interests to those of the other Members and therefore to reduce her revisionist program. But what she lost in this respect she might have gained by having a reduced program accepted and made permanent. As an integral part of a stable international order, a restored Germany could have exercised power without raising the anxieties that led others to treat her as a threat. The Germans, however, were never open to this reasoning.

Of course, Germany was not the only State to subscribe to such parochial interpretations of the League and its purpose. The British and the French were no less inclined to use the League to advance their own national interests, and they defined these as narrowly as the Germans. The British thought that the League should serve as a concert of the Powers for consultation and concilitation, and as a clearing house for irksome international problems. The French thought that the League should secure the *status quo* and supplement French security, especially against Germany. Neither was greatly concerned with the League's covenanted purposes. But Germany's parochialism was different. It put the League in jeopardy. As long as the League was linked to the Peace Treaty, Germany's revisionism was subversive of the League, and since Germany was a dynamic element among the more static elements of the League, her intense pursuit of revision implied that the League in its extant form would eventually be destroyed. Indeed, by undermining the League's attempts at cooperation for collective security and disarmament, Germany's activities during the years of membership contributed no little to the failure of the League in the interwar years.

Notes

1 For a contemporary statement of German attitudes, see the set of lectures delivered at the Geneva Graduate Institute of International Studies in the summer of 1932: Ernst Jäckh and Wolfgang Schwarz, *Die Politik Deutschlands im Völkerbund.* Geneva, Kundig, 1932. – 96 p. For a more extensive presentation of my own views, see my *Germany and the League of Nations.* Chicago, University of Chicago Press, 1976. – 266 p.

2 *ADAP,* B. I/1, no. 22, I/2, p. 665–69.

3 *ADAP,* B, VI, nos. 48, 71; VII, nos. 206, 246.

4 *ADAP,* B, I/2, nos. 76, 152; IV, nos. 253, 254; X, no. 52; Kimmich, *op. cit.* p. 98–100.

5 *ADAP,* B, VI, no. 221; VII, no. 9; Memorandum by Poensgen, 2 November 1927, Polititisches Archiv, Bonn: L1539/L466544–49; *Verhandlungen des Reichstags, Stenographische Berichte,* 392: 9814–15, 394:12558; Gustav Stresemann, *Vermächtnis: Nachlaß,* 3 vs., Henry Bernhard *et al.* editors, Berlin, Ullstein, 1932–1933, III, p. 73–75, 162–66.

6 *ADAP*, B, VII, no. 206; XI, no. 73; XII, no. 26; Weizsäcker (Berlin) to Missions, 24 June 1929, Politisches Archiv, Bonn: 3635/D805400–25; Helmut Pieper, *Die Minderheitenfrage und das Deutsche Reich, 1919–1933/34*. Hamburg, Institut für Internationale Angelegenheiten der Universität Hamburg, 1974. – 348 p.

7 *ADAP*, B, I/1, nos. 22, 45, 134; IV, no. 246; V, nos. 81, 136; VII, nos. 29, 84, 246; XI, no. 160; Köpke (Berlin) to Missions, 17 May 1929, Politisches Archiv, Bonn: 3147H/D659422–26.

8 *ADAP*, B, I/2, no. 152; V, no. 255; Dufour (Geneva) to Stresemann, 4 December 1928, Politisches Archiv, Bonn: 7381 H/H168675–82. In general, see F. P. Walters, *A History of the League of Nations*. London, Oxford University Press, 1952. – ch. 29, and Egon Ranshofen-Wertheimer, *The International Secretariat. A Great Experiment in International Administration*. Washington, Carnegie Endowment for International Peace, 1945. – 500 p.

9 *ADAP*, B, XII, no. 153; Weizsäcker (Berlin) to Dufour, 2 October 1929 and memorandum by Weizsäcker, April 1930, Politisches Archiv, Bonn: L1837/L532602–05, L532633–41; *Die Weizsäcker-Papiere, 1933–1950*. Leonidas E. Hill, editor. Frankfurt/M., Propyläen, 1974. – p. 66–67.

10 Memorandum by Eric Drummond, 14 May 1930, and Weizsäcker (Berlin) to Missions, 18 October 1930, Politisches Archiv, Bonn: 3147H/D661154–57, 3635/D805716–45. A milder version of Curtius's remarks in the Assembly is in LoN, *OJSS* no. 89, 1930. – p. 99–100.

11 Kimmich, *op. cit.* ch. 7; Pieper, *op. cit..*, *passim;* Müller (Berne) to Foreign Ministry, January 1931, Politisches Archiv, Bonn: 3635/D805828–41.

12 Shiva Kumar Sharma, *Der Völkerbund und die Großmächte: Ein Beitrag zur Geschichte der Völkerbundpolitik Großbritanniens, Frankreichs und Deutschlands, 1929–1933*. Frankfurt/M., Lang, 1978. – p. 13–68; Werner von Rheinbaben "Die Reform des Völkerbundsekretariats", *Zeitschrift für Politik*, v. 22, 1932–1933, p. 510–17; Kamphoevener (Berlin) to Missions, 1 November 1932, Politisches Archiv, Bonn: 3635/D806245–76.

13 Kimmich, *op. cit.*, ch. 8; Edward W. Bennet, *German Rearmament and the West, 1932–1933*. Princeton, Princeton University Press, 1979. – 569 p.

14 Dufour (Geneva) to Bülow, 31 May 1931, Köpke (Berlin) to Missions, 31 March 1932, and Kamphoevener (Berlin) to Missions, 1 November 1932, Politisches Archiv, Bonn: L1837/L532707–13, 3635/D806064–106, D806245–76; *Deutsche Allgemeine Zeitung*, 21 October, 1 November 1931; Deutsche Liga für Völkerbund, *Memorandum zur Vertrauenskrise des Völkerbundes*. Berlin, Juli 1932.

15 *ADAP*, C., I, no. 142; *Abrüstung und Sicherheit*, v. 2., Karl Schwendemann, editor, Berlin, 1935. – p. 467–80, 494–506; Günter Wollstein, *Vom Weimarer Revisionismus zu Hitler*. Bonn/Bad Godesberg, Verlag Wissenschaftliches Archiv, 1973. –

The United States and the League of Nations, 1919–1939

GARY B. OSTROWER
Alfred University, Alfred, New York

Co-operation between the United States and the League of Nations may have failed to achieve the major objectives of each side, but at least in the United States such cooperation rarely failed to evoke strong feelings. As late as 1935, a Senator could laud his predecessors who kept the nation out of the League. "They were God's instruments. They stood like Ajax defying the lightning, like Leonidas at the pass of Thermopylae, and headed off our being dragged into the League of Nations . . . To hell with Europe and the rest of the debt-cancelling nations," he continued. "Keep out of there; keep out of there."[1]

There were others, friends of the League, who felt equally certain that those same Senators were fools or worse. Yet, in reality, both sides exaggerated the consequences of American membership, and both underestimated the degree to which the United States had established regular contact with an organization that, formally, it did not recognize. By the thirties, the League and the United States had come to exert a significant influence on the policy of the other. Nevertheless, in large part because of American non-membership, the lines of this influence remained unclear. The historian is therefore required to search out the U.S.-League relationship as a sub-category of other topics: the Ethiopian Crisis, for example, or Neutrality policy.

There are four chronological phases to this story. The first involves the origin of the relationship from 1917 to 1920, including the organized efforts of the League to enforce peace during the war, Woodrow Wilson's efforts in Paris during 1919 to help draft the Covenant, and the Senate's well-publicized rejection of American membership. Because this first phase is so well-known, it will be only briefly surveyed in this paper. The other phases constitute the heart of the story: the second, from 1921 to 1931, when the United States evolved from literal non-recognition of the League to participation in League-sponsored technical and humanitarian activity; the third, which involved extensive though unproductive political involvement with the League during both the Manchurian and Ethiopian conflicts; and the final phase in which Washington's loss of interest in the organization mirrored the League's decline.

Phase I: The Beginnings

Although occasional American proposals for an international political organization predated the outbreak of the Great War, existing co-operation was limited to quasi-judicial work along the lines of the Hague Arbitration Conferences. The outbreak of war, however, and especially American entry into it in April 1917, greatly speeded up the demands for political co-operation. President Wilson's conversion to this cause eventually brought him to Paris where he became a principal author of the Covenant. Shortly thereafter, his domestic opposition skilfully undermined his work by proposing the so-called mild and strong reservations during the Senate debate over ratification. Since many historians have narrated and interpreted the fate of the Covenant during the Senate debate, I wish to make only a few brief points.

For one, we must bury the idea that the Treaty's defeat represented the resurgence of American isolationism. The vast majority of Senators supported the League in one form or another. So, too, did other organs of public opinion.[2] Certainly most Americans and their representatives favored at least an amended League.

Secondly, the few outright opponents of membership were greatly aided by serious (though largely unrecognized) differences of opinion within the internationalist community. The Treaty was therefore vulnerable once these differences were exploited, especially since Wilson had shifted the direction of international cooperation from juridical channels (which had been highly popular) to the political clauses embodied in Articles 10 to 16 (which raised the specter of force).[3]

Thirdly, Wilson, along with many other internationalists, remained ambivalent about the use of force during these years. He had not thought through the risks of collective security. Wilson at times demanded a League with "teeth," fearing that without Article 10 the organization would be "hardly more than an influential debating society." At other times, he feared substituting "international militarism for national militarism."[4] Indeed, Wilson was only one of many "Wilsonians" who suffered from intellectual confusion on these issues. Wilsonians generally insisted that the force provisions of the Covenant were essential to future peace (Wilson's refusal to compromise on Article 10 contributed directly to the Covenant's defeat in the Senate). At the same time, they were convinced that these provisions would never be utilized, for they believed that moral force – particularly the power of public opinion – would be sufficient to deter future aggressors. The latent contradictions in such thinking were not only exploited by League opponents in 1919 and 1920; they would also undermine American-League co-operation during the thirties.

Finally, the Senate's defeat of the Treaty demoralized the League's most ardent American supporters, emboldened its opponents, and left the State Department during the final weeks of the Wilson administration uncertain about how to relate to Geneva. Furthermore, the presidential election that brought Harding to office was soon interpreted as an anti-League mandate (in reality, Harding had been more anti-Article 10 than anti-League; his attitude toward international organization remained murky throughout the campaign). The myth of a popular referendum for isolation would, however, prove to be long-lasting.

Phase II: The first postwar decade, 1921–1931

During the 1920 campaign President Harding spoke vaguely of joining "an association of nations" in place of the League of Nations. However, he had no real interest in the idea, and his administration, despite the presence of a moderate internationalist as Secretary of State, generally side-stepped League-related issues. The earliest days of administration policy toward Geneva were actually characterized by extreme frigidity. The State Department did not even bother to reply to League correspondence, a practice altered (barely, by unsigned acknowledgments) only after a "leak" to the *New York Times* embarrassed the administration.[5] Thereafter, relations thawed, but so gradually as to lead to charges that the administration secretly hoped for the League's demise.[6] There may have been truth to the charges; to the extent that League success could embarrass the State Department in the light of U.S. non-membership, and to the degree that the League served as a rallying point for internationalist critics of the administration, Washington would not likely mourn the organization's disappearance. Nevertheless, we have no hard evidence on this matter. And, in fact, the record of American interaction with the League by the time of Harding's own death in December 1923 turned out to be rather mixed; this was mainly thanks to the growing recognition that the League would not disappear, and owing to some diplomatic successes (especially at the Washington Conference of 1921–1922) which in turn reduced U.S. anxiety about the League, as well as thanks to the efforts of Secretary of State Hughes, the chief American policymaker. A number of things by 1923 pointed toward non-co-operation: the already-mentioned mail issue, Secretary Hughes' refusal to permit the American panel of the Court of International Arbitration (technically a *non*-governmental group) from nominating candidates for judgeships on the World Court (the Permanent Court of International Justice), and the State Department's convoluted – indeed silly – efforts to have American information sent to League technical agencies appear unconnected to the League.[7] Furthermore, Hughes began a State Department tradition of refusing to comment about League activity, a tradition that would – with some important exceptions – continue throughout the interwar period. General requests for State Department views about the League were usually answered with perfunctory responses mindful of America's non-membership in the Organization.[8]

On the other hand – and of greater importance in the long run – Hughes endorsed co-operation with the technical and humanitarian work of League agencies, beginning with the League's Opium Committee in 1923. This initially involved sending an "unofficial observer" (something "between a guest and a spy," quipped one critic) who was, in fact, an official U.S. representative without voting rights.[9] Eventually, American delegates attended scores of meetings dealing with subjects as widely separated as technical aid to China and the white slave trade, and the U.S. Government financially supported the League in this work.[10] The money came directly from the State Department's emergency fund. The Department never asked for congressional appropriations, fearing that a general debate might lead to curtailment of *all* funds.[11]

Of importance in relation to U.S. involvement with the League during the 1920s was the decision to regularize diplomatic contact by appointing a consular official in Geneva whose *main* responsibility would be to report on League affairs. Although the Department exhibited its usual nervousness when it warned of the "appearance of accrediting him in any way to the League . . .", the reorganization of the Geneva consulate would pay significant dividends in later years.[12]

Financial contributions, the rearrangement of the consulate staff, participation in specialized non-political work: all were really secondary issues during the decade. About the political questions of greatest importance, the record of the 1920s contains little. The most significant U.S. foreign policy initiatives were almost invariably taken without reference to Geneva. Not only was this true of negotiations over the Dawes and Young Plans, Pan American co-operation (in which U.S. officials displayed uneasiness with Latin American membership in the League),[13] and the broad field of economic diplomacy geared to both European and Asian affairs, but also with phases of international co-operation that *directly* paralleled League activity. For instance, the 1921–22 Washington Conference that helped to limit navies and to frame a Far East détente might best be seen as providing a regional substitute for the League. Nor did the State Department consult the League about the Pact of Paris (Kellogg-Briand Pact), which some observers saw as contradicting the force provisions of the Covenant.[14] Concerning disarmament, the Americans participated in discussions which, though sponsored by the League, were preparatory to a general conference outside the League framework. And they surprisingly took little notice of Canadian and Scandinavian efforts during the early twenties to weaken the collective-security obligations of the Covenant (the Canadian initiative may have been designed to induce the Americans to reconsider League membership).[15]

Finally, although vigorous support for the League continued to exist among small segments of the American public, the larger public gradually lost interest in the old debate. By 1928, the Democratic Party platform had dropped its previous support for U.S. membership. By the same token, the waning of passions allowed the Republicans during the same year to endorse non-political co-operation.

The late twenties, then, represented a transition period. The early thirties, which would witness two Great Power challenges to the existing structure of peace, ushered in new initiatives for American-League co-operation. That these initiatives were unsuccessful tell us much about both League and U.S. policy.

Phase III: Collective Security: 1931–1935

A person seeking consistency in U.S.-League relations will not find it during the critical years of the League's history. Before 1931, White House and State Department officials had generally come to accept the importance of the League in non-political activity, but not in the areas of Latin American affairs, issues connected to possible American membership, and political measures involving not only force but consultation. This picture would become much less clear following the Japanese occupation of Manchuria.

American inconsistency in respect of the League during the Hoover Administration (1929–33) stemmed from at least four factors: 1) important policy and temperamental differences between the President and the Secretary of State; 2) American naval strength inadequate to allay anxiety about the sanctity of treaties;

3) confusion about the risks of collective security, including unrealistic expectations about the efficacy of moral pressure and public opinion; and 4) fear of popular isolationism at home.

By World War II, Secretary of State Henry L. Stimson (1929 to 1933) had become one of the leading collective security advocates in the U.S.[16] He, along with Charles Evans Hughes, had been one of the Republican proponents of American membership during the original Treaty debate, and he fit squarely into the internationalist tradition during the entire interwar period. But internationalism was not synonymous with support for collective security, and Stimson vacillated greatly on this issue. Even before becoming Secretary of State, he expressed misgivings about Article 10, emphasized the importance of international law over a formal political organization, and regretted his 1920 support for the League once it became politically controversial.[17] He did endorse U.S. membership in the World Court, and as Secretary he favored arms limitations talks both within and outside of the League. As late as 1931, he could write that the League furnished useful machinery "for the nations of Europe" while arguing that the U.S. would squander its influence and moral power if it joined the League in debating the "routine problems and squabbles" of the Continent.[18]

This was doubletalk. And when the Japanese Army occupied Mukden, idle chatter about Europe's routine squabbles gave way to serious consideration of conflict in Asia. The U.S. had traditionally been more willing to flex its political muscles in the Pacific to support the 'Open Door' and the Philippines.

Stimson, of course, did not make policy alone. President Herbert Hoover, preoccupied with the economic crisis at home, remained even more wary than Stimson of using economic or military power in any situation short of a direct invasion of American territory. Public attitudes also entered into policymaking. To the extent it can be measured, public opinion appeared hostile to Japan's aggression, fearful of war, yet tolerant of international co-operation not involving the use of force. This would have given Stimson plenty of room to co-operate with the League. But because public opinion could not be assessed with precision, State Department officials continued to worry about a hostile popular reaction.[19]

So Stimson groped during the early days of the crisis, offering the League tepid encouragement toward the end of September, but rejecting proposals for American participation at a Council meeting and for the creation of a League-sponsored commission of inquiry. His hesitations stemmed from two sources. He feared that combined American/League efforts might stimulate Japanese nationalism and therefore render a settlement of the conflict more difficult. He also suspected that the League might try to 'pass the buck' (in other words, shift the burden of responsibility) to the U.S., especially when officials in Geneva noted that Japan had violated not only the Covenant, but treaties which the U.S. had signed (such as the Nine-Power Treaty of 1922 and the Kellogg-Briand Pact).[20]

In October, his hesitations turned into outright inconsistency. Angered by broken Japanese promises and expanded military operations, Stimson, with Hoover's approval, surprisingly authorized U.S. representation at the October

Council session in order to dramatize international concern about the growing war. His decision to co-operate directly with the League created high hopes – and high drama. However, not only did he set exceedingly narrow limits to this co-operation – Consul Prentiss Gilbert, the U.S. representative, could only join discussion related to the Kellogg-Briand Pact – but Stimson ordered Gilbert to withdraw as soon as the Pact had been 'invoked.' This stunned the Council, for the general debate was far from over. Stimson therefore dashed these high hopes and came close to turning the drama into farce.[21]

It is impossible in a short paper to narrate adequately the subsequent course of American-League interaction during the crisis. However, certain points deserve special attention. For one, Stimson's fear that the League would 'pass the buck' to the Americans made him wary of co-operation during the *entire* crisis. Secondly, his inconsistent policy during the first month (cautious during September when he complained of League inaction while discouraging serious co-operation, such as the formation of a commission of inquiry or American representation; assertive when he ordered Gilbert to the Council table; cautious again when, fearing Japanese hostility, he ordered Gilbert away from the table) became the dominant motif of his policy until the day he left office. In November 1931, he again sent a representative to meet with the Council but this time permitted him to remain physically apart from the Chamber. Then, in January, he ignored co-operative action altogether by sending his nonrecognition note unilaterally. When others did not similarly protest, he became angry (later bitter), especially when he feared becoming isolated following the outbreak of fighting around Shanghai. Consequently, he again moved toward a cooperative policy, eventually secured Assembly endorsement of the nonrecognition policy in March 1932, followed by still another retreat from cooperation extending through midsummer. In August 1932, he swung back yet again toward co-operation, this time in his 8 August speech to the Council on Foreign Relations in which he asserted that the Kellogg-Briand Pact had made traditional concepts of isolation and neutrality obsolete. But with the American presidential election only months away, Stimson once more reverted to silence, offering "sympathetic consideration" to Drummond with respect to the upcoming debate over the Lytton Report while offering no specifics. Only *after* the Assembly acted on the Report and condemned Japan did he register his agreement. No wonder the British considered him unreliable.[22]

Furthermore, within this tale of erratic U.S.-League co-operation is another theme that deserves comment. Stimson has often been viewed as the one American official who seriously entertained the use of economic sanctions (an embargo) in support of the Covenant's Article 16. This is myth. The American Secretary *never* committed himself to sanctions, either publicly or privately. President Hoover *feared* that he would, and some of Stimson's subordinates probably favored the use of sanctions. Indeed, the State Department studied the probable impact of sanctions upon Japan, concluding that they would likely be highly effective.[23] A private American campaign for sanctions in February and March 1932 gathered support from prominent internationalists who saw themselves defending the principles of the Kellogg-Briand Pact, not the Covenant.[24]

Although Stimson did not discourage their effort, neither did he encourage them. It is true that he discussed a private boycott during the last weeks of 1931, but he soon settled on moral pressure (the nonrecognition statement) against Japan, not economic force. Similarly, Stimson may have sharply opposed Hoover's inclination to announce in *advance* that the U.S. would never have recourse to economic or military force (Stimson, unlike Hoover, understood the value of bluff), but his policy remained very restrained.[25] Like his President, he feared that economic pressure would lead to war. Nor did he even commit his government to consult with other Kellogg-Briand Pact signatories in case of aggression. In his 8 August speech, he spoke of consultation as "inevitable". But no guarantee.[26]

Finally, we should note that although Stimson wanted the Assembly to condemn Japan following the submission of the Lytton Report, and although he equally wanted to maintain the League's support for the nonrecognition of Manchukuo, he offered little meaningful support to the League following the 8 August speech. Perhaps his silence related to the upcoming presidential election, his general discouragement with the situation, or his fear that, should the U.S. encourage the League to condemn Japan after which Japan should leave the League, the U.S. might be held responsible.[27] His excessive caution became standard operating procedure. The upshot, of course, was that the League could never be sure about American intentions. In the long run, both the League and the U.S. would pay a high price for this uncertainty.

Which brings us to the heart of the matter. For Stimson – whose own caution was reinforced by his near-pacifist boss, who could excuse his own inaction by exaggerating isolationist influence during an election year, and who was frustrated by British unreliability not much different from his own – never came to grips with the fact that the League neither would *nor could* take effective action without knowing where his Government stood. The League would of course need British naval support to advance beyond moral pressure against Tokyo. But it equally would need American cooperation. The U.S. accounted for 40% of Japanese trade and had a fleet and merchant marine that could easily undermine League sanctions. The League had to know *in advance* whether the U.S. would co-operate; and Stimson therefore unintentionally guaranteed League inaction by demanding that the League take the initial steps.

*

Hoover and Stimson never really articulated a League policy. Neither did their successors, Franklin D. Roosevelt and Cordell Hull. Both Roosevelt and Hull had long been considered internationalists, and both had been active supporters of the League during the early debate over membership. Yet their foreign policy in respect to Geneva would be characterized by the same kind of inconsistency that beset Stimson's efforts, and for some of the same reasons. It might be added that Roosevelt never surrendered his basic internationalist sentiments, but his foreign policy, like that of his predecessors, placed the League well down on his scale of political priorities.

The Roosevelt Administration's ambivalence toward the League flowed naturally from the clash of Wilsonian sentiments and isolationist anxieties. This can be seen rather clearly in one of the Administration's first decisions concerning the League. A number of troublesome problems regarding U. S.-League communication had been exposed during the tense days of the Manchurian affair. To eliminate them, State Department personnel sympathetic to the League proposed a major reorganization of the U. S. Consulate in Geneva. This included the appointment of an ambassador to replace the lowly-ranking Consul then in charge of day-to-day contact with the Secretariat officials. Their plan, on the drawing board for months, had already been approved by Secretary of State Hull when the reorganization story broke in the *New York Herald Tribune*. Queried by reports, Hull quickly denied that the Department planned any change. "I was obliged categorically to deny the whole thing," he complained.[28] And although the plan lingered on for another year, Roosevelt withheld his necessary authorization as the European climate continued to deteriorate.[29]

The question of American membership in the International Labor Office likewise revealed the ambivalence. During 1934, the Administration sponsored a congressional resolution for membership in this body. Although the ILO was not a League organ, Administration officials feared it would be interpreted as such and therefore went to great lengths to differentiate the ILO from the League in the public mind. The White House, in fact, kept a tight rein on League enthusiasts in the State Department lest they upset the cart. Congressional approval was accomplished in part by having the Labor Department, not the State Department, carry the campaign to the public as an antidepression, not a foreign policy, measure.[30]

The campaign for American membership on the World Court equally illustrated ambivalence about the League. Americans probably had fewer reservations about the Court than about any other international body.[31] Even Harding had favored membership for the U. S.; so did Presidents Coolidge, Hoover and Roosevelt, along with all of their Secretaries of State. But when in January 1935 the Senate unexpectedly failed to ratify the Court Protocol following a sudden surge of isolationist opposition, the Roosevelt Administration became even more charry than usual about international cooperation. If it is not very surprising that Roosevelt flatly rejected the advice of two State Department aides who suggested - *before* the Court defeat - that the Administration campaign for League membership, it is even less surprising that the Administration ignored completely a League of Nations Association campaign for membership *after* the Court defeat.[32]

All in all, Americans by 1935 viewed cooperation with the League in much the same light as they had during the Manchurian crisis. Membership was out of the question; contact short of membership could be considered though anxiously. Ambivalent for over a decade, the pattern would be repeated throughout the last great crisis of the League's history - the Italian-Ethiopian dispute

When Mussolini marched his army into Ethiopia on 2 and 3 October 1935, the League had a different complexion than it had during the Manchurian crisis. The Germans and the Japanese had already departed; the Soviets had joined. According to Prentiss Gilbert who often reflected on the broad picture in Geneva, this made the League less universal and more partisan (in the sense of having become more of an anti-German agency). Futhermore Gilbert warned the Department that Sir Eric Drummond's successor had latinized the League. Not that Secretary-General Joseph Avenol was anti-American, claimed Gilbert; he was just pro-French.[33]

State Department officials seemed little affected by these observations. What seemed to impress them much more were the increasingly frequent cables from European capitals reporting that neither Britain nor France seriously contemplated action against Italy during the early months of the crisis. American observers viewed both Governments as more solicitous of Italian friendship (especially in the light of German revisionism) than Ethiopian sovereignty or the vitality of collective security. Combined with the growing pessimism about the prospects of European peace, fear of a Japaneses-Soviet conflict, the shock of the Senate's rejection of World Court membership, and Roosevelt's preoccupation with domestic affairs, the State Department kept a very low profile with respect to League activity. As early as December 1934, Secretary Hull informed the American Minister in Addis Abeba that the U.S. could not "usefully or properly take any action" because the dispute had been appealed by Ethiopia to the League.[34] This attitude prevailed until the summer of 1935. By then, evidence that the British Government (and to a lesser extent the French Government) contemplated some kind of League protest encouraged the State Department to dust off publicly the Kellogg-Briand Pact in a July message to Emperor Haile Selassie of Ethiopia.[35]

Although some U.S. supporters of the League applauded this latest use of the Kellogg-Briand Pact as an important step toward consultation, in fact it meant almost nothing at all. The Kellogg-Briand Pact had already proved to be merely a pious hope for peace. "American idealism has gone by the boards; it was never meant to be translated into reality," editorialized the *China Press* in reaction to the American note. Foreign reaction was generally cool. The State Department, anxious about international responsibility, was nonetheless stung by this unexpected criticism.[36] When, therefore, British Foreign Secretary Sir Samuel Hoare electrified the League in early September with, superficially, one of the more rousing speeches in support of collective security ever made by a representative of a Great Power, State Department officials were greatly encouraged to take an additional step of their own.[37] "A threat of hostilities anywhere cannot but be a threat to the interests . . . of all nations," warned Hull in a second - and stronger - statement of Kellogg-Briand Pact principles.[38] This time, however, American officials hoped to give the League more meaningful support. The Neutrality Act of 1935 had recently been passed by Congress. Although it mandated an embargo on trade in war items to *both* belligerents in a dispute (in other words, it worked against aggressor and victim alike), it would likely operate mainly against Italy since Ethiopia had never had much trade with the U.S.

Invocation of the Neutrality Act meant that, in a rough sort of way, an American embargo might be used to parallel League sanctions if later imposed against the aggressor. Since the Neutrality Act was, in reality, nondiscriminatory - that is, aimed against both parties to the dispute - it represented a very cautious brand of co-operation. Nevertheless, Americans expressed their usual nervousness.

When the Italians finally attacked, the Undersecretary of State even worried that the U.S. might look as if it were leading the League.[39] He need not have worried. Yet the decision to involve the Neutrality Act bore directly on co-operation with the League, and the Undersecretary wrote that while some of his colleagues felt that the U.S. "should pay no attention to Geneva," others felt that "we should be careful in not doing anything to upset the efforts of the world" assembled there.[40]

During the Manchurian affair, Hoover and Stimson had unintentionally undermined collective security. Hoping to deflect Japanese hostility away from themselves, they insisted that the League stake out its position before announcing their own. In 1935, their successors, aware that the 1931 and 1932 strategy had ultimately served neither League nor U.S. interests, resolved not to repeat the mistake. It was for this reason that the Roosevelt Administration, aware that the League would soon begin to discuss sanctions, resolved to invoke the Neutrality Act upon the outbreak of fighting.[41]

To be sure, there were some similarities with 1931. For instance, partisan considerations had not disappeared from the debate. Hull for example, argued that immediate invocation would protect the Administration from isolationist charges of following the League.[42] Similarly, formal American participation in sanctions under Article 16 were no more possible in 1935 than 1931. President Roosevelt explicitly ruled this out within a week after the outbreak of fighting.[43] Nor was the State Department in 1935 any more certain about the tactics of coordinating its efforts with the League than it had been four years earlier. For instance, on the matter of activating the provisions of the Neutrality Act, half of Hull's advisers recommended immediate action, half recommended delay until the Assembly acted.[44]

But there were also substantial differences with the 1931 crisis. For if Stimson's strategy contained a fatal contradiction - his sporadic turn toward Geneva were compromised by his obsessive need to appear independent of the League - American officials in 1935 were more genuinely concerned about the fate of collective security. This stemmed only in part from their earlier experience. The world in 1935 seemed to be a much more dangerous place than in 1931. Both Roosevelt and Hull received increasingly pessimistic prediction about the breakdown of peace on the Continent.[45] They consequently saw the future of collective security much more intimately tied to the crisis than had Hoover and Stimson four years earlier. Although the President had ruled out participation in sanctions, he nevertheless ordered Hull to consider expanding the list of embargoed goods covered by the Neutrality Act in order to support possible League sanctions. He also promised to "require drastic proof of non-transshipment" of American exports to nonsanctionist countries.[46]

Even disagreement within the State Department over the timing of the Neutrality Act embargo - before or after League sanctions - reflected increased concern about collective security. Officials on *each* side of the debate wanted to supplement Article 16. Those, like Hull and Roosevelt, who recommended immediate application of the embargo feared that isolationists might otherwise make it more difficult to parallel League action later. The advocates of delay, led by Hugh Wilson and including Undersecretary Phillips, Economic Advisor Herbert Feis, and division chiefs Wallace Murray (Near East) and Stanley Hornbeck (Far East), all expressed strong support for League efforts; they feared that a premature U.S. neutrality declaration might ironically induce wavering League members to declare their own neutrality rather than join the sanctionist front.[47]

As with Manchuria, it is impossible to provide an adequate narrative of the entire course of U.S.-League relations during the crisis. The co-operation of early October, described above, distills some of the more important similarities and differences in the diplomatic record. We might remember that American-League co-operation over Ethiopia benefitted from two conditions absent during the Far Eastern crisis. Unlike the occupation of Mukden, the Italian assault in October 1935 had been long expected; both League and U.S. officials had time to plan their response. Furthermore, there were few meaningful precedents for co-operation at the time of the Far Eastern crisis, whereas American and League officials in 1935 had allready learned from their earlier mistakes. The result was that American co-operation with the League appeared less erratic and less confused in 1935 than during 1931 and 1932. And with both the U.S. and the League more willing to consider economic pressure against Italy rather than the moral protests hurled at Japan, collective-security prospects should have been bright.

They were not. Collective security ultimately fared no better in Ethiopia than in Manchuria. There were many reasons for this, most unrelated to the failed promise of American-League co-operation. Some further words are in order, however, about the U.S.-League tie.

The diplomacy of October 1935 highlights the willingness of American officials to support the collective-security principle. Yet, during the most critical phases of the crisis, there existed less direct contact between U.S. and Secretariat officials than occurred during the Manchurian affair. American diplomats may have considered Sir Eric Drummond aloof and restrained, but they found him more approachable (and welcoming) than his more secretive successor.

Of even greater consequence was the caution that frequently seemed to undergird American policy. As with Stimson over Manchuria, the Americans really took few risks. Roosevelt and Hull undoubtedly thought themselves bold to co-operate with Geneva in the face of isolationist sentiment at home, especially when they announced a moral embargo on raw materials not specifically covered by the Neutrality Act. But they were not bold enough to add these raw materials (including oil) to the list of items formally included in the legal embargo. They *could* have done this (perhaps, months later, a court would have overruled them). They chose not to, for political reasons.[48] It is true that they inched closer to legal restraints on oil and other raw materials when it became clear during November 1935 that the moral embargo was less successful than they had originally hoped.[49] Nevertheless, their efforts came to nought after the Hoare-Laval Plan demoralized League enthusiasts both in Geneva and the U.S. Early in 1936 (an election year), Congress amended and extended the Neutrality Act in a way that barred the administration from applying an oil embargo. When Roosevelt decided not to challenge this isolationist attack on his policy prerogatives caution had become king.

It is highly unlikely that a more flexible Neutrality Act, permitting Roosevelt to embargo oil, would have "forced the reluctant hand of the League" into sanctions.[50] Even if Congress had not amended the Act, the British and French would probably have dragged their feet; after Hitler ordered the Wehrmacht into the Rhineland in early March, it is inconceivable that either country would have voted for sanctions, regardless of what the Americans said. Furthermore, Roosevelt's own reluctance to battle the amended Neutrality Act may have been reinforced by his knowledge that both Britain and France continued to discourage the use of sanctions. He was hardly about to squander his own political capital in the face of European ambivalence over the issue. From this point, U.S. officials increasingly noted the independence of American aims from those of the League.[51] Real cooperation, such that it was, gradually ended. The U.S. kept the embargo in force through the summer, but this merely camouflaged the wreckage of defeat.

Phase IV: The death of the League, 1936-39

There is virtually no evidence in either public or private American archives after the spring of 1936 that the League could fulfill its collective security purposes. Writing from Geneva as early as April, Prentiss Gilbert informed the State Department that Secretariat officials viewed the League as "suspended." "It is generally felt," he continued, "that for an indeterminate period, the League will in fact be left to one side."[52] Cables from London and Moscow, not to speak of those from Italy and Germany, addressed the League's impotence.[53] The American ambassador to Spain, a self-proclaimed "ardent League man since 1919," confessed that the League since the Ethiopian affair "only arouses my contempt."[54]

In circumstances like this, the Roosevelt Administration predictably kept the League at arms' length. The State Department undertook *no* serious initiatives with the League in respect of the Spanish Civil War, or the resumption of Sino-Japanese warfare, or the Brussels Conference. When Arthur Sweetser anxiously wrote the President about American-League co-operation during 1936 and concluded "I do not think the members of the Council themselves realized what an appreciable American association with the League they meant," Roosevelt carefully replied "I do not think that you should find in these contracts any greater significance than the fact that this country is continuing its cooperation in the League activities of an economic, humanitarian, and scientific nature in a friendly and sincere way."[55]

Outside official circles, pro-League internationalists generally continued their support for the organization. But the character of their activity changed. Instead of lobbying for American membership as they did as late as 1935, their work increasingly turned to schemes for League reorganization with less emphasis on political objectives and more on economic and social justice.[56] Moreover, they reverted back to linking the Covenant and the Kellogg-Briand Pact as a means of appealing to the Americans, and they frankly admitted what European proponents of reorganziation had long recognized: that Member States must have different security responsiblities.

However moderate and reasonable their suggestions, the Administration ignored them. The American embassy in London had already cabled that the Foreign Office was unenthusiastic about reorganization for fear that it would finally destroy the existing Covenant.[57] With the League increasingly moribund, this sort of information could only reinforce American fears that the U.S. might again be accused of trying to kill the organizaton.

Non-political cooperation continued, but without the enthusiasm of the twenties. When the Secretary-General in September 1938 welcomed further cooperation with non-Members, the State Department did not reply for five months.[58] By this time the war that the League had been designed to prevent was but a few months away. That the U.S. became the home of the League during that war is the final bittersweet irony of the interwar period.

Notes

1 Senator Thomas Schall. *Congressional Record,* p. 1117–22, 29 January 1935.

2 Denna Frank Fleming, *The United States and the League of Nations, 1918–1920.* New York, Putnam's Sons, 1932. – 559 p. (Surveys newspaper opinion)

3 See Warren F. Kuehl, *Seeking World Order: The United States and International Organization to 1920.* Nashville, Vanderbilt University Press, 1969. – chaps. 13–14.

4 These quotations appear in Marc Trachtenberg, "Versailles after Sixty Years," unpublished paper, 1980. – p. 14–15.

5 *New York Times,* 18 July 1921. Personal interview, 28 August 1968, with Arthur Sweetser, an American assigned to the League's information section, who leaked the information.

6 Denna Frank Fleming, *The United States and World Organization, 1920–1933.* New York, Columbia University Press, 1938. – p. 71 (Hereafter: *World Organization*).

7 Betty Glad, *Charles Evans Hughes and the Illusions of Innocence. A study in American Agency.* Urbana, University of Illinois Press, 1966. – chaps. 10 and 11; D. F. Fleming, *World Organization . . . op. cit.* p. 64–65; p. 72–73.

8 Many inquiries concerned Washington's views about League membership (or Council membership) of other States. See for instance. the cable to Ambassador Edwin Morgan, 14 September 1923, SD 500.C112/96 about Brazil's seat on the Council. This pattern continued into the 1930s. For instance, the Department refused comment on Soviet entry into the League. Memorandum, 11 September 1934, SD500.C001/991.

9 D. F. Fleming, *World Organization . . . op. cit.* p. 219–21.

10 Clarence A. Berdahl, *The Policy of the United States with Respect to the League of Nations.* Geneva, Kundig, 1932. – 129 p.; Ursula P. Hubbard, "The Co-operation of the United States with the League of Nations, 1931–1936", *International Conciliation,* p. 292–468 no. 329, April 1937; the issues of *League Special Studies* published during the early thirties; F. P. Walters, *A History of the League of Nations.* London, Oxford University Press, 1952. *passim;* and a State Department report listing 63 conference that the United States attended between 1925 and 1932 in SD124.54/35.

11 American financial contributions to the League remained fairly steady during the twenties, comparable to the British contribution. According to State Department sources, a decline in American contributions beginning in 1932 was due not to United States

financial resistance so much as the greater efficiency attained by the League in the organization of meetings. See memorandum of Theodore Achilles, 28 December 1937. SD500.C3/129.

12 Undersecretary of State Joseph Grew to Consul Pinckney Tuck, 9 September 1924, SD123.T79/103a, and correspondence with Ambassador Hugh Gibson, 25 April 1925, and 17 November 1925. SD125T79/116, and 500.C001/310.

13 Dana G. Munro to Kellogg, 12 December 1925, SD819.00/1246; Hughes to Ambassador Edwin W. Morgan, 15 January 1925. SD710.C2/166.

14 In fact, the League later sponsored efforts to reconcile the two: LoN, *Committee for the Amendment of the Covenant of the League of Nations in Order to Bring it into Harmony with the Pact of Paris.* Geneva, 25 February to 5th March 1930. LoN doc. C.160. M.69. 1930.V. James Barros, *Office Without Power: Secretary-General Sir Eric Drummond, 1919–1933.* Oxford, the Clarendon Press, 1979. – p. 31–37, deals perceptively with Drummond's concern that the Pact raised some problems for the League in respect to the general use of force, and in respect to the Monroe Doctrine. Drummond's efforts to enter the negotiations between the French and the Americans were rebuffed.

15 F. P. Walters, *op. cit.* v.1, 258–59, claims that the Canadian amendment of the Covenant aimed at American membership. The debates over the amendment can be traced in LoN, *Records of the First Assembly, Plenary Meetings*, 4 December 1920, p. 275; *Records of the Second Assembly. Minutes of the First Committee*, 30 September and 1 October 1921 p. 107–114; Records of the Fourth Assembly, Plenary Meetings, 25 September 1923, *OJSS*, no. 13, p. 86. The most recent discussion of this appears in Richard Veatch, *Canada and the League of Nations, 1919–1939.* Toronto, University of Toronto Press, 1975. – 224 p.

16 Henry L. Stimson and McGeorge Bundy, *On Active Service in War and Peace.* New York, Harper, 1947–1948, 2 v. The authors emphasize the Secretary's support for collective security.

17 Elting E. Morison, *Turmoil and Tradition: A Study of the Life and Times of Henry L. Stimson.* Boston, Hougthon Mefflin, 1960. – p. 206–07.

18 See E. E. Morison, *op. cit.* 206, 256–57; Stimson memorandum, 12 July 1931, *FRUS* 1931, I, p. 544–45.

19 Herbert C. Hoover, *The Memoirs of Herbert Hoover: The Cabinet and the Presidency, 1920–1933.* New York, Macmillan, 1952. – v.2 p., 366–70, 375; Justus D. Doenecke, "American Public Opinion and the Manchurian Crisis," unpublished PhD dissertation, Princeton University, 1966. – Gary B. Ostrower, "Henry L. Stimson and the League," *The Historian*, v. XLI, May 1979, 476–79 (hereafter: Ostrower, "Henry L. Stimson") adresses the question of public opinion and United States policy.

20 G. B. Ostrower, *Collective Insecurity: The United States and the League of Nations During the Early Thirties.* Lewisburg, Bucknell University Press, 1979. – p. 65–66 (hereafter: Ostrower, *Collective Insecurity*); and Christopher Thorne, *The Limits of Power: The West, the League, and the Far Eastern Crisis of 1931–1933.* London, Macmillan, 1972. – p. 152–58. The Secretary-General's reaction to American co-operation is covered in James Barros, *Office without Power, op. cit.* [see note 14] p. 322–25. Council debate appears in LoN, Minutes of the Sixty-fifth Session of the Council, 22 September 1931, *OJ*, December 1931, p. 2270–72. Stimson's reaction appears in his diary, 22 to 25 September 1931.

21 Stimson, after appeals from League and European officials, permitted his consul to remain at the Council table for a time. But Gilbert was to remain silent (to "keep his mouth shut," Stimson wrote acidly in his diary), and the damage was done. Appeals to reverse the withdrawal decision can be found in phone conversation, 19 October 1931, *FRUS*, 1931/III, p. 241–48; and phone conversation, 20 October, *FRUS, ibid.*

p. 267–68. This episode is covered in J. B. Donnelly, "Prentiss Gilbert's Mission to the League of Nations Council, October 1931," *Diplomatic History*, 2: 378–388, Fall 1978. Stimson was not the only one worried about American-League co-operation. Drummond feared that, by invoking the Kellogg-Briand Pact, a "dual jurisdiction" might be created that would weaken the League: J. Barros, *op. cit.* P. 330–32.

22 See, for instance, the note by Neville Charles as early as October 1931 in Foreign Office archives 371/15494/164. British complaints became much more frequent during the early months of 1932. Stimson, it might be added, did not think much better of the British.

23 Hoover, *op. cit.*, [see note 19], p. 366. State Department memorandum 6 December 1931, SD 793.94/4314.

24 Nicholas Murray Butler to Hoover, 7 March 1932. SD711.0012 Antiwar/1231.

25 Stimson's diary for the first week in December 1931 covers the private boycott. Also his diary for 24–25 February 1932. G. B. Ostrower, "Henry L. Stimson," *op. cit.*, [see note 19], p. 479–80.

26 For Stimson's own assessment of the speech, see Stimson and Bundy, *op. cit.*, [see note 16], p. 259.

27 Privately, Stimson stated that the United States would never clash with League action against a Kellogg-Briand violator. Memorandum 11 November 1932, SD 500. A15a4 Steering Committee/151.

28 Hull to Norman Davis, *op. cit.* 20 September 1933, Box 34, Cordell Hull Papers. The story of reorganization is mainly spelled out in Ostrower, *Collective Insecurity, op. cit.* p. 169–78.

29 See Memorandum of 13 February 1934, SD 124.54/36½; Dunn memorandum, 12 July 1934, SD124.54/39; Carr to Dunn, 12 July 1934, SD 124.54/40.

30 Ostrower, *Collective Insecurity, op. cit.* p. 179–88; and in my "The American Decision to Join the International Labor Organization," *Labor History* 16: 495–504, Fall 1975.

31 Denna F. Fleming, *The United States and the World Court, 1920–1966*, rev. ed. New York, Russell and Russell, 1968. – 233 p.; and Ostrower, *Collective Insecurity, op. cit.*, p. 188–98.

32 William Phillips Journal, 31 December 1934. The League of Nations Association campaign is thoroughly analyzed by Robert D. Accinelli, "Militant Internationalists: The League of Nations Association, The Peace Movement, and United States Foreign Policy, 1934–1938," *Diplomatic History* 4: 25–28, Winter 1980.

33 Gilbert to Hull, 13 November 1934 and 11 January 1935, SD500.C/179 and 725.

34 On French and British inaction, see, for instance, Gilbert to Hull, 24 May 1935, SD 765.332. The message to Addis Abeba is in Hull to George, 21 December 1934, SD 765.84/83.

35 Hull to George, 5 July 1935, *FRUS* I, 725.

36 Internationalist applause appears in Nichols to Hull, 9 July 1935, and statement by Senator James Pope, 6 July 1935, SD 765/84/475 and 476. Criticism appears in Cunningham to Hull, 11 July, and Hull to Kirk, 11 July 1935, SD765.84/480 and 495a; and Detzer to Hull, 7 Huly, SD 765.84/444.

37 LoN, Records of the Sixteenth Ordinary Session of the Assembly, Plenary Meetings, 11 September 1935, *OJSS* no. 138. p. 43; Hornbeck to Hull, 12 September 1935, FRUS I, 746.

38 Hull press statement, 12 September 1935, *FRUS* I, 746–49.

39 William Phillips Journal, 4 October 1935.

40 *Ibid.*, 7 October 1935. Also, Cordell Hull, *Memoirs of Cordell Hull*, v.1, New York, Macmillan, 1948. – p. 429.

41 The issue of timing is covered in the Roosevelt-Hull correspondence of 25 September and 5 October 1935, *FRUS* I, 797–800.
42 Hull, *op. cit.*, [see note 40], v.1, p. 429. William Phillips Journal, 16 September 1935.
43 Roosevelt to Hull, 10 October 1935, SD 711.00111 Armament Control/115.
44 Hull, *op. cit.*, [see note 40], v.1, p. 428–29.
45 Dodd to Roosevelt, 9 May 1935, – in: *Franklin D. Roosevelt and Foreign Affairs* Edgar B. Nixon, editor, Cambridge, Belknap Press of Harvard University Press, 1969. – v.2, p. 499–503. Wilson to Hull, 13 November 1935, Box 38, Cordell Hull Papers.
46 Roosevelt to Hull, 10 October 1935, SD 711.0011 Armament Control/115.
47 Wilson to Hull, 5 October 1935, *FRUS* I, p. 664–65; phone conversation, SD 765.84/1590½: Hull, v. I, 428–30; William Phillips Journal, 7 October. Brice Harris Jr., *The United States and the Italo-Ethiopian Crisis.* Standford, Stanford University Press, 1964. – p. 57–60 (Provides an overview of this issue)
48 Hull, *op. cit.*, [see note 40], v.1, p. 433; Roosevelt to Hull, 10 October 1935, *In:* Nixon, *op. cit.*, [see note 45], v.3, p. 19–20.
49 15 November 1935, *FRUS* I, 819; Hull, *op. cit.*, [see note 40], v.1, p. 435–36.
50 B. Harris Jr., *op. cit.*, [see note 47], p. 131, makes the argument that congressional revision of the Act killed League sanctions.
51 For instance, see the memorandum of William Phillips talk with the Rumanian ambassador, 13 February 1936, SD 765.84/3778.
52 Gilbert to Hull, 7 April 1936, SD 741.0011 Mutual Guarantee/613.
53 Atherton to Hull, 6 June 1936, SD 765.83/4624; Henderson (Moscow) to Hull, 26 May 1935, SD 765.83/4628.
54 Claude Bowers to Dodd, 1 October 1936. Box 48, Dodd Papers.
55 See exchange of correspondence, SD 500.C/854.
56 League of Nations plan, 11 May 1936, James T. Shotwell Papers, in Butler Library, Columbia Unviersity, LNA (League of Nations Association) Box. Eichelberger to Hull, 27 April 1936, SD 500.C/96.
57 Atherton to Hull, 9 June 1936, SD 765.84/4620.
58 The reply was mailed on 22 February 1939, SD 500.C/962.

The Soviet Union and the League of Nations

INGEBORG PLETTENBERG
Federal Republic of Germany

1. The Admission of the USSR to the League

On 15 September 1934 the Soviet Government with no surprise received a telegram from the representatives of 30 States members inviting the USSR to join the League of Nations and to give to it its "valuable collaboration".

Soviet acceptance followed on the spot, coupled with the formal "undertaking to observe all the international obligations and decisions binding upon members in conformity with Article 1 of the Covenant . . ." The Soviet reply contained a reservation to the effect that the methods of arbitration and judicial settlement provide for in Art. 12 and 13 of the Covenant "should not be applicable to conflicts regarding questions arising before its entry into the League."*

Following the majority recommendation made by its Sixth Committee the day before, the LoN Assembly on 18 September 1934 decided the admission on the basis of 39 votes, i. e. more than the two-thirds majority required. Three Members voted against, seven abstained. Formally unanimous (40 positive votes and 10 abstentions), the Assembly granted to the USSR a permanent seat on the LoN Council. Recommendations to this effect had been worked out by the Council on 9, 10, and 15 September 1934.[2]

In the evening of 18 September the Soviet delegates – the People's Commissar for Foreign Affairs M. M. Litvinov, and the Soviet ambassadors to Italy and Finland, V. P. Potemkin and B. E. Štejn, respectively – resumed their seats in the Assembly. Litvinov in his inaugural speech both motivated the Soviet entry into the LoN and outlined the basic ideas of the future activities of the new League of Nations Member. "The Soviet Government . . . could not but observe the increasing activity in the League of Nations of States interested in the preservation of peace and their struggle against aggressive militarist elements. Moreover, it noted that these aggressive elements themselves were finding the restrictions of the League embarrassing and were trying to shake them off . . . The organization of peace . . . must be set against the extremely active organization of war. Then, many believed that the spirit of war might be exorcised by adjurations, resolutions and declarations. Now, everybody knows the exponents of the idea of war – the open promulgators of the map of Europe and Asia by the sword – are not to be intimidated by paper obstacles. Members of the League know this

* Passages in double quotes frequently refer to translations into English of original Russian, French, German etc. texts.

by experience. We are now confronted with the task of averting war by more effective means . . . I am aware that the League does not possess the means for the complete abolition of war . . . I am, however, convinced that, with the firm will and close cooperation of all its members, a great deal could be done at any given moment for the utmost diminution of the danger of war . . . The Soviet Government has come here to combine its efforts with those of other States represented in the League . . ."[3]

The "most momentous event since the war"[4], the replacement of the "principle of homogeneous universality by that of heterogeneous universality«[5], the "final victory" of the "principle of peaceful co-existence of different social-political systems at a given historical stage«[6], did not fail to rouse much "partisan excitement" at the time.[7] In the course of nearly one month – from 7–29 August 1934[8] – the three permanent Members of the Council, Great Britain, France and Italy, had agreed jointly and actively to sponsor the Soviet case. Thus, the "wit of the Geneva jurists" could be brought into action in favour of the admission, the more so since there was "not the same overwhelming demand" for Soviet admission "as there was for Germany's"[10], and also that the single adverse vote sufficient to prevent a unanimous invitation to the USSR by the Assembly was available.

In admitting the USSR a procedure was adopted which followed the Mexican and Turkish precedents set up by the League itself a few years before. The gist of the procedure was that the Soviet Government was spared from explicitly submitting to the League as an applicant. This evoked at the Geneva quarters a sudden concern with the "dignity of the League"; concern that obtained even less expected support from the German national-socialist press which took the general line of "Russia being smuggled into Geneva by the back door."[11] The procedure, however, did not allow exclusively for Soviet susceptibilities. There still existed powerful tendencies on the one hand to hold off the USSR permanently on the ground that Communism and League principles were incompatible, and on the other hand at least to impose upon her entry political conditions other than those to be deduced from Article 1 of the Covenant.[12] Once the leading Powers of the Organization had come to the conclusion that integrating the USSR into the League system corresponded to their mutual political interest, the procedure served first and foremost as a means of avoiding risks.

That the Soviet Union would be admitted with "varying degrees of cordiality"[13] became evident when the 'private' invitation of the 30 League Members was drafted. The British sponsor took a particularly keen interest in a wording which would not imply "any certificate of good character" concerning the candidate.[14] Consequently from the French draft of 8 September 1934 the paragraph recognizing that the "Soviet Union fulfils general conditions laid down in Article 1 of the Covenant for a State to become a Member of the League of Nations«[15] was omitted. As an assurance given by the candidate, the same paragraph reappeared in paragraph 2 of the draft Soviet reply arrived at by Litvinov and the President of the Council, Beneš, in the course of "long and difficult negotiations" on 14 September 1934.[16]

The "varying degrees of cordiality" obviously reflected varying degrees of will to substantiate future co-operation with the USSR. Britain and France reached agreement on Soviet entry only on the basis of a minimum-formula: "Russia in the League was a lesser evil than Russia outside the League."[17] The mutual consent applied to formal Soviet membership only. This in turn to a certain extent, limited the prospects of an efficient future Soviet participation in the work of the LoN Assembly and Council.

Be that as it may – after 15 years of opposition the USSR had joined the Organization which, judging at least by the declarations of its founders, was created in order to safeguard general peace and to prevent a new world war. The League of Nations of 1919/1920 was a compromise and quite different from what originally its American, British, or French fathers specifically wanted it to be. But in its articles 10–17, the Covenant still echoed the main characteristics attributed to the Organization by the last of Wilson's Fourteen Points – "A general association of nations . . . for the purpose of affording mutual guarantees of political independence and territorial integrity to great and small States alike"[18]. Lloyd George's Fontainebleau memorandum of 25th March 1919 intended a League of Nations to be "a safeguard to those nations who are prepared for fair dealings with their neighbours and a menace to those who would trespass on the rights of their neighbours . . . the effective guardian of international right and international liberty throughout the world." Such a League, Lloyd George maintained, would be qualified to offer "an alternative to Bolševism".[19] Yet fifteen years later in explaining his country's turn towards the League of Nations the Bolševik M. M. Litvinov could give credit to the League's 'restrictions.'

In September 1934 the USSR became a Member with a permanent seat on the Council of the very Organization which had been appraised by the Comintern in 1919 as "a Holy Alliance of capitalists for the suppression of the workers' revolution.[20] In 1920 Lenin himself had called the League "a bubble", "a fraud"[21], and "a group of predacious animals."[22] From 1934–1938, however, the Foreign Minister of the first, and at the time the only State of Socialism did not cease to emphasize the role of the League as a "weapon of peace and a threat to the aggressor."[23]

2. *The Soviet concept of the League's rôle, 1919–1933*

The Soviet concept of the League's rôle, the difficulties which occurred in Soviet-League relations during 1919–1934, could not be imputed to the Soviet failure to recognize the principles of peace and international co-operation, principles which implied compromises to be made by the first socialist State with its capitalist 'environment.'

The first foreign policy action taken by the Soviet Government, the "decree on peace" of 8 November 1917, was both peaceful and co-operative in proposing to the nations and Governments "democratic and just peace without annexations . . . and contributions.[24] The inherent principle of "peace and security for all" re-appeared in Wilson's Fourteen Points and in the Covenant of the League of Nations.[25] But at the time the League excluded, amongst others, Soviet Russia; and the LoN was based upon peace-conditions which, not only in the Soviet view, were by no means just and democratic, and carried the germs of new wars.

Allied military intervention in Russia at the very moment when the 'peacemakers' at Paris adopted the Covenant, did not convince the Soviet Government of the Allies' sincerity. The founders of the League had in fact reserved a seat for Russia; but for a non-Bolševist Russia only, implying that the Soviet régime had to be abolished first.[26] The mistrust was deepened by Allied support of the Russian counter-revolutionary generals as well as a Poland, a League Member which, in spite of the pledges carried by such membership, invaded her Eastern neighbour. In those years of confrontation – when in Lenin's view[27] the Soviet State was a "fortress besieged", too busy just surviving, common aims and mutual interest – cornerstones of any future approchement with the League – did not seem to be the most urgent.

Soon, however, there was evidence that Soviet co-operation with League representatives or institutions – and *vice versa* – was possible and practicable. The humanitarian field offered the first opportunity for such co-operation. From 1920–1922 the Soviets, participating in the repatriation of prisoners of war, co-operated "to the utmost of their ability and resources"[28] with the League's High Commissioner F. Nansen. Nansen himself gave credit to this co-operation in his reports to the Council and to the Assembly; his personal integrity and good-will, in evidence particularly during the famine in Soviet Russia, contributed to Soviet co-operation with the League's Refugee Organization in repatriating those Russian refugees who wished to return to their homeland.[29] In 1922 co-operative contacts were taken up between Soviet health authorities and the League's Health Organization. A special commission set up by the latter obtained permission to investigate typhus conditions in Moscow.[30] During the following years, Soviet participation in 'technical' activities under the auspices of the League – activities in the economic, health, social, and humanitarian fields – gradually increased.[31]

When M. M. Litvinov at the head of a Soviet delegation arrived in Geneva in 1927 in order to participate in the work of the Preparatory Commission for the Disarmament Conference, this was, owing to the character of the work to be done, a first Soviet step towards the 'political' organization of the League of Nations.[32]

Soviet opposition to the League of Nations was not based upon divergences of views concerning communications and transit, drug traffic or the like. G. V. Čičerin in a statement to the press on 15 December 1925 hinted at this in declaring that the character of the League of Nations could not be deducted from its methods used to combat typhus.[33] The Soviet attitude towards the existing League of Nations was always subordinated to the general tasks of the foreign policy of the first State of Socialism, outlined by the 'peace-decree' of 1917. From the Soviet point of view, a League of Nations, in one way or another, had to fit into this concept.

When Čičerin in his note to Wilson on 24 October 1918 challenged the latter with the proposal that the League of Nations be "based on the expropriation of the capitalists of all countries",[34] Čičerin did not really expect that Wilson, or indeed any other head of Government of a capitalist State, would agree to this. However, in connection with the Genoa Conference, Čičerin, in 1922, elaborated along the lines of the 'peace-decree' the so-called 'pacifist programme'. This programme proposed a World Congress with a purely moral authority to promote, among other things, general and complete disarmament, assistance of the rich nations to the poor, emancipation of the peoples under colonial rule, and the participation of workers' associations in the activities of the said World Congress.[35] This programme was reflected in the Soviet attitude towards international organization, in general, but especially in terms of the Moscow Government declaring its readiness to participate in "an international organization in which and through which every nation could realize its national sovereign rights and all nations could settle the difference arising between them by peaceful and friendly means, on the basis of full equality, free of the artificially obtained preponderance of certain Powers and with the complete rejection of the principle of executive and coercive measures."[36] This statement implied that the existing League of Nations did not correspond to the Soviet view of such an organization.

On the other hand, Čičerin's 'pacifist' proposal was a compromise in that it did not, for practical purposes, require the pre-condition of 'expropriation of capitalists' – meaning that participants in the 'World Congress' would *ipso facto* subscribe to socialist revolution. Given the ambiguity of the values represented by the Preamble and the Covenant of the League of Nations, a close study might have shown that no unalterable antagonism existed between the declared principles of the League and those embodied in the Soviet counterproposal. However, at that time the Soviet Government was not yet prepared to base its judgment on the letter of the Covenant. It derived its criteria mainly from outside of it: that is to say, on the one hand, from what the Soviet Government perceived to be the foreign policy of the leading Great Powers of the League, and, on the other hand, from Lenin's appraisal of the interdependence of 'imperialism' and war, i. e. the main antagonisms which once had produced and could again produce a world war.[37]

Lenin, of course, concluded that under the given historical conditions the aims and efficiency of an international peace organization would necessarily be subjected to and limited by such antagonisms. On these grounds the Geneva Organization was regarded as a mere emanation of the Paris Peace Conference, and as the instrument for the maintenance of an unjust and undemocratic postwar order, or "with its present construction and physiognomy, a poorly-screened coalition of victor-Powers (sic!) created in order to secure their acquisitions and conquests."[38]

In the Soviet view the League, having admitted in 1926 as its Member the main vanquished power, Germany, represented an "instrument in the hands of a small group, a few powerful imperialist States, for their rule over all other States."[39] Arguing both from the view of socialism and from that of the "small and weak nations", the USSR did not "feel the slightest desire to . . . play the part either of hammer or anvil"[40], and did "not want to resume responsibility for . . . imperialist policy".[41]

The USSR ruled out the entry into such an international combination as long as no common aims were perceived, as long as it served exclusively 'imperialist interests', and as long as the USSR found reason to believe that in joining the

League the Soviet "new social-economic system" would renounce "and of its special features, and not "preserve intact" its "personality".[42] The position of the USSR representatives in the twenties was that "... the Soviet Government... thinks it impossible to find an arbiter who would observe sufficient objectivity in making decisions on differences between the Soviet Government and Governments of another 'type'. Consequently the Soviet Government considers it impossible to submit itself to the collection of Powers called the League of Nations, which partly adheres to the principle of arbitration, and partly applies the principle of majority decision with the consequent reprisals and punitive measures. The Soviet Government cannot submit its actions and decisions, which are based on the principles of the Soviet system, to the decisions of a majority of States which are based on wholly different foundations.«[43]

With a view to changing the Soviet attitude towards the existing League of Nations the solution mainly depended on how the Member States were prepared individually to come to terms with the Soviet Union. On the other hand, the decision which could be taken by the Soviet Government alone was whether or not and under what conditions, they would enter into 'combinations.'

Soviet diplomacy during the Twenties adopted the general line "to operate among these two categories of international combinations: the united front against us and the attempt by means of one combination or another to use us on a particular side."[44] In this way Soviet diplomacy followed the basic patterns of Lenin's carrying out the Brest-Litovsk Peace Treaty, by which Soviet Russia in "liberating" herself "to the utmost possible degree at present" from the "two belligerent imperialist groups", obtained a free hand, a "breathing space", in order to stabilize revolution at least in the one country in which it had succeeded.[45]

After the war, there were no more 'belligerent imperialist groups'. In the Leninist view the imperialist Powers were subsequently divided into the camps of the victors and the vanquished, with the victorious Powers progressivel antagonizing one another.

Pursuantly Soviet 'non-involvement' resulted in a series of bilateral treaties of non-aggression, friendship and neutrality for all of which the Treaty of Rapallo with its principles of full equality and mutual advantage served as a model.[46] As the Treaty had been adopted from the point of view "of the best conditions for the development and strengthening of socialist revolution", and not from the point of view "of the desirability of this or that imperialism"[47], this 'neutral policy' in the sense of non-participation in 'combinations' was not irrevocable. However, the prospects of these principles 'not being used on a particular side' were not entirely left at the discretion of the USSR. Russia had ceased to be an 'imperialist Power' in 1917, but she had not ceased to be a power factor. Even in 'isolating' herself from the concert of the traditional Great Powers she would deeply affect the mutual relations and the potential conflicts between the latter.

That the USSR would and could enter in one way or another into multilateral agreements aimed at the maintenance of general peace, was demonstrated by the Soviet Government not only in its adherence to the Briand-Kellogg Pact in 1928, but also in giving immediate effect to it by way of the Moscow Protocol of 9 February 1929[48], to which, apart from the USSR, Estonia, Latvia, Poland and Romania were contracting parties.

Next to the Soviet proposals in 1922 and 1927 of complete and immediate disarmament, their most prominent offer of multilateral agreement in terms of collective peace and security was made under conditions obviously reflecting the necessary reconsideration of 'neutrality'. On 6 February 1933 Litvinov presented to the General Commission of the Disarmament Conference a draft "definition of agression".[49] This marked the beginning of a process as a result of which – along with the breakdown of the Disarmament Conference and an accelerating Franco-Soviet rapprochement – the USSR would replace, but not altogether ultimately abandon, her conception of 'peace by disarmament' by a conception of 'peace by collective guarantees of security.' The process involved Soviet entry into the League of Nations; but prior to this, i. e. early in June 1934, the USSR – with a view to obtaining the USA participation, thereby securing a broader basis – proposed to turn the Disarmament Conference into a "Permanent Peace Conference."[50]

3. The League and the rise of an aggressive bloc

It was a whole complex of dangerous factors that urged the USSR into reconsidering her former 'neutral policy.' Japan's aggressive policy in Asia; in the midst of Europe, after the Fascists' acceded to power in Germany, the rise of a second centre of aggression; and the breakdown of the Disarmament Conference, all indicated to the Soviets that a new world war appeared iminent.[51] Of the Great Powers dissatisfied with the Paris and Washington Peace Treaties, two, or with Italy then already secretly preparing for the conquest of Ethiopia[52], three 'have-nots' were bent on war if not actually waging it. In the Leninist view, the 'inter-imperialist antagonisms' led to the breaking up of the 'imperialist system into two hostile 'camps' ultimately resulting in another struggle of 'two belligerent imperialist groups'. At the same time the ambition for conquest of Japanese militarism and German and Italian fascism threatened the Soviet Union as well as the 'small and weak nations.' The threat, however existed in varying degrees, which could not but affect the actions undertaken by an international organization for the maintenance of peace.

Japanese aggression in Asia constituted an immediate military threat to China, to the People's Republic of Mongolia and to the USSR. In the case of the USA, Britain and France, the maintenance of whose integrity was not jeopardized in the same way, colonial and economic interests were affected, the protection of which did not necessarily require efficient measures in defence of the victim of aggression.

Things in Europe looked different. The German Nazi régime – implacable enemy both of 'bolševism' and 'bourgeois democracy' – once it had recovered sufficient economic and military power could constitute a serious military danger not only to all of Germany's neighbouring States, but also to the USSR and Britain, neither of which had a frontier with Germany. The hard core of the Nazi scheme of conquest in Europe – outlined in Hitler's *Mein Kampf* and in his even more revealing 'Second book'[53] concerned the annihilation and subsequent colonization of the USSR and her western border States, Poland and the Baltic republics, as well as the reduction of France to a third-rate borderland under permanent military control by Germany.

When Hitler spoke of "Gleichberechtigung", he did not mean equality with France, Poland, or any other individual State. In fact, he meant "equality" – in terms of the superiority of a German "continental empire" compared to the British Empire and the "colossus" USA.[54] The 'decisive battle' with the latter two, as Hitler himself confessed, pointed to a very distant future – provided Britain and the USA would not intervene in the course of building the 'continental empire.'

No doubt these were mad ideas, and they could never be carried out by Germany alone. However, they constituted the foreign policy programme of the man who was allowed to become chancellor of Germany in 1933. The first item of such a programme to be put into practice, and settled in Hitler's mind in 1928[55], was the German withdrawal from the League of Nations.

The Nazi schemes of aggression implied the same two-front war which imperial Germany had lost once before. But Hitler had learnt the lesson. He would single out his adversaries, the majority of whom were organized in a potential alliance called the League of Nations. He tried to prevent the one combination which might most efficiently impede German expansions: the renewal of the "old entente" Britain-France-"Russia".[56] Fully aware both of the continuity of antagonisms and of the fears of Hitler, the Soviet People's Commissar for Foreign Affairs, M. M. Litvinov, in 1932 correspondingly instructed the new Soviet ambassador to Britain, I. M. Majsky, to do his utmost to improve Soviet-British relations, since their quality would be decisive for war or for peace.[57]

Hitler's assumption that the afore-mentioned combination would be avoidable was based in part on the fact that the vehement anti-bolševism of his programme to some extent 'camouflaged' the programme's potential for conflict with the Western Powers. And his assumption was also partly calculated in terms of continental power politics with the traditional Franco-British antagonism both *vis-à-vis* Germany and "Russia".[58]

How could the League face such a situation? What could it do, once its instruments of "peaceful conflict resolution" in the Far Eastern Crisis 1931–1933 had failed? According to the main Soviet criticisms, the League, no doubt, had undergone a change. Japan had shown that there was a rift among the 'Principal Allied and Associated Powers,' in control over the League by virtue of Art. 4 of the Covenant. As a result of this rift the League could not really act as a 'coalition of victorious Powers'. Furthermore, the withdrawal of Germany from the League also prevented it from acting as a 'coalition' or at least an instrument of conciliation between 'victors' and 'vanquished'. Accordingly, the League proved incapable of acting as an 'all-imperialist coalition' aginst the USSR.

But the 'principle of executive and coercive measures' still pertained in the Covenant. In other words: the League could still be 'a coalition.'

4. The Soviet concept of the League's rôle, 1933 and after

On 25 December 1933 Stalin in his famous interview with Walter Duranty of the *New York Times* indicated: "In spite of Germany's and Japan's withdrawal from the League of Nations – or possibly just because of it – the League may become a certain factor in retarding the outbreak of hostilities or in preventing them althogether . . ."[59]

Stalin's formula subsequently became the standard answer of Soviet diplomats questioned by their Western colleagues. In his report to the Central Executive Committee of the USSR (i. e. the Executive Committee, after 1936: the Presidency, of the Supreme Soviet of the USSR) on 28 December 1933, the head of the Soviet Government, V. M. Molotov, amplified the new Soviet concept of the League's rôle. Did the League become a "factor in retarding . . . or in preventing" the outbreak of hostilities, *in spite of* or *just because of* the withdrawal of Germany and Japan? The leaders of the USSR were obviously convinced that rather the *withdrawal* from the League of two aggressive Great Powers in order to obtain a free hand constituted the League's capacity of playing a "part . . . as a brake on the forces making for war".[60]

On 29 December 1933 Litvinov, also reporting to the Central Executive Committee of the USSR, went on further in explaining. In particular, he made an important distinction in his analysis of the 'capitalist environment' of the Soviet Union: ". . . not all capitalist States want war at all times, or always with the same intensity . . . there are bourgeois States, and they are not few, which are for the time being interested in the maintenance of peace and are prepared so to conduct their policy as to defend peace . . ."[61]

This distinction, according to the changed international conditions prepared the grounds for the USSR to abandon 'neutrality', to take sides in counteracting the threat of a new world war, and to this effect to enter into 'combinations' such as, amongst others, the League of Nations. Litvinov's distinction was preceded by another one stressed by the Executive Committee of the Communist International at its Thirteenth Plenum on 12 December 1933. By defining fascism as "the open terrorist dictatorship of the most chauvinistic and most imperialist elements of finance capital",[62] the ECCI prepared the grounds for the 'United-Front' policy, adopted by the Seventeenth Congress of the Comintern in 1935.

In his speech on 29 December 1933 Litvinov made it clear that the USSR would take the side of those States "which, like us, give proof of their sincere desire to maintain peace and are ready to resist those who break the peace."[63] This was not merely a reiteration of the principle of peaceful co-existence; it implied mutual assistance between a socialist State and capitalist or imperialist powers. The day before, the Soviet ambassador to France had handed to Paul-Boncour the proposal thus answering an initiative taken by the latter on 31 October 1933[64] – for a collective mutual assistance pact covering the USSR, France, Czechoslovakia, Poland, the Baltic States including Finland, and Belgium. The proposal also contained the Soviet agreement in principle to enter into the League of Nations, although a number of reservations were made against Articles 12, 13, 22 (mandates) and 23.[65] The plan had been officially approved by the Politbureau on 19 December 1933.

Thus, the foundations for future entry into the League and for the policy to be adopted therein had been laid officially, before Litvinov on 29 December 1933 stated that "we think that even hostilities which do not begin directly on the frontiers of our Union may threaten our security"[66], in this way elucidating the basic formula underlying the Soviet principle of "indivisibility of peace".[66a] But Litvinov in his statement that "the ensuring of peace cannot depend on our efforts alone; it requires the collaboration and cooperation of other states"[67] hinted at the limitations to future Soviet involvement in collective efforts of keeping in check the aggressive powers and preventing the outbreak of a new war.

The USSR definitely undertook to join the League in order to fulfill the precondition of the 'Eastern Locarno' Pact, Louis Barthou's counterproposal to the Soviet plan of 28 December 1933.[68]

The Soviet government on 26 July 1934 informed the French, British, Italian, Czechoslovak and Turkish governments that the USSR would not refuse joining the League if she were given an invitation and a permanent seat on the Council.[69] These confidential hints, inspired by the French, set in motion the work on procedural matters, ending successfully in September 1934.

Once in the League, the Soviet representatives followed the line adopted by the USSR in December 1933. They interpreted the Covenant in a way which resembled the post World War II view of the Western scholar seeing the League machinery as "a formidable deterrent to aggression" – "if the Members of the League really meant what they had covenanted."[70] Litvinov in his speech to the Assembly on 1 July 1936 put it this way: ". . . those who recognize the principle of collective security, who continue to regard the League Covenant as an instrument of peace, might blame the Covenant only if they could show either that the Covenant does not provide sufficiently effective means in support of Article 10, or that . . . all such means were utilised to the full; yet failed to achieve their aim . . . I assert that Article 16 equipped the League of Nations with such powerful weapons that, in the event of their being fully applied, every aggression can be broken. Moreover, the very conviction that they may be applied may rob the aggressor of his zeal to put his criminal intentions into practice . . ." In order to achieve these results, however, "every Member of the League" had "to realise its individual responsibility"[71].

Apart from the various cases of aggression the League was confronted with during the period of Soviet membership, an excellent opportunity for amplifying the Soviet view presented itself when, in 1936 – after the Ethiopia and Rhineland fiascos – the League Assembly set up a Special Committee mandated to 'study' the 'Application of the Principles of the Covenant'. This 'study' ended up with the 'separation of the Covenant from the Peace Treaties' in 1938, and did so at the same nineteenth Assembly that watched as a mere spectator[72] the dismemberment by the Munich Conference of a 'loyal member of the League', Czechoslovakia.

The Soviet Government in its proposals of 22 August 1936 on the 'League reform' rejected any action that could contribute to dismantling the provisions of Art. 10 and 16, and recommended measures for abbreviating and simplifying the procedures of the existing machinery.[73] All that might have been said by the defenders of a 'coercive League' in arguing with the partisans of a 'consultative' or an 'intermediate' League, was said by Litvinov in his Assembly speech of 28 September 1936, entirely dedicated to the question of the 'Application of the Principles of the Covenant': "... the aggressor, who is basing all his policy on superiority in brute material force, with only threatening demands, bluff, menaces and the tactics of *faits accomplis* in the arsenal of his diplomacy, is accessible only to the voice of a policy no less firm than his own, and to a cold calculation of the relative strength of forces ... the aggregate power of the peace-loving countries, both in the economic and in the military sense, their total resources in man-power and in the war industries, considerably surpass the strength of any possible combination of countries which the aggressor might rally around him. I am deeply convinced that it would be sufficient for these forces in some way to combine, to display merely the possibility of joint action, for the peril of war to be averted, and for the aggressor to be obliged to ask, sooner or later, to be admitted himself to the common system of collective security ... No, I am not asking for new *blocs*. I am prepared to be satisfied with a *bloc* which exists already, and which bears the name of the League of Nations, a *bloc* of countries that want peace and that have united for the purpose of mutual defence and mutual aid. All we ask is that this *bloc* should genuinely organise mutual aid: that it should draw up its plan of action well ahead, so as not to be taken by surprise, and that the organisation of war which is taking place outside this *bloc* should be answered by effective action for the organisation of collective resistance ..."[74]

A year before Stalin himself proffered in a more lapidary style these ideas to Anthony Eden during the latter's visit to Moscow on 29 March 1935: "We are six of us in this room; if Majsky choses (sic) to go for anyone of us then we must all fall on Majsky"[75]. The common core of the Litvinov and Stalin statements stressed a united-front proposal.

It goes without saying that in terms of the Soviet interpretation a League of Nations facing aggressors could be neither 'universal' nor 'neutral': "... A State which is governed by men who have incorporated into the programme of their foreign policy the conquest of other nations' territory, who ... before their people and the representatives of other States, enumerate the vast territories which they intend violently to separate from other countries, cannot sincerely accept Article 10, which ensures to all Member States their territorial integrity and political independence. A State which preaches the legality of so-called 'localised' wars cannot make its peace with Article 16 ... I would ask the supporters of 'universality at any price': must we sacrifice all the fundamental principles of the League in order to adapt it to the theory and practice of such a State, or must we invite the latter itself to adapt its principles to the present ideology of the League? My reply, at any rate, is: Better a League without universality than universality without League principles ..."[76]

Thus, along with the rise of a bloc of aggressive Powers – a bloc exemplified by the Anti-Comintern Pact of 1936/37 – the Soviet view of the potential and the fundamental tasks of the existing League of Nations was taking the founders of the League at their words, including their restricted notion of 'universality'.[77]

Thereby the USSR representatives displayed their unaltered appraisal of the League of Nations as a 'coalition' or 'combination'. But it was felt that the latter, under different historical-political conditions, and based on the distinction made between 'aggressive' and 'non-aggresive' powers, could now fit in with the Soviet conception of a united-front policy applicable to the field of foreign affairs and inter-State relations.

In connection with this, students of the historical continuity and discontinuity thesis may discover an additional source of contradiction in the fact that the leading Great Powers of the League – once guarantors of the political and territorial *status quo* of the world and, particularly, of Europe – exhibited tendencies to the contrary, the more so after 1933. To this effect a British Foreign Office memorandum of 5 September 1935 pointed to the 'danger' that "the League will be reduced . . . to an Anglo-French-Russian combine working together for the sole purpose of maintaining the *status quo* where and whenever possible. The letter of the Covenant would indeed have been preserved, but the fundamental idea of the League would have been definitely abandoned . . . Better surely a League with reduced powers of coercion than a League . . . reduced to a mere defensive alliance on the old model of the Sainte Alliance . . ."[78]

On 22 February 1938 Neville Chamberlain pointed out to the House of Commons: "If I am right, as I am confident I am, in saying that the League as constituted to-day is unable to provide collective security for anybody, then I say we must not try to delude small, weak nations, into thinking that they will be protected by the League against aggression and acting accordingly, when we know that nothing of the kind can be expected . . . the power of the League does not depend upon its nominal membership. It depends upon the conviction of its Members that it can carry out its functions . . . I say that to-day you will not find anywhere in the League any conviction that collective security can be provided by the League as now constituted . . . I would have it clearly understood, today, that . . . the nations in the League must not be saddled with liabilities or risks which they are not prepared to undertake. Nor must other nations expect that the League will provide that security which it was once hoped it would provide . . ."[79]

A few months later, during a visit to the British Foreign Office on 25 May 1938, the League's Secretary General could "foresse" a "more or less rapid diminution of the political significance of the League", on the grounds that "obligations existed on paper which no one had the faintest idea of carrying out."[80]

5. *The rôle of the USSR within the League*

The new Soviet approach to the League of Nations – seen as an instrument for the preservation of the security and the territorial integrity of all those States which, for one reason or another, were not interested in a 'revision' of the *status quo* by means of war – implied foremost concern with 'political' matters' – this was, in fact, a view displayed right from the beginning of Soviet participation in the political work of the League[81]. Soviet participation in, and their principal attitude towards the 'non-political', 'technical' activities of the Organization remained – as during the twenties – subordinate to the Soviet conception of what constituted the foremost political task of the League of Nations: "I do not dwell on the accessory, non-political work of the League. Far from denying the importance of such work, be it of an economic, social, or humanitarian character, I would not like to see too much League energy diverted in that direction at the expense of the fundamental task for which it has been founded."[82]

Soviet experts were appointed to the Economic, Financial and Health Committees in January 1935: Boris Danilovič Rozenbljum, head of the Economic Department of the People's Commissariat for Foreign Affairs; Aleksandr Svanidze, president of the Moscow Bank for Foreign Trade; Wolf Bronner, vice-president of the Medical Council of the People's Commissariat for Public Health.[83] Soviet experts or representatives were also appointed to the Committee for Communications and Transit (P. Kirsanov), to the International Committee for Intellectual Cooperation (V. Obolenskij-Osinskij, V. A. Socoline) and to the Supervisory Commission (Boris Štejn).

While Soviet non-participation in the Permanent Mandates Commission and in the Minorities Committees was motivated mainly by political opposition, the 'technical' Committees on the other hand did not always enthusiastically receive Soviet co-operation. For instance Aleksandr Svanidze, the "surprisingly popular and respected figure in the Financial Committee"[84] had difficulties in being appointed at all; some of the members of the Committee – the British fiscal expert Otto Niemeyer, in fact, resigned over this matter – felt that the representative of a socialist system should not be given the opportunity to meddle in capitalist affairs.[85]

From 1934–1938 M. M. Litvinov himself represented the USSR in the Sixth, Political, Committee of the Assembly. The five other main Committees, concerned with legal, economic, financial, humanitarian, health and social questions were frequently attended by Soviet ambassadors to France, Britain, Italy, Germany, and Sweden (Potemkin, Surić, Majsky, Štejn, Merekalov, Kollontaj) or by officials of the Moscow Narkomindel, such as V. V. Egor'ev, G. N. Laškevič, and E. Hoerschelmann[86]. Within the area of 'technical activities', Soviet cooperation during the thirties with the Health Committee remained as 'exceptional' as it had been during the twenties. The Bureau of the Health Committee was in fact the only League body ever to hold an official meeting in the Soviet Union.[87]

That the Soviet contribution to the Secretariat staff would be limited had already been pointed out by Litvinov to Avenol on 11 June 1934[88]. The two Under-Secretaries General, Marsel' Izrailovič Rozenberg (1935–1937) and Geneva-born Vladimir Aleksandrovič Socoline (1937–1939), obviously fulfilled a task of merely formal representation. At least once in his remarks to the Council Litvinov emphasized a sort of 'limited sovereignty' of the State Members of the League – ". . . The Government of a State which has become a Member of the League and accepted the Covenant has sacrified part of its sovereignty; there would be no purpose in international obligations if a Government could say, 'obligations, yes, but I am sovereign and can do what I like; I can break obligations as I wish . . ."[89] Yet it was out of the question that such 'sacrifice' of part of their 'sovereignty' had to be made by the governments of the Member States of the League, and not by the Geneva international Secretariat.

The USSR's financial contribution – the second largest next to Britain's[90] – as a Member of the Organization and as a permanent member of the Council contrasted considerably with the limited Soviet participation in the League's administration. This fact was soon appraised as a "somewhat ominous sign of lack of interest."[91] According to other views, however, even the limited Soviet share in the work of the Geneva apparatus seemed more than sufficient. The Nazi Government, detailing its conditions for a return to the League of Nations, included into the catalogue a "modification of the Secretariat of the League of Nations"[92]. A British official warned against "left wing tendencies" in the Secretariat: tendencies which would only transform the League into an "alliance of the so-called democratic against the so-called autocratic powers", and "influences" which, if not countered through "constant watching", would render it impossible for the League to become a home for aggressive Great Powers.[93]

Out of 44 political cases raised before the League of Nations during the whole period of its existence[94], 14 were dealt with during the period of Soviet membership; raising the very last case, in fact, ended the membership. In dealing with the 13 cases, the representatives of the USSR gave no evidence of 'lack of interest', but focused their attention on those cases involving, on the one hand, the security and integrity of League Members, and aggression, on the other. In the cases which involved the outbreak of hostilities, the Soviets argued right from the beginning in favour of alliance of League Members – and the deterrent potential of the League. In order to prove efficient against the "really dangerous aggressors", the League would have to bring its "authority" to bear even at remote "theatres of war". This was the essence of Litvinov's statement on 21 November 1934 to the Assembly in connection with the Chaco-war[95], and this would be the gist of any future statements on the outbreak of hostilities in other parts of the world.

F. P. Walters later gave particular credit to Litvinov by stating: "No contemporary statesman could point to such a record of ciriticisms justified and prophecies fulfilled."[96] Litvinov, however, was no more clairvoyant than, say, Sir Robert Vansittart, who in a memorandum on 7 April 1934 recognized that a Germany ruled by the fascists would be the "ultimate potential enemy" not only in the British view, but also in the view of "most of the political minds of Europe."[97] Consequently, it was not a problem of recognizing the Nazi threat, but a problem of how such threat could be accepted as the basis for the *anima societatis* i. e. collective action emanating from collective will and from the recognition of collective interests, without which the instruments of the League of Nations would never work.[98]

6. *The Soviet position towards selected political cases*

a) The Saar Plebiscite

When the USSR as a permanent member of the Council was confronted with taking practical decisions concerning the *Saar Plebiscite*, it had already been settled that the League would not become a 'third claimant'. In assuming the position of an interested party in terms of the Saar Annex to the Versailles Treaty, the League would have had to offer to the Saarlanders democratic self-government and the assurance that a *status quo* vote would not imply the permanent loss of their German nationality.

On 6 December 1934 Litvinov advocated both the 'delegation' of sovereign rights to the Saarlanders and a second plebiscite in case a majority vote supported the *status quo*[99] The USSR was not an 'intersted party' in the legal sense, in that she was not a signatory of the Versailles Treaty. But of course, behind the legally and diplomatically correct stand she took a lively interest in preventing the Nazi régime to achieve a 'democratic success'. That a plebiscite vote in favour of the 'Anschluß' would strengthen the Berlin régime morally, politically and economically, was by no means a secret. But Litvinov's attitude was deeply misunderstood: "It is clear that M. Litvinov regards the future of the Saar not in the light of its reaction on European peace so much as a possible means of injuring a régime in Germany which he detests."[100]

In the end, another spirit was allowed to inspire the work of the Council of the League: ". . . Looking at the whole of this question from the point of view of political expediency we feel that it is ultimately in the interests of Europe, and of France in particular, that the Saar problem should be eliminated as soon as possible by its complete and definite reversion to Germany, and that therefore any attempt to bring about a vote in favour of the maintenance of the present régime is to be deprecated, since it would only keep open a festering wound in the centre of Europe . . ."[101]

In a nutshell, this was the basic formula to all future British dealings with the territorial *status quo* in Europe, with which France in the end complied. The political potential offered by the USSR – the fourth permanent member of the Council – was turned down. This became evident when Laval on 5 December 1934 invited the Member States of the Council to participate in the drawing up of an 'international force' in order to maintain 'public security and order' in the Saar territory during the plebiscite. Even before the Soviet Government was able to take any decisions to this effect, Britain and Italy – also permanent members of the Council – had already settled that: ". . . it would be a great mistake to allow Russian, Czechoslovak and even Belgian participation . . . Red police or soldiers would inevitably be regarded as propagandists while Czechoslovak and Belgian contingents would be disliked in Germany . . ."[102] The Soviets did not insist on participation; Litvinov was not at all convinced of the necessity of an "international force"[103]. But: the spirit in which the force was drawn up; the off-stage complicity of two leading Great Power Members of the League with a régime that had openly challenged not only the Members but also the 'principles' of the Organization, and the dropping of all rules of collectivity set up a dangerous precedent.

b) German re-armament

The practice was continued in the case of the *unilateral repudiation of the military clauses of the Versailles Treaty by Germany.* When the Berlin Government on 10

March 1935 announced the existence of a German Air Force and on 16 March promulgated a law of conscription extending the German Army to 12 corps and 36 divisions – more than five times as much as the Versailles Treaty had originally conceded – this came as no surprise to any statesman in Europe, and consequently was no surprise to the League of Nations. Both Britain and France were so well informed on Hitler's plans that on 3 October 1934 Sir John Simon found it necessary to recommend that "much discretion will be needed to avoid becoming *particepts criminis*."[104] In November 1933, Britain turned down Paul Boncour's proposal for a joint British-French examination of the German breach of Part V of the Versailles Treaty[105]; as a result the French offered a mutual assistance pact to the USSR. That the London Government had brought its political authority to bear in order to 'moderate' the French became obvious, for instance, by Simon's written remarks of 21 March 1934 to the Cabinet on "Germany's illegal rearmament and its effect on British policy", namely that "... Part V is, for practical purposes, dead, and it would become a putrefying corpse which, if left unburried, would soon poison the political atmosphere of all Europe. Moreover, if there is to be a funeral, it is clearly better to arrange it while Hitler is still in a mood to pay the untertakers for their services .. "[106] Thus, when Hitler at last took action, he could at least rely on Britain doing nothing; furthermore, Laval was not Barthou, and Italy was already involved with Ethiopia. In the end, Hitler did not have to pay a farthing.

When on 16–17 April 1935 the Council discussed the German actions, the decision to be taken had once again been settled outside the League of Nations. The Stresa Conference, 11–13 April 1935, satisfied the British wish for a recommendation which "would probably secure a less provocative resolution than if the drafting was left to Geneva, where M. Beneš, M. Titulesco and Co. would be pressing for something violent ..."[107] And the Stresa Conference also convinced Mussolini that he would not run the risk of any serious League counter-measures when he came to deal with Ethiopia by military means.[108]

Litvinov's statement to the Council was firm but under the circumstances out of the running. Litvinov did not deny the principle of equality in armaments, but he pointed out that this principle could not be granted to "people who have announced to the whole world a program of foreign policy ... of unlimited conquests of foreign territory and the destruction of the independence of entire States ..." Litvinov's answer, re-affirming the offers made to Eden at Moscow in March, 1935[109], was a plea for common defensive measures in order to keep the potential aggressor in check. Litvinov emphasized the Soviet Government's aspirations "to collaborate in the creation of an international order under which the infringement of peace ... would be hampered to the utmost possible extent."[110]

There may have been reasons to doubt a solemn condemnation of the potential aggressor and the creation of a new committee as the proper means for safeguarding peace. But Litvinov voted for the resolution because, as he reminded the Council on another occasion, at least a "judgment" had been passed.[111] However, Litvinov's attempt to eliminate from the resolution an obvious, and – in view of the impending Italian attack on Ethiopia – dangerous limitation to

European affairs failed owing to the resistance of the British, French and Italian representatives.[112]

The Politbureau had first instructed Litvinov to abstain from voting in order to avoid an implicit consent to the Versailles Treaty. However, Litvinov convinced the 'Instancija' (i. e. the Politbureau) to withdraw this part of their instructions, since under the given circumstances to abstain from voting would have been "absolutely impossible." After this he received a free hand to vote as he thought best.[113] On the same day, 17 April 1935, Litvinov and Laval reached a preliminary agreement on the wording of the Franco-Soviet mutual assistance pact.[114] The mechanism of assistance was linked with Art 15 and 1 of the Covenant but not entirely dependent on them. The pact was signed on 2 May 1935 and followed on 16 May 1935 by a treaty along similar terms with Czechoslovakia.

However, the "conflicting strategies of peace"[115] once again became evident when Britain on 18 June 1935 separately concluded the Naval Agreement with Germany. This agreement, just as the French and Czechoslovak treaties of assistance with the USSR, attested to the existence of two antagonistic 'schools' within the League of Nations, and within the Council in particular; the rift even affected the permanent members of the Council. Although neither of the 'schools'-one partisan of collective resistance and for the establishment of a defensive front, the other aspiring to individual agreement with the aggressive power itself – had as yet been able to prevail, the Council resolution of 17 April 1935 reflected a unity which in fact did not exist. Hitler was allowed to gain the impression that isolating France and singling out his other adversaries would be practicable, and that because the leading Powers of the Council lacked collective determination, the League would not operate against him.

c) Italo-Ethiopian conflict

There would have been good reasons for the USSR to disinterest herself with regard to the Italo-Ethiopian conflict. The USSR was not a colonial power and thus in no competition either with Britain, France, Italy, or Germany – the latter having already begun with demands for colonial restitution[116] pressing Britain into European appeasement. The USSR had no diplomatic relations with Ethiopia, but maintained good political and economic relations with Italy on the basis of the bilateral treaty of friendship, non-aggression and neutrality of 2 September 1933. However, the USSR, in fulfilling her obligations as a Member of the League and as a permanent member of the Council took part in 'intervention', i. e. in the collective application of 'measures of coercion and reprisal' against the aggressor. This way the USSR continued to side with the "small and weak nations" which, "taking no part in the game of conquest", were "so to speak deprived to a considerable extent of that ready cash, that possibility of offering compensation, and of all those elements of diplomacy thanks to which, in the policy of imperialist States, the element of defense and the element of attack are intertwined . . ."[117]

And in this spirit Litvinov could denounce tendencies among the Council members to assist Italy in fulfilling her 'civilizing mission' versus Ethiopia. He rejected any attempt "to discriminate between Members of the League as to their internal regime, the colour of their skin, their racial distinctions or the stage of their civilisation."[118] But the anti-colonialist aspect was only one part of Litvinov's argumentation concerning the Italo-Ethiopian conflict. Litvinov stressed the wider political implications of the case when, about one month before the actual aggression took place, he warned the Council against the consequences of 'precedents', such as the Far Eastern conflict, during which the League's authority had not been brought into full play: "This is exactly a thing to be remembered now, for we all still feel in what measure that case weakened the League of Nation, diminished its authority and contributed to the creation of the politically unstable, menacing situation in which the world finds itself and even, maybe, to the arising of the present conflict. The repetition of that precedent would certainly have a cumulative effect and, in its turn, would stimulate new conflicts more directly affecting the whole of Europe . . ."[119]

In his statement to the Assembly on 14 September 1935 Litvinov resumed this thread; simultaneously he issued a warning that at one point the USSR might be compelled to recognize her expectations in the League of Nations as not being fulfilled: ". . . for the Soviet Union there is only one question of defending the Covenant of the League as an instrument of peace. This instrument has already been somewhat damaged by previous attempts, and we cannot allow a new attempt which would put it completely out of work. We may need it more than once and probably on still more serious occasions . . ."[120] It is rightly argued that Litvinov had the Nazi-régime in mind[121] when he pleaded for strong action on the part of the Leagues so as to create a precedent which, in turn, would be able to deter the really dangerous aggressors, i. e. those Powers, not only interested in, but also in terms of their economic, political and technological potential most capable of starting a new world war. But the actions taken in this instance served primarily to help Ethiopia resist the Italian aggression.

As for sanctions, actions outside the League limited the possible range of measure, i. e. a secret agreement by the two leading Powers of the Organization excluded a maritime blockade and a resulting complete and long-term embargo against Italy.[122] The Soviet representatives took the stand that "the measures which were now being elaborated in virtue of Article 16 should be rapid, firm and effective" and, consequently, "general".[123] And since the USSR "was prepared to go to any lengths in the measures aimed at shortening or stopping the war, provided that all other Members of the League did the same"[124], the representatives co-operated towards finding such measures. However, collective although not unanimous agreement was reached only on measures criticized on 19 October 1935 by Litvinov as not being 'exhaustive'.

The same statement also contained a warning. Litvinov pointed out that the USSR, having "no quarrel" with Italy and "no special interest in the case", "by agreeing to economic sanctions . . . was exposing herself to losses . . . It did so for reasons of solidarity and because of its desire to maintain peace and to fulfill all the obligations it had accepted under the Covenant. But these obligations held good only for so long as they were maintained and fulfilled by other Members of the League. Peace could not be based on voluntary contributions; it must be based on specific obligations undertaken by all the Nations. This was the true spirit of the League. No exemptions should be claimed, and no special cases should be put forward as a means to escape from these obligations." In view of such "exemptions" Litvinov reserved the right for his Government to re-"consider" participating in sanctions if the USSR came to the conclusion that a lack of collectivity would render the measures ineffective.[125] Thus, while taking part in collective measures, the representatives of the USSR left no doubt about the desirability under certain conditions of an alternative approach, namely the 'individual' or 'non-interventionist' way to deal with cases of aggression.

Soviet participation in the collectively adopted sanctions was loyal and correct. The recommendations were effected by decrees of the Council of People's Commissars on 17 October and 14 November 1935.[126] But Soviet participation, like that of any other Member State of the League, was no more 'exhaustive' nor more 'efficient' than the measures which had been collectively adopted.

Once again the Soviet attitude was "first and foremost realistic"[127] in that it did not intend to carry out unilaterally sanctions considered but not collectively agreed to. The USSR was, after Romania, Italy's largest supplier of oil. The USSR agreed to apply export sanctions to oil, coal, iron and steel, but the proposal was never put into practice. The closing of the Gibraltar Straits and of the Suez Canal would have rendered any discussion superfluous. But this measure was ruled out by the two leading Great Powers of the League while the prolonged 'neutrality act' of the USA did not preclude this potential supplier from interfering with an oil-embargo being adopted. Therefore, the USSR was not ready unilaterally to 'sacrifice' her individual economic interests; the less so since such a 'sacrifice' would not have had any effect on either shortening or stopping the war against Ethiopia. The Hoare-Laval plan[128], furthermore, did not fail to confirm the Soviet Government in its continued cautiousness. On 16 December 1935 Litvinov instructed Potemkin not to proceed with the extension of sanctions ahead of anyone else, but particularly not ahead of Britain and France.[129]

In his address to the Assembly on 1st July 1936 Litvinov not only discussed military sanctions, but also hinted at measures to be adopted as well as conditions to be fulfilled when dealing with future cases of aggression: "... Such measures could only be considered if one or several States could be found which, in virtue of their geographical position and special interests would agree to bear the main brunt of a military encounter. Such States were not to be found among us; and, even if they had been found, the other States, before deciding on any particular degree of co-operation in serious measures, would require guarantees that similar cc-operation could also be counted upon in other cases of opposing the aggressor.."[130]

d) Rhineland remilitarization

On the same occasion the Soviet representative displayed a somewhat shaken "belief that those guarantees ... could be immediately secured" alluding to the remilitarization of the Rhineland by Germany, 7 March 1936.[131] Quoting to the Council on 17 March 1936 passages from Hitler's *Mein Kampf*, Litvinov pointed out the immediate threat to France arising of the German action. In Litvinov's view, in spite of Hitler's attempts to legitimize his action in anti-Soviet terms, "his aggression may, in fact, aim at other countries in the immediate future. His attacks on the Soviet Union may, so far, serve merely as a smoke-screen for aggression which is being prepared against other States."[132]

The delegate of the USSR did not reject "negotiations and a peaceful settlement of the serious dispute which has arisen", but he insisted on imposing conditions: "We are resolutely against anything that might bring a war nearer by even a single month. But we are also against hasty decisions, directed rather by excessive fear and other emotions than by a sober reckoning of realities – decisions which, while represented as eliminating the causes of an imaginary war to-day, create all the premises for an actual war to-morrow. We stand for an international agreement which would not only consolidate the existing foundations of peace, but, if possible, would likewise create new foundations. We stand for the participation in such an agreement of all the countries which so desire. But we object to the idea that withdrawal from the League of Nations, brutal infringement of international treaties and sabre-rattling should confer upon a State of dictating to the whole of Europe its conditions for negotiations, of selecting the participants in those negotiations to suit its convenience, and of imposing its own scheme for an agreement. We are against negotiations proceeding on a basis which disorganizes the ranks of the sincere partisans of peace, and which must inevitably lead to the destruction of the only inter-State political organisation – the League of Nations . . ."[133]

On behalf of his government Litvinov declared that the USSR would be ready "to take part in all measures which may be proposed to the Council of the League by the Locarno Powers and will be acceptable to the other Members of the Council."[134] In doing so he, on the one hand, reiterated the offers of co-operation made to the British and French Governments on 9 March 1936[135]; on the other hand, he made it clear that the initiative for further dealings with the case would be left to the signatories and guarantors of the Locarno Treaty. On 19 March 1936 the USSR voted for the Council resolution condemning the German action. The Locarno Powers subsequently dismissed the case. From 3 May 1936 to 14 May 1938 the Council became familiar with the 'postponement of the question'.

e) Spanish Civil War

The application of the principle of 'non-intervention' to the Spanish Civil War no doubt contributed to a growing Soviet conviction that the Western democracies – although their security and strategic interests were seriously affected, not to speak of the price of letting down Governments of their own kind, and of democratic institutions such as the League of Nations – were inclined to capitulate to the threat emanating from the fascist powers.

The USSR had a first agreed to 'non-intervention' and to participation in the work of the London Committee, "because a friendly country feared the possibility otherwise of an international conflict."[136] It must not be forgotten that the French-Soviet accord on 'non-intervention', 23 August 1936,[137] was an accord between two Powers linked to each other by a pact of mutual assistance; and the

Soviets were well aware that "it's exactly what the left French Government doesn't want, to fight."[138] When it turned out that 'non-intervention' meant in fact to let the Spanish Republic face alone the Franco-Hitler-Mussolini coalition, the USSR – without openly intervening with regular forces – rendered military, financial and humanitarian aid to the Republic.[139] This help was given in accordance with the Covenant of the League of Nations, the more so after the legitimate Spanish Government had requested the League to abandon the policy of 'non-intervention'.[140] In practice, however, the aid was given without, or even in spite of, the League.

Litvinov in his comment on 21 September 1937 on the Secretary-General's report on the work of the League of Nations dealt at length with the 'anti-bolshevist' aspect both of the German-Italian intervention in Spain and the policy of 'non-intervention': ". . . We know three States which . . . in recent years have made attacks on other States. With all the difference between the regimes, ideologies, material and cultural levels of the objects of attack, all three States justify their aggression by one and the same motive: the struggle against Communism. The rulers of these States naively think, or rather pretend to think, that it is sufficient for them to utter the words 'anti-Communism', and all their international felonies and crimes will be forgiven them . . . any explanation of anti-Communism applied to the war against Republican Spain is all the more out of the question because Communism has not been and is not installed there, and because, so far as we are aware, the Spanish people are fighting to defend the democratic republican regime against the forces of reaction and military dictatorship . . . When people now speak of the Bolshevik regime which is to be wiped out, they often add the words 'and similar regimes'. We frequently hear that all democratic and parliamentary countries are on the eve of Bolševisation . . . Any country which may become the object of the appetites of aggressive States may be declared to be under suspicion of Bolševism, because no proofs are required . . ."[141]

Thus Litvinov did not only try to emphasize common interests between the 'democratic and parliamentary countries' and the USSR in face of the fascist threat, i. e. the very basis of the Soviet entry into the 'combination' represented by the League of Nations. He also implicitly reiterated the warning made to the Council on 28 May 1937: ". . . It should not be forgotten that Spain, at the time the rebellion began, had a Government similar in its programme to the Governments existing in many other States . . . As a State we have but little interest in the order which exists in Spain . . . All we want is that after the present events, just as it did before the rebellion, Spain would have the Government which it desired itself and which it voluntarily elected in accordance with the Constitution it has itself established . . ."[142] As he had done in connection with the Italo-Ethiopian war, here Litvinov again alluded to the possibility of a new Soviet 'isolationism', given the geographical realities on the one hand, and the lack of will or inability of the Western Powers to recognize the "varying degrees of military threat" on the other hand.[143]

f) Sino-Japanese War

While the war in Spain was going on, Japan embarked on a new war against China. Again, evidence of the 'cumulative effect' Litvinov had warned of. The Soviet representative in the Far East Advisory Committee supported the Chinese request of naming Japan the agressor[144], and appealed to the Assembly for more substantial assistance to China than was in fact being granted in the health, humanitarian and 'moral' fields[145], all the while in 1938 and 1939 the USSR supplied China with large quantities of arms, including 897 aircraft, and other war material.[146]

Political assistance to China by the USSR had been initiated when in 1933 Litvinov proposed to the USA a regional collective security system of the Pacific Powers[147], and when in March 1935 Stalin and Litvinov pointed out to the representatives of Britain that nothing could be done "to restrain Japan by Governments acting independently . . . The best solution would be a coalition of Pacific Powers."[148] On the other hand, the Soviet Government was determined to avoid a conflict in which the USSR would be isolated and alone against Japan. In other words, the Soviet Union, as long as she was not herself attacked by Japan, was not prepared *unilaterally* to tackle the Chinese problem – such as it was perceived by the League, Britain and the USA – while the Western Powers were staying out of the fight. There was a strong suspicion that the latter would try to settle their 'interimperialist' differences at the cost of the USSR. The same principle, of course, applied to Europe.

The Soviet attitude towards the League's stand on the new Far Eastern conflict was reflected in the instructions on 26 September 1937 by the Politbureau to Litvinov along the lines indicated above: motions for sanctions and for naming Japan the aggressor should be endorsed; but in case the leading powers of the League, namely Britain, continued to adopt a passive stand, Litvinov was not to play the rôle of the whip.[149] On 8 September 1938 the Soviet ambassador to China was instructed to inform the Chinese Government that the USSR – in absence of a mutual assistance pact with China – would enter into a war against Japan only under the following conditions: a) if Japan attacked the USSR; b) if Britain or the USA would join in a war against Japan; c) if the League of Nations would oblige the Pacific Powers to military actions against Japan.[150] This, on the other hand, did not preclude the USSR from taking efficient military counter-measures against Japan by way of fulfilling Soviet obligations towards the Mongolian People's Republic in terms of the mutual assistance pact of 1936 (battles at Lake Chassan, summer 1938, and Chalchin-Gol, summer 1939). To any interested member of the League, this could have indicated that the Soviet Union was able and willing to fulfil her treaty obligations.

g) The Czechoslovak crisis

The Czechoslovak crisis was not dealt with by the League of Nations. The particular form of 'peaceful conflict resolution', by which the crisis was settled outside the League, marked both the definite breakdown of the League as an instrument of 'collective security', and the turning point at which the USSR would start to drift again into 'isolationism', 'non-entanglement' and 'neutrality'.

Preparations for the Munich agreement of 29 September 1938 – itself a modified version of the disastrous Four Power Pact of 1933 – had begun in November 1937. While the League was occupied with 'non-intervention' in Spain and deployed a huge effort in only giving some 'moral' assistance to China, the Nazi régime singled out Austria and Czechoslovakia:[151] the first of a series of annexations and conquests openly to be committed by Germany. A few days later Lord Halifax travelled to Berchtesgaden to inform Hitler that Britain would not object to a revision of the territorial *status quo* in Central and Eastern Europe, if only Germany would bring this about by "peaceful development."[152] The story has been told and re-told; but somehow it became a neglected fact that at Berchtesgaden on 11 November 1957 the representative of a permanent member of the Council agrees to the revision of the frontiers of States themselves Members of the League of Nations. In Hitler's view, territorial revision could be brought about 'peacefully', if Britain and France and the USSR would not intervene, and if the States in question would not resist by military means. Hitler's speech on 5 November 1937 – protocolled by Colonel Hossbach – was based on the assumption that both Britain and France had already tacitly given away Czechoslovakia.[153] The proposals made by Halifax surely did not convince Hitler to the contrary.

Austria was annexed 'peacefully', for neither she herself nor the guarantors of the Versailles and St. Germain Treaties resisted. The 'peaceful' liquidation of the sovereignty and territorial integrity of Czechoslovakia, however, was brought about through the *active cooperation* between two permanent members of the Council and two professed League enemies and break-aways, already 'solemnly' condemned by the League as aggressors and breakers of international treaties. Two other Members of the League – Poland and Hungary – no less 'peacefully', could later on join in the dismemberment of Czechoslovakia.

In 'settling' the Czechoslovak crisis, the League's two leading Powers – earlier in a strong enough position to dictate the territorial *status quo* in Europe – promoted a solution which consciously disregarded Art. 10 of the Covenant and all the pledges derived therefrom. Once again, the Western democracies in the face of the fascist threat dropped the rules and principles they themselves had propagated as a means of safeguarding the general peace. The courageous plans developed in the social and economic fields of the League activities (Bruce reform) parallelly to the crises of 1938, could not really compensate for such political deficiencies.

The USSR, like France, was committed to Czechoslovakia both by the Covenant of the League of Nations and by a treaty of mutual assistance. When the latter was concluded, the Prague Government explicitly requested the inclusion of a clause making the implementation of the treaty depend on France's taking action first. Furthermore, in order to render immediate and efficient assistance, Soviet troops would have had to pass through Poland and/or Romania; therefore, the Soviet pacts with Czechoslovakia and Poland had been coupled with Art. 16 of the Covenant, the third paragraph of which provided for a certain legal basis to a right of passage of troops, but only in case Article 16 were implemented by the League.

From 17 March 1938 onwards, in public pronouncements and by diplomatic ways, the USSR advocated that the Czechoslovakian crisis be solved by strictly respecting Art. 10 of the Covenant. However, the Soviet proposal for a conference – the object of which would have been the adoption within or outside the League of collective and joint measures for the protection of Czechoslovakia,[154] was rejected.[155] In Chamberlain's view such a conference would have only contributed to the formation of "exclusive groups of Nations" in Europe.[156]

Bonnet in May 1938 simply ignored Litvinov's proposal for joint Soviet-French-Czechoslovak staff conversations which would have both taken into account particular geographical conditions and co-ordinated military measures in defence of Czechoslovakia.[157] On 2, 5 and 11 September 1938 Litvinov and Potemkin pointed out to the French that for such defence the following actions were necessary: 1. In accordance with Art. 11 of the Covenant, appeal to the League of Nations in order to state a German threat of war against Czechoslovakia; 2. a joint declaration by Britain, France and the USSR in order to warn Germany against an attack on Czechoslovakia; 3. joint Soviet-French-Czechoslovak staff conversations.[158]

Thus at the time the USSR was the only permanent member of the Council of the League of Nations to propose both the protection of Czechoslovakia's integrity and the application of the Leagus's 'instruments' to this effect. According to the existing treaty obligations, however, it was incumbent upon France to proceed with organizing the assistance of Czechoslovakia. French initiatives to this effect were considered by the Soviets as evidence that France really meant business. Given French tendencies to comply with the British line of disinteresting themselves in the territorial *status quo* of Central and Eastern Europe, Litvinov stated in a press interview on 25 December 1937: "C'est vous, Français, qui avez intérêt au respect des clauses territoriales de Versailles. Mais nous n'avons rien pris à Versailles. Nous n'avons donc rien à rendre . . . L'URSS ne serait pas atteinte par une révision territoriale. Nous pouvons donc nous desintéresser . . ."[159]

French initiatives, however, were not taken because France completely surrendered to British pressure. The Prague Government itself in the end complied with these pressures and capitulated. Prague neither requested Soviet assistance irrespective of French initiatives, nor did it request the League of Nations to state a German threat of war against Czechoslovakia.[160] In any case the two main conditions for implementing the Soviet-Czechoslovak Treaty of Mutual Assistance – conditions insisted on both by the Paris and Prague Governments themselves in 1935 – were not fulfilled: i. e. French initiatives and setting the machinery of the League of Nations to work.

On 21 September 1938 when Litvinov, in what turned out to be his 'farewell' to the Assembly, both confirmed Soviet loyalty to her treaty obligations and denounced the French manoeuvres of evading their own, the USSR was already left in complete isolation. Litvinov's last attempt to mobilize the forces of resistance inside and outside the League thus became a final verdict on the failure of the League, *viz.* its leading great powers failing to fulfil their historical mission: "It must not be forgotten that the League was created as a reaction to the World

War . . .; that its object was to make that the last war, to safeguard all nations against aggression, and to replace the system of military alliances by the collective organization of assistance to the victim of aggression. In this sphere the League has done nothing . . . A fire brigade was set up in the innocent hope that, by some lucky chance, there would be no fires. Things turned out differently, however. Fires have broken out in defiance of our hopes but luckily not in our immediate vicinity; so let us dissolve the fire-brigade – of course not forever, but merely temporarily. Directly the danger of any fire disappears, we shall reassemble the fire-brigade without a moment's delay . . . To avoid a problematic war to-day and receive in return a certain large-scale war to-morrow – moreover, at the price of assuaging the appetites of insatiable aggressors and of the destruction or mutilation of sovereign States – is not to act in the spirit of the Covenant of the League of Nations . . ."[161]

The Munich agreement, the "diminution of the political significance of the League"[162] along with the definite rejection of the Soviet proposal for a collective security policy marked the final victory of a particular British nation of 'peace'; of a 'pacifism' which merely misunderstood 'peace' as not having to resort to war, all the while letting the aggressors get what they wanted. This of course did not put an end to aggression, but created even more favourable conditions for it. With the creation in March 1939 of the 'Protectorate' of Bohemia and Moravia and with the foundation of a pro-Fascist Slovakian vassal-State the Munich agreement was dead; as dead as the British-French-Italian guarantee of the 'Munich-frontiers' of Czechoslovakia. On 22 March 1939 Germany annexed Memel; in April 1939 she completed military preparations for her attack on Poland, and repudiated both her non-aggression treaty with the latter and her naval agreement with Britain. In that same month, Italy annexed Albania.

The Council of the League of Nations in its 105th session in May 1939 merely took notice of the disappearance of two other Member States of the League. On the initiative of the Soviet representative, I. M. Majsky – who had to fight Avenol's procedural tricks with his own – the Pittsburgh appeal of Beneš was submitted in September 1939 to the Assembly for further discussion in September 1939.[163] Simultaneously, the negotiations opened in April by the three permanent members of the Council for a triple assistance pact continued. Litvinov's dismissal during the first days of May served as a warning that the USSR might reconsider her 'collective' policy in the face of aggression. V. M. Molotov, the head of the Soviet government and Litvinov's successor, however, in his foreign policy report to the Supreme Soviet, 31 May 1939, still emphasized the task of "creating a united front of peace-loving countries against further aggression."[164]

7. *Collective security: The last effort*

The April-August 1939 negotiations for a Soviet-British-French pact of mutual defence and a military convention were going on outside the League of Nations; the successful conclusion of these negotiations no doubt would have even been able to revive the 'political significance' of the Organization by emphasizing the 'alliance' and deterrent potential of the Covenant.

The last Soviet draft of a triple assistance pact, 2 June 1939, explicitly referred to the "principles of mutual support against aggression adopted by the League of Nations",[165] but rejected the British proposal of 27 May 1939, of introducing into the scheme the provisions of Art. 16, paragraphs 1 and 2, of the Covenant.[166] The Soviet Government considered this proposal as being "superfluous".[167] The British wish could easily be interpreted as an attempt to procrastinate the negotiations and to leave loopholes in the pact permitting Britain later on to evade her obligations. Firstly, because in referring to Art. 16 the British negotiators very obviously ignored its third paragraph, dealing with the question of passage of troops. Secondly, because the official British attitude towards the implementation of Art. 16 had not been revoked after Butler's statement to the Sixth Committee of the 19th Assembly on 22 September 1938, *viz.* that his government would not feel bound to apply economic or military sanctions.[168]

Thereagainst the Soviet draft made it clear that the USSR would not now be satisfied with vague promises, generalities and ambiguities. On the contrary, she would only enter into a multilateral mutual defence agreement if the latter a) imposed an equal share of action on *all* of the contracting parties and b) definitely and unmistakably fixed the commitments to be entered into by them. The Soviet proposals of 15 August 1939 for military commitments by the three contracting parties were based on the same principles[169], i. e. rapidly and efficiently stopping German aggression either in the East or in the West. This was not a new attitude, or at least not perceived as such by those who still remembered Litvinov's statements relative to the ending of the Italo-Ethiopian war in 1936.[170]

The British interest in a pact with the USSR was not so much based on the determination to stop aggression by any means, but was rather motivated by the desire "to ensure Russian participation in a Western war"[171] in case the secret British-German negotiations for a separate 'general settlement' were not successfully concluded. The Soviet proposals made no difference between an 'Eastern' and a 'Western war' but rather reflected the assumption that a Nazi aggression in Europe could be stopped in time if counteracted on two fronts. This implied for Britain having to enter into 'new engagements' after 'Locarno'. At no point in the negotiations did the British really give evidence that they were prepared thus to extend their obligations and consequently have their hands tied. The British refusal to participate in the joint guarantee for the Baltic States as proposed by the USSR and the London instructions to the British military mission for negotiations at Moscow[172] did not indicate determination to this effect.

The Baltic States for their part rejected any scheme of mutual defence in which the USSR would have been a party. Poland continued to oppose the passage of Soviet troops through Polish territory thereby rendering immediate and efficient military assistance either to Poland herself, or to France, Belgium and Britain and/or to all of them.

All possibilities of collective security and mutual defence had obviously been ruled out. At the same time the aggressiveness of the Nazi régime was not contained but rather increased; furthermore, not only the strategic position but also the economic and military potential of Germany's power improved considerably after 'Munich'. In view of her isolation and currently at war with Japan over the defense of Mongolia, the USSR now decided to deal exclusively with 'Soviet security'. Since co-operation with the other potential victims of German aggression had not proved feasible, the USSR no longer dwelled on the League's principle of 'peace and security for all'. Instead the USSR assumed 'neutrality' and 'non-involvement' by concluding the non-aggression treaty with Germany on 23 August 1939. Simultaneously the secret protocol to the treaty permitted the USSR to disinterest herself in the maintenance of the territorial *status quo* outside her own borders: the more so since the Great Powers, mainly responsible for the *status quo,* themselves had not shown any determination of defending it.

In practice the new Soviet withdrawal into 'non-involvement' considerably impaired the defensive positions of Poland, France and Britain vis-à-vis Germany. This was the inevitable consequence of the fact that the Western Powers had never taken seriously the Soviet position of 'indivisibility of peace' and 'collective security'.[173] Of course the geographic realities as well as the implications of a two-front war in the Nazi scheme of aggression were well known even in 1933. But the Western Powers counted too much on the 'anti-Bolševist' aspects of both the German and Japanese expansions allowing themselves to be misled by the assumption that it would be the USSR who would stand to gain most by collective security either within or outside the League of Nations. Thus, after the fall of Poland the old Locarno-conception of 'security in the West – insecurity in the East' ended up with 'truce in the East – war in the West.'

The Soviet attack on Finland, 30 November 1939, was part of the general USSR policy to make use of the 'breathing space' gained by the agreement of 23 August and to improve her strategic positions *vis-à-vis* Germany. With the Second World War going on in general and the 'phoney war' carried on in particular, i. e. with Britain and France doing nothing in defence of their Polish ally, but waiting in the West to see whither Hitler's armies – after having conquered Poland in only two weeks' time – would turn next, the USSR was even more determined not to let her North-Western neighbours become bases for an attack by Hitler's armies.

In order to come to peaceful terms with Finland, the USSR took up negotiations in April 1938; Finland broke off the negotiations on 13 November 1939. The Soviet demands in these negotiations had been: exchange of territory in order to improve the defensive position of Leningrad; a treaty of mutual defence; the sale or lease of a number of Finnish ports and islands for the establishment of Soviet military bases. In themselves the Soviet demands were not incompatible with the 'spirit of the Covenant of the League of Nations. However, any judgment on this case depended on the degree to which the fellow Members of the League would or would not accept the 'legitimacy' of Soviet security and its coincidence with their own.

The Finnish Government considered the Soviet proposals as a threat to Finnish neutrality, in fact Finland's position ever since the Eastern Locarno negotiations in 1934. If one believes the British representative at Helsingfors, Snow, Finnish neutrality was particular. Snow had alread pointed out to the Foreign Office in April 1939 "that the majority of the Finns and more particularly the Finnish military element, would be much better suited if Russia were the first Power to violate Finland's neutrality and not Germany", and that the Finns "would prefer to have to take up an anti-Russian attitude rather than an anti-German one.[174]

In the end the Soviets tried to obtain by military means what they had failed to obtain through negotiations. After the Mainila frontier incident on 26 November 1939 the USSR renounced the non-aggression treaty with Finland; on 29 November she broke off diplomatic relations and on 30 November she attacked. The Cajander government resigned; the Finnish Communists proclaimed a Democratic Republic at Terijoki on 1 December 1939, and the same day the Ryti/Tanner Government was formed. On 2 December the Kuusinen Government concluded a treaty of friendship and mutual assistance with the USSR, granting her what had previously been denied in the negotiations;[175] on 3 December the Ryti/Tanner government appealed to the League of Nations.[176] Subsequently the League Assembly and Council, after years of 'non-intervention', suddenly launched the last political action taken by the League – expulsion of the USSR.

Inspired by Avenol, himself co-operating with representatives of a non-Member of the League, the USA[177], a revival of the 'political significance of the League' took place, something which before neither the German attack on Poland nor the beginning of the Second World War had been able to bring about. Now, contrary to previous instances, there was no wavering between a 'consultative', an 'intermediate' or a 'coercive League'. Now noone considered the League's 'lack of universality' to be an obstacle to taking action. And the League machinery was set into motion with considerable speed: in the space of 9–14 December 1939 the whole business of expulsion was carried out, not only by the Council and the Assembly, but also by an *ad hoc* 'Committee of Thirteen' and a subcommittee.

The USSR remained absent both from the Council and the Assembly. Soviet representatives, however, – Suric and Gel'fand – participated in the work of the Fourth Committee of the Twentieth Session of the Assembly, dealing with budget questions. The Moscow Government refused to participate in the League's dealings with the Finnish appeal on 5 December 1939 on the grounds that "... The USSR is not at war with Finland and does not threaten the Finnish nation with war ... Soviet Union maintains peaceful relations with the Democratic Republic of Finland, whose Government signed with the USSR on December 2nd a pact of assistance and friendship. This pact settled all the questions which the Soviet Government had fruitlessly discussed with delegates (of) former Finnish Government now divested of its power ..."[178] But the Kuusinen Government, to which the Soviet statement referred, lacked a basis in Finland and consequently had no power. Thus the war went on until March 1940 when the USSR and the Ryti Government agreed to peace terms.

On 13 December 1939 the Assembly with formal unanimity (9 abstentions) adopted the report of the 'Committee of Thirteen'. The Assembly 'solemnly' condemned "the action taken by the Union of Soviet Socialist Republics against the State of Finland." It appealed to the Members of the League "to provide Finland with such material and humanitarian assistance as may be in its power and to refrain from any action which might weaken Finland's power of resistance." Finally it recommended the Council "to pronounce [itself] upon the question" arising from the fact that the USSR had "not merely violated a Covenant of the League, but has by its own action placed itself outside the Covenant..."[179] The Assembly based its verdict on a violation by the USSR of her non-aggression treaty with Finland, of Art. 12 of the Covenant of the League of Nations, and of the Briand-Kellogg Pact.

On 14 December the Council brought a decision along the lines of the Assembly recommendation. The resolution of the Council – voted for by seven out of 14 members, with four States abstaining and three being absent[180] – stated that "... by its act, the Union of Soviet Socialist Republics has placed itself outside the League of Nations. It follows that the Union of Soviet Socialist Republics is no longer a Member of the League."[181]

These were not only strong words, but also words unheard of in the previous activities of the League of Nations. Only a few years earlier Italy's aggression against Ethiopia had been condemned by the League, yet Italy was still allowed to participate in the condemning of the German action in the Rhineland. Furthermore, the explicit withdrawal from the League by Germany and Japan had not induced at the same time the majority of the League Members to advocate the strict implementation of the 'coercive' provisions of the Covenant; the course adopted was rather to 'separate' the Peace Treaties from the Covenant and to emphasize the 'optional' character of Art. 16, etc. The *volte-face* in the 'application of the principles of the Covenant' subsequently became even more evident when Britain and France, in giving assistance to Finland, also considered military intervention. Yet during the negotiations of the Eastern Locarno Pact (1934) and of the Triple Assistance Pact (summer 1939) the same two Powers consistently refused to enter into political or military commitments designed to maintain the independence and integrity of the States in North-East Europe.

But for all its firmness, the Council verdict of 14 December 1939 was also ambiguous. The verdict did not explicitly enact the expulsion of the USSR, but merely stated that the USSR through her actions had expelled herself. Regardless of whether the formal unanimity of the verdict rendered it legally valid – it has been argued that owing to the absence of Iran and Peru it was not[182] – it was all the more remarkable that none of the abstaining members of the Council was courageous enough openly to come up with a vote against the verdict. The representative of China – whose opposition had most likely been expected – was, on British initiative, to make "a promise . . . that he would lose [sic] his instructions", were these to arrive in time and to *contain an adverse vote.* "On this understanding the embarrassing ejection of China from the Council was avoided."[183]

Thus the League machinery was obviously allowed to function only in terms of the anti-Soviet basis on which it had been founded. To explain this with a 'moral and material support' given by the USSR to Germany would seem premature given the fact that the attitude of the League Members – particularly that of the permanent Council members – for excluding the USSR had existed before a treaty of non-aggression and a new Soviet-German trade agreement were concluded.

The expulsion of the USSR from the League at the outbreak of the Second World War could not conceal the fact that the political Organization failed to fulfill its foremost task – namely to avoid a new world war by 'peaceful conflict resolution' and 'collective guarantees of security'. In 1939 Europe was actually governed by the rules of war. Under such circumstances, implementing in a more determined fashion than ever before in the history of the League – the 'principles of the Covenant' could neither stop the war, nor prevent the "final destruction of the only inter-State political organisation."[185] On 14 December 1939 the worst was still abead: for the USSR, for France, for Britain, for the whole world.

However, the united front or collective security policy of the USSR – for which the League of Nations served as the main platform – was not a "lost cause".[186] Underlying this concept was the collective defence of all 'non-Fascist' Powers against 'Fascist imperialism'. Subsequently, the anti-Hitler coalition not only confirmed such a policy, but implemented it also by military means; a stand which, not only in the Soviet view, might have been reached a few years earlier by mere 'political' firmness. The opening of the second, 'western' front against Hitler was late, but it took place on 6 June 1944 – 10 years after Litvinov and Barthou had reached agreement on the Eastern Locarno Pact and on the entry of the USSR into the League of Nations.

Notes

1 LoN. Records of the Fifteenth Ordinary Session of the Assembly; Minutes of the Sixth Committee, Annex 1, September 1934, *OJSS* no. 130, p. 97. *Ibid.;* Plenary Meetings, 17 September 1934; *OJSS* no. 125, p. 59. cf. *DVP*, v. XVI, No. 331, p. 596 ff.

2 LoN, Records of the Fifteenth Ordinary Session of the Assembly; Minutes of the Sixth Committee, 17 September 1934; *OJSS* no. 130, p. 17–27. *Ibid.;* Plenary Meetings, 17 September 1934, *OJSS* no. 125, p. 59–65. LoN. Minutes of the Eighty-first Session of the Council, 15 September 1934, *OJ*, November 1934, p. 1394 ff. The 'informal' meetings of the members of the Council on 9 and 10 September 1934 were reported to the Foreign Office by Anthony Eden and William Strang, PRO, FO.371.18300 N 5226 and N 5352/2/38. – For an account of the admission cf. F. P. Walters, *A history of the League of Nations.* London, Oxford University Press, 1960. – p. 581–584.

3 LoN. Record of the Fifteenth Ordinary Session of the Assembly; Plenary Meetings, 18 September 1934; *OJSS* no. 125, p. 68 ff. *DVP*, v. XVII, No. 334.

4 F. P. Walters to W. Strang, 12 April 1934, *DBFP*, ser. 2, v. 7, No. 589, p. 677.

5 Georg Schwarzenberger. *The League of Nations and world order. A treatise on the principle of universality in the theory and practice of the League of Nations.* London, Constable, 1936. – p. 82 ff.

6 Litvinov speech, in LoN. Records of the Fifteenth Ordinary Session of the Assembly; Plenary Meetings, 18 September 1934; *OJSS* no. 125, p. 68.

7 F. P. Walters, *op. cit.* p. 583 [see note 2].

8 Cf. French note of 7th August 1934, *DBFP* ser. 2, vol. 7, No. 610, p. 712–714; British instructions of 29 August, *ibid.* no. 619, p. 727 ff. also cf. the French proposal on procedure to the Soviets and Soviet agreement on this, 31 July and 1 August, *DVP*, v. XVII, No. 289 and 290, p. 526 ff.

9 William E. Scott, *Alliance against Hitler. The origins of the Franco-Soviet pact.* Durham, Duke University Press, 1962. – p. 199.

10 Minute by W. Strang, Foreign Office, 20 August 1934, PRO, FO. 371. 18299. N 4761/2/38.

11 Sir Eric Phipps, Berlin, to the Foreign Office, 12 September 1934. *DBFP* 2, v. 7, No. 628, p. 736; the line was also taken by Eamon de Valera in his address to the Assembly the same day: LoN. Records of the Fifteenth Ordinary Session of the Assembly; Plenary Meetings, 12 September 1934; *OJSS* no. 125, p. 41 ff. Cf. also Barthou's complaint of calculated leakages disturbing the Geneva atmosphere, in LoN. Minutes of Eighty-first Session of the Council; *OJ*, November 1934, p. 1396.

12 Cf. the addresses to the Sixth Committee of the Portuguese, Swiss and Irish Free State representatives; LoN. Records of the Fifteenth Ordinary Session of the Assembly; Minutes of the Sixth Committee; 17 September 1934; *OJSS* no. 130, p. 17 ff. Letter by the French ambassador to the Holy See, Charles Roux to Louis Barthou, 30 May 1934, I/6, no. 258, p. 564–566; Sir John Simon's letter to the acting Prime Minister, Neville Chamberlain, August 1934, *DBFP* 2/7, No. 610, p. 711, note 1.

13 A. Eden's report to the Foreign Office, 17 September 1934, PRO, FO. 371.18300. N 5440/2/38.

14 Sir John Simon in an 'informal discussion' with the representatives of the Dominions, Geneva, 11 September 1934, *loc. cit.* N 5465/2/38.

15 Transmitted by A. Eden to the Foreign Office, *loc. cit.* N 5228/2/38.

16 Report of W. Strang, *loc. cit.* No 5386/3/38.

17 Sir John Simon to the Archbishop of Canterbury, 14 September 1934, *loc. cit.* N 5398/2/38.

18 *Documents of American History,*edited by H. S. Commager. 2nd ed. New York, F. S. Crofts and Co., 1942. – p. 319.

19 D. Lloyd George, *The truth about the Peace Treaties.* v. 1, London, Gollancz, 1938. – p. 404 ff.

20 *The Communist International, 1919–1943: Documents*, edited by Jane Degras. New York, Oxford University Press, 1956. – v. 1, p. 51.

21 Opening speech to the IXth Congress of the CPR (b), 29 March 1920, Lenin *Works*, German edition, v. 38, p. 439. (Translation into English by the author of this paper.)

22 Speech to the Conference on work in the country, 6 June 1920, *ibid.*, v. 31, p. 160. (Translation into English by the author of this paper.)

23 Litvinov's speech in: LoN. Records of the Seventeenth Ordinary Session of the Assembly. Plenary Meetings, 28 September 1936; *OJSS* no. 155, p. 61 ff.

24 Lenin-*Works,* German edition, v. 26, p. 240. (Translation into English by the author of this paper.)

25 The interdependence of Wilson's Fourteen Points with the 'peace-decree' has been pointed out by Georg Schwarzenberger, *Power Politics. A Study of World Society.* 3rd ed. London, Stevens, 1964. – p. 475.

26 Cf. D. I. Buzinkai, *Soviet-Leaguerelations, 1919–1939: A survey and analysis,* Ph. D. thesis, New York University, 1954. – (University Microfilms, Inc., Ann Arbor, Michigan), p. 10–23; D. H. Miller, *The drafting of the Covenant.* New York, G. P. Putnam's Sons, 1928. – v. 2, p. 61 ff.; G. Schwarzenberger, *The League of Nations and world order. op. cit.* p. 80 ff. [See note 5]

27 In his Letter to the American Workers, 20 August 1918, *Lenin Works,* German ed., v. 28, p. 62. (Translation into English by the author of this paper.)

28 Buzinkai, *op. cit.* p. 52.

29 *Ibid.*, p. 53–55.
30 *Ibid.*, p. 59 ff.
31 *Ibid.* p. 89–93; K. W. Davis, *The Soviets at Geneva. The USSR and the League of Nations, 1919–1933.* Geneva, 1934. – 315 p.
32 For the USSR and disarmament cf. Buzinkai, *op. cit.*, p. 100–146; Davis, *op. cit.*; Wilbur L. Mahaney, *The Soviets, the League, and disarmament, 1917–1935.* Ph.D. thesis, Philadelphia, 1940; for a Soviet account cf. V. A. Zorin's chapter *in: Istorija diplomatii* (Diplomatic History). Moskva, Politizdat, 1965. – v. 3, p. 557–572.
33 *DVP*, v. VIII, No. 412, p. 725.
34 *SDFP*, v. 2, p. 112–120; *DVP*, v. I, No. 374.
35 For the whole draft cf. V. I. Lenin, *Polnoe sobranie sočinenij*, 5 izd. (5th Russian ed. of Lenin's works), Moskva, Politizdat, 1965. v. 45, p. 34–40; for a German translation cf. *W. I. Lenin. Über die Politik der friedlichen Koexistenz; eine Auswahl* [edited by] Renate Hertzfeldt, Berlin, Dietz, 1977. – p. 164–170.
36 Čičerin's report to the Central Executive Committee, 18 October 1924; Engl. *SDFP*, v. 1, p. 464; Russ. *DVP*, v. VII, No. 237.
37 Cf. Lenin's study on Imperialism: *The highest stage of capitalism (1916)* and his remarks on *The United States of Europe Slogan* (1915).
38 Čičerin's report to the Central Executive Committee, 18 October 1924; *SDFP* v. 1, p. 464; *DVP* v. VII, No. 237.
39 Rykov's report to the IVth Soviet Congress, 18 April 1927; *SDFP* v. 2 p. 188.
40 Litvinov's statement to the press, 23 November 1925; *SDFP* v. 2, p. 65; *DVP* v. VII No. 394. – Litvinov was then Deputy to Čičerin.
41 Stalin to a foreign workers' delegation, 5 November 1927, *SDFP*, v. 2 p. 274 ff.
42 Litvinov speech, LoN. Records of the Fifteenth Ordinary Session of the Assembly, Plenary Meetings, 18 September 1934, *OJSS* no. 125, p. 68.
43 Čičerin in a press interview, 15 October 1925; *SDFP*, v. 2, p. 60; *DVP*, v. VIII, No. 351.
44 Čičeridin's report to the IIIrd Soviet Congress, 14 May 1925; *SDFP*, v. 2, p. 38; *DVP*, v. VIII, No. 140.
45 Cf. Lenin's stand on the conclusion of the Brest-Litovsk peace, January 1918; *Lenin Works*, German ed., v. 26, p. 450. (Translation into English by the author of this paper.)
46 Cf. Lenin's draft resolution of the All-Russian Central Executive Committee to the report of the Soviet delegation to the Genoa Conference, May 1922; *ibid.* v. 33, p. 342 ff.
47 *Ibid.* v. 26, p. 443–446; cf. also v. 27, p. 52–62. (Translation into English by the author of this paper.)
48 Cf. Rykov's report to the Vth Soviet Congress, 20 May 1929; *SDFP*, v. p. 373.
49 Conference for the Reduction and Limitation of Armaments. Records Ser. B., v. 2, Minutes of the General Commission, 14 December 1932 – 29 June 1933, LoN.doc. 1933, IX.10.
50 Doc. Conf. D./C.G. 163 in LoN doc. 1933. IX.10, v. 3, p. 684; *DVP*, v. XVII, No. 184; see also Litvinov's reiteration of the proposal in LoN. Records of the Fifteenth Ordinary Session of the Assembly, Plenary Meetings, 27 September 1934, *OJSS* no. 125, p. 76; *DVP*, v. XVII No. 342.
51 Cf. Stalin's report to the XVIIth Congress of the CPSU, 26 January 1934; Engl. *I. V. Stalin, Problems of Leninism.* Moscow, Foreign Languages Pub. House, 1954. – p. 583 ff.; Russ. *XVII s''ezd Vsesojuznoj kommunističeskoj partij* (b) . . . *Stenografičeskij otčet.* Moskva, 1934. – (Repr. 1975), p. 9.
52 J. Petersen, "Die Außenpolitik des faschistischen Italien als historiographisches Pro-

blem" *Vierteljahreshefte für Zeitgeschichte*, v. 22, no. 4, p. 417–457, 1974; V. A. Trefimov, "Ital' janskij fašizm i Efiopija" (Italian Fascism and Ethiopia) *Novaja i Novejšaja Istorija*, No. 6, p. 80–93, 1976.

53 The first volume of *Mein Kampf* was published in 1925, the second, containing 'foreign policy analysis', in 1927. This paper refers to the one-volume edition published in Munich in 1937, one of the numerous editions printed during the thirties. – The 'Second Book' was written in 1928, but then kept under lock and key. The text is printed in: *Hitlers Zweites Buch* [edited by] G. L. Weinberg, Stuttgart, Deutsche Verlagsanstalt, 1961.

54 *Mein Kampf, op. cit.*, p. 684–781, 722 *Hitler*, Weinberg *op. cit.* 108–110, 140, 173, 218.

55 *Ibid.* p. 135.

56 *Ibid.* p. 146, 218.

57 Cf. I. M. Majsky's memoirs, German ed., *Memoiren eines sowjetischen Botschafters.* Berlin, Dietz, 1975. – p. 24 ff.

58 *Hitler*, Weinberg, *op. cit.* p. 146, 151, 153–159, 173; *Mein Kampf, op. cit.* 694–699 *et pass.* (See note 54)

59 I. V. Stalin, *Works.* Vol. XIII. Moscow, Foreign Languages Publishing House, 1955 – p. 286.

60 *SDFP*, v. 3, p. 48; *DVP*, v. XVI, Annex 1, p. 780 ff.

61 *SDFP*, v. 3, p. 48 ff; *DVP*, v. XVI, Annex 2, p. 781–798.

62 *SDFP*, v. 3, p. 296; also cf. Kermit E. McKenzie, *Comintern and world revolution, 1928–1943. The shaping of doctrine.* New York, Columbia University Press, 1964. – p. 144 ff.

63 *SDFP*, v. 3, p. 51.

64 *DVP*, v. XVI, No. 332, p. 595; J. Paul-Boncour, *Entre Deux Guerres.* Paris, Plon, 1945. – v. 2, p. 364; *Les evènements survenus en France de 1933 à 1945.* Paris, Imprimerie de l'Assemblée nationale, 1951. – v. 3, p. 793 ff.

65 *DVP*, v. XVI, p. 876 ff.; *DDF*, I/5, No. 253.

66 *SDFP*, v. 3, p. 51.

66a LoN, Minutes of the Eighty-fourth Session of the Council, *OJ*, February 1935. – p. 136.

67 *SDFP*, v. 3, p. 51.

68 *DVP*, v. XVII, No. 254; *DDF*, I/6, No. 309.

69 *DVP*, v. XVII, Nos. 270 and 287.

70 G. Schwarzenberger, *Power Politics. op. cit.* p. 381. (See note 25)

71 LoN. Records of the Sixteenth Ordinary Session of the Assembly. Plenary Meetings, 1 July 1936; *OJSS* no. 151, p. 36 ff.; *DVP*, v. XIX, No. 206.

72 For 'League reform' cf. Walters, *loc. cit.* p. 709–720.

73 LoN. Documents relating to the Question of the Application of the Principles of the Covenant, 1936, p. 10 ff. *DVP.* v. XIX, No. 247.

74 LoN. Records of the Seventeenth Ordinary Session of the Assembly; Plenary Meetings, 28 September 1936, *OJSS* no. 155, p. 61–63; *DVP*, v. XIX, No. 280.

75 Participants in the conversation were: Stalin, Molotov, Litvinov and Majsky, as well as Eden, Strang and the British ambassador to Moscow, Lord Chilston. The quotation is taken from Eden's report to the Foreign Office, *DBFP, v. 2/12, No. 669, p. 767*; the Soviet record, *DVP* v. XVIII, No. 148, p. 248 ff. corresponds to the British one.

76 LoN. Records of the Seventeenth Ordinary Session of the Assembly; Plenary Meetings; 28 September 1936, *OJSS* no. 155, p. 61 ff.; cf. also Litvinov's controversy with the representative of Chile, in LoN. Records of the Eighteenth Ordinary Session of the Assembly; Plenary Meetings, 4 October 1937, *OJSS* no. 169. p. 111 ff.

77 Cf. *supra*, p. 4 ff.
78 The memorandum was written by Orne Sargent. – PRO.FO. 371.19687.W 8174/2304/98; to the same effect cf. also an earlier Foreign Office memorandum of 21 November 1933 by A. W. A. Leeper, *DBFP*, 2/6, Appendix *I*, p. 948, ff.
79 Quoted from PRO.FO.371.22509. W 2512/3/98.
80 Conversation Avenol – R. Skrine-Stevenson, *Ibid.* 22510. W 6793/3/98.
81 Cf. Litvinov's statement to the Assembly in connection with the Chaco dispute, in LoN. Dispute between Bolivia and Paraguay; Records of the Special Session of the Assembly, 21 November 1934, *OJSS* no. 132 p. 29; cf. also his instructions to the Soviet representative in the Chaco Comittee, Evgenij Giršfel'd 4 March 1935, *DVP*, v. XVIII, No. 96, p. 160 ff.
82 Litvinov's comment on the Secretary-General's report on the work of the League in LoN. Records of the Sixteenth Ordinary Session of the Assembly, Plenary Meetings, 14 September 1935, *OJSS* no. 138, p. 72; *DVP*, v. XVIII, No. 362, p. 509; cf. *supra*, p. 6.
83 LoN. Minutes of the Eighty-fourth Session of the Council; *OJ*, February 1935, p. 154; see also Avenol's list of nominations in LoN. Minutes of the Eighty-third (Extraordinary) Session of the Council, *OJ*, December 1934, p. 1761, which had been agreed upon with Litivnov; to this effect cf. Litvinov's letter to Boris Štejn, 20 January 1935, *DVP*, v. XVIII, No. 24, p. 36.
84 Walters, *op. cit.* p. 585. (See note 2)
85 Cf. Litvinov's letter to B. Šteijn, 20 January 1935, *DVP*, v. XVIII, No. 24, p. 36 and Henry Krisch, "Soviet Participation in the Non-Political Work of the League of Nations, 1934–1939", unpupblished manuscript (1969 ?), p. 17–19 (the manuscript may be consulted at the League of Nations Archives, UN Library Geneva).
86 Cf. the lists of members to the Committees I–VII, in LoN, Records of the Sessions of the Assembly, Minutes of the Committees, 1934–1938, *OJSS* nos 126–130, 139–143, 156–161, 170–175, 184–190.
87 Cf. the Bureau's official statement in: *OJ* 17 (1936), November, Annex 1613, p. 1239; Krisch, *op. cit.*, p. 50–52.
88 *DDF*, I/6, No. 324; *DBFP*, v. 2/7, No. 604.
89 In connection with the Soviet-Uruguay dispute, 1935/36, see LoN. Minutes of the Ninetieth Session of the Council, *OJ*, February 1936, p. 101.
90 Contributions for 1935: Britain 3,180,936,95 Goldfrs., USSR and France 2,393,376.35, Italy 1,817,678.25. – LoN. Budget for the Eighteenth Financial Period (including the Allocation of the Expenses for 1936) and Report of Financial Questions, *OJ*, October 1935, p. 1013. Contributions for 1938: Britain 2,407,209.50 Goldfrs., USSR 2,095,163.82, France 1,783,118.20. LoN. Records of the Nineteenth Ordinary Session of the Assembly; Members of the Fourth Committee, Annex no. 6, September 1938, *OJSS* no. 187, p. 103.
91 Statement made by the French representative to the Fourth Committee, LoN. Records of the Seventeenth Ordinary Session of the Assembly, Minutes of the Fourth Committee, 8 October 1936, *OJSS* no. 159, p. 64.
92 Memo handed to Sir Eric Phipps by the RAM Legal adviser, Dr. Gaus, on 14 March 1935, PRO.FO.371.19687. W 2304/2304/98.
93 Memo of R. Skrine-Stevenson on 'left wing tendencies at Geneva', 21 October 1937, approved by A. Cadogan and Lord Cranbourne. *ibid.* 21243. W 19456/250/98.
94 Cf. *ibid.*, p. 306–328, and Victor-Yves Ghebali, *A Repertoire of League of Nations' serial documents, 1919–1947*. New York, Oceana Publications, 1973. – v. 1, p. 266–289.

95 LoN, Dispute between Bolivia and Paraguay; Records of the Special Session of the Assembly, 21 November 1934, *OJSS* no. 132, p. 29.
96 Walters, *op. cit.* p. 712. (See note 2)
97 *DBFP*, v.2/6, p. 981.
98 Cf. G. Schwarzenberger, *Power polities op. cit.* p. 95 and 274 ff. *The League of Nations and world order, op. cit.*, p. 176. (See notes 25 and 5)
99 LoN. Minutes of the Eighty-third Session of the Council, *OJ*, December 1934. p. 1709 ff.
100 A. Eden to the Foreign Office, *DBFP*, v. 2/12, No. 199, p. 255; see also Laval's remarks to this effect. *ibid.* No. 200, p. 228.
101 Sir John Simon's instructions to the British ambassador to France, 15 November 1934, *ibid.* No. 185, p. 211.
102 *Ibid.*, No. 362, p. 302, No. 273, p. 313.
103 LoN. Minutes of the Eighty-third Session of the Council, *OJ*, December 1934. p. 1707.
104 *DBFP*, v.2/12, No. 135, p. 150, note.
105 *DDF*, I/4, No. 65, and I/5, No. 60.
106 *DBFP*, v. 2/6, No. 363, p. 578.
107 Simon's memo of 5 April 1935 on the positions to be taken by Britain at Stresa was approved by the Cabinet on 8 April. *Ibid.* 2/12, No. 696, p. 826.
108 For the records cf. *ibid.*, No. 722, p. 862–914.
109 *Ibid.* Nos. 669 and 673; *DVP*, v. XVIII, Nos. 145–148, No. 155.
110 LoN. Minutes of the Eighty-fifth (Extraordinary) Session of the Council, *OJ*. May 1935. p. 556.
111 Statement by Litvinov in connection with the relations between the Soviet Union and Uruguay, LoN. Minutes of the Ninetieth Session of the Council, *OJ*, February 1936. p. 105.
112 LoN. Minutes of the Eighty-fifth (Extraordinary) Session of the Council, *OJ*, May 1935, p. 553 ff.
113 *DVP*, v. XVIII, Nos. 180–182, p. 284–286, 14 April 1935.
114 *Ibid.* No. 187, p. 292 ff.
115 With reference to the sub-title of Arnold Wolfers, *Britain and France between two wars. Conflicting strategies of peace since Versailles.* New York, Harcourt, 1940. – 467 p. (repr. 1966).
116 Cf. *DBFP*, v. 2/12, No. 294. *op. cit.* No. 651 (record of Simon's conversations with Hitler, March 1935); C, III, No. 549.
117 Čičerin's report to the 3rd Soviet Congress, 14 May 1925, *SDFP*, v. 2, p. 34 ff.; *DVP*, v. VIII, No. 140.
118 LoN. Minutes of the Eighty-eighth Session of the Council, *OJ*, November 1935. p. 1142; *DVP*, v. XVIII, No. 357.
119 *Ibid. ibid.*
120 LoN. Records of the Sixteenth Ordinary Session of the Assembly; Plenary Meetings, 14 September 1935, *OJSS* no. 138, p. 73; *DVP*, v. XVIII, No. 362.
121 Cf. Buzinkai, *op. cit.* p. 168. (See note 26)
122 Apart from the Stresa records, which reflect the British-French differences in the sanctions question (see note 109) cf. also the records of the British-French talks at Geneva, 9–11 September 1935, *DBFP* v.2/14, Nos 553–554.
123 LoN. Dispute between Ethiopia and Italy; Coordination of Measures under Article 16 of the Covenant; Committee of Eighteen, Minutes, 12 October 1935, *OJSS* no. 145, p. 40.
124 *Ibid.* Sub-Committee on Economic Measures, Minutes, 16 October 1935, *OJSS* no.

145, p. 97; see also Litvinov's instructions to Potemkin, 4 October, *DVP*, v. XVIII, no. 372, p. 523.

125 LoN. Dispute between Ethiopia and Italy; Coordination of Measures under Article 16 of the Covenant; Coordination Committee, Minutes, 19 October 1935, *OJSS* no. 145, p. 27.

126 *Ibid.;* Proposals and Resolutions of the Coordination Committee and the Committee of Eighteen, and Official Correspondence and Communications Relating Thereto, 1936, *OJSS* no. 150, p. 296–300.

127 Buzinkai, *op. cit.*, p. 168 (see note 26); cf. thereagainst Lowell R. Tillett, "The Soviet Role in League Sanctions against Italy, 1935–36". *The American Slavic and East European Review*, v. 15, p. 11–16, July 1956.

128 8 December 1935. cf. *DBFP*, v.2/15, Nos. 336 and 338.

129 *DVP*, v. XVIII, Nos 447–448, p. 591 ff.

130 LoN. Records of the Sixteenth Ordinary Session of the Assembly, Plenary Meetings, 1 July 1936, *OJSS* no. 151, p. 36.

131 Ibid.

132 LoN, Minutes of the Ninety-First (Extraordinary) Session of the Council, *OJ*, April 1936, p. 321; *DVP*, v. XIX, No. 87.

133 *Ibid.*, p. 323.

134 *Ibid.*

135 *DVP*, v. XIX, Nos. 70, 71, 76; *DBFP*, v. 2/15, No. 71.

136 LoN. Records of the Seventeenth Ordinary Session of the Assembly, Plenary Meetings, 28 September 1936, *OJSS* no. 155, p. 64; *DVP*, v. XI No. 280, p. 446.

137 *DVP*, v. XIX, No. 249.

138 *Ibid.* No. 292, p. 459, Krestinskij to Kagan, 4 October 1936.

139 For figures cf. *Istorija vtoroj mirovoj vojny* (History of the Second World War, in 12 v.) Moscow, Voenizdat, 1974. – v. 2, p. 54.

140 See Alvarez del Vayo's arguments, Minutes of the Ninety-Fifth (Extraordinary) Session of the Council, *OJ*, January 1937, p. 8 ff.

141 LoN. Records of the Eighteenth Ordinary Session of the Assembly, Plenary Meetings, 21 September 1937, *OJSS* no. 169, p. 79 ff.; *DVP*, v. XX, No. 337.

142 LoN. Minutes of the Ninety-seventh Session of the Council, *OJ*, May–June 1937, p. 321 ff.; *DVP*, v. XX, No. 180, p. 276.

143 Cf. *supra*, p. 133 ff.

144 LoN. Sino-Japanese Conflict; Appeal by the Chinese Government; Minutes of the Third Session of the Far-East Advisory Committee, 21 September to 5 October 1937, *OJSS* no. 177, p. 7–26.

145 LoN. Records of the Eighteenth Ordinary Session of the Assembly, Plenary Meetings, 5 October 1937, *OJSS* no. 169, p. 122 ff.

146 Cf. *Soviet peace efforts on the eve of World War II* (Documents) v. 2, Moscow, Novesti Press Agency Publications House, 1973. – Nos. 335 notes 5, p. 278 ff. 126, p. 314 ff; *DVP*, v. XXI, No. 60, p. 102–106.

147 *DVP*, v. XVI, Nos. 425 and 434; *FRUS*, *The Soviet Union 1933–1939*, ed. by US Department of State, Wachington, Govt. Printing Office, 1952. – p. 53,61.

148 28 March 1935. *DBFP*, v. 2/12, No. 673, p. 738; No. 669; *DVP*, v. XVIII No. 146, p. 239, No. 148.

149 *DVP*, v. XX, note 197, p. 752 ff.; *ibid.* No. 341, p. 552.

150 *DVP*, v. XXI, No. 336, p. 482.

151 *ADAP*, D,I, No. 19, 5 November 1937. (Hossbach Protocol)

152 *Ibid.* No. 31, 11 November 1937.

153 *Ibid.* No. 19, p. 30.

154 *SDEP*, v. III, p. 276 ff.; *DBFP*, v. III/1, Nos 90 and 92; *DVP*, v. XXI, No. 82, p. 128 ff.
155 *DBFP*, v. III/1, No. 116, p. 101.
156 *Documents of international affairs, 1938*, edited by Monica Curtis. London, Oxford University Press, 1942. – v. 1, p. 47 ff.
157 *New documents on the history of Munich*, edited by the Ministry of Foreign Affairs of the CSSR and by the Ministry of Foreign Affairs of the USSR, Prague, Orbis, 1958. – No. 14, p. 39 ff.; *DVP*, v. XXI, No. 182, p. 262 ff.; *DDF*, v. II/9, (13 May 1938).
158 *New documents ... op. cit.* Nos. 26, 27 and 30; *DVP*, v. XXI, Nos. 324, 343.
159 Statement to Luciani, the Moscow correspondent of *Le Temps*. *DDF*, II/I, No. 390, Annexe.
160 *New documents ... op. cit.* Nos. 36, 38 and 39; *DVP*, v. XXI, Nos. 354, 355, 356.
161 LoN. Records of the Nineteenth Ordinary Session of the Assembly; Plenary Meetings, 21 September 1938, *OJSS* no. 183, p. 74–78; *DVP*, v. XXI, No. 357.
162 Cf. *supra*, p. 129.
163 LoN. Minutes of the Hundred and Fifth-Session of the Council, *OJ*, May-June 1939, p. 248; LoN. doc. A.15.1939.VII.
164 *Soviet peace efforts. op. cit.* (See note 146) v. II, No. 314, p. 67–75; p. 74.
165 *Ibid.*, No. 315, p. 75–76; *DBFP* v. III/5, No. 697; *SDFP*, v. III, 340 ff.
166 *DBFP*, ser. 3, vol. V., No. 624, p. 679.
167 Aide-mémoire by *Molotov*, 16 June 1939, *Soviet peace efforts. Op. cit.* II, No. 331, p. 96; *DBFP*, ser. 3, vol. VI, No. 69, p. 86.
168 Records of the VI. Committee, 19th Assembly. – 4th Meeting, 22. Sept. 1938. *OJSS* No. 189, p. 24 f.
169 *Soviet peace efforts. Op. cit.* II, No. 417, p. 212–215; *DBFP*, v. III App. II, No. 1–2, p. 561–595.
170 Cf. *supra*, p. 133 ff.
171 Statement of the British Minister for Co-Ordination of Defence, Foreign Policy Committee, Meeting of 16 May 1930, PRO. FO. 371. 23066. C 7401/G/3356/18.
172 DBFP, ser. 3, vol. VI, App. V, pp. 762 ff.
173 Cf. *supra*, p. 127.
174 Mr. Snow to Sir L. Oliphant, 11 April 1939, PRO. FO. 371.23650. N 1993/26/63.
175 Cf. Vaïno A. Tanner, *The Winter War. Finland Against Russia 1939–1940*, Stanford, Stanford University Press, 1957. – p. 101–103.
176 LoN doc. C 370. M 283.1939. VII.
177 Cf. Victor-Yves Ghebali, *Organisation internationale et guerre mondiale. Le cas de la Société des Nations et de l'Organisation Internationale du travail pendant la seconde guerre mondiale.* 2 v. Unpublished diss. Grenoble, 1975. – v. 1, p. 129. James Barros, *Betrayal from within: Joseph Avenol, Secretary-General of the League of Nations 1933–1940.* New Haven, Yale University Press, 1969. – p. 198 ff. Arthur W. Rovine, *The first fifty years. The Secretary-General in world politics, 1920–1970.* Leyden, Sijthof, 1970. – p. 149 ff. For the whole Soviet-Finnish conflict cf. J. Hevakivi, *The Appeal that was never made. The Allies, Scandinavia and the Finnish Winter War 1939–1940.* London, Hurst, 1976. – Anthony F. Upton, *Finland 1939–1940.* London, Davis-Poynter, 1974. – p. 19–50; for the Soviet view: *Istorija diplomati* (Diplomatic History). Moscow 1975, v. IV, p. 5–38 and *Istorija vtoroj mirovoj vojny*, Moscow 1975, v. IV.
178 LoN. Doc. C.375.M.288.1939.VII.
179 LoN. Minutes of the Hundred-and-Seventh Session of the Council, Annex: Report of the Assembly, provided for in Article 15, Paragraphs 4 and 10, of the Covenant, submitted by Special Committee of the Assembly. *OJ*, November–De-

cember 1939, p. 540. LoN doc. A. 46.1939.VII (Report of the Committee of Thirteen).

180 France, Britain, South Africa, Egypt, Belgium, Bolivia, and the Dominican Republic voted for the resolution. Finland, China, Greece and Yugoslavia abstained. The USSR, Peru and Iran were absent.

181 LoN. Minutes of the Hundred-and-Seventh Session of the Council, *O. J.*, November–December 1939, p. 506.

182 Cf. Leo Gross, "Was the Soviet Union Expelled from the League of Nations?" *The American Journal of International Law,* v. 39, January 1945, p. 35–44. A. S. Protopopov, *SSSR, Liga Nacij i OON* (The USSR, the League of Nations and the United Nations). Moskva, Izd. vo "Mysl", 1968. – p. 62–68.

183 Confidential report of the British delegate, R. Butler, to Viscount Halifax, 22. December 1939, PRO.FO. 371. 24045. W 19159/17958/98.

184 Walters, *op. cit.* p. 805. (See note 2)

185 Cf. *supra*, p. 135 ff.

186 H. L. Roberts, "Maxim Litvinov" in *The diplomats, 1919–1939* [edited by] Gordon A. Craig [and] Felix Gilbert. Princeton, Princeton University Press, 1953. – p. 344.

La Suisse et la Société des Nations

Roland Ruffieux
Universités de Fribourg et de Lausanne

Pendant un quart de siècle, la SdN a marqué plus que tout autre élément d'origine étrangère la politique générale de la Suisse. Au niveau le plus élevé et de manière très apparente, elle a entraîné une redéfinition de la neutralité[1] et, de ce fait, une réorientation de la politique extérieure de la Suisse[2], terrain où son influence s'est exercée en concurrence avec les efforts plus généraux accomplis à la fin de la Première Guerre mondiale: naissance d'un nouvel ordre européen, issu des traités de 1918–1920; modification dans l'équilibre des puissances, changements dans les opinions publiques et les mentalités collectives. Elle a également accéléré une mutation, commencée avant la guerre, dans l'instrumentation de cette politique étrangère, touchant l'élargissement de la démocratie semi-directe, c'est-à-dire la ratification populaire des engagements internationaux de longue durée[3].

Par cette voie oblique, la participation à la SdN et, plus généralement aux affaires du monde, est devenue véritablement un enjeu de politique intérieure, ne déterminant pas seulement l'apparition de mouvements et d'associations militantes pour la cause internationaliste ou, à l'inverse, en faveur de l'isolationnisme[4]. Elle a entraîné encore un reclassement des partis face aux affaires étrangères dont ils s'occupent désormais beaucoup plus que par le passé. Celles-ci vont enfin influer – fait également nouveau – sur les rapports entre les diverses forces organisées de la vie politique, approfondissant, par exemple, le fossé séparant la gauche pacifiste et la droite nationaliste.

Dans l'impossibilité de traiter tous les aspects, au surplus très complexes, de cette participation, la présente communication n'en retiendra que trois. Tout d'abord l'accession de la Suisse à la nouvelle ligue, en rapport avec les troubles qui, dans ce pays, comme ailleurs, marquent la fin de la guerre, décision facilitée par une volonté de rompre avec la tradition mais dont les modes ont un caractère particulier. Puis, les effets qu'exerce en Suisse une des crises les plus graves que la SdN a connues, celle des sanctions contre l'Italie lors de l'agression contre l'Ethiopie. Le principal des ces effets, est d'ébranler l'autorité de Motta, inamovible chef du Département politique fédéral[5] et de le pousser à faire revenir le pays à la neutralité intégrale. Enfin, à la fin de la Seconde Guerre mondiale, le rôle joué par la Suisse dans la liquidation de la SdN, opération difficile parce qu'elle coïncide à nouveau avec un passage délicat pour la neutralité helvétique, honnie par les vainqueurs, ce qui explique l'abstention durable à l'égard de l'ONU.[6] A cette occasion, comme dans les précédentes, l'appréciation de la valeur des expériences faites avec la SdN joue un rôle décisif dans le choix de la ligne de conduite ultérieure du pays. D'autant plus qu'en 1944–1946, comme en 1918–1920, l'on assiste à deux des très rares réorientations de la diplomatie helvétique coïncidant avec des changements de titulaire au Département politique fédéral, aujourd'hui Département fédéral des affaires étrangères.

*

Les rapports entre la Suisse et la SdN en formation posent plusieurs problèmes importants dont un seul sera retenu ici. La démarche insolite, suivie par un pays dont la neutralité a été reconnue et garantie en 1815 par le concert européen et que la guerre a épargné sur le plan militaire, fait-elle de la Suisse un membre à part entière, capable de remplir ses engagements et d'adhérer vraiment à »l'esprit de Genève« qui commence bientôt à souffler? Dès les premières approches de la paix, tardives si elles sont comparées à la démarche des pays belligérants, le gouvernement qui, jusqu'à l'affaire Grimm-Hoffmann, avait espéré jouer un rôle de médiateur[7], adopte une attitude essentiellement pragmatique, qui l'amènera à une erreur d'appréciation. Ne se contente-t-il pas, en septembre 1917, de mettre en chantier une analyse préparatoire de l'après-guerre? La priorité étant donnée aux questions économiques en raison de la situation difficile de la Suisse entre les belligérants, il inscrit les problèmes posés par l'organisation future de la paix, dans la suite des travaux préparatoires pour la IIIe Conférence de La Haye, ajournée en 1914,[8] sous-estimant l'importance des préparatifs en cours, spécialement dans les pays anglo-saxons. En juin 1918, Calonder répond en termes vagues à une interpellation parlementaire et se contente de former un groupe d'experts chargés d'étudier le projet d'une Ligue des Nations à laquelle Wilson a décidé d'attacher son nom. Dans leurs travaux menés à l'automne, ceux-ci se bornent à réclamer de la future organisation qu'elle applique les principes d'universalité et d'égalité entre les Etats.[9] Dans cet esprit, le gouvernement adresse, le 20 novembre, aux puissances alliées et associées une demande d'invitation à la Conférence de la paix où il pense présenter un projet de Ligue des Nations, conçu sur le modèle confédéral.

Aussi, l'ouverture de la Conférence de Paris, l'orientation que le Conseil des Quatre lui donne et la rapidité avec laquelle elle traite les problèmes d'organisation de la paix surprennent-elles la Suisse qui, dans un premier temps, essaie d'expliquer l'importance européenne de sa neutralité et de constituer même un front des neutres.[10] Heureusement, en parallèle de la diplomatie officielle et grâce aux contacts que W. Rappard entretient avec le Colonel House,[11] Genève est choisie comme siège de la future organisation internationale à condition que la Suisse admette un nécessaire aménagement de sa neutralité, surtout en raison de l'article 16 du Pacte prévoyant des sanctions contre l'Etat qui rompt des engagements. Les premiers pourparlers, menés à ce propos à l'occasion de deux voyages d'un membre du gouvernement helvétique à Paris, font apparaître une divergence irréductible sur les sanctions militaires mais une reconnaissance possible de la neutralité de la Suisse en rapport avec l'article 21 du Pacte. L'appui de la France est prévisible, en contrepartie de l'abandon de la neutralisation de la Savoie du Nord et de la suppression du régime des zones.

Au moment où le Conseil suprême adopte le projet du Pacte et remet à l'Allemagne les conditions de paix (7 mai 1919), l'opinion suisse prend conscience du lien qui relie les deux problèmes. Malgré la protestation des milieux hostiles à ce qui sera bientôt qualifié de »diktat«, le gouvernement s'engage publiquement en faveur d'une adhésion à la SdN, assortie d'un aménagement de la neutralité.[12] La hâte subite avec laquelle un message aux Chambres est préparé et publié, le 4 août, s'explique certes par le fait que si la Suisse veut bénéficier de la qualité de membre originaire et voir se fixer chez elle le siège de la SdN, désiré par la Belgique, elle doit ratifier promptement le Traité de Versailles dont le Pacte de la SdN fait partie intégrante. Pour la première fois dans le chapitre III du message et grâce à son rédacteur Max Huber, une distinction claire est établie entre le principe juridique de la neutralité – "le droit pur" – et la politique de neutralité qui consiste à l'apprécier là où les intérêts supérieurs du pays sont en jeu[13].

Mais avant même que commence la phase parlementaire, les dissensions qui affectent les partis, les associations économiques, les organisations à but idéal et la presse font sentir leur influence dans le prolongement du fossé moral qui a coupé la Suisse en deux, voire en trois, devant et en rapport même avec les perspectives que la paix a de se développer en Europe. Comme le Conseil fédéral a choisi pour l'adhésion à la SdN la voie d'un arrêté constitutionnel soumis au referendum obligatoire, des comités se constituent en vue de la campagne populaire, au moment où les hésitations de plusieurs parlements étrangers, spécialement du Sénat américain, commencent à entraver le mouvement.

Le gouvernement n'en aborde pas moins les Chambres qui, après un premier ajournement en septembre acceptent, au terme de débats très disputés (11–21 novembre 1919) l'adhésion à la SdN, moyennant quelques concessions mineures. L'opposition réunit paradoxalement les socialistes et les défenseurs d'une neutralité intégrale. Pour désamorcer les objections, particulièrement celle de la »clause américaine« préconisant d'attendre le verdict du Sénat, il décide alors d'obtenir des puissances alliées et associées une reconnaissance solennelle de la neutralité différentielle, lui permettant d'aborder ensuite le peuple souverain avec plus de chances de succès[14].

Commence un intermède diplomatique qui s'annonce d'abord mal, puisque le Conseil suprême refuse à la fois, le 2 janvier 1920, une reconnaissance explicite de la neutralité helvétique et une prolongation du délai d'adhésion jugée nécessaire par la procédure exceptionnelle que la démocratie semi-directe, elle-même en revision sur la ratification des traités internationaux, impose à la Suisse. Cette décision négative, Rappard l'interprète comme un »arrêt de mort«[15]. En effet, au terme des deux premières phases – l'approche maladroite de 1917–18, les négociations plus heureuses de 1919 – la question de la SdN en Suisse semble dans l'impasse.

Le redressement imprévu de la situation qui s'opère dans les mois suivants est l'œuvre de Giuseppe Motta, qui vient de reprendre la direction des affaires étrangères[16]. Seul représentant de la Suisse italienne au Conseil fédéral, partisan convaincu de la neutralité différentielle, le Tessinois entreprend d'exploiter ses idées sur la place de la Suisse dans l'Europe et le rôle directeur de celle-ci dans les affaires mondiales. Utilisant à la fois les thèmes de la démocratie modèle, de la réconciliation entre les grandes cultures et de la fonction humanitaire de la Suisse, concrétisée par le Comité international de la Croix-Rouge, il ouvre les voies à une politique nouvelle.

Pour l'immédiat, le plan de Motta consiste à dissiper le trouble qui s'accroît dans les esprits, surtout en raison des difficultés rencontrées par Wilson, en faisant reconnaître explicitement la thèse suisse sur la neutralité perpétuelle et la compatibilité de celle-ci avec les engagements requis par la SdN. La seconde habileté consiste à la réclamer du Conseil suprême sur la base de l'article 435 du Traité de Versailles et du Conseil de la SdN en application de l'article 21 du Pacte. Le 13 février 1920, après avoir entendu la délégation suisse, ce dernier adopte la déclaration dite de Londres. Après avoir rappelé l'incompatibilité entre la neutralité et l'appartenance à la SdN, il accepte une dérogation pour la tradition séculaire de la neutralité suisse »implicitement incorporée dans le droit des gens« et reconnue par le Traité de Versailles[17].

Ce succès diplomatique permet de débloquer la question. Un message complémentaire est adressé aux Chambres qui, du 27 février au 4 mars, reprennent à fond l'ensemble du problème. Les assurances données à Londres épaulent les partisans, l'éloignement définitif des Etats-Unis affaiblit les adversaires. Finalement, de larges majorités se déclarent pour proposer la ratification au peuple. En fait, la campagne pour le plébiscite, fixée au 16 mai, était engagée depuis plusieurs mois déjà. Le comité du oui, disposant de moyens financiers importants, multiplia les assemblées et les appels, recourant à des moyens originaux de propagande[18]. En revanche, les adversaires ne parvinrent pas à faire l'unité, car les milieux traditionnalistes et souvent germanophiles refusèrent d'agir avec les socialistes qui étaient leurs adversaires sur le terrain de la politique intérieure.

Au terme d'une campagne menée de façon intensive par l'écrit et la parole, les trois quarts de l'électorat helvétique se rendirent aux urnes pour donner 416 870 oui et 323 719 non, la majorité des cantons étant plus étroite[19]. Si le clivage entre une Suisse alémanique hésitante et une Suisse latine résolue – cette dernière ayant emporté l'adhésion – est évident, il faut le compléter par l'influence du facteur confessionnel et l'importance de la structure socio-professionnelle[20]. En fait, comme il n'y a eu nulle part un raz-de-marée ou un rejet massif, l'argumentation du oui plus affective mais plus persuasive a mieux fixé le vote flottant. Le 15 novembre suivant, Motta ouvrait en sa qualité de président de la Confédération, la première assemblée de la SdN à Genève et déclarait que la collaboration entre vainqueurs et vaincus était une »nécessité vitale«. Cette affirmation a également une valeur sur le plan intérieur, puisque l'éventail des opinions, ouvert par le grand tournant de 1918–20, ne se referme pas, créant une conscience nationale originale dans le domaine jusqu'alors délaissé des affaires étrangères.

*

Après une quinzaine d'années d'activité de la SdN, la Suisse pouvait juger positif le bilan de son engagement: abstention militaire acceptée lors de l'affaire de Vilna (1921), participation financière appréciée aux deux protocoles d'aide à l'Autriche (1922); réserve commune à plusieurs Etats membres envers le Protocole de Genève (1924); soutien actif à l'entrée de l'Allemagne (1926) après celle de l'Autriche; réaction prudente devant le projet Briand de créer les Etats-Unis d'Europe (1929–31); déception également partagée ailleurs devant l'enlisement progressif de la Conférence du désarmement (à partir de 1932); hostilité déclarée à l'entrée de l'URSS (1934)[21]. De cette interprétation, assez restrictive, de la politique de neutralité différentielle, Motta, qui dirige alors la diplomatie helvétique, était souvent personnellement responsable. Ne combinait-il pas une vision particulière des relations internationales, et particulièrement de l'avenir européen, avec le souci de maintenir, dans l'opinion suisse, une balance qui, à vrai dire, tenait compte plus de l'opposition durable de la droite nationaliste que du railliement conditionnel de la gauche socialiste?[22]

Une composante majeure de la politique extérieure de Motta restait, malgré les incidents passagers, »l'amitié« de Mussolini dans laquelle le Tessinois voyait, à tort ou à raison, une garantie de l'indépendance du pays et de sa stabilité intérieure. Aussi, cherchait-il constamment à modérer les attaques d'une partie de la presse suisse contre le Duce, qui d'ailleurs en tirait l'argument principal de ses protestations à Berne[23]. Il minimisait également les incidents provoqués, dans le pays même, par les faisceaux italiens qui, à partir de 1933, trouvèrent des partisans plus nombreux, au moment du »printemps des fronts«[24]. Durant l'année 1934, les sautes d'humeur du Duce à qui Motta rendit visite à l'occasion du renouvellement du traité de conciliation et d'arbitrage entre les deux pays, se multiplièrent, si bien que le conflit italo-éthiopien éclata dans une évolution en train de se détériorer.

Au fur et à mesure d'ailleurs que s'approchait l'heure où la Suisse se trouverait, pour la première fois, dans l'obligation d'appliquer les sanctions prévues à l'article 16 et qui avaient fait l'objet de réserves théoriques en 1919–21, l'inquiétude de Motta croissait. D'autant plus qu'il s'agissait du voisin de la Suisse, à ses yeux, le plus important. L'incident d'Oual-Oual (5 décembre 1932) réveilla, dans la presse suisse, des discordances intermittentes depuis 1922. L'accord passé entre Laval et Mussolini les aggrava, obligeant Motta à prêcher la modération aux journaux en s'appuyant sur la doctrine de la »double thèse« qu'il venait de mettre au point pour les différends avec l'Allemagne[25].

Lorsqu' une large majorité se dégagea à la SdN pour désigner l'Italie comme agresseur, Motta déclara, le 9 octobre 1935, que son pays n'avait ni l'intention ni les moyens d'appliquer intégralement les sanctions réclamées, mais qu'il y participerait. Finalement, le Conseil fédéral interdit toute livraison ou transit d'armes en direction des deux pays, égalité de traitement qui fut critiquée à Genève et dans le pays. S'associant aux sanctions financières, il limita les échanges commerciaux avec les deux adversaires au »courant normal« de 1934[26]. Selon les milieux anti-sanctionnistes, la Suisse pouvait redouter des mesures de représailles contre ses 18 000 nationaux résidant en Italie, le contrecoup d'un blocus sur son économie en crise et peut-être même la guerre. Les partisans de la sévérité, quant à eux, citaient les pays neutres, tels la Belgique et la Suède, qui avaient répondu à l'injonction du comité de Londres[27].

La crise fournit une bonne occasion d'esquisser la configuration initiale de l'opinion publique exprimée et son évolution au cours des principales étapes de la crise. Particulièrement attentive à ce qui se passait à Genève et dans la péninsule, la presse romande intervient très tôt, avant même l'éclatement du conflit militaire et la mise en place des sanctions. Durant l'hiver 1934–35, elle se divise entre une gauche pacifiste, partenaire de la sévérité envers un régime qu'elle dénonce depuis son avènement et ralliée à la SdN à qui elle prêche la fermeté et une droite plus soucieuse des intérêts nationaux de la Suisse et de l'Italie, nations d'ancienne civilisation. En effet, le clivage se complique bientôt d'un débat sur la colonisation. Selon les uns, peut-on désavouer l'Italie, au surplus maltraitée lors du partage des dépouilles en 1919–20, de vouloir répandre les bienfaits de la civilisation européenne en Afrique? Pour d'autres, l'Ethiopie n'a-t-elle pas été reçue membre de plein droit de la SdN, sans jugement de valeur sur son régime politique et social?[28]

A partir d'octobre 1935, le débat autour des sanctions se complique de divergences quant aux raisons de la Suisse de soutenir une organisation dont la réforme à l'étude, paraît problématique. D'une manière générale, les journaux qui appuient la majorité gouvernementale du pays,[29] approuvent le »point de vue suisse«, cherchant à concilier les exigences de la neutralité et la participation aux sanctions. La proximité entre le discours de Motta à Genève (10 octobre 1935) et les élections pour le renouvellement du Conseil national exerce aussi une influence, puisque le bloc national subit alors les pressions conjuguées des frontistes et de l'opposition socialiste. Celle-ci est à peu près la seule à considérer que la Suisse doit appliquer intégralement les sanctions si elle veut respecter ses engagements, préserver son »capital moral« face à des risques économiques jugés minimes[30]. On retrouve un partage analogue, lors des débats aux Chambres (28 janvier 1936) qui ratifient massivement les positions officielles. L'approche de la victoire italienne renforce l'argumentation des journaux anti-sanctionnistes qui réclament la levée de mesures inefficaces parce qu'elles ont manqué leur but. Même si elle est presque seule à le faire, la presse de gauche insiste sur les horreurs de la guerre, salue l'héroïsme de la résistance et souligne le fossé que l'attentisme helvétique a creusé entre le public et les dirigeants.[31]

Outre le poids de l'opinion exprimée, la diplomatie helvétique subissait alors un double handicap. Mussolini, en effet, fit à nouveau pression sur Berne pour que la Suisse devançât même la liquidation générale de l'appareil des sanctions. Motta poussa la délégation suisse à travailler en faveur d'une décision favorable, l'échéance étant fixée finalement au 15 juillet 1936. La conclusion, le 20 juin 1936, d'un accord de compensation italo-suisse n'est peut-être pas étrangère à une complaisance qui, après avoir poussé le Conseil fédéral à refuser au Négus l'établissement en Suisse, précipite la reconnaissance *de jure* de l'annexion de l'Ethiopie (23 décembre 1936). Il est vrai que, le 4 septembre précédent, la Suisse avait remis au Secrétariat de la SdN sa réponse concernant la réforme du Pacte. Elle contenait une critique sévère de l'institution genevoise destinée surtout à justifier la position très particulière de la Suisse.[32] L'homme, qui avait milité en 1920 pour l'admission, était donc en train de réviser son jugement et le thème dominant de sa diplomatie: la neutralité différentielle.

Au début de 1938, l'affaiblissement de la SdN et les risques accrus d'une conflagration générale formaient un contraste suffisant pour que le gouvernement suisse se décide d'agir. Il y était également contraint par les dissensions de l'opinion publique, mises en évidence par la guerre d'Espagne, et par la menace des milieux isolationnistes de lancer une initiative constitutionnelle pour le retour à la neutralité intégrale, qui aurait obligé la Suisse à quitter la SdN. Ecartant l'idée de dénoncer la Déclaration de Londres, le groupe des Sages constitué par Motta lui conseilla de demander au Conseil de la SdN de la réinterpréter de façon à libérer purement et simplement la Suisse d'appliquer l'article 16.[33] Cette issue paraissait possible du fait que, dans la question toujours à l'étude de la réforme du Pacte, une proposition suédoise prévoyait de rendre facultative l'application des sanctions.

La démarche tourna court, mais l'Anschluss de l'Autriche reposa le problème dans toute son acuité. En reconnaissant précipitamment le fait accompli, Motta démontra qu'il ne croyait plus aux mécanismes de la sécurité collective. Le memorandum que le Conseil fédéral fit préparer à l'intention de la SdN invoquait, en effet, la clause *rebus sic stantibus* pour constater l'impossibilité de la Suisse d'appliquer désormais la Déclaration de Londres. Le 6 mai 1938, Motta en personne plaida le dossier à Genève. Le 14 mai suivant, le Conseil, à »la presque totalité de ses membres«[34], adopte un rapport et une résolution prenant acte des intentions suisses. Berne obtint encore, le 21 juin, des notes conjointes de l'Allemagne et de l'Italie exprimant leur satisfaction, bien compréhensible, de voir la Suisse se libérer d'engagements pouvant compromettre sa neutralité.[35]

*

La guerre n'interrompit pas les activités de la SdN et, par conséquent, ne délia pas sur le plan juridique la Suisse de ses engagements. Comme l'obstacle politique qu'elle avait opposé, au début des années 1930, à l'expansionnisme des Etats opposés à l'Europe de Versailles et aux manquements à la paix était maintenant levé, la tâche de ses partisans en Suisse devient de plus en plus malaisée. D'autant plus que, entre 1939 et 1945, l'organisation genevoise eut à affronter des difficultés majeures aggravant un contentieux déjà ancien, qui allait faciliter une probable liquidation.[36]

Au début des hostilités, un accord tacite fut passé entre les autorités de Berne et le Secrétariat afin de faciliter l'observation par la Suisse de ses devoirs de neutralité.[37] L'application s'en révéla malaisée, comme on le vit à propos de l'intervention de la SdN dans la guerre russo-finlandaise. L'opinion helvétique sympathisa ouvertement, mise à part la presse frontiste, avec le petit Etat. Pourtant, dans les débats qui débouchèrent sur l'exclusion de l'URSS, la Suisse reste sur la réserve et sa délégation s'abstient lors du vote du 14 décembre 1939, position qui contrastait avec l'engagement de Motta en 1934.[38]

La défaite de la France et les vicissitudes de la guerre entraînèrent la dispersion des services, la réduction des effectifs et la limitation des tâches. La démission de Joseph Avenol et son remplacement par un Irlandais fut suivie du retrait de plusieurs Etats membres, dont l'Etat français. Devant cet affaiblissement de l'institution dont elle restait membre mais surtout à cause des pressions allemandes renouvelées, la Suisse réduisit au minimum ses liens avec la SdN: suspension du paiement des cotisations, refus de tout contact officiel avec le Secrétariat, dénonciation de la convention règlant les activités de Radio-Nations,[39] avatar de la guerre des ondes qui sévissait partout en Europe.

Exception faite de la présence de fonctionnaires de nationalité helvétique, dont le quota élevé au départ subit le effets des mesures d'austérité, la Suisse ne participa pour ainsi dire pas aux activités à court terme ni à la préparation de l'après-guerre. Les études publiées sur ce dernier point n'en rencontrèrent pas moins de l'intérêt dans l'opinion helvétique, où elles furent utilisées contre les thèses de la »nouvelle Europe«.[40] De son côté, l'Association suisse pour la SdN faisait une pause de plusieurs années.

Quand furent signées la Charte de l'Atlantique (14 août 1941) et la Déclaration des Nations Unies (1er janvier 1942), les perspectives changèrent et l'opinion suisse put enregistrer la volonté des Alliés de remplacer la SdN par une organisation nouvelle. Très lent, le mouvement d'opinion se limita d'abord à quelques cercles. Ainsi en est-il des positions en 1942–43 par Paul Guggenheim et Hans Wehberg sur l'impossibilité de réformer le Pacte de la SdN.[41] Une revue comme *Suisse contemporaine*, qu'on pouvait considérer comme favorable à la cause alliée, ne tablait pas non plus sur l'institution genevoise,[42] quoique de manière générale, on continue à utiliser son titre pour désigner l'institution à venir.

Dans l'été 1944, parallèlement à la Conférence de Dumbarton Oaks, l'Association suisse pour la SdN s'exprime à nouveau en public.[43] Lors de l'assemblée tenue à Zürich, son secrétaire général place la reconnaissance de la neutralité suisse parmi les préalables à l'organisation de la paix future.[44] Suit une campagne de conférences où sont examinés les divers aspects de la confrontation entre la Suisse et les plans des Nations Unies. P. Guggenheim s'inspira de 1920 pour chercher une compatibilité jugée possible si l'on reconnaissait le caractère spécifique de la neutralité suisse.[45] En revanche, Rappard penchait vers le maintien de la neutralité traditionnelle et l'attentisme tout en soulignant la nécessité de régulariser les rapports avec l'URSS. On ne s'étonne guère de percevoir chez lui une réaction très vive aux projets de Dumbarton Oaks. N'estime-t-il pas, en effet, que la Suisse ne saurait collaborer avec le Conseil de Sécurité, qui ressemble peu au Conseil de la SdN, alors que sa participation au Conseil économique et social n'est nullement à exclure?[46]

Si elle n'influe pas directement sur l'attitude de la Suisse envers la SdN, la crise de novembre-décembre 1944 n'en précipite pas moins une évolution qui lui est défavorable. La démission forcée de M. Pilet-Golaz, chef du Département politique fédéral, et l'arrivée de Max Petitpierre entraînent moins une rupture dans la politique étrangère du pays que la recherche plus active de solutions aux problèmes dont la guerre a bloqué l'évolution.[47] Le nouveau chef de la diplomatie helvétique dut affronter aussitôt une crise grave de la neutralité attaquée de plusieurs côtés à la fois. Mise en cause pour la période de guerre lors des négociations économiques de Berne avec la mission Currie (12 février – 8 mars 1945), elle est fortement contestée dans les milieux qui travaillent à préparer la nouvelle organisation internationale et spécialement par les Grands, à l'exception de la Grande-Bretagne.[48]

Au début de son séjour à Berne, l'émissaire de Roosevelt a remis au Conseil fédéral une lettre du Président exprimant l'espoir de voir la Suisse s'associer aux puissances alliées. Une première réponse est donnée, le 6 mars 1945, par le Conseil fédéral, lorsqu'il refuse d'entrer en guerre contre l'Axe, condition mise pour recevoir une invitation à la prochaine Conférence de San Francisco. Toutefois, afin de permettre une prise de position plus circonstanciée, la délégation du Conseil fédéral pour les affaires étrangères se réunit, le 12 avril, avec quelques experts. Parmi les points à l'ordre du jour, on note, en rapport avec la possibilité d'une installation du Conseil de Sécurité aux portes de Genève, l'éventualité d'une exterritorialisation des installations de la SdN. Mais l'idée exprimée par Rappard de chercher une voie analogue à celle de 1919 n'est pas retenue et le Conseil fédéral renonce finalement à participer à la Conférence de San Francisco. Quant à l'hypothèse d'un accord d'exterritorialité, elle n'est pas jugée plausible.[49]

Pour des raisons de politique intérieure, autant que de politique extérieure, les partis et la presse approuvent, à quelques exceptions près,[50] la réserve officielle quand ils ne surenchérissent pas sur elle. Dès l'ouverture de la conférence chargée de mettre sur pied la nouvelle organisation, la proposition française, présentée par Paul-Boncour, d'interdire la participation à l'ONU de la Suisse, de l'Espagne et de la Suède provoque une émotion qui retombe lorsqu'elle est refusée.[51] Le 9 juin, la question de l'adhésion est évoquée devant l'Association suisse pour la SdN qui se divise entre partisans d'une limitation de la neutralité et attentistes.[52]

De même, devant le Conseil national les 19 et 20 juin 1945, l'essai tenté par A. Lachenal de passer à une politique plus active en vue de poser éventuellement la candidature de Genève comme siège de l'ONU, se heurte à une réserve générale.[53] La reprise, dans le *Journal de Genève* du 11 juin 1945, d'un projet de »Cité des Nations« datant de 1930 et proche de l'éventualité examinée par le Conseil fédéral deux mois plus tôt, ne retient guère l'attention. On est donc très loin en Suisse de croire à une répétition des événements heureux de 1919–20. En effet, la signature de la Charte de l'ONU, le 26 juin 1945, saluée comme un événement historique ne suscite pas un intérêt profond en Suisse.[54]

L'attitude adoptée au moment de la Conférence de Potsdam, les résultats d'un sondage d'opinion chiffrant l'attachement des Suisses à la neutralité intégrale même si elle entraînait des inconvénients d'ordre économique, les travaux des experts mandatés en été pour ouvrir la voie à une consultation plus étendue, l'acceptation par le Parlement d'étendre le réseau diplomatique helvétique: tout concourt à renforcer la constatation que, tenue à l'écart par les grandes puissances et par sa volonté de mener une politique indépendante, la Suisse risque de se replier sur elle-même. Bien placée pour percevoir les dangers d'un isolationnisme, l'Association suisse pour la SdN propose d'illustrer la politique active de neutralité qui s'amorcerait, par l'adhésion à la Cour internationale de justice et la collaboration aux activités non-politiques de l'ONU.[55] Les 14–15 novembre, la commission consultative, chargée d'étudier l'ensemble des problèmes, se borne, en ce qui touche le sort le la SdN, à recommander d'offrir l'hospitalité de Genève aux nouvelles institutions techniques et administratives que pourraient créer les Nations Unies.[56]

L'année 1945 fut également marquée par un regain d'activité de la SdN mais il avait pour principal objectif d'ouvrir la voie à l'ONU. En effet, ni l'URSS ni les Etats-Unis n'entendent maintenir en vie une institution à laquelle ils ne participent pas. Bien que la Charte de San Francisco puisse être interprétée comme une version plus précise et plus avancée du Pacte, toute mise en rapport est évitée. L'hostilité à l'ancienne organisation dicte les mesures que propose la commission spéciale désignée à San Francisco pour préparer l'entrée en vigueur de la Charte. Finalement, grâce au gouvernement britannique, le soin de la liquidation fut confié à l'assemblée générale de la SdN qui se réunit une dernière fois à Genève, du 8 au 18 avril 1946.[57]

La double réserve de la Suisse – envers la SdN pendant la guerre, face à la nouvelle organisation qui se préparait – facilita sa préparation à cette ultime assemblée. Pour tourner la page, la Suisse régla d'abord ses contributions arriérées depuis 1941, ceci à la fin de 1945. Les instructions de la délégation helvétique ne divergeaient pas de celles des puissances qui avaient animé la vie de l'institution genevoise. Tout au plus par le biais du maintien des »droits acquis« s'efforça-t-elle de rappeler la situation spéciale du pays et de souligner son désir de rester associée aux activités techniques de la SdN qui seront reprises par les Nations Unies.[58]

L'idée de continuité, exprimée à cette occasion, ne fut pourtant réalisée que de façon incomplète. Le 19 avril 1946 fut signé un arrangement provisoire relatif aux privilèges et immunités des Nations Unies réglant le statut des fonctionnaires internationaux dont le maintien à Genève s'expliquait par l'acquisition dès le ler août 1945 par l'ONU, des bâtiments et installations de la SdN. L'adoption d'un statut fut préjugée par l'accord passé, le 11 mars 1946, entre la Suisse et l'OIT dans lequel une clause de sauvegarde garantissait l'indépendance et la neutralité du pays hôte. Elle s'exprimait à la fois par la non-responsabilité du pays hôte touchant les actes de l'organisaiton et par le droit du Conseil fédéral de prendre les précautions utiles »dans l'intérêt de la sécurité de la Suisse.«[59]

Or, la délégation de l'ONU, chargée de négocier un accord, refusa ce précédent, tandis que le gouvernement fédéral tenait à cette clause de sauvegarde. Au terme de pourparlers ouverts à Berne et poursuivis à New York, la Suisse finit par se contenter d'une déclaration dégageant sa responsabilité et interdisant à l'ONU de conduire des opérations militaires à partir de Genève. Fixées dans une lettre de Max Petitpierre au secrétaire général Trygve Lie, ces conditions furent approuvées par l'assemblée générale de l'ONU, le 14 décembre 1946.[60] En 1946, comme en 1919, la neutralité donnait l'impression d'un noeud gordien dans les rapports de la Suisse avec les organisations internationales de nature politique. Pourtant, entre ces deux bornes et surtout avant 1938, cette neutralité aménagée avait influé de façon positive sur les relations avec la SdN. Au sortir de la guerre et durant de longues années encore, il semblait pourtant que cette expérience, en soi féconde, ne pût infléchir les attitudes face à l'ONU.

Au total, quel bilan peut-on dresser de ce quart de siècle de participation de la Suisse à la première organisation internationale politique disposant d'organes permanents et dépassant le stade ancien de la diplomatie multilatérale? Au XVIIIe siècle, les voyageurs parcourant la Suisse remarquaient dans plusieurs cantons non seulement l'engagement des élites politiques pour une participation à la vie internationale, liée à des intérêts précis, mais également le fait que des assemblées démocratiques débattaient, par exemple, de l'alliance avec la France. Durant la première moitié du XIXe siècle, ces diplomaties cantonales continuèrent de se manifester en l'absence d'un Etat fédéral, aggravant même les crises internes. Quand celui-ci parut en 1848, ses organes encore faibles ne purent d'emblée imposer une politique étrangère digne de ce nom. Jusqu'à la Première Guerre mondiale, cette politique de la Confédération tout en étendant son champ d'action, ne se manifesta que de façon intermittente et, à son tour, conflictuelle.

C'est le mérite de la SdN d'avoir obligé la Suisse en tant qu'Etat fédéral, à donner une réelle continuité à sa politique fédérale envers la communauté internationale. La reconnaissance du caractère particulier de la neutralité helvétique joua, à cet égard, un rôle déterminant. Mais également – conséquence de la Première Guerre mondiale – l' ouverture de l'opinion vers les affaires de l'Europe et du monde. A ces opinions fortement régionalisées, la présence de la SdN à Genève donna, même aux journaux qui la critiquaient, un motif tangible de suivre et de juger l'actualité internationale. Enfin, les principes placés à la base du Pacte, les modes d'action de la SdN coïncidaient avec la démarche helvétique dans le domaine du droit international public. En raison de l'évolution des événements, la période d'une collaboration large fut relativement brève et la Suisse se replia dans un isolement qu'imposait la neutralité intégrale. Mais l'habitude d'appréhender les problèmes dans une perspective européenne, voire mondiale, survécut à la disparition de la SdN qui en avait favorisé l'apparition. De ce fait, même absente de l'ONU en 1945, la Suisse put appliquer plus aisément le principe d'universalité à ses relations, postulat dont la SdN avait contribué à faire connaître l'utilité.

Notes

1 Edgar Bonjour, »Geschichte der schweizerischen Außenpolitik in ihren Grundzügen.« *In:* Handbuch der schweizerischen Außenpolitik. Bern, Stuttgart, Paul Haupt, 1975.-p. 57–80. Edgar Bonjour, *Geschichte der schweizerischen Neutralität.* Band 2, 5. Aufl., Basel Helbing und Lichtenhahn, 1965. – Camille Gorgé, *La neutralité helvétique. Son évolution politique et juridique des origines à la Seconde Guerre mondiale.* Zürich, Editions Polygraphiques, 1947.-485 p. Alphonse Morel, *La neutralité de la Suisse et la Société des Nations. Deux conceptions de la paix.* Lausanne, F. Rouge, 1931.-p. 87–149. Dietrich Schindler, »Die schweizerische Neutralität (1920–1928)«, *Zeitschrift für öffentliches Recht und Volksrecht* 8: 413–444, Nr. 3, 1938.

2 R. Soiron, *Der Beitrag der Schweizer Außenpolitik zum Problem der Friedensorganisation am Ende des Ersten Weltkrieges.* Basel, Stuttgart, Helbing und Lichtenhahn, 1973. – P. Stettler, *Das außenpolitische Bewußtsein in der Schweiz (1920–1930).* Zürich, Leemann, 1969.

3 Roland Ruffieux, »L'entrée de la Suisse dans la Société des Nations. Analyse d'une décision, »*Revue suisse d'histoire* 11: 157–192, 1961. Roland Ruffieux, *L' entrée de la Suisse dans la Société des Nations (1918–1920). La démocratie référendaire en Suisse au XXe siècle.* T.1: Analyse de cas. Fribourg, 1972.-p. 39–118. Sergio Stupan, *Comment la Suisse a adhéré au Pacte de la Société des Nations.* Lausanne, Imprimerie Centrale, 1943.-175 p.

4 H. Ch. Binswanger, »Schweizerische Staatsidee und Außenpolitik«, *In:* Handbuch der schweizerischen Außenpolitik, *op. cit.* [voir note 1] p. 121–146.

5 E. Bonjour, *Geschichte der schweizerischen Neutralität.* Band 3, p. 203–281. Jean Rodolphe von Salis, *Giuseppe Motta. 30 Jahre eidgenössische Politik.* Zürich, Orell und Füssli, 1941. – B. Stettler, *Die Stellung der Schweiz zum Sanktionssystem des Völkerbundes. Von 1919 bis zur Anwendung gegen Italien 1935/36.* Bern, P. Lang, 1977.-307 p. »Zum 100. Geburtstag von Giuseppe Motta«. Beiträge von C. J. Burckhardt, E. Celio, C. Doka (u. a.). *Schweizer Rundschau* 6: 370–464, November/Dezember 1971.

6 Reinhart Ehni, *Die Schweiz und die Vereinten Nationen von 1944-1947.* Tübingen, J.C.B. Mohr (Paul Siebeck), 1967.-p. 10–29. Max Petitpierre, *Politique étrangère. La Suisse depuis 1945.* Bern, Francke, 1971.-p. 154–174.

7 Edgar Bonjour, *Geschichte der schweizerischen Neutralität,* Band 2, p. 612–637. P. Stauffer, »Die Affäre Hoffmann/Grimm«, *Schweizer Monatshefte,* Sonderbeilage, Hft. 1, p. 1–30, April 1930.

8 Edgar Bonjour, *Geschichte der schweizerischen Neutralität,* Band 2, p. 507–522. M. Huber, *Rückblick auf die Haager Konferenz. Rückblick und Ausblick.* Zürich, Atlantis Verlag, 1957.-p. 405–410. A. Rebsamen, »Die diplomatische Vertretung der Schweiz von 1800–1914«, *Neue Zürcher Zeitung* Nr. 31, 7. Januar 1954.

9 William E. Rappard, *L'entrée de la Suisse dans la Société des Nations.* Genève, Editions Sonor, 1924.-p. 6–13. Roland Ruffieux, »L'entrée de la Suisse dans la Société des Nations (1918–1920)«, *op. cit.* [voir note 3], p. 77–96.

10 R. Soiron, *op. cit.* [voir note 2], p. 108–118. B. Stettler, *op. cit.* [voir note 5], p. 35–45.

11 William E. Rappard, *Woodrow Wilson. La Suisse et Genève. Centenaire W. Wilson 1856–1956.* Genève, 1956.-p. 29–74.

12 Pierre Renouvin, *Le traité de Versailles.* Paris, Flammarion, 1969.

13 E. Bonjour, *Geschichte der schweizerischen Neutralität.* Band 2, p. 741–769. »Message du Conseil fédéral à l'Assemblée fédérale concernant la question de l'accession de la Suisse à la Société des Nations du 4 août 1919«. *Feuille Fédérale* 4: 567–681, 1919. »Message complémentaire du Conseil fédéral à l'Assemblée fédérale concernant l'accession de la Suisse à la Société des Nations du 21 juin 1920«. *Feuille Fédérale* 3: 827–836, 1920.

14 W. E. Rappard, *L'entrée de la Suisse dans la Société des Nations, op. cit.* [voir note 9], p. 42–48. R. Ruffieux, *L'entrée de la Suisse dans la Société des Nations (1918–1920), op. cit.* [voir note 3], p. 96–105.

15 W.E. Rappard, *L'entrée de la Suisse dans la Société des Nations, op. cit.* [voir note 9], p. 44.

16 S. Stupan, *Comment la Suisse a adhéré au Pacte de la Société des Nations. Op. cit.* [voir note 3], p. 97–126. R. Ruffieux, »L'entrée de la Suisse dans la Société des Nations. Analyse d'une décision.« *op. cit.* [voir note 3] p. 167–170. J. R. von Salis, *Giuseppe Motta. 30 Jahre eidgenössische Politik. Op. cit.* [voir note 5]. »Zum 100. Geburtstag von Giuseppe Motta«, *op. cit.* [voir note 5] p. 423–427.

17 C. Gorgé, *La neutralité helvétique. Son évolution politique et juridique des origines à la Seconde Guerre mondiale. Op. cit.* [voir note 1] p. 199–215.

18 W.E. Rappard, *L'entrée de la Suisse dans la Société des Nations, op. cit.* [voir note 9], p. 58–79. R. Ruffieux, *L'entrée de la Suisse dans la Société des nations (1918–1920), op. cit.* [voir note 3], p. 109–117. R. Ruffieux, »L'entrée de la Suisse dans la Société des Nations. Analyse d'une décision.« *Op. cit.* [voir note 3], p. 170–182.

19 Explication de la campagne plébiscitaire: le cas du demi-canton d'Appenzell.

20 R. Ruffieux, *L'entrée de la Suisse dans la Société des Nations (1918–1920), op. cit.*, [voir note 3] p. 182–190.

21 E. Bonjour, *Geschichte der schweizerischen Neutralität. Op. cit.* [voir note 1], Band 2,

p. 771–803. C. Gorgé, *La neutralité helvétique. Op. cit.*, p. 261–372. Giuseppe Motta, *Testimonia Temporum.* v. 1. et 2. *Discorsi e scritti scelti.* Bellinzona, Istituto editoriale ticinese, 1931/1936. B. Stettler, *Die Stellung der Schweiz zum Sanktionssystem des Völkerbundes, op. cit.* [5] p. 178–201. P. Stettler, *op. cit.* [voir note 2] p. 243–286 et p. 294–335.

22 E. Bonjour, *Geschichte der schweizerischen Neutralität. Op. cit.* [voir note 1]. Bd. 3, 1970. p. 11, 37. Wolf Ukena, *Die Rückkehr der Schweiz zur integralen Neutralität.* Berlin, Nicolaische Verlagsbuchhandlung, 1941.-p. 16–50.

23 Katharina Spindler, *Die Schweiz und der italienische Fascismus.* Basel, Stuttgart, Helbing und Lichtenhahn, 1976. – G. Motta, *op. cit.* [voir note 21], v. 1, p. 343–351. E. Bonjour, *op. cit.* [voir note 22], p. 143–161.

24 Glaus, Beat, *Die nationale Front. Eine Schweizer faschistische Bewegung 1930–1940.* Zürich, Benziger, 1969. – p. 96–104. Walter Wolf, *Faschismus in der Schweiz. Die Geschichte der Frontenbewegung in der deutschen Schweiz.* Zürich, Flamberg, 1969. – p. 15–27 et 57–106.

25 W. Ukena, *op. cit.* [voir note 22], p. 51–69. B. Stettler, *op. cit.* [voir note 5], p. 221–232. G. Motta, *op. cit.* [voir note 21], v.2, p. 116–119.

26 G. Motta, *op. cit.* [voir note 21], v.2, p. 140–160 et p. 218–222. E. Bonjour, *op. cit.* [voir note 22], p. 161–187. C. Gorgé, *op. cit.* [voir note 1], p. 341–366. B. Stettler, *op. cit.* [voir note 5], p. 201–250.

27 Armand Cohen, *La Société des Nations devant le Conflit italo-éthiopien. Politique et procédure.* Genève, Droz, 1960. – p. 39–49 et p. 111–130. B. Stettler, *op. cit.* [voir note 5], p. 201–219.

28 "Les sanctions moribondes." *Journal de Genève,* 12. 5. 36. "La Suisse et sa politique extérieure." *Journal de Genève,* 17. 6. 36. "Renoncement aux sanctions." *Journal de Genève,* 18. 6. 36. "Contre les sanctions." *Le Pays,* 12. 5. 36. "En Abyssinie – L'occupation italienne". *La Sentinelle,* 9. 5. 36. B. Stettler, *op. cit.* [voir note 5], p. 271–284.

29 M. de Boccard, *La Suisse devant le conflit italo-éthiopien. Rôle de l'opinion publique dans un problème de politique étrangère.* Fribourg, Mémoire Lettres, 1962. – p. 45–69. Kurt Semmler, *Kirche und Völkerbund.* Zürich, Juvis-Verlag, 1973. – p. 159–176.

30 M. de Boccard, *op. cit.* [voir note 29], p. 45–69. G. Motta, *op. cit.* [voir note 21], v.2, p. 140–162 et p. 218–219. B. Stettler, *op. cit.* [voir note 5], p. 232–294. W. Ukena, *op. cit.* [voir note 22], p. 47–50.

31 M. de Boccard, *op. cit.* [voir note 29], p. 45–69. G. Motta, *op. cit.* [voir note 21], v.2, p. 140–162.

32 "La réponse de la SdN et la Suisse". *Le Pays,* 7. 9. 36. "A la SdN – La réponse de la Suisse". *La Sentinelle,* 8. 9. 36. "Le Conseil fédéral et la réforme du Pacte", *Journal de Genève,* 6. 9. 1936. La Suisse reconnaît la souveraineté italienne sur l'Ethiopie. *Journal de Genève,* 25. 12. 36. "Il fallait s'y attendre, M. Motta reconnaît la souveraineté italienne sur l'Ethiopie." *La Sentinelle,* 24. 12. 36. E. Bonjour, *Geschichte der schweizerischen Neutralität. Op. cit.* [voir note 1] Band 3, p. 161–187 et p. 188–201. G. Motta, *op. cit.* [voir note 21], v. 2, p. 220–222, v. 3, 1941, p. 167–178.

33 E. Bonjour, *Geschichte der schweizerischen Neutralität, op. cit.* [voir note 1], Band 2, p. 242–263. C. Gorgé, *op. cit.* [voir note 1], p. 373–428. W. Ukena, *op. cit.* [voir note 22], p. 70–83.

34 E. Bonjour, *Geschichte der schweizerischen Neutralität. Op. cit.* [voir note 1], Band 2, p. 263–281, G. Motta, *op. cit.* [voir note 21], v.3, p. 226–229.

35 E. Bonjour, "Die Befreiung der Schweiz von den Sanktionspflichten des Völkerbundes 1938," *Revue Suisse d'Histoire,* Hft. 1/2, 1978 p. 51–61. C. Gorgé, *op. cit.* [voir note 1] p. 412–428. W. Ukena, *op. cit.* [voir note 22], p. 83–93.

36 Pour l'ensemble de la guerre voir Pierre Gerbet, Victor-Yves Ghebali, Marie-Renée Mouton, *Les palais de la paix. Société des nations et organisation des Nations unies.* Paris, Richelieu, 1973, spécialement le chap. 4.

37 *ibid.* p. 147.

38 *ibid.* p. 147–157.

39 *ibid.* p. 160.

40 On peut signaler, par exemple, l'intérêt des milieux syndicaux attesté par la publication dans la *Revue syndicale suisse* de plusieurs articles.

41 Paul Guggenheim, "Problème de la fédération internationale de l'avenir," *Suisse contemporaine,* décembre 1942, p. 1001–1009; voir également son article dans la *Neue Zürcher Zeitung* du 14 février 1943 et celui de Hans Wehberg dans *Die Friedenswarte* 2: 115–118, 1943.

42 Les nombreuses études consacrées à l'organisation future de la paix, y sont signées de William E. Rappard, Laszlo Ledermann, Paul Guggenheim; Jacques Freymond y fait allusion dans ses chroniques de politique étrangère.

43 Pour la période qui commence alors, l'étude de base est celle de R. Ehni, *op. cit.* [voir note 6].

44 *Bulletin de l'Association suisse pour une SdN,* 1944. 22:90, No. 5, 1944.

45 Paul Guggenheim, *Völkerbund, Dumbarton Oaks und die schweizerische Neutralität.* Zürich und New York, Europaverlag, 1945.

46 William E. Rappard, *Perspectives d'après-guerre.* Glaris, Eduard Tschudi, 1944. – "Dumbarton Oaks et nous", "*La Suisse*-Annuaire national", éditée par la Nouvelle Société Helvétique, année 16, 1945. – p. 7–25.

47 Outre la littérature générale, P. Favre, *La Suisse après la Deuxième Guerre mondiale – 1944/1946 – Politique extérieure et opinion publique.* Fribourg, Mémoire Lettres, 1979. Dans une déclaration au Conseil national en 1944, le démissionnaire n'avait pas exclu l'adhésion de la Suisse à la nouvelle SdN. *Bulletin sténographique officiel du Conseil National.* 1944. – p. 480–489.

48 Sur ce point voir Edgar Bonjour, *La neutralité suisse. Synthèse de son histoire.* Neuchâtel, Editions de la Baconnière, 1979. – p. 224–228. R. Ehni, *op. cit.* [voir note 6], p. 10–40.

49 Le protocole de la séance de la Délégation est utilisé par Favre, *op. cit.* [voir note 47], p. 66–69.

50 Le Parti suisse du Travail, d'allégeance communiste, en est une. Ses organes, *Vorwärts* et *Vie ouvrière* condamnent la neutralité, un exemple dans le numéro du 12 avril 1945.

51 R. Ehni, *op. cit.* [voir note 6], p. 32–36.

52 *Bulletin de l'Association pour une SdN,* v. 23, avril 1945.

53 *Bulletin sténographique officiel du Conseil National,* 1945. – p. 250–252.

54 Par exemple, le *Journal de Genève* du 27 juin 1945.

55 *Bulletin de l'Association pour une SdN,* v. 23, novembre 1945, p. 107.

56 P. Favre, *op. cit.* [voir note 47], p. 114 citant le rapport de la commission.

57 P. Gerbet, V. Y. Ghebali et M. R. Mouton, *op. cit.* [voir note 36], p. 164–166.

58 Rapport du Conseil fédéral à l'Assemblée fédérale sur la XXIe session de l'Assemblée de la Société des Nations du 19 avril 1946. *Feuille fédérale* 98: 1177–1201, II, 1946.

59 Le cas est évoqué dans un Message concernant le statut juridique de l'ONU et de ses organisations spécialisées, daté du 28 juillet 1955. *Feuille fédérale* 2, p. 423, 1955.

60 *ibid.* p. 416. R. Ehni, *op. cit.* [voir note 6], p. 107–111.

La Suisse et Radio Nations

ANTOINE FLEURY
Université de Genève

S'il est une affaire qui reflète bien les attitudes des autorités suisses à l'égard de la Société des Nations, leur changement de comportement à son sujet et d'appréciation de sa fonction au gré de la conjoncture internationale, c'est le projet et la création d'une station radiotélégraphique au service de la nouvelle organisation mondiale. Dès le départ, le gouvernement suisse a été concerné par la réalisation d'une telle entreprise d'une façon toute particulière du seul fait que la station en question devait être établie sur son territoire. A ce titre, aucun autre gouvernement n'a eu à se préoccuper de cet instrument de la SdN d'une manière aussi intense. Sa mise en oeuvre a constitué pour la Suisse – mais aurait sans doute suscité un problème analogue à tout autre pays qui l'eût assumée – un véritable test pour sa conception des devoirs qui lui incombaient en tant qu'Etat, siège de la SdN; elle a révélé en outre l'importance que le gouvernement fédéral attachait à l'institution genevoise par rapport à sa politique générale.

I. Origine du premier projet d'un poste radiotélégraphique et son abandon

Dans le jaillissement des idées les plus grandioses et parfois utopiques qui accompagna la naissance de la SdN, un projet de doter la future organisation de la paix mondiale d'un instrument de diffusion et de communication de ses idées et de ses activités fut avancé par des membres de la délégation américaine à la Conférence de la Paix, à Paris. Le Colonel House qui s'occupait activement du siège de la SdN s'enquit dès mars 1919 auprès de William Rappard, délégué officieux du Conseil fédéral à la Conférence de la Paix, de la possibilité d'ériger en Suisse une station radioélectrique à la proximité des terrains où s'installera la SdN.[1]

Toutefois avant que le projet ne puisse être poursuivi, deux conditions devaient être remplies au préalable. D'abord que la Suisse soit choisie comme siège de la SdN – ce qui fut acquis en un premier temps le 10 avril 1919 à la commission chargée de préparer le Pacte, et définitivement à la Conférence de la Paix le 28 avril qui fixa dans l'article 7 du Pacte le siège de la SdN à Genève. Ensuite que le Conseil fédéral accepte le principe d'une telle installation sur son territoire. Or, avant même que l'acquisition du siège ne fût définitive, le Conseil fédéral s'était empressé d'acquiescer aux désirs formulés par House. Dans sa séance du 5 avril 1919, il accepte – simultanément à l'octroi de l'exterritoritalité aux terrains destinés à la SdN, le projet de l'installation d'une station radiotélégraphique[2] non sans avoir examiné la compatibilité de ce projet avec la convention de La Haye de 1907 sur les droits et les devoirs des neutres en cas de guerre terrestre, qui dans son article trois interdit la création et l'utilisation en territoire neutre de stations radiotélégraphiques à fins exclusivement militaires. Convaincu que la station de la SdN ne sera pas édifiée à des fins exclusivement militaires, le Conseil fédéral n'en est pas moins conscient qu'en temps de guerre les Etats de la SdN pourraient s'en servir, ce qui serait préjudiciable à la neutralité suisse. Mais, argumente le Conseil fédéral, puisqu'il s'agira de guerre collective de la SdN, la neutralité s'en trouvera forcément modifiée dans le sens d'un traitement différentiel de la part de la Suisse des parties en guerre.

La déduction qu'on peut tirer de cette interprétation du nouveau statut de la neutralité de la Suisse au sein de la SdN, c'est qu'en mars-avril 1919, le gouvernement fédéral voulait éviter à tout prix de dresser des obstacles au moment où il déployait toutes ses énergies à obtenir quelque chose de beaucoup plus important: la confirmation par les Puissances du choix de Genève comme siège de la SdN.[3] Car, comme l'a dit Georges Clemenceau á Gustave Ador, on pouvait considérer »le choix de Genève comme assurant la neutralité de la Suisse.«[4]

Dans l'esprit des dirigeants helvétiques, il n'y avait pas lieu, en l'occurrence, de dresser l'inventaire de toutes les conséquences qui résulteraient pour la Suisse de l'installation éventuelle d'une station de radio sur son territoire; d'ailleurs elles ne pourraient être identifiées qu' à la suite de l'arrangement qui interviendra entre la SdN et l'Etat-hôte. Aussi l'étude de l'installation d'une station radiotélégraphique est-elle poursuivie tant du côté américain que du côté suisse. Déjà en avril 1919, le Colonel House envoie à Rappard l'homme appelé à être la cheville ouvrière de l'entreprise, un certain M. Rogers »qui, en temps ordinaire s'occupe . . . à la fois d'information et de publicité d'une part, et de télégraphie avec ou sans fil de l'autre«.[5] Rogers fait part de l'intérêt de la Ligue, selon les vues du gouvernement américain »d'établir en Suisse une station de radiotélégraphie munie d'appareils assez puissants pour lui permettre d'être en contact avec le monde entier«. Car,poursuit-il, »dans l'idée du Président Wilson, il serait extrêmement important, pour le développement de la SdN et pour l'avenir pacifique de l'humanité, que Genève devînt, en partie grâce à cette station de radiotélégraphie, le centre mondial d'informations en matière politique internationale«. Rogers propose à Rappard de prier les autorités suisses d'adresser au gouvernement américain une invitation pour deux ou trois experts qui viendraient en Suisse et se mettraient en rapport avec les hauts fonctionnaires des télégraphes afin de procéder avec eux aux reconnaissances nécessaires. Il précise en outre que l'établissement de la station »serait fait aux frais et risques du gouvernement américain, qui serait ensuite disposé à le céder, à des conditions à débattre, soit au gouvernement suisse, soit à la Ligue des Nations«.[6]

Les propositions pressantes du délégué américain incitent le Département politique fédéral à solliciter immédiatement l'avis des départements concernés.[7] Si les autorités fédérales déclarent qu'il ne sied guère, après que la Suisse a tant lutté pour obtenir le siège de la SdN, de faire des objections au projet américain, elles signalent néanmoins la nécessité de bien mesurer les implications qui pourraient en résulter; ainsi le Chef du Département militaire fédéral, Camille Décoppet, estime que cette station devra être placée sous le contrôle des autorités suisses et que pour des raisons militaires, il ne saurait être question d'accorder l'exterritorialité à cette station.[8] Pour sa part, le Département des Postes ... suggère la construction d'une telle station aux frais de la Suisse.[9]

En dépit de ces réserves, le Conseil fédéral décide le 2 août 1919 de poursuivre la discussion avec les Américains puisque ce sont eux qui insistent; il charge Rappard qui se rend à Londres de dire au Colonel House que la Suisse est prête à accueillir les experts américains et qu'elle reste ouverte aux solutions envisagées. En fait, dès l'été 1919, les autorités suisses expriment leur préférence pour une station suisse qui serait mise à disposition de la SdN,[10] mais elles hésitent quant à l'opportunité d'exprimer leur point de vue à ce sujet tant que le projet américain ne se précise pas davantage.

Dans l'intervalle, en effet, l'intérêt américain pour le projet en question a considérablement diminué. Devant les réticences du Sénat américain à accepter le Pacte, le Colonel House confie à Rappard que le gouvernement du Président Wilson a momentanément intérêt à ne pas trop s'engager dans la mise en œuvre de la SdN; c'est la raison pour laquelle il a renoncé pour l'instant à envoyer une mission d'experts en Suisse. De fait, les experts ne viendront jamais, car le refus américain de ratifier le Pacte a privé la SdN naissante des idées et des ressources qui avaient si magistralement contribué à la propulser à l'issue de la guerre.

Si l'abandon du projet américain procura un évident soulagement aux autorités suisses, celles-ci n'en pensèrent pas moins que l'idée d'une station radio sera reprise tôt ou tard, qu'il fallait par conséquent s'y préparer, notamment du point de vue de la neutralité.[11] Ainsi dans son *Message à l'Assemblée fédérale concernant la question de l'accession de la Suisse à la SdN* du 4 août 1919,[12] le Conseil fédéral admet que »l'établissement du siège en Suisse entraînera aussi, très probablement, l'installation d'une station radio-télégraphique sur notre territoire. Car il est d'une grande importance pour la SdN, d'avoir un service de nouvelles bien organisé et indépendant« (P. 52).

En fait, le projet était quasi mort-né. Si des particuliers, notamment à Genève, ont occasionnellement avancé des propositions, soit aux autorités suisses soit à la SdN,[13] il faudra attendre plusieurs années avant que l'idée ne soit reprise au sein de la SdN.

Du côté suisse, pourtant, on ne va pas rester inactif. Que l'on étudie l'origine de *Radio-Suisse*[14] ou l'état des télécommunications dans notre pays au début des années vingt,[15] on constate le coup de fouet qu'a donné aux milieux suisses concernés l'arrivée de la SdN à Genève et le défi que les autorités helvétiques ont dû relever pour lui procurer les moyens de communications adéquats. Si, dès la 1ère assemblée de la SdN en novembre 1920, la société britannique *Marconi* a réalisé des performances, en se servant d'installations provisoires, afin d'assurer la diffusion à travers le monde des travaux de la SdN, une solution de continuité s'imposait.

Dans le souci d'éviter toute critique des prestations offertes par la Suisse en faveur du bon fonctionnement de la SdN, le gouvernement fédéral encourage la création d'une *Société suisse de radiotélégraphie* qui aura la concession pour l'ensemble du pays; c'est ainsi qu'est née le 11 mars 1921, la *Marconi-Radio-Station, S. A.* avec siège à Berne; la raison sociale de cette société ne sera modifiée qu'en 1928, sous le nom de *Radio-Suisse, S. A.* Ce nouvel arrangement entre les autorités suisses et la grande firme britannique qui annonçait le développement des télécommunications entre la Suisse et l' étranger intéressa vivement la SdN. En tout cas, son Secrétaire général, le britannique Drummond se réjouit dans une lettre qu'il adresse le 17 mars 1921 au Conseiller fédéral Haab, Chef du Département fédéral des Postes et des Chemins de fer, de la promesse d'un service plus régulier entre Genève et l'extérieur; il se permet en outre de préciser: »bien que la question n'ait pas été discutée d'une manière officielle, on a fréquemment envisagé, dans des entretiens privés entre gens qui s'intéressent aux communications, la possibilité de créer un jour une station de télégraphie sans fil propre à la Société. Cette idée ne me paraît pas réalisable, mais j'estime que nous devons songer à toutes les éventualités: en effet, plus de la moitié des Membres de la Société se trouve hors d'Europe, et une puissante station TSF, plus puissante que n'en serait sans doute disposée à créer une compagnie commerciale, peut devenir absolument nécessaire pour la Société«.[16] Dans sa réponse, le Conseiller fédéral Haab reconnaît explicitement que dans l'accord avec Marconi »il a été tenu compte dans une large mesure des intérêts du service d' information de la SdN«.[17]

Et de fait, pendant toutes les années vingt, les administrations et les milieux suisses concernés par les communications ne vont plus cesser de travailler à doter la Suisse d'un instrument de communications qu'exigeaient les tâches exceptionnelles qui incombaient à l'Etat, siège de la SdN. Un défi était à tenir face aux efforts des grandes compagnies étrangères de télécommunications qui s'évertuaient à tirer parti du forum international sans égal que représentait Genève. Mais, le dévelopement continu et approprié des télécommunications suisses – tant en fonction des besoins propre du pays et de la SdN que des innovations techniques en constante évolution-semblait devoir satisfaire les utilisateurs internationaux. Mais c'est un autre défi qu'auront à relever les autorités de la Confédération!

II. A la recherche d'un instrument de communications sûr entre la SdN et ses Membres

C'est dans le cadre même des activités de la SdN que l'organisation de communications sûres et rapides est à nouveau évoquée. C'est notamment le Comité de la SdN, chargé des travaux préparatoires relatifs à la réduction des armements, qui se préoccupe dès 1925 de l'ensemble du problème relatif aux principales communications intéressant la SdN en période de crise.[18] Il s'agit en particulier de pouvoir assurer aussi bien la convocation rapide du Conseil que »les relations de toute nature entre les Membres de la Société intéressés, le Conseil, le Secrétaire général et les missions qui pourraient être envoyées par le Conseil«. A ce propos, le Conseil venait d'entendre la commission d'enquête sur le différend grécobulgare; elle recommandait »qu'il y aurait lieu d'envisager que des facilités spéciales de transmission et de transit fussent accordées aux gouvernements et au Secrétariat de la SdN en cas de danger de guerre, en particulier l'emploi de la TSF«.[19]

La suggestion allait être entendue. Le 8 décembre 1926, le Conseil de la SdN invite la Commission consultative et technique des communications et du transit »à engager immédiatement, en collaboration avec le Secrétaire général, en vue de présenter un rapport au Conseil à la date la plus rapprochée possible, les études nécessaires pour que la Société puisse avoir à sa disposition une station radiotélégraphique à elle suffisamment puissante lui permettant de communiquer, par ses propres moyens, avec le plus grand nombre possible d'Etats membres de la Société«.[20] La dite commission va se mettre au travail sans tarder; elle dépose le 10 septembre 1927 son premier rapport au Conseil.[21] A son avis, la tâche la plus importante qui incombera à cette future station serait d'émettre et de recevoir en temps de crise les télégrammes et d'assurer leur réception dans les divers pays. Face à cette intention manifeste des instances de la SdN d'établir une station radiotélégraphique à proximité du siège, on va assister à une réaction en chaîne dans les milieux suisses concernés.

Dans un premier temps, on se montre sceptique au sujet de la réalisation d'un projet aussi ambitieux et aussi coûteux pour la SdN. Mais afin de parer à toute éventualité, les autorités suisses doivent se préparer; désormais, il s'agit pour elles qu'elles arrivent à prendre de vitesse les initiatives de la SdN de manière à éviter l'installation d'une station indépendante sur territoire suisse; éventualité que le gouvernement fédéral estime ne pas pouvoir tolérer. En l'occurrence, plutôt que de devoir heurter de front le Conseil ou l'Assemblée de la SdN à la suite d'une décision qui entérinerait la création d'une station, mieux vaut évaluer toutes les possibilités qui s'offrent à la Suisse pour courcircuiter le projet en cours, par exemple en allant au-devant des désirs et des besoins exprimés par la SdN.

A ce sujet, la documentation consultée montre que l'inspiration des attitudes et des mesures à prendre n'émanait pas tant des sphères gouvernementales, mais surtout de la direction de la *Station Radio Marconi S. A.* Son directeur, Fritz Rothen, fixe en effet dans un mémoire du 26 février 1927,[22] l'articulation des principaux arguments dont la Suisse doit se prévaloir dans cette affaire. Tout d'abord, il évalue les intentions et les besoins de la SdN, c'est-à-dire la préoccupation, justifiée politiquement, de disposer de moyens de communications sûrs en temps de crise. Cela est légitime et souhaitable; la Suisse ne doit nullement s'y opposer et d'autant moins si les mesures prises dans cette intention peuvent contribuer à éviter la guerre. Mais, interroge Rothen, quelles seraient les activités de la station de la SdN en temps normal? Le trafic du Secrétariat – à part les périodes de conférences et de sessions de l'Assemblée – n'est pas suffisant pour justifier l'installation d'une station par la SdN elle-même. En revanche, les besoins des institutions internationales peuvent être pleinement satisfaits par la station de Berne que la société Marconi continue à équiper et à développer. En tout cas, estime Rothen, la Suisse doit rester attentive à l'égard de ce projet; elle ne peut s'y opposer, mais elle doit faire comprende à la SdN les difficultés et les inconvénients d'une station indépendante et surtout lui signifier tous les efforts que la Suisse est en train de fournir et qu'elle apportera dans l'avenir pour répondre aux exigences de la SdN.

Pour sa part, le chef du Département politique fédéral, Giuseppe Motta, pense que la Suisse devra intervenir auprès de la commission chargée de préparer le projet; il s'étonne d'ailleurs qu'aucune autorité n'ait été invitée à y envoyer un expert qui aurait pu d'emblée exposer le point de vue de la Confédération, qui est bien le premier Etat concerné par ce projet. A son avis, la question sera soumise tôt ou tard à l'Assemblée de la SdN; or, »pour ne pas être pris au dépourvu, il s'agirait maintenant d'étudier, sous toutes ses faces, à tête reposée, mais sans perdre de temps, une question sur laquelle nous pouvons être appelés à nous prononcer à plus ou moins bref délai«.[23] Enfin, Motta formule la question qui s'impose, en dépit des avis sceptiques de certains au sujet de la réalisation du projet: »La Suisse peut-elle autoriser la création sur son territoire d'une station radiotélégraphique soustraite à tout contrôle de sa part et réservée à l'usage exclusif de la SdN?«[24] Il reprend finalement les arguments qui avaient déjà été avancés en 1919 au sujet de la difficile compatibilité d'une telle station avec la neutralité en regard de la convention de La Haye de 1907; il se demande si »les exigences de notre armée et de la défense nationale autoriseraient la présence sur notre sol, d'une station radiotélégraphique dont les émissions ne seraient pas contrôlées«.[25]

C'est dans une note du 5 août 1927 que le Département politique fédéral fait connaître sa position au Secrétariat de la SdN. Faisant sienne la préoccupation d'ensemble formulée par le Conseil de la SdN, dans sa résolution du 8 décembre 1926, le gouvernement fédéral prend volontiers l'engagement d'assurer, pour sapart, par tous les moyens à sa disposition, »un fonctionnement rapide et efficace des organismes de la SdN en cas de crise«.[26] La note énumère tout ce que la Suisse fait pour améliorer les liaisons ferroviaires et aériennes, elle décrit l'état des communications télégraphiques, radiotélégraphiques et téléphoniques ainsi que les possibilités de développement dans ce domaine; mais elle n'aborde pas directement la question d'une station radiotélégraphique indépendante, qui serait construite par la SdN. Au lieu de parler de la question du statut de cette station, les Suisses mettent l'accent sur les services réels qu'ils rendent et sont capables de rendre encore à la SdN. Tant que le projet ne prend pas des formes plus précises, ils en restent là. Ce n'est que lorsqu'il prendra forme qu'il conviendra, estiment-ils, de faire connaître la véritable position de la Suisse. Ce moment ne va pas tarder.

Le 26 septembre 1927, l'Assemblée de la SdN félicite le Conseil d'avoir mis rapidement à l'étude la question des communications en cas de crise et le prie de poursuivre ces études, »notamment en ce qui concerne les communications téléphoniques entre le siège de la Société et les diverses capitales, l'identification des avions effectuant des transports intéressant la SdN en temps de crise, l'établissement d'une station radiotélégraphique au siège de la Société, l'aménagement d'un terrain d'atterrissage, etc. . . .«

Placé ainsi devant la certitude que la SdN veut assurer des communications en cas de crise, le gouvernement helvétique ne peut plus rester sur la réserve. C'est encore le directeur de la *Station-Radio Marconi SA*, Rothen, qui prend les devants.[27] A son avis, la Suisse doit éviter d'être placée devant un fait accompli. Le projet de la SdN représente un double danger. Tout d'abord, la station sera dans la zone exterritoriale, gérée par un personnel international; elle échappera donc à tout contrôle suisse. Le chef de la section des communications et du transit de la SdN, le français Robert Haas le lui a confirmé. Deuxièmement, cette station internationale représentera une concurrence certaine pour l'administration suisse des PTT et pour la station suisse. Aussi Rothen suggère-t-il au Conseil fédéral d'empêcher par tous les moyens que ce projet se réalise. Pour sa part, il propose un renforcement de la station suisse et de ses prestations, en la dotant d'un nouvel émetteur et d'un bureau d'exploitation à Genève.[29] Pourtant Rothen se demande si ces mesures suffiront à convaincre les instances de la SdN que la station suisse – dont l'émetteur est situé à Münchenbuchsee et le récepteur à Riedern près de Berne – offre toutes les garanties de fonctionnement au service de la SdN et qu'il est par conséquent inutile d'établir une station indépendante à Genève. Peut-être conviendrait-il d'édifier une station émettrice de la société suisse dans les environs de Genève si cela pouvait aider à convaincre les instances internationales qui auraient ainsi sous leurs yeux une station à disposition. Placés de cette façon devant le fait accompli d'une station suisse à proximité de la SdN, ses dirigeants seraient sans doute dissuadés de construire une deuxième station. Certes, l'édification d'une station suisse dans les environs de Genève est financièrement coûteuse et la société *Marconi* suisse ne peut assumer tous les frais qu'elle occasionnerait. Mais, si pour des raisons politiques, il faut construire cette station qui doit empêcher la construction d'une station internationale, c'est aux autorités de faire un effort financier approprié, conclut Rothen.

Les propositions du directeur de la Marconi sont discutées dans une séance interdépartamentale de l'administration fédérale, le 10 novembre 1927;[28] Motta la préside. On y décide l'envoi d'une note à la SdN, disant que »le projet . . . ne présente pas seulement des inconvénients d'ordre technique, mais soulève également des problèmes de nature juridique et militaire«. Cette note envoyée le 13 janvier 1928[30] reprend aussi les arguments avancés par Rothen en faveur des prestations satisfaisantes fournies par la société Marconi; elle suggère enfin l'établissement de garanties spéciales de fonctionnement des communications qu'assurerait la station suisse dans les périodes de crise.

Quelle va être la réaction des instances concernées de la SdN devant ce qui est à la fois une offre généreuse et une réserve? Au sein de la commission consultative et technique, la thèse et la démonstration helvétiques -notamment les économies que la solution suisse apporterait à la SdN- marquent rapidement des points. Dans sa séance du 27 février au 2 mars 1928, la commission pose toute une série de conditions pour le cas où la SdN décidait à entrer dans les vues suisses:

1. la station suisse proposée devrait pouvoir fournir toutes les prestations techniques demandées à la station de la SdN prévue.
2. la SdN devrait pouvoir en tout temps requérir l'adaptation de la station à tous les progrès techniques.
3. la station doit être proche du siège
4. la station doit fonctionner en permanence et comme une station d'intérêt international: les considérations d'intérêt général doivent l'emporter sur les considérations de rendement commercial
5. le Secrétaire général dès qu'il l'estime nécessaire, en temps de crise, doit pouvoir mettre la station à la disposition de la SdN et la placer sous son contrôle exclusif.

Enfin, la commission admet que si de tels arrangements pouvaient aboutir, il en résulterait pour la SdN des sacrifices financiers importants, mais moindres que ceux de la construction d'un poste indépendant.[31]

Comment en est-on arrivé, pratiquement en une séance, à cette ébauche de solution jusqu'alors inédite et si contraire aux désirs des promoteurs du projet au sein de la SdN? Tout d'abord, on trouve parmi ces derniers avant tout des Français qui n'étaient pas désintéressés par l'affaire. Depuis des années, la Compagnie générale de TSF française faisait sentir sa présence à Genève, notamment lors des assemblées. Par ailleurs, le chef de la section des communications, Haas, semble s'être fait un devoir de réaliser cette station indépendante, en tout cas, c'est lui qui s'y accrochera le plus longtemps; il avait même eu l'idée qu'au cas où la Suisse ferait des difficultés pour lui accorder l'exterritorialité, il serait possible de trouver un terrain en France voisine.[32]

Mais il n'y a pas que les Français que se soient montrés intéressés à la construction d'une station de prestige à Genève. D'autres ne le furent pas moins. Aussi les Suisses, conscients des rivalités entre grandes sociétés européennes, voire américaines, ne restent-ils pas inactifs. Les liens entre la SA Marconi, Berne et la grande société britannique ne sont-ils pas intimes? Est-ce pour les camoufler quelque peu qu'on décide justement en 1928 de changer la raison sociale en *Radio-Suisse, SA*, modification qui n'empêche d'ailleurs nullement la présence de délégués de la Marconi au sein du conseil d'administration de la société suisse.[33] Des signes évidents de cette concurrence entre firmes spécialisées dans les télécommunications on en trouve dans certaines démarches dont parle le directeur de Radio-Suisse. Rothen mentionne ainsi celles qu'aurait entreprises la firme britannique Marconi auprès du gouvernement de Londres afin que son délégué à la commission de la SdN intervienne contre le projet d'une station indépendante. Rothen indique aussi la conversation qu'il a eue dans le même sens avec le délégué allemand et il suggère que le gouvernement italien soit informé de la position suisse: Mussolini, pense-t-il, sera tout disposé à intervenir quand on lui dira que ce sont les Français qui poussent à la création d'un poste radio-émetteur de la SdN.[34] Enfin, ce qui lui paraît rassurant, c'est qu'on lui a fait savoir que le Secrétaire général de la SdN, Drummond, serait personnellement opposé au projet.

Dans ces conditions, il n'y a rien d'étonnant de voir le délégué britannique au sein de la commission consultative, le colonel Lee, reprendre à son compte les arguments avancés par la Suisse. Pourtant, la position britannique ne suffit pas à modifier la proposition initiale du Conseil de la SdN, c'est plutôt au niveau des modalités concrètes de la réalisation du projet que les avis de la Grand-Bretagne seront favorables à la proposition suisse. Cependant, dans le rapport que la commission adresse au Conseil et aux Membres de la SdN, le 14 mars 1928, il est encore surtout question du profil général de la future station, sans préjuger des conditions de sa construction. Cette station, pour remplir les tâches que la SdN lui confiera, doit comprendre »un poste d'émission à ondes courtes, permettant d'émettre à la fois sur deux longueurs d'ondes, et complété, le cas échéant, par un poste d'émission à ondes moyennes«, qui »serait techniquement en état, de l'avis unanime des experts, de donner de très bonnes relations avec tous les postes du monde«.[35] Le coût de construction avec les terrains a été estimé à 1 250 000.– francs suisses et les dépenses annuelles de fonctionnement à 200 000.– frcs, tandis que les recettes tourneraient autour des 100 à 150 000.– frcs par année au début.

Ayant pris connaissance de ces données, le Conseil de la SdN décide le 8 juin 1928 de porter à l'ordre du jour de la prochaine assemblée »la création d'une station de TSF de la SdN«.[36] Désormais, le projet prend forme; les autorités suisses doivent se hâter si elles veulent éviter la construction d'une station qui leur a paru trop longtemps utopique.

A défaut de pouvoir agir au niveau de la commission consultative au sein de laquelle domine le chef de la Section des communications et du transit, partisan de la réalisation de ce qui avait été une idée de son compatriote Paul-Boncour, le gouvernment fédéral s'adresse directement au Secrétaire général. Un haut fonctionnaire helvétique de la Section politique du Secrétariat, Jean-Daniel de Montenach servira d'intermédiaire. Grâce à lui, Drummond va être directement informé de la solution suisse: à savoir la construction aux frais de la Confédération d'une nouvelle station qui pourrait s'appeler *Radio-Suisse* et qui serait distincte de la *Marconi Radio-Station SA* – en fait, celle-ci changea simplement de dénomination le 10 mai 1928 – et qui serait à la disposition de la SdN; mais en échange de cette offre, la SdN renoncera à la construction d'une autre station. La seule question qu'il conviendra d'approfondir, en cas de prise en considération de la proposition suisse, c'est celle de l'utilisation de la station suisse par la SdN, en temps de crise, sans que cela n'implique des conséquences contraires à la neutralité.[37]

Le gouvernement suisse se déclare prêt à entrer immédiatement en discussion avec la SdN, offre qu'accepte le Secrétaire général qui estime d'emblée que les propositions suisses pourraient aboutir à une solution très satisfaisante.[38] Mais son collaborateur, le chef de la Section des communications, chargée de l'étude de ce projet avancé par le Conseil de la SdN réagit tout différemment. Prenant position au sujet des propositions suisses transmises par Montenach, celles-ci lui paraissent »renverser la situation«.[39] A son avis, il n'y a que le solution envisagée officiellement par la SdN qui doit être l'objet d'un examen; les propositions de Berne présentent quelque chose de nouveau qui n'entre pas dans le cadre de la mission confiée par le Conseil de la SdN à la commission consultative. »Si les Autorités suisses estiment pour des raisons politiques cette solution impossible, elles doivent le dire d'abord, expliquer pourquoi, et prendre la responsabilité de leurs objections politiques devant le Conseil et devant l'Assemblée; mais il est impossible de traiter en quelque sorte par prétérition une question soumise déjà à de longues études et ayant encore récemment fait l'objet de demandes de solution de la part du comité de sécurité et de la commission du Désarmement«. – »Je ne crois pas, en conséquence, que le secrétaire général puisse se prêter à une conversation sur une solution autre que celle envisagée jusqu'à présent par le Conseil, l'Assemblée et la Commission du Désarmement, s'il ne peut pas connaître les objections politiques qu'aurait le gouvernement suisse à cette solution«. En tout cas, toute solution, à son avis, doit contenir le principe »que la station quelle que soit l'autorité qui la construise ou qui en soit propriétaire, doit en temps de crise être entièrement indépendante de tout contrôle autre que celui du secrétariat et de la SdN«. Ce principe conclut Haas est une condition qui ne peut pas être discutée comme le suggère le gouvernement suisse. »A défaut de l'acceptation de cette condition, la seule alternative possible est alors la construction d'une station par la Société elle-même«.

Si Haas a sans doute raison quant au fond, il a totalement sous-évalué au départ, notamment dans les études préliminaires, la position du gouvernement suisse sur le territoire duquel la station serait érigée. C'est ce que lui donne à entendre son collègue Montenach.[40] Celui-ci relève l'identité des questions essentielles quelle que soit la solution définitive. »Si la station est construite et gérée par le gouvernement suisse, il n'est point douteux que la SdN aura des conditions à formuler. Si, au contraire, la station est construite et gérée par la SdN, le gouvernement suisse jugera utile d'obtenir des garanties en vertu d'un droit de souveraineté qu'il est difficile de lui contester«. Quoiqu'il en soit, fait encore remarquer Montenach, la Suisse restera fidèle à son devoir d'Etat-hôte tel qu'il avait été précisé le 11 février 1920 à Londres par Lord Balfour »that if the permanent seat of the League of Nations were at Geneva, the League would be able to operate in full liberty and to make use of all the resources of which it might be in need«. Mais, pour sa part, la SdN doit respecter la neutralité militaire de la Suisse et c'est bien là l'aspect le plus délicat qu'implique l'installation sur son sol d'une station radio-électrique.

Ainsi, à la veille de la rencontre prévue entre les délégués du gouvernement fédéral et le Secrétariat, les questions de fond et les solutions possibles ont été ouvertement discutées entre les principaux intéressés. Mais, il faut constater que la solution suisse avancée à la dernière heure vient bousculer non seulement des projets déjà bien élaborés au sein de la SdN, mais aussi la procédure établie.

Aussi, n'est-il pas surprenant que c'est au plus haut niveau que la discussion va se poursuivre. Le 31 mai 1928, deux membres du gouvernement suisse se rendent à Genève, Motta, Chef du Département des Affaires étrangères et Haab, Chef du Département des Postes et des Chemins de fer, accompagné du Directeur général de l'administration des Télégraphes et des Postes, Reinhold Furrer; ils sont reçus par le Secrétaire général Drummond qui s'est entouré pour la circonstance de quelques hauts fonctionnaires de la SdN: Sugimura, Hiam et Montenach.[41] On notera l'absence justement de R. Haas, l'homme chargé de l'étude du projet.

Le Conseiller fédéral Motta qui expose le projet suisse de construire une station TSF voulue par la SdN, juge opportun d'envisager une solution qui tiendrait compte des préoccupations de la SdN et qui comporterait, tant pour elle que pour le gouvernement suisse des avantages indéniables. En échange des Services que rendrait la station TSF suisse à la SdN, l'administration suisse serait en droit d'attendre en retour quelques prestations de sa part, sous la forme d'une subvention déterminée par des services techniques compétents. En revanche, et cela est plus important, »le Conseil fédéral voudrait qu'il fût tenu compte, lors de l'utilisation de cette station en temps de crise, de la situation spéciale de la Suisse du point de vue de sa neutralité militaire«. Mais poursuit Motta faisant montre d'un bel optimisme: »La situation politique s'améliore chaque année et on peut espérer que les périodes de crise auront un caractère de plus en plus exceptionnel«. Et que »dans ces conditions, la meilleure solution paraîtrait être celle qui, étant la moins onéreuse en temps normal, comporterait cependant les mêmes avantages en temps de crise«. En tout cas, il faut que le fonctionnement de cette station ne puisse placer le gouvernement fédéral dans une situation incompatible avec ses devoirs de neutralité. Aussi, »ce que la Suisse s'estime en droit d'obtenir, conclut Motta, c'est d'avoir l'assurance la plus formelle que la neutralité de la Suisse ne saurait être mise en cause en cas de crise par la libre utilisation de la station par la SdN«.

Prenant la parole, Drummond revient sur le point essentiel de toute l'affaire dès l'origine: assurer l'entière indépendance des communications de la Société en temps de crise. Il rappelle que dans ce cas la station puisse fonctionner sous l'autorité exclusive de la SdN. Et qu'en l'occurrence, l'idée d'un certain contrôle des autorités suisses sur l'usage de la station en temps de crise est inacceptable. »Par contre, il serait aisé de donner à la Suisse l'assurance que l'utilisation de cette station par la Société ne saurait en aucun cas compromettre la neutralité suisse«. Invitant les autorités suisses à faire preuve d'une nécessaire flexibilité, il leur déclare que la SdN préfère une station chère, mais indépendante qu'une station peu coûteuse pour elle et dont l'indépendance ne serait pas assurée.

Ceci dit, Drummond propose la solution suivante: »Lorsque, en temps de crise, la station se trouverait mise entièrement à la disposition de la Société et fonctionnerait sous son autorité, les autorités fédérales pourraient détacher un observateur qui, sans doute, n'aurait pas le droit de s'opposer à l'envoi de messages ni de les censurer, mais qui aurait pour tâche de renseigner régulièrement l'administration fédérale«. Par ailleurs, la Suisse devrait solliciter une déclaration des Membres de la Société à teneur de laquelle l'utilisation de la station ne saurait en aucune manière être jugée incompatible avec la neutralité; pour sa part, le gouvernement suisse devrait préciser la nature des garanties qu'il souhaite obtenir à ce sujet. En conclusion, le Secrétaire général indique les principaux points du mémoire que le gouvernement fédéral devrait porter à la connaissance des diverses instances de la SdN.

La préparation de ce mémoire va prendre quelques mois; le 21 août 1928, le Département politique fédéral est enfin en mesure de transmettre le texte définitif à la SdN;[42] il contient un projet de statut de la station en temps normal où elle serait propriété suisse avec utilisation prioritaire pour les besoins de la SdN, et en temps de crise où la station passerait sous la gestion de la SdN, celle-ci supportant les frais qui en résulteraient. Quant à la note remise simultanément, elle signale le côté politique de toute l'affaire, notamment: »Un Etat ne saurait ignorer donc l'activité déployée par une installation de ce genre sur son territoire, cette activité pouvant avoir, dans des circonstances données, des répercussions dont il est impossible d'apprécier à l'avance la nature et la portée. Si le besoin qu'éprouve la SdN de disposer, en temps de crise, d'une station radiotélégraphique lui donnant toutes garanties de fonctionnement est des plus légitimes, il n'est pas moins légitime que le pays où s'installe cette station demande des garanties indispensables à la sauvegarde de sa souveraineté«. Sans oublier que »l'exploitation de stations radiotélégraphiques touche directement aux intérêts de la défense nationale«.

Prudence ou sens des engagements de longue durée! Quoi qu'il en soit, le gouvernement suisse sachant qu'il ne pouvait s'opposer à un projet voulu par la SdN doit convaincre non seulement que son contre-projet répond aux préoccupations de la SdN, mais encore que la Suisse a droit à des garanties pour son statut de neutralité tel qu'il a été reconnu par la déclaration de Londres du 13 février 1920.

Placés en septembre 1928 devant deux solutions, l'Assemblée de la SdN estime ne pas être en mesure de trancher définitivement; elle renvoie sa décision, pour complément d'information et pour une meilleure étude des conditions suisses, à la 10e Assemblée.

Si la prise en considération du projet suisse constitue un retournement déjà considérable des perspectives de départ, les desiderata, les précautions, les demandes de garanties que formulent les autorités suisses depuis bientôt une année et qui vont en s'accroissant depuis qu'elles ont obtenu un premier succès devant l'Assemblée en septembre 1928, tout cela semble dépasser la mesure. Du moins, c'est le sentiment qui se propage dans les milieux de la SdN, au point qu'un Eric Drummond, pourtant si bien disposé à l'égard de la proposition suisse, fait part à Motta, le ler mars 1929, de sa déception devant certaines attitudes helvétiques; il rappelle »qu'il a toujours été l'un des partisans les plus chaleureux et les plus convaincus du maintien du siège de la SdN à Genève. Il ne lui est venu qu'une seule fois un doute sur les avantages que présentait le choix d'un tel siège pour la SdN: ce fut en prenant connaissance de la lettre adressée au conseiller juridique du Secrétaire général en réponse à sa communication relative à la station radiotélégraphique. Cette réponse traduit une telle méfiance à l'égard du Secrétaire général et paraît inspirée de si grands doutes quant à la loyauté de ses actes et de ses sentiments qu'il n'en peut attribuer la teneur qu'à un malentendu«.[43]

En fait, le point litigieux qui reste à résoudre est celui de l'observateur suisse au sein de la station quand celle-ci passera sous contrôle de la SdN en temps de crise. Sur les responsabilités de cet observateur qui pourraient aller du droit de regard au droit de veto dans la transmission des messages, c'est encore Drummond qui suggère un compromis acceptable: le Conseil fédéral pourra chaque fois qu'il l'estimera nécessaire en appeler au Conseil de la SdN, mais le texte des communications officielles transmises par la station restera secret.

Ces bases d'accord une fois acquises de part et d'autre, les choses avancent. Dans sa séance du 9 mars 1929, le Conseil de la SdN[44] semble avoir déjà entériné la solution suisse; il recommande d'accepter en temps de crise la présence d'un observateur suisse qui aurait pour seule compétence de connaître l'origine et la destination des messages. Il recommande à la commission consultative de préparer un modus vivendi entre le gouvernement de Berne et la SdN. Durant tout l'été 1929, les négociations vont se poursuivre entre les autorités suisses et celles de la SdN.[45]

Finalement, ce sont trois solutions qui sont envisagées:

1. une station indépendante construite par la SdN et gérée par elle en tout temps. La Suisse n'en veut pas.
2. la solution dite mixte: la Suisse et la SdN équipent ensemble une station. En temps normal, c'est la Suisse qui administre et qui exploite. En temps de crise, la station passe sous contrôle de la SdN. Dans ce cas, le gouvernement suisse désire avoir un observateur dans la station et sollicite une déclaration des Membres de la SdN qui dégagerait la Suisse de toute responsabilité quant à l'usage de

la station. Cette solution serait l'expression de l'esprit de mutuelle confiance et du désir de collaboration entre la SdN et la Confédération.

3. la solution suisse: la station est entièrement équipée et exploitée par la Suisse en temps normal comme en temps de crise. Le gouvernement fédéral donnerait toutes les garanties à la SdN pour l'indépendance et la sécurité de ses communications. La SdN déléguerait un observateur dans la station. Cette solution a bien entendu la préférence de Berne; elle aurait l'avantage de ne rien coûter à la SdN et elle illustrerait l'aide que la Suisse accorde à son œuvre.

Tels sont les éléments qui sont soumis aux diverses commissions de la SdN à l'occasion de sa 10e Assemblée. La solution qui aura la préférence des délégués des Etats, ce sera la formule mixte. Dans son rapport du 21 septembre 1929,[46] René Cassin, président de la 3e Commission s'en explique. »La solution qui comporte l'exploitation du poste par la Société Radio-Suisse en temps normal et le passage sous la gestion exclusive de la SdN en temps de crise, offre actuellement des avantages sérieux de nature à orienter dans ce sens l'Assemblée . . . En résumé, conclut-il, la solution soumise . . . paraît, en tenant compte de l'indépendance de la SdN et de la situation particulière de la Suisse, concilier heureusement les intérêts en cause«. Et il estime que par cet arrangement, »la SdN sort consolidée disposant d'un poste de portée mondiale«.

La solution mixte est adoptée par l'Assemblée le 24 septembre 1929.

Cette étape franchie, il reste à négocier la mise en œuvre d'une solution qui fait appel à deux stratégies commerciales différentes. La Suisse a été prête à faire un sacrifice, en prenant à ses frais la construction d'une station radiotélégraphique, pour éviter une station indépendante concurrente. Elle offre en effet les terrains et les bâtiments, l'équipement d'un bureau central d'exploitation, l'installation non loin de Genève d'un émetteur à ondes moyennes à Prangins et d'une station réceptrice à Colovrex. Fritz Rothen, Directeur de la Radio-Suisse déclare ouvertement que »cette station n'aurait jamais été construite à Genève si nous n'avions pas eu à servir la SdN«.[47] »C'est parce que nous sommes des amis de la Ligue et nous considérons comme un privilège de faciliter sa mission que Radio-Suisse, conclut Rothen, s'est fait l'honneur d'établir le plus grand nombre possible de liaisons internationales«. En fin de compte, il se déclare heureux de collaborer avec la SdN à la construction d'une station qui doit satisfaire des besoins au-delà de ce qu'une station nationale eût pu assumer seule.

En effet, si la Suisse fournit une partie de l'équipement – l'émetteur à ondes moyennes – la SdN se charge de fournir à ses frais deux émetteurs de télégraphie et de radiophonie à ondes courtes, permettant d'assurer en toutes circonstances les liaisons avec toutes les parties du monde.

L'ensemble des arrangements et des conditions négocié entre les autorités suisses et la SdN figure dans deux textes signés le 21 mai 1930:[48]

a) un accord entre la SdN et le gouvernement suisse stipule les arrangements intervenus, les garanties mutuellement consenties: respect de la neutralité de la Confédération et dégagement de sa responsabilité en cas de crise d'une part et indépendance des communications pour la SdN en tout temps en dépit de la présence d'un observateur suisse dans la station en temps de crise d'autre part.

b) une convention entre la SdN et Radio-Suisse réglant toutes les questions de compétences, d'installation, d'administration et de partage des charges et bénéfices de l'entreprise.

L'arrangement est conclu pour une durée de dix ans. En septembre 1930, l'Assemblée de la SdN approuve un budget d'équipement à la charge de la SdN de 2 330 264.– francs suisses. Les travaux d'installation peuvent commencer.

Ici apparaît un autre aspect des raisons profondes du compromis intervenu en faveur de la solution mixte: c'est la possibilité d'une véritable contribution internationale à l'édification de *Radio-Nations:* celle-ci ne doit pas être de par sa vocation et sa dénomination l'œuvre d'une seule société. Elle doit être le reflet de la coopération technologique et industrielle au sein de la SdN. Aussi quatre grandes compagnies participent-elles à la construction: Bell Tel. Cpy., Marconi S. W. Cpy., Cie générale de TSF, Paris et Telefunken.

Sous cet angle, Radio-Suisse a acquis une expérience incomparable dans la concertation de l'ensemble des travaux et dans la connaissance des dernières performances technologiques des diverses sociétés qui ont concouru à cette installation qui coûta 2.45 millions de francs à la SdN et 1.3 millions à Radio-Suisse. En dépit de quelque retard dans le montage de certains équipements, la station a pu être inaugurée le 2 février 1932. Les autorités de la SdN invitèrent les Etats, les délégués, etc. à utiliser les services de Radio-Nations, car il dépendait d'eux que cette station souhaitable politiquement fût viable financièrement.

L'appel était en effet bien nécessaire; il sera peu efficace, car si en 1929–1930, on pouvait escompter un développement des activités de la SdN et de la coopération internationale, il n'en était déjà plus de même le jour de la mise en action de Radio-Nations. Dès son inauguration, la station accusa le contrecoup du déclin de la SdN. Certes, elle rendit quelques précieux services lors de la Conférence du Désarmement et dans l'affaire de Mandchourie notamment,[49] mais elle restera en déficit. Fort heureusement, le développement du secteur commercial va compenser quelque peu la faiblesse de l'apport de la SdN en messages émanant de ses services. Vers la fin des années trente Radio-Nations sert essentiellement aux télécommunications privées. Elle accroît considérablement ses recettes en transmettant des émissions en radiophonie pour le compte des grandes sociétés américaines – NBC, CBS, MBC – et de la société suisse de radiodiffusion.

A cette étape de la vie de Radio-Nations, la Suisse peut tout de même être satisfaite. Grâce à ses initiatives prises unilatéralement – la construction d'une station à ondes moyennes à Prangins dès 1929 – elle a pu éviter l'établissement d'une station internationale dont le contrôle lui aurait échappé. La solution mixte estime Rothen lui-même est »le maximum de ce que la Suisse pouvait espérer«,[50] étant donné les forces en présence, en particulier l'intérêt des sociétés françaises – Société française radioéléctrique – et allemandes – Telefunken – qui envisageaient par ce biais de concurrencer l'emprise de Marconi en Suisse.

Pour sa part, la SdN peut se déclarer satisfaite. Elle dispose tout près de son siège d'un instrument de communications capable de rivaliser avec les dernières performances des stations nationales de grands pays et d'une garantie d'utilisation en tout temps. C'est du moins dans cet esprit et dans cette perspective que fut inaugurée Radio-Nations. Mais à quelques brèves années de fructueuse coopération suisse-esdénienne allait succéder la mise à mort progressive non seulement de la SdN, mais aussi de sa station radiotélégraphique.

III. Le retour à la neutralité intégrale et l'avenir de Radio-Nations

Il n'est pas dans notre propos d'analyser ici l'évolution de l'attitude de la Suisse à l'égard de la SdN, ni d'expliquer les raisons de son progressif éloignement des engagements souscrits en 1919–1920, éloignement ou abandon qui aboutit, le 14 mai 1938 à la reconnaissance par le Conseil de la SdN du retour de la Suisse à sa neutralité intégrale.[51]

Dans ce contexte, la station Radio-Nations prend une signification tout autre que celle qu'on eût pu imaginer à la fin des années vingt. Aux yeux des responsables helvétiques, cette station apparaît, à la fin des années trente, comme une tache qui macule le drapeau restauré de la neutralité traditionnelle de la Confédération, et qu'il convient d'éliminer au plus vite si l'on désire que ce drapeau soit encore respecté par les deux grands voisins – le Reich de Hitler et l'Italie de Mussolini – qui ont juré la mort de la SdN.

En effet, dès le retrait italien de la SdN (11 décembre 1937) on se préoccupe sérieusement à Berne du retour à la neutralité intégrale et notamment des dangers que peut représenter Radio-Nations pour une politique de neutralité. Dans sa séance de janvier 1938, le Conseil d'administration de Radio-Suisse évoque déjà la chose et suppute les menaces qui pourraient effectivement résulter des émissions de Radio-Nations pour la neutralité en cas de véritables crises; éventualité qui impliquerait selon les accords de 1930 la mise de toute la station sous le contrôle de la SdN.[52] Or, le retour à la neutralité intégrale qu'est en train de préparer le Conseil fédéral[53] va placer les obligations découlant des arrangements de 1930 sous un jour tout-à-fait différent; ne serait-il pas indiqué, pense-t-on à Berne, de songer à dénoncer l'accord qui arrive à echéance en février 1942.

Ce qui est frappant dans cette affaire, c'est que les aspects politiques du statut de Radio-Nations semblent hautement préoccuper une instance »technique« – le conseil d'administration de Radio-Suisse – au point que comme dix ans auparavant, les suggestions sur la conduite à suivre n'émanent pas du Département politique, chargé en principe d' assumer la dimension politique des engagements pris par la Suisse envers la SdN, mais justement d'individus tels que Fritz Rothen très soucieux des conséquences politiques du statut de Radio-Nations. Cela ne veut pas dire que l'instance politique n'a pas perçu la chose. Ainsi, dans une prise de position au sujet des vues exprimées par les milieux de Radio-Suisse et du Département des Postes et des Chemins de fer, le chef de la diplomatie suisse, Motta signale que son Département »n'a pas perdu de vue la question des modifications à apporter au statut actuel de la station Radio-Nations lorsque nous aurons recouvré notre neutralité entière . . . Il nous est apparu cependant qu'il serait prématuré de soulever cette question dès maintenant. Elle ne ferait que compliquer notre tâche, qui est suffisamment difficile en ce moment . . . Aussi longtemps que notre position d'Etat neutre dans la SdN n'aura pas été clairement définie au point de vue politique, il serait assez peu opportun d'entreprendre une action parallèle dans le domaine technique. Le principe de la neutralité intégrale posé et reconnu, les conséquences suivront. Une des premières sera la revision de l'accord du 21 mai 1930«.[54]

Autrement dit, »techniciens« et »politiques« sont d'accord sur l'objectif: tôt ou tard, il faut couler Radio-Nations! Dans une notice du 9 avril 1938,[55] Camille Gorgé, le zélé collaborateur de Motta et l'homme de liaison du Département politique fédéral avec les milieux internationaux de Genève, analyse déjà les conséquences du retour à la neutralité pour le statut de Radio-Nations et les diverses possibilités de dénonciation de l'accord de 1930 ou de sa modification. Arguant du fait nouveau – le changement de statut de la Suisse au sein de la SdN – toute la situation juridique des arrangements de 1930 s'en trouve modifiée au point que la Confédération »n'est plus en état de se conformer aux obligations prévues par l'accord« et qu'en conséquence, elle peut se prévaloir de la clause »rebus sic stantibus«. En conclusion de son exposé, Gorgé estime que »le mieux serait de dénoncer l'accord du 21 mai 1930 aussitôt que possible, soit dès que la question de notre neutralité aura été élucidée devant le Conseil«.

Telle était la disposition d'esprit des plus hauts dirigeants helvétiques; seul un sursaut de scrupule et sans doute la prudence de Motta, les retinrent de s'exécuter immédiatement. Mais, dans ce cas, comme dans beaucoup d'autres affaires, la proverbiale lenteur helvétique dans la prise de décision va être bénéfique. En effet, les circonstances vont évoluer favorablement dans le sens des desseins des responsables de Berne. Au cours de 1938, la décomposition croissante de la SdN incite le gouvernement suisse à temporiser; il mise en quelque sorte sur une dégradation de la situation de la SdN; »car, il est bien certain que, dans les présentes circonstances, la SdN serait incapable de décréter l'»état de crise«, qui nous obligerait à lui abandonner l'exploitation exclusive de la station sur notre territoire. L'accord du 21 mai 1930 est pratiquement déchu, pour le moment de toute virtualité politique« écrit Motta en Novembre 1938.[56] Ainsi, la Suisse n'aura pas à endosser la responsabilité d'une dénonciation d'accords la liant à la SdN. Les circonstances y pourvoiront!.

En regard des événements tragiques de cette année 1938, les propos de Motta ne dénotent rien d'une amère désillusion ni d'un léger sursaut de fidélité à la SdN, mais une sorte de cynisme – qui ne lui ressemble guère, mais plutôt à certains de ses collaborateurs – qui lui fait voir l'intérêt que peut retirer son pays de la déconfiture de ce qui fut »la grande idée«. Chose plus stupéfiante encore, cette progressive politique d'abandon des liens avec la SdN que justifie une politique délibérée d'apaisement et de ménagement des voisins allemand et italien, va pouvoir compter sur une aide inattendue: celle de responsables de la SdN qui se découvrent irréalistes, mesquins et prétentieux.

Tout prêts à dénoncer la convention de 1930, dès le début de 1938, réticents à faire le geste pour des raisons d'opportunité, – car une telle dénonciation aurait constitué un coup d'éclat qui aurait été fortement applaudi à Berlin et à Rome, mais qui n'aurait certainement pas rehaussé le prestige de la neutralité intégrale aux yeux des puissances démocratiques – jugeant enfin inutile de créer des problèmes à une institution en décrépitude, les responsables de Berne accueillent avec soulagement les suggestions inattendues de révision des arrangements de 1930 que leur fait parvenir le Secrétariat de la SdN; ce dernier estime que le régime de Radio-Nations serait financièrement trop favorable à Radio-Suisse.[57] Se basant sur un examen inexact des bilans de Radio-Nations, il sollicite une revision de la convention qui devrait procurer à la SdN des ressources financières supplémentaires. Quoi qu'il en soit de l'aspect financier qui semble seul intéresser les dirigeants de la SdN, les responsables suisses y voient d'emblée »une occasion toute trouvée pour nous de nous libérer d'engagements politiques que nous ne serions plus à même d'assumer en temps de crise«.[58] Motta suggère qu'une nouvelle convention intervînt entre Radio-Suisse et la SdN et qu'un nouvel accord soit conclu entre la SdN et le gouvernement suisse, à la condition, bien entendu, qu'il ne contienne plus rien d'inconciliable avec notre neutralité«.

A vrai dire, la demande du Secrétariat a surpris les responsables suisses, notamment ceux de Radio-Suisse qui avaient espéré qu'au vu des charges financières incombant à la SdN, celle-ci, face à ses difficultés de trésorerie, lâcherait d'elle-même sa part dans Radio-Nations. Le Conseil d'administration de Radio-Suisse ne venait-il pas d'évoquer la possibilité soit de récupérer l'ensemble des installations contre un léger dédommagement à la SdN, soit d'augmenter sa part dans la perception des taxes, convaincu que les conditions financières de la convention de 1930 s'étaient révélées défavorables pour les comptes de Radio-Suisse.[59]

Dans ces conditions, il n'est pas étonnant que le directeur de Radio-Suisse s'attache à démontrer l'erreur d'appréciation du Secrétariat quant à la rentabilité de la station et »qu'en tant qu'instrument politique et de propagande, Radio-Nations constitue certainement pour l'un des deux propriétaires, la SdN, l'exploitation radioéléctrique la meilleur marché qui existe au monde«.[60] En l'occurrence, si révision il doit y avoir, elle ne doit pas se faire au profit de la SdN, mais en faveur de Radio-Suisse, argumente Rothen.

Saisi de l'affaire, le Conseil fédéral prend position, le 4 février 1939;[61] à son avis, du moment que le Secrétariat demande une révision de la convention technique, »on ne saurait pas ne pas demander la révision de l'accord politique, ce dernier étant incompatible avec la neutralité intégrale« . . . »On peut même, en un certain sens, se féliciter que le Secrétariat ait formulé sa demande de révision. Elle permettra de sortir au plus vite d'une situation quelque peu embarrassante«.

On le voit, le Secrétariat a procuré ainsi aux autorités suisses l'opportunité qu'elles recherchaient pour faire connaître à la SdN leurs intentions relatives aux clauses politiques de l'accord de 1930 qu'elles considèrent pratiquement dépourvues de toute portée depuis le retour à la neutralité intégrale. C'est ce qu'elles font dans la note que le Département politique fédéral transmet à Genève,[62] en guise de réponse à la demande du Secrétariat de réviser la convention de 1930 formulée le 3 novembre 1938; dans sa note, le Conseil fédéral accepte la proposition d'une révision de la convention technique de 1930, mais il ajoute qu' »il attacherait également le plus grand prix à ce que l'Accord de la même date . . . fût aussi révisé. Certaines de ses stipulations ne correspondent plus, en effet, à la situation issue du fait que la Confédération a recouvré sa neutralité traditionnelle«.

L'offre de négociation est acceptée de part et d'autre et sur les deux objets.[63] Des pourparlers qui s'ensuivent au cours de l'été 1939, il résulte qu'en ce qui concerne l'accord politique, Avenol déclare s' abstenir de toute initiative personnelle dans ce domaine;[64] mais la Suisse donne clairement à entendre que la révision doit porter sur le statut de Radio-Nations pendant la guerre, que son contrôle en particulier doit revenir entièrement aux autorités de la Confédération. Certes, cette revendication est en contradiction directe avec les engagements pris par le Conseil fédéral en 1930; elle s'oppose notamment à l'article 3 de l'Accord qui stipule: »Le gouvernement suisse assurera en tout temps à la station et aux installations qui en dépendent même protection et même sécurité qu'aux immeubles de la SdN. Le statut juridique de la station, en temps de crise, sera le même que celui des immeubles de la SdN«.[65] Mais au point où se trouve la SdN, le Secrétariat vent éviter d'inutiles tensions avec le gouvernement fédéral; de fait, il renonce le 4 septembre 1939 à diffuser des émissions de propagande et déclare éviter tout ce qui serait susceptible de procurer des difficultés au gouvernement suisse.[66]

En ce qui concerne la convention technique, les positions du Secrétariat et de Radio-Suisse rendent un arrangement très difficile, les arguments des uns et des autres étant diamétralement opposés. Pour les délégués suisses, »la SdN qui souhaite alléger ses charges à Radio-Nations n'a droit à aucune compensation . . . et il ne peut être question de l'indemniser du fait que son matériel s'est déprécié . . . et que la station n'a pas eu, pour la SdN, le développement qu'elle escomptait. Ce n'est peut-être pas sa faute si la Radio-Nations a souffert directement du déclin de la SdN; c'est encore moins la nôtre«, conclut Gorgé qui suggére de dénoncer l'accord à bref délai.

Devant le piétinement des négociations et, sans doute aucun, devant l'aggravation de la situation de guerre, le Conseil fédéral se résoud[67] à dénoncer les accords pour le 2 février 1940, étant entendu, d'après les clauses de 1930, que l'accord n'est dénonçable qu'après un délai de 10 ans suivant l'inauguration de la station, à savoir au 2 février 1942. Du point de vue suisse, cette mesure s'impose avec urgence puisque la SdN n'est plus l'organisation pacifique qu'elle devait être, qu'elle est impuissante et que contrairement à 1930 où la Suisse était entourée entièrement d'Etats membres de la SdN, en 1940 les trois quarts de ses voisins sont ennemis de la SdN. C'est ainsi qu'argumente le gouvernement suisse, conscient que l'accord de 1930 prévoyant la mise sous contrôle de la SdN de Radio-Nations en temps de crise est incompatible avec la neutralité traditionnelle du pays. Le 27 janvier 1940, le Département politique féderal fait part à la SdN de la décision du gouvernement suisse de dénoncer les arrangements de 1930, avec effet à partir du 2 février 1942.[68]

En raison des circonstances, la proposition suisse de revision n'avait pas pu être soumise à l'Assemblée de la SdN qui ne se réunit plus depuis décembre 1939. A défaut de pouvoir proposer l'affaire aux organes compétents de la SdN, le Secrétariat tente de laisser subsister l'accord, de maintenir en pratique le statu quo, ce qui équivalait, il est vrai, à une solution minimale par rapport à la clause de l'accord de 1932 qui prévoyait le passage de Radio-Nations sous le contrôle de la SdN en cas de crise. Le Secrétariat renouvelle ses assurances de ne rien entreprendre qui puisse léser les intérêts de la neutralité. Or, en dépit de ces précautions le gouvernement de Berne juge nécessaire de créer une situation nette; il annonce la 8 juillet 1941,[69] que son offre de négociation en vue d'un nouvel accord doit être considéré comme caduque. Il a été poussé à cette décision, écrit-il, en raison des circonstances internationales qui font que la Suisse se trouve être un des derniers Etats du continent à être membre de la SdN.[70]

La dénonciation de l'accord entraînait à terme, par voie de conséquence, l'élimination de la station Radio-Nations.[71] En effet, de pénibles négociations vont s'ensuivrent au sujet du rachat des installations payées à l'origine par la SdN.[72] Tandis que le Secrétariat les évaluait à un million et demi de francs, Radio-Suisse les estiment à peine à 300 000 francs.[73] Devant l'impossibilité de s'entendre sur le montant, il a fallu instaurer un arbitrage confié à une commission d' experts – ce qu'avait prévu la convention de 1930 –. Les experts s'arrêtèrent à un montant proche de l'estimation suisse, puisqu'ils attribuèrent les installations de Radio-Nations à Radio Suisse pour la somme de 265 530 francs, le 13 janvier 1942.

Ce règlement ne liquide pas encore l'affaire; un nouveau différend surgit au sujet du partage de certains stocks, notamment de quelque 58 tonnes de gasoil entreposées à Prangins; le Secrétariat de la SdN confie le contentieux à Jacques Secrétan, l'avocat-conseil du B.I.T., qui suggère un arrangement à l'amiable. Tandis que la direction de Radio-Suisse souhaitait soumettre l'affaire à un nouvel arbitrage qui lui aurait donné gain de cause dans la jouissance de cet entrepôt, le Département politique fédéral approuva une formule de compromis avancée par l'avocat du Secrétariat; celle-ci ne sera acceptée de part et d'autre que le 30 juillet 1943.[74] Sur le stock de 58 tonnes de gasoil, la SdN en reprend 48 et Radio Suisse 10 tonnes; Berne avait appugée cette transaction du fait que le Secrétariat souhaitait récupérer ce gasoil pour chauffer durant le prochain hiver le Palais des Nations.[75] Mais, conclut un des hauts fonctionnaires du Département politique fédéral, »toute cette affaire est due, en somme, au dépit de la SdN, qui désavouée par la sentence arbitrale fixant le prix de vente des installations au niveau, à peu près, de l'offre de Radio-Suisse, a donné une importance exagérée à l'insignifiante divergence de vue née à propos du droit de disposition des 58 tonnes de gasoil«.[76]

Dans l'intervalle, il est vrai que la station de Prangins a connu un beau développement des communications et pour ainsi dire dès le début des hostilités. Cette évolution favorable des affaires de la station incitait d'autant plus les dirigeants de Radio-Suisse à disposer librement de cette station durant le conflit. La menace de la voir place sous contrôle international au moment où elle devenait rentable[77] préoccupait a fortiori la direction de Radio-Suisse dont les avis contribuèrent à accélérer les initiatives pour écarter ce risque.[78] Si la station de Prangins a cessé de fonctionner comme station de la SdN, le ler février 1942 à minuit, elle poursuivra néanmoins ses activités et les développera rendant de précieux services notamment au Comité international de la Croix Rouge; mais l'expérience »Radio-Nations« avait vécu!

Quelles conclusions tirer de cette affaire?

Une première remarque s'impose. Dès les tout premiers projets d'établissement d'une station radiotélégraphique sur sol helvétique, le gouvernement fédéral a mesuré les dangers qu'impliquerait pour sa politique de neutralité l'acceptation de cette station. Les réserves avancées en 1919–1920, on les retrouve formulées dès 1926 quand l'idée est reprise. En 1920, cependant,les autorités fédérales prenaient le risque d'entrer dans les vues du gouvernement américain, parce que ce projet mettait d'emblée en jeu les relations avec les représentants d'un Etat qui avaient tant contribué à ce que la Suisse devienne le siège de la SdN. En outre, il ne fallait pas offusquer les Etats qui avaient fait ce choix et il fallait aussi éviter d'alimenter la propagande contre l'installation de la SdN à Genève, en dressant des obstacles à propos d'un projet auquel d'ailleurs la Suisse pourrait prendre une part active lors de sa réalisation. De fait, le projet ne s'étant pas réalisé, la Suisse décide toute une série de mesures qui doivent assurer à la SdN les télécommunications qu'elle est en droit d'exiger.

Cette première expérience nous conduit à une deuxième remarque. Manifestement, le gouvernement de Berne espère par une politique de faits accomplis aller au-devant des désirs de la SdN; c'est sa ligne de conduite jusqu'à la conclusion des arrangements de 1930. Car, l'objectif constamment recherché, c'est de rester maître chez soi, de garder en tout cas sa liberté d'action. Il ne l'obtient pas sur le fond, il est vrai, puisque les accords de 1930 hypothèquent en cas de crise la station »Radio-Nations« au profit de la SdN, mais il en jouit en pratique tant que l'état de crise n'est pas déclaré. C'est là le sens de la déclaration optimiste de Motta qui conjure l'état de crise comme probablement impossible, afin de justifier au niveau des principes l'acceptation de cette épée de Damoclès qui pèse sur la neutralité suisse en cas de crise. D'ailleurs, n'est-ce pas pour réduire le plus possible l'influence effective de la SdN dans Radio-Nations, que le gouvernement fédéral a contribué à la construction de la station de Prangins – construction totalement injustifiée tant techniquement que financièrement selon les dirigeants de Radio-Suisse; il s'agit en l'occurrence d'une aide totalement disproportionnée par rapport aux besoins réels de la SdN, aide décidée uniquement dans le souci d'éviter l'érection d'une »station internationale«. C'est le prix payé pour »rester maître chez soi«.

Or, cette attitude des autorités suisses qui les porte à aller au-devant des risques d'empiètements de la part de puissances étrangères, sans doute a-t-elle été bénéfique à la SdN durant les premières années, mais elle va se retourner contre elle dès 1938. En effet, dans le souci de prévenir toute récrimination qui pourrait venir de Berlin ou de Rome qui donnent d'ailleurs à entendre qu'elles ne toléreraient pas que la Suisse serve de base à une propagande dirigée contre elles, Berne estime de plus en plus urgent au fur et à mesure que la crise européenne évolue vers un conflit ouvert, d'éliminer Radio-Nations, ou en tout cas, d'éviter que la station ne passe sous le contrôle exclusif de la SdN comme le prévoit l'accord de 1930. Le Secrétaire général n'ayant pu se résoudre à la placer sous son contrôle, en dépit de l'état de crise, la station ne devenait pas menaçante pour la neutralité helvétique. Cette situation aurait dû persuader les dirigeants suisses de »laisser les choses en état«. Or, pourquoi ne l'ont-ils pas fait?

C'est la troisième remarque que nous aimerions faire. Elle concerne les responsables de la SdN. Pourquoi ceux-ci se sont-ils laissés aller à un quasi sabordage en septembre 1939? L'embarras dans lequel ils se trouvent à la suite du refus des Etats membres de se rendre à Genève pour condamner une Allemagne à laquelle venait de se lier une Union soviétique, membre de la SdN. Enfin, les velléités exprimées par certains d'entre eux d'utiliser la SdN dans un conflit qui la dépassait totalement; en ce qui concerne Radio-Nations, leur maladresse à vouloir tirer quelques maigres profits d'une station qui se mit à florir dès le déclenchement des hostilités, grâce aux messages d'ordre commercial et divers qu'on lui confiait. Ce sont là autant de facteurs qui ont incontestablement fourni au gouvernement suisse l'opportunité recherchée depuis le début de 1938 pour se retirer d'un engagement qu'il jugeait en totale disproportion au vu de l'effondrement de la SdN et du peu de cas qu'en faisaient les autres Etats membres.

L'affaire de »Radio-Nations« et l'attitude des autoritées suisses à son sujet reflètent assez fidèlement l'évolution de la politique suisse à l'égard de la SdN. Disponibilité au départ, tant qu'il n'y a pas de risques, qu'il y a même du prestige à recueillir, puis abandon progressif qu'on n'exprime pas ouvertement, mais qu'on indique d'une façon suffisamment claire par des mesures techniques, particulièrement mesquines (refus d'acueillir à Berne le successeur d'Avenol, refus de payer les cotisations dès 1941, contrôle des télégrammes et téléphones, etc.) mesures propres à faire comprendre aux responsables internationaux de Genève que la SdN ne compte plus.

Certes, il ne revenait pas à la Suisse de sauver la SdN, mais en tant qu'Etat hôte et vu le rôle exceptionnel que la Suisse a joué à ce titre dans la politique international durant une grande partie de l'entre-deux-guerres,[79] on est en droit de s'interroger sur le zèle que déployèrent certains hauts fonctionnaires helvétiques à rompre les liens avec l' institution internationale. Quant aux fonctionnaires rescapés de la SdN ils étaient en droit de rencontrer sinon plus de retenue et de dignité de la part de leurs interlocuteurs suisses, du moins d'être informés ouvertement des lignes directrices de la nouvelle politique étrangère de la Suisse résultant du retour à la neutralité intégrale. Que celle-ci impliquerait notamment une modification profonde des engagements et des devoirs de l'Etat – siège à l'égard non seulement des activités de la SdN en général, mais du statut de son Secrétariat et singulièrement de sa station de télécommunications. Aussi l'élimination de Radio-Nations, souhaitée par Berne dès 1938 et achevée en février 1942, s'inscrit-elle dans une politique beaucoup plus vaste et représente-t-elle un enjeu politique bien plus important que la matérialité de son existence et de son fonctionnement!

Notes

1 *DDS*, Berne, Benteli, 1979. v. 7,1, no 294, p. 566–568.
2 *DDS*, 7,1, no. 305, p. 585–586.
3 Cf. les propos du Conseiller fédéral Ador, *ibid.*, no. 289, p. 558 et de Rappard, *ibid.*, no. 297, p. 577 et no. 355, p. 710.
4 *Ibid., no. 369, A., p. 741.*
5 *Ibid., no. 369, p. 730 et ss.*
6 *Ibid.*, p. 731.
7 Cf. Lettre de Felix Calonder, chef du DPF au Département des Postes, Télégraphes et Chemins de fer du 5 mai 1919, AF, E 2001 (c) 5, v. 47.
8 *Ibid.*, Lettre du 28 mai 1919.

9 D'après un rapport cité dans la publication *Radio-Suisse SA. 50 ans, 1922–1971*, Berne, 1971, p. 8, les autorités fédérales auraient posé le principe suivant: »notre station radio doit être financée par la Suisse et doit être exploitée par l'administration suisse des télégraphes et téléphones. Il ne saurait être question de reconnaître un droit de regard à des étrangers ou à un fournisseur.«

10 Télégr. du DPF à Rappard du 2 août 1919, AF, E 2001 (c) 5, v. 47.

11 Lettre du DPF au Département des Postes . . . du 10 février 1920, *ibid.*

12 Ce message a été publié en 1919 evec en annexe les principaux documents relatifs à la participation de la Suise à la SdN, en français chez Wyss à Berne, en allemand chez Stämpfli à Berne, en italien chez Grassi à Bellinzone et en anglais par l'University press de Cambridge.

13 Ainsi le projet esquissé par les ingénieurs genevois Rambert et Rambal dans une lettre à E. Drummond du 24 octobre 1923. ASdN, 1919–1927/40/32308/11641 (R 1583).

14 Cf. la publication *Radio-Suisse SA. 50 Ans: 1922–1971*, Berne, 1971.

15 Pour un bilan de l'équipement au début des années vingt tant en Suisse qu'à Genève dans le domaine des communications télégraphiques et téléphoniques, ainsi que des efforts entrepris jusqu'en 1927 pour les développer, cf. le rapport du 26 février 1927 qu'adresse le Département fédéral des Postes . . . au DPF, AF, 2001 (c) 5, v. 17. On trouve aussi des descriptions détaillées sur l'état d'équipement de Genève dans d'autres domaines tels que les liaisons ferroviaires (le pitoyable état de la gare Cornavin), aériennes et dans l'hôtellerie, dans les notes prises sur le vif par Guillaume Fatio, chargé par le Secrétaire général de la SdN, d'organiser l'installation du secrétariat et de l'accueil de la première assemblée à Genève ainsi que de tous les aménagements ultérieurs au profit de la SdN. (Papiers personnels de G. Fatio prêtés aimablement par M. Olivier Fatio, Céligny).

16 ASdN, 1919–1927/40/11641 x (R 1583),

17 *Ibid.*, Lettre du Conseiller fédéral Haab à Drummond du 24 mars 1921.

18 Doc. SdN, C.677.M.268.1926.IX.

19 Doc. SdN, A.58.1927.IX.

20 *Ibid.*

21 *Ibid.*

22 AF, E 2001 (c) 5, v. 17: »Memorandum betreffend die Errichtung und den Betrieb einer eigenen Radio-Sendestation durch den VB.«

23 AF, E 2001 (c) 5, v. 47. Lettre de Motta au Département militaire fédéral du ler avril 1927.

24 *Ibid.*

25 Faut-il rappeler qu'en 1920, le Département militaire fédéral avait exclu la possibilité de doter la station envisagée alors du statut d'exterritorialité accordée aux bâtiments de la SdN.

26 *Ibid.*

27 AF, E 2001 (c) 5, v. 47: »Bemerkungen zum Bericht des Völkerbundssekretariats vom 10. September 1927 über die Erstellung einer eigenen drahtlosen Völkerbundsstation in Genf. Bern, den 14. Oktober 1927.«

28 *Ibid.*, Dans une lettre du 10 novembre 1927 à la section des communications et du transit, Rothen offre toutes ces améliorations des prestations de sa societé qui rendront superflu »l'établissement et l'exploitation d'une station TSF par la SdN elle-même« – »solution irrationnelle tant au point de vue technique que financier.«

29 *Ibid.*, »Protokoll der interdepartementalen Konferenz betreffend Radiostation des Völkerbundes.«

30 *Ibid.*, Extrait du procès-verbal de la séance du Conseil fédéral du 13 janvier 1928, ou aussi ASdN, 1928–1932/9G/639/225 (R 2590).

31 ASdN, 1928–1932/9G/639/225 (R 2590) ou doc. SdN. C.142.M.33,1928.VIII.

32 AF, E 2001 (c) 5, v. 17: »Memorandum betreffend die Errichtung und den Betrieb einer eigenen Radio-Sendestation durch den Völkerbund« signé Rothen, le 26 février 1927.

33 Voici les membres britanniques, les seuls étrangers, qui ont fait partie du conseil d'administration de Radio-Suisse, de 1922 à 1965: H. W. Allen de 1922 à 1931, H. A. White de 1922 à 1941, A. W. Hibberdine de 1932 à 1934, A. Sabater de 1944 à 1946 et L. B. Nicholls de 1947 à 1965, cf. *Radio-Suisse op. cit.*, p. 25.

34 AF, E 2001 (c) 5, v. 47: Lettres de Fritz Rothen des 20 et 27 décembre 1927 au Département fédéral des Postes . . .

35 Doc., SdN, C. 141.M.32.1928.VIII.

36 *Ibid.*

37 ASdN, 1928–1932/9G/3935/225(R2590): voir la note du ler mai 1928 de Montenach rendant compte d'une séance qui a eu lieu à Berne le 28 avril 1928, réunissant Motta, Haab, Dinichert, Furrer et Secrétan au cours de laquelle on fixa l'offre suisse susmentionnée.

38 *Ibid.*, Note de Drummond du 2 mai 1928: »At first sight«, écrit-il, »the suggestion made by the Swiss Authorities seem to me to offer prospects of a very satisfactory solution.«

39 *Ibid.*, dans une note interne de Robert Haas, du 26 mai 1928.

40 *Ibid.*, »Remarques sur la note de M. Haas en date du 26 mai concernant la question de la station radiotélégraphique«, note datée du 30 mai 1928.

41 *Ibid.*, Compte-rendu de l'entretien du 31 mai 1928 au secrétariat de la SdN.

42 *Ibid.*, Le mémoire et la note ont été distribués le 23 août 1928 au Conseil et à l'Assemblée, sous doc. SdN, A.31.1928.VIII.

43 ASdN, 1928–1932/9G/10502/225 (R2591): Note sur l'entretien du ler mars 1929 entre Drummond, Motta et C. Gorgée. La lettre incriminée est celle qu'envoya le DPF, le 22 février 1929, signé: Motta.

44 *Ibid.*

45 Doc. SdN, A.31.1929.VIII.

46 ASdN, 1928–32/9G/14215/225 (R2591).

47 ASdN, 1928–32/9G/16832/225 (R2591): note sur la séance de négociation à Genève, le 3 février 1930.

48 Doc. SdN. C.192.M.92.1930.VIII.

49 Sur les services rendus à la SdN par Radio-Nations, cf. Victor-Yves Ghebali, *Organisation internationale et Guerre mondiale.* Thèse de l'Université de Grenoble, 1975, Tome 1, p. 350.

50 Cf., la publication *Radio-Suisse SA, op. cit.* [voir note 14], p. 118.

51 *Journal officiel de la SdN*, 1938, p. 375; sur l'influence de la diplomatie hitlérienne dans ce retour à la neutralité intégrale, cf. Bourgeois, Daniel. *Le Troisième Reich et la Suisse 1933–1941.* Neuchâtel, La Baconnière, 1974, p. 75 ff. Pour d'autres aspects, cf. Ghebali, *op. cit., passim.*

52 AF. E 2001 (D) 4, v. 78: cf. la lettre qu'adresse le 26 janvier 1938, Rothen au Département fédéral des Postes et Chemins de fer. Dans une autre séance du conseil d'administration de Radio-Suisse du 9 nov. 1938, Rothen constate avec regret que la SdN est devenue désormais un bloc de puissances qui s'oppose à un autre bloc. Dès lors, il est temps d'en tirer les conséquences pour Radio-Nations qu'il faut détacher rapidement de la SdN.

53 Sur le contexte général, cf. Roland Ruffieux. *La Suisse de l'entre-deux-guerres.* Lausanne, Payot, 1974, p. 339 ff.

54 AF, E 2001 (D) 4, v. 78: Lettre de Motta du 18 février 1938 au Département des Postes et des Chemins de fer.

55 *Ibid.*
56 *Ibid.*, Lettre de Motta du 7 novembre 1938 au Département des Postes et des Chemins de fer.
57 *Ibid.*, Lettre de J. Avenol à Motta du 3 novembre 1938.
58 *Ibid.*, Lettre de Motta du 7 nov. 1938 au Département des Postes
59 *Ibid.*, Auszug aus dem Protokoll der Sitzung des Verwaltungsrates der Radio-Schweiz AG vom 9. November 1938.
60 *Ibid.*, Lettre de Rothen à la Direction générale des PTT, du 16 décembre 1938.
61 Procés-verbal de la séance du Conseil fédéral du 4 février 1939.
62 *Ibid.*, Lettre de Motta au Secrétaire général du 13 février 1939.
63 *Ibid.*, Lettre d'Avenol au DPF du 7 juin 1939 et Procès-verbal de la séance du Conseil fédéral du 14 juillet 1939.
64 *Ibid.*, »Notice concernant Radio-Nations« du 30 août 1939, rédigée par Camille Gorgé, qui rend compte du premier »round« qu'il a eu avec les hauts fonctionnaires de la SdN. L'atmosphère dans laquelle se déroulent les pourparlers atteste la dégradation des relations entre Berne et Genève. Gorgé parle d'une tentative de chantage de la part d'Avenol qui lui fit entendre qu'un consortium étranger s'intéresserait au matériel appartenant à la SdN; ce qui lui valut une verte réplique de Gorgé, disant que si la SdN trouve un acquéreur pour ses installations, »elle ne devrait pas hésiter à vendre à n'importe quel prix« . . . »en réalité, ce beau matériel . . . ne vaut, commercialement parlant, plus un liard.« Gorgé aurait encore dit à Avenol et ses collaborateurs: »Ce n'est pas nous qui avons voulu cette station, et j'ai insisté là-dessus dans mon exposé initial. Nous offrions gratuitement une station à la SdN. Elle n'a pas voulu notre présent. Elle a tenu au contraire, à faire certaines dépenses pour être elle-même maîtresse de la station en temps de crise. Il est juste qu'elle en supporte les conséquences.«
65 Il est vrai que parallélement à ces démarches suisses visant à éliminer »Radio-Nations«, on étudie sérieusement à Berne l'hypothèse d'un retrait de la Suisse de la SdN. Cf. AF, E 2001 (D) 4 v. 52, dossier »Sortie éventuelle de la Suisse de la SdN.«
66 *Ibid.*, v. 61, cf. Note de Gorgé pour l'Etat-Major de l'Armée Suisse, du 3 septembre 1939 et Notice interne du 5 septembre 1939, dans laquelle Gorgé rapporte qu'il a »remercié le Secrétaire général du fait qu'il avait renoncé à toute émission pour des fins de propagande. Je lui ai dit qu'il nous sortait d'un grand embarras« . . . car »il est à peu près certain que des émissions régulières de la SdN par la station de Prangins nous auraient valu bien des difficultés.« Voir aussi la lettre de remerciement de Motta à Avenol du 6 décembre 1939, *ibid.*, v. 6.
67 Dans sa séance du 23 janvier 1940.
68 Pour cette correspondance, cf. doc. SdN C.56.M.53.1941, et Ghébali, *op. cit.* [voir note 14], p. 353.
69 Lettre du Ministre Bonna du 8 juillet 1941, reproduite sous SdN, doc. 56.M.53.1941, et communiquée au Conseil et aux Membres de la SdN, ou AF, E 2001 (D) 4, v. 78.
70 Sur la décomposition de la SdN à partir de l'effondrement de la France et sur »l'asservissement de la majorité des Etats membres européens« au nouvel ordre hitlérien, cf. Ghébali, *op. cit.*, p. 164 ff. Parmi les derniers Etats libres de l'Europe restés membres, on comptait la Grande-Bretagne et cinq neutres: Grèce, Irlande, Portugal, Suisse et Turquie.
71 Dans une lettre au DPF du 28 juin 1941, Rothen estime que »la liquidation de Radio-Nations comme station internationale s'impose.« AF, E 2001 (D) 4, v. 78.
72 La SdN avait investi quelque deux millions et demi de francs dans l'installation de Radio-Nations.
73 Dans une lettre du 25 août 1941 au Secrétaire général de la SdN, Rothen énumère tous les éléments d'appréciation qui aboutirent à l'offre de rachat de 250 000 francs. *ibid.*

74 Sur l'ensemble de cette affaire, cf. la notice de Kohli du 11 octobre 1943: »Différend entre la SdN et Radio-Suisse au sujet d'un stock de gasoil de 58 tonnes.« *Ibid.*

75 Selon la communication faite par Jacques Secrétan lors de son entretien à Berne avec les responsables de l'Administration fédérale; note sur cet entretien du 25 mars 1943. *Ibid.*

76 *Ibid.*, Notice de Kohli du 11 octobre 1943.

77 Pour l'année 1940, selon la convention de 1930, Radio-Suisse dut verser à la SdN une participation aux bénéfices de Radio-Nations d'un montant de 345 000 francs et on l'estime à 400 000 pour 1941, augmentation des activités et du chiffre d'affaires qui n'est pas provoquée par le Secrétariat de la SdN dont les activités sont considérablement réduites. cf. »Notiz für Herrn Minister Bonna« préparée par Zurlinden, du 7 novembre 1941. AF, E 2001 (4), v. 61.

78 Cf. La lettre qu'adresse Rothen au DPF, le 28 juin 1941. AF, E 2001 (D) 4, v. 78.

79 Sur »L'enjeu du choix de Genève comme siège de la Société des Nations«, cf. notre contribution, *In:* L'Historien et les relations internationales. Recueil d'études en hommage à Jacques Freymond. – Genève, Institut universitaire de hautes études internationales, 1981. – pp. 251–278.

William E. Rappard and the League of Nations

A Swiss contribution to international organization

ANIA PETER
Oberwil/Basle

The Genevese William E. Rappard (1883–1958) was "by personal inclination and over a long period of time . . . above all a man of learning, a researcher and an academic teacher. In the first place, he was an economist and, as such, by virtue of intellect and temperament, an economist of a pronouncedly liberal character."[1] From 1913 on Rappard lectured at the University of Geneva on economic history and public finance: In addition, he was the author of over 300 publications;[2] a number of these deal with his special subject, but the majority concern international organization as such. During the decisive early years, when the League of Nations had just begun its activities, Rappard was a member of the League Secretariat, functioning as Director of the Mandates Section. He belonged to those »Pioneers in World Order«[3] who strove to put Woodrow Wilson's conception of the League of Nations into practice.

During World War I and at the Paris Peace Conference in the course of which the League of Nations Covenant was elaborated, much had been written about the League, its significance and organization: but there was no precedent for the practical establishment of this first international organization. Thus, much depended on the way in which the leading members of the only permanent League authority, the Secretariat, conceived their tasks and on how they influenced the League of Nations policy. If the League of Nations attained international importance and did not become the mere plaything for its Member States, if the idea of the international organization has survived the breakdown of the League, it was the merit of men such as Salvador de Madariaga, Paul Mantoux, Jean Monnet, Ludwik Rajchman, Sir Arthur Salter and – last, not least – William Rappard.[4]

*

However, there is another aspect of the work of William Rappard in connection with the League of Nations which cannot go unmentioned: Rappard, together with his friend Paul Mantoux, the first director of the Political Section of the League of Nations Secretariat (1920–1927) in 1928 founded the Graduate Institute of International Studies.

Here, too, Rappard was a pioneer. The Institute was to be bilingual and help train the leading personnel required by democratically based international organizations.[5] Rappard was also convinced of the need for studying peace – like war with its own strategy – in order to safeguard it. In his view, and given international relations the extreme complexity of the desire of the peoples of the world for peace was not enough in itself. It is much easier to excite the masses by offering them a distorted version of reality rather than to calm them by an objective examination of the facts.[6] The Institute, directed by Rappard from 1928 to 1955, was to work out a scientific basis for the avoidance of war, and to encourage the study of international relations and institutions.[7] It is a tribute to the soundness of his conception that the Institute has survived both the League of Nations and Rappard himself.

I. Rappard's role in establishing the League in Geneva

We must also look at the role played by Rappard at the time of Switzerland's entry into the League of Nations. Already during the summer of 1917 when the American wheat supplies to Switzerland were at stake, Rappard had met the creator of the League of Nations, Woodrow Wilson, and his adviser Colonel House.[8] During a further meeting in 1918, House encouraged Rappard to contact him whenever he had news of something important in Swiss or international politics.[9] Thus, Rappard wrote to House that the Swiss Federal Counsellor Calonder (head of the Political Department from 1918 to 1920) was ready to do anything short of endangering the national security of Switzerland for the sake of the League of Nations' idea.

Many Swiss hoped, as Rappard stressed, ,,that Switzerland, uniting, as it does, in the heart of warring Europa, three different races on the basis of free and federative democracy, may be of some true aid in helping the United States contribute to the solution of Europe's problem in the spirit of our common ideals."[10]

Following a suggestion of House[11], the Federal Council sent Rappard as a contact man to the Paris Peace Conference where he was in close contact first of all with Calonder, and with the Genevese Gustave Ador, head of the Department of the Interior, as well as with Edmund Schulthess, who directed the Department of National Economy. An aide mémoire of the Political Department to the Berne embassies of the Allied Powers describes Rappard's task as follows: »Le Conseil fédéral a envoyé M. le Professeur Rappard à Paris à titre non officiel, comme son homme de confiance pour maintenir avec les Délégations des Etats Alliés un contact utile à la résolution des questions intéressant la Suisse.«[12]

It is clear that Rappard did not wish to become just another official diplomat. He had written to Calonder: »Moins on mettra de forme à tout cela et plus je serai satisfait, car je tiens essentiellement, dans l'intérêt même des démarches dont je suis chargé, à la plus grande liberté convenus de la diplomatie tend du même coup à restreindre cette liberté«.[13]

What was the reason for Rappard's special mission and of what nature were the functions? The explanation is to be found in the person of Rappard himself. He had grown up in the United States, had studied at various universities, including Harvard where he lectured from 1911 to 1913. He knew English as well as French, was familiar with the American mentality and had many friends who had contacts within the State Department and with President Wilson himself. Hence, he was well placed to assist the Federal Council in 1917 and in 1918 when the food supplies to Switzerland were in jeopardy; in 1919 he was the obvious choice as the Swiss representative in Paris, whose mandate it was to facilitate Switzerland's entry into the League of Nations.

The standing of Rappard, who could speak in confidence,[14] unconventionally and as an equal with the Americans and the British – the architects of the League of Nations[15] – was of the greatest importance in overcoming difficulties caused by Switzerland's neutrality.

Rappard attempted unsuccessfully, however, to influence the League of Nations' Covernant in Switzerland's favour and to obtain for her a special status akin to Article 16.[16] But the Federal Council did not follow Rappard's suggestion to declare officially, towards the middle of March 1919 that Switzerland wanted to join the League and Rappard feared that the historical hour might be missed[17] because of timidity and a lack of political imagination and determination. Moreover, the Federal Council let go by over a month before reacting to Rappard's admonition of June 1919 that Switzerland's hesitation was disappointing House and Cecil, estranging them from Switzerland.[18] However, it was Rappard who gave first-hand reports to Berne on the progress of the negotiations; thus, for instance, he was the first Swiss whom House allowed a glimpse of the draft Covenant of the League of Nations, two days before its publication on 14 February.[19] Rappard, as an official and 'non-American', could unlike others ask the opinions not only of House and Wilson, but also of Cecil and could report their remarks and verbal assurances to Berne.[20] It was Rappard who counselled other Swiss delegations in Paris and also introduced other negotiators, such as Max Huber, to their American and English partners.[21] Rappard tried to convey Switzerland's difficult position in the negotiations; for instance he fought the optimism of Colonel House who did not believe that without a guarantee of neutrality the Swiss electorate would vote against Switzerland's entry into the League.[22] In view of the ill-humour in League of Nations circles, Rappard took it upon himself to inform Drummond privately that the Federal Council had recommended to Parliament Switzerland's entry into the League, once again explaining to the Secretary-General the special situation of Switzerland.[23] And it was Rappard who greatly contributed towards bringing the League of Nations to Geneva.

*

Early in 1919 Rappard had heard the rumour that the Anglo-Americans were considering the possibility of establishing the League of Nations in Geneva.[24] Apart from its general significance for Switzerland such a prospect could not but appeal to the Genevese Rappard. He shared the scepticism prevailing in French Switzerland as to whether, in view of the newly created League, traditional neutrality could be rigidly adhered to, and he would have been ready to forgo neutrality in exchange for having the League's seat in Geneva. When it appeared that Switzerland would have to choose between neutrality or this seat, he urged Ador, close to him as a Genevese and former President of the ICRC: » . . . J'espère que vous userez de toute votre autorité auprès de vos collégues et du peuple suisse, pour leur montrer que nous devons préférer la participation à la

Société des Nations et la possession du siège, à notre neutralité traditionelle.«[25]

However, quite apart from the question of neutrality, the candidature of Geneva as the seat of the League was not uncontested. There was no danger from Lausanne, which House had preferred as a seat for a time, although this possibility created rather a stir among the Genevese in the Political Department.[26] But things were different as far as Brussels was concerned. Wilson and Cecil were against Brussels which, as Miller wrote, had not really been supported anywhere but in Belgium, whereas the advantages of Geneva as a neutral , centrally situated and international city were obvious.[27] However, because of Switzerland's reserve with regard to her neutrality, the question was not quite as simple as Miller suggested.

Rappard's reports frequently give the impression that negotiations were about to be broken off. It is also possible that the uncertainty as to which country should ultimately become the home of the League of Nations was made use of in order to exert some pressure on the Swiss Government so that it would declare itself for the League. Still, the situation had its absurd side: the seat of the League was to be established in a country which would join the League only with the reservation as to country's neutrality; yet even so this country's entry was still anything but assured. That Rappard's fears had substance can be seen in the fact that the movement in favour of Brussels did not cease after the definitive choice of Geneva as the seat of the League and after Switzerland's joining it.

To convene the first Assembly of the League of Nations was according to the Covenant Woodrow Wilson's privilege – in spite of the withdrawal of the USA; – the League Council, at the suggestion of the Secretariat asked Wilson to convene the first Assembly in Brussels. But according to Rappard, Wilson refused the request and made sure that Geneva became the seat of the League.[28]

In Paris the negotiations about the establishment of the League of Nations in Switzerland had gone through Colonel House, called by Rappard "le grand artisan de notre succès."[29] However, Rappard also had two meetings with Wilson, who, as he assured Rappard definitely favoured Geneva.[30] Rappard, knowing the Paris scene, was able to give the Swiss Federal Council tactical advice[31] concerning the competition of Brussels. Virtually compelled by Cecil and House to sign on behalf of the Federal Council an understanding that a convenient site should be made available and the necessary facilities granted, Rappard even had to act for his Government. It was not really in Rappard's competence to give his signature, but in view of the efforts made by the Belgians he believed that he had no other choice: »Je ne voudrais pas qu'une hésitation ou qu'une timidité de ma part puisse réduire nos chances de succès en face de cette redoutable concurrence.«[32]

This line of argument shows how much Rappard's thinking differed from what is usual in diplomatic circles. He was ready to take the initiative and to assume political responsibility – as, indeed, he continued to do later when he was in the Secretariat of the League of Nations. The official Swiss Ambassador in Paris had advised Rappard to go to Berne immediately and to consult Calonder. Rappard did not do this; two days later, when there had still been no instructions from

Berne, he signed. In a letter to Calonder, who the next day confirmed by wire Rappard's signature on behalf of the Federal Council[33], Rappard justified himself: »L'insistance de nos amis anglais et américains, et le désir de ne négliger aucune possibilité de succès, par une absence de 48 heures, m'ont décidé à aller de l'avant.«[34]

How correct Rappard's summing up of the situation had been emerged shortly afterwards. On 11 April the League of Nations Commission of the Paris Peace Conference made the decision to recommend the choice of Geneva as seat of the League of Nations, albeit with a 12 to 7 majority.[35]

Various authorities praise Rappard for his work in championing the candidature of Geneva. There is a pompous ring, however, about the words of Arthur N. Holcombe, a Harvard colleague of Rappard's, in the brochure presented the latter on his 70th birthday: that the deep impression Rappard had made on Wilson in 1917 and in 1918 had helped "when Rappard was persuading Wilson to locate the seat of the League in Geneva".[36] Albert Picot is rather more discreet when, in his obituary of Rappard, he states: »On peut dire que l'influence de Rappard à été déterminante pour que Wilson reste ferme jusqu'au dernier jour en faveur du siège de Genève, malgré l'opposition tenace de plusieurs Etats qui souhaitaient la désignation de Bruxelles.«[37]

It was Max Huber, himself a participant in the Paris negotiations on Switzerland and the League of Nations, who paid the most adequate tribute to Rappard. He wrote to him on the day after the choice of Geneva: 'My dear Colleague, last evening, when the cable concerning the choice of Geneva as seat of the League of Nations had finally been decoded and communicated to me, my first thought was that a first merit goes to you for this, as I hope, happy decision for Switzerland and for the League.'

There had been much in favour of Geneva and of Switzerland, Huber continued. 'But no one but you was able to gather and increase the forces favourable to Switzerland and to bring about the objectively right decision against the counterplay of subjective, human and all too human interests. Pictet de Rochemont, after all, had just put on record the past and what already existed. You have helped to build the future.'[38]

Let us add that the medal which Rappard received as token of gratitude from the Federal Council bore the following inscription:

A William E. Rappard,
qui, en des temps difficiles,
a consacré ses aptitudes et ses forces
au service de la patrie.[39]

And, on the occasion of the 50th anniversary of the choice of Geneva as seat of the League of Nations, the Government of the Canton of Geneva decided to name the street leading to Rappard's former residence at Valavran "chemin William Rappard".[40]

*

Throughout his life and on behalf of his country Rappard continued to be deeply involved in international organization. From 1928 onwards he was a member of the Swiss delegation to the League of Nations Assembly; and from 1927 onwards and again from 1945 to 1956 he was a member of the Swiss Government's delegation to the ILO. In these functions he was basically a Swiss delegate amongst others, true, with the best knowledge of international organizations, but nevertheless just someone who, above all, followed the instructions of his Government. By contrast, Rappard played a more personal role as a member of the League Secretariat from 1920 to 1925; and his thoughts on international organizations, as contained in his writings, are considerably influenced by the experience gained in this office. The second part of this paper, accordingly, shall deal with Rappard's work as director of the Mandates Section of the League Secretariat and with his conception of international cooperation.

II. Rappard in the Secretariat of the League

Rappard did not owe his appointment to the League Secretariat to the fact that he was Swiss, but to the name he had made for himself in League circles. Since, however, this name had been achieved in the service of Switzerland, his activity in the League of Nations may be considered as a Swiss contribution to international cooperation. In another sense, too, Rappard did remain a Swiss in the League of Nations. As he himself explained, the Swiss officials had been called into the League of Nations as private persons and on account of their personal abilities. However, Switzerland's reputation for impartiality and political maturity had been helpful to them. In this way, they were the bearers of the moral authority of their country and had to safeguard its prestige by acting in an unprejudiced and balanced manner.[41] Rappard himself had occasion to follow these principles during his four years as director of the Mandates section of the League of Nations Secretariat.

The management of the Mandates Section had actually been intended for the American colonial expert George Louis Beer and, on his death, had been taken over temporarily by the Englishman Baker. Then, Drummond offered this position to Rappard. There had been an earlier attempt to give Rappard an office in the Secretariat, but it had failed. Drummond had modified his first offer to such an extent that it no longer was of any interest to Rappard.[42] Rappard was also rather reserved with regard to this new offer, even though Drummond had wrapped it in very flattering terms: "Broadness of outlook, tact, energy and keenness, plus brains, are the real qualifications needed. Will you not, therefore, accept?"[43]

It seems that Rappard was afraid of being only a stop-gap. He may have suspected that after the withdrawal of the Americans, Drummond aimed at reducing the importance of the mandates system, which was a thorn in the side of the colonial Powers, by choosing an inexperienced director without national support. Some evidence points in this direction[44], but the statements of later colleagues of Rappard's in the Secretariat contradict it. So, for instance, Walters: "Rappards qualifications for a high Secretariat post were outstanding in almost every respect and his name was inevitably the first that Drummond would think of. The vacancy at the head of the Mandates Section was clearly 'made to measure' for him, if he was ready to accept it."[45]

And Madariaga pointed out: "Rappard has excellent language qualifications, was the citizen of a non-colonial country and his intellectual ability was first-class. Should not this be sufficient?"[46]

When examining in detail Rappard's work in the Secretariat and the reasons for his resignation, as well as the reaction of the members of the Mandates Committee to his resignation[47], it must be concluded that both suspicion and praise were justified.[48] In fact, Rappard appeared to be the ideal candidate for this post. The mandates system was one of the most disputed institutions of the League of Nations. It was capable of raising the League's prestige as much as it would have harmed it, if it had revealed itself as a fraud and merely the masking of colonial annexation. Clearly, as a director of the Mandates Section Drummond needed someone whose impartiality and integrity were beyond doubt. While many members of the Secretariat were chosen with a view to their being not only loyal servants of the League of Nations but also capable to serve as a liaison to their countries – the League could not function without those countries' cooperation –, the nationality of the director of the Mandates Section was dictated by the need for his impartiality.[49] Who then could be better suited than a Swiss whose country had never possessed any colonies? In short, Rappard was in every respect the right man in the right job, the more so since he also brought administrative experience to his task[50]; or, in the words of House: "Inevitably, such a man was drafted by the League of Nations to help in the work of bringing order out of chaos and in maintaining world peace."[51]

On 1 November, 1920, Rappard joined the Secretariat of the League of Nations as director of the Mandates Section and quickly became an expert in respect of mandates, problems of colonial administration and international law.[52] He saw himself as a servant of the League of Nations and considered it his duty to see the mandates article fulfilled not only literally, but also faithfully in keeping with Wilson's conception of the League. During his period of office in the Secretariat Rappard urged that everything should be avoided that could shake public confidence in the mandates system and, thus, in the League of Nations as a whole.[53]

At this point it should be explained what the mandates system meant to Rappard. It seemed to him important not only for the credibility of the League of Nations but also as a way towards universal peace and world government at some time in the future. Contrary to popular opinion today, Rappard thought that colonization was necessary. He was against colonization in the sense of exploitation by an economically and politically stronger Power, and against colonization camouflaged as a human obligation; but he believed that the modern world could not survive without the raw materials located in countries whose populations were unable to exploit these resources themselves. This view, Rappard emphasized, implied a responsible approach both towards native populations and towards the nations of the world.[54] In the mandates system this double responsibility had been institutionalised; what had started as an emergency solution had become an unhoped for chance for securing peace. For centuries rivalry for military bases and trade advantages in overseas territories had been one of the most dangerous reasons of international conflict. By making the colonial Powers trustees, if only in certain areas, this was eliminated. Wars which had been fought for possession and monopoly would hardly flare up for the sake of the distribution of international responsibility.[55] And the mandates system helped to avoid war yet in another respect by the gradual and disinterested preparation of underdeveloped peoples for independence, in short, by responsible and justified decolonization. Rappard wrote in 1932: »N'est-il pas concevable que l'institution des mandats fournisse au XXe siècle un moyen de concilier les besoins d'émancipation nationale, qui sont déjà sensibles et qui peuvent devenir irrépressibles chez tous les peuples primitifs, avec la nécessité d'un utile apprentissage politique et d'une bonne organisation économique, tant que ces peuples sont encore incapables de se gouverner eux-mêmes et de s'assurer les avantages matériels et moraux d'une administration bien ordonnée?«[56]

Certainly, these words recall the self-confidence of a Europe we have lost, and it cannot be denied that Rappard had illusions about the 'teachers'. At most he feared their egotism and he did not conceive the possibility of a flight from reason. Yet his thoughts show a tempting alternative to the situation of today. Were his ideas realistic or was this the utopia of a thinker with roots in the 19th century, and who, as a Swiss, did not understand enough of power politics in general, and colonial politics in particular and, who as an economist, knew not enough of ethnology and psychology? – In any case, Rappard did manage the Mandates Section for four years and, as is universally acknowledged, carried out this difficult work with "unusual tact and unusual ability".[57] And the Mandates Commission, which counted a number of recognized experts amongst its members, wanted Rappard to join them, "considering the thorough knowledge acquired by M. Rappard, director of the Mandates Section, not only as regards the situation existing in each of the mandated territories but also as regards the general principles of the mandates system and of its relations with the League, and having, moreover, derived great benefit since the creation of the Commission from M. Rappard's able and sound advice".[58]

Rappard's optimism, and his hope that the mandates system would be effective over and beyond the limits set by the Covenant, was sustained by his experience with the League of Nations and particularly the work of the Mandates Commission.

Due to its integrity and competence, the Mandates Commission, originally created as a mere consultative body, attained a real international or even a supernational reputation.[59] The result was that the Council of the League of Nations as well as the mandatory Powers followed its recommendations – in the opinion not only of Rappard, but also of other authorities on the mandates system.[60] Another important condition for this success was the tenor of the Commission's reports. It laid more stress on consultation and co-operation than on criticism and surveillance[61], proceeding with a maximum of tact and heeding the sensitivity of the mandatory Powers. The members of the Mandates Commission did not form a tribunal, but were, as a rule, in Rappard's words, "content to express their hope that they would be privileged to find in the next statement of the mandatory Power information calculated to allay their misgivings."[62] Such language would be considered today an empty diplomatic formula, but at the time of the League of Nations courtesy and emphasis were not mutually exclusive, with pressure displayed in a polite way. For Rappard this was the only way to achieve success. Harsh criticism, even if justified, would have inevitably irritated not only the executive, but also the parliament as well as the general public of the country concerned, and would thus have had a purely negative effect.[63] In this light, the reproaches of too much leniency[64] levelled against the Mandates Commission can be seen as quite the opposite. From the working of the Mandates Commission, Rappard even derived guidelines for the working of international organization itself. The starting point had to be mutual confidence and voluntary co-operation, secured by publicity, persuasion and emulation. Coercive and direct intervention was subject to political arbitrariness and might prove destructive of international confidence. Only the pressure applied by public and parliamentary opinion could bring the national Governments to sacrifice the dogma of sovereignty to the principle of world unity. To win public support the League of Nations had to become the true representative of the world community. The Mandates Commission offered a good example as to how this was to be achieved: "The great lesson which this experiment (the mandates system) has taught is that of the pacifying virtue of true impartiality, as opposed to the irritating influence of national partiality. As nothing excites nationalism as nationalism itself, the best method of allaying feelings of hatred between states is, whenever possible, to eliminate politics from the settlement of disputes between them. The experience of the Mandates Commisison, as well as that gained by several other instances in which individuals, released from all bonds of national allegiance, have been associated in the execution of the peace treaties, has been extraordinarily enlightening. As perhaps no other single incident in the course of the last ten years, it has served to open new vistas for the future of world government."[65]

Two years after Rappard had written these words, excessive nationalism led to World War II altering the general situation to such an extent that a World Government, based on the experience of the League of Nations, is no longer considered a serious possibility. Indeed, today the whole League of Nations seems to have been based on myth rather than on reality. However, one should not forget that Rappard's point of departure was always the League Wilson had founded "to make the world safe for democracy". Rappard's confidence in public opinion will be discused further on; for the moment the focus remains on his role in the League Secretariat.

As already mentioned, Rappard did everything in his power to raise the prestige of the mandates system. He strove to interest the members of the Mandates Commission in their task and to give them the feeling of doing important work.[66] He took the initiative not only in order to achieve the true objectives of the mandates system, but also smooth the Council decisions at variance with those recommended by the Commission.[67] In doing this, he always encountered the resistance of Drummond. The views of the two men on the role of the Secretariat differed greatly. Rappard considered the Secretariat to be the guardian of the League's principles, which had not only to carry out the wishes of the Member States but, if necessary, to see that these States fulfilled their obligations. Thus, he was in favour of the Secretariat going its own particular way, however discreetly. Drummond, on the other hand, always insisted on adhering closely to the regulations when directing the work of the Secretariat.[68] He consciously restrained his leading collaborators and did not let them participate in the League's policy to the extent Rappard would have desired in the interest of the League of Nations itself. Evidence of this can be found in the minutes of the directors' meetings. The argument that the members of the League of Nations Secretariat were only servants of the League's Council and as such, on principle, without any opinion of their own, was countered by Rappard with: Its servants they were but as they had to prepare the Council's decisions, the Council no doubt would wish them to be its intelligent and responsible servants. Therefore, it was indispensable and in the interest of the League of Nations that the directors be kept thoroughly informed on day-to-day problems. This was not done – despite the fact that the meetings were well conceived – because of the attitude of the participants of the directors' meetings and because of that of the 'presidium'. Without wanting to call into question the prerogatives of the Secretary-General as stipulated in the Covenant, Rappard asked Drummond to show more confidence in the directors' meetings. After all, they all worked towards the same end and in spite of all risks, mutual trust had to be the basis of their work.[69]

The main risk was indeed the fact that Drummond's foremost collaborators were of such a calibre that they were badly suited for his policy of keeping the Secretariat in the background and not letting it take any real responsibility.[70] His conduct "was inspired by the traditions of the British Civil Service, by his own sense of constitutional propriety and by a certain tendency to avoid responsibility and to distrust enthusiasm"[71]. However, too many of his early directors were not 'civil servants' but were more akin to statesmen, or international politicians.[72] Sooner or later it had to come to a break between these men and the Secretary-General – or to a modification of the Secretariat's policy. As we know, it was Drummond who prevailed and the place of the 'pioneers' – who had established the League of Nations as a centre of international relations – was increasingly taken over by professional diplomats. There was no secret about the reason for this change. In a contemporary essay on the League of Nations Morley stated: "Some (of the members of the Secretariat) are too individualistic to sink themselves happily in a bureaucracy which is destined to become increasingly more anonymous"[73] and a participant at the Carnegie Conference of 1942 on the League of Nations Secretariat stated openly: »M. Monnet, M. Rappard, M. Madariaga and Sir Arthur Salter, for example, they are persons who, I think, took certain initiatives. They were defeated and resigned, and were followed up . . . by people of quite a different type, who took orders but did not undertake to take such initiative in the matter of the broad policy."[74] Its author called this statement a "broad generalisation" which "would probably have to be supported with certain facts"; – as regards Rappard, in the archives of the League of Nations Secretariat there is sufficient evidence to support the statement.

Perhaps a change was inevitable, perhaps Drummond's policy was the only realistic one. However that may be, after the international successes of the first few years, this development led to the decline of the Secretariat. Drummond was responsible for this, as well as for the successes. Madariaga expresses it in these terms: "He tolerated what he felt unable to repress" and speaks of Drummond's pragmatical trend towards compromise and defeatism.[75] Looking back on the League, it is easy to call this trend towards compromise wisdom, and such defeatism common sense. The bias is towards what did happen and call that which had not come off a myth.

*

As the reason for his resignation from the Secretariat Rappard gave his election as Vice-Rector of the University of Geneva. The real reason, however, was doubtless the working conditions at the Secretariat. Whatever he could achieve in the Secretariat was no longer worth the rules he had to submit to. Above all, he was restricted as to freedom of speech, a fact which greatly hindered him as a publicist – a fact to which he himself draws attention: "A League official was precluded from writing anything which, if wrongly interpreted or even willfully misinterpreted, might offend one of the fifty nations whose servant he was. His wings and his talons were, so to speak, clipped. As a writer he was therefore reduced to impotence.«[76]

On the other hand, as a member of the Mandates Commission and as a Swiss delegate to the League of Nations, nothing stopped him from taking up publicly the cause of the League and to develop his own opinions concerning international organization.

III. Rappard as a Swiss delegate to the League

As Swiss delegate Rappard once again had occasion to concern himself with the situation in the Secretariat. The question was that of the adequate representation of small States in the Secretariat, becoming more and more the domain of the Great Powers. Rappard put forward the point of view of Berne, although his arguments derived from his own experience and conviction.

On the occasion of the annual budget debates, Rappard had called the contributions to the League "an extremely light insurance premium against an extremely grave risk"[77] and the hesitation of the Member States to accept their financial obligations "perhaps a reason for future historians to despair of peace"[78]. But Rappard also gave the reason for this reluctance to pay: "33 million (the 1933 budget) is a trifle to pay for acts, but it is a great deal to pay for mere words"[79]. It was, he continued, the fault of its Members that the work of the League consisted in mere words, since they were exclusively engaged in cultivating their sovereignty and refused to subordinate their special interests to the interests of all. Like all communities, the League could prosper, or merely exist, only if its Members respected the laws, Rappard was in favour of steps being taken against debtors and he recommended the publication of a "barometer of international solvency"[80]; but he also requested that the League of Nations should prove that it was worth the money it asked.[81] The Members needed to have confidence in the League and to recognize it as their own concern. To this end, they needed to be adequately represented. This meant, amongst other things, that the small States should have the same number of members in the

Secretariat as the Great Powers.[82] Rappard recognized the advantage the nationals of the Great Powers had in their capacity of liaison officers within and outside the Secretariat. However, he saw the difference in political influence of small States compared with that of the Great Powers as a matter of degree rather than of substance.[83] Moreover, nationals of small States were often in a position to serve the League without prejudice since, as a rule, their countries were less involved in conflicts, thus making impartiality easier.[84] On the principle whether impartiality was at all possible, Rappard's answer was an unqualified yes. In his view, the really international official, however rarely encountered, did exist without being a 'psychological monster'; and Rappard's examples included, apart from historical figures, the International Judges at The Hague and the Director of the ILO, Albert Thomas. But conditions suitable for the existence of such impartial officials had to be created. As long as persons were appointed to the Secretariat only on the basis of national criteria, and merely spent some part of their national career in this post, one could not expect them to become truly international officials. But as soon as it was recognized that to serve the League of Nations also meant to serve one's own country, such an international outlook would become possible. It was paramount to develop this new mentality, if the League was to survive and secure peace and international justice.[85]

Although in favour of the equal representation of small States and Great Powers, Rappard was against a rigid quota system as an impediment towards securing truly international officials of the first order. He was "too keen a believer in the future of the League of Nations to be tempted ever to subordinate its interests to those of any one country, not even (his) own".[86] He was too convinced of the seriousness, the responsibility and the necessity of international co-operation to accept a semblance – i. e. a quantitatively just distribution of international officials from amongst the Member nations – for the real thing, i. e. valuable and efficient cooperation from all concerned. Therefore, he insisted: "It would be far better to have international organizations which, although constituted on a faulty model, were inspired by a high international spirit, attentive to the claims of justice, than organizations with a model constitution which were diseased and selfinterested."[87]

Rappard did not consider the credibility of the League as the sole responsibility of the Secretariat. On the basis of the day-to-day working of the League he made precise demands on the Council and of the Assembly, the underlying principle being the just balance between responsibility and power.

In the Council of the League of Nations real power was to correspond to real responsibility. If too many of the smaller Powers forced their way into the Council, Rappard warned, the Great Powers would begin to discuss important questions among themselves and then force their decisions upon the others. The Council would be discredited, the international organization weakened.[88]

For the Assembly of the League of Nations, too, Rappard demanded a realistic relationship between real influence and theoretical rights. In particular he warned against the pseudo-democratic 'one-man-one-vote' formula. Was it acceptable if a majority of small States imposed their will upon the Great Powers whose contributions financed the major part of the international organization? Would not the Great Powers, here, too, turn away from a game whose rules were determined by others, but for which they paid the stakes? Words like these, from a Swiss, a national of a small State and an uncompromising democrat, should be noticed: "Si la justice, en effet, exige toujours l'égalité devant la loi, elle ne commande nullement, elle condamne au contraire, l'attribution de fonctions et d'avantages égaux à des sujets d'inégale importance et partant d'inégale utilité sociale."[89]

As an alternative, Rappard recommended a system such as had been realised by the International Monetary Fund[90], an "equivalence de prestations et de pouvoirs."[91]

While these thoughts of Rappard's have no doubt remained relevant, another of his recommendations can be understood only against the background of the intellectual climate prevailing during the first half of the century. This recommendation, too, concerns the relationship between responsibility and power, but in a very different way.

According to Rappard, the Assembly of the League of Nations had attained something akin to international leadership, seeing how the Member States sent delegates who were not only politicians but individuals of European stature; Rappard named in particular Fridtjof Nansen, Gilbert Murray and Lord Robert Cecil. When these men gave their own opinions, they pronounced the hopes, the fears and the desires of the world more genuinely and effectively than their diplomatic colleagues could have done.[92] For the Assembly to be, the "Parliament of Nations"[93] of the future Rappard wished to see even more delegates of this kind, proposing Albert Einstein, H. G. Wells and the French historian Aulard.[94]

An international parliament as a kind of world conscience, as a moral authority? Would not such an institution have to suffer the same fate as, for instance, St. Paul's Cathedral in Francfort? No, Rappard would reply, for times had changed. The Assembly was no longer at the mercy of absolutist monarchies, but supported mostly be democratic States. The work of the League of Nations was public, with radio and the press at its disposal. Publicity, Rappard concluded from the example of the mandates system and of other League of Nations activities, was an incentive to international good conduct[95], provided, of course, it found an interested as well as democratically active audience. This second presupposition Rappard, perhaps too optimistically, took for granted, and he did what he could to inform the public and enlist its interest in the League. As a professor and as a publicist he made the League of Nations his subject, explained its functions and its problems. He was convinced that in terms of propaganda truth would always in the end triumph, while exaggerations and lies would reveal themselves as such.[96] Such confidence, too, is difficult to grasp in Orwell's "newspeak" of today. Did Rappard, the international practician and scientist, succumb to wishful thinking? Well, as always, he states the reasons for his opinion and here again shows his Swiss origins: he points to Switzerland's experience with the nationalist propaganda of her neighbours, directed against Switzerland. Yes, he speaks not only of the special case of Switzerland, but of the League of Nations itself, more particularly of the circumstances of its downfall. The moral authority of the League had been unable to restrain Japan, Germany or the Soviet Union from their schemes, but these same countries were so noticeably disturbed by this authority that, after a vain attempt to justify themselves, they resigned from the League of Nations.[97] Rappard concludes: »Ne peut-on pas en conclure qu'une organisation internationale, même lorsque la solidarité qui unit ses membres pacifiques n'est pas assez active et résolue pour assurer le respect de sa charte et pour contraindre leurs associés belliqueux, constitue cependant par elle-même, du seul fait de son existance et notamment de la publicité de ses délibérations, une précieuse alliée de la paix?«[98]

Rappard also participated in international co-operation during the post-war period. From 1945 to 1956, two years before his death, he headed the Swiss Government delegation at the International Labour Conferences and in 1951 presided its meeting in Geneva – which speaks for his international standing. While Rappard thus supported the ILO where, at the time, work was not hampered by an automatic majority and political rituals, he could not reconcile himself to the United Nations as a whole. It was too similar to what, in his view, an international organization should not be.

Certainly, the UN had the advantage of being supported by the USA; Rappard understood the lack of universality of the League of Nations, exemplified by the non-participation of the USA, as a decisive reason for the League's failure.[99] But the other important reason, the retention of their national sovereignty by the individual States[100], had become a basic principle of the UN. The victors of 1945, by their right of veto, blatantly disregarded their obligations according to the UN Charter. Rappard was willing to weigh but not to count the votes; but this principle was no justification for carrying over the structure of a wartime alliance into a peacetime institution. The architects of the UN had created a hierarchy of rights and obligations[101], and demanded that the other Member States sacrifice their sovereignty without guarantees offered for their own security. Worse still: while the UN Charter, as Rappard said, protected its signatories against rather imaginary dangers, it left them unprotected against that very real danger, "to which small states remain exposed by such aggressive action as may be undertaken with impunity, not only by any one of the Great Powers, but by any other state with the approval, or even without the expressed and active disapproval, of any one of the Great Powers."[102]

Here, too, Rappard has shown himself a clearsighted analyst, though he was spared seeing how right he had been. In any case, he obviously could not advise Switzerland to join the UN in 1945.[103] "La destinée de la Suisse est . . . manifestement de vivre internationalement"[104], he stresses as before. But the UN was neither the liberal nor the efficient organization which was needed, nor did it hold the promise of resolving the foremost problem of world politics: how to combine national freedom with international security.[105] Thus he wrote as late as 1951: "Tant que la communauté internationale est organisée ou désorganisée au point qu'elle ne possède aucune police pour maintenir l'ordre, ni aucun tribunal pour dire le droit, ni même aucune loi qui serait l'expression collective de ce droit, la neutralité n'est assurément la négation d'aucune obligation morale."[106]

But, Rappard also recognised that Switzerland could not altogether turn her back on the UN.[107] There had to be found ways and means for practical co-operation, as long as the UN's attitude to neutrality excluded full membership, and as long as its structure excluded the waiver of neutrality. Switzerland could – and this in the interest of both parties – have the status of an 'ally'.[108]

For all his idealism, Rappard was a realist. He was ready to accept a faulty model if it was inspired by a high international spirit and promised to function efficiently. But how could he tolerate it if it discredited the idea of international organization as such? Was he to console himself with the argument that, while the League of Nations had failed on account of the high principles of its Covenant and the inability of its Members to live up to them, the UN promised greater stability for having been conceived in such a way that its Charter could be violated without shaking it to its foundations?[109] Rappard could be mocking and ironical, often to the point of hurting, but he was innately honest and aware of his responsibilities. He was in no way a cynic and certainly not a cynic on the subject of international co-operation. The suggestion that the inefficiency of the sanction clauses would in effect secure neutrality within the UN and thus render superfluous a legal guarantee was not unknown to him. As early as 1946 he had pointed out that the disunity of the Great Powers conditioned the freedom of the underprivileged Members of the UN.[110] But he considered it unacceptable to let Switzerland join the UN under such conditions.

In his view, the international organization of the post-war period had to use the experience of the League of Nations in spite of the changed circumstances. The possible success of the UN could not dispel Rappard's scepticism: such a success was merely a side-issue and of no lasting value. At the time, describing the activities of the League of Nations, Rappard had coined the phrase "Three Leagues in One"[111] and defined these Leagues as follows: the execution of the Peace Treaties, the promotion of international co-operation, and the outlawing of war. Whatever progress the League of Nations might have achieved in the first two instances, the third was decisive for the future of the whole organization: "L'idée fondamentale de la Société des Nations était celle de la paix par le droit et par la solidarité internationale. A tous les différends une solution pacifique, à toutes les aggressions une sancton tutélaire, telle était sa formule. Arbitrage et sécurité collective, voilà donc le double objectif dont la recherche occupait le théâtre principal de ses opérations. Tout le reste – désarmement, protection du travail, défense des minorités, administration des mandats coloniaux, collobaration internationalé à des tâches techniques – si intéressantes, si importantes, si prometteuses souvent qu'aient été ces activités, était d'ordre accessoire."[112]

Rappard and the League of Nations both have their roots in the 'World of Yesterday'[113], in the liberal tradition of the 18th and the 19th century. As has already been stated, this world has been transformed by World War II. The West, although still economically in the lead, was outwitted by the Second, the Third and the Fourth Worlds within the international organizations themselves – with all the consequences Rappard had foreseen stemming from inequality in respect of representation and influence. A 'world conscience' as described by Stefan Zweig and assumed by Rappard as fundamental to any international organization, no longer exists. No longer can we have confidence in the spoken or the written word, for organised lies and brutality have become socially acceptable – even in international organizations. In more ways than one Wilson's world of a secure democracy has moved too close to 1984. Under the circumstances the UN in its present form is perhaps the most we can hope for.

Be that as it may, for Rappard the League of Nations represented the realisation of most of his hopes. He did not feel that World War II had proved either the idea of 'international organization' or the concept of the League of Nations to be invalid. In 1940, in an analysis of the failure of the League he wrote: "Ceux qui avaient mis leurs espoirs dans la Société des Nations n'ont donc ni à; s'en repentir ni à s'en humilier. Ils n'ont eu que le tort de trop présumer de la sagesse de leur génération. Ceux-là seuls ont le droit de les condamner qui préfèrent les affres de la réalité présente aux promesses d'un avenir incertain, certes, mais dont nul ne peut dire ni qu'il était ni qu'il demeure inconcevable et utopique."[114]

There would be no peace in freedom, Rappard stressed, except at the end of the path along which the founders and the friends of the League of Nations had begun to make their way.[115]

Meanwhile, as Rappard recognized, an international organization as the UN, although imperfect, was better than no international organization at all. He was ready to further the "common cause of international peace and goodwill critically but full of sympathy" within the framework of the UN.[116] However, the UN always remained for him a second best. "Good will without illusions" was in the end his attitude towards international cooperation.[117] His model was and remained the League of Nations, the end of which – as Max Huber says – caused him to lose "a hope, but not the conviction of having wanted the right thing."[118]

Notes

1 »Article de Max Huber, Neue Züricher Zeitung, 2 Mai 1958« *In: William E. Rappard, 22 avril 1883–29 avril 1958. In Memoriam.* – Valavren (Genève), [Mme. William Rappard], 1961. – p. 54–56.

2 For the complete bibliography until 1953 see *Varia politica* publiés ou réimprimés à l'occasion du soixante-dixième anniversaire de William Rappard. Zürich, ed. Polygraphiques, p. 340–352, 1953.

3 *Pioneers in World Order. An American Appraisal of the League of Nations.* Harriet E. Davis, editor. New York, Columbia University Press, 1944. – 272 p. (hereafter *Pioneers*).

4 The relevant studies are unanimous on the importance of the first members of the Secretariat; the above names continue to be mentioned. See in particular Frank G. Boudreau, "International Civil Service", *Pioneers,* p. 76–86; Helen Moats, *The Secretariat of the League of Nations. International Civil Service or Diplomatic Conference.* Diss., Chicago, 1936. – p. 262; Felix Morley, *The Society of Nations. Its Organization and Constitutional Development.* Washington, Brookings Institution, 1932. – p. 250 f. Jean Siotis, *Essai sur le secrétariat international.* Genève, Droz, 1963. – p. 51, 80, 101.

5 »Allocution de M. de professeur Jacques Freymond, directeur de l'Institut universi-

taire de hautes études internationales.« *In: William E. Rappard. In Memoriam., op. cit.*, p. 22–24.

6 William E. Rappard, *Le problème des colonies et des mandats.* Bucarest, Impr. nationale, 1932. – ü. 4 f.

7 Michael A. Heilperin, "William Rappard, Universitaire". *In: William E. Rappard. In Memoriam, op. cit.* p. 65–72.

8 See also, William E. Rappard, »La mission suisse aux Etats-Unis, août-novembre 1917«. *Opinions suisses,* 1918. – p. 72.

9 Correspondence Rappard – Colonel House. 1918. – unpublished. Private Archives Rappard. Rappard to House, 31. 1. 1918. Now: AF, Berne.

10 *Ibid.*, Rappard to House, 9. 7. 1918.

11 Correspondence Rappard – Hans Sulzer, 1917–1919, unpublished. Rappard to Sulzer 13. 2. 1919. Private Archives Rappard.

12 Correspondence Rappard – Lardy (Polit. Department), 1919, unpublished. Lardy to Rappard 6. 3. 1919. Private Archives Rappard.

13 Correspondence Rappard – Felix Calonder, 1919. Rappard to Calonder, 24. 2. 1919. Private Archives Rappard. Rappard's reports to Berne and the official letters addressed to him can also be consulted in the Federal Archives in Berne.

14 Rappard wrote to the Swiss Ambassador in the United States, Hans Sulzer: Wilson, House, Lansing ». . . et tous leurs collaborateurs subalternes, parmi lesquels je compte beaucoup d'anciens collègues et amis, ont vraiment mis et mettent toujours à nouveau un empressement touchant à aider la Suisse de toute façon.« Rappard to Sulzer, 13. 2. 1919. AF

15 Rappard to Calonder, 17. 3. 1919, Lord Robert Cecil to Rappard. AF

16 Miller writes on this subject: "The Swiss representative, Professor Rappard, labored eloquently to induce me to advise President Wilson in accordance with the Swiss view; but I feared the effect of such a clause upon neutral and American opinion, and the President maintained his position. While the Swiss obtained a recognition in the treaty of their special position and while the Council has since passed a resolution to the same effect, the Covenant was not changed to meet the opinion of Switzerland." David Hunter Miller "The Making of the League of Nations." *In: What really happened at Paris. Story of the Peace Conference 1918–1919 by American Delegates.* Edward M. House and Charles Seymour editors, New York, C. Scribner's Sons, 1921. – p. 415.

17 Rappard to Calonder, 13. 3. 1919. AF

18 Rappard to Calonder, 28. 6. 1919. *ibid.*

19 Rappard to Calonder, 12. 2. 1919. *ibid.*

20 Cecil, Wilson and House repeatedly assured Rappard of their sympathy for Swiss neutrality. House authorised the Swiss Government to quote him as saying that he considered neutrality compatible with entry into the League of Nations. Wilson used similar words and declared that he would not oppose a reserve of neutrality. See also, Rappard to Calonder, 11. 4., 14. 4., 24. 4., 28. 4. 22. 4. 1919, as well as exchange of letters Rappard – Sulzer, Rappard to Sulzer, 13. 2. 1919. AF

21 See also, Ania Peter, *William E. Rappard und der Völkerbund. Ein Schweizer Pionier der internationalen Verständigung.* Bern, H. Lang, 1973. – p. 43 f., 54 f.

22 Rappard to Calonder, 14 and 28. 4. 1919. AF

23 Letter of Rappard to Drummond, 18. 8. 1919. LNA 1919 – 1927/28/834/44 (R 1445).

24 Correspondence Rappard – Max Huber, 1919. Rappard to Huber, 31. 1. 1919. AF.

25 Correspondence Rappard – Gustave Ador, 1919. Rappard to Ador, 26. 3. 1919. AF.

As appears from his handwritten reply, Ador was in complete agreement with Rappard; Ador to Rappard 29. 3. 1919. *ibid.*

26 See also Peter, *op. cit.* p. 63 f.

27 Miller, *The Making, op. cit.* [see. note 16]p. 417.

28 William E. Rappard, "Woodrow Wilson, la Suisse et Genève. D'après des papiers inédits" *In: Centenaire Woodrow Wilson*, 1856–1956. Genève, Centre européen de la Dotation Carnegie, 1956. – p. 74. I want to thank Mr. Breycha-Vautier for calling to my attention the correspondence on this point between Walters and Rappard. Walters challenged Rappard's view in 1956 after the publication of Rappard's paper on 'Woodrow Wilson, Switzerland and Geneva', and tried to prove that the Secretariat never intended to bring the League of Nations to Brussels. Rappard remained unconvinced – and, indeed, his argumentation is more convincing than Walters'. The correspondence is attached to the copy of the above-mentioned publication available at the UN Library in Geneva.

29 Rappard to Calonder, 10. 4. 1919. AF

30 William E. Rappard, »Wie Genf Völkerbundstadt wurde«, *Nord und Süd*, Jahrgang 52, Oktober 1929. – p. 888.

31 See also, Huber to Rappard, 1. 4. 1919; Rappard to Calonder, 7. and 9. 4. 1919. AF

32 Rappard to Calonder, 2. 4. 1919. *ibid.*

33 Calonder to Rappard, 5. 4. 1919. *ibid.*

34 Rappard to Calonder, 4. 4. 1919. *ibid.*

35 See also, Rappard, *Woodrow Wilson, op. cit.*, [see Note 28] p. 58 f.

36 Arthur N. Holcombe in the introduction to *Varia Politica, op. cit.*, [see note 2] p. ix f.

37 Albert Picot, *Portrait de William Rappard,* Neuchâtel, Editions de la Baconnière, 1963. – p. 58.

38 Huber to Rappard, 12. 4. 1919. AF

39 Calonder to Rappard, 1. 11. 1919. ibid.

40 *Journal de Genève*, 30. 4. 1969, p. 17.

41 William E. Rappard, *La politique de la Suisse dans la Société des Nations. Un premier bilan.* Genève, Editions Forum, 1925. – p. 5, 58 f.

42 According to Rappard, Drummond had offered him at first the post that Fosdick should have had, but – for financial and administrative reasons – with the title of "Director" instead of "Under-Secretary General". Drummond's final offer, however, was that of some sort of quartermaster and head of personnel, "primarily occupied with questions of internal administration and organization of a material nature«, with the title of "Director of Internal Administration". Rappard to Drummond, 18. 6. 1920. Drummond to Rappard, 10. 6. 1920. AF

43 Drummond to Rappard, 9. 10. 1920. *ibid.*

44 Peter, *op. cit.*, p. 78.

45 Walters, letter dated 20. 2. 1969, Paris in connection with Peter, *op. cit.* [see note 21]

46 Madariaga, letter of 1. 4. 1968, Oxford, in connection with Peter, *op. cit.*

47 They requested that Rappard's successor should be of equal quality, that the Mandates Section should not be weakened, and they also obtained Rappard's nomination as an extraordinary member of the Commission. LoN, Minutes of the Permanent Mandates Commission, (hereafter: Min. PMC) LoN doc. A.13.1924.VI. LoN, Records of the Fifth Ordinary Session of the Assembly, Minutes of the Sixth Committee, 24 September 1924, *OJSS*, no. 29, p. 15. LNA, 1919–1927/1/40493/248 (R8). LoN, Minutes of the Thirty-second Session of the Council, 11 December 1924, *OJ*, February 1925.

48 Peter, *op. cit.*, p. 84 f.
49 Moats, *op. cit.*, [see Note 4] p. 340; Siotis, *op. cit.* [see Note 4], p. 98, 113 f.
50 Rappard was for one year Secretary of the »Internationales Arbeitsamt« in Basle and for another year Secretary General of the League of Red Cross Societies in Geneva.
51 Colonel House, Introduction to William E. Rappard, *Uniting Europe. The Trend of International Cooperation since the War.*, New Haven, Yale University Press, 1930. – p. vii.
52 Rappard practically 'was' his section. Until March 1921 he was alone with one secretary, then he temporarily had two collaborators, until finally, in March 1923, the section grew to two collaborators, apart from the secretarial staff. Peter, *op. cit.*, p. 83 n. 37.
53 *Ibid.*, p. 84 f.
54 LoN, Min. PMC, in LoN doc. C.386.M.132.1925.VI, p. 48 f. William E. Rappard, "The Practical Working of the Mandates System". *Journal of the Royal Institute of International Affairs,* v. 4, September 1925, p. 205–224, *Varia Politica, op. cit.* p. 163–180, p. 168.
55 Rappard, »*Le problème des colonies . . .*« *op. cit.*, p. 13.
56 *Ibid.*
57 Nansen Speech; LoN. Records of the Fifth Assembly, Plenary Meetings, Text of the Debates, *OJSS,* no. 23, p. 126.
58 LNA, 1919–1927/1/40493/248 (R8). In connection with Rappard's work in the Mandates Commission, his special concern for Palestine and his relationship to Lord Lugard and also to Chaim Weizmann must be mentioned.
59 William E. Rappard, "The Mandates and the International Trusteeship Systems". *Political Science Quarterly,* v.61/3, September 1946, p. 408–419; *Varia Politica, op. cit.*, [see note 2]), p. 184.
60 Pierre Orts, »Le système des mandats de la Sociétée des Nations«. *Revue de l'Université de Bruxelles,* 32; 4, 494–524; 1927. Campbell L. Upthegrove, *Empire by Mandate. A History of the Relations of Great Britain with the Permanent Mandates Commission of the League of Nations.* New York, Bookman Associates, 1954. – p. 30; Daniel F. W. Van Rees, *Les mandats internationaux. Le contrôle international de l'administration mandataire.* Paris, Rousseau, 1927. – p. 137; William E. Rappard, »Zur Soziologie des Mandatssystems«. *Zeitschrift für Politik,* Heft 1, p. 16, 1928. – William E. Rappard, *International Relations as Viewed from Geneva,* New Haven, Yale University Press, p. 36, 1925.
61 Rappard, "The Practical Working . . ." *In: Varia Politica, op. cit.*, p. 171 f.
62 Rappard, *International Relations, op. cit.*, p. 36.
63 Rappard, »Zur Soziologie . . .«, *op. cit.*, p. 16.
64 See also R. N. Chowdhuri, *International Mandates and Trusteeship Systems. A Comparative Study. The Hague, Nijthoff, 1955.* – p. 185, 200.
65 William E. Rappard, *The Geneva Experiment.* London, Oxford University, p. 78 f. See also, Rappard »Zur Soziologie . . .« *op. cit.*, p. 17. Rappard, "The Mandates, and the International . . .", *op. cit.*, p. 189 f. Rappard, The *Geneva Experiment, op. cit.*, p. 66.
66 LNA, 1919–1927/1/23063/16844 (R 57). Rappard to Drummond, 7. 2. 1921.
67 See in particular Peter, *op. cit.*, p. 107 f.
68 Siotis, *op. cit.*, p. 80.
69 LoN doc., Director's Meeting, 28 February 1923, p. 8 f., 10 f.
70 Siotis, *op. cit.*, p. 80.
71 F. P. Walters, *A History of the League of Nations,* London, Oxford University Press, 1952. – p. 559.

72 In this connection it is interesting to note how Rappard judged Drummond on meeting him for the first time. He wrote to Calonder from Paris: »Il a certainement pour lui une culture étendue, sinon très profonde, une connaissance suffisante des langues et une expérience politique et diplomatique très riche. Il m'a donné l'impression d'un esprit assez vif, d'un caractère plutôt facile et d'une humeur très enjouée. J'ai eu le sentiment de me trouver en présence d'un bon fonctionnaire, bien plus que d'un homme d'état, aux vues larges et au caractère indépendant.« Rappard to Calonder, 2. 5. 1919. AF

73 Morley, *op. cit.*, [see note 4] p. 291.

74 *Proceedings of the Exploratory Conference on the League of Nations Secretariat*, Washington, Carnegie Endowment for International Peace, 1942, 130 p. Siotis, *op. cit.*, [see Note 5] p. 101.

75 Salvador de Madariaga, *Morning without Noon, Memoirs*. Westmead, Saxon House, 1973. – p. 278; cf. also Jean Rudolf von Salis, *Grenzüberschreitungen*, Ein Lebensbericht, Zweiter Teil 1939–1978. Zürich, Orell & Füssli, 1978. – p. 125.

76 LoN, Records of the Nineteenth Ordinary Session of the Assembly; Minutes of the Fourth Committee, 19 September 1938, *OJSS*, no. 187, p. 25.

77 LoN, Records of the Fourteenth Ordinary Session of the Assembly, Minutes of the Fourth Committee, 30 September 1933, *OJSS*, no. 118, p. 29.

78 LoN, Records of the Thirteenth Ordinary Session of the Assembly, Minutes of the Fourth Committee, 1 October 1932, *OJSS*, no. 107, p. 24.

79 LoN, Records of the Thirteenth Ordinary Session of the Assembly, Plenary Meetings, 17 October 1932, *OJSS*, no. 104, p. 93.

80 LoN. Records of the Fifteenth Ordinary Session of the Assembly, Minutes of the Fourth Committee, 24 September 1934, *OJSS*, no. 128, p. 56.

81 LoN, Records of the Thirteenth Ordinary Session of the Assembly, Plenary Meetings, 17 October 1932, *OJSS*, no. 104, p. 94.

82 LoN, Records of the Tenth Ordinary Session of the Assembly, Minutes of the Fourth Committee, 19 September 1929, *OJSS*, no. 79, p. 65.

83 LoN, Records of the Thirteenth Ordinary Session of the Assembly, Minutes of the Fourth Committee, 5 October 1932, *OJSS*, no. 107, p. 57.

84 LoN, Records of the Eleventh Ordinary Session of the Assembly, Minutes of the Fourth Committee, 22 September 1930, *OJSS*, no. 88, p. 75.

85 LoN, Records of the Tenth Ordinary Session of the Assembly, Minutes of the Fourth Committee, 20 September 1929, *OJSS*, no. 79, p. 73.

86 Rappard to Drummond, 30. 6. 1920. AF

87 LoN, Records of the Tenth Ordinary Session of the Assembly, Minutes of the Fourth Committee, 16 September 1929, *OJSS*, no. 79, p. 45.

88 William E. Rappard, »The Evolution of the League of Nations«, *The American Political Science Revue*, v. XXI; 4, November 1927, p. 801 ff.

89 William E. Rappard, »La Suisse et les organisations internationales d'après-guerre«. *L'Echo* octobre 1946. – p. 43–51.

90 Rappard, »Vues rétrospectives sur la Societé des Nations«, *RCADI*, v. 71, 1947. – p. 151.

91 Rappard, »La Suisse . . . d'après-guerre«, *op. cit.*, p. 7.

92 Rappard, »The Evolution . . .« *op. cit.*, p. 808.

93 Walters, *A History of the League of Nations*, *op. cit.*, p. 118 f.

94 Rappard, »The Evolution . . .«, *op. cit.*, p. 808.

95 Rappard, *The Geneva Experiment*, *op. cit.*, p. 96.

96 LoN, Records of the Ninth Ordinary Session of the Assembly, Minutes of the Fourth Committee, 6 September 1928, *OJSS*, no. 68, p. 12.

97 *Loc. cit.*
98 Rappard, »Vues rétrospectives . . .«, *op. cit.*, p. 207.
99 Rappard, »La Suisse . . . d'après guerre«, *op. cit.*, p. 6.
100 Rappard, *The Geneva Experiment, op. cit.*, [see Note 65], p. 102.
101 Rappard, »La Suisse . . . d'après-guerre«, *op. cit.*, p. 6. Rappard, »La Suisse et la Charte de San Francisco«. *La Suisse. Un annuaire national,* 1946. – p. 2.
102 William E. Rappard, "The United Nations as Viewed from Geneva". *The American Political Science Review,* 40/3 June 1946. – p. 545–551; *Varia Politica, op. cit.* p. 203. Elsewhere Rappard also includes the Great Powers in this danger: »Mais ni les petits ni les grands ne sont protégées contre les grands ou contre un de leurs satellites«. Rappard, »La Suisse . . . d'après-guerre«, *op. cit.*, p. 6.
103 Rappard, »La Suisse . . . San Francisco«, *op. cit.*, p. 13. William E. Rappard, »La neutralité suisse et l'Union européenne«. Conférence inédite faite à la Section zurioise de la Société de Zofingue, le 28 mai 1951. *Varia Politica, op. cit.*, p. 250 f.
104 Rappard, »La Suisse . . . d'après-guerre«, *op. cit.*, p. 7.
105 William E. Rappard, "The United Nations from a European Point of View". *The Yale Law Journal,* 55, p. 1047. August 1946.
106 Rappard, »La neutralitée suisse«, *op. cit.*, p. 249.
107 Rappard, »La Suisse . . . San Francisco«, *op. cit.*, p. 5 f.
108 *Ibid.* p. 16
Rappard, »La Suisse . . . d'après-guerre«, [see Note 89] p. 8. Rappard, speaking in front of a Swiss audience, used the term of ›Zugewandter Ort‹ which means a state of restricted membership to the ancient Swiss Confederacy.
109 Rappard, "The United Nations . . . in *Varia Politica, oü. cit.* p. 204.
110 *ibid.*, p. 202.
111 Rappard, *International Relations, op. cit.*, p. 9.
112 William E. Rappard, »A propos de l'agonie de la Société des Nations«. *La Suisse. Un annuaire national,* 1940–1941, p. 233–241.
113 Stefan Zweig, *Die Welt von Gestern. Erinnerungen eines Europäers,* Stockholm, Bermann-Fischer, 1944.
114 Rappard, »A propos de l'agonie . . .«, *op. cit.*, p. 6 f.
115 Rappard, "The United Nations from a European Point of View«, *op. cit.*, p. 1043.
116 Rappard, "The United Nations as viewed from Geneva" *In:* Varia Politica, *op. cit.*, p. 200.
117 Dinner at the Hotel Richemond, Geneva, 9 July 1955, on the occasion of Rappard's resignation as Head of the 'Institute'. Hommage à William Rappard, 1956. – p. 84; Picot, *op. cit.*, [cf. Note 37] p. 50.
118 Message (of the Federal Council to the National Assembly concerning entry into the League of Nations) of 4 August 1919, Berne 1919, p. 105; in the sense here quoted referred to by Rappard in Rappard, »La neutralité suisse«, *Varia Politica, op. cit.*, [see. Note 2], p. 252.

Chapter/Chapitre III

Security problems

Les problèmes de la sécurité

La Société des Nations et le désarmement

Maurice Vaïsse
Université de Paris I

Parmi tous les espoirs que soulevaient la création et l'existence de la SdN, le plus grand était sans aucun doute celui de réduire le fardeau des armements nationaux et de mettre fin à la course aux armements jugée responsable du déclenchement de la Grande Guerre. A tort ou à raison, la réduction des armements était considérée non seulement comme le test du succès de la SdN mais aussi comme l'objet même de son existence.[1] Or la SdN échoue. Le désarmement réalisé »sur le tas« dans les années 20 pour des raisons financières n'est pas valable aux yeux du Pacte.[2] Ces réductions d'armement, décidées en toute souveraineté par chaque pays, ne sont pas prises en application d'un plan général de désarmement, et ne sont soumises à aucun contrôle international. Si le désarmement naval enregistre des succès aux conférences de Washington et de Londres, c'est qu'il est de loin le plus facile à mettre en oeuvre et à contrôler. Les trois plus grandes puissances navales s'entendent entre elles pour mettre fin à une course aux armements ruineuse, tout en consolidant aux moindres frais leur suprématie navale. Surtout, ce désarmement naval n'est pas entrepris dans le cadre de la SdN. Non seulement la SdN échoue, mais le désarmement attendu se transforme en réarmement et aboutit à la seconde guerre mondiale. Nous nous proposons d'expliquer pourquoi il y a eu échec du désarmement dans le cadre de la SdN.[3]

Il y a échec parce que le Pacte est un instrument imparfait pour aboutir au désarmement. Il est le fruit d'un compromis entre des tendances opposées, et il est lié aux traités de paix dont le maintien suppose le *statu quo*, c'est-à-dire la coexistence d'Etats armés et désarmés. Entre les projets et les textes, la SdN perd en efficacité et le désarmement en force résolutoire.

A l'encontre du projet Wilson, Clemenceau fait prévaloir une conception non restrictive de la sécurité. Mais lorsqu'il s'agit d' organiser la sécurité, il en est tout autrement. Le projet Léon Bourgeois d'un désarmement contrôlé dont les manquements seraient sanctionnés à l'aide d'une force internationale se heurte à l'hostilité des Anglo-Saxons qui repoussent aussi le contrôle.[4] Effort sans précédent pour l'organisation de la paix, le Pacte pèche par le caractère trop vague de ses clauses, comme le montre l'article 8, charte du désarmement. L'adhésion au Pacte entraîne la reconnaissance que le maintien de la paix exige la réduction des armements. Bien que le Pacte ne mette pas en cause la légitimité des armements, il limite le droit d'entretenir une armée. Ce droit subsiste seulement pour des buts nettement définis: sauvegarder la sécurité ou exécuter des obligations internationales. Il faut donc laisser à la disposition des Etats des forces armées pour qu'ils puissent s'acquitter de leurs engagements. *Ainsi le Pacte écarte le désarmement complet; il se borne à imposer le devoir de réduire les armements.* L'expression est très vague quant au niveau des armements, car il est extrêmement difficile de déterminer »le minimum compatible avec la sécurité nationale«. L'article 8 définit aussi le rôle du Conseil: il ne peut pas imposer aux membres le devoir de réduire leurs armements; il ne s'occupe que de la préparation des plans qu'il soumet aux gouvernements, qui sont libres de les accepter ou de les repousser.

Le Pacte, qui invite à la réduction des armements donc à l'égalisation de statut militaire entre les vainqueurs et les vaincus, est lié aux traités et en particulier au traité de Versailles, dont la partie V fixe les effectifs de l'armée allemande à 100 000 hommes et prescrit son organisation dans les moindres détails.[5] Mais le désarmement de l'Allemagne doit, aux termes du préambule de la partie V, servir de modèle et de prélude au désarmement général.[6] La concession de Clemenceau à l'idéal wilsonien est purement formelle, car elle subordonne à l'exécution des engagements de l'Allemagne le désarmement des autres puissances, et elle est dangereuse car elle introduit dans le traité une imprécision supplémentaire, source de conflits pour les années à venir.[7]

Conformément au Pacte (article 9), le Conseil crée la Commission permanente consultative dont les membres – officiers désignés par leur gouvernement – devaient établir des plans de réduction d'armements prévus à l'article 8. A la demande de l'Assemblée, dont la troisième Commission s'occupe activement du désarmement, le Conseil crée la Commission temporaire mixte, composée en majorité de personnalités civiles. Dans le cadre du Secrétariat, une Section du désarmement est créée.[8] La mise en place des nouvelles institutions nées du Pacte est lente. C'est »la phase théorique et sentimentale« à un moment où la paix se révèle plus précaire que prévu.[9]

Le désarmement est un échec parce que la SdN n'est pas universelle: à ses débuts elle ne compte ni l'Allemagne, ni l'URSS, ni les Etats-Unis d'Amérique. L'absence des »grands Etats militaires« est même le prétexte invoqué par la première Assemblée pour ajourner tout examen sérieux du désarmement, mais elle a des effets bien plus nocifs. Le refus du Sénat américain de ratifier le traité de Versailles affaiblit la SdN sur le plan moral, puisque le principal maître d'oeuvre s'abstient; il diminue son importance sur le plan matériel: comment serait-elle un »instrument efficace à l'échelle mondiale« sans la coopération des Etats-Unis?[10] Comment concevoir un plan de désarmement sans la participation américaine?[11] Surtout, il enlève à la France la garantie de sécurité que Wilson et Lloyd George avaient accordée à Clemenceau en compensation de la renonciation française à la formation d'un Etat rhénan. En raison de la défection anglo-saxonne, la France est dans la situation paradoxale d'un vainqueur qui a peur du vaincu. Faute d'une assistance anglo-américaine, la France subordonne tout désarmement à l'obtention de garanties de sécurité.

Dès les origines, la responsabilité américaine est très grande. Avoir promu la SdN et l'avoir ensuite abandonnée vaut aux Etats-Unis d'être, selon Madariaga, "the blackest obstacle on the path towards disarmament".[12] Au cours des années 20, la politique américaine affaiblit le travail collectif de la SdN en prenant des initiatives, par la Conférence de Washington et par la Conférence Coolidge. Le succès relatif de la Conférence de Washington revient ainsi au pays qui a rendu le désarmement impossible à travers la SdN. Ces initiatives apparaissent même comme un défi à la SdN. C'est particulièrement vrai lors de la Conférence Coolidge, dont la tenue à Genève[13] semble incongrue alors que se tiennent les débats de la CPD.[14] Protégés par deux océans, les Etats-Unis qui n'ont rien à craindre de leurs voisins refusent de prendre en considération le besoin de sécurité de la France, et ils ne comprennent pas les dépenses militaires faites par des Etats débiteurs.[15] Puissance navale, ils ont tendance à voir dans les grosses unités navales d'inoffensifs jouets.[16] Très susceptibles, ils refusent tout contrôle de leurs armements.[17] Même quand ils ne sont pas un obstacle au désarmement, les Américains peuvent (par aveuglement ou par surenchère), nuire à la cause dont ils se veulent les champions. »Mus par une vanité illimitée à se déclarer compétents à propos de toute question internationale, les Etats-Unis sont dans l'incapacité d'apporter leur contribution à la solution des problèmes internationaux.«[18]

Quant à l'Union Soviétique, elle constitute aux yeux des pays d'Europe occidentale un danger et un facteur d'instabilité qui justifient à eux seuls de rester armés. De plus, dès la Conférence de Gênes, mais surtout de 1927 à 1932, l'Union Soviétique se pose en champion du désarmement intégral et adopte donc une attitude de surenchère qui nuit aux efforts de la SdN dont la charte en matière de désarmement évoque seulement la réduction des armements, et implique le maintien d'un minimum d'armement afin de concourir aux sanctions militaires. Il est symptomatique que c'est à travers la conférence du désarmement que l'Union Soviétique est amenée à coopérer de plus en plus à l'oeuvre de la SdN et finit par y rentrer. Malgré l'absence de certaines grandes puissances, la SdN aurait pu agir si elle n'avait pas été paralysée par le désaccord franco-britannique.

Or tout le débat sur le désarmement dans les années 1920 se résume à une confrontation entre le Grande-Bretagne et la France. »L'une veut désarmer d'abord . . . L'autre veut pacifier d'abord.[19] Les premières discussions font apparaître le lien entre la réduction des armements et un système d'assistance mutuelle. C'est l'origine de la résolution XIV adoptée par la troisième Assemblée le 27 septembre 1922. Cette résolution, qui subordonne le désarmement à l'assistance mutuelle, est la clef de voûte du système de sécurité collective. Elle doit servir de base à l'élaboration d'un traité d'assistance mutuelle, qui donne lieu à une confrontation entre le projet de Robert Cecil et celui du colonel Réquin.[20] Le pacte de garantie, combinaison des deux projets, est proposé à la quatrième Assemblée dans une conjoncture délicate: l'Allemagne est contrainte à céder dans la Ruhr occupée par les troupes françaises depuis janvier 1923. La Grande-Bretagne et les Dominions sont plus que réticents.[21]

L'échec du Traité d'assistance mutuelle est un rude coup pour la SdN. Mais la coïncidence au pouvoir en France et en Angleterre de Edouard Herriot et de Ramsay MacDonald semble augurer une ère de succès pour la sécurité collective, au moment où les accords de Londres (août 1924) marquent un tournant dans la vie diplomatique de l'après-guerre.[22] Pour rompre le cercle vicieux: Sécurité – Désarmement ne peut-on avoir recours à l'arbitrage? propose MacDonald; Herriot accepte et énonce la fameuse trilogie: Arbitrage – Sécurité – Désarmement. La résolution franco-britannique qui sert de base pour l'élaboration du *Protocole pour le règlement pacifique des différends internationaux* est adoptée à l'unanimité le 2 octobre 1924. Ce protocole met en place un système de règlement pacifique de tous les différends pouvant surgir entre Etats qui doivent alors s'en remettre à l'arbitrage international. L'interdépendance entre la sécurité et la réduction des armements y est réglée et prévue dans les moindres dispositions. Malgré son adoption dans l'enthousiasme, le Protocole reste lettre morte.[23] En novembre 1924 en effet, le gouvernement travailliste de MacDonald est remplacé par un gouvernement conservateur qui décide d'en ajourner la signature.[24] Le 12 mars 1925, par sa déclaration devant le Conseil de la SdN, Austen Chamberlain donne le coup de grâce au projet. La même année, les accords de Locarno, dans l'esprit du Protocole,[25] situent bien les positions: au contraire de la France qui y voit le commencement de l'organisation de la sécurité, ils en sont pour l'Angleterre: »l'achèvement, la dispensant de toute autre précision«.[26]

Une fois de plus l'entreprise de désarmement est remise en chantier par la SdN qui la confie, en décembre 1925, à une Commission préparatoire pour la conférence du désarmement (CPD) ouverte à la fois à des représentants des Etats membres de la SdN et à des pays non membres comme les Etats-Unis et l'URSS. A un moment où les relations internationales, propices à des accords bilatéraux et multilatéraux (Pacte Briand-Kellogg), connaissent une réelle détente, la CPD met quatre ans à définir un projet de convention du désarmement. Embarrassée dans des considérations techniques, la CPD est surtout paralysée par le désaccord franco-britannique. Il apparaît dans les projets de convention Cecil et Paul-Boncour, présentés lors de la troisième session (21 mars–26 avril 1927). Celui de R. Cecil prône l'étude séparée des armements terrestre et naval, la publicité des dépenses d'armement, la limitation des effectifs du temps de paix, la limitation navale par catégorie de bâtiments, la limitation des armements aériens par le nombre des appareils et une vague formule de surveillance. Le projet de Paul-Boncour, au contraire, insiste sur l'interdépendance des armements et sur la liaison sécurité-désarmement. Il préconise une organisation préalable et précise de l'assistance militaire dont ne veulent pas les Anglais qui soutiennent que les sanctions économiques, obligatoires aux termes de l'article 16 du Pacte, suffiraient à décourager l'agression ou à la faire cesser. Il recommande la limitation des dépenses des armements navals et aériens, et le contrôle de ces dispositions par une commission. L'opposition est si tranchée que tout compromis paraît impossible. Les plus graves divergences portent sur les réserves instruites,[27] les stocks de mobilisation, la limitation des dépenses militaires, le contrôle international des armements, et sur les armements navals. Cette divergence de vues, tant sur l'interprétation sociologique des armements que sur la méthode de désarmement,[28] cache en fait une opposition beaucoup plus profonde sur le maintien de la paix dans l'Europe de Versailles. Pour les Britanniques, les armements sont la cause directe des guerres. Réduire les armements, c'est diminuer le nombre des hommes en état de combattre; limiter directement le matériel de guerre, c'est écarter la possibilité d'une guerre, retarder son déclenchement, empêcher sa prolongation. Du désarmement sort la sécurité. Pour les Français, c'est l'insécurité qui crée un besoin de défense et d'armements. Désarmer, c'est priver les nations pacifiques d'armes qui dissuaderaient les agresseurs éventuels.

Ce contraste entre la position britannique et la position française sur le désarmement provient d'une différence d'attitude fondamentale sur la sécurité. Une fois l'ennemi disparu, la flotte allemande anéantie, la Grande-Bretagne à l'abri dans son île ne comprend pas le besoin de sécurité des Etats continentaux qui lui semble une obsession. A la différence des Français, qui ne se sentent pas en sécurité, les Britanniques estiment leur sécurité assurée par la victoire et font pression en faveur du désarmement. Certes, le désarmement britannique correspond à un besoin d'économie, mais il est aussi effectué en connaissance de cause. Au Comité de Défense Impériale, au début des années 20, les responsables politiques avertissent les chefs des forces armées qu'ils n'ont pas à prévoir de grand conflit avant dix ans.[29] Conséquences: l'armée britannique démobilise rapidement, ses effectifs diminuent régulièrement, et l'aviation néglige son équipement; quant à la Royal Navy, elle accepte la parité avec la marine américaine lors des accords de Washington, et une limitation générale lors des accords de Londres.

En fait, la divergence de vues entre la France et la Grande-Bretagne en matière de désarmement camoufle un désaccord bien plus profond sur le maintien de la paix dans l'Europe de Versailles.[30] Si l'on se prononce pour l'exécution, la paix doit être assurée par les sanctions et par la force. Prône-t-on la révision? Le désarmement qui met fin à l'inégalité du statut militaire en Europe est un objectif prioritaire. D'ailleurs, le pacifisme de l'opinion britannique, hostile à des engagements sur le continent pour perpétuer un règlement territorial injuste en Europe rejoint le souci des hommes d'Etat britanniques de ne souscrire aucun engagement contraignant[31] et de ne pas être le gendarme de la SdN.[32]

Le reproche le plus fréquemment adressé à la politique britannique est de n'avoir pas su faire le geste adéquat au moment opportun. Robert Cecil n'est pas seul à le déplorer.[33] Plus tard, Thanassis Aghnides interpellera Eden: »Pourquoi ne faites-vous pas quelque chose? Parce que si vous ne faites rien, il n'y aura pas de désarmement, c'est clair, il n'y en aura pas.«[34] Faute d'un accord franco-britannique, le CPD doit s'ajourner en 1927 après avoir consigné les résultats de la première lecture du projet de convention. Ce n'est qu'en 1929 qu'une convergence des points de vue anglais, français et américain permet à la CPD d'aboutir à un projet de convention (novembre-décembre 1930).

Le projet de convention témoigne à la fois du sérieux de l'entreprise de la CPD et de ses difficultés. La CPD n'est pas restée au niveau théorique ou général. Tout est prévu, mais rien n'est fixé. Le projet de convention ne contient en effet aucun chiffre. La CPD s'est contentée de dresser un cadre. A la Conférence de faire l'essentiel, c'est-à-dire, d'une part adopter ou rejeter tout ou partie de ce cadre, d'autre part de choisir des chiffres tant pour les effectifs que pour le matériel. Le projet de convention est un projet de limitation, non de réduction. Les mesures les plus audacieuses de désarmement ont été soigneusement ramenées à des modestes propositions de publicité des armements. Au lieu de mener au désarmement, le projet de convention gèle les armements existants. Constituant un succès pour la France qui a réussi à écarter la limitation des réserves instruites et la limitation directe du matériel, le projet est vivement contesté par les puissances désarmées qui critiquent son hypocrisie et refusent de souscrire à un texte qui pérennise leur infériorité militaire.[35] Quant à la complicité franco-britannique, elle est éphémère: la Grande-Bretagne qui reproche à la France de ne pas adhérer à la partie III du traité naval de Londres, adopte une attitude d'arbitre et refuse tout nouvel engagement lors de la Conférence du désarmement. Alors, plus que jamais, la discorde franco-britannique s'exaspère, avant de mener à l'alignement français dans *l'appeasement*.

Le désarmement est un échec parce que dans les principaux pays il existe des forces hostiles au désarmement, pour des raisons diverses.[36] Voulant expliquer l'échec de la conférence du désarmement, Philip Noël-Baker s'en prend dans son dernier livre aux *faucons;*[37] selon lui, les négociations ont échoué »because men in positions of authority or influence have wanted them to fail, and have striven successfully to make them do so«.[38] Avant les faucons, Noël-Baker avait attiré l'attention sur le rôle des marchands de canons.[39] Le caractère polémique de telles affirmations, les qualificatifs journalistiques utilisés et les erreurs historiques[40] ne doivent pas nous faire oublier que Philip Noël-Baker a mis l'accent sur des obstacles majeurs au désarmement. Que des hommes (défendant des intérêts) aient tenté de nuire aux négociations du désarmement, c'est indéniable. Mais autant il est difficile de prouver l'action des marchands de canon,[41] autant les preuves abondent sur le rôle des Etats-majors.

Confier le désarmement à des militaires, c'était aller au-devant d'un échec. Non parce qu'ils ne peuvent eux-mêmes abolir leur instrument de travail, mais parce que leur existence consiste à assurer la sécurité de leur pays.[42] Or les experts militaires ont toujours été nombreux à Genève. A commencer par la Commission permanente consultative[43]: elle comprenait des officiers dont le métier était de faire ce que leurs supérieurs disaient, c'est-à-dire rien, et empêcher si possible quiconque de faire quelque chose.[44] Aussi, à la demande expresse de l'Assemblée, le Conseil crée-t-il, le 25 février 1921, une autre commission qui doit envisager la question du désarmement dans ses aspects généraux en liaison avec la sécurité collective, la Commission temporaire mixte largement ouverte aux civils. Néanmoins, à l'intérieur de chaque pays, les militaires continuent d'intervenir; la préparation des négociations est laissée à la seule charge des Etats-majors qui définissent la politique de leur pays et donnent des instructions strictes. La Conférence Coolidge en est un exemple parfait.[45] Hugh Wilson le constate à la conférence navale de Londres.[46] D'autre part, les militaires sont eux-mêmes chargés de participer aux négociations. L'Amirauté britannique influence les gouvernements anglais, à tel point que Cecil donne sa démission.[47] L'Etat-major français pèse de tout son poids pour éviter les réductions d'armement, en particulier de matériel. Le général Gamelin intervient en pleine discussion à Genève pour rappeler à Tardieu que la France ne peut accepter aucune réduction de ses armements. Le général Weygand oppose une résistance ferme au plan Paul-Boncour.

La toute-puissance des experts présente de graves inconvénients pour le fonctionnement de la diplomatie en régime démocratique.[48] "The officials should be, as the Americans say, always on tap and never on top."[49] Au cours des conversations de décembre 1932, pressé par MacDonald de se prononcer sur la possibilité d'un accord naval franco-italien, Herriot répond qu'il a besoin des avis du ministre de la Marine et de ses experts.[50] MacDonald lui rétorque alors que »c'est une erreur de s'en remettre pour les décisions aux experts; il faut leur demander leur avis et décider soi-même«. Mais le recours aux experts sert parfois de prétexte aux hommes politiques pour refuser ou enterrer une question. »Chaque fois que les délégués se trouvaient devant un problème insoluble ou qu'ils désiraient gagner du temps, ils nommaient une commission d'experts qu'ils critiquaient ensuite parce qu'elle n'avait pas résolu la difficulté.« Au fond, les experts sont parfois les boucs-émissaires des impasses auxquelles ont mené les hommes politiques par leur scepticisme. Robert Cecil le constate en Angleterre. En France, la diplomatie genevoise est loin de faire l'unanimité. Même chez un homme comme Briand, on trouve du scepticisme à l'égard du désarmement.[51]

Echec parce que la conférence du désarmement, convoquée trop tard et sous de mauvais auspices, n'a pas fait l'objet d'une préparation diplomatique suffisante. Le problème politique fondamental reste l'antagonisme franco-allemand. A l'exigence allemande de révision du système de Versailles, s'oppose la volonté française de maintien du *statu quo*. Au moment où la dynamique des relations internationales dans ces années de crise économique[52] remet en question l'Europe de 1919, la France et ses alliés s'accrochent à la stabilisation politique du continent. Sur le plan militaire, celle-ci suppose l'inégalité d'armements entre la France et l'Allemagne, qu'avantagent une population plus nombreuse et un potentiel de guerre plus considérable. Pour l'Etat-major français, la sécurité de la France, une fois la Rhénanie évacuée, ne repose plus que sur l'inégalité d'armements entre la France et l'Allemagne, dont la nécessité est réaffirmée par le mémorandum du 15 juillet 1931.

Avec Brüning, la révision négociée du système de Versailles demeure le leitmotiv de la diplomatie allemande dont l'objectif est d'obtenir l'annulation des réparations, et la concession de l'égalité des droits.[53] En fait, il s'agit de transformer la Reichswehr et de substituer une nouvelle convention à la partie V du traité de Versailles.

Toute une année s'écoule encore avant l'ouverture de la Conférence du désarmement. Or cette occasion n'est pas mise à profit pour résoudre les problèmes politiques. Au contraire, ceux-ci s'aggravent au cours de »l'année terrible«: le projet douanier austro-allemand et le moratoire Hoover opposent la France à l'Allemagne, alors que la Grande-Bretagne connaît une grave crise interne. Les circonstances dans lesquelles la conférence se réunit sont loin d'être favorables, et cependant sa tenue (cause ou hasard?) coïncide avec une pause dans la course aux armements. Pour les années 1931, 1932, 1933,[54] sur le plan naval le désarmement est réel, même s'il est partiel. Quant au désarmement terrestre, on a assisté à des réductions considérables depuis la guerre. Les grandes armées anglaise et américaine, mises sur pied pour combattre en France, ont été démobilisées. L'armée française elle-même, qui subit pendant les années 20 une réduction substantielle des effectifs et de la durée du service, un laisser-aller dans l'équipement et une mentalité défensive, représente une puissance militaire très peu menaçante.

En ce qui concerne les dépenses d'armements, la tendance générale est au freinage en 1931 et en 1932. Si les six grandes puissances qui totalisent à elles seules 75% des dépenses mondiales ont peu diminué (de l'ordre de 2,5%), les petites ont réduit leurs dépenses dans des proportions plus considérables: 14%

entre 1930 et 1932. Il y avait une chance sérieuse de succès si les grandes puissances se mettaient d'accord, à un moment où la tendance générale était à la baisse. Certes la pause dans la course aux armements constatée en 1931–1932 n'est pas entièrement due à la tenue de la conférence du désarmement. La grande crise économique qui secoue le monde joue à coup sûr un rôle prépondérant. La réduction des dépenses militaires est un remède tout trouvé aux problèmes financiers. On ne peut donc pas dire que la conférence tombait au pire moment.[55]

D'autres indices sont beaucoup moins encourageants. La démocratie, qui avait paru sortir fortifiée du premier conflit mondial, semble en déclin: des régimes dictatoriaux naissent et se consolident en Italie, au Japon; la démocratie est menacée en Allemagne. Surtout le conflit sino-japonais, né à l'automne 1931, est de fâcheux augure pour une conférence du désarmement. A la suite d'attentats commis dans la région de Moukden dans l'été 1931, l'armée japonaise garante de la sécurité ferroviaire étend son emprise sur toute la Mandchourie, occupe Changhaï en janvier 1932 et provoque la création d'un nouvel Etat en mars 1932. Devant ce coup de force déguisé en opération de police, la SdN et les Etats membres manifestent leur impuissance. Certes, dès le début, la SdN demande l'évacuation des territoires occupés et la collaboration de toutes les puissances, y compris les Etats-Unis, car l'enjeu apparaît clairement.[56] Si le système de sécurité collective réussit à faire échec à l'agression japonaise et prouve par là son efficacité, l'autorité de la SdN s'en trouvera considérablement renforcée.[57] Malgré cet enjeu, il ne sort rien des délibérations de l'Assemblée et du Conseil de la SdN[59], en raison des réticences des grandes puissances à s'opposer au Japon, et à risquer leur autorité dans une affaire lointaine à un moment où le mot d'ordre est à l'économie.[60] C'est le premier échec de la sécurité collective, d'autant plus grave qu'il intervient à la veille puis au cours de la conférence du désarmement, car l'écho des combats qui se déroulent en Chine se répercute fâcheusement à Genève. »On ne peut imaginer de loin l'extraordinaire jeu de va-et-vient entre la série de réunions cherchant désespérement à arrêter la guerre en Chine et l'autre série de réunions cherchant presque aussi désespérément à amener les nations à réduire leurs armements.«[61]

D'autres facteurs tiennent à des questions d'hommes ou de dispositions. On a mis en cause le rôle du Secrétariat,[62] d'Avenol[63] et d'Henderson: Henderson est choisi comme président alors qu'il est secrétaire au Foreign Office. En février 1932, il n'est plus rien: son autorité s'en ressent. Il fait l'admiration par sa gentillesse et sa disponibilité, mais il est de santé fragile, il ne parle ni ne comprend le français, et ses désaccords avec Ramsay MacDonald sont notoires.[64] Bien que le Secrétariat de la SdN et les autorités helvétiques aient tout fait pour que les conditions matérielles de la Conférence soient propices, certains regrettent l'atmosphère névrosée,[65] artificielle[66] ou abrutissante[67] de Genève.[68]

On constate l'omniprésence des experts et des militaires dans une Conférence dont les implications sont surtout politiques. Les experts ont sur les hommes politiques un double avantage: la compétence et la présence. Pour des raisons électorales ou parlementaires, les seconds ne font que passer, et souvent même changent.[69] De ce point de vue-là l'année 1932 est une année particulièrement chargée.[70] Les effets de ces joutes électorales à répétition sont considérables: ils éloignent les hommes politiques de Genève pendant les périodes électorales, ils influencent les débats et incitent aux spéculations.[71] A cela s'ajoute l'annonce par l'Allemagne qu'elle ne pourra reprendre le paiement des réparations, ce qui traduit en fait une volonté d'annuler purement et simplement les réparations. Cette annonce, faite dans des conditions ambiguës, jette un doute sérieux sur le degré de confiance à accorder à l'Allemagne.[72] L'atmosphère internationale est tellement lourde qu'on envisage l'ajournement de la conférence du désarmement. Mais personne n'ose le proposer. La conférence va alors se dérouler comme une tragédie grecque. La seule différence est qu'il n'y aura pas de *deus ex machina* à la conférence de Genève.[73]

Echec parce que la conférence du désarmement tourne à l'épreuve de force franco-allemande. L'enjeu de la conférence pour la réduction et la limitation des armements[74] qui s'ouvre le 2 février 1932, est l'équilibre des forces en Europe. La France, considérée comme la plus grande puissance militaire, paraît directement visée par la conférence. L'Allemagne, officiellement désarmée, a tout à y gagner. Que les autres puissances désarment, elle y gagnera par le nivellement des armements; que les puissances victorieuses refusent d'abandonner les instruments de la victoire, et elle sera en droit de réclamer des armes. Dès le début, le sort de la conférence est suspendu à l'issue du duel franco-allemand. Devant la revendication allemande de l'égalité des droits, la France contre-attaque en accusant l'Allemagne de réarmer clandestinement, et elle en tire argument pour refuser de désarmer, sans garantie supplémentaire de sécurité. Aussi fait-elle figure d'obstacle au désarmement: »Chaque fois que nous – Henderson et Aghnides – voulions avancer un peu plus loin, nous étions très mal vus, et par une certaine délégation que vous devinez, qui ne voulait pas du désarmement, les pressions étaient constantes et pénibles«.[75] D'entrée de jeu, le premier délégué français, André Tardieu, soumet un plan destiné à ajourner indéfiniment toute concession d'une égalité des droits à l'Allemagne, et à faire porter la responsabilité de l'échec aux puissances qui refuseraient d'accroître les garanties de sécurité. Tardieu propose en effet la mise à la disposition de la SdN de l'aéronautique civile de transport et de l'aviation de bombardement, de certains matériels terrestres et navals, la création d'une force internationale et des garanties de sécurité. Du plan Tardieu on retient seulement le principe du désarmement qualitatif qui plaît à l'Allemagne, et dont les avantages humanitaires et financiers sont évidents. Le 20 avril, la Commission générale adopte le principe du désarmement qualitatif, et confie son étude aux commissions spécialisées qui sont chargées de dire quelles sont les armes les plus spécifiquement offensives.[76] Cet épisode tourne à la farce. Les discussions font surtout apparaître le talent des experts et les égoïsmes nationaux. Chaque grande puissance propose d'enthousiasme l'abolition des armes auxquelles elle ne tient pas, alors que sa rivale y possède une supériorité incontestée.

Les conversations privées entreprises fin avril à Bessinges autour du Secrétaire d'Etat Stimson et du Premier ministre britannique MacDonald dans l'espoir de parvenir à une solution politique ne débouchent pas sur un résultat.[77] Le chancelier Brüning demande à ses interlocuteurs de transférer la partie V du traité de Versailles dans la future convention du désarmement et d'autoriser l'Allemagne à modifier certaines clauses.[78] Si la laryngite que prétexte Tardieu pour décliner l'invitation à se rendre à Bessinges n'est pas une maladie diplomatique,[79] elle est particulièrement opportune. Comment Tardieu aurait-il pu, à la veille d'élections générales, accepter une transformation de la Reichswehr?[80] Selon Temperley, »un accord aurait signifié la paix pour une génération«.[81] La réalité est tout autre. L'arrangement était ambigu. Ni les Américains ni les Anglais n'étaient disposés à offrir de nouvelles garanties de sécurité. D'ailleurs, les Allemands n'attendent pas le résultat des négociations pour mettre en oeuvre le réarmement soigneusement dissimulé par la collaboration des hommes politiques et militaires.[82] C'est en avril 1932 précisément que le commandement allemand approuve les préparatifs du plan *Umbau.*

Alors qu'une conférence est réunie à Lausanne pour débattre des réparations et mettre pratiquement fin à leur paiement par l'Allemagne qui plaide l'insolvabilité, le président américain lance, le 22 juin 1932, de façon impromptue, un plan draconien fondé sur la distinction entre les forces défensives et les forces d'agression.[83] Si ces propositions concrètes paraissent donner »un élan nouveau«[84] à la conférence, en revanche le plan Hoover néglige d'apporter une solution au problème de la sécurité. Surtout, il apparaît comme une manifestation à caractère électoral,[85] comme un geste spectaculaire »sorti tout droit d'Alice au Pays des Merveilles«. Le plan Hoover crée une situation confuse, car ni la France ni la Grande-Bretagne ne peuvent l'accepter. Les réserves en rendent impossible l'application pratique ou immédiate. C'est pourquoi l'idée de synthétiser les points d'accord dans une résolution de caractère général fait son chemin.

Votée le 23 juillet 1932 par 41 voix contre 2 (Allemagne et URSS) et 8 abstentions, la résolution Bénès non seulement ne règle rien, mais elle met au premier plan le problème de l'égalité des droits, puisque la délégation allemande a fait savoir qu'elle ne pouvait continuer à participer à la Conférence que si cette égalité était reconnue. En fait, le 7 novembre 1932, la Reichswehr passe aux actes et décide d'appliquer le plan *Umbau* à partir du ler avril 1933: il s'agit de détripler la Reichswehr et de mettre sur pied une armée de campagne de vingt-et-une divisions modernes pour le ler avril 1938.[86]

Inquiet du réarmement allemand et de la menace hitlérienne,[87] le gouvernement Herriot refuse de prendre en considération une demande allemande de négociation bilatérale, et il propose de donner satisfaction à l'Allemagne dans le cadre d'un règlement global. Fondé sur le plan Hoover, le plan Herriot-Paul-Boncour consiste à réduire les forces d'agression tout en insistant sur une organisation souple de la sécurité, permettant ainsi aux Etats-Unis et à la Grande-Bretagne de ne s'engager qu'en partie.[88] Les Etats de l'Europe continentale liés par un pacte d'assistance mutuelle pourraient ramener leurs fores armées à des milices, à effectifs et temps de service réduits.[89] A l'égard de l'Allemagne, les dispositions du plan constructif ont un caractère équivoque. D'un côté, elles mettent l'Allemagne à égalité avec les autres nations européennes par l'uniformisation des forces armées continentales: c'est l'égalité des droits; de l'autre, elles mettent l'Allemagne à l'épreuve en la contraignant à sacrifier la Reichswehr: c'est la manoeuvre destinée à faire apparaître la volonté de réarmement de l'Allemagne. De son côté, le Royaume-Uni présente, le 17 novembre 1932, une série de propositions destinées à donner également satisfaction à l'Allemagne, dans la mesure où cela n'impliquerait pas le réarmement. Surtout, le Foreign Office multiplie les démarches diplomatiques pour obtenir le retour de l'Allemagne à la Conférence.[90]

Réunis à Genève du 3 au 12 décembre 1932, les représentants des Etats-Unis, du Royaume-Uni, de la France, de l'Allemagne et de l'Italie, aboutissent à un accord et conviennent que l'un des principes de la Conférence du désarmement doit être l'octroi à l'Allemagne de l'égalité des droits dans un régime de sécurité. Cet accord permet le retour de l'Allemagne à la Conférence, mais il est ambigu. Que serait ce régime de sécurité? L'égalité des droits est-elle un point de départ ou un point d'aboutissement? De plus il n'apporte aucun résultat positif dans le domaine du désarmement.[91] Enfin, l'accord du 11 décembre 1932 est considéré comme la porte ouverte à la révision des traités.[92]

Quand la Conférence reprend ses travaux, le 2 février 1932, Hitler est devenu chancelier, et l'atmosphère de guerre réapparaît un peu partout: en Extrême-Orient et en Amérique du Sud, mais aussi en Europe. Le Japon qui a réussi à détacher la Mandchourie de la Chine, rejette le rapport Lytton et annonce, le 27 mars 1933, son intention de quitter la SdN.[93] Le conflit du Chaco dégénère en guerre entre le Paraguay et la Bolivie. La tension germano-polonaise et franco-allemande fait craindre à plusieurs reprises une guerre préventive. En Allemagne, Hitler poursuit avec plus de vigueur la politique révisionniste de la République de Weimar contre le traité de Versailles[94] et donne toute latitude à la Reichswehr pour son réarmement.[95] Il a une profonde aversion pour la SdN et n'escompte rien de bon des négociations, mais il lui faut gagner du temps pour renforcer l'Allemagne. C'est pourquoi il ne rompt pas tout de suite. »La négociation de Genève est un ballet d'avant-scène chargé de dissimuler ce qui se passe en profondeur, c'est-à-dire l'*Umbau* de la Reichswehr«.[96] Ce double jeu allemand réussit d' autant mieux qu'il bénéficie de la complicité italienne et de l'*appeasement* britannique.[97]

L'examen par la Commission générale du plan constructif français mène rapidement à une impasse. L'Allemagne et l'Italie rejettent le pacte d'assistance mutuelle. L'échec du plan constructif est acquis. Dès lors, on ne négocie plus pour aboutir. Les dialogues entre Paul-Boncour et Massigli d'une part, Nadolny d'autre part, tournent à la passe d'armes destinée à mettre l'adversaire en difficulté devant l'opinion internationale.[98] De fait, en raison de la radicalisation de son régime politique (incendie du Reichstag le 27 février, élections du 5 mars, pleins pouvoirs, persécutions antisémites), l'Allemagne perd du terrain: plusieurs pays se prononcent pour une organisation rigoureuse de la sécurité. L'impasse est telle que la délégation britannique prépare, à l'initiative du »captain« Eden, un projet de convention destiné à synthétiser toutes les propositions.[99] Le Premier ministre britannique, Ramsay MacDonald, vient lui-même proposer ce plan, volontairement modeste dans ses objectifs et balancé dans ses dispositions.[100] Prévu pour une durée de cinq ans, comme une première étape, il comprend l'établissement d'un contrôle international, d'une Commission permanente du désarmement et d'une procédure consultative, comme garantie de sécurité. Il adopte le système de l'uniformisation des armées d'Europe continentale, assigne des chiffres aux effectifs et des limites pour les matériels.[101] Aux termes du projet britannique, l'Allemagne se voit attribuer une armée de 200 000 hommes et une certaine quantité d'armes. Malgré les réticences françaises[102] et allemandes, le 27 mars 1933 la Commission générale adopte à l'unanimité[103] le projet de convention comme *base de discussion,* mais réserve la possiblilité d'amender le plan lors de son examen détaillé, ajourné d'un mois en raison du projet de Pacte à Quatre lancé par Mussolini. Une fois de plus, la Conférence est menacée et le projet mussolinien propose clairement de substituer à la Conférence du désarmement et à la SdN un directoire des quatre grandes puissances européennes: Italie, Grande-Bretagne, Allemagne, France. L'article 3 prévoit d'autoriser l'Allemagne à réaliser une égalité des droits par degré, en cas d'échec de la Conférence du désarmement. L'émotion des pays de la Petite Entente et de la Pologne devant un pacte ouvertement révisionniste amène la France à faire modifier profondément le projet et à lui ôter quasiment toute nocivité.[104] Néanmoins, pendant un mois, toute l'attention diplomatique a été détournée de Genève.

La première lecture du projet de convention britannique, qui dure du 30 avril au 8 juin 1933, est marquée d'abord par une phase de tension croissante jusqu'à la mi-mai où la délégation allemande fait de l'obstruction.

Dans cette conjoncture, la détente intervient à la suite de deux discours. Le 16 mai, le président Roosevelt s'adresse aux chefs d'Etat représentés à la Conférence de Genève et à la conférence économique de Londres. Approuvant le plan MacDonald, il les adjure de ne pas augmenter leurs armements et il propose un pacte solennel de non-agression. Le 17 mai, le chancelier Hitler, apparaissant comme un chef d'Etat parlant au monde et non comme un chef de bande haranguant ses troupes,[105] excelle à donner de l'Allemagne l'image d'une nation désarmée et de bonne volonté. Il accepte le plan MacDonald comme base de discussion. En fait, il s'agit d'une manoeuvre tactique destinée à rejeter la responsabilité de l'échec sur les adversaires de l'Allemagne.[106] Dès lors la première lecture est menée sans encombre. Finalement, la Commission générale accepte, le 8 juin 1933, le projet britannique comme base de la future convention du désarmement, sous réserve d'amendements ultérieurs. En fait, cette nouvelle session de la Commission générale tourne court en raison de la Conférence économique de Londres, dont l'échec pèse d'ailleurs sur le climat de coopération internationale, et se répercute sur l'évolution de la question du désarmement.[107] Aussi la Commission générale décide-t-elle le 29 juin de s'ajourner jusqu'au 16 octobre 1933, tout en autorisant le président Henderson à mener des négociations afin de régler les problèmes en suspens.

Si les illusions sur le pacifisme hitlérien sont encore partagées par des responsables,[108] et si de toute façon l'*appeasement* est déjà assez répandu, l'inquiétude devant le réarmement allemand justifie le rôle nouveau accordé au contrôle, à l'occasion de conversations anglo-franco-américaines (juin-septembre 1933), le gouvernement français propose et fait accepter une importante modification du projet britannique, consistant à porter la période d'application de cinq à huit ans, et à la séparer en deux phases: la première verrait la transformation des armées continentales en armées de service à court terme, et la mise en œuvre d'un système adéquat de contrôle par l'intermédiaire de la Commission permanente de désarmement; avec la seconde, on passerait au désarmement proprement dit. Même le gouvernement italien se rallie à ces propositions à l'occasion des conversations bilatérales franco-italiennes. Au cours d'une réunion du Bureau, le 14 octobre 1933, sir John Simon rend compte de l'accord intervenu, en insistant sur le fait qu'on ne peut accepter une convention qui comporterait un réarmement immédiat.

Placé devant un front commun et mis devant la nécessité d'accepter un contrôle, le gouvernement hitlérien ne se contente pas de repousser la modification du projet britannique et de rejeter la responsabilité de l'échec sur les Etats puissamment armés. Il annonce sa décision de quitter la conférence et la SdN.[109] La propagande allemande réussit à camoufler ce premier coup de force de la diplomatie hitlérienne.[110] Par une véritable »offensive de paix«, elle dissocie le front commun, neutralise la France par des offres de négociation directe et paralyse la conférence. La Commission générale, troublée par la décision allemande et la désunion des autres puissances, ajourne alors ses travaux, laissant au Bureau la tâche de poursuivre la mise au point du projet de convention. C'est en fait la mise en sommeil de la Conférence et la porte ouverte aux négociations diplomatiques parallèles, de novembre 1933 à avril 1934.

Cette négociation prend la forme d'un échange de notes entre l'Allemagne, la France, la Grande-Bretagne et l'Italie, communiquées par l'entremise de leurs ambassadeurs. La diplomatie traditionnelle ressurgit. Genève n'en est plus le centre, mais un des objets. Aussi le désarmement aboutit-il à remettre en question le rôle de la SdN. Les Allemands veulent bien négocier, mais en dehors de Genève; les Français acceptent de discuter, mais à condition que les conversations facilitent un accord, qui se ferait à Genève. Entre ces positions diamétralement opposées, Anglais et Italiens formulent eux aussi des voeux sur le rôle de Genève et de la SdN, au point que la question de désarmement se double de la question de savoir si les problèmes européens seront réglés par la SdN ou en dehors d'elle. Après quatre mois de discussions, les grandes puissances ont des points de vue plus divergents que jamais. Les exigences allemandes n'ont cessé de croître, profitant de l'*appeasement* de la Grande-Bretagne et de l'Italie. La Grande-Bretagne accorde à l'Allemagne un réarmement sensiblement égal à celui qu'elle réclame (sauf sur le plan aérien) et désarme la France, mais elle lui propose de reconsidérer la question des garanties. Dans cette perspective, elle presse le nouveau gouvernement français présidé par Gaston Doumergue de dire si, dans le cas où on aboutirait à un accord sur les garanties d'exécution, il accepterait comme base de convention le mémorandum britannique du 29 janvier 1934, modifié à la suite de la visite d'Eden à Berlin. Dans ce cas, quelle serait la nature exacte des garanties d'exécution proposées par le gouvernement français? Après avoir beaucoup hésité, le gouvernement français, par la note du 17 avril 1934, souligne que le gouvernement allemand a proclamé sa volonté de poursuivre son réarmement et rend ainsi impossible toute nouvelle négociation. Dans ces conditions, la France a le devoir de pourvoir à sa sécurité, qu'elle ne sépare d'ailleurs pas de la sécurité des autres puissances. Aussi exprime-t-elle l'avis que la Conférence devrait reprendre ses travaux.

A la session de la Commission générale ouverte le 29 mai, l'impasse est totale. Mais personne ne veut prendre l'initiative de proposer un ajournement, de peur de paraître responsable de l'échec de la Conférence. Surtout, le désarmement n'est plus de saison, le réarmement est partout à l'ordre du jour; d'où l'accent mis sur l'organisation de la sécurité par le président Henderson et les délégations française, soviétique, turque et de la Petite Entente. D'autres délégations comme celles de Grande-Bretagne et d'Italie, mettent au premier plan la solution des problèmes politiques, et en particulier le retour de l'Allemagne à Genève. A la suite des réunions du Bureau et de conversations entre délégations, la Commission générale adopte, le 8 juin, une résolution invitant le Bureau à résoudre les problèmes en suspens (dont le retour de l'Allemagne), et privilégiant certaines questions: la sécurité, les garanties d'exécution, l'aviation, la fabrication et le commerce des armes, confiés à des comités. Le Bureau devait encore se réunir en novembre 1934 puis en mai 1937, et différents comités se préoccuper de problèmes particuliers. Mais la Commission générale, c'est-à-dire la Conférence de désarmement, avait tenu sa dernière réunion.

Echec enfin en raison des problèmes. Il est permis de se demander si une conférence investie du programme que l'on sait, universelle par les Etats représentés et par l'étendue de ses préoccupations, n'était pas trop ambitieuse. Peut-être même ce type de réunions facilite-t-il l'obstruction. »Chacun se met à l'avance en position de bataille. On part armé jusqu'aux dents. Les difficultés s'enveniment, les antagonismes s'accusent. Les possibilités d'entente se rétrécissent.«[111] Si bien que, la presse et l'opinion publique aidant, on ne négocie plus pour aboutir mais pour rejeter la responsabilité de l'échec sur l'adversaire.[112] En s'attaquant au principe de la souveraineté nationale, la SdN avait affaire à forte partie. La puissance militaire procure du prestige international, de la prépondérance politique. "The kernel of the problem of disarmament lies in the fact that armaments are instruments of power".[113] De ce point de vue, aucune des grandes puissances ne semble prête à abandonner un pouce de sa souveraineté nationale[114] et ne s'intéresse à la SdN que dans la mesure où elle sert ses intérêts.[115] La responsabilité des grandes puissances est à cet égard écrasante.[116] "The smaller powers were left to stand and watch as a chorus often inactive and dumb, while the big powers pow-wowed in secret over their guns, aircraft and navies".[117] Le Pacte à Quatre en est l'illustration.[118]

Enfin, la question est de savoir si le problème du désarmament n'est pas mal posé. "In fact, the problem of disarmament is not the problem of disarmament. It really is the problem of organization of the world community".[119] Réduire ou limiter les armements, est-ce un objectif réalisable, en dehors de la création d'un nouvel état d'esprit dans l'humanité?[120] N'inverse-t-on pas les problèmes en voulant d'abord se débarrasser des armements avant de s'attaquer au problème de la sécurité?[121] Faute d'avoir résolu le problème de la sécurité, toute activité de désarmement se transforme automatiquement en activité d'armement.[122] C'est le sort, malheureusement, qui s'est abattu sur la conférence du désarmement puisque, lors des dernières réunions de la Commission générale, les différents Etats prenaient, les uns après les autres, des mesures de réarmement.

L'échec de la SdN dans la question du désarmement ne peut donc lui être imputé. Les obstacles et difficultés de tous ordres étaient assez nombreux pour l'expliquer. En revanche, on peut dire que l'échec du désarmement a porté un discrédit considérable à la SdN. Il cause l'amoindrissement de l'institution de

Genève par le désintérêt de certains de ses membres, par les exigences de réforme des autres, enfin par le tort causé à l'esprit sociétaire. Si le Japon ne quitte pas la SdN en raison du désarmement, il est manifestement en désaccord avec le but poursuivi; mais l'Allemagne quitte la SdN en raison de l'impasse de la Conférence du désarmement, et déclare ne vouloir y revenir que lorsque l'égalité des droits lui aura été effectivement reconnue. Quant à l'Italie, le remplacement de Grandi par Italo Balbo annonce une nouvelle étape des relations tendues entre la SdN et l'Italie. Celle-ci ne cache pas son mépris pour l'institution de Genève, et son projet de Pacte à Quatre est ouvertement dirigé contre la SdN. Après le 14 octobre, l'Italie prend une position d'observateur que d'autres pays, par résignation ou désespoir, adoptent lors de la dernière session de la Commission générale. L'Italie en prend même acte pour réclamer une réforme de la SdN, symptôme révélateur des répercussions de l'échec du désarmement sur la SdN. La lucidité ne manque pas à Joseph Avenol qui a vu le danger. Au cours d'une conversation avec les représentants américains, en mai 1934, il estime que la Conférence du désarmement est dans une impasse totale, et confie son inquiétude pour l'avenir de la SdN: dans l'opinion publique, le destin de la SdN est lié au destin de la Conférence du désarmement; plus tôt la SdN sera débarrassée de ce fardeau, plus tôt elle prouvera sa vitalité dans d'autres domaines.[123] A son prédécesseur de juger l'influence du désarmement sur la SdN: faute de pouvoir redresser la situation, écrit Jean Monnet: »La machine se bloqua définitivement sur le problème le plus brûlant, le plus capable de mobiliser l'opinion, celui du désarmement«.[124]

Notes

1 F. P. Walters, *A History of the League of Nations,* London, Oxford University Press, 1960, p. 500.

2 Robert Cecil, *A Great Experiment. An Autobiography,* London, J. Cape, 1941, p. 84.

3 On voudra bien excuser le caractère formel de ces explications. Le cadre limité de cette étude ne permettait pas de nuancer beaucoup et de tout traiter. Quant à notre information, elle provient – outre l'étude de F. Walters, *op. cit.*, et des acteurs – de notre thèse de doctorat sur *La politique française en matière de désarmement entre les deux guerres* (parue en 1981 aux Editions Pedone sous le titre *Sécurité d'abord*).

4 Ce qui explique l'intervention solennelle de Léon Bourgeois lors de la séance plénière du 28 avril 1919: »Ce que nous redouterions le plus pour l'institution internationale, c'est qu'elle apparût un jour inefficace et impuissante«; cf. David Hunter Miller, »My Diary of the Conference of Paris«, v. 20, p. 78.

5 Armée de métier recrutée par voie d'engagement volontaire à long terme (12 ans), conscription abolie, fortifications démantelées, marine réduite, aviation interdite, matériel limité (artillerie lourde inférieure à 105 mm).

6 »En vue de rendre possible la préparation d'une limitation générale des armements de toutes les nations, l'Allemagne s'engage . . .«

7 W. M. Jordan, "*Great Britain, France and the German Problem, 1918–1939. A study of Anglo-French Relations in the Making and Maintenance of the Versailles Settlement*", London, Oxford University Press, 1943. – p. 135.

8 Cf. Salvador de Madariaga, *Disarmament,* London, Oxford University Press, 1929. –

317 p., et *Morning without Noon*, Westmead, Saxon House, 1974. – 411 p.; ASdN, Souvenirs de Thanassis Aghnides.

9 Article de William Martin, in *Journal de Genève*, 23 septembre 1926 cité dans: *William Martin, un grand journaliste à Genève*, Genève, publié sous la direction de Pablo de Azcárate, Centre européen de la Dotation Carnegie pour la paix internationale, 1970. – p. 119.

10 Lettre de Drummond à Sweetser, 25 novembre 1921, citée in Terry Deibel: *Le Secrétariat de la SdN et l'internationalisme américain*, Centre européen de la Dotation Carnegie pour la paix internationale, 1970. – p. 13.

11 »La Réserve Dix, exemptant les Etats-Unis des mesures de désarmement prises par la SdN en cas de guerre ou de menace d'intervention . . . ferait de toute tentative de désarmement de la SdN une moquerie et une farce«. Mémorandum Fosdick, Hudson, Sweetser, 7 novembre 1919, *ibid.*, p. 24.

12 Salvador de Madariaga, *Disarmament, op. cit.*, p. 255, cf. aussi *Morning without Noon, op. cit.*, p. 90.

13 Hugh Wilson in *Diplomat between Wars*, London, Longmans Green, 1941. p. 215 veut y voir un signe de collaboration entre les Etats-Unis et la SdN contrairement à Madariaga, *Morning without Noon, op. cit.*, p. 87–90.

14 "An orchestra is playing Beethoven's Ninth Symphony, under the direction of an experienced conductor; another less experienced conductor turns up between two of the movements and suggests that the five principal executants retire in order to perform a Bach quintet", in Madariaga, *Disarmament, op. cit.*, p. 191.

15 Cf. Hugh Wilson, *Diplomat between Wars, op. cit.*, p. 269 et 273.

16 *Ibid.*, p. 268.

17 Robert Cecil, *A Great Experiment, op. cit.*, 213.

18 Gordon Craig, "The Hoover Administration and the Disarmament Conference" communication au colloque d'Augsburg, mars 1979.

19 Article de William Martin, in *Journal de Genève*, 4 septembre 1924, cité dans *William Martin, un grand journaliste à Genève, op. cit.*, p. 104.

20 Réquin, Edouard, *D'une guerre à l'autre. 1919–1938 – Souvenirs*, Paris, Charles-Lavauzelle, 1949, p. 65–68.

21 Michael Howard, *The Continental Commitment. The Dilemma of British Defense Policy in the Era of the two World Wars.* The Ford lectures in the University of Oxford; London, Maurice Temple Smith, 1971.

22 Cf. Jacques Bariéty, *Les relations franco-allemandes après la première guerre mondiale: 10 novembre 1918 – 10 janvier 1925: de l'exécution à la négociation*, Paris, A. Pedone, 1977. – p. 505–732.

23 Seuls quatorze membres, dont la France, le signent.

24 En fait, avant même le changement de gouvernement, les réticences sont nettes à Londres. cf. David Marquand, *Ramsay MacDonald* London, J. Cape, 1977. p. 353–355.

25 Voir à ce propos Jon Jacobson. *Locarno Diplomacy. Germany and the West*, 1925–1929, Princeton University Press, 1972. – 420 p.

26 Lettre Paul-Boncour/Briand, 10 décembre 1925, Service historique de l'Armée, 7 N 3559-1.

27 Cf. Réquin, *D'une guerre à l'autre, op. cit.*, p. 98: »Il suffisait de jeter dans la discussion les mots de ›réserves instruites‹ pour réveiller instantanément l'Angleterre . . . et les Etats-Unis, prêts à l'attaque«.

28 Sur ce débat franco-britannique, voir l'ouvrage classique de Jordan, *Great Britain, France and the German Problem, op. cit.*, et David Carlton, "The Anglo-French Compromise on Arms Limitation, 1928" *Journal of British Studies* v. 8, 1969, p. 151–162;

"Disarmament with Guarantees: Lord Cecil, 1922–1927", *Disarmament and Arms Control*, v. III.

29 Robert Shay, *British Rearmament in the Thirties: Politics and Profit*, Princeton, Princeton University Press, 1977. – p. 22; Michael Howard, *The Continental Commitment*, *op. cit.*, p. 70.

30 Cf. Jordan, *Great Britain, France and the German Problem*, *op. cit.*, p. 169.

31 Michael Howard, *The Continental Commitment*, *op. cit.*, p. 74–95.

32 "As you know very well, we have never believed very strongly in the League as a policeman". Letter Sargent/Campbell, 22 janvier 1933, DBFP 2/IV no. 196.

33 Robert Cecil, *A Great Experiment*, *op. cit.*, p. 229 et 238.

34 ASdN, Souvenirs de Th. Aghnides, p. 142.

35 L'article 53 maintient en vigueur »les dispositions des traités intérieurs limitant les armements de certaines puissances«.

36 De passage à Genève, Stimson constate les interférences entre politique extérieure et politique intérieure: "Over here nobody is thinking about anything except the domestic side of it", extrait du Stimson Diary, juin 1932, cité par Elting Morison, *Turmoil and Tradition. A study of the Life and Times of Henry L. Stimson*, Boston, Houghton Mifflin, 1960, p. 410–414.

37 Philip Noël-Baker, *The First World Disarmament Conference 1932–1933, and Why it Failed*, Pergamon Press, 1979. – 147 p.

38 *Ibid.*, p. XIII.

39 Philip Noël-Baker, *The Private Manufacture of Arms*, v. I, London, Gollancz, 1936. – 574 p.

40 Exemples: selon Noël-Baker (*The First World Disarmament Conference*, *op. cit.*, p. 86–87) qui place au pinacle le plan Hoover: "if it had come into force, Germany would have remained totally disarmed in fulfilment of the Treaty of Versailles". Quand on connaît le degré de réarmement clandestin de l'Allemagne, on ne peut que constater les illusions de Philip Noël-Baker. Celui-ci affirme que les marchands de canon ont fait élire Lebrun, candidat du Comité des Forges, à la place de Briand (*ibid.*, p. 63). Mais Lebrun n'était pas le candidat du Comité des Forges et c'est Paul Doumer qui a battu Briand. A trop vouloir prouver . . .

41 Le professeur Becker cite les propos du ministre Treviranus approché par un des responsables de la firma Skoda qui, au nom de Schneider aurait proposé que si sa firme se voyait accorder 50% de commandes d'armement, les limitations militaires du traité de Versailles seraient levées pour permettre à l'Allemagne d'avoir une armée égale à 80% de celle de la France; cf. J. Becker, La politique révisioniste du Reich, de la mort de Stresemann à l'avènement de Hitler. *La France et l'Allemagne, 1932–1936. Communication présentée au Colloque franco-allemand à Paris, mars 1977;* Editions du Centre National de la Recherche Scientifique, Paris, 1980. – p. 24, note 26.

42 Madariaga, *Disarmament*, *op. cit.*, p. 79.

43 La CPC, créée le 17 mai 1920 pour remplir les dispositions du Pacte (article 9) est composée d'éléments militaires relevant uniquement de leurs gouvernements.

44 Cecil, *A Great Experiment*, *op. cit.*, p. 78–79; Madariaga, *Morning without Noon*, p. 23–25.

45 "The American delegation was dominated by the Navy Board at Washington" . . .; lettre Sweetser/Noël-Baker, *The First World Disarmament Conference*, *op. cit.*, p. 32.

46 Hugh Wilson, *Diplomat between Wars*, *op. cit.*, p. 248.

47 Cecil, *A Great Experiment*, *op. cit.*, p. 358–363.

48 Edward Hallett Carr, *The Twenty Years Crisis, 1919–1939. An Introduction to the Study of International Relations*, London, Macmillan, 1939. – p. 18.

49 Cecil, *A Great Experiment, op. cit.*, p. 95–96.

50 Conversation de décembre 1932, in *DDF* t. 2, no. 68.

51 »Les contacts créés par les négociants traversant les frontières . . . c'est plus efficace que la destruction de mille canons. Cela rapproche les peuples . . .« déclaration à la Commission des Affaires étrangères de la Chambre, 23 novembre 1928.

52 Le colloque d'Augsburg (mars 1979) »Internationale Beziehungen in der Weltwirtschaftskrise 1929–1933« a très utilement mis l'accent sur ces questions.

53 Heinrich Brüning, *Mémoires*, Paris, Gallimard, 1974. – p. 309–312.

54 Ces indications statistiques sond fondées sur les annuaires statistiques de la SdN et sur l'ouvrage de N. M. Sloutzki, *The World's Armament Race 1919–1939*, Geneva, Geneva Research Centre, (Geneva Studies, v. XII, no. 9) 1941. – 129 p.

55 En fait, la crise économique était équivoque: elle aurait pu aboutir à une réduction des dépenses de défense nationale. Cet effet a été de courte durée. Le réarmement l'a emporté.

56 Pour Joseph Avenol: »C'est une secousse de l'assise fondamentale de la SdN . . .« et il situe clairement le danger: »La tactique du Japon peut inspirer ou illusionner des téméraires«. Dans sa réponse, Sir Eric Drummond évalue les menaces potentielles du conflit sino-japonais: "If the League fails in this matter, not only is the value of the peace-making clauses of the Covenant destroyed . . . but also the success of the Disarmament Conference is seriously endangered since if no security is afforded by the Covenant and other international conditions, each country can rightly say that she is bound to depend on her armed forces«. (Lettres du 5 et 6 novembre 1931. Correspondance Avenol/Drummond, v. 35, AD Papiers Avenol).

57 »Aucun gouvernement n'oserait plus à l'avenir courir les énormes risques d'une guerre d'aggression et les Etats désormais assurés d'un soutien collectif en cas de danger se montreraient accommodants sur la question du désarmement« in Jean Schwoebel, *L'Angleterre et la sécurité collective*, Paris, Recueil Sirey, 1938. – p. 222.

58 Cf. Paul-Boncour, *Entre deux guerres, souvenirs sur la IIIème République*, t. 2, *Les lendemains de la victoire*, 1919–1934, Paris, Plon, 1946. – p. 201.

59 Christopher Thorne, *The Limits of Foreign Policy: the West, the League and the Far Eastern Crisis of 1931–1933*, London, Macmillan, 1972. – 442 p.

60 C'est à cette occasion que le cabinet britannique décide de suspendre la règle de la paix de dix ans. Mais tout réarmement est ajourné "The services had won the right to plan but not to spend", *in:* Shay, *British Rearmament in the Thirties, op. cit.*, p. 24.

61 Lettre d'Arthur Sweetser/Hornbeck, 24 mars 1932, citée par Thorne, *The Limits of Foreign Policy, op. cit.*, p. 321.

62 »Le Secrétariat de la Société concourut de toutes ses forces au plus énorme avortement de l'histoire . . . Dissimuler la mésentente des délégations, ignorer leurs réticences, leurs atermoiements, revenait à se rendre à une politique d'illusions« dit Louise Weiss in *Mémoires d'une Européenne*, t. 2, Paris, Payot, 1968. – p. 216.

63 James Barros (in *Betrayal from Within, Joseph Avenol, Secretary General of the League of Nations 1933–1940*, New Haven, Yale University Press, 1969. – 289 p.) a mis en cause, à la suite de Thanassis Aghnides (ASdN, Souvenirs de Th. Aghnides) le rôle de Joseph Avenol, jugé trop inactif et trop mou face aux pressions extérieures. Jean Monnet (*Mémoires*, Paris, Fayard, 1976. – p. 100) reproche aussi à Avenol son manque d'imagination et de courage.

64 Salvador de Madariaga, *Morning without Noon, op. cit.*, p. 24; A. C. Temperley, *The Whispering Gallery of Europe*, London, Collins, 1938. – p. 281; ASdN, Mémoires de Th. Aghnides, p. 26, 77, 97.

65 Samuel Templewood, *Nine Troubled Years*, London, Collins, 1954. – p. 123.

66 Colonel Joseph Beck, *Dernier rapport. Politique polonaise, 1926–1939.* Neuchâtel, Edition de la Baconnière, 1951. – p. 258.
67 Lettre Tardieu/Laval, 9 février 1932, AD Papiers Tardieu, 643.
68 Que défendent en revanche Paul-Boncour (*Entre deux guerres, op. cit.*, p. 166) et Temperley (*The Whispering Gallery of Europe, op, cit.*, p. 233).
69 Quatre délégués français se succèdent: Tardieu, Paul-Boncour, Herriot, Barthou. Anthony Eden remplace progressivement Sir John Simon. Neurath succède à Brüning.
70 Des élections législatives ont lieu en Albanie, Belgique, Danemark, France, Allemagne, Grèce, Irlande, Japon, Roumanie et aux Etats-Unis. En outre, des élections présidentielles sont prévues en Equateur, Allemagne, Nicaragua, Panama, Etats-Unis. Rien qu'en Allemagne, du 2 février 1932 au 5 mars 1933, il y a trois élections générales, deux tours d'élections présidentielles sans compter les nombreuses élections dans les Länder.
71 Brüning, *Mémoires, op. cit.*, p. 353–354.
72 Cf. *Troubled Neighbours, Franco-British Relations in the Twentieth Century*, Neville Waites, editor, London, Weidenfeld and Nicolson, 1971. – p. 156.
73 ASdN, Souvenirs de Th. Aghnides.
74 Elle réunit 60 Etats, parmi lesquels 6 Etats non-membres de la SdN. ASdN, Souvenirs de Th. Aghnides, p. 139; cf. rapport Henderson, doc. SdN, Conf. D-171 (1), p. 147.
75 A. V. Temperley, *The Whispering Gallery of Europe, op. cit.*, p. 276–277.
76 Résolution du 22 avril 1932, doc. SdN, Conf. D/C.G 28(2).
77 Elting Morison, *Turmoil and Tradition, op. cit.*, p. 403–423.
78 La réduction du temps de service, le droit pour l'Allemagne de fabriquer des munitions, la possession d'armes défensives lourdes.
79 Edward Bennett, *German Rearmament and the West*, Princeton, Princeton University Press, 1979. – p. 150.
80 François Le Grix, *Vingt jours chez Hitler. Tableaux d'une révolution.* Paris, Grasset, 1933. – p. 84.
81 A. C. Temperley, *The Whispering Gallery of Europe, op. cit.*, p. 200–204.
82 Hans Wilhelm Gatske, *Stresemann and the Rearmament of Germany*, Baltimore, John Hopkins Press, 1954. – p. 92 et 104; Brüning, *Mémoires, op. cit.*, p. 53–54; Michael Geyer, »Das Zweite Rüstungsprogramm 1930–1934«, *Revue Internationale d'histoire militaire*, 1975. – no. 33.
83 Doc. SdN, Conf. D.126. Le plan propose de réduire d'$^1/_3$ les armements mondiaux, d'abolir les chars, la guerre chimique, l'artillerie lourde mobile, l'aviation de bombardements; de réduire d'$^1/_3$ le nombre et le tonnage des cuirassés et de sous-marins, d'$^1/_4$ les nazis passent de 107 à 230 sièges.
84 Rapport Henderson, doc. SdN, Conf. D.171(I).
85 Cf. Bulletin du jour du *Temps*, 24 juin 1932.
86 Bennett, *German Rearmament and the West, op. cit.*, p. 256–257.
87 Discours du général von Schleicher (26 juillet). Aux élections allemandes du 31 juillet, les nazis passent de 107 à 230 sièges.
88 Tous les Etats devraient se mobiliser contre une guerre entreprise en violation du Pacte Briand-Kellog. Les Etats membres de la SdN devraient s'acquitter de leurs obligations en vertu de l'article 16 du Pacte.
89 Leurs armements seraient limités. Ils devraient entretenir des unités spécialisées dotées d'un matériel puissant, à la disposition de la SdN.
90 Bennett, *German Rearmament and the West, op. cit.*, p. 220–230.
91 Norman Davis avait bien essayé de faire au monde »un cadeau de Noël« sous la forme d'une convention préliminaire. En vain.

92 Cf. communication d'Eliza Campus: »La Petite Entente et la sécurité collective« (colloque de Poznan, novembre 1973).

93 Néanmoins le Japon demeure membre de la Conférence du désarmement où on peut d'ailleurs se demander ce qu'il fait depuis que le gouvernement japonais a estimé nécessaire de réarmer.

94 K. Hildebrand fait l'état des travaux dans »La politique française d'Hitler jusqu'en 1936«, in *La France et L'Allemagne 1932–1936, op. cit.*, p. 339–372.

95 Bennett, *German Rearmament and the West, op. cit.*, p. 338.

96 Georges Castellan, *Le réarmement clandestin du Reich, 1930–1935 vu par le Deuxiéme Bureau de l'Etat major français*, Paris, Plon, 1954. –

97 Voir à ce propos Jens Petersen, *Hitler-Mussolini, Die Entstehung der Achse Berlin–Rom 1933–1936*, Tübingen, Niemeyer, 1973. – 559 p.; *Maurice Cowling, The Impact of Hitler, British Politics and British Policy 1933–1940.* Chicago, University of Chicago Press, 1977, 445 p.

98 Cf. Sten Nadolny, *Abrüstungsdiplomatie 1932/33, Deutschland auf der Genfer Konferenz im Übergang von Weimar zu Hitler*, München, tuduv-Studie, 1978. – p. 264–270.

99 Temperley, *The Whispering Gallery of Europe, op. cit.*, p. 234; Marquand, *Ramsay McDonald, op. cit.*, p. 752; Sir Anthony Eden, *Facing the Dictators*, London, Cassell, 1962. – p. 45.

100 Doc. SdN. Conf. D.157.

101 Par exemple, au cours de la convention, le nombre des avions devrait être réduit à 500 pour le Royaume-Uni, la France, l'Italie, le Japon, l'URSS, les Etats-Unis. Mais les Etats-Unis ne possédant pas d'aviation au 1er janvier 1933 devraient respecter le statu quo jusqu'à la fin de la convention.

102 La marine française est particulièrement hostile au plan MacDonald.

103 Par 42 voix pour, l'URSS, l'Allemagne et l'Autriche s'abstenant.

104 Cf. Konrad Jarausch, *The Four-Power Pact*, Madison, University of Wisconsin, 1965, et notre article, »La mission de Jouvenel à Rome«, in *Italia e Francia dal 1919 al 1939*, a cura di Jean Baptiste Duroselle e di Enrico Serra, Istituto per gli Studi di politica internazionale, Milano, 1981, pp. 85–99.

105 D'après la formule pittoresque de Gordon, chargé d'affaires américain à Berlin, in Télégramme 2421, 20 mai 1933, Gordon/Cordell Hull, FRUS, 1933, v. I, p. 159.

106 Le document capital est le procès-verbal du Conseil de Cabinet du 12 mai 1933, in ADAP 1/I no. 266; cf. aussi Christoph Kimmich, *Germany and the League of Nations*, Chicago, University of Chicago Press, 1976. – p. 179.

107 Colonel Beck, *Politique polonaise, op. cit.*, p. 48.

108 Cf. ASdN, Mémoires de Th. Aghnides, p. 79–80, 89–90, 96, 103–104, 117; voir aussi la conversation J. Paul-Boncour/A. Henderson, 19 septembre 1933, AE/AD-SdN, sous-série II, v. 882.

109 Cf. Bennett, *German Rearmament, op. cit.*, p. 470; G. Weinberg, *Diplomatic Revolution*, Chicago, University of Chicago Press, 1976, p. 165; Kimmich, *op. cit.*, p. 187; Michael Geyer, »Militär, Rüstung und Außenpolitik. Aspekte militärischer Revisionspolitik in der Zwischen-Kriegszeit«. *In:* Manfred Funke, *Hitler, Deutschland und die Mächte*, Düsseldorf, Droste, 1976.

110 Bennett, *op. cit.*, p. 486, parle à ce propos de la première des »Saturday surprises«.

111 Wladimir d'Ormesson, »Libres opinions« in *Le Temps*, 10 juin 1933.

112 Cf. exemples dans George Scott, *The Rise and Fall of the League of Nations*, London, Hutchinson, 1973. – p. 198; Wilson, *Diplomat between Wars, op. cit.*, p. 259–260.

113 Madariaga, *Disarmament, op. cit.*, p. 224.

114 Madariaga, *Morning without Noon, op. cit.*, p. 101.

115 Cecil, *A Great Experiment, op. cit.*, p. 256.
116 Walters, *A History of the League of Nations, op. cit.*, p. 550. cf. aussi Madariaga, *Morning without Noon, op. cit.*, p. 275.
117 Madariaga, *ibid.*, p. 252.
118 "It was therefore again an idea essentially contrary to the Covenant, a League of physical power versus moral power and therefore the very reverse of the spirit of disarmament". Madariaga, *Morning without Noon, op. cit.*
119 Madariaga, *Disarmament, op. cit.*, p. 48.
120 *Ibid*, p. 304.
121 "Let fear of war vanish and armaments will soon be discarded. No one goes about with a revolver in his pocket in the streets of Geneva, but one does sometimes in Shangai or in Chicago". Madariaga, *Morning without Noon, op. cit.*, p. 31.
122 *Ibid.*, p. 252.
123 Cf. Lettre Hugh Wilson à Cordell Hall, *FRUS*, 1934. – v. I, p. 63–65.
124 Jean Monnet, *Mémoires, op. cit.*, p. 100.

La sécurité régionale et la Société des Nations

Constantin Svolopoulos
Université de Thessalonique, Thessalonique

Le souci constant des Etats de s'assurer les moyens de renforcer leur sécurité face à toute menace extérieure a toujours profondément conditionné l'évolution des rapports internationaux. Conséquence pratique de ce souci: la tentative d'organiser la vie internationale sur une base rationnelle et qui constitua un tournant décisif. La consécration finale de cette aspiration dans le Pacte de la Société des Nations a été ainsi saluée comme le début d'une ère nouvelle de »paix par la sécurité«. Mais la doctrine de la sécurité collective, qui se substituait à la conception traditionnelle de l'équilibre des forces, allait-elle vraiment mener à la consolidation de la paix à l'échelle mondiale? Et, dans le cas contraire, le recours des Etats à l'ancienne pratique des coalitions et des alliances aurait-il été la seule solution de rechange? N'était-il pas possible de promouvoir l'œuvre générale de la paix à travers un système de garanties basé sur l'idée de la décentralisation internationale? Un tel système ne pouvait-il, vraiment, que contredire les dispositions du Pacte?

Historiens et juristes – et parmi les plus éminents – se sont de bonne heure penchés sur ce problème épineux[1]. Sans prétendre approfondir tous les aspects du sujet ou de proposer une formule adéquate, nous nous contenterons ici de fournir un aperçu récapitulatif des ses éléments de base.

I. A la recherche d'un processus de décentralisation internationale

L'instauration du système de la sécurité collective allait, au lendemain de la Première Guerre mondiale, faire naître l'espérance d'une ère nouvelle, celle d'une paix solide. Néanmoins, cet optimisme ne s'avéra pas bien fondé. Rappelons schématiquement les données fondamentales du problème: l'article 16 du Pacte précisait que le recours à la guerre »illicite« (c'est-à-dire menée en violation des engagements prévus par les articles 12, 13 et 15, destinés à prévenir le recours à la force) entraînerait des sanctions (obligatoires) d'ordre économique et des sanctions (facultatives) d'ordre militaire. Néanmoins, la prise de telles mesures coercitives contre l'agresseur restait conditionnée par l'accord, sinon de tous les autres membres de la Société, du moins des grandes puissances. L'attitude des Etats révisionnistes, le pacifisme négatif et les divisions politiques au sein du camp des défenseurs du régime des Traités, allaient en fait entraver fatalement toute décision unanime et toute action efficace.

Ces inquiétudes se manifestèrent très tôt, non seulement chez les Etats membres les moins puissants de la SdN, mais également au sein des milieux dirigeants attachés à l'esprit et aux méthodes de la Société. Ces derniers, sans toujours recourir au jeu de l'équilibre des forces et à la pratique des groupements et des alliances, se trouvèrent néanmoins aux prises avec la nécessité de remédier aux insuffisances des mécanismes juridiques de Genève par certains procédés classiques. Dès le début des années vingt, on faisait remarquer que la vocation universelle de la Société des Nations n'interdisait pas des liens de solidarité particulière entre certains membres de la communauté internationale.

La source de cette thèse se trouvait dans l'idée qu'à côté d'un droit international universel et d'une organisation mondiale pour le maintien de la paix, existaient des »droits particuliers« pour les Etats et les hommes d'une région donnée ainsi que pour les organismes continentaux et régionaux, créés dans ce même but.[2] Sur un plan pratique, cela signifiait que les Etats d'une région géographique bien déterminée pouvaient, en vue de garantir leur sécurité, conclure entre eux des ententes que le Pacte ne saurait prohiber. Ce besoin pouvant se manifester de façon impérieuse,il eût été imprudent d'obliger les gouvernements à choisir entre la liberté de traiter entre eux et la fidélité à la Société. »Il s'agit de savoir – remarquait Georges Scelle – si la forme actuelle de la juxtaposition des Etats, qui est celle de la Société des Nations, ne compromet pas son extension nécessaire, ne constitue pas un obstacle à son évolution vers l'universalité«.[3]

Or, la conclusion des traités de garantie mutuelle à base régionale ou même continentale, était-elle compatible avec les dispositions correspondantes du Pacte? Le problème se trouva déjà posé du seul fait du libellé sybillin de l'article 21: »Les engagements internationaux, tels que les traités d'arbitrage, et les ententes régionales, comme la doctrine de Monroe, qui assurent le maintien de la paix, ne sont considérés comme incompatibles avec aucune des dispositions du présent Pacte«[4]. Cette formulation ambiguë de ce texte a donné lieu à diverses interprétations: certains ont ainsi soutenu que le régionalisme était le seul moyen de résoudre les stipulations contradictoires de l'article 21, c'est-à-dire de concilier les dispositions du Pacte avec la réserve relative à la doctrine Monroe. Sans se pencher sur les arguments développés de part et d'autre, contentons-nous de reprendre la remarque concluante de Georges Scelle: »Le problème n'avait pas échappé à la Commission (spéciale de la Conférence de la Paix) et nous savons que celle-ci se demanda si les alliances particulières étaient compatibles avec le Pacte. C'était tout de suite aller au point vital et sensible, car l'alliance est la forme extrême de l'Entente. La Commission n'osa pas se prononcer; elle sentit bien qu'il était impossible de porter une prohibition, mais comme l'idéologie wilsonienne, assez imprécise, ambitionnait de substituer une alliance générale aux alliances particulières, on ne voulut pas dire que celles-ci étaient compatibles avec le Pacte, et l'on se borna à faire allusion à certaines ententes et à employer une expression négative pour marquer qu'elles n'étaient pas incompatibles avec le Pacte«.[5] Mais, même dans ce cas, quelles ententes régionales pouvaient être jugées compatibles avec les dispositions du Pacte? Quelle aurait dû être l'ampleur ou le contenu des futurs accords qui allaient tomber sous cette dénomination? Il y avait là un problème préalable de définition, difficile à resoudre.

La mise à l'épreuve de la conception universaliste monolithique par l'adoption d'un procédé de décentralisation au sein de la Société des Nations se manifesta dès le début des années vingt. La Commission temporaire mixte, chargée d'envisager le problème de la réduction des armements proposa à l'Assemblée un projet dont l'essentiel se résumait ainsi: »Mettre les Etats à même de réduire leurs armements tout en leur assurant des moyens de sécurité au moins aussi grands que ceux dont ils jouissent à présent«.[6] La mise en discussion de ces principes de base ne tarda pas à soulever une question cruciale: faut-il s'en tenir à l'idée d'un traité général ou envisager aussi la conclusion des traités régionaux? Selon leurs défenseurs, les accords régionaux tiendraient mieux compte des facteurs concrets du problème de la sécurité, des données historiques, géographiques, économiques et également des conditions particulières de chaque pays. Pour les »universalistes«, au contraire, la pratique des accords régionaux risquait de dévaloriser le Pacte et de disloquer la Société des Nations – en un mot, d'annoncer le retour aux antagonismes du passé. La querelle entre ces deux tendances, telle qu'elle se reflète des débats de la IIIe Assemblée, n'empêcha toutefois pas celle-ci d'adopter la »résolution XIV«, qui prévoyait, notamment, la conclusion d'un accord défensif »accessible à tous les pays, qui engagerait les parties à porter assistance effective et immédiate et suivant un plan préétabli au cas où l'une d'elles serait attaquée, pourvu que l'obligation de venir en aide à un pays attaqué soit limitée, en principe, aux pays situés dans la même partie du globe«.[6bis] La résolution en question représentait une tentative de conciliation entre les deux thèses en présence: la réduction des armements pouvait s'opérer »soit sous la forme, qui serait la plus souhaitable, d'un traité général, soit sous la forme de traités particuliers, mais destinés à s'élargir et demeurant accessibles à tous les pays . . .«[6ter]. La Résolution XIV introduisait ainsi certains principes de base ayant directement trait à l'idée d'une décentralisation internationale opérée sous l'égide de la Société des Nations, – principes qui allaient régir les dispositions du Traité d'assistance mutuelle (qu'adoptera la IVe Assemblée), le Protocole de Genève de 1924, et, enfin, les Traités de Locarno.[7]

Le Traité d'assistance mutuelle fut élaboré et discuté par l'Assemblée de 1923. A cette occasion, l'opposition très vive entre »universalistes« et »régionalistes« se manifesta à nouveau. Face au projet d'un traité de garantie générale (soumis par Lord Robert Cecil) assurant à l'Etat attaqué l'appui de tous les membres de la Société des Nations, se dressa un second projet, rédigé par le colonel français Réquin prévoyant que les parties contractantes pourraient conclure »soit deux à deux, soit entre un plus grand nombre, des accords créant des groupements dans un but exclusif de défense mutuelle et réglant à l'avance l'assistance qu'elles se prêteraient mutuellement, conformément à l'article 10 du Pacte, dans des éventualités d'agression qu'elles estimeraient possibles contre l'une quelconque d'entre elles«.[8] Malgré la fusion apparente des deux thèses, le texte du projet finalement soumis à l'Assemblée était pro-régionaliste sur au moins trois points: l'article 4 autorisait la présence aux délibérations du Conseil alors chargé d'arrêter les hostilités ou de prévenir l'agression, des Etats considérés comme »spécialement intéressés«; l'article 5 prévoyait que »la participation aux opérations militaires, navales et aériennes ne sera pas, en principe, demandée aux autres parties contractantes situées dans un continent autre que celui dans lequel les opérations doivent avoir lieu«; enfin les articles 6, 7 et 8 sanctionnaient la conclusion d'»accords complémentaires défensifs«, à deux ou à plusieurs, destinés »à faciliter l'exécution des mesures prescrites par le Traité en réglant, à l'avance, l'assistance dans des éventualités d'agression déterminées«.[9] Ces accords complémentaires pouvaient être négociés et conclus sous les auspices de la Société des Nations mais auraient été, obligatoirement, examinés par le Conseil avant tout enregistrement du point de vue de leur conformité avec le Pacte et le Traité; des Etats tiers (qui se seraient sentis visés) pouvaient y adhérer – mais avec le consentement des premiers signataires.

Cette tendance en faveur d'une certaine décentralisation internationale souleva des oppositions assez vives qui expliquent en partie l'échec final du projet de traité d'assistance mutuelle. Dans sa réponse nettement défavorable, Ramsay MacDonald évoqua, au nom du gouvernement britannique, »la superposition à un traité général d'un système de traités particuliers« propres à ramener à l'ancienne pratique des groupements et des alliances. Sans trop schématiser, on pourrait observer que, parmi les Etats appelés à donner leur adhésion, ne s'exprimèrent favorablement – à part la France – que ceux qui couraient le risque d'être attaqués par des voisins plus puissants: Pologne, Tchécoslovaquie, Belgique, Etats baltes, Finlande. Fallait-il en conclure que tout accord capable de réduire effectivement les inquiétudes de ces derniers serait rejeté par les membres de la société internationale qui se sentaient à l'abri de tout danger imminent? En réalité, un certain accord entre les deux »camps« ne tarda pas à se produire. La réaction d'une partie de l'opinion publique anglaise contre la position prise par le Premier ministre travailliste, jugée susceptible de mettre en échec l'œuvre accomplie par trois Assemblées consécutives et, aussi, l'esprit de détente et le rapprochement entre Paris et Londres aboutit à la mise au point d'une nouveau projet: le Protocole pour le règlement pacifique des différends internationaux, plus connu sous le nom de Protocole de Genève, adopté par l'Assemblée en octobre 1924.

Les principes sanctionnant la possibilité d'une certaine décentralisation internationale dans le cadre de l'application du Pacte, dépendait au premier chef de la finalité ainsi que des priorités du Protocole. Ainsi, dans le contexte d'un programme plus vaste impliquant l'interdépendance de l'arbitrage, de la sécurité et du désarmement, les pactes de garantie subsistèrent sous le contrôle accentué du Conseil. La décision de ce dernier d'appliquer les sanctions, après avoir déterminé l'agresseur, constituait la condition de l'action entreprise en vertu des dispositions de tout accord particulier. Mais, parallèlement, on admettait le principe du droit d'accession à celui-ci pour tout autre Etat qui pouvait se considérer comme directement concerné par ses dispositions. Cette faculté étendue à ceux même contre qui la pointe était en principe dirigée – pointe dissimulée dans tout procédé classique d'alliance, permettait d'arriver à »un équilibre particulier« et d'assurer »une garantie régionale ou locale de sécurité«.[10] Les défenseurs des principes »régionalistes« insérés dans le texte du Protocole évoquaient, désormais, la nécessité d'établir, en face de toute menace d'agression, des plans d'action préalablement coordonnés. Le recours à des organismes régionaux prêts à parer à toute menace contre la paix, permettait d'entreprendre une action efficace sans qu'il ait à déclencher immédiatement et dans tous les cas le mécanisme universel.

L'adoption initiale du Protocole de Genève et, même, son rejet final – avant toute espèce d'application – marquent les limites et font ressortir les difficultés contre lesquelles se heurtait toute tentative de combler les lacunes du Pacte par le recours au procédé de la décentralisation sous l'égide et dans le cadre de la Société des Nations. On ne doit toutefois pas omettre d'observer que cette double tentative, par ses très rudes assauts portés contre la formule universaliste en matière d'assistance mutuelle, renforça la tendance régionaliste. En effet, du moment où l'on se posait la question de savoir si la formule de la juxtaposition des Etats – qui était celle de la Société des Nations – ne constituait pas un obstacle à son évolution vers l'universalité, on admettait plus facilement l'idée énoncée par les régionalistes dès le début des années vingt: »le régionalisme condition de l'universalisme«. C'est dans ce sens que les milieux dirigeants et l'opinion publique internationale saluèrent la conclusion des accords de Locarno comme un pas positif vers la consolidation de la paix par le sécurité, réalisé sous l'égide bénéfique de Genève.

II. La conclusion des accords de Locarno: débuts d'une ère nouvelle de sécurité basée sur l'idée de décentralisation internationale?

La conclusion des accords de Locarno constitua un pas décisif dans la voie d'un système d'ententes régionales, patronné par la Société des Nations. D'une manière générale, la mise en œuvre des éléments insérés dans le Pacte et, ensuite, dans une série de traités d'arbitrage, de conciliation, de non-agression et de garantie, dépendait de certaines stipulations du Protocole de Genève; mais les accords de Locarno furent davantage: »la première de ces ententes régionales en quoi se décompose le Protocole de Genève qui n'est lui-même qu'un vaste traité d'assistance mutuelle«.[11]

Les actes de Locarno, conclus le 16 octobre 1925, visaient à pourvoir au règlement pacifique des conflits de toute nature et à donner aux »Puissances signataires intéressées des garanties complémentaires dans le cadre du Pacte de la Société des Nations et des Traités en vigueur«. La pièce capitale, pivot de tout le système, fut le Traité de garantie mutuelle, passé entre l'Allemagne, d'une part, et de l'autre par la France et la Belgique sous la garantie conjointe de l'Angleterre et de l'Italie. Il stipulait l'inviolabilité des frontières entre l'Allemagne, la Belgique et la France, l'interdiction totale de toute guerre d'agression et l'assistance, de la part des puissances garantes, à la partie contractante qui aurait été victime d'une agression. Le Pacte rhénan s'accompagnait de quatre conventions d'arbitrage, conclues entre l'Allemagne d'une part, et la Belgique, la France, la Pologne et la Tchécoslovaquie d'autre part, ainsi que de deux accords bilatéraux de garantie – franco-polonais et franco-tchécoslovaque. Dans le cadre de ces accords supplémentaires se trouvait notamment prévue l'institution d'une commission permanente de concilitaion, chargée d'aplanir tout différend contre les pays signataires et, dans certain cas, l'intervention de la Cour permanente de justice internationale.

Les stipulations des textes signés à Locarno, bien que résultant de négociations menées par les gouvernements intéressés en dehors de la Société des Nations, ne contredisaient pas les dispositions du Pacte; bien au contraire, ces textes consacraient l'adoption de la solution régionaliste par les milieux genevois. Déjà la mise en application de certains principes de base sanctionnés dans le cadre de l'activité menée par la Société des Nations au cours de ses premières années suffisait à confirmer cette constatation. Mais, plus encore, la soumission de l'exécution des accords au contrôle permanent du Conseil était assez révélatrice. On pouvait aisément, dans ces conditions, admettre que leur application ne se concevrait pas sans l'existence et le fonctionnement de la Société des Nations.

La conclusion des accords le Locarno marqua donc un tournant décisif dans l'évolution de la Société des Nations. L'attachement au principe de l'»universalité« de l'organisme genevois semblait devoir se concilier avec une pratique de décentralisation internationale, étendue d'ailleurs au – delà du domaine politique – en matière de justice ou d'économie. Mais, cette tendance trouvait son terrain d'application le plus propice dans le cadre bien concret de l'organisation régionale de la sécurité. De ce point de vue, la conclusion des accords de Locarno se présentait comme le premier pas vers la généralisation de la pratique des ententes régionales. C'est ainsi que les organes principaux de la Société des Nations s'orientèrent vers l'application des procédés et l'extension des garanties de Locarno à d'autres parties du monde. La VIIe Assemblée adopta une résolution selon laquelle la conclusion d'accords calqués sur le modèle de Locarno serait de nature à favoriser l'établissement de la confiance et de la sécurité et, par là, à contribuer à la consolidation de la paix; le Conseil était censé »offrir éventuellement ses bons offices pour la conclusion d'accords appropriés«. Dans le sillage de ces même principes, le Comité d'arbitrage et de sécurité, constitué au cours de 1927, établit des modèles de traités de non-agression et d'assistance mutuelle, largement inspirés de l'esprit de Locarno; l'Assemblée de 1928 n'hésita pas à recommander aux Etats – membres ou non de la Société – leur mise en application.[12]

L'adoption par les milieux genevois des idées régionalistes, élaborées par les organes de la Société et déjà contenues dans le texte des accords de Locarno, répondait à une nécessité d'importance accrue: combiner l'autonomie d'une action locale, toujours plus efficace, avec un contrôle susceptible de permettre de rétablir l'unité difficile. Mais, en réalité, les garanties de sécurité assurées à Locarno ne couvraient qu'une partie seulement du continent européen. Certes, les accords bilatéraux passés entre la France, d'une part, et la Pologne et la Tchécoslovaquie d'autre part, et surtout, les conventions d'arbitrage signées par l'Allemagne et ces deux derniers Etats, visaient à étendre les garanties assurées pour la région rhénane, grâce au Traité à cinq, aux frontières orientales de l'Allemagne: l'observation des procédures pacifiques pour la solution des différends surgis entre les parties contractantes; le respect des droits établis par les traités ou résultant du droit des gens, et, enfin, la non-modification des droits d'un Etat sans son consentement, constituaient les principes de base qui allaient, désormais, régir les rapports entre ces pays. Néanmoins, à défaut des garanties contenues dans le Pacte rhénan, les voisins orientaux de l'Allemagne restaient exposés à une attaque éventuelle de cette dernière sans avoir même la certitude d'être pleinement secourus. Ne pouvait-on pas, donc, compléter le système instauré à Locarno par une série d'actes similaires au Pacte rhénan? Une fois conclu, ce dernier n'ouvrait-il pas la voie à un système de garanties propre à combler de la même manière les lacunes du Pacte en matière de sécurité?

L'adoption par la Société des Nations d'une position favorable touchant l'extension des garanties de Locarno à d'autres régions du monde, constituait une réponse positive des milieux genevois. En réalité, ce plan d'action avait été conçu dès 1921 par le principal artisan des actes de Locarno, Aristide Briand: la paix assurée sur le Rhin aurait été le point de départ d'une organisation plus générale de sécurité.[13] Toutefois, les facteurs qui s'étaient avérés propres à empêcher l'Allemagne de s'engager préalablement à respecter toutes ses frontières, allaient, continuellement, entraver toute tentative d'extension des garanties de Locarno à l'Europe orientale. Le gouvernement de Berlin, bien disposé à composer avec la France en vue d'obtenir – entre autre – l'évacuation du territoire rhénan, n'avait aucune raison de renoncer définitivment à ses revendications à l'Est. Devant l'obstination de Stresemann, renforcée par l'attitude complaisante de Chamberlain, Briand se contenta des acquis de Locarno – accompagnés de l'entrée allemande à la Société des Nations – tout en espérant que ceux-ci ouvriraient la voie à une généralisation des garanties déjà assurées à l'échelle restreinte de l'espace rhénan. L'échec de toutes les tentatives entreprises en vue de répondre aux impératifs de cette stratégie, confirmait la persistance menaçante d'une fissure par où la guerre pouvait s'engouffrer dans un avenir proche ou lointain . . . En réalité, il y avait là encore ce facteur marquant des relations internationales de l'entre-deux-guerres: l'opposition, très souvent vive, entre les Etats défenseurs des Traités de paix et les Etats tenants du révisionnisme.

L'évolution, également négative, dans une autre partie du continent européen, les Balkans, confirme cette hypothèse. Certes, l'application de la formule de Locarno dans le sud-est européen impliquait certaines difficultés au moins d'ordre technique, selon une remarque pénétrante d'André Michalakopoulos, homme politique très attaché à l'esprit de Genève:

»Vous parlez d'un Locarno balkanique? Mais voyons de plus près en quoi effectivement consistent les accords de Locarno. Deux peuples, la France et l'Allemagne, en lutte depuis des siècles l'un contre l'autre, ont pris l'engagement de ne pas s'attaquer mutuellement et deux autres nations, l'Angleterre et l'Italie, se sont portées garantes de cet engagement auquel a également participé la Belgique. Voudriez-vous me dire quel Etat balkanique jouera le rôle de la France, quel autre celui de l'Allemagne et quels seront les garants? Il me semble que les formules séduisantes du genre de la formule locarnienne ont pour résultat de faire naître en nous des désirs qui, à défaut d'autre chose, nous entraînent à méconnaître la diversité des circonstances et des conditions particulières . . .«[14] Mais, outre ces réserves, la réalisation d'un Locarno balkanique se heurtait, principalement, à la stratégie révisionniste du gouvernement bulgare. David Mitrany, chargé par la Société des Nations d'enquêter sur les possibilités d'un accord qui regrouperait tous les Etats de la Péninsule, pouvait conclure: »Puisque [la Bulgarie] nie la frontière, elle n'obtiendra pas de concessions et sans concessions un Locarno balkanique sera impossible ou inutile«.[15]

C'est ainsi que par son refus de négocier sur la base du *statu quo* que la Bulgarie mina les tentatives entreprises par ses voisins en vue d'aboutir à un accord politique calqué sur modèle de Locarno. De même, par sa liaison étroite avec les Etats du camp révisionniste – l'Italie, la Hongrie et, plus tard, l'Allemagne – la Bulgarie renforça les tendances centrifuges dans le Sud-Est européen.

L'échec des efforts déployés pour élargir le champ d'application des garanties offertes par le Pacte rhénan au moyen d'autres accords régionaux calqués sur son modèle, se confirma au terme des années vingt, par le rejet du fameux projet d'organisation d'un régime d'Union fédérale européenne«. A vrai dire, les Européens n'étaient pas les premiers à envisager la »continentalisation« comme solution propre à promouvoir l'œuvre de la paix. Le panaméricanisme sous forme d'Union de tous les Etats du continent, existait bien avant l'instauration de la Société des Nations; c'est sous l'influence de ce phénomène, que d'éminents juristes parlèrent, dès 1927, d'une »européanisation« de la Société des Nations, avant que Briand, animé par le »sentiment de la responsabilité collective de tout le continent en présence des dangers qui menaçaient la paix européenne«, ne finisse par penser qu'il était nécessaire de donner à l'organisme genevois des bases continentales.[16] Néanmoins, l'homme politique français ne s'inspirait que de très loin du modèle américain. Dans le cadre de son projet »d'un régime d'union fédérale européenne« les systèmes d'arbitrage et de sécurité, préconisés au sein de l'organisme de Genève, auraient été développés et la politique de Locarno aurait abouti à l'intégration d'une série d'accords particuliers dans un système plus général; les garanties, plus précisement celles assurées par le Pacte rhénan auraient été étendues à l'Europe orientale et cette fois-ci, renforcées par une solidarité économique à l'échelle continentale.[17]

III. Les accords régionaux incompatibles avec les dispositions du Pacte?

La mise en cause du système de la sécurité collective aboutit à renforcer, à l'échelle universelle, la tendance des gouvernements à chercher des garanties de sécurité dans le jeu traditionnel des groupements et des alliances. A défaut de pallier les insuffisances des mécanismes du Pacte au moyen d'un système d'accords régionaux calqués sur le modèle de Locarno, les Etats les plus directement concernés esquissaient déjà un réseau d'accords particuliers, bilatéraux ou multilatéraux, pour renforcer leur position face à toute menace d'agression. Parmi les cas que l'on pourrait citer, en Europe ou hors de celle-ci, le plus révélateur est celui de la Petite Entente.

La Petite Entente fut fondée par trois conventions bilatérales, conclues en 1920–1921 entre la Yougoslavie, la Roumanie et la Tchécoslovaquie; elle instituait une alliance défensive qui impliquait l'obligation de concourir à la défense de la partie attaquée; néanmoins, grâce au Traité collectif de 1929 et au Pacte d'organisation de 1933, les trois partenaires arrivèrent progressivement à une forme beaucoup plus évoluée: celle d'une »union politique d'Etats«.[18] Aussi bien dans sa forme initiale que dans sa forme la plus évoluée, la Petite Entente se définit toujours par opposition au courant révisionniste de l'Europe orientale lui ayant attribué comme mission de faire respecter les Traités de paix placés sous l'égide de la Société des Nations, ses partisans la présentaient comme l'auxiliaire et le soutien le plus ferme de l'organisation de Genève en Europe orientale. »Il ne paraîtrait point oiseux« – soulignait M. Spalaikovitch – »d'affirmer aujourd' hui que, sans une France forte à l'Occident, les Traités de paix ainsi que l'institution même de la SdN eussent été déjà depuis longtemps bafoués. Le souci devant un tel danger a suscité également, dans la partie orientale de l'Europe, la formation d'une combinaison politique des plus utiles. Assurer leur propre sécurité, faciliter la tâche de la France et sauvegarder l'institution de la SdN, voilà une triple fin qui poussa spontanément le royaume des Serbes-Croates et Slovènes, la Tchécoslovaquie et la Roumanie à s'unir dans un accord politique.«[19]

La formation de la Petite Entente fut à l'origine d'une controverse qui marqua profondément la vie internationale pendant presque toute l'entre-deux-guerres. Une entente régionale, vouée à la sauvegarde de la légitimité internationale mais fondée sur la conception de l'équilibre des forces, était-elle compatible avec le système de la sécurité collective ou révélait-elle plutôt le retour aux antagonismes et aux alliances du passé? Au risque de schématiser, on pourrait soutenir que, désormais, deux tendances bien distinctes se dégageaient: la première était basée sur la conception wilsonienne selon laquelle dans le cadre de la SdN »il ne pouvait exister ni alliances, ni réunions, ni ententes, ni accords diplomatiques«; la deuxième, découlant d'une conception plus souple et réaliste, visait à intégrer les accords régionaux au sein du système prescrit par l'organisation de Genève. Les dispositions du Pacte – et surtout l'article 21 déjà mentionné – étaient trop confuses pour permettre de trouver une solution mutuellement acceptable.

C'est ainsi que l'un des artisans principaux de la Petite Entente, Edouard Bénèš, porta devant la SdN le problème général posé par la conclusion des accords régionaux. Il proposa d'ajouter à l'article 21 deux alinéas ainsi conçus: »Toutes conventions entre deux ou plusieurs Membres de la SdN tendant à préciser ou à compléter les engagements en vue du maintien de la paix ou de la collaboration internationale tels qu'ils sont stipulés dans ce Pacte, pourront être non seulement approuvées par le Conseil ou l'Assemblée, mais encouragées par eux et négociées sous leurs auspices; ces dispositions peuvent s'appliquer aux engagements internationaux tels que les traités d'arbitrage, aux conventions complémentaires en vue d'étendre la compétence de la Cour de justice, aux ententes régionales comme la doctrine de Monroe, ou à toutes autres qui seront jugées, par le Conseil ou l'Assemblée, comme étant en accord avec le paragraphe Ier de cet article.

Le Conseil ou l'Assemblée pourront, en vue de ces fins, et à la demande d'un nombre suffisant des membres de la Société, provoquer la réunion de conférences spéciales ouvertes à tous les membres qui se jugeront intéressés.[19 bis]«

Les thèses alors développées par le représentant tchèque faisaient ressortir les arguments évoqués, depuis lors, à plusieurs reprises, en faveur d'une »conciliation de la décentralisation inévitable et de l'unitarisme indispensable« pour reprendre une expression caractéristique. Toutefois, la proposition tchèque, prise dans un cercle vicieux d'opinions contradictoires, ne parvint finalement pas à revêtir la forme d'un amendement, ni même d'une déclaration interprétative du Pacte par l'Assemblée. L'entreprise n'aboutit qu'à la rédaction d'un texte, adopté à l'unanimité par la deuxième Assemblée, selon lequel les accords »tendant à préciser ou à compléter les engagements en vue du maintien de la paix ou de la collaboration internationale, tels qu'ils sont stipulés par le Pacte, peuvent être considérés comme de nature à contribuer aux progrès de la Société dans la voie des réalisations pratiques.«[20]

L'idée de placer les accords régionaux sous l'égide de la SdN ne paraissant pas devoir obtenir gain de cause à travers un amendement ou une déclaration interprétative du Pacte, les membres de la Petite Entente d'abord, puis d'autres Etats, n'hésitèrent pas à recourir aux méthodes traditionnelles afin de consolider leur sécurité. Loin de mépriser ou de défier l'œuvre accomplie à Genève, les animateurs de cette politique furent motivés dans leurs efforts par un souci bien constant: »Comment dans une situation comme celle d'aujourd'hui, où la plupart des nations préfèrent la violation du droit à l'emploi de la force pour le défendre, où la mauvaise foi de certains gouvernements et l'indifférence des autres paralysent l'œuvre de reconstitution générale, comment demander aux peuples de renoncer à toute sauvegarde personnelle, avant de leur avoir fourni une organisation internationale propre à leur garantir la vie et le droit? Tant que la sécurité des nations demeurera précaire, et tant que les gouvernements ne se seront mis d'accord sur les mesures à prendre en commun contre celui qui essaye de se soustraire à ses obligations, nous devons conserver des armes avec le droit de nous en servir.« L'Entente balkanique, l'Union balte et, enfin, le Pacte oriental (ou Pacte de Saadabad) conclus dans la même perspective que la Petite Entente illustrèrent les types d'accords régionaux les plus caractéristiques de la période de l'entre-deux-guerres.[21]

Le Pacte d'Entente balkanique fut conclu à Athènes, le 9 février 1934, entre la Roumanie, la Grèce, la Turquie et la Yougoslavie. Les Etats balkaniques avaient vu les premiers s'évanouir leurs espoirs d'assurer à Genève une garantie de leur indépendance politique et de leur intégrité territoriale. Bien que pour la plupart défenseurs résolus de l'esprit de la SdN, leurs dirigeants se sont ainsi vus obligés de recourir au jeu traditionnel de l'équilibre des forces afin de s'assurer les garanties nécessaires à leur sécurité. Après avoir établi, entre 1928 et 1933, un réseau d'accords bilatéraux, ils se décidèrent, devant l'aggravation menaçante pour eux, de la crise européenne à chercher dans un pacte multilatéral une garantie supplémentaire contre les pressions extérieures et contre la menace des révisionnismes locaux. L'adhésion du gouvernement bulgare, constamment déterminé dans ses choix par les pressions d'une opinion publique largement animée par l'esprit révisionniste, s'avérant impossible, les quatre Etats balkaniques, attachés à l'idée de la sauvegarde des Traités de Paix, n'hésitèrent plus à signer un pacte de garantie mutuelle, de sept ans – avec possibilité de dénonciation au bout des deux premières années – ouvert à l'adhésion de tout autre pays de la Péninsule.[22]

Quant à l'Union balte, elle fut conclue le 12 décembre 1934, entre trois des dix Etats riverains de la mer Baltique – l'Esthonie, la Lettonie et la Lithuanie. Les parties contractantes s'engageaient à contribuer »au maintien et à la garantie de la paix«, prévoyaient une action concertée sur les questions de politique extérieure »d'importance commune« et prévoyaient une aide mutuelle »dans leurs relations internationales«. Le traité de l'Union balte soulignait la conformité de ses dispositions avec celles du Pacte de la SdN. Enfin, tout comme l'Entente balkanique, il restait ouvert à l'adhésion d'autres Etats et était d'une durée de dix ans.[23]

Enfin, le Pacte oriental fut signé au palais de Saadabad à Téhéran, le 8 juillet 1937, entre l'Afghanistan, l'Irak, l'Iran, et la Turquie. Les termes dans lesquels il était conçu révélait toutes les caractéristiques d'une »entente régionale«: son but était »d'assurer la paix et la sécurité dans le Proche-Orient au moyen de garanties additionnelles dans le cadre de la SdN et de contribuer ainsi à la paix générale«. Reprenant la définition de l'agression formulée par la Conférence du désarmement en 1932, le Pacte prévoyait que dans le cas où l'une des parties contractante estimerait qu'une agression avait été ou était sur le point d'être commise, elle porterait la question devant le Conseil de la Société »sans préjudice de prendre toutes les mesures qu'elle jugerait nécessaires dans ces circonstances«. Les principes régissant la coopération instaurée par cet acte (non-ingérence dans les affaires intérieures, inviolabilité des frontières communes, dénonciation du traité vis-à-vis d'un des signataires qui se serait livré à une agression contre une tierce puissance, etc.) se trouvaient renforcés par la confirmation des obligations assumées en vertu du Pacte de la SdN et du Traité de Paris du 27 août 1928.[24]

La querelle au sujet de la compatibilité des accords régionaux avec les dispositions du Pacte se déroula devant la IIe Assemblée et aboutit à la formation de deux groupes distincts, les »universalistes« et les »régionalistes«. Face à l'obstination des doctrinaires de l'»unitarisme«, se dressa la conception plus souple exprimée par les partisans d'une »décentralisation« internationale opérée sous l'égide et le patronage de la SdN. Les représentants des Etats menacés dans leur propre voisinage, ainsi que la plupart des juristes ou des publicistes n'hésitaient pas à adopter, à l'exemple d'Alejandro Alvarez, la thèse selon laquelle les ententes régionales pouvaient, dans certaines conditions, contribuer à la consolidation de la sécurité et de la paix. Cette tendance connut un regain de vigueur dans les années trente à partir des premiers signes de la crise mondiale. La Conférence du désarmement décida ainsi d'établir un comité spécial de sécurité chargé de dégager les principes susceptibles de régir la formation des ententes régionales. Les conclusions correspondantes qui en résultèrent, plutôt limitatives, s'énonçaient ainsi: »Les accords régionaux de sécurité ne doivent pas être dirigés contre une puissance ou un groupe de puissances. Ainsi que l'avait établi en 1928 le Comité d'arbitrage et de sécurité, les traités d'assistance mutuelle auront plus de valeur et mériteront d'autant mieux l'appui de la SdN que, suivant le précédent rhénan de Locarno, ils seront conclus entre les Etats qui faisaient partie dans un passé récent de groupes rivaux ou dont les différends seraient susceptibles de mettre en danger la paix du monde.«[25]

Les initiatives prises depuis lors dans ce sens se heurtèrent à l'enchaînement des événements qui révélaient la décomposition totale du système de la sécurité collective aussi bien que de l'équilibre de forces à l'échelle mondiale. Au cours même de l'année critique 1936, la cause du régionalisme fut plaidée, encore une fois, avec beaucoup d'éloquence devant l'Assemblée de Genève. Les représentants français, Léon Blum et Yvon Delbos, proposèrent même une définition des ententes régionales qui allait trop loin: »Selon nous, c'est dans l'organisation des nouvelles ententes régionales ou dans le resserrement de celles qui existent déjà, que la solution peut être trouvée. Et par ›ententes régionales‹, nous voulons dire tout groupement de puissances dont l'union se fonde sur la situation géographique ou sur la communauté d'intérêts . . .«[26]

Certes, cette tendance se trouvait contredite par les symptômes de la crise qui sévissait au sein des relations internationales. Mais d'autre part, ce même phénomène procédait encore une fois du souci de promouvoir la solution »régionaliste« au niveau aussi bien politique qu'institutionnel.

Les tentatives de la diplomatie française d'ajouter au »Locarno de l'Ouest« un »Locarno de l'Est« furent renouvelées. A l'aspiration briandiste et, ensuite, au projet de Pacte oriental, se succédèrent les efforts déployés par Delbos dans le but d'étendre les garanties de 1925 à l'Est européen sous la forme d'un »Locarno généralisé«. Mais, si cette tentative se heurtait à nouveau à des difficultés insurmontables, n'était-il pas encore concevable de prévoir, dans le cadre d'une réorganisation de la SdN, la possibilité de conclure des accords régionaux? En effet, parmi les propositions avancées lors des discussions ouvertes à ce propos, à partir de 1936, le recours aux pactes régionaux en tant que solution pratique au problème de la sécurité fut avancé. Toutefois, cette proposition ne fut pas retenue par le comité spécial chargé par l'Assemblée d'étudier la réforme éventuelle de la Société . . . Le débat fut clos en septembre 1939, avec le déclenchement de la guerre, lequel mit un terme aux derniers espoirs et illusions.

Conclusion

Pour porter un jugement final sur les pactes régionaux, il serait superficiel de se contenter de répéter les principes énoncés par certains juristes, même des plus éminents. Abstraction faite de toute théorie, l'évolution du phénomène régionaliste fut largement conditionnée par l'influence de critères politiques proprement dits. La querelle entre »universalistes« et »régionalistes«, mais surtout la controverse entre défenseurs du régime des Traités au moyen d'un réseau des pactes régionaux d'une part, et révisionnistes, opposés à toute coalition vouée à la défense du *statu quo* territorial d'autre part, se trouvait inextricablement liée à des choix politiques. Les Etats membres de la Société des Nations, attachés continuellement à leurs prérogatives nationales, finirent par transposer au sein de l'organisme de Genève leurs intérêts antagonistes et leur divergence de vues. C'est ainsi que tous les efforts déployés dans le but de concilier »l'unitarisme indispensable et la décentralisation inévitable« se heurtèrent finalement à des résistances insurmontables.

Dans ces conditions, peut-on dire que les ententes régionales, dans leur forme la plus répandue, tendaient à promouvoir l'œuvre de la paix? Ont-elles, au contraire et selon l'opinion de leurs adversaires, contribué à la détérioration du climat international? Etant donné que la conclusion d'accords régionaux non conformes au modèle de Locarno ne fut pas généralement reconnue comme compatible avec les dispositions du Pacte, se prononcer pour l'une ou l'autre thèse équivaudrait à prendre position en faveur d'un camp politique bien déterminé. On ne saurait, toutefois, ne pas se rendre compte du fait qu'à défaut d'un mécanisme capable de consolider la paix à l'échelle universelle, la tendance régionaliste, dans la mesure où elle se soumettait à l'ordre international et proclamait une fidélité sincère envers la Société des Nations, constituait une solution de rechange dont l'adoption générale aurait pu, sous certaines conditions, amener à des résultats positifs pour la paix.

Notes

1 Voir sur ce sujet spécifique: Jesus Maria Yepes, »Les accords régionaux et le droit international«, *Recueil des cours de l'Académie de droit international* (ci-après: R.C.A.D.I.) 71: 227–344, 1947.

J.R. de Orue y Arregui, »Le régionalisme dans l'organisation internationale; *R.C.A.D.I.* 53: 1–95, 1935.

Axel von Freytagh-Loringhoven, »Les ententes régionales«, *R.C.A.D.I.* 56: 585–677, 1936.

Octavian Stefanovici, *Le régionalisme en droit international.* Paris, Recueil Sirey, 1935. 239 p.

A. Randle Elliott, *Regionalism in the League of Nations to the Outbreak of World War II.* Cambridge, Harvard University Press, 1949. 254 p. On se référera également à un témoignage classique, celui d'Alejandro Alvarez, *L'Organisation internationale; Précédents de la Société des Nations et de l'Union fédérale européenne.* Paris, Editions internationales, 1931. 357 p. Sur les divers aspects du problème, voir aussi *Dix ans de coopération internationale.* Genève, Secrétariat de la SdN, 1930. 628 p.

George Scelle, *Une crise de la Société des Nations. La réforme du Conseil et l'entrée de l'Allemagne à Genève (mars-septembre 1926).* Paris, Presses universitaires de France, 1927. 254 p.

Maurice Bourquin, »Le problème de la sécurité internationale«, *R.C.A.D.I.* 49: 469–542, 1934.

2 J. M. Yepes, *op. cit.* p. 246.

3 George Scelle, *op. cit.* p. 201.

4 Pour compliquer le problème, il y avait le fait additionnel que le texte anglais ne correspondait pas exactement au texte français de l'article. Le premier »envisageait le problème sous son aspect plutôt positif, l'autre n'en voyait que l'aspect négatif et l'éxégèse des deux textes pouvait mener à des conclusions différentes« (Yepes, *op. cit*, p. 259). Sur l'article 21, voir Vladislav Mirkovitch, *Des rapports entre l'article l et l'article 21 du Pacte de la Société des Nations.* Paris, les Editions internationales, 1932, 202 p.

5 George Scelle, *op. cit.* p. 182.

6 *Dix ans de coopération internationale.* – Genève, *op. cit.* 1930. p. St.

6bis SdN, *Actes de la Troisième Assemblée,* Séances plénières, vol. I, p. 291.

6ter *Ibid.*

7 *Dix ans de coopération internationale, op. cit.* p. 84–85.

8 *Ibid.*, p. 86. Voir aussi Edouard Réquin, »Traité d'assistance mutuelle et réduction des armements«, *Revue militaire française* 93: 226–237, 19 novembre 1923.

Rafaël Erich, »Les rapports entre le Pacte de la Société des Nations et le projet de traité d'assistance mutuelle«, *Revue de droit international et de législation comparée* 5: 1–12, ;–2, 1924.

9 George Scelle, *op. cit.* p. 191–192.

10 *Ibid.* p. 193.

11 *Ibid.*, p. 194. Sur Locarno, voir, *Les accords de Locarno et la Société des Nations.* Genève, SdN, 1925. 26 p. (Supplément au *Résumé mensuel des activités de la Société des Nations,* décembre 1925) *Locarno Treaties, 1925.* Washington, Carnegie Endowment for International Peace, 1925.

George Glasgow, *From Dawes to Locarno.* London, Benn 1925. 186 p. Gabriel Péri, *Genève–Locarno. La SdN et le pacte de garantie.* Paris, Librarie de l'Humanité, 1925. 164 p.

René Cassin, *Les Accords de Locarno et la Société des Nations.* Paris, Association française pour la Société des Nations, 1926. 12 p. Nicolas Politis, »Les Accords de Locarno.« *Revue de droit international et de législation comparée* 6: 713–731, 1925. No. 6.

Charles G. Fenwick, "The Legal Significance of the Locarno Agreements«, *American Journal of International Law* 20: 108–111, January 1925.

James T. Shotwell, "A Turning Point in History«, *International Conciliation* 229: 149–161, April 1927.

E. Grigg, "The Merits and Defects of the Locarno Treaty as a Guarantee of World Peace, *International Affairs* 14: 176–197, March–April 1935.

12 Voir surtout *Dix ans de coopération internationale, op. cit.* p. 118–130.

13 N. Politis, »Les Accords de Locarno«, *op. cit.* p. 718 *et seq.*

14 A. Michalakopoulos, *Logo koinobouleutikoi* [Discours parlementaires] Athéna, vol. 2, 1964, p. 274–5. De l'avis du Ministre grec des Affaires Etrangères, les Etats balkaniques auraient dû se contenter de contracter, deux par deux, des accords politiques garantissant la paix et consacrant la conciliation, l'arbitrage et l'aide mutuelle.

15 David Mitrany, "The Possiblity of Balkan Locarno", *International Conciliation* 229: 167–168, 1 April 1927.

D'autres publications contemporaines sur les efforts de rapprochement balkanique au lendemain de Locarno: Auguste Gauvain, »Les projets de rapprochement balkanique«, *L'esprit international* 1: 30–43, janvier 1927.

P. Loew, »Das Locarno des Balkans«, *Neues Europa* 13: 22–26, Januar–Februar 1927.

H. H. M. Macartney, "Towards a Balkan Bloc", *Fortnightly Review* 123: 311–322, March 1928.

L. Maccas, »Les conditions de l'entente Balkanique«, *Revue des Nations* 112–124, avril 1927.

David Mitrany, »A Balkan Locarno«, *Living Age* 331: 394–397, Decembre 1926.

Albert Mousset, »L'Europe balkanique et danubienne de 1925 à 1928«.

16 Très caractéristique, A. Alvarez, *L'organisation internationale. op. cit.*

17 Voir surtout: Aristide Briand, *Discours et écrits de politique étrangère: la paix, l'Union européenne, la SdN.* Paris, Plon, 1965. 302 p. Sur le projet Briand, quelques points de vue très intéressants: Richard Coudenhove-Kalergi, »Die Aktion Briands und die Paneuropa-Bewegung«, *Paneuropa* 6: 258–263, Juni–Juli 1930.

Auguste Gauvain, »Le projet d'une Union fédérale européenne de M. Briand«, *L'esprit international* 4: 375–386, 1930.

Henry de Jouvenel, »Le projet de fédération européenne«, *L'esprit international* 4: 483–490, 1930.

Albert de La Pradelle, »L'Union juridique et le projet de M. Briand«, *Revue de droit international* 4: 360–3, 1930.

Nicolas Politis, »Le projet d'union européenne et la SdN«, – *Revue de droit international* 8: 201–211, 1930.

Caarel Pusta, »L'idée de l'Union européenne devant les gouvernements et la SdN«, *Revue de droit international et de législation comparée* 12: 150–162, 1931.

George Scelle, »Le mémorandum Briand et la fédération européenne«, *Revue politique et parlementaire* 143: 376–96, 10 juin 1930.

18 Sur la Petite Entente, entre autres: E. Benès, *Le Pacte d'Organisation de la Petite Entente et l'état actuel de la politique internationale.* Prague, 1933.

A. Hobza, »La Petite Entente«, *Revue de droit international et de législation comparée* 14: 216–234, 1933.

Stefan Osusky, »La Genèse de la Petite Entente«. *Revue d'histoire diplomatique* 46: 131–142, avril–juin 1932. Du même, "The Little Entente and the League of Nations", *International Affairs* 13: 378–393, May–June 1934.

V. M. Radovanowitch, »La Petite Entente«. *Revue générale de droit international public* 40: 716–778, novembre–décembre 1933.

R. W. Seton-Watson, "The Little and the Balkan Entente." *Slavonic Review* 75: 553–576, April 1937. Du même, »La Petite Entente.« *L'esprit international* 5: 592–613, octobre 1931.

M. Spalaikovitch, *La Société des Nations et la Petite Entente*. Paris, s.e., 1923. 15p.

Etudes plus récentes: Piotr S. Wandysz, *France and her Eastern Allies, 1919–1925, French–Czechoslovak–Polish Relations from the Paris Peace Conference to Locarno*. Minneapolis, University of Minnesota Press, 1962. 454 p.

Nicolae Iordache, *La Petite Entente et l'Europe*. Genève, I.U.H.E.I., 1977. 397 p.

E. Campus, *The Little Entente and the Balkan Alliance*, Bucarest, Editura Academiei Republicii Socialiste România, 1978.

19 M. Spalaikovitch, *op. cit.* p. 12–13.

19bis Amendement proposé par le gouvernement tchécoslovaque, 30 mars 1921. Doc. SdN, A.C.5.

20 George Scelle, *op. cit.* p. 183–8.

21 M. Spalaikovitch, *op. cit.* p. 8–9.

22 Sur les efforts de rapprochement balkanique dans les années trente: Michel Dendias, *L'organisation du Proche-Orient et le mouvement de rapprochement balkanique*. Paris, Rodstein, 1935. 182p.

Norman Padelford, *Peace in the Balkans. The Mouvement towards International Organization in the Balkans*. New York, Oxford University Press, 1935. 209 p.

R. Kerner, H. Howard, *The Balkan Conferences and the Balkan Entente* 1930–1935. Berkeley, University of California Press, 1936. 271 p.

T. I. Geshkoff, *Balkan Union. A Road to Peace in South-Eastern Europe*. New York, Columbia University Press, 1940. 345 p.

Publications plus récentes:

K. Svolopoulos, »Le problème de la sécurité dans le Sud-Est européen de l'entre-deux-guerres: A la recherche des origines du Pacte Balkanique de 1934«, *Balkan Studies* 14: 247–282, 1973. Du même, To Balkanikon Symphōnon kai hē hellēnikē exōterikē politikē, 1928–1934: anekdoton keimenon ton Elefterion Veniszelou. [Le Pacte Balkanique et la politique extérieure de la Grèce. 1928–1934: texte inédit de Elefterion Venizelou] Athēna, »ESTIA«, 1974.

E. Campus, *Intelegerea balkanica*. Bucuresti, Academiei Republicii Socialiste România, 1972. – 394 p.

D. Kitsikis, »Les projets d'Entente Balkanique, 1930–1934«, *Revue Historique* 241: 117–140, 1969.

23 Bronias Kaziuskas, *L'Entente Baltique*. Paris, Recueil Sirey, 1939. 327 p.

Robert Machray, "The Baltic Pact, Vilna and Memel«, – *Nineteenth Century* 117: 585–596, May 1935.

V. M. Radovanovitch, »L'Entente Baltique devant le droit international.« – *Revue générale de droit international public* 62: 688–735, 1935.

Michel Romeris, »L'Entente Baltique et la Solidarité régionale«. *Conciliation Internationale* Bulletin: 485–503, no 5–6–7 1936. Du même, »L'organisation de l'Est européen par voie de solidarité régionale.« *Revue de droit international* 20: 64–91, 1937.

24 A. Fleury, »La constitution d'un ›Bloc oriental‹ le pacte de Saadabad – comme contribution à la sécurité collective dans les années trente«, *Revue d'histoire de la Deuxième Guerre Mondiale* 106: 1–18, avril 1977. Sur les pactes régionaux conclus pendant cette période, voir J.R. de Orue y Arregui, *op. cit.* p. 65–74.
A. v. Freytagh-Loringhoven, *op. cit.* op. 456–66.
25 J. M. Yepes, *op. cit.* p. 263.
26 *ibid.* p. 253.

Leticia and Ethiopia before the League

George W. Baer
University of California, Santa Cruz

The League had certain minor attributes of an independent actor, but it was, essentially, an association of sovereign States, each acting in particularist national interests. Adherence to the Covenant was not a guarantee of co-operation. Collective action rested on independent estimations of the legitimacy, competence, status, and benefits of the League. Decisions of its Members might be in systemic accord with the terms of the Covenant but their judgments, basically, were made from unilateral evaluations of their own interests, their independent determinations of risks and opportunities. In each case, political decisions were dependent on the existing pattern of interaction between sovereign States, in which the value of cooperating as the League of Nations in terms of the Covenant was but one of the features of international life to be assessed.[1]

In a review of Walters's *A History of the League of Nations*, Gerhart Niemeyer called for an approach that viewed the League "not merely in terms of an ideal goal but above all as an institution situated in the mainstream of world politics and intended to affect the conditions of war and peace."[2] In like vein, Inis Claude urged a recognition of international institutions as "not participants in, or masters over, but as adjuncts to the multi-state system."[3] We must avoid discussions that narrowly evaluate decisions in terms of the degree of their fidelity to the Covenant, or to the hopes of the League's founders. Such proprietary analyses are marked by a debilitating isolation from broad political realities, and are soon exhausted as historical explanations. Such thinking has led League partisans to misplaced anger when the League was ignored or manipulated, and has given critics the opportunity to dismiss the League as a fantasy doomed to superficiality and failure, an organization that confused form with substance.

In the case of Leticia, the League served the primary policy interests of all States associated with the dispute. Therefore the League had value, and League methods worked. In the case of Ethiopia, these conditions for success were absent. Therefore League methods failed.

I. The occupation of Leticia was not an act of policy by the Peruvian government. Whether it was a filibuster of Lorentanos in their local interest or an act to embarrass the government by the Aprista opposition, it only became a matter of state when the president, Sánchez Cerro, supported it as a patriotic action. Sánchez Cerro based his administration on an appeal to popular patriotism, on an assertion of national independence. On this occasion, he saw an opportunity to call into question the validity of the treaty of 1927 that had given up the Leticia territory to Colombia, and to reopen border talks. Where the previous Government had buckled to strong American pressure in signing the treaty, Sánchez Cerro stood opposed to any external interference, and he rejected American entreaties and Brazilian offers of mediation as meddling with Peru's right of self-determination. Neither of these Powers had a direct stake in the dispute. Although the Government in Rio had some worry about another war breaking out on Brazil's border, and the army raised doubts as to whether Brazil could remain neutral, the Government, its offer of mediation rejected in Lima, withdrew it. The fact that Colombia proposed to invoke the Kellogg-Briand pact, and that the United States denounced Peru as an aggressor merely exacerbated the anti-American attitude of Sánchez Cerro's national populist Government, and rendered any intra-American representations futile.[4] The immediate political stakes lay between Bogotá and Lima.

Both states, however, were Members of the League, and Geneva decisively dismissed Peru's claim to reopen unilaterally the question of the Leticia's sovereignty. At the League the occupation was considered an unambiguous violation of a valid international agreement. Some in the League milieu urged a hard and narrow line of principle against Peru, seeking a precedent with regard to frontier violations for collective action in Europe and the Far East. For the major European powers, however, and for the United States, the dispute was too distant and, ultimately, too inconsequential to pursue as a test case. The Council's Advisory Committee worked within the terms of the Covenant, naturally, but without pushing principle, cognizant always of the limited capacity of the League to determine events in the upper Amazon Valley. Neither the United States nor Brazil belonged to the League, but with their advice ignored in Lima, and themselves unable to act to prevent a war, both were willing to leave the League the task of searching for a settlement. In Madariaga's words, the League works "unmolested."[5]

It acted under Article 15. The job of the Advisory Committee under Sean Lester was to find terms of settlement. The Council warned the parties to accept its recommendations, but it had no certainty that the threat of sanctions could be carried out if they did not. A new American Government under Roosevelt was willing to co-operate to an extent, seeing the League's initiative as a logical next step to the failure of its own influence in Lima. A representative from the United States, and also one from Brazil, attended meetings of the Advisory Committee. But Roosevelt was not willing to consider an embargo in case of war. Most Latin American States remained determinedly neutral.

During the critical early months of 1933 the Advisory Committee was the planning center. It listened to the advice of European ambassadors in Lima and Bogotá, notably the British. The Council started from the position that Peru was in the wrong, that Colombia held sovereignty over Leticia, and that the *sine qua non* was Peruvian withdrawal. The Committee took the Brazilian idea of a third-party peacekeeping mission and recommended that Leticia be placed under the administration of a League-controlled international commission for one year, during which time direct negotiations between the parties would take place. In their final formulation, however, the Committee's recommendation did not state that if negotiations failed Colombia would resume its sovereignty. Colombia demanded prior recognition of its abiding treaty right as a condition of the talks. The Government in Bogotá was alarmed. Peru was accused of treaty violation, yet the so-called Lester modifications now seemed to imply that Peru could reopen the issue of that treaty's legitimacy. The formula did not guarantee to Colombia the right of reversion of Leticia if negotiations failed. The Committee, it seems, was making a concession on British advice to Peruvian sensitivities to stop the drift to war, but it should be noted that despite Colombian dismay at this point the Council never intimated that the current treaty was invalid, nor did it ever put pressure on Colombia to consider revision.

The object of the recommendations was to get the parties to the table. At this point, in mid-April 1933, with the imminent threat of war, European and American envoys turned their attention to overcoming the objections in Bogotá. The Council had unanimously warned Peru against war, and called on it to withdraw. Peru hat not, and Colombia, despite its early co-operation and sound position, now balked at acceptance as well. It was an impasse. The armed forces of both States converged on Leticia. Both sides were so poorly prepared that extensive military operations were unlikely, but combat was taking place, Colombians held forts in Peruvian territory, and the outbreak of war seemed at hand.

It was the assassination of Sánchez Cerro on 30 April, and the accommodating stance taken by the Benavide's new Administration that changed the situation. Benavide's authority did not rest on mass appeal, on flamboyant xenophobia. He was concerned about the financial and political strains a war would cause, and the possibility of additional trouble with Ecuador. He reportedly stated to the Peruvian Congress: "Peru is not in a position to carry on a war with Colombia with any hope of a satisfactory conclusion. We will probably not be able to withstand the Colombian drive now being made on Puerto Arturo. We are isolated among the countries of the world and our diplomatic position is even worse than our military one. The ships that we have just sent to Pará have had a most unfortunate trip, owing to the united action of the countries at whose ports these ships stop for provisions and fuel. This shows that these countries are united against Peru. I fear that all the countries belonging to the League will shortly withdraw their diplomatic representatives from Lima as a sign of protest; that there may likewise be an embargo on arms and possibly an economic boycott."[6]

Whether he used the possibility of League action as a convenient excuse, or whether his concern about international opposition was as genuine as this suggests, there came a dramatic turn in Peruvian policy. Benavides had cordial personal relations with A. López, leader of the antimilitarist Liberal party in Colombia and who, in February 1934, was to become president of the state. This, with the support of the Peruvian Congress, led almost immediately to an agreement between the Governments to accept the Council's recommendations.

Hostilities ceased, troops of both sides withdrew from occupied territory, and for a year a League "Commission for the Administration of the Territory of Leticia," flying a League flag and in command of a force of Colombian soldiers, held the trapezium. Peru and Colombia met in Rio under the auspices of the

Brazilian Government in direct negotiations in which the League played no part. These talks did not go smoothly. All the old questions of treaty rights and revisionist claims for frontier modification reemerged, and a breakdown appeared likely. Preparations for war got under way again in both countries.

Peru asked the Council to extend its control for an additional six months. To this Colombia stood unalterably opposed. So did the Council. The Council insisted that the two parties take responsibility for a settlement within the year as originally accepted, and, after much hemming and hawing, at the last moment, a "Protocol of Peace, Friendship, and Cooperation" was signed. It made no mention of either Leticia or the League, beyond the statement that "Peru sincerely deplores, as she has previously declared, the events which have taken place since September 1, 1932, which have disturbed her relations with Colombia." But this, with the establishment of a demilitarized frontier, border agreements, a free trade zone, and a statement that disputes henceforth would be put under discussion, settled the conflict over Leticia. After one year the League Commission withdrew, and Colombian troops took control of the territory.

This bilateral conclusion does not detract from the League's decisive role in defusing the dispute. In consultation with interested Powers the Council provided the mechanism of the Administrative Commission for separating the contestants and stopping the drift of war.[7] The Council's action under article 15, its insistence on Peruvian withdrawal and on negotiation as a requirement of League participation, and its threat of possible action if its recommendations were rejected, gave a breathing space and direction to both parties, and a rationale to negotiation as a means of settlement. With Brazilian co-operation, with persistent British and American diplomatic encouragement, and faced at a decisive moment with an unyielding League Council, the disputants had the means and the need to work out their differences. The League did not seek, nor was it empowered, to impose a final settlement. It could and did hold the ring and pointed, even perhaps at the last moment shoved, the disputants towards peaceful resolution. There was, in this circumstance, enough of the carrot of neutral good offices and the stick of international disapproval, to make the parties think twice about going to war.

II. With Ethiopia, as with Leticia, the problem was that the dispute was not initially susceptible to mediation. The League's capacity for conciliation depended on agreement by all parties to accept limitations on their political ambitions. Without such cooperation League agencies could do little until the Covenant was violated, article 16 invoked, and the process of collective enforcement begun. With Leticia, this climacteric was fortuitously avoided, and the reconciliationist recommendations of the League were put to use. With Ethiopia, Mussolini rejected all alternatives other than war. His aim, he had declared in December 1934, was "the destruction of the Abyssinian armed forces and the total conquest of Ethiopia."[8] This uncompromising stance posed a dilemma for League Members. Their leaders, Britain and France, preferred to avoid Geneva's involvement altogether. A collectivist response in this case went against their growing, if yet unformed, impulse to appeasement, part of their search for security outside the framework of the League. For instance, Gaines Post noted that ministers in Britain "distinguished both politically and procedurally between emergency and long-term planning. They treated the quarrel with Italy as a separate and temporary problem of policy, one that had to be quickly and peacefully solved because it upset the machinery as well as the timetable of long-term rearmament."[9] This applied similarly to France, which – weak and anxious about Germany, and above all fearing another European war – wanted no conflict with its southern neighbour. Yet these Governments could not ignore the League entirely, partly because they had to acknowledge the pro-League sentiment among their electorates, and partly because at this time they had no alternative plan for security in Europe. It seemed, therefore, to the British and French Governments that the only realistic response was a dual policy, direct negotiations to settle the Ethiopian question by territorial agreement (which they hoped would be validated at Geneva) combined with limited support for the Covenant (enough to maintain a semblance of solidarity without provoking Mussolini). The search was for a way to avoid exposing the disorder of European affairs. The affair was to be got through with as little cost as possible, kept from being escalated to a test of principle at Geneva, so that Britain and France could avoid a call for action beyond their military or political capacity.

One sees how conditional this policy was in support of the League. It exemplified what Emile Giraud bitterly excoriated as the use of the technicalities of League procedure to avoid confronting essential political realities.[10] In London, it was held such evasion was in the League's interest. For the League to act decisively against Italy was impossible, as neither Britain or France would do so. The Ethiopian affair need not directly affect European security. Any confrontation at Geneva would only reveal the impotence of the machinery of collective security, and expose the disarray of the putative western allies, that is, the badly strained relations between Britain and France. At first the affair was minimized and isolated. The border incident at Walwal was subjected to arbitration, but the League was given no part. This arbitration, like the Walwal dispute, was a charade. The border incident was removed from its context, from the larger issue of war preparation by both sides. It was Italy's red herring, a tactic of delay and distraction, accepted by the other Powers. Similarly, the British and French co-operated with Italy, outside the League and with no reference to the Ethiopian Government, to find a territorial concession in the manner of old colonial settlements, an imperialist throw-back but one that could not succeed as it could not deliver to Mussolini what he wanted, namely a war. What such behavior did deliver was a blow to League confidence, legitimacy, and presumptive authority. But there was nothing the bulk of Members could do if its leading States were loath to use League methods.

Such temporizing showed Mussolini he had nothing to fear from Geneva. He knew that neither Britain nor France had a vital interest in maintaining the independence of Ethiopia, and he saw that neither would risk war in Europe over it either, not just for the League. Haile Selassie understood this too, and saw his fate. Yet a League policy was his only hope, for Britain's connection to Geneva, however ambivalent, was what kept London from deserting him entirely. It was a weak reed. The British discouraged Ethiopia from invoking article 15, for instance, during the months of Italian military preparation, while they pursued a territorial settlement. When article 15 was at last invoked, on the eve of the war, the Council Committee proposed, in Madariaga's phrase, an "international mandate."[11] Unbacked by any determination to enforce it, this recommendation was at once rejected by Mussolini. He did not want influence in Ethiopia, he did not want to be part of an internationalized administration. What he wanted was a war of conquest. It is as simple as that. "What am I to do with my army of a million?" he asked, and this was the question.[12] He was confident of victory. He dismissed the anxieties of his general staff that Italy could not face a determined opposition. He relied on his diplomacy to keep Europe docile through *his* threat of war. He certainly did not care what happened to the Covenant's norms of international conduct. To him they were a conservative ideology meant to serve the haves, to protect the *status quo*, the doctrine of a dog in the manger. He was prepared to withdraw from Geneva. Basically, he just did not care.

The invasion, and the invocation of article 16, laid down the challenge to the League. The question became: were the political system of the League and the norms of the Covenant valued more highly than the maintenance of autonomy by its parts?[13] The answer was, essentially 'no.' There was no stable pattern of co-operation by powerful States intent upon maintaining the international law the Covenant proclaimed. The system remained theoretical; it did not reflect the political reality on which the nation-States based their decisions. Therefore, to what purpose was it to be defended? Powerful States remained outside, some fervently revisionist. Among Members there was discord, divergent priorities. Even if a spark of support for the Covenant existed, lack of military preparedness made the cost of conflict with Italy too high for governments to consider, when it seemed this might be the only way to stop the invasion. Enforcement of the terms of the Covenant, then, could not be an end in itself.

To the British Government it mattered less that the League process succeed than that it *appear* to be tried. Faced with popular internationalist expectations, which the Government had not discouraged, British leaders feared that if they gave no support to sanctions, if, ultimately, an oil embargo was not at least proposed, the electorate would turn, disillusioned, to isolation, and the Government would be unable to begin rearmament.[14] The double policy contained troublesome paradoxes. It involved support for a system of collective security in which the Government had no faith against a State with whom they sought good relations, or at least the avoidance of conflict. It involved seeling, or responding to, domestic support in order, ultimately, to avoid having to rely in the end on this very system of collective security. Lastly, the Government's support was intrinsically partial, aimed at avoiding a provocation it was the purpose of collective security to, if necessary, confront.

There was some talk that the line of enforcement should be a means to a further end, that opposition to Italy's aggression might lead to the creation of an anti-German coalition through the League. Baldwin, no Leaguer, had called the League 'the sheet anchor' of British policy, and Eden spoke of the Italian invasion as the 'test case' of the League. These were false images, deceptive, really, when one sees how little was done. A crucial limitation was the distrust between the British and the French. Their lack of mutual support made joint resolve at Geneva impossible. This vitiated the notion of a test case. The French got no assurance of help in Europe and so saw no reason to oppose Italy. France could not afford an enemy over the Alps without a friend across the Channel. Their unwillingness was in fact a relief to the British, who made it the excuse for their own inaction.

The logic of the situation, therefore, argued for a continuation of the double policy. This is reflected in the sanctions. Recall that application of the terms of article 16 was neither automatic or enforceable. Nothing affected the freedom of States to co-operate, or not, with terms of action the Council could only recommend. Collective action could take place only to the extent participants saw value in supporting the League's norms and forms (a League at this point standing with its leaders hesitant, its utility in doubt) or had a sense of further or mutual advantage (a condition never present, for it would have meant more precise commitments to a set of new power relations in Europe than either the French or the British would make). The result was minimal action at Geneva.

Sanctions in 1935 were imposed not to punish the Italian people, or to destroy fascism, or to topple Mussolini. Military action against Italy was never considered. Indeed, all conservative governments, and the Pope, feared that if Mussolini fell bolshevism would sweep the peninsula. Sanctions were limited to economic and financial measures, a political solution was sought through economic means. The idea was to weaken the Italian economy just enough to inspire political opposition to the war. Mussolini might then find it too costly to continue. This pressure was to be limited so as not to provoke an act of retaliation. Sanctions, in effect, were to make Mussolini amenable to settlement. In this form they were compatible with the continued search for a negotiated peace, and this could be pursued outside the League. Sanctions, thus, were made part of the dual policy.

In the beginning it seemed this formula stood a chance. Everyone thought an Italian victory would take two years, time enough, perhaps, for graduated economic pressure to work. Whether from honor, fear, hope, or despair over fifty states applied, if only partially, the provisions of article 16. For the first and only time sanctions were systematically brought into force against a Member State, and this a significant European Power. It seemed a moment of triumph for the League. There were problems. The burdens fell unequally. This was expected, if lamented, becoming a problem when sanctions were perceived to be sacrifices without predictable benefits. This gave way to backsliding, as states hedged their bets. The list of goods sanctioned was incomplete. It did not include essential materials, notably oil. America did not participate, and the prospect of American supplies to Italy made it hard to argue for a comprehensive prohibition by League Members, a fatal limitation to the universalistic assumptions of article 16. The arms embargo was in effect discriminatory. Applied to both belligerents, it in fact favored the aggressor, who had access to the world arms market, and deprived the victim who needed arms the most, especially if the war was to be drawn out. The success of economic sanctions depended on a prolonged conflict. The biggest problem for the sanctionist position was that it soon appeared evident the war might end much sooner than expected.

A continuation of the policy of negotiation seemed the only way to prevent the humiliation of the League. An arranged territorial settlement might save some remnant of Ethiopia's independence while satisfying Mussolini's colonial ambition. This was the thinking behind the Hoare-Laval proposals. Mussolini saw no reason to accept them. Defeat for the League as well as Ethiopia was now his goal. But even before he rejected them the Hoare-Laval proposals collapsed through their own contradictions. The dual policy made sense to the Governments of Britain and France, but the gap between public expectations following from the proclaimed policy of support for the League, and the dismay at the reality of the practice of concession to the aggressor, was too wide for the democratic states to endure. An outpouring of Outrage in Great Britain, the stunned disbelief of minor League States, the dismay of the Americans, left this attempt at territorial settlement in ruins. And, within weeks. Mussolini was sure of victory in the field. He had no need to string the idea of compromise along any further. Unexpectedly he was deriving great advantage from the opposition, turning it to a cause of patriotic support. The cry of 'Italia contra mundum' rallied national support for his regime, which he used to consolidate his dictatorship and harden his resolve. Sanctions were good for fascism.

The Geneva front was upset further by startling developments in Europe. The post-war settlement was collapsing. German rearmament and remilitarization of the Rhineland presented a more serious threat to League Members than the loss of Ethiopia's independence. The Rhineland crisis came at the moment when the British at last proposed an oil embargo, and it buried that proposal completely. The absence of League action against the German violation of the Versailles Treaty, the absence of French or British action, destroyed the idea that sanctions against Italy might lead to a united stand in defense of treaties in Europe.

The Rhineland crisis also came just at the moment when Mussolini announced his armies had broken the Ethiopian northern front. The collapse of Ethiopian resistance destroyed the sanctionist timetable and the rationale for sanctions themselves. Instead of lasting two years the war lasted seven months.

For the Italians it was a two front victory. For Geneva, and for Ethiopia, it was a disaster. It also revealed the disarray of Europe. Britain and France had not settled their differences. Indeed, they were now further apart than ever. Their lack of resolve, their pursuit of accommodation, discredited all hope for a system of collective security. This Avenol acknowledged, in his despairing and passive fashion, when he called the Ethiopian affair "a European poison."[15] What was not discredited was appeasement. For Britain and France appeasement got them through this dangerous time; it prevented war with Italy. Appeasement worked, and could be practiced on one's own. There seemed no further use for the Covenant. A realistic response to the incoherence and instability of international affairs lay, it seemed, in new, particular accommodations, and preparations for war. States drifted apart, into neutralism, ad hoc connections, and rearmament. After 1936 statecraft reverted to the enduring principle of international disorder: save oneself and the devil take the hindmost. Indeed, statesmen had never given up this principle. That, for a history of the League, is one lesson of the Ethiopian affair.

III. It is clear that the League's methods of settling disputes could only work when political ambitions at odds with the Covenant could be limited, and when disputants were willing to work out a compromise through negotiation.[16] This did not occur in the crises we have examined during the nationalist, integrative, xenophobic, and belligerent regimes of Sánchez Cerro and Mussolini. Both men rejected the Covenant's values, dismissed efforts at League intervention, and asserted their political independence regardless of international opposition. The failure of conciliation left the League with the problem of enforcement.

Sanctions capable of stopping a war were difficult to apply in the upper Amazon. It was fortunate for the League that Benevides took advantage of the League's proposals to lay the groundwork for a peaceful settlement. As we saw, sanctions against Italy were based on complex considerations by the Great Powers, particularly the assumption that graduated economic pressure would be sufficient to force Mussolini to end the war but not drive him out of the reconciliationist framework of the League. Looking back we see that the moderation, the ambiguity, of the 'dual policy' involved a decision not to target sanctions in a manner calculated to stop the invasion at once, for example by closing the Suez Canal, or immediately imposing an oil embargo. Finally, Mussolini's totalitarian regime and the Italian economy were neither of them as susceptible to international pressure as was imagined. Quite the contrary, the highly public censure fomented a siege mentality in Italy that Mussolini exploited to foster national solidarity and opposition to the League. This effect was precisely opposite to the one sanctions were meant to produce.[17]

These conclusions have a general relevance to questions concerning the coercive capacity of international organizations. The purpose of this paper, however, was to understand each case in its historical context, stressing particularly the dependence of the League on the existing political nature and power relations of the nations of the world, that is, its position in the incoherent state of international affairs in the mid-1930s.

Notes

1 Margarte P. Doxey, *Economic Sanctions and International Enforcement.* London, Oxford University Press, 1971. – p. 138–139.

2 Gerhart Niemeyer, "The Balance-Sheet of the League Experiment". *International Organization,* v. 6, 1952. – p. 557.

3 Inis Claude Jr., "The Growth of International Institutions". *In: The Aberystwyth Papers; International Politics, 1919–1969.* Brian Porter, editor, London, Oxford University Press, 1972. – p. 293.

4 R. St. John, "The End of Innocence: Peruvian Foreign Policy and the United States, 1918–1942". *Journal of Latin American Studies,* v. 8, 1976. – p. 336–340.

5 Salvador de Madariaga, *Memorias, 1921–1936.* Madrid, Espasa-Calpe, 1974. – p. 361.

6 Bryce Wood, *The United States and Latin American Wars, 1932–1942.* New York, Columbia University Press, 1966. – p. 230.

7 Stan Windass, "The League and Territorial Disputes". *In: The International Regulation of Frontier Disputes.* Evan Luard, editor, New York, Praeger, 1970, p. 82.
8 Giorgio Rochat, *Militari e politici nella preparazione della campagna d'Etiopia: Studi e documenti, 1932–1936.* Milano, F. Angeli, 1971. – p. 376–379.
9 Gaines Post Jr., "The Machinery of British Policy in the Ethiopian Crisis". *The International History Review,* v. I, 1979. – p. 541.
10 Emile Giraud, *La nullité de la politique international des grandes démocraties, 1919–1939.* Paris, Recueil Sirey, 1948. – p. 155.
11 Robert F. Dell, *The Geneva Racket, 1920–1939.* London, R. Hale, 1940. – p. 123.
12 *FRUS 1935.* v. 1, p. 756.
13 Margaret P. Doxey, *op. cit.,* p. 138.
14 George W. Baer, *Test Case: Italy, Ethiopia and the League of Nations.* Stanford, Hoover Institution Press, 1976. – p. 211–212.
15 *DDF,* 1964. – ser. 2, v. 2, no. 72.
16 Ernst B. Haas, *Collective Security and the Future International System.* Denver, Colorado University, 1968. – p. 11–12 (Social Science Foundation. Monograph Series in World Affairs, v. 5, no. 1). George W. Baer, "Sanctions and Security: The League of Nations and the Italian-Ethiopian War, 1935–1936". *International Organization,* v. XXVII, 1973, p. 172–174.
17 Richard Stuart Olson, "Economic Coercion in World Politics: With a Focus on North-South Relations". *World Politics,* v. 31, 1979. – p. 484.

Chapter/Chapitre IV

The League of Nations: aspects of financial, economic, social and humanitarian cooperation

La coopération financière, économique, sociale et humanitaire de la Société des Nations

Technical assistance and the League of Nations

A. ALEXANDER MENZIES
Canadian Department of Finance
Ottawa, Ontario

In looking back over the past sixty years a student of economic history cannot help but note the emergence of consistent and comparable international and national economic data following the founding of the League of Nations. The League provided a focal point where Governments could discuss commercial problems which had been handled on an *ad hoc* basis prior to World War I and where multilateral, as opposed to bilateral, solutions could be developed. Throughout the 1920's the technical assistance provided by the League had two major influences on both the League and international order. In 1920 the League faced the problem of how to establish its competence and gain the confidence of Member States in a general, ongoing manner in order to be able to exercise political influence. Second, there was the problem of how to make the League meaningful to the Member States so as to involve them on a continuous basis in the work of the League. In the early 1920's the League concentrated much of its efforts on commercial and financial assistance through the Economic and Financial Committee.

In practice the Economic and Financial Committee operated as two committees – the Economic Committee and the Financial Committee. The two committees met jointly only on rare occasions. In present day terms the work of the Economic Committee corresponds to that of the General Agreement on Tariff and Trade (GATT) and the work of the Financial Committee corresponds to that of the International Monetary Fund/World Bank organization. This paper concentrates on the technical assistance of the Economic Comittee.

I. Structure and Organization

The basis for the League's work in the economic field had its origin in the Third of President Wilson's Fourteen Points and was incorporated in Article 23(e) of the Covenant which stated that the League's Member Governments would make: "provision to secure and maintain freedom of communications and of transit and equitable treatment for the commerce of all Members of the League. In this connection, the special necessities of the regions devastated during the war of 1914–1918 shall be borne in mind".[1]

The Secretariat's plan of work under this Article was developed during the summer of 1919 by the Secretary-General and Arthur Salter, head of the Economic and Financial Section. They agreed that the first tasks would be the supply of physical relief to the devastated areas of Europe and the reconstruction of national finances. It was agreed that the Economic and Financial Section should arrange for statistical research and the general collation and publication of economic statistics on a comprehensive scale. This would include the publication of all national regulations relating to import and export prohibitions and restrictions. In starting this work the Secretariat decided to cooperate closely with existing international bureaux and organizations, both governmental and non-governmental. This cooperation would avoid duplication and hopefully earn the Secretariat wider public acceptance and prestige by being seen to have been accepted by established international organizations. The Secretariat also hoped that the Council would appoint an economic advisory body to work with the Secretariat on international economic and financial investigations. Such a body was viewed as being the most effective means of establishing both official and unofficial direct consultation with Member Governments.[2]

In May 1920 the Council laid down the following rules for the constitution of its technical advisory committees. "The technical organizations of the League now in process of formulation are established for the purpose of facilitating the task of the Assembly and the Council . . . and . . . to assist the Members of the League . . . to fulfil their international duties.

They [the technical committees] must keep enough independence and flexibility to make them effectively useful to the Members of the League, and yet they must remain under the control of the responsible organizations which the general business of the League, with a view to verifying whether the proposals are in conformity with the principles and spirit of the Covenant.«[3]

In November 1920 the Council established the Joint Provisional Economic and Financial Committee.[4] The Committee, and its members, were to be responsible to the Council and not to national Governments. However, as one of the primary purposes of the advisory committees was to establish and pursue close co-operation between the League and its Member Governments, it was necessary that the individual members should have the support and confidence of their Governments. This was achieved in a roundabout manner. Governments, through their Council delegates, proposed nationals who were acceptable to them and these were then confirmed by the Council. Since the Economic and Financial Committee was to be a technical advisory organ of the League and not a political body for direct inter-governmental discussions, the Government nominees were generally drawn from the senior civil service, national professional bodies and the diplomatic corps. In an age of slow travel, the choice of nominees was often influenced by the availability of suitable persons. Subject to these constraints the financial advisors were generally senior members of central banks, international merchant banks and treasury officials. The economic advisors were generally drawn from government departments of trade and commercial relations. This choice was due to the fact that during the 1920's central banks were still independent with the result that international financial co-operation was carried out on an extra-governmental basis. On the other hand economic and commercial relations were carried out on a more direct inter-governmental basis.

The original members of the Economic Committee represented Brazil, France, Great Britain, Italy, Japan and Switzerland. By June 1922 the Committee had been expanded to include representatives of Australia, Belgium, Czechoslovakia, Denmark, Poland and Roumania. In 1927 the final composition of the Economic Committee was completed with the addition of representatives from Austria and Germany. One of the reasons for the success of the Committee, and one of its strengths, was probably due to the continuity of its membership. In 1927 four of the six original members were still serving. Over the years this continuity of membership created a 'club' atmosphere within the Committee and this strengthened its position in dealing with the Council, Assembly and the Member Governments. The Committee reported annually to the Assembly and received its instructions for the following year. The membership of the Assembly tended to change from year to year and given the comprehensive nature of the Committee's reports and the continuity of its membership, its authority and prestige grew each year until the late 1920's. A reading of the Assembly's discussions shows that the 'governing' body gradually came to accept the Committee's reports and was prepared to readily endorse its proposals.[5]

There was another factor which helped to establish the authority that the Economic Committee enjoyed within the League. In theory the Committee members served in a personal and private capacity being appointed by, and responsible to, the Council. But the members, especially those from European states, were senior civil servants from departments of trade or commercial relations. For example, the British member was Chief Economic Advisor to the British Government while the French, Italian, German and Austrian members were their Governments' senior advisors on commercial relations. At the early Council meetings Goverments were represented by senior ministers but there developed a habit of sending retired politicians. This custom was reversed when Austen Chamberlain, the British Foreign Secretary, started to attend and other Foreign Ministers were compelled to attend as well.[6] From then on the Council was a 'political' body concerned mainly with political rather than technical questions and required sound advice on which to base its actions. At home these politicians were advised by their senior civil servants and when they moved to an international forum they assured themselves of the same sound advice by appointing their national advisors to the Economic and Financial Committee. Having appointed this particular group of experts the Council Members were unlikely to be given conflicting views as between their national positions and that of the League. This close connection between the 'political' and the 'technical' bodies of the League eased the way to international compromise and agreement. When any question appeared on the Committee's agenda members could clarify their Governments' position in advance and a compromise could be worked out in Committee without bringing the matter into the open before an agreed solution had been reached. This broadened the scope for bargaining among the Great Powers and allowed them to carry some of the lesser States with them so that when a question became public there was a solid body of committed States behind the proposed solution. This made opposition by individual States less effective or possible.

The formal structure of the League of Nations was embodied in the Covenant. All Members States of the League had a seat in the Assembly which met for several weeks each autumn to discuss world problems in general, and the work of League in particular. The Assembly would endorse the work which had been carried out during the previous year, approve a work agenda for the coming year and vote the funds which were deemed necessary for this purpose. The Council acted as the League's executive and met at intervals throughout the year. The Secretary-General was directly responsible to the Council and the Secretariat derived its authority for action through the Secretary-General from the Council. The Secretariat was divided into sections with responsibility for the administration of specific articles of the Covenant.

The development of the League's technical advisory committees followed the formal establishment of the League and were not specifically provided for in the Covenant. The Covenant did provide, in a general way, for the establishment of such committees in the general powers of the Council. The Council appointed the various advisory committees for practical reasons. The Assembly met only annually and was too large to carry out efficiently the detailed studies of particular problems. The Council met more frequently but, although a smaller body, it lacked both the expertise and the time to prepare detailed technical studies and proposals. The Secretariat might have been staffed for this work but the cost would have been great and its proposals could have been blocked by the Assembly's refusal to provide funds if some states did not agree with the Secretariat's proposals. Therefore, the League needed independent expert advisors to draft solutions on the basis of continuous consultation with Governments so that when the Council recommended the implementation of such proposals they would already have the support of several interested Governments. The Economic Committee fulfilled this role.

In 1923 Salter wrote the following defence of the Economic and Financial Organization of the League. "The essential method of these organizations is, with the aid of a small secretariat, to get the main expert work done by means of experts drawn from the outside economic and financial world and from treasuries and boards of trade. This method had the triple advantages of securing better expert assistance than the League could easily command on its own staff; of securing assistance which is not only expert but which remains in constant and daily contact with the organizations which control action in different countries; and also that of being extremely economical, since the experts in question give their services without fee and the only cost to the League consists of travelling and subsistance allowances."[7]

II. Defining the Tasks

The problems which the Economic Committee faced in defining its technical tasks and in achieving a mandate to carry them out illustrate the relative impotence of the League in the early years. Initially many of the meaningful technical tasks, such as food supplies and distribution, remained under the control of the Supreme Economic Council. By the summer of 1919 it was evident that this would not last because of the attitude of the United States. In January 1920 the

Secretariats of the League and the Supreme Economic Council reached a resolution on the future economic work of the League which Member Governments of the Supreme Economic Council would support at the First Assembly of the League. Throughout 1920 the Supreme Economic Council gave technical advice but had no authority to direct the operations of the League's Secretariat.[8] This arrangement gave the League two main advantages. First, in practical terms, it provided the Secretariat with a vast amount of statistical data and expertise on international economic conditions. Second, in political terms, the Secretariat gained political stature and prestige by cooperating with the Supreme Economic Council even though it was only an informal arrangement.

The first real challenge for the embryonic Economic and Financial Organization of the League came in January 1920 with the call for a conference to consider the international financial crisis. The preparation and organization of the subsequent Brussels Financial Conference was the prototype for all future League conferences. One of the initial problems was how to provide for participation by the United States. The League had to rely on an American member of the Reparations Commission but the problem with this arrangement was that the American data was confidential and could not be referred to publically. In the end the League enlisted the assistance of various American bankers who happened to be in Europe. As a result all representatives at the Conference were unofficial delegates invited by the League's Council. This method of convening the Conference meant that it was really just an assembly of experts who came together to discuss the financial situation rather than a properly constituted intergovernmental conference attended by delegates with plenipotentiary powers to sign binding agreements.

The Brussels Financial Conference (September 1920) was accepted by the public at the time as a success because of the apparent unanimity of its recommendations. It was a shallow success, however, because on issues of importance where there had not been unanimity there were no recommendations. The issues not referred to covered such items as commercial credits and guarantees, arbitration, tariffs, import and export prohibitions and restrictions and, of course, reparations. The report of the Brussels Financial Conference to the League Council provided a work agenda for the new Economic and Financial Committee but most of the items fell on the financial side.

In June 1921 the Economic Committee informed the Council that there were three main areas of economic policy which should be investigated.[9] These were:

(1) import and export restrictions;
(2) monopolies;
(3) unfair competition.

But the Committee's work was not settled and in August the economic section informed the Secretary-General that: "At the present time an attempt to ensure the Equitable Treatment of Commerce would be carried out in the light of many interests and criticisms, which were not in the minds of the authors of the Covenant, it would almost certainly fail. No doubt, as the political power of the League grows, its attempts to promote Disarmament, or political harmony may lead the nations into the examination of the policies which govern armaments, and so into an examination of commercial policies: the Equitable Treatment of Commerce, the Blockade, etc. But until this time arrives, the League, although it may justifiably prepare its staff and accumulate material, would be unwise to try to force such questions as these to the point of international decision.

Comparatively small questions, involving international action, will always exist in large numbers. And Governments will always be glad to be relieved of the nuisance of them. The Economy Organization can, if it wishes, occupy itself entirely with lost securities, the treatment of Branches of Foreign Banks, Finishing Credits, trade marks, unfair competitition and so on. Some of these are perhaps important enough, and pressing enough, to merit action forthwith. But none of them are considerable.

The big questions of international moment may be summarized as: –

1. Russia
2. South-Eastern Europe
3. Reparations
4. Inter-Allied debts
5. Inflated currencies; deflation and devaluation; and the problems that arise therefrom.

If the Economic Organization of the League is to be more than an International waste-paper basket, it must become the authority for dealing with one or more of these questions.

The present position in *Economics*, therefore, is one of inactivity. The Economic Section may engineer an international agreement about trade marks. This in itself would hardly justify an Economic Conference. Nevertheless, if it is useful work, it should be done by the League. It is not likely to be done otherwise."[10]

This memorandum is hardly one of glowing hope for future success in the field of international economic policy. But this was a period when the financial problems of Central and South-Eastern Europe were at their worst. The main effort of the Financial Section was concentrated on implementing the International Credits Scheme which had been recommended by the International Financial Conference. Austria and Hungaria were in a state of almost total financial and economic collapse and approaching anarchy. There was still fighting between Greece, Bulgaria and Turkey, and the League was trying to solve the refugee problem and to raise funds for this purpose. The reparations problem was becoming worse with each passing month. The five major problems mentioned by the Secretariat were all really 'political' and 'financial' in nature. It is difficult to draw a clear distinction between international 'financial' and 'economic' problems – they are the two sides of the same coin – but in the summer of 1921 one would have had to agree that the 'political' and 'financial' problems were paramount and of such a nature as to rule out any hope, in the near future, of any international agreement on the improvement of commercial relations, particularly in Europe.

The final external source of tasks for the Economic Committee, and a further step in establishing the competence of the League, was the Genoa Conference in the spring of 1922. The Genoa Conference was called by the Supreme Council on the instigation of Lloyd George to negotiate international agreements on economic and financial problems. It was the Supreme Council's intention to exclude the League because it was hoped that the United States and Germany would attend. This would not have been possible if it had been a League conference as these two States were not Members of the League. In the end the Supreme Council was forced to call on the League for technical assistance because the Governments at the Conference were unwilling to set up and finance the machinery necessary for its conduct and to implement its recommendations. They had no alternative but to turn to the League for assistance.

The reasons for the failure of the Genoa Conference are not relevant to this paper. Its importance lies in the additional areas of possible technical assistance which were referred to the League. The Conference discussed but failed to reach agreement on issues such as consular agreements, treatment of foreign nationals and enterprises, unconditional most-favoured-nation treatment, freedom of trade in raw materials and dumping or differential prices. In the end the Conference recommended:

1. That customs tariffs should be published promptly and clearly.
2. That steps should be taken to render tariff nomenclature as comparable as possible.
3. That common principles should be adopted for economic statistics.
4. The condemnation of import and export prohibitions and restrictions.
5. That states should inform the League of all tariff modifications and of all changes in import and export prohibitions and restrictions.[11]

These were passed unanimously and it was agreed that the League of Nations was the proper body to continue the work of the Conference.

The commercial matters referred to the League by the Brussels International Financial Conference had given some guidance on government attitudes towards the application of equitable treatment for commerce. The Genoa Conference recommendations, although vague generalities, gave an even broader expression of opinion from which the League could draw its own conclusions as to the possibilities before it. With minor exceptions these two conferences were the source of the commercial questions which the Economic Committee was to consider until the World Economic Conference in 1927.

These two conferences also influenced the Economic Committee's decisions on which international commercial problems were 'ripe' for action. The euphemism 'ripe' is frequently used in League documents and should be elucidated. Basically, the Economic Committee established its priorities on the basis of ist subjective evaluation of the willingness of Governments to alter their laws and administrative regulations in order to obviate commercial problems. When the Committee had, by a variety of means, determined that Governments were willing to make the necessary changes they said that a particular problem was 'ripe' for action. Article 23(e) directed the League to secure the equitable treatment of commerce among the League's Members but this direction was extremely vague. The Brussels Conference and the Genoa Conference expanded and illustrated what Governments considered to fall within the realm of equitable treatment. Some problems were directed to the Economic Committee for immediate action.

On others it was clear that no immediate action was possible and that they had been directed to the Committee as a means of avoiding a diplomatic conflict. Thus, depending on the source of any problem the Committee was able to judge its 'ripeness'. For example, the Brussels Conference made it clear that there could be no early action for the reduction of tariffs and the Genoa Conference had done the same concerning import and export prohibitions and restrictions. Over time the 'ripeness' of the economic problems studied by the League changed and shifted but the political difficulties encountered by the Genoa Conference ruled out an early assault on national impediments to international trade. In these circumstances the Economic Committee had to be content during the early 1920's with solving a variety of legal and administrative problems which were an annoyance rather than a direct impediment to trade.

III. Tackling the Issues

The experience of the Brussels International Financial Conference and the Genoa Conference made it clear that the time was not 'ripe' for a frontal attack on any of the major technical impediments to international trade in the immediate post-war period. If the most pressing individual problems were not susceptible to resolution at this time then the suggestion by some that the League should convene a general international economic conference certainly had no hope of success. Despite these constraints the Economic Committee had to be seen to be doing something and preferably something useful. There was a general desire in the early post-war period for a return to what was perceived to have been the order of the pre-war period. It is not surprising, therefore, that in seeking soluable tasks the Economic Committee looked to the issues which had been dealt with in the pre-war period. As a generality these issues were of a legal or administrative nature covering bills of exchange, commercial arbitration, the simplification of customs formalities and the standardization of statistical methods and customs nomenclature.

1. The Unification of Laws on Bills of Exchange, Promissory Notes and Cheques

A number of international bodies and congresses had studied the difficulties for traders arising from the existence of different legal systems concerning bills of exchange since 1863 and there had been two international conferences at the Hague in 1910 and 1912.[12] The 1912 Convention established a uniform law but, although signed by twenty-seven States, its ratification had been interrupted by the war. The Convention stipulated that if it was not ratified the Netherlands Government should reconvene the Conference but before this could be done the International Financial Conference referred the whole question to the League. In view of the high degree of international agreement which had been possible in 1912 the Economic Committee decided at its first session to prepare a questionnaire to Governments to ascertain their opinions on the usefulness of holding another conference.[13] But the Committee was reminded by the Dutch that they had a continuing interest in the problem.[14] The preparation of the questionnaire was left to the Secretariat which used the opportunity to show some concrete action by the Economic Committee even if nothing came of it.[15] The bills of exchange question was also used for wider political purposes by the Secretary-General who used the questionnaire in an attempt to interest the United States in the technical work of the League. The United States responded, however, that it was only interested "as a most remote aspiration".[16]

In March 1922, 18 States had indicated they would attend a conference but the British Dominions and Switzerland objected. The British indicated that they would change their law if necessary but the French were not in favour of changes although French commercial and banking opinion were in favour. Japan was in favour of a conference but had a problem because their commercial policy followed the British pattern while their legal system was based on the 'continental' system.[17] The Committee agreed to plan a conference for the autuumn of 1923 based on the experts, reports and the 1912 Convention. The preliminary work was completed by December 1922 and this was communicated to Governments.[18] The preparation of the conference was left to the Secretariat which reported in March 1922 that there was a desire in England and America for progress on the question and that they had secured a very elastic formula with the Dutch over the convening and organization of the conference but this had been difficult.[19]

In the years which followed there was considerable action but no progress. In 1923 the Committee authorized the Secretariat to obtain expert reports from four law professors. The professors were unable to produce a common solution and suggested that the least that could be hoped for was a unification of the 'continental' system based on French law. The issue was revived in 1925 with a French proposal that a special committee composed of businessmen and jurists should study the problem. This, too, failed to produce a solution but did have the beneficial side effect of establishing a continuing liaison between the Secretariat and the International Chamber of Commerce. Action on the report of the special committee was then interrupted by the World Economic Conference. Clearly the unification of laws on bills of exchange was not 'ripe' for solution!

In January 1930 the Council finally gave approval for a conference. In the end the Conference concluded three Conventions affecting the 'continental' laws on bills of exchange which were signed by twenty-six States.[20] The regulation of the laws on cheques was referred to a second session of the Conference which met in 1931 and concluded three further Conventions which were signed by the same twenty-six States plus the Unites Kingdom.[21] The Conventions on Bills of Exchange were to be ratified by 31 August 1932 and the Convention on Cheques by 1 September 1933. In September 1932 the Economic Committee reported to the Assembly that the Conventions on Bills of Exchange had been ratified by Austria, Belgium, Finland, Greece, Italy, Japan, the Netherlands, Norway, Sweden and Switzerland. To enter into force the Conventions required ratification by seven States including three permanent Members of the Council and this condition had not been realised. However, the French and German Governments had placed the Conventions before their Parliaments and it was expected that the Conventions would soon be in force.[22]

The problem of bills of exchange had been the subject of two pre-war conferences and were under consideration by the League for thirteen years before anything ressembling success was achieved. The 'Anglo-Saxon' system was unchanged and the 'continental' system was standardized but not unified. What do these protracted negotiations reveal about the League's role in commercial diplomacy?

The Economic Committee discussions illustrate the fact that technical points were seldom raised but they did provide reasons for not proceeding. The British position was inconsistent but showed a willingness to compromise on the technical points raised by business interests. Basically there were no problems within the 'Anglo-Saxon' system since the commercial laws of the countries adhering to it were based on British common law which allowed for gradual change to meet changing commercial needs more easily than the codified 'continental' system. Within the 'continental' system France alone raised objections which was surprising since the system was based on French law. The changes recommended by the experts required few changes in French law since their aim was to bring the rest of the continent into line with French practice.

The chronicle of events and the varying degree of interest in the problem may give a more accurate explanation for the delays. It was the Secretariat which urged the Economic Committee into action in the early 1920's when the Committee was reluctant. Later the Secretariat was prepared to allow the Committee to proceed at its own pace. In the early period the Secretariat probably thought that since the 1912 Hague Convention had come so close to success that the bills of exchange question offered a vehicle with which the Committee could make itself felt in international relations. A similar opinion by the Dutch would explain why they wished to maintain control of the question. The Secretariat's zeal became manifest when in Januar 1923 the Committee left the future of the problem to the Secretariat. The Secretariat though it could carry forward on its own and failed to realize that the Committee had dropped the question because no immediate solution was possible. Another indication of the Committee's view of the problem was the choice of a Brazilian as its rapporteur. France and Britain were the main Powers on the Committee who mattered on questions of commercial policy. Major problems had French or British representatives as rapporteurs and minor or peripheral problems were given to the representatives of the smaller States.[23] Brazil was unlikely to have much influence on European commercial policy despite the good intentions and ability of its representatives.

The crux of the problem was never clearly stated at the time – bills of exchange provided short-term finance for international trade. Once this aspect of the question is recognized many of the problems and delays take on a new significance. The failure of Governments to ratify the 1912 Convention can be explained on the grounds of national security during a period of rearmament and international tension which culminated in the World War I. The situation before unification was that bills drawn on, say, Berlin could not have been discounted in Paris or London because the discounting banks required the signature of client banks which acted as guarantors for the principals. But once an international convention on the unification of the laws on bills of exchange was in force these legal impediments to the international discounting of bills would be removed. This would have allowed German merchants to purchase goods on the world market and to finance their imports by discounting the bills in Paris or London. During a period of rearmament or a re-stocking boom such action could have restricted French and British ability to finance their own imports and would have also increased the interest rates for short-term credits. Governments were unwilling, therefore, to support the unification of the laws on bills of exchange for reasons of national security. The question was also important to national monetary authorities as all credit instruments affected the money supply, and in periods of international tension financial institutions did not wish to be creditors of unfriendly states while Governments preferred to maintain a system which allowed them to act in a discriminatory fashion. The financial and commercial systems before the war did not necessarily permit such discounting but the unification of the laws on bills of exchange would have increased the possibility.

When the post-war re-stocking boom finished there were a range of international financial problems which ruled out agreement on credit instruments. The pound was still below its pre-war parity and British deflation and monetary controls meant a tight money policy in the London capital market. For European trade London was the most important market for bills of exchange and it was not surprising that the British were reluctant to change the law on bills of exchange which might have given others access to the London market. The exchange rate was an important consideration before April 1925 when Britain returned to the pre-war parity and was to continue to be a consideration for the rest of the 1920's. But the important disturbances were reparations and the financial instability of Germany, Austria and Hungary. While these countries were on the verge of financial collapse there was no hope of achieving stability in international commodity and money markets which was necessary to an agreement on bills of exchange. The Economic Committee was unable to hope for success until 1926 when the financial reconstruction of Austria and Hungary had been completed, Britain had returned to the gold standard and the reparations problem had been settled by the Dawes Plan. The Economic Committee recognized this situation when they left the problem to the Secretariat in 1923 and this explains why all the early efforts were fruitless.

The financial and trade implications of the bills of exchange problem, although unspoken, explains its long history under the League. The fact that bills of exchange were credit instruments for the financing of international trade meant that their legal foundations and applications were fundamental to national commercial policy and, therefore, Governments were most unwilling to accept unification by international conventions which would have limited their freedom of action.

2. *The Development of Commercial Arbitration*

Commercial arbitration between private parties within a State was well established prior to the First World War and its international application had depended largely on British hegemony. As with bills of exchange the international application of commercial arbitration was of direct concern to the business community rather than Governments but it also raised problems of national security and sovereignty which could only be settled by inter-governmental agreement. The problem of commercial arbitration was introduced to the Economic Committee by the British representative in November 1921.[24]

The British noted that an arbitration clause was frequently inserted in private commercial contracts and thousands of arbitration cases had been settled in London. Problems occasionally arose when one party appealed to their national courts on matters which should have gone to arbitration. In addition, some Governments imposed restrictions on arbitration and this could have made an international convention difficult. As a solution the Economic Committee suggested that Members of the League should agree to exclude intervention by their courts where the parties to a private contract voluntarily agreed to submit disagreements to arbitration with the Method of arbitration stated in the contract. Failing this the League's Members should allow for intervention by their courts only in the country where the arbitration was to take place. Both of these proposals were submitted to a committee of jurists. Central European opinion favoured leaving commercial problems to the courts as there were examples where the courts had ruled that exchange fluctuations could be a case of 'force majeure' which a court of arbitration could not take into consideration. The British were also concerned with the problem of the execution of arbitration awards and the Committee agreed that this problem should be studied by the experts. The British Government supported the League's study of commercial arbitration at the Genoa Conference by a resolution supporting the League's work in this area.[25]

The Committee named a group of experts and the Secretariat arranged for the group to be assisted in its work with practical and technical advice by the International Chamber of Commerce. The experts reported in the autumn of 1922 that there was general agreement on the principle of arbitration but that they had been unable to solve the problem of how an award granted in one country could be executed by the courts of another country. As a result, the Committee decided to proceed by way of a protocol rather than a convention. Further, they decided that the terms of the protocol could apply between any two States which signed it.[26] The Committee circulated the draft Protocol to Member Governments and it was submitted to the Council and Assembly in September 1923. The Protocol provided for the recognition of the authority of arbitration courts and the execution of awards by the courts of the country of arbitration.[27]

In October 1925 the Secretariat returned to the problem of the execution of foreign awards and presented a report to the Committee. The momentum for dealing with this issue had been assisted in 1925 by resolutions from the Hague Conference on International Private Law and the International Chamber of Commerce Congress. In August 1926 the Committee prepared a draft convention which was approved in principle by the Council and a further group of experts was appointed to prepare a final text. Again the International Chamber of Commerce participated in the group of experts. This draft was presented to the Assembly in September 1927, approved and opened for signature by those Governments which had signed the 1923 Protocol.[28]

As with the 1923 Protocol, the 1927 Convention required only two ratifications to enter into force as its application depended on reciprocity. In May 1929 the Secretary-General notified the League's Members that the Convention had been ratified by Zealand and Denmark and was therefore in force.[29] By September 1929 the Convention had only been ratified by five Governments.

The development of the legality of private commercial arbitration in essence was similar to the unification of the laws on bills of exchange as both were generally the concern of private individuals rather than Governments. But government recognition was necessary for the international application of arbitration. The fact that the League's sponsorhip of commercial arbitration produced agreements as early as 1923 and again in 1927 indicates that government interests and national sovereignty were not directly affected. This was because arbitration could affect the supply of specific shipments of goods but did not interrupt access by one state's nationals to the products of another. These agreements also indicate the differences between a protocol and a convention. By the 1923 Protocol on Commerical Arbitration States simply undertook to recognize the inclusion of arbitration clauses in private contracts and agreed not to interfere in the process of such arbitration. The Protocol was a statement of intent but did not bind governments to take any action. The term convention was applied to the 1927 agreement for the execution of arbitral awards because it established the conditions under which the courts of one country would recognize and enforce awards made in another country. This was a binding agreement which implied action and was therefore called a convention.

These two agreements also give an excellent indication of the 'modus operandi' of international commerial diplomacy during the early 1920's. The agreements had been sponsored by the League and were in theory multilateral in application but, in fact, they entered into force when signed by only two States; in practice, they were bilateral agreements whereby the benefits were granted on the basis of reciprocity. Compared with some of the most-favoured-nation commercial agreements which the League sponsored the recognition of arbitration and the execution of foreign arbitral awards on the basis of bilateral reciprocity was much easier to complete.

Beyond the sphere of commercial diplomacy the agreements on arbitration were advantageous for the League as the Covenant supported the general application of arbitration for the preservation of world peace. The international recognition of commercial arbitration did not directly affect the use of arbitration in political disagreements but it strengthened the League's moral support of the principle.

3. The Simplification of Customs Formalities

The simplification of customs formalities was of general concern to businessmen but was a direct concern of Governments since it was an administrative problem directly connected to national commercial policy. Customs formalities could constitute administrative protection but customs formalities, customs nomenclature and national statistical methods did not originate from conscious policies of protection but arose from the haphasard development of customs systems during the nineteenth century. This is confirmed by the fact that Governments were prepared to discuss customs formalities in the early 1920's at a time when they were not prepared to discuss other trade restrictions or tariffs.

The Economic Committee's interest in customs formalities developed from within rather than being referred to it from outside sources. The importance which the Committee attached to the issue is illustrated by that fact that the sub-committee established to deal with customs formalities was chaired by the British representative. The Committee's original goal was to reduce the discriminatory use of customs formalities, provide for the rapid passage of goods through customs and to establish common treatment for travellers' luggage, temporary entries and goods in bond. From the beginning the Committee planned to have those issues dealt with by a League sponsored customs conference. By the end of 1922 the Committee had completed the heads of a draft convention and these were approved by the Assembly. As on other technical issues the Committee and Secretariat worked closely with the International Chamber of Commerce. One of the benefits of this co-operation was that any agreement would be granted *de facto*, if not *de jure*, recognition by the United States. As in its treatment of other technical issues the Committee appointed a group of experts to prepare the conference documentation.

The experts appointed to prepare for the Customs Conference were all nationals of the same 14 States represented on the Economic Committee. This was probably a tactical error. The issue of customs formalities had been generated within the Committee and, therefore, did not necessarily have wide support outside that forum. The choice of experts could have been used to broaden interest in the subject and generate support for the Committee's proposals. This weakness in the organization of the Conference was only partially offset by the active participation of the International Chamber of Commerce. It was hoped that national chambers of commerce would urge their Governments to support the League's convention on customs formalities.

The International Conference for the Simplification of Customs Formalities met in October 1923 and was attended by 31 Members of the League, 4 non-Members and an American observer.[30] Several members of the Economic Committee attended as their countrys' representatives and the League's Secretariat acted as the Conference staff. The Committee's draft Convention was agreed to and signed but the Conference was unable to agree on a method for settling disputes or on how *ad valorem* duties should be calculated. The issues were not openly discussed until 1926 at which time Governments were prepared to allow a general discussion of their tariff and commercial policy. Until Governments took this step the Economic Committee was unable to come to grips with the calculation of customs duties. Many of the calculation problems were the result of statistical disagreements about such matters as gross and net weights and measures, and the exact definition of commodities which determined the applicable tariff. The uneven application of Customs regulations opened the way for discrimination by customs authorities against particular countries or importers which was not necessarily deliberate. During the early 1920's the Economic

Committee decided that these statistical and nomenclature irregularities could be treated as technical rather than policy problems, and that international standardization could eventually form a common language for the discussion of tariffs.

4. *The Standardization of Statistical Methods and Customs Nomenclature*

The growing need, both nationally and internationally, for statistical data on employment, agricultural and industrial production, trade and national finances led to the Economic Committee's interest in the standardization of statistical methods. Within the Secretariat this work was carried out by the Economic Intelligence Unit. During the 1920's the standardization of statistics was quite successful but the policy relationship between customs nomenclature and commerical policy made standardization difficult in this area.

From its inception the Secretariat had taken over from the Supreme Economic Council the publication of the *Monthly Bulletin of Statistics*. The Secretariat also co-operated in the publication of data collected by the International Institute of Agriculture. In September 1932 the Economic Committee instructed the Secretariat to prepare statistical schedules and tables for use by Governments when submitting data to the League. For the time being it was decided that the League should not duplicate the work of the International Office for the Publication of Customs Tariffs which had been established in Brussels since 1890.[31] Pressure for the non-discriminatory administration of customs nomenclature was given further support in the resolutions of the Genoa Conference. The main constraint against formal action on customs nomenclature during the early 1920's arose because Governments were unwilling to discuss tariffs or any issue directly related to tariffs.

By early 1923 the Council had approved a proposal by the Committee for a Statistical Conference. The Conference was to deal with the scope and definition of 'imports' and 'exports', the classification of imports and exports, categories of commodities and the calculation of quantities, values, periods, etc.[32] There was no mention of customs nomenclature. A group of experts was appointed to prepare the Conference documents. This work was carried out in co-operation with the International Institute of Statistics, the International Institute of Agriculture and the International Labour Office.

In December 1925 the Committee instructed the Secretariat to prepare a small Statistical Year Book. The Secretariat arranged with the London and Cambridge Statistical Services for the League to be able to use their data and this was expanded in 1927 when Harvard University allowed the League to reproduce its statistical publications.

All of this statistical work and the agenda for the Statistical Conference was fed into the preparation of the World Economic Conference. The Committee hoped to use the World Economic Conference in 1927 as a sounding board for the most likely areas of success on statistical methods. It was also hoped that following the Economic Conference it would be possible for the Committee to deal openly with the question of customs nomenclature. In the end all of the Committee's statistical recommendations were unanimously adopted by the World Economic

Conference. In addition, the Conference resolution concerning customs nomenclature was ranked second only to that on the liberty of trade.[33]

The immediate result was that the Council convened a special session of the Economic Committee in June 1927 to instigate immediate action on tariffs and customs nomenclature.[34] Experts were again appointed and by December 1927 they had prepared a general framework and a detailed and systematic classification system. In the end the League discarded the idea of calling a conference with the aim of drawing up a convention as it had been found that the methods of classifying commodities entering trade varied even more widely than the economic system which produced them. The Economic Committee found a solution in a nomenclature which could be extended or compressed, according to need, in such a way that each separate item would always correspond to a given number in the tariff schedule. The draft nomenclature included three types of items: principle items, numbering about 1000, which appeared in every tariff; secondary items, being subdivisions of the main classifications; and finally, tertiary items introducing further distinctions. For example:

Principle Item	butcher's meat
Secondary Item	beef
Tertiary Item	frozen or fresh

The onset of The Great Depression made it impossible to contemplate a diplomatic conference for the implementation of the new nomenclature. The League recommended the nomenclature to Governments and left it to them to adopt if they could, or would. This method was not conducive to universal success and few States applied the new Customs Nomenclature but it did have its uses in the preparation of commercial agreements by providing a common language for all sides.

The League's Statistics Conference was held in November and December 1928 and was attended by the representatives of forty-two States. The Convention prepared by the Conference involved definite obligations regarding the scope of economic statistics and the methods to be employed in compiling international statistics. In particular, the Convention provided for the adoption of principles for the compilation of mineral, metallurgical and fisheries statistics and established rules concerning the indices of industrial activity and censuses of industrial and agricultural production.

IV. Conclusion

The technical assistance provided by the League during the 1920's as illustrated by some of the work of the Economic Committee provided three main benefits. First, it provided a standard technical background against which future commercial negotiations took place. Second, these technical issues provided vehicles which the League could use to establish its competence during a period when discussion of broader commercial policy issues was blocked by national positions on reparations, tariffs, trade restrictions, etc. Finally, the pursuit of these technical issues established broad contacts between the League and government civil services and with a wide range of international agencies. This contact was important to the whole range of the League's work as it directly involved a large number of persons who then felt that they had a personal commitment to the success of the League.

Notes

1 Hans Aufricht, *Guide to League of Nations Publications. A Bibliographical Survey of the Work of the League, 1920–1947.* New York, Columbia University Press, 1951, p. 416.
2 LNA, 1919–27/10/243/243 (R. 291) Memo from Salter to Drummond and Drummond's reply, 10–11/VII/19.
3 Martin Hill, *A Survey of Twenty-Fice Years' Experience. Washington, Carnegie Endowment of International Peace, 1946.* – p. 21.
4 LNA., 1919–27/10/8338/8338 (R. 310) Council Memorandum, 14/XI/20.
5 This impression was supported by Dr. V. Stencek, Oral interview, Geneva, 6/VII/72.
6 LNA, S. 118. Letter from Sir Otto Niemeyer to Salter, 7/V/27. "I regarded it as so important for Foreign Secretaries to attend Council meetings that I was prepared to face a good deal of inconvenience, if necessary, for that object. (The real importance of Foreign Secretaries is not that they are particularly gifted or useful at the Council but that it means that the Foreign Offices have got to face up to the League and not regard it as a poor relation)." Niemeyer as Permanent Under-Secretary at the British Foreign Office, had become involved with the League very early on as a member of the Financial Committee and in the light of its reconstruction work was in a position to judge the value of the Economic and Financial Committee's work both for the world and, perhaps more important, as an instrument for carrying out the policies of the Foreign Office in an era of uncertainty and realignment. It is clear that over the period 1920 to 1927 Niemeyer and Llewellyn Smith were among the Committee's most active and influential members.
7 LNA, S. 115. No. 1.23. Minute, 5/VII/23.
8 LNA, 1919–27/10/2996/2101 (R 293) Memo from Drummond to Salter, –/I/20.
9 LNA, 1919–27/10/13791/10512 (R 319) Economic Committee Report to the Council, 28/VI/21, p. 1.
10 LNA, S. 123. Secretariat memo, 23/VIII/21.
11 LoN doc., C. 423.M.257.1922. The Genoa Conference and the League of Nations: Memorandum by the Secretary-General, 26/VI/22.
12 LoN doc., E.F. S. 11. Report by M.J.A. Barboza-Carneiro on the Unification of Bills of Exchange Law, –/II.
13 LNA, 1919–27/10/11493/11493 (R 322) Provisional Economic Committee Minutes, 2nd Session, 2nd Meeting, 23/II/21.
14 LNA, 1919–27/10/12020/12019 (R 348) Provisional Economic and Financial Committee Minutes, 4th Joint Meeting, 2nd Session, 25/II/21.
15 LNA, S. 126. Secretariat memo, 13/VII/21.
16 LoN doc., E.F.S. 145. Reply to the Secretary-General from C. E. McGuire, Assistent Secretary of the United States Section of the Inter-American High Commission, 10/VIII/21, p. 2.

17 LoN doc. E.F. S. 11. Report to the Economic Committee on the Unification of the Laws on Bills of Exchange by M. Barboza-Carneiro, –/III/22.
18 LNA, 1919–27/10/20382/11493 (R 323) Provisional Economic Committee Minutes, 4th Session, 3rd & 4th Meetings, 21–22/III/22.
19 LNA, S. 116. Letter from Nixon to Drummond, 22/IV/22.
20 LoN doc., A. 79.1930.II. Report and Draft Resolutions Presented by the Second Committee to the Assembly, –/IX/30, p. 3.
21 LoN doc., A. 75.1931.II.B. Report and Draft Resolutions Submitted by the Second Committee to the Assembly, –/IX/31, p. 8.
22 LoN doc., A.79.1930.II. *loc. cit.*
23 This organization of the system of committee rapporteurs has been substantiated by Dr. V. Stencek. Oral interview, Geneva, 6/VII/72.
24 LNA, S. 127. Letter from Llewellyn Smith, 1/XI/21.
25 LNA, 1919–27/10/20382/11493. (R 323) Provisional Economic Committee Minutes, 4th Session, 2nd Meeting, 21/III/21.
26 LNA, S. 127. Secretariat memo, 14/XII/22.
27 LoN doc., A.83.1923.II. Protocol on Arbitration Clauses, Geneva, 24/IX/23. It was signed originally by Belgium, Lithuania, Greece, Britain, Brazil, Uruguay, France, Panama, Italy, the Principality of Monaco, Germany, Roumania, Japan, Spain, Holland, Finland. During 1924 it was signed by Denmark, Norway, Switzerland, Latvia, Salvador, Chile, the Netherlands' colonies, Paraguay, Austria. By 1930 it had been signed by Siam, Poland, New Zealand, the Free City of Danzig, Nicaragua, Estonia, Sweden, Luxemburg, Czechoslovakia, Peru, Portugal and Bolivia.
28 LoN doc., E. 335. Note by the Secretariat on the Opening of a Convention Relating to the Execution of Foreign Arbitral Awards, 8/X/27.
29 LoN doc., C.L.83.1929.II. Letter from the Secretary-General to Member States, 10/V/29.
30 LNA, 1919–27/50/31637/26832 (R 1802) Report by Lord Buxton, 15/X/23.
31 LNA, 1919–27/10/21387/11493 (R 323) Provisional Economic Committee Minutes, 5th Session, 3rd Meeting, 9/VI/22.
32 LoN doc. C. 75(1).M.81.1923.II. Economic Committee Report to the Council, 8/II/23, p. 8.
33 LNA, 1919–27/10c/59914/46431. (R 531) Note on the results of the World Economic Conference prepared for the British Press by Sir Arthur Salter, –/V/27.
34 LNA, 1919–27/10/60079/11493. (R 329) Letters recalling of the 22nd (Extraordinary) Session of the Economic Committee, –/VI/27.

China and the League of Nations

NORBERT MEIENBERGER
University of Zurich

The League of Nations was organized in order to prevent war and to promote international co-operation. At the beginning, international co-operation was considered to be of minor importance. In the course of time, however, the League's social and economic activities developed to the point of equalling its work in the political field.

One of the reasons for this shift was the recognition by politicians and civil servants of the interdependence between prosperity and peace, the close connexion between the socio-economic and the political situation.

In 1939 the 'Bruce-Report'[1] pointed to this state of affairs as follows: "The experience of the last twenty years has shown the growing extent to which the progress of civilisation is dependent upon economic and human values. State policies are determined in increasing measure by such social and economic aims as the prevention of unemployment, the prevention of wide fluctuations in economic activity, the provision of better housing, the suppression and cure of disease. These matters, which affect the daily lives of every man, woman and child, are among the principal preoccupations of statesmen and politicians in all countries, whatever their political structure."[2] In order to solve these problems, international co-operation was thought to be necessary: "Modern experience has also shown with increasing clearness that none of these problems can be entirely solved by purely national action," the report concluded.[3]

Among the so-called non-political activities, the technical co-operation between the League and China is of particular interest. In the following pages, I shall try to shed some light on this kind of international co-operation. Before taking up the matter, however, it would be useful to sketch the setting within which this co-operation took place.

The China of the inter-war period was characterized by three distinct features: First: China's economy was stagnant; progress was very slow; living conditions for the great majority of the people were almost unbearable. Second: during the whole period, the country was not really unified. When China entered the League, the Central Government in Beijing claimed to represent the whole of China, although large parts of the country were beyond its control; and after the establishment of the National Government in Nanjing in 1927, various regions remained virtually independent of the Guomindang Government, although they belonged nominally to it.[4] In other words: The inter-war period in China was a time of civil war with three groups fighting each other: the Guomindang, the

Gongchandang – or Communist Party – and the different war lords throughout the country. Third: China was further weakened during this period through aggression from without: In 1931, Japan began to occupy Manchuria and launched a full-scale offensive in 1937.

It was under these circumstances that the League initiated technical assistance. That assistance was much needed, was obvious; that it was possible to realize it, was almost a miracle; and that, under the circumstances, help could be only very limited, was unquestioned. This background must be kept in mind in dealing with the League's and China's collaboration.

The League's assistance to China was unique not only because it was effected so early and under terribly adverse conditions, but also because of the concept underlying it: The documents speak not of "technical assistance" but of "technical collaboration." This terminological detail should be emphasized because it is most significant for understanding the League's and China's work done in this field.

The term 'collaboration' implies that the facilities the League's technical organizations could provide should not be considered as an act of benevolence granted from above, but as one of the possible, quite natural relations between the international organization and one of this Members.

The League's assistance should not give the impression that China was dependent – that the League was the benefactor and China the recipient. It should be viewed in a different light. As a Member – obliged to contribute its share to the League's expenses in the form of membership dues – China was entitled to ask for help of the League's technical organizations.

The above mentioned 'Bruce-Report' described this state of affairs as "finally and perhaps most important of all, Governments which desire expert advice or help can get this, not from outside or as a favour, but from an institution which they themselves maintain and on whose services they have a right to call."[5]

Wang Cheng-t'ing, one of the Chinese plenipotentiaries at the Paris Peace Conference clearly stated – before the League came into existence – that China expected, among other things, that the new international organization would furnish his country "with expert knowledge and capital."[6]

The gap between "Wunsch und Wirklichkeit", between desire and realization, was, however, enormous. In the twenties, Norman White, Ludwik Rajchman, and Albert Thomas went to China. They all returned without tangible results. All they could do was to prepare the ground.[7]

The formal technical co-operation between the League and China began in 1929 in the field of public health at the request of the National Government located in Nanjing. Drummond's response was positive; and the Council unanimously endorsed the proposal.

Arthur Henderson, the representative of Great Britain, supported the idea to assist China most energetically: "He thought it a very good testimony to the standard of efficiency which the League had attained that countries should be requesting technical assistance in the way which was indicated in the report. It was also, he thought, a source of great satisfaction that China should now feel that her position was becoming so stabilised that she could ask the League to assist her in applying the more humanitarian ideals and ideas of the League, not only in connection with the condition of her ports, but he hoped shortly, in connection with the homes of her people. He was sure the Council would be prepared to say that all the assistance which the League could give to China, in the great efforts she was making to bring about her own development, would be only too gladly given."[8]

Two experts of the League – L. Rajchman and F. G. Boudreau – arrived in China in November 1929. They dealt with China's quarantine service in certain ports and with the organization and the activities of medical and hygienic institutions in selected regions.

In December 1929 the Chinese Government proposed a plan of co-operation with the League in the field of health service; the Council of the League approved this program in May 1930.

The program entailed the dispatch of further League experts, the invitation of Chinese specialists to study sanitary conditions in Europe and America, and the establishment of a group of experts at the League's headquarters in Geneva, trying to solve the problem of cholera and smallpox in the region of Shanghai.[9]

The League's technical collaboration was limited to the solution of health questions only during a short time. Early in 1931 China asked the League to send an expert to discuss financial and economic problems. At this request Sir Arthur Salter went to China, where he stayed six weeks.

Salter saw clearly that essentially the solution of China's problems was not a question of know-how. It was in his opinion not difficult to solve the problems of a purely technical nature. He thought, however, that it was an illusion to believe that this could be done under the existing political conditions. He wrote: "The indispensable basis was peace, external and internal, and a reasonably good government. Without this all financial and economic schemes were useless. And to this end the technician could contribute nothing. The first step must be political and military; economic reconstruction might then be consolidated; but it could not be initiated."[10]

Along with Arthur Salter there were in China two other high ranking League officials – Robert Haas and Ludwik Rajchman. The discussions of these three League directors with the Chinese authorities would have far-reaching consequences. Hoe, an expert in East Asian Affairs, remarked: "The part played by this triumvirate of League Directors in consultation with the Chinese Government will always be remembered as marking a new epoch in the history of China's National reconstruction; for the outcome of their conference and plans was the program of continuous collaboration between China and the League."[11]

The immediate result of the talks was the announcement to establish a National Economic Council, an organ envisaged to be responsible for the coordination of the various reconstruction schemes. The League was asked to assist the Chinese authorities in carrying out this program. In a telegram of 25 April 1931, the League of Nations was informed of this new development: "Referring our telegram 7th January and resulting conversations with your three Directors in

China am instructed by Chairman Chiang Kai-shek to state Chinese Government having set up National Economic Council for planning reconstruction requests collaboration League. For this purpose ask that League's technical organisations assist as advisers above Council for drawing up and carrying out reconstruction plans as follows:

1. First, in the initial planning and organisation stage the League might be able to send someone – as it has already done in the special domain of health work – for such a limited period as might be practicable and convenient to the Government, in order to provide it with both as to the plan itself and as to any subsequent methods.
2. Second, in the execution of particular projects the League might, at the request of the Government, send or propose officials, representatives or experts who, apart from their own competence, could also maintain contact with the relevant technical organization in Geneva.
3. Third, in appropriate special cases a League Committee – whether standing or *ad hoc* – might, at the requests of the Government, assist it in drawing up and/or improving a given scheme.
4. Fourth, the League might in several ways help in the training of China's own officals required in later years for more extended work. In the domain of health the League, sometimes with the aid of fellowships, has already been able to arrange practical work.
5. Furthermore, the League might help the Government to find advisers to assist in the development of the Chinese educational system and facilitate the relations between the centres of intellectual activity in China and abroad.
6. Lastly, China might at times wish to initiate League action concerning the international coordination of policies of certain countries, as a prerequisite for removing some obstacles to China's development. In this way, the technical organisations of the League could continuously advise the Government and/or the National Economic Council in connection with reconstruction plans.

T. V. Soong, Vice-Chairman Executive Yuan."[12]

In short, the Chinese Government requested: 1. one League official to assist the Chinese authorities with the establishment of the National Economic Council, and with information on the possibilities of technical assistance; 2. officials and experts for carrying out special projects; 3. if necessary, a committee of specialists for setting up, or improving, special programs; 4. assistance for the training of Chinese specialists; 5. experts for the development of the Chinese educational system and, assistance towards improving the relations with intellectual centers abroad; 6. assistance for removing obstacles of an international character. The Council dealt with these proposals on 19 May 1931. All the members were determined to promote the desired collaboration with China. Arthur Henderson "realised very fully the tremendous difficulties with which the Chinese Government was faced in attempting to consolidate and reorganize a country with so ancient a civilisation, so vast a territory and so numerous a population. He had the deepest admiration for the way in which the leaders of the Chinese Government had begun to grapple with these difficulties, and would express his warmest wishes for its continued success, and his hope that extended collaboration with the League might lead to the beneficient results desired by all."[13]

In the following years, technical collaboration between the League and China developed rapidly. It lasted until 1941 when the World War II made further assistance impossible.

During the period between 1929 and 1941 about 30 League officials and experts once or several times went to China in order to assist the Chinese authorities in their efforts towards economic and social reconstruction. These advisers were most active in the fields of hygiene and education, transportation and agricultural questions in particular organizing rural co-operatives.

The League did also assist the Chinese Government in times of emergency: in 1931, a flood-disaster necessitated help while in 1938 widespread epidemics required the League's assistance; in order to fight disease, three groups were sent to China.

Through the good offices of the League, China was able to obtain firstclass specialists; among these three professors went to Nanjing in 1932 and began to teach at the university. The League was also instrumental in training Chinese students, officials and technicians.

The League's technical assistance to China was intended to be completely non-political. The clear distinction between 'technical' collaboration and 'political' support was due to the strained relationship between Japan and China. The League repeatedly emphasized that its good offices were of a purely technical nature; since certain influential Member States wanted to be on good terms with Japan, the League's attitude was quite understandable.

In practical terms the situation was different. The 'technical' assistance of the League automatically carried political implications, for any kind of assistance towards social and economic reconstruction necessarily strengthened the national Government. For example, the League's providing experts certainly heightened the prestige of the Guomindang.

It should be stressed that the League's assistance was by no means an act of curtailing the independence of China. The League provided only experts at China's request; and these experts had no executive power, for their task was to advise, not to decide.

The picture would be distorted, however, if one tried to forget the important part played by certain League officials. Without the initiative of Ludwik Raichman – the head of the League's Health Organization – and the dedication of Robert Haas – the head of the League's Organization for Communications and Transit – the collaboration with China would not have been quite so intense.

And finally, the technical collaboration between the League and China was only a part of the overall relationship between the international organization and of its Member States. In the early twenties, the emphasis was not on technical co-operation, but on the question of the 'unequal treaties'; the central question in the thirties was the conflict between China and Japan. In both instances the League was unable to bring about a solution. Yet the knowledge of the League's failure in this respect does not curtail the value of the League's technical assistance. On the contrary: in my opinion the League was only really successful in its activities with China; and the fact that the League could play such a positive role was less the merit of the Assembly and of the Council than the merit of the Secretariat, i. e. the merit of the initiative of a few officials within the League's Secretariat.[14]

Notes

1 Cf. also Dubin's contribution in the Symposium *Proceedings*, p. 42.
2 The Development of International Co-operation in Economic and Social Affairs. Report of the Special Committee. LoNdoc.A.23.1939. – p. 6 (Hereafter: Bruce Report).
3 *Ibid.*, p. 6.
4 Cf. Lloyd E. Eastman, *The Abortive Revolution – China under Nationalist Rule, 1927–1937.* Cambridge, Harvard University Press, 1974. – *passim.*
5 Bruce Report, *op. cit.*, p. 17.
6 Wang Cheng-t'ing, China's Aspirations. *In:* Koo, V. K. Wellington, *China and the League of Nations.* London, Allen and Unwin, 1919. – p. 11.
7 Norbert Meienberger, *Entwicklungshilfe unter dem Völkerbund – Ein Beitrag zur Geschichte der internationalen Zusammenarbeit in der Zwischenkriegszeit unter besonderer Berücksichtigung der technischen Hilfe an China.* Winterthur, Verlag P. Keller, 1965. – p. 43–50.
8 *Ibid.*, p. 57.
9 *Ibid.*, p. 61.
10 *Ibid.*, p. 59.
11 *Ibid.*, p. 61.
12 *Ibid.*, p. 62.
13 *Ibid.*, p. 53.
14 *Ibid.*, p. 132–135.

L'œuvre d'un organisme technique de la Société des Nations: Le comité financier et la reconstruction de l'Autriche (1921–1926)

Nicole Pietri
Université de Poitiers

La reconstruction financière de l'Autriche fut la première des opérations de stabilisation monétaire et de remise en ordre des finances publiques réalisée sous l'égide de la SdN et sous la pression d'un système de contrôle international exercé, au nom de l'institution genevoise, par le ressortissant d'une puissance neutre, le Commissaire général néerlandais Zimmerman. La responsabilité de l'élaboration d'un plan de reconstruction, avec le concours du gouvernement autrichien, ainsi que la surveillance de son exécution incomba au Comité financier. Celui-ci s'avéra constituer, en outre, un garant sérieux de la réussite de l'émission de l'emprunt international de restauration.

La monnaie autrichienne avait commencé à se déprécier au cours du premier conflit mondial et elle avait perdu les 2/3 de sa parité or d'avant-guerre au moment de l'armistice. La dépréciation atteignit, cependant, son paroxysme, après la guerre, mais la débâcle monétaire proprement dite ne débuta pas avant l'automne 1921 au cours duquel l'Autriche prit conscience de la nécessité d'assurer elle-même son propre salut. La question de l'aide extérieure s'était posée, néanmoins, dès 1919, année de pénurie pendant laquelle la valeur extérieure de la couronne avait subi une forte réduction. La dépréciation s'exprima, cependant, plus fortement dans les prix intérieurs que dans le cours de la devise nationale sur le marché des changes. En ce qui concernait l'aide extérieure, il s'était avéré qu'il ne s'agissait pas, exclusivement, de consentir des avances à l'Autriche. La nécessité de procéder à une reconstruction financière à laquelle seraient liés, à la fois, l'exercice d'un contrôle sur les finances publiques et la gestion des gages offerts en garantie ne tarda pas, en effet, à s'imposer. Toutefois, aucun plan d'ensemble ne fut appliqué dans l'immédiat. Les »crédits de relèvement« d'un montant total de 27 à 30 millions de livres dont bénéficia l'Autriche furent utilisés pour se procurer des produits alimentaires et des matières premières en provenance de l'extérieur.

La deuxième phase de la période de dépréciation de la monnaie autrichienne débuta après la signature du Traité de Saint-Germain et s'acheva pendant l'été 1921. Le cours du change fut soumis à une série de fluctuations. Il subit une baisse qui se précipita entre décembre 1919 et janvier 1920. Il se releva pendant le premier semestre de cette dernière année puis s'abaissa dans sa seconde moitié. Il demeura relativement stable au cours des six premiers mois de 1921, pendant lesquels fut élaboré le premier plan du Comité financier. Les fluctuations de l'indice des prix ne furent pas exactement similaires à celles de la devise nationale et il y eut un écart entre les valeurs intérieure et extérieure de la couronne qui fut assez fortement marqué en 1921. L'augmentation constante et progressive de la circulation fiduciaire caractérisa également cette période. Or, si l'on fait abstraction des crédits extérieurs destinés à l'acquisition des produits alimentaires, le poste le plus élevé de la dette publique était représenté par des bons du Trésor à 2½% qui constituaient la base même de l'émission fiduciaire. Cette inflation pour besoins d'Etat était déterminée, en partie, par le financement des subventions publiques pour les produits alimentaires. Ceux-ci étaient, en effet, rationnés et vendus aux consommateurs à un prix inférieur à celui du marché, la différence étant réglée par l'Etat. Ces subventions représentaient à la fin de l'année 1920, 25% de la totalité des dépenses publiques. Elles constituaient 58% de ce total, au terme de l' année suivante, et contribuaient à renforcer les tendances inflationnistes.

Le premier plan du Comité financier fut élaboré pendant cette seconde phase de l'histoire de l'inflation autrichienne. L'idée du recours à la SdN était apparue pour la première fois dans l'énoncé d'une décision du Cabinet britannique, adoptée le 30 décembre 1920. Tout en refusant d'accorder à l'Autriche de nouveaux crédits gouvernementaux, le Cabinet faisait observer que le plan adopté, récemment par la SdN, offrait un cadre plus approprié pour traiter la question autrichienne que celui de la Commission des Réparations.[1] Le plan de crédits internationaux auquel le Cabinet faisait allusion avait été présenté par le banquier néerlandais Ter Meulen à l'issue de la Conférence financière internationale de Bruxelles et il avait été adopté par le Conseil de la SdN. Son application requérait la constitution de gages. Les actifs autrichiens étant hypothéqués au titre des réparations et des crédits de relèvement, le Cabinet demandait donc à la France et aux autres gouvernements alliés s'ils étaient prêts à suspendre ces hypothèques constituées en leur faveur.[2] Cette suggestion devait se matérialiser dans la déclaration interalliée aux ministres autrichiens du 17 mars 1921. Elle fut élaborée au cours d'une réunion semi-officielle qui eut lieu dans les locaux du *Treasury* sous la présidence de Basil Blackett et en présence de Joseph Avenol. Aux termes de cette déclaration les gouvernements français, italien, britannique et japonais se déclaraient prêts à suspendre les hypothèques qu'ils détenaient sur les actifs autrichiens au titre des armées d'occupation, des crédits de relèvement et des réparations à condition que les autres gouvernements intéressés procèdent à cette suspension. Les quatre puissances alliées étaient également disposées à reculer l'échéance des paiements au titre des réparations et des avances consenties à l'Autriche depuis l'armistice, la dette du gouvernement autrichien demeurant, toutefois, entière. Il était, enfin, entendu que le gouvernement souhaitait la mise en oeuvre dans son pays du plan Ter Meulen, et qu'il était prêt à confier la gestion des actifs assignés en gages au Comité financier de la SdN.

A l'origine, le plan Ter Meulen était destiné à faciliter l'octroi des crédits nécessaires au financement des importations de matières premières afin de permettre la restauration de la capacité productive et exportatrice des pays emprunteurs. Ce plan tentait de pallier les difficultés auxquelles se heurtaient, après la guerre, les industriels pour se procurer les matières premières nécessaires en raison du manque de capitaux et de devises. Ces difficultés étaient particulièrement ressenties en Europe centrale. L'accent avait donc été mis à Bruxelles sur la nécessité de substituer le crédit international au crédit national défaillant, au cours du processus de transformation des matières premières en produits fabriqués. Le plan Ter Meulen devait permettre aux nations appauvries d'inspirer une confiance suffisante pour obtenir des crédits. Il était donc prévu de créer à cette fin, dans les pays auxquels les crédits commerciaux étaient nécessaires, un »réservoir de gages« dans lequel serait puisée la garantie d'un paiement ultérieur.[3] Aussi, les gouvernements désireux de bénéficier du plan Ter Meulen seraient-ils tenus de dresser, en premier lieu, la liste de ces gages et de la communiquer à une Commission internationale désignée par le Conseil de la SdN. Ce Comité déterminerait la valeur or des crédits susceptibles d'être accordés. Le gouvernement concerné serait alors autorisé à émettre des obligations de la valeur or fixée par la Commission. Les recettes provenant des gages seraient affectées au service de ces titres. La gestion de ces gages pourrait être assurée par la Commission internationale. Les obligations émises et contresignées par celle-ci devaient être offertes en nantissement, en priorité, pour obtenir les crédits nécessaires à l'importation de matières premières et de produits de première nécessité.

Or, le Comité financier de la SdN remplissait provisiorement les fonctions dévolues à la Commission internationale prévue par le plan Ter Meulen et l'affaire autrichienne fut, ainsi, déférée, par ce biais, à l'institution genevoise probablement pour ces deux raisons invoquées par Joseph Avenol. Les gouvernements alliés se refusaient à assurer eux-mêmes le contrôle des finances autrichiennes d'une part, et l'intervention de la SdN donnait à ces derniers une garantie très forte contre le rattachement de l'Autriche à l'Allemagne d'autre part.[4] Le fait de subordonner la suspension des hypothèques à l'adoption du plan Ter Meulen impliquait, en effet, l'instauration d'un contrôle sur les revenus autrichiens affectés en gage qui devait être confié au Comité financier. Le rôle de ce dernier pouvait, d'ailleurs, être étendu à celui de conseiller financier pour l'Autriche, cette dernière devant accepter aisément l'intervention d'un organisme technique neutre et international.

Le Comité financier procéda à un premier examen du problème autrichien à la fin du mois de mars 1921. Il fixa à vingt ans la durée de suspension des hypothèques. Les emprunts émis au cours des cinq premières années, avec son approbation, devaient, à son avis, bénéficier pour leur service et jusqu'à leur total amortissement d'une priorité absolue par rapport aux droits et privilèges mis en suspens. Le Comité avait cherché, par ailleurs, à donner aux Autrichiens le sentiment que l'ouverture des crédits étrangers pourrait dépendre de leur propre action.[5] Ainsi, un emprunt extérieur ou l'application du plan Ter Meulen ne leur apporteraient dans l'immédiat aucun concours utile tant que les réformes destinées à »l'assainissement« de la situation financière n'auraient pas été adoptées. Ces mesures indispensables et urgentes étaient selon le Comité au nombre de quatre: l'émission dans l'immédiat d'un emprunt intérieur, la réduction des dépenses publiques, l'affectation au service des emprunts de certains gages acceptés par la Commission genevoise, la réalisation des opérations d'émission et d'escompte par la Banque d'Autriche- Hongrie. Au cas où ces conditions seraient réalisées, le Comité financier pourrait être appelé à contrôler, à la fois, les gages et l'utilisation du produit des emprunts.[6]

Une délégation de la Commission se rendit à Vienne entre le 15 avril et le 10 mai 1921. Elle comprenait deux de ses membres, Joseph Avenol et Emile Glückstadt, directeur de la *Landmandsbank* danoise, ainsi que l'organisateur du plan Ter Meulen, le Britannique Sir Drummond Fraser. Les délégués évitèrent de formuler eux-mêmes un programme de reconstruction, laissant au gouvernement autrichien le soin de l'élaborer et de le soumettre à l'adhésion des différents partis politiques. Après avoir procédé à une enquête auprès de différentes personnalités du monde politique et économique, ils se livrèrent à une analyse de la situation autrichienne. Ils insistèrent sur la »viabilité« de ce pays dont Vienne et l'industrie constituaient deux atouts majeurs. Ils étudièrent les composantes de l'inflation: baisse constante du cours de la couronne, chute des prix, ruine des finances publiques, spéculation effrénée, thésaurisation et donc immobilisation des devises étrangères. L'Autriche recelait, néanmoins, des ressources financières importantes. Leur utilisation dans le pays dépendait, toutefois, de la remise en ordre de ses finances. Le remède consistait à »assainir« le change en réduisant sa valeur intérieure et en fixant »un rapport solide avec l'or ou avec son équivalent la devise américaine«. La délicate question du choix du niveau auquel devrait être stabilisée la couronne fit l'objet d'échanges de vue entre les délégués et les représentants des milieux économiques et financiers. Les avis étaient très partagés: »financiers« et industriels présentaient des points de vue divergents n'estimant »ni possible ni nécessaire l'obligation légale du remboursement en or«; les délégués pensaient qu'il suffirait de disposer, en permanence, du stock de devises nécessaires pour pouvoir faire face à toute demande de remboursement. La création d'une nouvelle banque d'émission allait de pair, selon eux, avec la réforme monétaire. Cet institut serait une société privée par actions, totalement indépendant à l'égard de l'Etat. La moitié du capital devrait être souscrite à l'étranger. A côté du Conseil d'administration siégerait une Commission de contrôle désignée par le Comité financier qui pourrait surveiller la réalisation du programme de réformes.

L'Autriche devrait contracter un emprunt extérieur d'un montant élevé, soit 150 millions de dollars. Son produit serait destiné à couvrir les dépenses dues à l'importation des produits alimentaires pendant deux ans et à constituer une réserve. Il devait être garanti par la propriété privée autrichienne. Il serait par ailleurs nécessaire de recourir à un emprunt intérieur forcé afin de combler le solde du déficit budgétaire ne résultant pas des achats de vivres à l'extérieur. Il permettrait également d'adapter la circulation fiduciaire aux besoins réels du pays. Cet emprunt qui porterait sur la propriété immobilière autrichienne devrait atteindre 2% de la valeur réelle de celle-ci.

L'adoption de mesures aussi importantes que la réduction du nombre des fonctionnaires, la simplification de l'appareil administratif, la réforme de la fiscalité et des entreprises publiques apparaissait, enfin, comme indispensable.[7] En prenant acte des résultats de cette enquête, le Comité financier insista sur la nécessité absolue de mettre fin, en tout premier lieu, à l'émission fiduciaire, en lançant dans l'immédiat un emprunt intérieur d'un montant suffisant. La reconstruction était subordonnée à la réalisation de celui-ci et à celle de l'équilibre budgétaire, ainsi qu'à la création de la Banque d'émission, ces trois mesures constituant les parties solidaires d'un même programme. En créant ce nouvel institut dont la moitié du capital aurait été réservée aux souscripteurs étrangers, il n'était, cependant, pas nécessaire de réaliser simultanément la réforme monétaire. Un certain temps devrait s'écouler entre le moment de cette fondation et celui où serait créée une »unité monétaire entièrement nouvelle ayant une valeur déterminée«. A cet égard, Basil Blackett avait déjà précisé qu'il serait impossible de ramener la couronne autrichienne à sa valeur d'avant-guerre par rapport à l'or.[8]

Il était prévu que l'octroi des avances temporaires se ferait dans le cadre du plan Ter Meulen. Ces dernières seraient gagées sur les actifs donnés en nantissement. Le Comité financier devait être autorisé à nommer une commission spéciale pour l'Autriche et à déléguer à Vienne un représentant permanent. Il avait été, par ailleurs, clairement spécifié que l'obtention par l'Autriche des crédits extérieurs, sous forme de tranches successives, serait subordonnée à la réalisation graduelle des mesures de réforme prévues dans son programme financier.

Ce premier plan connut un début de réalisation. Grâce à l'appui du gouverneur de la Banque d'Angleterre, le Comité financier avait réussi à assurer à l'Autriche l'ouverture d'un crédit de 5 millions de livres. Les démarches en vue d'obtenir l'adhésion des dix-huit gouvernements concernés par la suspension des hypothèques et le recul de l'échéance des paiements n'aboutirent cependant pas, en raison, notamment, de la résistance opposée par les pays de la Petite Entente. Tout effort pour assurer l'octroi de ces avances temporaires fut, de ce fait, rendu stérile. Or, à partir de l'automne 1921, l'Autriche entra dans la troisième phase de la période d'inflation qui devait s'achever avec la débâcle monétaire de l'été 1922. Des périodes de stabilité relative alternèrent avec des phases de dépréciation si violente que la machine de l'Etat parut sur le point de se briser. Après la Conférence de Gênes dont les résultats furent décevants pour l'Autriche et en dépit de l'arrivée au pouvoir de Monseigneur Seipel, la chute de la valeur extérieure de la couronne se précipita. Les prix, les salaires et les dépenses publiques subirent une très forte majoration. Le plan financier du gouvernement Seipel et le contrôle draconien des changes instauré en juillet 1922 ne purent arrêter la course à l'abîme. Le point le plus bas fut atteint le 25 août, la cote du dollar s'élevant ce jour à 83.600 couronnes. La courbe de l'indice des prix ne cessa de suivre celle du change dans sa marche ascendante. L'accroissement continu et régulier de la circulation fiduciaire doit être mis, enfin, en relation avec la progression constante des émissions de bons du Trésor servant à financer les besoins d'un Etat qui accumulait, de ce fait, une énorme dette flottante.

Dans ces conditions, les Alliés réunis à Londres du 7 au 17 août 1922, pour examiner le problème des réparations allemandes, répondirent à l'appel angoissé du gouvernement autrichien, en renvoyant cette question à la Société des Nations pour »examen et rapport«. L'institution genevoise devait proposer un plan qui permettrait à l'Autriche d'obtenir des crédits d'origine privée, ceux-ci devant, toutefois, bénéficier de garanties gouvernementales. L'action diplomatique remarquable de Monseigneur Seipel qui se rendit successivement à Prague, Berlin et Vérone[9] ouvrit la voie à une concertation qui eut lieu à Genève entre les représentants des gouvernements français, britannique, italien et tchécoslovaque. Elle aboutit à la signature des Protocoles du 4 octobre 1922 qui contenaient un plan de reconstruction élaboré sur la base des accords péniblement négociés de ces quatre gouvernements[10] et sur les garanties politiques et financières qui leur avaient été progressivement arrachées.[11] Or, le Comité financier fut directement responsable de la partie technique du plan. Il convient donc de s'interroger sur la composition de cette commission.

Celle-ci subit relativement peu de changement entre 1921 et 1926, en ce qui concernait, tout au moins, ses membres les plus marquants. Toutefois, à la fin de l'année 1922, Basil Blackett fut remplacé par Otto Niemeyer et l'année suivante Joseph Avenol abandonna son siège à Parmentier. En 1925 et 1926, ce dernier fut remplacé par de Chalendar. A l'exception de Joseph Avenol, les Français ne jouèrent, cependant, pas le rôle principal au sein du Comité, bien que leur influence se soit exercée, à la fin de l'année 1925, en faveur de la suppression graduelle du contrôle financier. Les Britanniques Blackett, Niemeyer et Strakosch jouèrent, par contre, un rôle déterminant.

– *Basil Blackett* était né, le 8 janvier 1882, à Calcutta, ses parents étant l'un et l'autre missionnaires en Inde. Il fit ses études à Oxford et entra dans l'administration du Trésor. Il remplit, également, les fonctions de secrétaire de la Commission royale des finances et de la monnaie indiennes. Il se rendit aux Etats-Unis successivement en 1914 et en 1915, la seconde fois en tant que membre de la Commission financière franco-britannique. Il représenta le *Treasury* à Washington de 1917 à 1919. A son retour il devint le premier contrôleur des Finances du Trésor. En 1922, il fut nommé membre du Conseil du vice-roi de l'Inde. Il demeura cinq années dans ce pays où il fit preuve de qualités remarquables dans la gestion des finances publiques. De retour en Grande-Bretagne, en 1928, Blackett ne tarda pas à quitter le Trésor. Son ami Montagu Norman facilita son élection à un poste de directeur de la Banque d'Angleterre et il fut appelé à la présidence de la nouvelle Compagnie de communications impériales et internationales. Il la quitta en 1932 pour entrer au Conseil d'administration de la société De Beers. Il fit partie du Comité international qui élabora le plan Young. S'intéressant beaucoup à l'Allemagne, Blackett devait mourir dans ce pays, en 1935, des suites d'un accident d'automobile.[12]

– *Otto Ernst Niemeyer*, qui fit également partie du Comité de contrôle des Etats garants de l'emprunt autrichien, eut à ses débuts la même carrière que Blackett. Il était né en 1883. Son père originaire de l'Allemagne du Nord, avait émigré en Grande-Bretagne et était devenu citoyen britannique. Classé premier au concours de l'administration civile, comme Blackett, il choisit également d'entrer au Trésor et devint contrôleur des Finances en 1922. Il était chargé, à ce titre, du contrôle technique des finances nationales et notamment des questions relatives aux dettes et à la monnaie. Il fut pendant quinze ans membre du Comité financier et joua, ainsi, un rôle de premier plan dans la reconstruction économique et financière de l'Europe. En 1927, il quitta le Trésor pour la Banque d'Angleterre. Cet institut s'intéressait, alors, particulièrement au réaménagement des secteurs déprimés de l'économie britannique et Niemeyer fut un des principaux auteurs des plans de reconstruction de ces derniers. Il devint l'un des directeurs de la Banque des règlements internationaux de Bâle dont il présida le Conseil d'administration de 1937 à 1940. Il demeura vice-président de cette institution jusqu'à l'âge de quatre-vingts ans. Il acquit, par ailleurs, une grande notoriété entre 1930 et 1933 au cours de ses missions extérieures répondant à l'appel des gouvernements australien, brésilien, grec, égyptien et indien désireux de connaître son avis sur leurs problèmes monétaires et financiers. En Grande-Bretagne il faisait partie du Comité des porteurs de valeurs étrangères et représentait la Banque d'Angleterre, dont il était l'un des directeurs, à la Commission des émissions de capital. Il conserva ses fonctions de directeur exécutif lors de la nationalisation de l'institut d'émission, en 1946. Il devait jouer un rôle important, en 1952, au cours des négociations qui aboutirent à l'accord international sur la dette allemande. Il mourut, en 1971, à l'âge de quatre-vingt sept ans. Sir Otto Niemeyer appliquait une grande intelligence doublée d'un solide bon sens à l'étude des problèmes financiers nationaux et internationaux. Ne cherchant à dissimuler ni la vérité ni son pessimisme à l'égard de l'Autriche, il pouvait, à l'occasion, paraître cassant lorsqu'il préconisait des solutions rigoureuses.[13]

– La carrière de *Sir Henry Strakosch* qui fut membre du Comité financier de 1920 à 1937, diffère des deux précédentes. Né en 1871, à Hohenau, en Autriche, Strakosch avait acquis la nationalité britannique en 1907. Il fit ses études à Vienne puis en Grande-Bretagne et se fixa à Londres où il entreprit de faire carrière dans la banque. Il fut étroitement associé au développement industriel de l'Afrique du Sud et notamment à l'exploitation des gisements aurifères. Auteur, en 1920, de la loi bancaire et monétaire de ce pays, il le représenta cette même année à la Conférence financière internationale de Bruxelles. Il joua le rôle de conseiller financier du gouvernement sud-africain aux Assemblées de l'institution genevoise, à la Conférence de Gênes et à la consultation impériale de 1923. Il fut délégué de l'Afrique du Sud aux Assemblées de la SdN en 1923 et 1924. De 1925 à 1926, il fut membre de la Commission royale sur les finances et la monnaie indiennes, et appartint au Conseil de l'Inde entre 1930 et 1937. Il fut le délégué de ce pays à la consultation impériale d'Ottawa, en 1932, ainsi qu'à la Conférence économique de 1933. Sir Henry Strakosch est l'auteur de plusieurs ouvrages sur les questions monétaires et la crise économique.[14]

– Les trois membres français qui se succédèrent au Comité financier eurent en commun leur appartenance au corps de l'inspection des Finances. *Joseph Avenol*, né à Melle, en 1879, était issu d'une famille de la vieille bourgeoisie poitevine. Il fit des études juridiques et de sciences politiques à Poitiers et à Paris. Il devint inspecteur des Finances, en 1905. Il fut délégué financier du gouvernement français, à Londres, à la fin de la Première Guerre mondiale. Membre du Comité financier de la SdN de 1920 à 1923, il sera appelé à remplacer Jean Monnet au poste de Secrétaire général adjoint de l'institution genevoise de 1923 à 1933. Il assumera les fonctions de Secrétaire général entre 1933 et 1940.[15] Joseph Avenol s'intéressa particulièrement à la question autrichienne, en 1921 et 1922 notamment. Il lui arriva de dénoncer la politique des milieux financiers britanniques.

– *Jean Parmentier* et *Louis de Chalendar* commencèrent leur carrière en tant qu'adjoints à l'Inspection générale des finances. Ceux-ci étaient recrutés par concours parmi les licenciés en droit, ès sciences ou ès lettres et les anciens élèves de l'Ecole Polytechnique. Ils gravirent par la suite les différents échelons de l'inspectorat. Parmentier fut directeur général adjoint des finances du protectorat marocain en 1913. Mobilisé au début de la Grande Guerre, blessé au cours des combats, il accomplit par la suite une mission au Maroc en 1915, et une autre en Roumanie en 1916. Il fut sous-directeur auprès de l'administration centrale en 1919 et directeur du mouvement général des fonds à partir du 11 janvier 1921. Il fut nommé directeur général honoraire du Ministère des Finances en 1923. Il fit partie de la Commission des transferts créée par le plan Dawes. Le comte de Chalendar également blessé au cours de la Grande Guerre, accéda au grade d'inspecteur de quatrième classe en 1923. Il fut chargé de mission auprès du Cabinet du Ministre, cette même année. Il se rendit en Pologne, en 1924, et fut par la suite attaché financier auprès de l'Ambassade de France à Londres.[16]

– L'Italie fut représentée, généralement, par *Giuseppe Bianchini.* Né à Cremone en 1876, avocat, journaliste, député au Parlement, il fonda et dirigea la *Rivista Bancaria.* Il était également l'auteur de plusieurs publications juridiques. A partir de 1916, il assuma la direction de l'Association bancaire italienne. Il présida la Confédération nationale fasciste du Crédit et des Assurances entre 1926 et 1933. Il fut secrétaire de l'Association pour la liberté économique fondée à l'initiative de Pareto et présida de nombreuses associations culturelles et de bienfaisance, notamment l'Institut fasciste pour la Culture. Il fut membre du Conseil supérieur du Crédit et du Conseil national des Corporations. Il participa à la Conférence de Gênes et fut membre de la Commission des réparations et du Comité du plan Dawes. Il fut vice-président de la Corporation de la Chimie et sous-secrétaire d'Etat aux Finances, en 1935.

– Le Suisse *Léopold Dubois* auquel fut confié, en 1926, la gestion du reliquat de l'emprunt autrichien, avait été instituteur avant de diriger l'Ecole de commerce de Neuchâtel entre 1883 et 1890. Il fut placé à la direction de la Banque cantonale neuchâteloise de 1890 à 1901. A partir de cette date, il appartint à la direction générale des Chemins de fer suisses. Tout d'abord délégué de la Société de Banques de Suisse il devait assurer la présidence du Conseil d'administration de cet institut, à partir de 1920. Il avait accompagné la délégation suisse à la Conférence de Gênes en 1922.

– Le Tchèque *Vilém Pospisil* représentait également son pays aux conférences financières internationales. Né en 1873, il acquit une formation juridique et appartint aux services judiciaires avant d'entrer, en 1902, à la Caisse d'épargne municipale de Prague dont il devint directeur. Il fut proche du ministre des Finances Rasin. En 1926, il devint gouverneur de la Banque nationale tchécoslovaque. L'Union des Caisses d'épargne de ce pays et le Fonds général des instituts financiers de Tchécoslovaquie furent créés à son instigation. Pospisil appartenait à la franc-maçonnerie. Il devait s'intéresser vivement à la reconstruction autrichienne.

– *Marcus Wallenberg* appartenait à la grande dynastie financière de Suède qui avait fondé son »empire« sur un certain nombre de grandes firmes suédoises et norvégiennes créés ou reconstituées sous sa direction ainsi que sur l'*Enskilda*

Bank. Marcus Wallenberg était né en 1864. Il fit des études juridiques à Uppsala, renonça à la carrière judiciaire, et entra à l'*Enskilda Bank* de Stockholm dont il devint vice-président en 1920. Il était, également, président ou membre du Conseil d'administration de plusieurs sociétés bancaires et industrielles suédoises et étrangères. En 1910, il créa l'Association du patronat industriel de Suède avec la collaboration d'E. J. Ljunberg. Pendant la guerre, son gouvernement mit à profit ses qualités de négociateur, notamment au cours des pourparlers avec les représentants de l'Entente. Pendant la Conférence de la Paix, il fut chargé de sauvegarder les intérêts financiers de son pays et fit partie de la délégation suédoise aux Conférences de Bruxelles et de Gênes. Il participa à l'exécution du plan Dawes et présida le Comité qui élabora le plan Young. Il fut membre des cours d'arbitrage créées dans le cadre de l'application de ces deux plans et fut appelé à participer à la réorganisation du système bancaire allemand ébranlé par la grande crise.

Wallenberg était commissaire fiduciaire de l'emprunt autrichien ainsi que l'Américain Jay et son ami de longue date, Albert Edouard Janssen. Ce dernier, qui dirigea la délégation du Comité financier à Vienne, en novembre 1922, avait été sollicité par Montagu Norman pour exercer les fonctions de président de la Banque nationale d'Autriche.

– *Albert Edouard Janssen* naquit à Anvers en 1883. Il fit des études juridiques et philosophiques et manifesta, sans tarder, un grand intérêt pour les questions financières. Sa thèse, parue en 1911, portait sur les conventions monétaires. Il entra à la Banque nationale de Belgique en 1908 en tant qu'avocat-conseil. Attaché au contentieux, chargé des études économiques, il fut également le premier bibliothécaire de cet institut. Il accéda en 1911 au grade de docteur ès sciences politiques et économiques. Il fut nommé professeur à l'Université catholique de Louvain et poursuivit son enseignement dans cette Faculté pendant quarante-deux ans. Il fut également l'auteur de nombreuses publications. Secrétaire du Conseil de la Banque nationale de Belgique, à partir de 1914, il devait diriger cet institut jusqu'en 1925. Son service d'Etudes économiques fut créé à son initiative en 1922. Composé d'économistes qui s'inspiraient des théories de Gustav Cassel, ce service renonça progressivement au retour du franc belge à sa parité or d'avant-guerre et il conféra à la politique de la banque une grande unité.

Janssen fit partie de la Commission des réparations entre 1919 et 1924 et fut membre du Comité financier de la SdN, de 1921 à 1940. Il siégea également dans le Comité de contrôle des Etats garants de l'emprunt autrichien. Commissaire fiduciaire de ce dernier (et de l'emprunt de la République estonienne également, émis sous les auspices de la SdN), il accomplit plusieurs missions dans les pays dont les finances furent »reconstruites« sous l'égide de l'institution genevoise. Il participa à l'exécution du plan Dawes en tant qu'expert et à titre de membre du Comité des transferts. Ministre des Finances, en 1925 et 1926, dans le Cabinet Poullet-Vandewelde, c'est sous ce ministère qu'échoua la tentative d'assainissement monétaire dont le plan avait été conçu par la Banque nationale. Il abandonna la direction de cet institut et revint à la Société nationale de Crédit à l'Industrie dont il était administrateur-délégué depuis 1924. En 1932, il assura la vice-présidence de la Société belge de Banque. Il fut président du Conseil d'administration de cet institut de 1935 à 1964. Il assuma également la présidence de plusieurs comités et instituts, tout en administrant pendant de longues années l'Union chimique de Belgique et deux grandes compagnies d'assurances. Sur le plan international, il poursuivit son action au sein de la SdN, représentant notamment le Comité financier à la Conférence économique de Londres en 1933. Il fut administrateur de la Banque des règlements internationaux de 1949 à 1956. La liste serait longue, par ailleurs, des activités diverses d'Albert Edouard Janssen, notamment dans le domaine social. Sur le plan politique, le portefeuille des Finances lui fut à nouveau confié dans le Cabinet Spaak (1938 et 1939) et dans le ministère Van Houtte (1952 à 1954), et il fut nommé ministre d'Etat en 1949. Il occupa à la fin de sa vie, entre 1956 et 1965, un siège de sénateur et fit partie de la Commission des finances de cette institution. Albert Edouard Janssen parvint au terme de cette existence particulièrement active en 1966. Cet homme affable, tolérant, catholique convaincu, doté d'un solide équilibre et d'un esprit méthodique se préoccupait de connaître les réactions de l'opinion publique et s'attachait à maintenir de bonnes relations avec ses collaborateurs et ses subordonnés.[17]

– Le nom du banquier néerlandais *Carel Eliza Ter Meulen* est également associé à la reconstruction des finances autrichiennes. Il appartint à la maison Van Hope et Co. d'Amsterdam de 1901 à 1937. Cet institut était l'agent de la Banque d'Angleterre aux Pays-Bas. A partir du 22 juillet 1933, il devint second vice-président de la *Credit Anstalt*.[18]

Les membres du Comité financier[19] appartenaient donc à deux catégories différentes. L'on peut ranger dans la première les hauts fonctionnaires du ministère des Finances et du Trésor, et dans la seconde ceux qui seront désignés commodément sous le terme de »banquiers«. La plupart d'entre eux participèrent aux conférences financières internationales de Bruxelles et de Gênes qui fixèrent les principes directeurs de la reconstruction européenne. Ils contribuèrent, également, dans leur majorité à l'élaboration et à l'application des plans Dawes et Young et certains devaient appartenir à la Banque des règlements internationaux. A l'exception de Blackett et d'Avenol, ils furent commissaires fiduciaires des différents emprunts émis sous les auspices de la Société des Nations. L'intervention du Comité financier dans la reconstruction européenne avait d'ailleurs introduit à un double titre un élément nouveau et essentiel dans le marché des prêts extérieurs. La *City* avait, en effet, toujours conseillé aux gouvernements étrangers le recours à l'institution genevoise s'il s'était avéré qu'ils n'inspiraient pas une confiance suffisante aux marchés financiers de Londres et de New York.[20] La caution du Comité financier facilitait incontestablement l'émission des emprunts de reconstruction et cela était apparu à l'évidence pour la première fois en Autriche. Le Comité n'était cependant pas préparé, dans son ensemble, à aborder les problèmes complexes et spécifiques posés par les finances publiques, l'administration, les conditions politiques et économiques autrichiennes. Strakosch et Pospisil étaient peut-être plus aptes que les autres à les comprendre de par leurs origines et Janssen avait déjà abordé la question de la liquidation de la Banque d'Autriche-Hongrie. Mais une connaissance suffisante des conditions régnant dans l'ancien Empire faisait, généralement, défaut aux membres du Comité.

Au cours de l'élaboration des Protocoles de Genève, Blackett joua un rôle déterminant (ainsi que Jean Monnet et Arthur Salter) en intervenant fréquemment au cours des débats, en participant, dans une large mesure, à la conception du plan de reconstruction et en contribuant à obtenir de son gouvernement, au départ très réticent, une promesse de garantie du futur emprunt autrichien. Le Comité financier insista, d'ailleurs, fortement sur la nécessité de ces garanties gouvernementales car l'Autriche n'inspirait pas, à l'époque, une confiance suffisante aux marchés financiers. Or, l'exécution du plan de reconstruction devait être assurée par un fonds de réserve considérable constitué par l'emprunt extérieur.

Le plan lui même, qui devait être complété sur place, était inspiré par les jugements sévères portés sur l'Autriche par les Britanniques, Blackett notamment. Dans un projet de rapport, celui-ci imputa le chaos monétaire et le désordre des finances publiques à l'esprit qui présidait à l'établissement du budget destiné, selon lui, à maintenir dans la fonction publique le nombre le plus élevé possible de citoyens autrichiens. Craignant, par ailleurs, une augmentation du coût de la vie et de l'index, le gouvernement majorait impôts et tarifs avec hésitation et timidité. Les prix des produits des monopoles étaient, en grand partie, responsables du déficit budgétaire. Les raisons des pertes colossales subies par les chemins de fer étaient l'hypertrophie de leur personnel, l'augmentation automatique des salaires selon l'indice du coût de la vie, le prix élevé du charbon et l'insuffisance notoire des majorations tarifaires.[21] Lord Robert Cecil,[22] comme Basil Blackett, rendait l'Autriche responsable, en premier lieu, de ses difficultés présentes. C'est pourquoi elle devrait se soumettre à un contrôle rigoureux destiné à assister son gouvernement et à collaborer avec lui dans l'exécution du programme de réformes radicales de l'exécution desquelles dépendait la possibilité d'emprunter«.[23] Le terme »radicales« vaut d'être noté de même que le lien établi, à l'instigation probable de Blackett, entre l'exécution des réformes et le lancement de l'emprunt. Strakosch se prononça en faveur d'un contrôleur unique, formule à laquelle se rallièrent les autres membres du Comité. Il devait être désigné par le Conseil de la SdN et exercé au nom de cette institution. Les fonctions du contrôleur seraient définies par le Comité financier et il devrait être doté d'une autorité étendue. Les autres points sur lesquels insista la Commission furent la réalisation de l'équilibre budgétaire dans un délai de deux années et la réforme des entreprises industrielles de l'Etat. Celles-ci devaient être soit supprimées, soit gérées par l'Etat selon des principes commerciaux, soit cédées à des concessionnaires privés. Les causes du déficit des chemins de fer étaient, selon le Comité, celles qui avaient été dégagées par Blackett dans son projet de rapport. La nécessité de réduire le nombre des fonctionnaires plus élevé qu'à l'époque impériale s'inspirait également des conclusions de Blackett.

La question de la Banque d'Emission qui était un des »piliers« de tous les plans antérieurs de reconstruction avait, par ailleurs, longuement retenu l'attention du Comité. Se conformant à une résolution des conférences de Bruxelles et de Gênes, il souhaitait qu'elle soit libérée de toute influence gouvernementale. Il insistait sur la nécessité de centraliser auprès d'elle toutes les opérations comptables de recettes et de dépenses publiques. L'importance extrême accordée par le Comité à la réalisation de l'équilibre budgétaire, condition de la stabilisation monétaire dans les limites d'une période bien définie (ici deux années), ainsi qu'à la réduction des dépenses publiques, était également conforme aux résolutions adoptées à Gênes quelques mois auparavant.

Blackett, faisant preuve à cet égard d'une certaine connaissance des réalités autrichiennes, évoqua par ailleurs la nécessité de procéder à une réforme administrative en signalant la coexistence dans les *Länder* des deux administrations parallèles de la Confédération et de la Province.

La question monétaire fit, enfin, l'objet de longs débats au cours desquels Strakosch et Blackett tracèrent la voie à l'institut d'émission autrichien. Ils considérèrent en effet comme désastreuse une hausse éventuelle du cours de la couronne et ils suggérèrent à la future banque de maintenir la stabilité de ce dernier en procédant suivant le cas à des achats ou à des ventes de devises étrangères. Le plan de la SdN était, ainsi, fondé sur la stabilisation de l'unité monétaire et non sur une hausse de la valeur de celle-ci.

Bien qu'il ait tenu compte de la balance autrichienne des paiements et donc de l'énorme passif du bilan commercial susceptible d'être compensé, il est vrai, par des exportations invisibles qualifiées de »considérables«, le Comité avait accordé trop peu d'importance à la situation économique. Il subordonnait l'amélioration de cette dernière à la poursuite d'une »politique financière appropriée«. Il semble, enfin, qu'il ait cherché à éviter à l'Autriche les inconvénients d'une déflation brutale tout en l'invitant à adopter une politique d'austérité en restreignant, notamment, sa consommation afin de l'adapter à sa capacité de production.[24]

Après la signature des Protocoles, le Comité financier se rendit en délégation à Vienne, sur la proposition du chancelier autrichien, Monseigneur Seipel. Il se peut que celui-ci ait désiré s'appuyer sur son autorité lors de la mise en œuvre de l'action d'assainissement. La délégation présidée par Janssen comprenait Joseph Avenol, le sénateur italien Maggiorino Ferraris, Vilém Pospisil, le banquier suisse Alfred Sarasin, Sir Henry Strakosch et Sir Otto Niemeyer; Sir Arthur Salter participait aux travaux de la Délégation ainsi qu'Adrian Pelt, membre de la section d'Information du Secrétariat de la SdN.

La mission de la Délégation était définie dans le Protocole III de Genève. Elle devait collaborer avec le gouvernement autrichien à l'élaboration d'un programme de réforme et d'assainissement. Elle veillerait, également, à ce qu'il soumette à la fois au Parlement un projet de loi des pleins pouvoirs et la ratification de la convention de Genève.

Dans l'atmosphère de la capitale viennoise, avec l'aide d'Adrian Pelt et à l'instigation probable de Joseph Avenol, les délégués mesurèrent l'influence exercée par les sociaux-démocrates sur une partie non négligeable de la population. Ayant pris conscience de l'hostilité foncière de ces derniers à l'égard de l'œuvre genevoise et ayant constaté qu'ils étaient incapables de formuler un autre plan, ils tentèrent de les associer à l'œuvre de reconstruction. Ils entrèrent en contact avec leurs leaders et la cinquante-deuxième réunion de la Délégation se tint même chez Karl Seitz, en présence de Karl Renner et d'Otto Bauer.[25]

Les socialistes étaient surtout violemment hostiles aux »pleins pouvoirs« qui semblaient dépouiller le Parlement de la totalité de ses attributions. En effet, aux termes du Protocole III de Genève, le gouvernement devait être doté de pleins pouvoirs lui permettant de prendre dans les limites du programme de réformes et d'assainissement, toutes les dispositions nécessaires au rétablissement de l'équilibre budgétaire en deux ans, sans recourir à une sanction ultérieure du Parlement. Ces »pleins pouvoirs« devaient faire l'objet d'une loi et la Délégation exigea qu'elle soit dotée du caractère constitutionnel. Requérant, de ce fait, la majorité des deux tiers, elle ne pouvait être votée qu'avec l'appoint des voix socialistes. Or, cette solution avait, aux yeux des délégués, un triple avantage. Elle éviterait de rendre irréductible l'opposition sociale-démocrate; elle obligerait cette dernière à se prononcer clairement sur l'adoption ou le rejet de la loi; elle permettrait, enfin, de ne pas recourir à de nouvelles élections législatives. Tout en s'efforçant de réaliser un compromis avec l'opposition, les délégués cherchèrent, cependant, à respecter l'esprit dans lequel avait été conçue cette disposition du Protocole III de Genève. C'est pourquoi ils repoussèrent le premier projet dans lequel l'exécutif n'était aucunement soustrait au contrôle du législatif et imposèrent une série d'amendements successifs. Le texte final fut, ainsi, le résultat d'un compromis savamment dosé entre le gouvernement, l'opposition et les délégués du Comité financier de la SdN. Considérée comme un succès par les socialistes, cette forme affaiblie des pleins pouvoirs devait faire hésiter le Néerlandais Zimmermann à accepter de remplir les fonctions de Commissaire général. Cette loi constitutionnelle des pleins pouvoirs votée, le 26 novembre 1922, à la quasi unanimité créait un Conseil extraordinaire de Cabinet comprenant le chancelier fédéral, les membres du gouvernement et vingt-six conseillers d'Etat élus par le Conseil national parmi les députés des deux chambres sur la base de la représentation proportionnelle. Il comprendrait donc des socialistes.

1. – Ce Conseil était appelé à prendre les décisions dites »gouvernementales particulières« dans deux cas dûment précisés:

a) Il s'agissait, tout d'abord, des mesures d'exécution du programme de réformes à prendre par voie d'ordonnance qui n'étaient pas juridiquement formulées dans les dispositions de la loi d'assainissement.

b) Ces »décisions gouvernementales particulières« s'appliquaient, également, aux modifications du programme de réformes au cas où ce dernier s'avérerait insuffisant pour rétablir l'équilibre permanent du budget en l'espace de deux ans et s'il était impossible d'introduire ces amendements par la voie administrative ou par la promulgation des ordonnances prévues dans les dispositions législatives existantes.

2. – Le Conseil extraordinaire de Cabinet se prononcerait également sur les motions du Conseil national tendant à modifier les prévisions budgétaires et les lois de finances dans le sens d'une augmentation des dépenses ou d'une diminution des recettes contraires au programme de réformes ou aux ordonnances promulguées sur la base des »décisions gouvernementales particulières«.

3. – Il appartiendrait, désormais, au Conseil extraordinaire de Cabinet de fixer les tarifs ferroviaires et postaux, les prix des produits des entreprises publiques. Ces attributions appartenaient jusqu'alors à la Commission centrale du Conseil national.

Les socialistes qui avaient craint de voir le gouvernement user des pleins pouvoirs pour exécuter le plan financier dans un esprit partisan, obtenaient de ce fait droit de regard sur l'application de celui-ci. En facilitant la conclusion de ce compromis avec l'opposition, les délégués du Comité financier s'étaient vus dans l'obligation de s'immiscer, à titre exceptionnel, dans la politique intérieure autrichienne. Une telle intervention ne devait plus se renouveler ultérieurement. Sans doute la Délégation avait-elle tenté de faciliter l'adoption d'un programme d'économies sévères qui devaient affecter toutes les couches de la population autrichienne.

Les délégués avaient établi, avec l'aide du ministère autrichien des Finances, un programme budgétaire pour les années 1923 et 1924 qui était divisé en quatre périodes semestrielles. Les dépenses et les recettes de la Confédération avaient été évaluées pour chacune d'entre elles selon un plan clair et simple dont la présentation différait de celle du budget fédéral autrichien. Le déficit mensuel moyen avait été également fixé pour chaque semestre. Selon ces prévisions, le rétablissement de l'équilibre budgétaire en deux ans devait être assuré, en première ligne, par la réduction des dépenses et en second lieu par l'accroissement des recettes. Ainsi, entre le 1er octobre 1922 et l'année 1925, les dépenses militaires et celles des autres services administratifs devaient être réduites de moitié et celles de la Prévoyance sociale d'un tiers. Les prêts de la Confédération aux *Länder* devaient cesser d'être attribués et la participation de cette dernière aux dépenses »personnel« des provinces était appelée à diminuer des deux tiers. Le déficit des entreprises fédérales, y compris celle des chemins de fer, devait être entièrement comblé en 1925. Les seules dépenses qui étaient appelées à s'accroître étaient celles du service de la dette en raison de l'émission future de l'emprunt SdN ainsi que la charge des retraites et indemnités consécutives aux compressions de personnel. Le gouvernement autrichien s'était, en effet, engagé à licencier 100 000 fonctionnaires d'ici le 1er janvier 1925. Les dépenses d'investissement, enfin, n'avaient pas été distinguées des dépenses courantes comme elles auraient dû l'être.

Une partie du déficit devait être comblée grâce à l'augmentation du bénéfice net des monopoles et du produit des impôts. Entre la fin de l'année 1922 et 1925, les recettes douanières devaient s'élever de 40 à 100 millions de couronnes or, celles des impôts de consommation de 1,6 à 31,9 millions, celles des impôts directs de 24 à 65,4 millions, celles des taxes de 21,3 à 114 millions.[26] Ces évaluations avaient été établies sur la base d'une charge fiscale supportable n'excédant pas 75 couronnes or par tête d'habitant, y compris les impôts. Au cours du deuxième semestre de l'année 1924, dernière étape du plan, un excédent budgétaire aurait été ainsi dégagé. Il semblait toutefois difficile de pouvoir chiffrer avec précision la charge des pensions; comment évaluer, d'autre part, les conséquences financières de la réforme des chemins de fer? L'extension éventuelle du chômage pourrait créer une source de dépenses supplémentaires. Les prix et les salaires maintenus à un niveau inférieur au cours de la période de dépréciation devraient tendre à rejoindre la parité mondiale. La question des investissements publics n'avait semble-t-il pas été sérieusement abordée. Les résultats budgétaires prévus par la Délégation supposaient enfin la réalisation de trois conditions: l'exécution de la totalité des réformes projetées, qui faisaient l'objet de la loi dite »d'assainissement«,[27] la disparition du passif des chemins de fer fédéraux, l'adaptation de l'économie autrichienne à une charge fiscale accrue.[28]

La Délégation accorda, par ailleurs, la plus grande attention à la révision des statuts de la nouvelle banque d'émission dont elle recommanda instamment la création immédiate. Les délégués s'efforcèrent d'assurer l'indépendance de cet institut vis-à-vis du gouvernement. Ils tentèrent de limiter l'influence que pourraient exercer les dirigeants des autres instituts de crédit sur la conduite des affaires de la banque. Ils contribuèrent à faire adopter, au sujet de la couverture de la circulation fiduciaire, des dispositions suffisamment souples et adaptées à la situation économique de l'Autriche. Une distinction fut établie, à cette fin, entre la partie de cette circulation couverte par l'encaisse or et devises (selon le principe du *Gold Exchange Standard*) et celle qui l'était par le crédit et notamment par les traites escomptées. Les délégués insistèrent, par ailleurs, pour que le capital actions soit d'origine exclusivement nationale. Se conformant aux désirs londoniens, ils conseillèrent au chancelier de confier les fonctions de président à un étranger agréé par les milieux financiers occidentaux.

Dans leur désir d'inspirer confiance aux futurs prêteurs, ils instaurèrent les premiers linéaments du contrôle avant l'arrivée du commissaire général dans la capitale autrichienne.

Dans l'intervalle des missions et des sessions du Comité, ses membres britanniques étaient tenus au courant de l'évolution de la situation autrichienne. Ils correspondaient avec le Commissariat général de la SdN à Vienne, avec le conseiller étranger auprès de la Banque nationale d'Autriche, avec Sir Arthur Salter qui dirigeait la Section économique et financière du Secrétariat de l'institution genevoise et avec le gouverneur de la Banque d'Angleterre, Montagu Norman. L'émission des deux emprunts autrichiens à court et à long terme fut véritablement l'œuvre de ce dernier et, dans une moindre mesure, celle de Niemeyer et de Strakosch. Celui-ci intervint en Belgique et aux Pays-Bas au cours des négociations de l'emprunt à court terme. Les »conseils« de Niemeyer concernant la composition de la commission tripartite de négociation du prêt à long terme furent par ailleurs suivis. Les efforts de cette commission furent constamment soutenus et aidés par Norman, Niemeyer et Strakosch. Ces derniers discutèrent, également entre eux, les termes de »l'Engagement général«, mis au point par les juristes de la Banque d'Angleterre, qui contenait les conditions de l'emprunt. C'est sous la pression de Norman et de Niemeyer que les négociations avec les banquiers français reprirent après avoir été momentanément interrompues.

Tout en contribuant à réaliser ainsi une des conditions essentielles du succès du plan de Genève, Norman, Niemeyer et Strakosch très irrités par la désignation d'un Autrichien à la présidence de la Banque nationale, tentèrent de diriger la politique de cet institut dans le sens qu'ils souhaitaient. Son président, Reisch, s'engagea envers Norman à suivre une politique restrictive d'escompte et crédit. Niemeyer invita Strakosch à exiger de lui qu'il s'abstînt de laisser s'élever le cours de la couronne stabilisé »de facto«. Il pouvait être tenté de le faire, en effet, en raison de l'afflux des prêts extérieurs et de l'abondance de l'offre de devises sur le marché national.[29] En dépit des critiques dont elle fut l'objet en Autriche, cette politique fut, d'ailleurs, suivie et l'institut d'émission maintint le cours de la couronne rigoureusement stable par rapport au dollar. Par contre, il ne fut pas en mesure d'éviter une hausse des prix qui signifiait probablement un processus d'adaptation de l'Autriche au niveau des prix mondiaux. Cette hausse pouvait servir d'argument au ministre autrichien des Finances pour justifier le dépassement des prévisions de dépenses fixées par la Délégation.

Cette évolution de la gestion budgétaire devait, d'ailleurs, inciter le gouvernement autrichien à présenter à la SdN, en mars 1924, une double requête. Il demandait à bénéficier de la latitude qui lui avait été laissée de modifier le plafond de dépenses de 350 millions de couronnes or fixé en accord avec la Délégation provisoire, s'il s'avérait qu'un dépassement de ce montant était sans danger. Pour répondre à un souhait très largement répandu, il désirait, en second lieu, être autorisé à utiliser le reliquat de l'emprunt de restauration à des fins économiques. Celui-ci avait été émis, en effet, dans le but de combler le déficit budgétaire. Son montant avait été fixé par le Comité financier sur la base de l'évaluation de celui-ci. L'évolution de la gestion budgétaire avait été, cependant, très différente de celle qui avait été prévue par la Délégation. Ses résultats étaient apparemment très satisfaisants en raison d'un accroissement des recettes qui avait largement dépassé les prévisions. Il était à craindre, toutefois, que leur niveau ne puisse se maintenir alors que les dépenses, en fait difficilement compressibles, avaient tendance à s'accroître. Or, le système de contrôle qui s'exerçait essentiellement sur la gestion budgétaire présentait alors de grosses lacunes. Il est vrai que son exercice était rendu plus difficile par le fait que la Banque nationale n'était pas devenue le »caissier de l'Etat« comme le lui recommandaient les Protocoles de Genève. En fait la plupart des recettes étaient encaissées par la Caisse d'Epargne postale qui réglait également les dépenses de l'administration centrale. Il y eut, d'ailleurs, toujours là un point faible du contrôle en dépit des améliorations incontestables apportées, en 1925, sous la pression du Comité financier. Celui-ci avait donc des motifs d'inquiètude quand lui parvint la double requête du gouvernement autrichien. C'est pourquoi il recommanda au Conseil, à l'instigation de Niemeyer (et de Salter), d'ajourner la discussion sur ce document jusqu'à la session de juin 1924. Cet ajournement fut effectivement décidé par le Conseil dans les termes mêmes du projet rédigé par Niemeyer qui constituait pour l'Autriche un sérieux avertissement.

La crise financière qui éclata à Vienne au cours du printemps 1924 acheva de persuader celui-ci que la prospérité récente de ce pays était plus apparente que réelle. Il parut ne pas envisager que cette crise pouvait être considérée comme une séquelle de l'inflation. Il dénonçait, par contre, le poids excessif de la fiscalité autrichienne. Le Commissaire général et le Comité financier mettaient alors l'accent sur celle-ci. A cet égard, trois questions pouvaient être posées:

1. Le montant de l'imposition par tête d'habitant était-il déjà supérieur à la capacité fiscale de celui-ci?

2. Le système des impôts autrichiens n'était-il pas préjudiciable à l'activité économique?

3. Ne convenait-il pas de tenir compte de l'imposition provinciale et communale? Quel était le poids de cette dernière? La Confédération disposait-elle d'un droit de veto à l'égard du pouvoir local de taxation? Comment était réglée la question du partage des impôts communs entre le *Bund* et les *Länder*? Il s'avéra, en effet, que le problème des relations financières entre la Confédération, les Provinces et les Communes ne pouvait être éludé. Il passa même au premier plan

des préoccupations alors qu'il n'avait pas retenu réellement l'attention du Comité avant la signature des Protocoles de Genève.

Les travaux de la Commission, qui se réunit au siège de l'institution genevoise en juin 1924, furent dominés par Niemeyer, Strakosch et Salter. Le premier se fit l'interprète des inquiètudes des milieux financiers londoniens. Il traduisait, également, les préoccupations des prêteurs américains. Le Comité adopta, par ailleurs, les conclusions de Janssen sur les conséquences de la crise boursière du printemps 1924[30] qui devait retarder, selon lui, d'une année l'achèvement de la reconstruction financière. Le solde de l'emprunt de restauration devait donc être conservé pour couvrir d'éventuels déficits budgétaires. Dans un rapport confidentiel qui n'était pas destiné à la publication, afin de ne pas ébranler la confiance des milieux financiers étrangers, le Comité insista sur le fait que, depuis le mois de novembre 1922, les dépenses n'avaient pas été réduites. A la lumière de l'expérience, il mit l'accent sur les dépenses et la fiscalité des organismes autonomes[31] de même que sur leurs relations financières avec la Confédération. Les Britanniques, Norman, Niemeyer et Strakosch notamment, ne devaient d'ailleurs plus cesser d'accorder à cette dernière question la plus grande importance. Elle posait néanmoins sur le plan politique un double problème: celui des relations entre *Bund* et *Länder* et celui des rapports entre majorité et opposition. Enfin, avant de se prononcer définitivement sur les deux requêtes présentées au mois de mars par le gouvernement autrichien, les membres du Comité décidèrent de poursuivre leur enquête à Vienne.[32]

Sur place, le Comité dut se rendre à l'évidence. Les données du problème autrichien s'étaient transformées sous l'influence de facteurs internes et externes. A l'intérieur, l'évolution de la situation budgétaire n'avait pas été conforme aux prévisions. La crise boursière avait entraîné faillites et liquidations tout en ébranlant fortement la position de la Banque nationale. En raison de l'existence d'un fort courant fédéraliste et à cause de l'opposition sociale-démocrate, la mise en œuvre de certaines réformes avait été différée et de nombreux compromis avaient été réalisés. La clause des Protocoles de Genève sur les »pleins pouvoirs« était demeurée lettre morte et, cependant, le bilan des réformes était loin d'être négligeable. A l'extérieur, l'adoption du plan Dawes pourrait contribuer à aggraver, pour l'Autriche, la concurrence allemande. La jeune république alpine avait bénéficié de deux années d'avance mais celles-ci avaient-elles été, réellement, mises à profit? Pour être en mesure de répondre à cette question, les délégués entrèrent en contact avec les représentants des milieux économiques autrichiens et accordèrent dans leur étude une grande importance à l'économie qui avait été fort négligée à l'automne 1922. Le rapport commun rédigé, en septembre 1924, par le Comité financier et le Commissaire général, différait ainsi profondément de celui qu'ils avaient publié en juin. Les considérations sur la dernière crise financière et les données économiques y tenaient la plus grande place. Le texte d'un accord, qui constituait une nouvelle charte pour la reconstruction, était annexé au rapport. Il contenait un certain nombre de mesures fiscales et monétaires que le gouvernement autrichien s'engageait à exécuter. Elles étaient destinées à »assainir la vie économique« et à faciliter à l'Autriche l'obtention des crédits extérieurs, qui lui étaient indispensables.[33] Selon le voeu exprimé par les associations de banquiers et d'industriels, et afin de limiter le coût déjà trop élevé du capital, les taxes sur les transactions bancaires et celles portant sur les devises devaient être réduites à un forfait nominal et le taux de l'impôt sur les sociétés abaissé à 25%. La législation fiscale devait être modifiée de façon à faciliter l'émission d'obligations. Les milieux économiques se plaignaient, en effet, d'obtenir avec difficulté des crédits à long terme. L'introduction de bilans or qui seuls permettraient aux prêteurs étrangers d'appréhender la situation réelle des sociétés autrichiennes, devait être, par ailleurs, fortement encouragée. La Délégation avait fait sienne à cet égard, une suggestion présentée par l'Association centrale de l'industrie autrichienne. Le gouvernement de ce pays s'engageait, par ailleurs, »à attirer l'attention des autorités responsables sur le fait qu'il était souhaitable d'établir à bref délai une relation légale entre la couronne autrichienne et un poids d'or déterminé«. La stabilisation légale n'était, en effet, pas encore intervenue. Deux clauses de l'accord dit »de septembre« concernaient directement l'institut d'émission. L'engagement pris par le gouvernement autrichien »d'obtenir la création à la Banque nationale d'un comité exécutif restreint pour les mesures d'urgence« répondait aux préoccupations de Montagu Norman et des milieux financiers londoniens concernant le taux d'escompte de l'institut d'émission autrichien. Ce taux était fixé, en effet, par le Conseil général de la Banque qui se réunissait une fois par mois et comprenait des représentants des milieux économiques peu favorables à une majoration de ce taux. Or, il était reproché vivement à la Banque de n'avoir pas relevé à temps le taux officiel, sans que cela ait été implicitement compris dans »les mesures d'urgence«. Le gouvernement autrichien s'engageait également à user de son influence auprès de la Banque nationale afin qu'elle conduise »sa politique d'escompte de façon à maintenir la stabilité de la couronne, non seulement par rapport à l'or, mais encore par rapport aux marchandises«. Cette disposition répondait aussi aux préoccupations de Norman, Niemeyer et Strakosch concernant la hausse des prix en Autriche. Le troisième établissait, en outre, un rapport direct entre la montée des prix et l'inflation de crédit.

En ce qui concernait le budget, le gouvernement autrichien avait obtenu que la limite maximale des dépenses courantes, pour 1925, soit fixée à 495 millions de couronnes or et celle des investissements à 50 millions (au lieu des 350 millions prévus par la Délégation en novembre 1922). Les Autrichiens auraient désiré, néanmoins, un plafond plus élevé. Les investissements dits »nettement productifs« pourraient être financés, par ailleurs, à l'aide des fonds prélevés sur le reliquat de l'emprunt de restauration.

Le gouvernement autrichien s'engageait, d'autre part, à réaliser un certain nombre de réformes administratives, notamment la fusion des deux administrations parallèles, celle de la Confédération et celle de la Province qui coexistaient au sein des *Länder*. Un choix avait été fait parmi les vingt mesures contenues dans la loi »d'assainissement« de novembre 1922 qui n'avaient pas été encore adoptées. Le Comité avait pu renoncer à exiger la réalisation de réformes soulevant des difficultés d'ordre politique et touchant, notamment, à l'armée et à l'enseignement.

Le Comité financier, au sein duquel Otto Niemeyer avait joué un rôle déterminant, avait ainsi cherché à obtenir du gouvernement autrichien qu'il s'engageât à prendre les mesures propres à restaurer le crédit et la position de l'Autriche. Il avait subordonné la suppression du contrôle à l'exécution des mesures de l'accord et au maintien des chiffres du budget à l'intérieur des limites fixées. Il avait concédé la mise en place d'un dispositif de contrôle »allégé« afin de faciliter la tâche du gouvernement autrichien et la mise en œuvre du nouveau programme de réformes. Le chancelier autrichien s'était, enfin, engagé à négocier avec les dirigeants des *Länder* les bases d'une réforme de leurs relations financières avec la Confédération.[34]

Ces derniers engagements furent, cependant, à l'origine d'une crise politique. En tentant de régler en vain, sous la pression de Genève, la question des relations financières entre le *Bund* et les *Länder*, le chancelier Seipel se vit contraint d'abandonner le pouvoir après avoir mesuré la force du courant fédéraliste au sein de son propre parti. Des difficultés étaient également apparues concernant le contrôle. Des différences considérables s'étaient fait jour, en effet, entre les comptes clos arrêtés par la Cour des comptes et ceux qui avaient été communiqués au Commissaire général. Un compte séparé, soustrait au contrôle, dont l'existence était depuis longtemps soupçonnée venait d'être découvert. Des différences s'étaient, enfin, manifestées entre la Banque d'Angleterre et l'institut d'émission autrichien. Les critiques des Britanniques portaient sur les variations du taux d'escompte, la hausse des prix en Autriche, les opérations au comptant et à terme sur les devises étrangères et la suppression du contrôle des changes.

Selon l'optique londonienne le taux officiel aurait dû être relevé beaucoup plus tôt. La Banque nationale avait également trop tardé à exercer une censure rigoureuse sur les traites qui étaient présentées. Le portefeuille d'escompte contenait, en outre, selon Strakosch, une quantité excessive de papiers de médiocre valeur qui n'étaient pas de véritables traites commerciales.

Les Britanniques avaient un second sujet d'inquiétude: la politique de crédit trop libérale de la Banque nationale n'était-elle pas responsable de la hausse des prix en Autriche? Pour Montagu Norman, il appartenait à l'institut d'émission de juguler cette élévation en réduisant la circulation fiduciaire et en restreignant les crédits d'escompte.

La reprise par la Banque nationale à l'automne 1924 des opérations consistant à acheter des devises étrangères au comptant et à les vendre à terme était également vivement critiquée par Londres. Elles encourageaient, cependant, les banques autrichiennes à accepter des crédits extérieurs à court terme. La question cruciale du crédit était, ainsi, en partie résolue. Les Britanniques souhaitaient néanmoins que le volume de ces devises »en report« soit réduit et qu'elles cessent de figurer dans l'encaisse de la Banque.

Les débats du Comité financier lors de sa session de février 1925 et le rapport qui en est issu reflétèrent ces préoccupations. L'accent fut mis sur quatre points essentiels: la nécessité de développer un système de contrôle national efficace, l'importance d'un règlement satisfaisant des relations financières et fiscales entre la Confédération et les Provinces, la politique de la Banque nationale d'Autriche, les insuffisances constatées dans l'exécution de l'Accord de septembre 1924. Le Comité se fit l'écho de certaines préoccupations londoniennes. Il s'inquiéta du développement exagérément rapide des opérations de report des devises; il demanda à l'institut d'émission autrichien de prévenir toute inflation de crédit; il l'invita à poursuivre la liquidation de la crise boursière qui avait affaibli sa position. Il recommanda l'abolition, vivement souhaitée à Londres, du contrôle des changes. Il reprit une idée très chère à Montagu Norman en soulignant l'intérêt de l'instauration d'une collaboration entre les banques centrales. Il invita, enfin, l'institut d'émission à user très prudemment du nouvel article 86 de ses statuts, très mal accueilli à Londres, qui permettait d'élargir la base de l'émission fiduciaire.

Peu avant la session de septembre 1925, Salter estima que le contrôle pourrait être supprimé à condition de mettre en place un dispositif national efficace de supervision et d'imposer à l'Autriche deux clauses de sauvegarde. Celles-ci visaient à rétablir éventuellement le contrôle au cas où la stabilité financière du pays serait menacée après le départ de Vienne du Commissaire général et à maintenir dans ses fonctions le conseiller étranger auprès de la Banque nationale. Niemeyer donna à ces deux dernières conditions un caractère impératif et les Autrichiens furent contraints de les accepter, en dépit de leurs réticences initiales. La situation autrichienne éveillait, en effet, chez lui certaines inquiétudes partagées par Strakosch et Ter Meulen. Celles-ci portaient sur le budget qui n'avait pas été maintenu dans les limites fixées, sur la situation véritable des sociétés qui serait révélée par l'établissement des bilans or mais surtout sur la précarité d'une stabilisation assurée par des crédits extérieurs à court terme, provenant notamment des Etats-Unis, et dont une partie était immobilisée dans des placements à long terme.[35]

En décembre 1925, le Comité dut traiter la question délicate du contrôle de l'emploi du solde important de l'emprunt de restauration. Au risque de décevoir le gouvernement autrichien, Niemeyer s'entendit avec le Secrétariat de la SdN et avec Rome pour que le reliquat fût conservé sous forme liquide sur un compte bloqué afin de pouvoir combler d'éventuels déficits budgétaires. La situation autrichienne ne lui inspirait pas encore une confiance absolue. En juin 1926, il considéra comme trop ambitieux le projet du gouvernement autrichien d'un emprunt de 200 millions de schillings destiné aux travaux d'extension des câbles téléphoniques à grande distance. A son instigation, le Comité se limita à approuver le prélèvement d'un montant de 27 millions se schillings sur le reliquat de l'emprunt pour la construction des lignes téléphoniques reliant Vienne à la frontière suisse et Linz à la Suisse.

La politique autrichienne de Niemeyer était ainsi toujours empreinte d'un certain pessimisme, d'ailleurs assez fondé, à l'égard de l'avenir de l'Autriche. Il souhaitait que ce pays adapte ses besoins à ses possibilités. En contact avec les prêteurs anglo-saxons, il évitait de nuire à son crédit tout en tentant de favoriser l'épargne nationale.

Joseph Avenol n'avait donc pas tort qui mettait l'accent sur »la très haute action des membres anglais du Comité financier«. Il ajoutait qu'ils agissaient »en collaboration parfaite avec le *Foreign Office* et surtout avec la Banque d'Angleterre.«[36]

Le rôle joué par cette dernière dans l' »anglicisation« de la Banque anglo-autrichienne en 1921, l'intérêt manifesté dès le début par son gouverneur à l'égard de l'affaire autrichienne, le mérite qui lui revenait de l'émission réussie des emprunts, les liens établis avec la *Credit Anstalt*, prouvent que Montagu Norman avait une politique à l'égard de l'Europe centrale et de l'Autriche en particulier. Il avait, par ailleurs, le souci d'instaurer une collaboration entre les banques centrales et souhaitait diriger la politique bancaire et monétaire des pays en voie de reconstruction. A cet égard, il paraissait déçu par le manque de contacts avec la Banque nationale d'Autriche, qui constituait peut-être son principal grief à l'égard de son président Richard Reisch.

Or, par l'intermédiaire de Niemeyer et de Strakosch qui assistèrent notamment, en mars 1925, aux entretiens entre Reisch et Norman, ce dernier exerça une certaine influence sur la politique du Comité financier. Mais plutôt que d'influence, il serait préférable de parler d'accord entre Norman, Niemeyer et Strakosch, accord réalisé et maintenu sur la base de quelques principes très simples: stabilité de la monnaie non seulement par rapport à l'or, mais encore dans le maintien de son pouvoir d'achat, nécessité absolue d'éviter le recours à l'inflation de crédit, restriction de l'autonomie financière des *Länder*, adaptation des dépenses publiques et de la consommation des particuliers à la superficie et à la production réduites d'un Etat appauvri par les déperditions successives de capital qu'il avait subies.

Cette politique avait été à certains égards une réussite. La monnaie était demeurée stable bien que l'on puisse s'interroger sur le niveau auquel avait été réalisé cette stabilisation. Le budget était équilibré. Une part très importante du produit de l'emprunt avait été utilisée non pour combler le déficit budgétaire mais pour financer des dépenses de capital. Le contrôle de la Cour des comptes avait été renforcé. Le ministère des Finances avait adopté des mesures tendant à faire de la Banque nationale le caissier de l'Etat. Sous la pression extérieure, l'Autriche avait procédé à des compressions de personnel ainsi qu'à une simplification relative de ses rouages et de ses méthodes administratives. Elle avait adopté, sous cette même pression, en juillet 1925, au prix d'inévitables compromis politiques, une série de réformes importantes. Cette nouvelle législation précisait les attributions respectives de la Confédération et des Provinces aux plans législatif et exécutif; elle assurait la prise en charge par les Provinces de l'administration de l'Etat et la réforme des instances agraires; elle devait permettre une certaine unification de la politique fiscale sur l'ensemble du territoire fédéral. Elle étendait le contrôle de la Cour des comptes à la gestion des *Länder*, à l'exception majeure de la province de Vienne. Elle devait assurer ce contrôle plus efficace des dépenses provinciales qui était souhaité par Genève et par Londres, au prix, il est vrai, d'une décentralisation accrue des tâches administratives.

La politique du Comité financier soutenue par le contrôle n'avait pas permis seule d'obtenir ces résultats. La conjoncture avait facilité l'accroissement des recettes qui avait permis de réaliser l'équilibre budgétaire. Vienne, place bancaire, centre commercial et industriel, avait également joué un rôle important.

L'œuvre demeurait néanmoins inachevée. La situation économique était mauvaise en 1926. On ne pouvait en conclure, cependant, que l'Autriche n'était pas »viable«. Il est vrai que l'examen de la balance des paiements ne permet pas à lui seul de donner à cette question une réponse satisfaisante. L'absence de statistiques sur la totalité des »postes invisibles« ne permet pas de mesurer, en effet, avec précision de quelle manière était comblé le lourd passif du bilan commercial.

La situation de l'institut d'émission paraissait très solide quant au pourcentage de couverture de la circulation fiduciaire et au stock de devises mais l'importance des crédits à court terme pouvait être inquiétante.

L'appareil bancaire très alourdi depuis l'armistice était loin, par ailleurs, d'avoir pansé toutes les blessures que lui avaient infligées la guerre, l'inflation et la crise financière de 1924.

Les dépenses publiques avaient, en fait, augmenté notamment au chapitre »personnel« et la question des traitements des fonctionnaires n'avait pas été définitivement résolue.

La situation de l'entreprise des chemins de fer, devenue une »Corporation économique autonome«, demeurait enfin difficile, en dépit des progrès de l'électrification dont le financement était assuré en partie au moyen du produit de l'emprunt de restauration. Le Comité financier ne pouvait, toutefois, être rendu responsable de ces difficultés. Il avait tenté de prouver, contre les tenants du rattachement à l'Allemagne, que l'Autriche était »viable« et l'avenir devait lui donner raison, après la Seconde Guerre mondiale.

Notes

1 Les Britanniques opposaient ainsi une fin de non recevoir aux propositions françaises qui suggéraient de confier à nouveau à la Commission des réparations le soin d'étudier la question autrichienne. Selon Otto Niemeyer, ce Comité n'était également pas l'organe adéquat pour exercer un contrôle sur les finances de ce pays.

2 PRO, Londres, T. 160/57/2073/2 et TO. 371. 5739 C. 2479/75/3. Mémoire sur la position du Trésor; CAB. 23/23, c. 80/20(6). Cabinet, 30 décembre 1920; PRO, Londres, T. 160/57/2073/2. Note de Niemeyer sur les propositions françaises destinées au Chancelier de l'Echiquier (29 décembre 1920) et projet de réponse au gouvernement français adressé par Niemeyer au Foreign Office (ler janvier 1921); MF, Paris, F 30 637. Memorandum du Foreign Office (ler janvier 1921). Les auteurs de ces idées appartenaient vraisemblablement au Trésor.

3 AE, SdN, 1318. Note sur le Crédit international et Mémoire de Ter Meulen (28 octobre 1920).

4 MF, F 30 637. Rapport d'Avenol, Paris, 21 juin 1921.

5 Doc., SdN, Directors' Meetings, 11 avril 1921.

6 ASdN, S. 143, doc. EFS 68 (a) A.40 (a) Réponse du Comité financier de la SdN aux gouvernements alliés.

7 BM für Finanzen. SIV A /42.466/1921. Projet d'un plan d'assainissement de la situation monétaire et financière de l'Autriche communiqué par les délégués de la SdN; doc., SdN, C. 103. M.56. 1921.II

8 Doc., SdN, F/P.V. Procès-verbal de la 4ème session du Comité financier (24–25 mai 1921).

9 L'inspirateur de cette politique aurait été Sir Basil Blackett.

10 Ces quatre gouvernements étaient représentés dans une commission *ad hoc,* le sous-comité autrichien du Conseil, qui traita les questions politiques et assura la coordination nécessaire.

11 ASdN, S. 107., A. Salter à Mac Fadyan, 4 octobre 1922.
12 *The Dictionary of National Biography* (1931–1940), London, Oxford University Press, 1950, p. 83–84.
13 *The Times*, 8 février 1971, p. 12.
14 *The Dictionary of National Biography* (1941–1950). London, Oxford University Press, 1959, p. 846–847.
15 James Barros, *Betrayal from within. Joseph Avenol, Secretary General of the League of Nations 1933–1940.* New Haven, Yale University Press, 1969. 289 p.
16 *Annuaire général des Finances* 1925–1926 et 1933–1934. Nancy, Berger-Levrault, 1926 et 1934.
17 Comtesse Plater Zyberk, *Albert-Edouard Janssen raconté par sa fille* Bruxelles, Oyez, 1976, p. 296; H. Van der Wee et K. Tavernier, *La Banque nationale de Belgique et l'histoire monétaire entre les deux guerres mondiales.* Bruxelles, Banque nationale de Belgique, 1975, p. 542.
18 *Ein Jahrhundert Creditanstalt-Bankverein.* Wien, herausgegeben von der Creditanstalt-Bankverein, 1957, p. 392.
19 Nous n'avons pas dressé une liste exhaustive de tous les membres ayant appartenu au Comité financier entre 1921 et 1926, nous bornant à retracer la carrière des personnalités les plus marquantes et de ceux qui avaient réellement participé à la reconstruction autrichienne.
20 PRO, T/175/34. Montagu Norman, gouverneur de la Banque d'Angleterre au Foreign Office (mars 1929).
21 ASdN, S. 59. Projet de rapport par Sir Basil Blackett.
22 British Museum. Londres. Cecil Papers. v. 5163, Cecil à Lady Gladstone (16 septembre 1922).
23 Réponse du Comité financier aux questions qui lui ont été adressées par le Comité d'Autriche du Conseil (question 6) dans: *La reconstruction financière de l'Autriche. Exposé général des documents principaux.* doc. SdN. C. 568. M. 232, 1926, II., p. 197.
24 ASdN, C. 36 et S. 107. Procès-verbaux de la neuvième session du Comité financier (septembre 1922). Réponses du Comité financier aux questions qui lui ont été adressées par le Comité d'Autriche du Conseil (septembre 1922).
25 ASdN, C. 34. Procès-verbal de la 52ème séance de la Délégation provisoire (21 novembre 1922).
26 BM, Präs: 988/1922. Tableau des recettes annuelles sur la base du plan de réforme. ASdN, S. 107. doc. C/S.C.A./17 Annexe C; *ibid.*, C. 20. Tableau. Base mensuelle des dépenses et des recettes autrichiennes d'après le plan de réformes par étapes arrêté entre le gouvernement et la délégation provisoire de la SdN.
27 L'élaboration de ce plan de réformes et d'assainissement demeura une affaire intérieure.
28 BM, Präs /988/1922. Réponses aux questions posées par le Comité financier de la SdN (25 et 30 octobre 1922).
29 PRO, FO. 371 8539 C. 3603/16/3. Niemeyer à Zimmerman (24 février 1923).
30 Janssen, assisté de Pierre Denis, venait d'achever une enquête dans la capitale autrichienne sur les conséquences de cette crise grave des finances privées.
31 Provinces et Communes *(Länder und Gemeinden).*
32 Doc. SdN, F/15 ème session/P.V.Comité financier. Procès-verbaux de la 15e session; doc. SdN, F 162, Rapport confidentiel du Comité financier (Genève, 15 juin 1924); Rapport du Comité financier et du Commissaire général communiqué par le Comité autrichien au Conseil le 14 juin 1924 dans *La reconstruction financière de l'Autriche, op. cit.*, p. 228–232.

33 Cette délégation du Comité financier comprenait Niemeyer, Ter Meulen, Parmentier, Janssen, Dubois, Pospisil et Mazzucchelli qui remplaçait Bianchini.

34 ASdN, 1919–1927/IOB/24461 (R 511–514). Rapport commun du Comité financier et du Commissaire général du 15 septembre 1924, texte de l'accord de septembre et de ses deux annexes dans *La reconstruction financière de l'Autriche, op. cit.*, p. 233–247.

35 Doc. SdN, F/19 ème session, P. V., Procès-verbaux des séances de la 19e session du Comité financier (5–9 septembre 1925).

36 Archives nationales, Paris. Fonds privé Pierre Quesnay. Note d'Avenol (décembre 1926); AE, Paris, Papiers Avenol 37. Avenol à Quesnay (17 février 1928). Avenol à Salter (9 février 1928).

La conférence économique internationale de 1927

Jean Halperin
Nations Unies, Genève

Lorsque s'ouvrit, le 4 mai 1927, dans la Salle de la Réformation à Genève, la Conférence économique internationale, qui avait été convoquée à la suite d'une résolution adoptée par l'Assemblée de la SdN le 26 septembre 1925, sur la proposition de la délégation française et malgré l'opposition à peine dissimulée de l'Empire britannique, elle fut aussitôt saluée de toutes parts comme un événement sans précédent et d'importance majeure. Disons tout de suite que cette Conférence qui a siégé pendant trois semaines, jusqu'au 23 mai[1], se distinguait par le nombre des Etats participants (50, y compris les Etats-Unis, l'Union soviétique et la Turquie qui ne faisaient pas partie de la SdN), l'importance des délégations (194 membres et 226 experts), le soin avec lequel elle avait été préparée et l'ampleur de son programme.

Bien sûr, au regard des réunions internationales de caractère économique que nous connaissons aujourd'hui, la Conférence de 1927 paraîtra à certains comme relativement modeste. Mais, à l'époque, on n'avait effectivement rien vu de pareil jusqu'alors. Il faut donc la situer à la fois dans son temps et dans l'histoire pour mieux mesurer ce qu'elle pouvait représenter de nouveau et pour apprécier, le cas échéant, le chemin qui a été parcouru depuis lors. Nous devons savoir éviter les pièges d'une lecture anachronique qui consisterait à interpréter la situation de 1927 *comme si* nous étions en 1980, ou à lire le paysage international de 1980 sous les couleurs de 1927. En d'autres termes, il faut veiller à ne pas projeter dans l'analyse du climat de 1927 les mentalités, les réflexes, le style ou les arrière-pensées d'aujourd'hui.

A l'organisation économique de la communauté internationale, les traités de paix et le Pacte de la Société des Nations n'avaient fait qu'une place symbolique. Dans l'ordre social, le Traité de Versailles avait, en sa partie XIII, créé l'Organisation internationale du travail, mais dans l'ordre économique, le seul texte est celui de l'alinéa e) de l'article 23 du Pacte, souvent cité, mais peu explicite: »Sous la réserve, et en conformité des dispositions des conventions internationales actuellement existantes ou qui seront ultérieurement conclues, les Membres de la Société (des Nations) . . . prendront les dispositions nécessaires pour assurer la garantie et le maintien de la liberté des communications et du transit, ainsi qu'un équitable traitement du commerce de tous les Membres de la Société, étant entendu que les nécessités spéciales des régions dévastées pendant la guerre 1914–1918 devront être prises en considération.«[2] (Il convient d'ajouter qu'aux termes de l'alinéa a) du même article 23, les Membres »s'efforceront d'assurer et de maintenir des conditions de travail équitables et humaines pour l'homme, la femme et l'enfant . . . Aux termes de l'alinéa f), ils »s'efforceront de prendre des mesures d'ordre international pour prévenir et combattre les maladies«.) Ces dispositions ne définissaient directement aucune mesure précise à prendre dans l'immédiat: elles n'empêchaient pas les initiatives ambitieuses, pas plus qu'elles n'interdisaient une action rudimentaire et limitée. Ce n'est donc pas par la force des textes, mais de façon plus ou moins empirique, sous la pression des événements, que les modalités de la coopération économique se sont précisées. Bien plus nettes, à cet égard, seront les dispositions de la Charte des Nations Unies.[3]

Assez vite, l'action entreprise dans le cadre de la Société des Nations a revêtu trois formes différentes: une action continue exercée par les organes permanents constituant l'Organisation économique et financière ainsi que l'Organisation des communications et du transit; une action directe entreprise pour remédier à telle ou telle situation déterminée – restauration financière de l'Autriche, de la Hongrie et aide apportée à d'autres pays (Grèce, Bulgarie, Estonie, Dantzig, Albanie, Sarre); et les conférences économiques, générales et spéciales.

La première conférence internationale de caractère économique avait eu lieu à Bruxelles en septembre–octobre 1920, en vertu d'une décision prise en février 1920 par le Conseil de la SdN à sa deuxième session sur la proposition du représentant britannique. Préoccupé, en effet, par la situation financière en Europe, le Conseil avait jugé utile de »convoquer une conférence internationale en vue d'étudier la crise financière et de rechercher les moyens d'en conjurer et d'en atténuer les dangereuses conséquences«. A cette conférence, 86 hauts fonctionnaires, parlementaires, hommes d'affaires et banquiers privés participaient »en qualité d'experts et non pas comme porte-parole d'une politique officielle«; ils représentaient 39 Etats, dont les Etats-Unis et l'Allemagne. Cette conférence était à la fois la première grande conférence internationale convoquée par la SdN et la première conférence de ce genre spécialement consacrée aux problèmes financiers et monétaires qui ait jamais eu lieu dans l'histoire.[4] Pour la première fois aussi, les débats auxquels cette conférence a donné lieu ont été rendus pleinement publics. La circonstance était d'autant plus remarquable qu'au lendemain même de la guerre, rigoureusement rien n'avait été entrepris de façon concertée pour assurer la restauration économique et financière de l'Europe. C'est à croire que, las de la coopération intergouvernementale que les nécessités de la guerre avaient imposée aux Alliés et satisfaits de la victoire militaire acquise, chacun d'eux n'avait rien de plus pressé à faire que de revenir à une politique économique étroitement nationale et isolée sans se préoccuper des répercussions que cette politique pouvait avoir pour l'ensemble de la communauté européenne et internationale. Les tentatives, somme toute fort timides, que le Conseil de la SdN avait ébauchées pour créer les rudiments d'une organisation économique internationale s'étaient heurtées à une vive opposition: le danger commun et immédiat paraissait avoir disparu, or, c'est là, comme chacun sait, le stimulant le plus efficace de toute coopération. Non seulement tout contrôle international, même discret, mais encore tout accord impliquant quelque action concertée sur le plan économique et financier suscitait, de la part des gouvernements, la réserve la plus extrême, voire l'hostilité.[5] C'est d'ailleurs l'une des raisons pour lesquelles les aspects non politiques de l'organisation internationale ont si peu retenu l'attention à l'origine. Cette attitude caractérise l'orientation générale de la coopération économique à ce moment-là.

Les recommandations de Bruxelles étaient empreintes d'une parfaite orthodoxie financière et monétaire. Leurs auteurs ne s'en sont pas cachés: comme le dit le rapport de la Conférence, certaines de ces recommandations »peuvent avoir l'apparence de vérités élémentaires plutôt que de contributions originales au problème financier du monde. Leur adoption impliquerait cependant un changement fondamental dans la politique de la plupart des pays d'Europe«. Ces recommandations marquent aussi une volonté de retour au libéralisme le plus complet sur le plan intérieur, au sens, du moins, où ce terme correspond à l'absence de toute intervention de l'Etat dans la vie économique du pays.

Mais si, sur le plan national, les experts réunis à Bruxelles ont préconisé avec tant de chaleur le retour à la libre initiative privée, ils n'en ont pas moins posé, sur le plan international, les bases d'une véritable collaboration. Non seulement, ils ont demandé la création d'organismes permanents au sein de la SdN – organismes qui deviendront le Comité économique et le Comité financier – avec un secrétariat plus important, mais encore ils ont insisté sur la valeur qui s'attache à la confrontation internationale des politiques économiques et financières nationales, à la publication internationale et sous une forme comparable des renseignements essentiels, et même, sur certains points, à une action concertée de tous les Etats. Dans la conclusion de son rapport, la Conférence est formelle:

»La coopération internationale, dont la Conférence est la première manifestation tangible, doit se continuer et se développer. Il appartient à la SdN de prendre les initiatives nécessaires pour parvenir à ce résultat. Les propositions concrètes qui ont été présentées, telles que le projet de création d'un organisme international de crédits, ne sont que des exemples de cette coopération et d'autres mesures doivent être élaborées en détail.«[6]

Sur le papier, de semblables recommandations paraissent aujourd'hui banales (bien qu'encore utopiques à certains égards); en fait, elles étaient alors presque révolutionnaires. Et d'ailleurs, l'ampleur prise en réalité par la coopération économique internationale pendant les années qui ont suivi n'a sans doute pas répondu entièrement aux espérances des experts de Bruxelles. Ceux-ci avaient été unanimes à déplorer et même à condamner la politique des gouvernements qui les avaient désignés et il leur était difficile de remporter aussitôt la victoire dans la lutte qu'ils avaient entrepris de mener contre le nationalisme économique.[7] Après quelques semaines d'euphorie, il fallut se rendre à l'évidence dès novembre 1920, lors de la première Assemblée de la SdN: une tentative faite par plusieurs délégations, et notamment par Tittoni, délégué de l'Italie, pour élargir la compétence de la SdN dans le domaine économique, en particulier en vue d'assurer l'égalité d'accès aux matières premières, se heurta à une oppostion vigoureuse. Cet antagonisme est résumé avec une parfaite netteté par William E. Rappard:

»D'un côté – du côté américain[8] – l'affirmation d'une intransigeante volonté d'indépendance nationale s'opposait tant à toute velléité de gouvernement international qu'à toute velléité d'internationalisme économique. Du côté européen, d'autre part, et par la bouche du représentant d'un grand pays, pauvre et surpeuplé, l'exposé d'une doctrine de mise en commun des richesses naturelles de la planète, sous l'autorité d'une Société des Nations représentant la collectivité internationale tout entière et administrée selon les principes de l'intérêt général.«[9]

Ce débat a été d'autant plus important que de son issue devait dépendre toute l'orientation de l'action économique internationale. En fait, il se termina »par le triomphe apparent de l'internationalisme, mais par la victoire effective de ses adversaires«. Une enquête sur les matières premières fut bien entreprise, mais elle n'aboutit à aucun résultat.

Dorénavant, la doctrine est fixée par la force même des choses: comme l'a dit Hanotaux à la deuxième Assemblée de la SdN, »c'est par la persuasion qu'il faut arriver à la coopération«.

Le mandat de la Conférence de 1927 devait être beaucoup plus large.

Un Comité préparatoire constitué par le Conseil de la SdN et comprenant trente-cinq personnes choisies parmi les ressortissants de 21 pays »à titre d'experts, comme étant les mieux qualifiées par leurs titres et leur expérience personelle«, (»industriels, négociants, agriculteurs, financiers, fonctionnaires compétents en matière de politique commerciale, économistes, représentants des organisations d'ouvriers et de consommateurs«) a siégé à deux reprises, en avril et en novembre 1926, pour préparer l'ordre du jour de la Conférence et arrêter la documentation qui devait être élaborée à son intention. Cette documentation a été l'œuvre de la Section économique et financière du Secrétariat de la SdN – dirigée par Arthur Salter – et elle comprend aussi des monographies préparées par le Bureau international du travail, la Chambre de commerce internationale, l'Institut international d'agriculture et par des personnalités compétentes à la demande spéciale du Comité, au total près de 70 volumes. Parmi ces monographies, il faut citer une étude d'Eugène Grossmann sur les »systèmes de rapprochement économique«,[10] un mémorandum sur le »dumping« par Jacob Viner,[11] une étude de William Oualid sur »les ententes industrielles internationales et leurs conséquences sociales«,[12] et une autre étude de Gustave Cassel sur »les tendances monopolisatrices dans l'industrie et le commerce au cours de ces dernières années – Caractères et causes de l'appauvrissement des nations«.[13] Comme à Bruxelles, les participants n'étaient pas à proprement parler *mandatés* par les gouvernements qui les avaient désignés.

A ce titre, ils jouissaient d'une plus grande liberté de pensée et d'expression, ils pouvaient mieux servir de relais vis-à-vis des groupes d'opinion et d'intérêt, mais ils étaient sans doute moins en prise directe sur les centres de décision politique.

L'ordre du jour de la Conférence était très vaste: examen de la situation économique mondiale; liberté du commerce, tarifs douaniers et traités de commerce, moyens indirects de protéger le commerce national et la navigation nationale, répercussion sur le commerce international de la diminution du pouvoir d'achat, situation des principales industries et de l'agriculture, leurs difficultés et les possibilités d'action internationale. Aussi la Conférence s'est-elle scindée en trois commissions plénières, celles du commerce, de l'industrie et de l'agriculture.

Mais à la faveur d'un vaste débat général, qui n'a d'ailleurs duré que 4 jours, et des résolutions adoptées, il est possible de dégager les grandes lignes du travail accompli. Et d'abord, ce fut l'occasion de dresser un tableau général de la structure de l'économie mondiale et d'établir une manière de diagnostic.

A cet égard, il faut citer en premier lieu le discours du représentant de l'Empire britannique, Walther T. Layton, alors rédacteur en chef de l'*Economist*, en raison de la valeur propre de ses observations et parce qu'elles ont été reprises en partie dans le rapport final de la Conférence elle-même.[14] Une constatation de fait, d'abord: alors que la production industrielle a augmenté relativement vite après la fin de la guerre, le commerce intereuropéen n'a point accusé les mêmes progrès: si le commerce mondial est passé de l'indice 100 en 1913 à l'indice 105 en 1925, le commerce européen était encore à l'indice 89 en 1925; dans le même temps, le nombre des unités douanières est passé de 20 à 27 et les cordons douaniers en Europe se sont allongés de près de 11.000 km; quant au nombre des monnaies nationales en Europe, il est passé de 13 à 27. D'autre part, le rétablissement des échanges, sous réserve de quelques exceptions importantes, s'est fait surtout en suivant les courants qui existaient avant la guerre, ce qui permet de croire que les grands courants du commerce international ne sont pas simplement fortuits, et qu'ils dépendent de différences profondes, d'ordre physique et économique, entre les divers pays. Mais cela ne signifie pas que la structure économique de l'Europe et du monde en 1927 soit restée ce qu'elle était avant. Non seulement, il existe, à ce moment, en Europe au moins quatre millions de chômeurs, mais encore, d'une façon générale, »l'Europe est en présence d'une situation mondiale qui, à de nombreux égards, a subi, par rapport à la situation de 1913, des changements de caractère permanent«. Ce serait un jugement un peu sommaire que d'admettre qu'il suffirait de laisser aller le cours des choses pour que l'Europe regagnât le retard révélé par les statistiques. C'est donc une erreur de viser seulement à rétablir »les conditions d'avant la guerre« (comme on avait voulu le faire à Bruxelles et à Gênes) et de penser que si l'on y parvient, tout sera bien. Point de départ utile au cours des années qui ont suivi immédiatement la guerre, alors qu'il fallait parer au plus urgent, la conception du »retour à l'avant-guerre« est désormais »non seulement futile, mais donnerait une idée complètement fausse des problèmes en face desquels se trouve le monde«.[15] Le rapport de la Conférence sur ce point est à citer:

»C'est la tendance instinctive des hommes de se tourner vers le passé plutôt que vers l'avenir et, au moment où sont en train de naître des ordres nouveaux, de se retourner de préférence vers les conditions antérieures pour essayer de les faire revivre.«[16]

Parmi les transformations survenues, Layton en relève trois, et l'on peut observer que son diagnostic n'est point encore périmé. C'est, d'abord, le développement de l'industrialisation dans le monde entier qui, d'alleurs, est de nature à entraîner un accroissement considérable du volume du commerce international, accroissement dont l'Europe aura sa part, à condition, toutefois, d'envisager un équilibre entièrement nouveau. Au reste, cette répartition nouvelle de l'activité productrice du monde n'est pas une simple conséquence de la guerre qui n'a fait qu'accélérer un mouvement qui avait commencé vingt ou trente années auparavant. Il est intéressant, à ce propos, de citer l'observation suivante de Valerian Obolenski-Ossinski, délégué de l'Union soviétique: »Même les pays les plus arriérés se sont éveillés de leur sommeil séculaire. Tous aspirent à l'égalité économique et sociale. Celui qui n'a pas saisi cette vérité ne possède pas la clef de la psychologie sociale de l'époque.«[17]

A noter qu'en dehors des Etats-Unis et de dominions comme l'Afrique du Sud, l'Australie, le Canada et la Nouvelle-Zélande, les pays non européens représentés à la Conférence étaient au nombre de 17: le Brésil, le Chili, la Chine, la Colombie, Cuba, l'Egypte, l'Ethiopie, le Guatemala, l'Inde, le Japon, le Nicaragua, le Paraguay, la Perse, Salvador, le Siam, l'Uruguay et le Venezuela – soit le tiers seulement de l'ensemble des Etats participants.[18] Entendue rétrospectivement, la déclaration soviétique, qui n'avait guère eu d'écho sur le moment, prend valeur d'avertissement. A la Conférence de 1927, manifestement, le souci prédominant restait largement localisé en Europe, même si les termes de l'échange ont bien été évoqués, notamment par Gustav Cassel: »L'orientation générale de l'évolution est marquée par une chute des prix des produits coloniaux, par rapport aux prix des articles manufacturés que l'Europe peut offrir en échange. On peut citer de nombreux exemples des prix très bas atteints à l'heure actuelle par les produits coloniaux. Pour une grande quantité de ces produits, les prix absolus sont, à l'heure actuelle, à peu près aussi bas et, dans certains cas, considérablement plus bas même qu'avant la guerre. Par contre, les produits que le monde colonial est obligé d'importer ont, en général, atteint des niveaux bien supérieurs au niveau général des prix de gros.«[19]

La seconde modification importante est l'apparition, parmi les pays exportateurs de capitaux, des Etats-Unis, qui, de pays débiteur, sont devenus l'un des principaux créanciers du monde. »La fourniture abondante et opportune de capitaux par les Etats-Unis, au cours de ces dernières années, a été un facteur extrêmement important qui a hâté la restauration économique d'après guerre.« Mais les conditions dans lesquelles s'est effectuée cette exportation de capitaux sont tout à fait différentes de celles auxquelles la Grande-Bretagne, par exemple, exerçait ce rôle avant 1913, puisqu'en effet, sa balance commerciale a toujours accusé un excédent sensible de ses importations de marchandises. Tel n'est pas le cas des Etats-Unis dont la balance commerciale est créditrice et qui »en ce qui concerne tout au moins l'Europe, prennent des mesures pour exclure les produits des pays dont leurs capitaux assurent le développement ou le rétablissement«[20]. Layton se demande, non sans inquiétude, si les Etats-Unis continueront à avancer libéralement des capitaux, mais sans rien acheter à l'Europe. »Dans ce cas, est-il probable qu'aux yeux des Etats-Unis, un nouvel équilibre pourra être réalisé, dans lequel l'Amérique achètera les produits naturels des pays tropicaux en quantités suffisantes pour permettre la liquidation de sa situation de créancier par un système de commerce que l'on peut appeler triangulaire?«.[21]

Enfin, le morcellement économique et politique de l'Europe centrale a provoqué la création de nouvelles petites unités économiques qui, dans les conditions actuelles de la production, sont devenues un anachronisme. Aussi bien, l'idée qui semble avoir été évoquée le plus souvent au cours de la Conférence, avec la nécessité de développer les échanges commerciaux et d'abaisser les barrières, est celle-ci: l'interdépendance des nations de l'Europe est si étroite que leur prospérité économique constitue un tout indivisible. Il faut parvenir à un degré croissant de solidarité économique et développer, dans un grand nombre de domaines, une collaboration beaucoup plus étroite qu'elle n'a existé dans le passé.

Parmi les nombreuses questions qui ont été discutées dans les commissions et en séances plénières, deux surtout ont occupé une place importante: la politique commerciale et les ententes internationales de producteurs.

En matière de politique commerciale, il suffit de rappeler que, depuis la guerre, les barrières douanières étaient devenues à la fois plus nombreuses, plus élevées et plus instables, les accords commerciaux étant conclus pour une durée de plus en plus brève et les tarifs étant constamment modifiés. Aussi la Conférence, après avoir déclaré que le moment était venu »de mettre fin à l'accroissement des tarifs douaniers et de s'orienter dans une direction opposée[22]«, a-t-elle recommandé aux Etats de ne pas apporter aux droits de douane des modifications brusques et préconisé l'établissement de traités de commerce de longue durée et la consolidation des droits. Ces recommandations n'ont pas eu une grande portée pratique et des résultats plus précis ont été obtenus par la généralisation de la clause de la nation la plus favorisée. Ce qui est important, surtout, c'est, si l'on peut ainsi écrire, l'entrée des tarifs douaniers et de la politique commerciale dans l'ordre international. Jusqu'alors, en effet, on considérait très généralement la question douanière comme relevant exclusivement de la compétence des souverainetés nationales; la communauté internationale, en tant que telle, n'avait pas à en connaître. Le président de la Conférence, Georges Theunis, n'a pas manqué de souligner, à juste titre, que c'était là »une étape considérable dans l'évolution des idées« dans ce domaine.

Si la politique commerciale a pratiquement été au centre des préoccupations de la Conférence, il semble qu'à l'origine, ses promoteurs, et notamment la délégation française dirigée par Loucheur et Serruys, aient voulu réserver une place de choix à la question des ententes industrielles internationales. Aussi bien, cette question a fait l'objet d'un ample et parfois violent débat qui, toutefois, n'a pas tout à fait évolué dans le sens que certains avaient souhaité. Dès l'ouverture de la discussion générale, le professeur Cassel s'était élevé avec véhémence contre le malthusianisme économique et il avait fait le procès des monopoles sous toutes leurs formes, ceux des grandes entreprises industrielles comme ceux des syndicats ouvriers »lorsqu'ils tâchent d'établir un niveau de salaires artificiellement élevé«. De multiples arguments furent invoqués de part et d'autre, pour et contre les cartels. Finalement, la Conférence a constaté que le phénomène des ententes était un fait »dont on doit enregistrer le développement et qui . . . peut être considéré comme bon ou mauvais selon l'esprit qui préside à la constitution et au fonctionnement de ces ententes, notamment selon la mesure dans laquelle leurs dirigeants s'inspirent de l'intérêt général«.[23] Après que des propositions de contrôle international des ententes eussent été rejetées, la Conférence demanda que des études économiques et juridiques fussent entreprises par la SdN. Alors que le professeur Oualid, notamment, avait proposé d'obliger les cartels internationaux à se faire enregistrer auprès des services qualifiés de la SdN, la Conférence s'est contentée de faire valoir que l'un des moyens les plus efficaces pour empêcher les abus éventuels était de donner toute la publicité voulue à la nature et à l'activité des ententes. On reconnaissait aussi que, sur le terrain international, comme sur le plan national, les mesures d'interdiction pures et simples étaient impuissantes. Par la suite, conformément à la recommandation de la Conférence, la question des ententes est restée à l'ordre du jour du Comité économique et a fait l'objet de plusieurs études. On pourrait à cet égard tenter un parallèle avec l'attitude qui sera adoptée bien plus tard à l'ONU vis-à-vis des entreprises transnationales.

Comme en matière de politique douanière, le fait même que la SdN ait ainsi été saisie du problème des cartels et des trusts est significatif, puisque les ententes industrielles ne constituent pas une réalité étatique, mais des organisations privées. On s'achemine ainsi, en fait, sinon en doctrine vers une notion d'ordre public international, alors même, d'ailleurs, que l'on constate entre les deux guerres une tendance assez constante des conférences à défendre les intérêts des producteurs plutôt que ceux des consommateurs.[24] Quant à l'initiative des gouvernements en la matière, c'était, alors comme aujourd'hui, affaire de conjoncture. Ainsi, comme le note René Courtin dans l'important article précité, »en 1920, en période de sous-production, l'Italie consommatrice de charbon demanda la création, à son profit, d'un office international de répartition. En 1928, en période de surproduction, l'Angleterre, productrice, demande, toujours à son profit, la même mesure«.[25] On a pu récemment observer le même parallélisme à propos des principaux produits de base.

Sur un autre point, on découvre, par rapport à la situation actuelle, une certaine analogie: il s'agit de l'attitude de l'Union soviétique. La délégation de ce pays (qui comprenait entre autres l'économiste Varga) a pris une part très active à la Conférence et il importe de relever la déclaration de Grégoire Sokolnikoff:

»Les systèmes politiques et économiques de l'URSS et des pays capitalistes diffèrent profondément. Néanmoins, leur collaboration est parfaitement possible, comme l'a prouvé l'expérience des années passées . . . Une entente avec l'Union soviétique ouvrirait à l'industrie étrangère un marché durable, stable et solidement garanti . . . Le rétablissement des relations normales en matière de crédit peut donner, à bref délai, un élan aux importations à destination de l'URSS tout en renforçant ses exportations. L'Union soviétique donne aussi au capital étranger la possibilité de participer à la vie économique du pays sous forme de concessions. . . . Enfin, l'URSS a besoin de forces techniques que le monde capitaliste possède en quantité considérable.«[26]

La doctrine de la coexistence pacifique a donc été affirmée avec force pour la première fois à l'occasion de cette Conférence. Celle-ci a d'ailleurs adopté une résolution en ce sens:

»La Conférence, reconnaissant l'importance de la reprise du commerce mondial; s'abstenant entièrement de tout empiètement dans le domaine politique; considère la participation des membres de tous les pays présents – indépendamment de toute différence dans leurs systèmes économiques – comme un heureux présage en vue d'une coopération commerciale pacifique entre toutes les nations.«[27]

De l'autre côté, l'attitude du principal délégué des Etats-Unis, Henry M. Robinson, président de la First National Bank, était symptomatique aussi. Parlant au nom d'un »pays neuf«, il dit mal connaître les difficultés de l'Europe et avoir peu d'expérience des affaires mondiales[28].

La presse mondiale et les milieux économiques de tous bords avaient suivi la Conférence avec un intérêt extrême. Sur le moment, on avait pu avoir l'impression que la Conférence constituait en soi un événement de portée majeure, et cela pour trois séries de raisons: elle marquait l'entrée du facteur économique dans l'orbite des décisions politiques au sens large du terme; elle offrait la première tentative d'introduire dans la sphère de la coopération internationale une recherche déclarée de rationalité et de solidarité qui devait se substituer à l'arbitraire national et au chacun pour soi; elle devait être le point de départ d'une série d'initiatives concrètes et de travaux de longue haleine dont on pensait qu'ils finiraient par créer un climat propre à susciter de façon quasi continue la discussion, voire la négociation sur un vaste ensemble de sujets dont il aurait été désormais reconnu qu'ils étaient véritablement d'intérêt commun.

Comme le dira, lors de la séance de clôture, le président de la Conférence, »la Conférence économique doit être considérée non pas comme un événement isolé, mais comme une étape du travail continu de collaboration internationale dans le domaine économique, qui avait commencé avant que le projet d'une conférence générale eût été formulé et qui se prolongera après la fin de cette conférence . . . Nous pouvons être fiers de cet effort. Mais n'oublions point qu'il n'aura de sens que dans la mesure où nous serons persévérants . . . En contribuant à l'élaboration et à l'adoption des recommandations que nous avons établies, nous avons contracté un véritable engagement moral de propager, de défendre, de faire triompher les vérités que nous avons solennellement proclamées. Elles finiront par s'imposer, graduellement sans doute, par fragments«.[29]

En sens inverse, et très vite, on notera un jugement désabusé, marqué de déception, de la part de l'économiste suédois, Per Jacobson, qui appartenait alors au Secrétariat de la Société des Nations.

S'il est vrai qu'au cours de la session du Conseil de la SdN qui suivit la Conférence et de l'Assemblée de 1927, divers gouvernements annoncèrent expressément leur intention de s'inspirer de ces recommandations, il faut reconnaître que cet espoir allait être déçu. Tout au plus, peut-on enregistrer que, conformément à l'une des résolutions de la Conférence, le Conseil de la SdN institua en 1928 le Comité économique consultatif qui devait comprendre environ 70 membres représentant une grande diversité d'intérêts et dont certains devaient appartenir aux groupes travailleurs et employeurs du Conseil d'administration du Bureau international du travail. En réalité, la délégation française à la Conférence, notamment par la voix de Léon Jouhaux, préconisait la mise en place d'une organisation économique autonome dans le cadre de la SdN.

»1. Une Conférence consultative constituée par des membres nommés par les différents gouvernements en vertu de leur compétence dans les différentes branches de l'économie: finance, industrie, agriculture, commerce, travail, coopération, consommation, mais n'ayant reçu de ces gouvernements aucun mandat impératif.

La Conférence consultative se réunira périodiquement au moins une fois tous les trois ans. Elle indiquera à l'organisme exécutif, dont il sera parlé ci-dessous, les directives de son action au moyen de résolutions et de recommandations.

2. Un Conseil économique international, composé de 18 membres. Douze de ces membres seront désignés par le Conseil de la Société des Nations et devront représenter les diverses nationalités et les divers intérêts qui constituent l'économie du monde. Six de ces membres seront recrutés par le Conseil d'administration du Bureau international du travail, en proportion égale dans son groupe patronal et dans son groupe ouvrier.

3. Le Conseil économique international constituera tous les comités techniques nécessaires pour étudier les diverses questions de l'économie qui lui paraîtront susceptibles d'être mises tôt ou tard à l'ordre du jour des travaux de l'organisation. Il convoquera, sur avis de ses comités techniques, des conférences techniques particulières dont les membres seront désignés ou mandatés par les gouvernements et qui pourront établir des conventions internationales, portant sur les questions mises à l'ordre du jour par le Conseil économique international.

4. Le Conseil économique international aura sous sa direction un bureau ou secrétariat ayant à sa tête un directeur nommé par lui. Le Conseil et son bureau se tiendront en liaison étroite avec le Secrétariat de la Société des Nations et le Bureau international du travail. Ils se tiendront également en relations constantes d'information avec les conseils économiques nationaux déjà existants ou qui seront créés dans l'avenir.«[30]

En réalité, il faudra attendre le rapport de la Commission Bruce à la veille de la Deuxième Guerre mondiale, puis la Charte des Nations Unies, avec la création du Conseil économique et social et de ses organes subsidiaires, pour que ce projet prenne une forme concrète. A cet égard, il est permis de penser que certains au moins des protagonistes de la Conférence de 1927 étaient visiblement en avance sur leur temps. Dans une déclaration, les représentants des organisations de travailleurs signalent, mais sans en traiter, »le problème de la mise en valeur économique et des conditions de travail dans les territoires qui n'ont pas atteint leur plein développement, comme les pays sous mandat ou les territoires administrés comme colonies sous forme d'occupation ou de concession«.[31] Il est intéressant aussi de noter que l'un des représentants de l'Empire britannique, Arthur Pugh, vice-président des *Trade-Unions*, avait proposé que la Société des Nations »soit développée selon des principes à peu près analogues à ceux qui régissent l'Organisation internationale du travail. Il serait créé un Conseil économique auquel les Etats, les producteurs et les consommateurs seraient représentés. Ce Conseil examinerait les études et les rapports élaborés de temps à autre par le Secrétariat économique. Il formulerait la politique à suivre dans des conventions économiques internationales au moyen de recommandations«.[32] Au Conseil de la SdN, le représentant de l'Italie, Vittorio Scialoja, avait souligné fermement que la SdN devait »demeurer fondamentalement une organisation des Etats«.[33] Finalement, devant l'opposition vigoureuse à laquelle se sont heurtés les partisans de l'établissement d'un mécanisme institutionnel nouveau, la Conférence a dû se contenter d'un texte parfaitement anodin ainsi conçu: »En ce qui concerne la suite à donner à ses recommandations, la Conférence, sans présenter aucune suggestion quant à une organisation définitive, ne peut mieux faire que d'attirer l'attention du Conseil sur les conditions de composition et d'équilibre du Comité préparatoire qui ont déjà donné d'excellents résultats dans la préparation de la Conférence«.[34]

Après l'échec de la Conférence de Londres de 1933, aucune autre conférence économique générale ne fut plus convoquée jusqu'à la guerre. Faut-il, dans ces conditions, établir un procès-verbal de carence? Il ne semble pas.

Et cela, d'abord, pour deux raisons élémentaires. En premier lieu, un travail considérable, qui avait commencé dès le lendemain de la Conférence de Bruxelles, a été poursuivi, sur un autre plan et sous des formes plus modestes, assurément, mais avec une efficacité certaine. La recherche de solutions universelles et générales a cédé la place à des efforts plus délimités. Ce travail, jalonné par une série de conférences et de réunions spécialisées (consacrées aux statistiques, aux problèmes de transports, aux questions fiscales, à la nomenclature douanière, au logement, à l'hygiène et à la vie rurale, à la nutrition, etc.) a été l'œuvre des services techniques de la SdN, comme les questions de main-d'oeuvre ont continué d'être traitées par le BIT. A maints égards, ces travaux spéciaux ont une valeur plus grande et plus constructive que les conférences générales. En second lieu, et en tout état de cause, il est dangereux et illusoire d'attendre des conférences générales des résultats immédiats et concrets. Indépendamment de leur valeur de témoignage pour ce qui est de l'état d'esprit, sinon de l'opinion publique en général du moins de celui des dirigeants et des experts, elles servent surtout à des confrontations d'idées et à des prises de contact qui, en dernière analyse, ne peuvent manquer d'être fructueuses. Elles facilitent la prise de conscience des problèmes et des difficultés. Centres de propagande à large résonance, ce sont aussi (et l'on voudrait ajouter: surtout) d'utiles réunions d'enseignement mutuel. Quant à leur succès proprement dit, il convient de le mesurer à l'orientation que les débats et les recommandations de ces conférences sont susceptibles de donner, sous l'angle de la coopération, aux mesures d'ordre national et international prises par la suite, parfois sensiblement plus tard. C'est donc là un élément qu'il est souvent malaisé d'apprécier à sa juste valeur.

Au nombre des grandes idées perçues à l'époque comme radicalement neuves et mises en relief dans le rapport de la Conférence, adopté à l'unanimité avec les seules abstentions de l'URSS et de la Turquie, on peut citer:

»— Le commerce international constitue non pas une victoire ou une défaite des uns aux dépens des autres, mais l'assurance d'avantages réciproques pour les intéressés«.[35]

»— Le maintien de la paix du monde dépend, pour une large part, des principes sur lesquels sont basées les politiques économiques des diverses nations et dont elles sont l'application; les gouvernements et les peuples de tous les pays devraient constamment se consulter mutuellement quant à cet aspect du problème économique«.[36]

»— Les conflits économiques et les divergences d'intérêts économiques sont peut-être les plus sérieux et les plus permanents de tous les dangers qui sont susceptibles de menacer la paix du monde. On ne peut compter, en vue de maintenir la paix, sur aucun organisme pour le règlement des différends internationaux, si les politiques économiques du monde se développent de telle manière qu'il en résulte non seulement de profondes divergences d'intérêts économiques entre les divers groupes de la population mondiale, mais encore un sentiment de préjudice et d'injustice intolérables.«[37]

»– L'acceptation et l'application des principes contenus dans les résolutions de la Conférence, pour être couronnées de succès, dépendent non seulement de la bonne volonté des gouvernements et des administrations, mais aussi d'une opinion publique bien informée et favorable dans le monde entier; à cette fin, elle accueillerait avec satisfaction le développement d'une coopération internationale plus étroite de la part des institutions scientifiques et éducatives dans le domaine économique aussi bien que dans les autres domaines, ainsi que la collaboration de la presse et d'autres facteurs importants pour renseigner et éclairer l'opinion publique.«[38]

»– Considérant que le monde, dans son ensemble, continue à consacrer aux armements et à la préparation de la guerre des sommes considérables qui réduisent les disponibilités pour le développement de l'industrie, du commerce et de l'agriculture et constituent un lourd fardeau pour les finances des différents Etats, en entraînant de lourds impôts dont la répercussion se fait sentir sur l'ensemble de leur vie économique et abaisse leur niveau d'existence.

La Conférence exprime l'ardent espoir que tous les efforts – notamment ceux qui se poursuivent sous les auspices de la Société des Nations – tendant à réaliser, par des accords entre Etats, la limitation et la réduction des armements, seront couronnés de succès et pourront amener ainsi l'allégement des fardeaux ci-dessus rappelés.«[39]

Le président de la Conférence souligne dans son discours d'ouverture:

»– L'œuvre politique de la SdN ne serait rien si elle ne reposait sur une substructure économique appropriée. L'action politique et l'action économique (. . .) sont solidaires (. . .). L'interdépendance des intérêts est un fait.«[40] Il précisera la même idée à la clôture des travaux du Comité préparatoire: »Trop de gens croient encore que le domaine politique et le domaine économique sont entièrement différents; c'est là une erreur profonde et dangereuse, car toute grosse question économique est par le fait même, une question politique. A l'œuvre de paix politique et de désarmement doivent correspondre la paix et le désarmement économiques«[41]. Vérités d'évidence, penseront certains. Reconnaissons du moins aujourd'hui qu'il a fallu beaucoup de temps, depuis lors, pour qu'elles soient acceptées comme telles. Et ceci encore de G. Theunis à la clôture de la première session du Comité préparatoire de la Conférence, le ler mai 1926: »Il faudra montrer également qu'il est impossible, à l'heure actuelle, qu'une nation quelconque vive dans la prospérité si d'autres nations vivent dans l'indigence et le malaise.«[42]

Incontestablement, on attendait beaucoup et avec une conviction certaine de la SdN. Ainsi, Loucheur: »Genève deviendra, si elle ne l'est déjà en quelque sorte, le poste central des sonnettes d'alarme du monde. Il faudrait que nous y installions la sonnette d'alarme de la vie économique«, une sorte de poste d'informations et d'observations.[43]

Peut-être faut-il noter aussi l'intervention de la déléguée de l'Autriche, Mme Emmy Freundlich qui regrettait qu'un seul gouvernement ait compté une femme parmi ses délégués et qu'une seule femme ait siégé au Comité préparatoire. Et d'ajouter, plus d'un demi-siècle avant la récente Conférence de Copenhague:[44] »Les femmes constituent plus de la moitié du genre humain et nous devons leur laisser, dans toutes les décisions à prendre, la part qui leur revient«. Si elles étaient plus nombreuses à se faire entendre, il y aurait plus de solidarité.[45]

Le 16 juin 1927, intervenant en qualité de rapporteur pour les questions économiques devant le Conseil de la SdN, Stresemann n'avait pas hésité à qualifier la Conférence comme étant »l'une des plus remarquables et des plus fécondes qui aient jamais encore été convoquées par la SdN«. Il avait souligné aussi que les membres de la Conférence avaient représenté »à peu près toutes les compétences, tous les intérêts et toutes les opinions possibles«.[46] Il y a lieu de noter, en effet, que, dans nombre de délégations, l'éventail des partis politiques et des positions socio-économiques et idéologiques avait été très ouvert.

Les bilans établis peu après la Conférence font bien apparaître les espoirs point seulement rhétoriques qu'elle a suscités[47]. Peut-on dire aujourd'hui, pour autant, qu'elle a marqué vraiment une ère nouvelle des relations économiques internationales? Elle constitue à coup sûr un important jalon sur la route longue et difficile d'une action internationale concertée, comme instrument de prise de conscience, par sa valeur éducative et pédagogique et par le sens de la durée dont elle témoigne dans la mesure où elle refusait la tentation des solutions factices immédiates.

Notes

1 La date de clôture avait initialement été fixée au 21 mai, mais l'on s'était réservé la possibilité d'aller, en cas de besoin, jusqu'au 28.

2 Ce texte allait moins loin encore que le troisième des quatorze points du Président Wilson: »Suppression aussi complète que possible de toutes les barrières économiques et établissement de conditions commerciales égales pour toutes les nations consentant à assurer la paix du monde et s'associant pour son maintien«. Cf. W. E. Rappard, L'origine de la clause dite »de l'équitable traitement du commerce« dans le Pacte de la Société des Nations, dans *Mélanges d'économie politique et sociale offerts à M. Edgard Milhaud,* Paris P. U. F. 1934. – p. 276–295.

3 Quatrième et huitième alinéa du Préambule de la Charte, paragraphe 3 de l'article premier et chapitres IX et X, surtout articles 55 et 56.

4 Le Secrétariat de la Conférence fut dirigé par Jean Monnet, alors secrétaire général adjoint de la SdN.

5 Martin Hill, *The Economic and Financial Organization of the League of Nations,* Washington, Carnegie Endowment for International Peace, 1946, – p. 23.

6 Conférence financière internationale, Bruxelles, 1920. Comptes rendus de la Conférence, tome I. Rapport p. 11.

7 Il faut relire à ce sujet le cours professé à La Haye par William E. Rappard, »Le nationalisme économique et la Société des Nations«, *Recueil des cours de l'Académie de droit international,* 1937, tome 61, p. 97–252.

8 Ce point de vue a été exprimé surtout par le délégué du Canada, soutenu par les représentants des autres dominions britanniques.

9 Rappard, *op. cit.* (voir note no. 7), p. 167.

10 Eugène Grossmann, Methods of Economic Rapprochement. Geneva, 1926.; doc. SdN C.E.C.P. 24(1) 1926, II, 69.
11 Jacob Viner, Memorandum on Dumping, Geneva, 1926; doc. SdN, C.E.C.P. 36(1), 1926.II.63.
12 William Oualid, The Social Effects of International Industrial Agreements: The Protection of Workers and Consumers, Geneva, 1926; doc. SdN C.E.C.P. 94.
13 Gustav Cassel, Recent Monopolistic Tendencies in Industry and Trade: Being an Analysis of the Nature and Causes of the Poverty of Nations, Geneva, 1927, doc. SdN, C.E.P.C. 98 1927.II.36.
14 Actes de la Conférence économique internationale, doc. SdN C.356.M.129.1927.II., v. I. p. 110–113. (Ci-après: *Actes*)
15 *Actes*, p. 111.
16 *Ibid.*, p. 31.
17 *Ibid*, p. 132.
18 Les Etats européens représentés étaient: Albanie, Allemagne, Autriche, Belgique, Empire britannique, Bulgarie, Danemark, Ville libre de Dantzig, Estonie, Finlande, France, Grèce, Hongrie, Etat libre d'Irlande, Italie, Lettonie, Luxembourg, Norvège, Pays-Bas, Pologne, Portugal, Roumanie, Royaume des Serbes, Croates et Slovènes, Suède, Suisse, Tchécoslovaquie, Turquie et URSS.
19 *Actes*, p. 69.
20 Dans son discours, le délégué de la France, Louis Loucheur, avait également souligné l'importance de ce changement et noté que, malgré l'accroissement de puissance d'absorption du marché intérieur des Etats-Unis, »le producteur américain devient chaque jour plus exportateur: il ne peut l'être qu'aux dépens de l'Europe«. *Actes*, p. 138.
21 *Ibid.*, p. 112.
22 Cela par un triple effort: »Action individuelle des Etats sur leurs propres tarifs; action bilatérale, par la conclusion de traités de commerce appropriés; action collective, à l'aide d'une enquête tendant à encourager l'extension du commerce international sur une base équitable, en éliminant ou réduisant les barrières que des tarifs de douane excessifs opposent aux échanges internationaux.« *Actes*, p. 39.
23 *Ibid.*, p. 50.
24 René Courtin, »Essai sur l'organisation et l'activité économique de la Société des Nations«, *Revue d'économie politique*, v. 45, 1929, p. 1314.
25 *Ibid*, p. 1318.
26 *Actes*, p. 128–129.
27 *Ibid.*, p. 56.
28 *Ibid.*, p. 98–101.
29 *Ibid.*, p. 11–17.
30 *Ibid.*, p. 90–91.
31 *Ibid.*, p. 241.
32 *Ibid.*, p. 186.
33 Quarante-cinquième Session du Conseil, 16 juin 1927, SdN, *J.O.* p. 785.
34 *Actes*, p. 57.
35 *Ibid.*, p. 12.
36 *Ibid.*
37 *Ibid.*, p. 13.
38 *Ibid.*, p. 56.
39 *Ibid.*
40 *Ibid.*, p. 65–66.
41 *Ibid.*, p. 228.
42 *Ibid.*, p. 221.

43 *Ibid.*, p. 139.

44 »Conférence mondiale de la décennie des Nations Unies pour la Femme: Egalité, Développement et Paix«, juillet 1980.

45 *Actes*, p. 78.

46 Quarante-cinquième Session du Conseil, 16 juin 1927, SdN, *J.O.* p. 782 et 783.

47 *Cf. entre autres Elmer Hantos, Die Weltwirtschafts-Konferenz.* Probleme und Ergebnisse, Leipzig, G. A. Gloeckner, 1928. – 205 p. (à signaler la bibliographie considérable fournie dans cet ouvrage); *The Economic Consequences of the League. The World Economic Conference, with an Introduction by Sir Arthur Salter,* London, Europa Publishing Co., 1927. 235 p. *World Prosperity and Peace,* with an Introduction by F. C. Goodenough, London, P. S. King & Son, Ltd., 1928, 188 p.

The League of Nations and the refugees

Atle Grahl-Madsen
University of Bergen and Uppsala University

The drafters of the Covenant of the League of Nations were not entirely blind to the importance of social and economic conditions for the maintenance of international peace and security.

Article 23 of the Covenant sets forth, inter alia, that the Members of the League will endeavour to improve labour conditions, secure just treatment of the native inhabitants of territories under their control, entrust the League with general supervision over the execution of agreements with regard to the traffic in women and children and the traffic in opium and other dangerous drugs, and also will endeavour to take steps in matters of international concern for the prevention and control of disease.

But protection of and assistance to refugees are not included in this enumeration. One did not think of refugees in Versailles in 1919.

Yet one of the really pressing problems which arose in the wake of the First World War and the ensuing great revolutions, was the exodus of great masses of human beings seeking refuge in foreign countries. Around 800 000 fled from Russia alone, invading all the countries bordering on their homeland. Some also found their way to Western Europe.[1] For new and old States alike, with their war-devastated economies, this influx created a serious problem. The refugees were compelled to live in miserable conditions; their lack of recognizable identity papers being an added obstacle both to integration and resettlement.

The plight of the refugees was a challenge to the consciences of public-spirited persons in many countries. But by the end of 1920, it had become obvious that the task of assisting refugees was far beyond the capabilities of charitable organizations working on their own.

However, by the terms of Article 25 of the Convenant of the League of Nations, the Members of the League were pledged to co-operate with Red Cross organizations, having as their purposes the improvement of health, the prevention of disease, and the mitigation of suffering throughout the world.

This Article provided an opening.

It was therefore not by chance that Gustave Ador, President of the International Committee of the Red Cross (ICRC), after consultation with other important organizations, in a famous letter of 20 February 1921 appealed to the Council of the League of Nations; his premise was that the League was "the only supernational political authority capable of solving a problem which is beyond the power of exclusively humanitarian organizations".

In his letter, the Red Cross President proposed that the League should appoint a Commissioner for Russian Refugees; the Commissioner would provide a measure of protection for refugees at the same time as he would promote their repatriation, resettlement, or integration and co-ordinate the efforts already being undertaken for the material relief of the refugees.[2]

This was setting the torch to a burning matter. Already six days later, on 26 February 1921, the Council passed its first resolution on refugees.[3] Throughout the lifespan of the League questions relating to refugees were to become a recurrent theme on the agendas of the Council, and of the Assembly as well.

On 27 June 1921 the Council decided to convoke a Conference on the Question of Russian Refugees, and to authorize the President of the Council to appoint – "after obtaining the approval of his colleagues" – a High Commissioner for Russian Refugees.[4]

The Conference was convened at Geneva in August 1921. A few days later, Fridtjof Nansen, whose name was already mentioned in Gustave Ador's letter, accepted the appointment as High Commissioner. This meant another very important humanitarian task heaped on the Norwegian explorer, scientist, and statesman.

In April 1920 Nansen had reluctantly accepted to be the League's High Commissioner for the repatriation of prisoners of war. By early 1921 the bulk of this task had been performed, and upon completion of the work in the autumn of 1922, Nansen could report to the League of Nations that 430 000 prisoners of war had been brought back to their homelands at a minimal cost.[5]

Parallel with his task of repatriating prisoners of war, Nansen had involved himself in the efforts to bring food to the starving millions in the Soviet Union. Delegates of 48 voluntary agencies and 12 Governments met in Geneva on 15 and 16 August 1921, where they elected Nansen and his friend, Herbert Hoover (who subsequently became President of the United States 1929–33), High Commissioners for the relief action. Hoover, who shortly before had been appointed U.S. Secretary of Commerce, declined, but Nansen could not say no.

The Soviet authorities refused to enter into any agreement with the League of Nations or other international organizations, but they recognized Nansen, the humanitarian, and on 27 August 1921 two agreements were concluded between Georgij Čičerin, People's Commissar for Foreign Affairs of the Russian Socialist Federative Soviet Republic, and "Dr. Fridtjof Nansen, High Commissioner for Aid to Russia, appointed by the Geneva Conference". These agreements provided the framework for a relief operation of gigantic dimensions, lasting until the summer of 1923, which not only brought Nansen the Nobel Prize for Peace (in 1922) but, more important, saved millions of human lives.[6]

One can only marvel at how it was possible for one person to perform – almost simultaneously – three such momentous tasks. Nansen's courage and integrity, as well as his mental and physical strength, were legendary. His prestige was beyond comparison. Yet the funds and the means at his disposal were utterly meagre.

However, the fact remains that from the moment of his appointment, the name of Fridtjof Nansen was inextricably linked with the League of Nations' activities for refugees throughout the period of the League's existence. For almost nine years, until his death in 1930, Nansen was the League of Nations High Commissioner for Refugees. And after his death to honour his memory the office created to carry on the good work Nansen started was named after him: The Nansen International Office for Refugees, generally referred to as the Nansen Office. Moreover, one of the great legal inventions of the period carried his name, the 'Nansen passport', and refugees benefitting from it became known as 'Nansen refugees'. The post-World War II International Refugee Organization (IRO), in taking over refugees from the League of Nations referred to their national status simply as 'Nansen'.

By selecting Nansen for the post of High Commissioner for Russian Refugees, the League of Nations was assured of the highest degree of integrity, impartiality, initiative, and deep humanitarian concern in its refugee operation. All around, the humanitarian and non-political character of the High Commissioner's efforts was recognized. It is symptomatic that the same man who did his utmost to help Russian refugees could be elected an honorary member of the Soviet of the City of Moscow (January 1922), an honour which he declined in order to maintain his neutrality and impartiality, but which was nevertheless confirmed.[7]

Refugee law was no novelty in 1921. To make the point, it is sufficient to mention such highlights as the Edict of Potsdam of 1685, the numerous British Acts concerning the naturalization of 'Foreign Protestants' in the Colonies in America throughout the eighteenth century, and the French law concerning foreign refugees residing in France of 1832. But apart from the extradition treaties adopted since about 1830 and certain resolutions of the International Institute of International Law, the creation of an 'international refugee law' my be credited to the first High Commissioner for Refugees.

Fridtjof Nansen was a professor of zoology, later of oceanography, but he was no lawyer. And yet this man, used to snow and ice from his ski-treks across Greenland and the Polar ice-cap, started a legal avalanche.

The High Commissioner appointed representatives in many capitals, to keep in touch with Governments, but also with charitable organizations; and many Governments appointed officials to communicate directly with the High Commissioner.

In his capacity as organizer of the repatriation of prisoners of war and of Russian famine relief, Nansen even had a permanent representative in Moscow, through whom he could sound the possibilites for repatriation of Russian émigrés and for the guarantees required in that connexion.[8]

On 5 July 1922, an international Conference, called by the High Commissioner, adopted an "Arrangement with regard to the Issue of Certificates of Identity to Russian Refugees".[9] This Arrangement was eventually acceded to by 53 States. Thus, the 'Nansen passport' came into being.

How much of an innovation this was, is apparent from the fact that only five years later the Third General Conference on Communications and Transit adopted a Recommendation relating to Identity and Travelling Documents for Persons Without or of Doubtful Nationality;[10] the Recommendation signalled the inception of issuing passports to aliens.[11]

In 1924 the High Commissioner and his staff drafted a "Plan for the Issue of a Certificate of Identity to Armenian Refugees". No conference was called. The Plan was simply circulated to Governments and acceded to by 39 States.[12]

The Arrangement of 1922 and the Plan of 1924 were supplemented and amended by an Arrangement, dated 12 May 1926,[13] which in turn was supplemented by an Arrangement of 30 June 1928 to the categories of refugees to include Assyrian, Assyro-Chaldean, and Assimilated (Syrian and Kurdish) refugees, and Turkish refugees (the latter category being limited to a list of 150 persons named in the Protocol of Lausanne of 24 July 1923).[14] Thus, 'Nansen passports' became available to all these categories of refugees.

The arrangements of 1926 and 1928 were adopted by international conferences. The 1928 Conference also adopted a couple of other agreements, one concerning the functions of the representatives of the High Commissioner[15] (ratified by Belgium and France), and one relating to the legal status of Russian and Armenian refugees.[16]

The former laid the foundation for the unique set-up, still existing, whereby the High Commissioner's representative in Brussels determined the eligibility for refugee status and thereby, in fact, the question of asylum on behalf of the Belgian Government;[17] the agreement also defined the participation of the High Commissioner's representative in the French Office for the Protection of Refugees and Stateless Persons (OFPRA).[18]

The 1928 Arrangement relative to the Legal Status of Russian Refugees, apart from laying the foundation for the activities of the High Commissioner's representatives in different countries, contained provisions concerning the personal status of refugees; exemption from reciprocity, *cautio judicatum solvi*, and restrictions on foreign labour; expulsion; taxation; freedom of residence; and travel documents.[19] This Arrangement thus was a forerunner for the Refugee Conventions of 1933 and 1938, and consequently for the present Refugee Convention of 1951 and its 1967 Protocol.

The refugees could not be helped by legal measures alone. There were emergency situations in several of the countries bordering on the Soviet Union, and notably in Constantinople, where famine threatened. From the outset Nansen was faced with the need of finding funds for the maintenance of the refugees and offers for their resettlement in other countries. Apart from fund-raising, the High Commissioner enlisted the active assistance of voluntary organizations and some Governments, of which especially the British and the French Governments deserve to be mentioned.

The High Commissioner had to intervene with Governments to prevent expulsion of refugees until other solutions could be found. In the beginning Nansen hoped that the Russian refugees could return to their homeland, and some were actually repatriated, but by 1923 this scheme came to its definitive end.[20]

By this time Nansen had deleted the word 'Russian' from his title. He was now the straightforward 'High Commissioner for Refugees', for in the meantime the problem of Greek and Armenian refugees had arisen. The settlement of Greek refugees in Western Thrace and the exchange of Greeks from Turkey and Turks from Greece, involving some two million persons, were highlights of Nansen's and his colleagues' achievements in this area.[21]

Eventually the work for Greeks was taken over by another body under the authority of the League: the Greek Settlement Commission; and the work for Bulgarian refugees was also singled out and placed under a League Commissioner.[22]

By 1924 it was clear that the refugee problems could not be resolved as quickly as the task of repatriating prisoners of war. It was therefore decided to transfer the technical problems of employment, settlement, and migration to the International Labour Organisation (ILO). The High Commissioner's staff, headed by the Assistant High Commissioner, Major T. F. Johnson, was transferred from the League Secretariat to the ILO, here becoming the Refugee Service.[23]

Nansen remained High Commissioner, but his attention was increasingly absorbed by a scheme for resettling Armenian refugees in Erevan in Soviet Armenia.

The fate of the Armenian people was one of Nansen's major preoccupations during the last few years of his life, and the unwillingness of politicians to find a solution was one of his great disappointments: " Woe to the Armenian people! It had been better if its name had never been uttered by any European diplomat!" With these words Nansen expressed his bitterness.[24]

The financing of the refugee operations was a continuous problem. The League of Nations paid only for administrative expenses. For the ten years 1921–1930, the administrative budget totalled less than 2.8 million Swiss gold francs. So tight was the budget that it was even a problem to raise the 100 Swiss francs needed for the printing of the 1924 Plan to provide Armenian refugees with identity certificates.

The League assumed on the whole no responsibility for the funding of aid for refugees. Funds had to be solicited from Governments, voluntary organizations, and private individuals, largely on an ad hoc basis. The only regular, if modest, source of revenue were the five gold francs paid by the refugees (except the most destitute) for the Nansen stamp on their identity certificates. From 1926 up to 31 July 1930 the sale of Nansen stamps brought a total revenue of 406 775 gold francs.[25]

Encouraged by ILO's Director, Albert Thomas, the Refugee Service within the ILO did much towards the resettlement and integration of refugees, although the initial high hopes fell short of fulfilment. The dual allegiance of the staff, to ILO and to the High Commissioner, also created certain problems. By the end of 1929 it was found practical and opportune that the functions undertaken by the ILO should be transferred back to the High Commissioner.[26]

On 13 May 1930 Fridtjof Nansen died at the age of 68 years. It was an irreparable loss. The German cartoon magazine Simplicissimus wrote the perhaps most fitting epitaph: "Norwegen hat ihn geboren – die Menschheit hat ihn verloren." (Norway bore him – Mankind suffered his loss.)[27]

The League Assembly decided in 1930 to entrust the legal and political protection of refugees to the regular organs of the League. At the same time an autonomous Nansen International Office for Refugees was established to take charge of the humanitarian work for a limited period and scheduled to terminate by the end of 1938.

The Nansen Office was placed under the authority of the League in conformity with Article 24 of the League Convenant; the Article dealt with bureaux and commissions for the regulation of matters of international interest.

The Nansen Office began its work on 1 April 1931, with Dr. Max Huber, President of the ICRC, as its first President, and Major T. F. Johnson as Secretary-General.

Max Huber resigned for reasons of health in 1933. He was succeeded by Judge Georges Werner, Vice-Chairman of the ICRC. On his death in January 1935, the presidency was vacant for a year, until in January 1936 the Norwegian Judge Michael Hansson assumed the duties of President.[28]

The division between political and legal protection on one hand, and the humanitarian work on the other hand, could not be strictly maintained in practice. It was the Nansen Office, not the Secretariat of the League, which had representatives in different capitals and thus could intervene in specific cases.[29]

The Convention concerning the International Status of Refugees of 1933[30] was in fact largely prepared by the Nansen Office. This Convention, which was ratified by a handful of States only, created a legal status for those categories of refugees covered by the 'Nansen passport' arrangement of 1928.

Like the former High Commissioner, the Nansen Office had to operate on a shoestring budget. The administrative budget for the six years period of 1931–1936 totalled less than two million Swiss francs. The total receipts of the so-called Humanitarian Fund for this six year period amounted to 2.6 million Swiss francs. Within this total, the Nansen stamps contributed 875 000 francs, and the surcharged postage stamps sold in Norway and later also in France brought 72 000 francs. In addition there was a Near East Fund totalling 6.8 million francs. Even if the buying power of the Swiss franc was considerably greater than today, the need for economizing was striking.[31]

The Nansen Office had only been in operation for two years when political events in Germany gave rise to another refugee problem. Germany was still a member of the League, and this was probably the main reason why the Assembly in 1933 decided to vest responsibility for the new problem in an autonomous High Commissioner for Refugees coming from Germany, who had to report to a separate Governing Body rather than to the Council of the League.[32]

However, when as a result of the plebiscite which returned the Saar territory to Germany francophile persons and other opponents of the National Socialist regime fled the Saar territory, the League Assembly entrusted their protection and care in May 1935 to the Nansen Office, and not to the High Commissioner. The arrangement of 24 May 1935, extending the issuance of 'Nansen passports' to Saar refugees, was acceded to by seventeen States.[33]

It soon became clear to the then High Commissioner, the American James G. McDonald, that he was left out in the cold. He had managed to achieve a good deal but the German refugee problem could not be tackled solely by relief measures: without a closer link to the League, the High Commissioner found that he could not command sufficient authority vis-à-vis Governments.

A proposal by the Foreign Minister in Norway's new Labour Government, Professor Halvdan Koht, that the League should create a central organization with responsibility for all refugees, whatever their origin, was met with singularly little enthusiasm in the 1935 Assembly.[34]

Consequently, several categories of refugees remained without League protection; notably refugees from the Fascist regime in Italy and from other dictatorial regimes established in European countries.[35]

Mr. McDonald was left to strive as best he could, and in December 1935 he resigned. His letter of resignation remains an important public document clearly illuminating the situation.[36]

In October 1935 Germany left the League; when early in 1936 Sir Neill Malcolm was appointed High Commissioner for Refugees, his status was very similar to that of the first High Commissioner in the nineteen-twenties.[37]

As the German refugees were neither covered by the previous Arrangements nor the 1933 Convention, they could at first only get aliens' passports in conformity with the Recommendation of the Communications and Transit Conference of 1927. But in 1936 a Provisional Arrangement concerning identity and travel documents for German refugees was adopted,[38] and this was followed by a Convention relating to the Status of Refugees coming from Germany in 1938.[39]

By Council resolutions in 1938 and 1939 and Additional Protocols of 7 July and 14 September 1939, the benefits of the 1936 Arrangement and the 1938 Convention were extended to refugees coming from "the territory which formerly constituted Austria"[40] and from Sudentenland (the German-speaking part of Czechoslovakia annexed by Germany).[41]

The Assembly concerned itself with other refugee questions as well. In annual resolutions it complained about the practice of certain States punishing refugees for illegal entry and residence, and pushing them across frontiers into neighbouring countries, where history repeated itself. Only in 1937 could the Assembly note, with some satisfaction, a certain improvement of this unworthy situation.[42]

In accordance with an Assembly decision of 1931, the Nansen Office was to close down by the end of 1938. In September of that year, the Assembly decided to merge the Nansen Office and the Office of the High Commissioner for German Refugees under a single 'High Commissioner for Refugees under the Protection of the League of Nations', with a mandate for five years. Sir Herbert Emerson was appointed High Commissioner with effect from 1 January 1939. He was to be responsible for the Russian, Armenian, Saar, and German refugees, interpreting this to comprise also refugees from Austria and the Sudetenland.[43]

The work of the League suffered from the fact that the United States of America was not a Member. This shortcoming came fully into the open as the refugee-producing effects of the Nazi take-over in Germany were faced. On the initiative of President Franklin D. Roosevelt, an important meeting took place in Evian, France, in July 1938. The outcome of this meeting was the creation of an Intergovernmental Committee on Refugees (IGCR) with headquarters in London, with the purpose of aiding potential and actual refugees from Germany (including Austria). Twenty-seven States were represented on the Committee from the beginning.[44]

An American, Mr. George Rublee, was appointed Director of the Committee's permanent secretariat. The idea was that he, not connected with the League, could negotiate with the German Government in order to secure an orderly emigration of persons unwanted in the Third *Reich*. However, increasing international tension, culminating in the outbreak of the war, ruled out this possibility. Mr. Rublee resigned in February 1939, and Sir Herbert Emerson, the League's High Commissioner, also became Director of the IGCR.

The war spelt the virtual end of the League of Nations. Therefore, the IGCR became the more important instrument for aid to refugees during the war years. The Committee was able to assist some thousand refugees from German and German-occupied territories and bring them to safety. In 1943 the mandate and the membership of the Committee were broadened; and as parts of Europe were liberated in 1944, the Committee found its place beside the Allied armed forces and the United Nations Relief and Rehabilitation Administration (UNRRA), and it assumed the task of protecting and assisting refugees in liberated territories.[45] But that is another story.[46]

By 1946 there were still about a quarter of a million Russian, Armenian, Assyrian, and Saar refugees demanding international care; and also some 110 000 German refugees and 212 000 Spanish refugees who were the concern of the IGCR.[47]

The work of the League of Nations High Commissioner for Refugees was terminated on 31 December 1946. Responsibility for the remaining Russian, Armenian, Assyrian, and Saar refugees was formally assumed by the IGCR until 1 July 1947, when the Preparatory Commission for the International Refugee Organization (PCIRO) could commence operations; PCIRO took over not only IGCR activities, but also the responsibility for the great number of people uprooted by the war, the so-called displaced persons, who until 30 June 1947 had been in the care of UNRRA.[48]

The refugee work of the League of Nations stretched over almost twenty-six years. It covered a period of fateful events in European and world history; marked by uneasy recovery, unfulfilled hopes, disenchantment with the new world 'fit for heroes'; economic crash, mass unemployment; the rise of dictatorial regimes in important countries such as Russia, Italy, and Germany; collapse of the idea of collective security, and finally, frantic rearmament leading up to the most devastating war in world history so far.

The refugee work falls into three distinct phases of about equal length.

The formative first phase of 8½ years was marked by Fridtjof Nansen as High Commissioner (1921–1930) and by the Refugee Service within the ILO (1925–1929). It was a period of great disasters, deep emotions, *ad hoc* solutions, but also a period of relative optimism. There was hope, perhaps against reason, that the refugee problem could be solved or that at least it would fade away within a relatively short time; but the hope dwindled towards the end of the decade of the twenties.

The second phase covered the lifespan of the Nansen International Office for

Refugees (1931–1938) and of the Office of the High Commissioner for Refugees coming from Germany (1933–1938). The refugee organization had gained a new lease of life, but there was an expressed will on the part of the politicians in the League to keep at a safe distance the embarassing questions posed by the presence of refugees and to terminate such work within a reasonable time.

The third phase commenced with the creation (outside the League) of the Intergovernmental Committee on Refugees (1938–1947) and the establishment of the single High Commissioner for Refugees under the protection of the League of Nations (1939–1946). It was a period characterized by the decline of the League, increased international tension, rearmament, and finally war. The new organs were born out of the realization that it had not been possible to achieve the complete integration of the 'Nansen refugees', and that the new regime established in the midst of Europe had given rise to a new refugee problem of unassessable proportions.

In trying to characterize the League of Nations' effort in caring for refugees, one may revert to the main principles laid down expressly or tacitly on Fridtjof Nansen's appointment in 1921. As summarized by Sir John Hope Simpson these principles were:

(a) The League had accepted responsibility for political and legal protection of certain classes of refugees; at no time had suggestions for the extension of League protection to all classes of refugees been officially encouraged.

(b) League intervention was on a temporary basis;

(c) League funds might be used for the administrative expenses of the Central Office and in some cases for local offices;

(d) League organizations were expected to co-ordinate relief and settlement efforts, but League funds for such purposes might not be spent.[49]

These principles held good for the entire League period. But if the official involvement of the League was half-hearted, the selfless enthusiasm and compassion of certain individuals in leading positions turned the operation into one of importance and consequence . . . not only for the hundreds of thousands of fellow men, women, and children directly affected, but also for posterity, since the endeavour created an international humanitarian model of proven worth.

If mention is made of those who gave inspiration and leadership to the refugee effort, men of six nations come to mind: the Swiss Gustave Ador, Max Huber, and Georges Werner; the Norwegians Fridtjof Nansen and Michael Hansson; the British Lord Robert Cecil, Gilbert Murray, Sir Philip Noel-Baker, Sir Samuel Hoare, Thomas Frank Johnson, Sir Neill Malcolm, and Sir Herbert Emerson; the Frenchman Albert Thomas; the Belgian Paul Hymans; the Americans James G. McDonald, Myron Taylor, George Rublee, and last, but not least, Franklin Delano Roosevelt – although the three last-mentioned were not officially linked to the League, they must not be forgotten in any account of the refugee work throughout the period between the two World Wars.[50] One refugee should also be mentioned, namely Maître J. Rubinstein, for he played a decisive role first in the preparation of the 1928 Arrangements and subsequently preparing the first Refugee Convention; he also became a member of the Governing Body of the Nansen Office.[51] The fact that some are named, however, detracts nothing from the efforts and achievements of all the others whose names cannot be mentioned but who made the refugee work possible.

It cannot be emphasized strongly enough that voluntary organizations and generous donors of many nations played a vital part. In fact, when it came to material assistance, the organs of the League of Nations could only assume a planning and co-ordinating role: they were totally dependent on outside financing and on others doing the actual work in the field.[52]

Last but not least, let us remember that refugees themselves contributed to the solution of the problems, by taking part in the work of organizations large and small, down to the purchase of the Nansen stamp affixed to their certificates of identity.

The League of Nations never promised the refugees very much, but thanks to the whole-hearted efforts of its servants and other individuals, it more than kept its pledge.

Notes

1 Cf. John Hope Simpson, *The Refugee Problem.* Report of a Survey, London, Oxford University Press, 1939. – p. 62, in particular p. 82.
2 LoN, Minutes of the Thirteenth Session of the Council, June 1921, Annex 218, *OJ.* p. 227.
3 LoN, Minutes of the Twelfth Session of the Council, Febr. 1921, *OJ.* p. 19, Annex 168, p. 117.
4 LoN, Minutes of the Thirteenth Session of the Council, June 1921, *OJ.* p. 53.
5 Tim Greve, *Fridtjof Nansen. 1905–1930.* Oslo, Gyldendal, 1974. – p. 148; E. E. Reynolds, *Nansen,* Hammondsworth, Penguin Books, 1949. – p. 215.
6 Greve, *op. cit.*, p. 165.
7 *Ibid.*, p. 175.
8 Simpson, *op. cit.*, p. 200.
9 LoN, Treaty Series, v. 13, p. 237.
10 2 September 1927, LoN doc. C.558(b).M.200(b).1927.VIII, p. 57, cf. p. 33 and 62.
11 Cf. also LoN. Passport Conference (Geneva, 12 to 18 May 1926). Final Act of the Conference, 18 May 1926, *OJ.* p. 1088.
12 LoN doc. C.L. 72 (a). 1924.
13 LoN, Treaty Series, v. 89, p. 47.
14 LoN, Treaty Series, v. 36, p. 145; see also Atle Grahl-Madsen, *The Status of Refugees in International Law, vol. I: Refugee Character,* Leiden, Sijthoff, 1966. – p. 129.
15 LoN, Treaty Series, v. 93, p. 377.
16 LoN, Treaty Series, v. 89, p. 53.
17 Grahl-Madsen, *op. cit.*, p. 343.
18 *Ibid.*, p. 345.
19 Text and preparatory work to be found in LoN publication 1930.XIII.1.
20 Louise W. Holborn, "The League of Nations and the Refugee Problem", *The Annals of the American Academy of Political and Social Science* (hereafter: AAAPSS) 203, May 1939, p. 129.
21 Simpson, *op. cit.*, p. 11 ff. and 202.
22 Paul Frings, *Das internationale Flüchtlingsproblem 1919–1950,* Frankfurt am Main, Verlag der Frankfurter Hefte, 1951. – p. 27 and 29; Werner von Schmieden, Die

Flüchtlingshilfe des Völkerbundes. *Handbuch des internationalen Flüchtlingsrechts,* Wien, Braumüller, 1960. – (Abhandlungen zu Flüchtlingsfragen, Band I), p. 235 and 238.

23 Simpson, *op. cit.*, p. 197 and 203.

24 Liv Nansen Høyer, *Nansen og verden,* Oslo, Cappelen, 1955. – p. 280 ff.; Reynolds, *op. cit.*, p. 247.

25 Simpson, *op. cit.*, p. 209.

26 Holborn, *AAAPSS* p. 130; Simpson, *op. cit.*, p. 206.

27 *Simplicissimus,* 9 June 1930: Drawing by Olaf Gulbrandsson. Facsimile in Jon Sørensen, *Friedtjof Nansen saga,* Oslo, Dybwad, 1931. – p. 339.

28 Frings, *op. cit.*, p. 30; Holborn, *Annals,* p. 131; von Schmieden, *op. cit.*, p. 223; Simpson, *op. cit.*, p. 207 ff.

29 Simpson, *op. cit.*, p. 211.

30 LoN, Treaty Series, v. 159, p. 199.

31 von Schmieden, *op. cit.*, p. 225; Simpson, *op. cit.*, p. 212 f.

32 von Schmieden, *op. cit.*, p. 239 ff.; Simpson, *op. cit.*, p. 214.

33 LoN, Minutes of Eighty-Sixth Session of the Council, 24 May 1935, *OJ.* p. 633; cf. Simpson, *op. cit.*, p. 211.

34 Simpson, *op. cit.*, p. 216.

35 Holborn, *AAAPSS,* p. 135.

36 LoN doc. C.13.M.12.1936.XII – Annex; cf. von Schmieden, *op. cit.*, 240; Simpson, *op. cit.*, p. 217 f.

37 Holborn, *AAAPSS,* p. 133; Simpson, *op. cit.*, p. 217 f.

38 LoN, Treaty Series, v. 171, p. 75.

39 LoN, Treaty Series, v. 192, p. 59.

40 This is the wording found in the Protocol, 9 September 1939, in LoN, Treaty Series. v. 198, p. 141.

41 Grahl-Madsen, *op. cit.*, p. 131 ff. p. 135.

42 Simpson, *op. cit.*, p. 246 ff.

43 Louise W. Holborn, *The International Refugee Organization: A Specialized Agency of the United Nations, Its History and Work, 1946–1952* (hereafter: IRO) London, Oxford University Press, 1956. – p. 9; von Schmieden, *op. cit.*, p. 242 ff.

44 Frings, *op. cit.*, p. 44 ff.; Holborn, IRO, p. 11; Simpson, *op. cit.*, p. 223 ff.

45 Holborn, IRO, p. 12 ff. and p. 215 ff.

46 The IGCR sponsored the conference which adopted the London Agreement relating to the Issue of a Travel Document to Refugees who were the concern of the Intergovernmental Committee on Refugees, 1946 (United Nations, Treaty Series, v. 11, p. 73).

47 Holborn, IRO, p. 198.

48 *Ibid.*, p. 15 ff.

49 Simpson, *op. cit.*, p. 192.

50 Holborn, IRO, p. 9.

51 Michael Hansson, *Flyktningsproblemet og Folkeforbundet.* Foredrag i Nobelinstituttet, Oslo, 7 januar 1937, Oslo, Cammermeyer, 1938, p. 26; LoN publication 1930.XIII.1, p. 7.

52 Frings, *op. cit.*, p. 88 ff.; Simpson, *op. cit.* p. 172 ff.

Minorities and the League of Nations

RICHARD VEATCH
University of Winnipeg, Manitoba, Canada

On 13 February 1920 the Council of the League of Nations adopted a resolution placing under the guarantee of the League the provisions of a treaty of 28 June 1919, between Poland and the Principal Allied and Associated Powers, "so far as they affect persons belonging to racial, religious or linguistic minorities".[1] The following October the Council adopted the procedural resolutions necessary for the implementation of this guarantee, recognizing a right of petition to the League "with regard to an infraction or danger of infraction" of the minorities provisions, a right which had not been mentioned in the treaty, and providing for consideration of petitions by three-member minorities committees of the Council.[2] Thus began an experiment in the international protection of minorities, which was eventually extended to fifteen States and which lasted for some twenty years, until the final meeting of the League Council in December 1939.

Normally, under international law, questions regarding the rights of minorities within a State's own population had been within the exclusive jurisdiction of that State. There had already been some deviations from that principle in the nineteenth century, with regard to the new States in the Balkans, but no international enforcement machinery had been set up.[3] Beginning at the Paris Peace Conference, those same States plus other eastern European States were obliged by the major Powers to become parties to new treaties bringing their treatment of minorities under a degree of international supervision. The treaties had, in effect, been imposed on these States following defeat in the World War, or as a condition of receiving additions to territory or recognition of independence. By 1924 minorities treaties or agreements were in effect with regard to thirteen States (Albania, Austria, Bulgaria, Czechoslovakia, Estonia, Greece, Hungary, Latvia, Lithuania, Poland, Romania, Turkey and Yugoslavia), plus the Upper Silesian province of Germany, in each case placing them under the guarantee of the League of Nations, with procedures which included a right of individual petition. The only subsequent addition to the system came in 1932, when at the time it achieved independence Iraq became a party to a minorities agreement.[4]

One striking, and much criticized, feature of the minorities protection system was its limited applicability, essentially to the eastern European States. This was officially explained and defended by the French premier Clemenceau, as president of the Peace Conference, in a 24 June 1919 letter to Polish premier Paderewski, asserting that conditions peculiar to eastern Europe justified the minorities guarantees: "The situation with which the Powers have now to deal is new, and experience has shown that new provisions are necessary. The territories now being transferred both to Poland and to other States inevitably include a large population, speaking languages and belonging to races different from that of the people with whom they will be incorporated. Unfortunately, the races have been estranged by long years of bitter hostility. It is believed that these populations will be more easily reconciled to their new position if they know that from the very beginning they have assured protection and adequate guarantees against any danger of unjust treatment or oppression."[5]

In effect, special protective measures for the minorities in eastern Europe were claimed to be justified for reasons that were primarily political, rather than humanitarian. If the minorities were treated in an unjust and oppressive manner, new political crises and conflicts could be expected, threatening to engulf all States in yet another war. If, on the other hand, they were treated fairly and humanly, they could be expected to become reconciled to the new political situation and an explosion could be avoided.

Whatever merits this argument might have, many, at least, of the States on whom minorities obligations were imposed bitterly resented being singled out for this purpose. Nevertheless, there was no intent, so far as the major Powers were concerned, to establish a universally applicable minority protection system, or one which was applicable to themselves. In contrast, the obligations of the eastern European States were of indefinite duration (except for German Upper Silesia, where a 15-year transitional arrangement was to expire in 1937).

The provisions of the Polish treaty, and of the subsequent treaties and agreements for which it served as a model, were applicable to all nationals of the State concerned who belonged to 'racial, religious or lingustic minorities'. No additional definition was given of what constituted a minority. The term 'race' was used, in effect, as a synonym for ethnic group (e.g., German race or Polish race). As such groups were normally identifiable through differences in either language or religion, in practice the two latter criteria served as a basis for identifying a minority. There was, therefore, rarely any difficulty in determining whether any given individual or group was or was not part of a protected minority.

One controversy which did arise was over whether a minority "must belong to the country . . . by origin", and "must be sufficiently numerous to constitute an appreciable percentage of the countrys's population", in order to be eligible for protection by the League. Lithuania contended that both questions should be answered affirmatively, in contesting in 1928 the receivability of a petition from twenty-one persons of Ukrainian origin, resident in Lithuania for some sixteen to eighteen years, claiming discriminatory treatment in the expropriation of land. The Council rapporteur rejected Lithuania's claims, on the grounds that no such criteria were found in its minorities declaration, and the Council found the petition receivable.[6]

The only other substantial problem to arise as to the existence or nonexistence of a minority had to do with a series of petitions, dealt with by minorities committees from 1924 to 1933, from or on behalf of an alleged Bulgarian minority in Yugoslav Macedonia. Yugoslavia persistently denied the existence of any such minority, claiming that the inhabitants of Macedonia, even though their language might differ from standard Serbo-Croat, were all 'south Slavs' and therefore part of the Yugoslav majority, and ineligible for treatment by the League as a minority. It would appear that Council members were sympathetic toward Yugoslavia's claim, but unwilling to accept in principle that a Bulgarian minority in Yugoslavia was impossible. Through the years, the various minorities committees considering these petitions successfully evaded giving an answer to the basic question of the existence of the alleged minority, always finding some other reason for rejecting the petitions without taking them to the Council for a public airing.

The rights protected by the minorities treaties were defined in sweeping and unequivocal terms. In general, they required the States concerned to give their nationals equal civil and political rights, without distinction as to race, language, or religion. In addition to individual rights, group rights were also protected, whereby minorities would be able to maintain their own religious, social and educational institutions, and to receive an equitable share of state funds provided for such activites.

In addition, individual minorities treaties often contained provisions peculiar to the State concerned. For example, the Czechoslovak treaty provided for an autonomous local government for the Ruthene (Ukrainian) province of that country; the Greek treaty provided for maintenance of the traditional rights of the non-Greek monastic communities of Mount Athos; many provisions of the Turkish treaty applied to non-Moslem minorities only.[7]

The treaties notably did not contain guarantees of 'human rights' as such, applicable to all individuals, whether members of the majority or of the minority. Thus they provided no guarantees against repressive actions by Governments, unless directed in a discriminatory way against members of a minority. This was brought out clearly, for example, in action by a minorites committee of the Council in considering a petition on behalf of the White Russian minority in Poland, alleging abuses and irregularities in connection with the Polish elections of 1930. It was clear, in fact, that these elections had been held in an atmosphere of repression and intimidation directed at suspected opponents of the Government in power. The Minorities Committee (France, Norway and Yugoslavia) decided at its first meeting on the petition not to pursue the matter, reporting to the Council that it "did not find that the electoral irregularities in question were of a character specifically connected with minorities, . . .; it had the impression rather that the facts in question occured in connection with the general political life of the country".[8]

Only in the case of more extreme abuses were the Council members prepared to deviate from this approach, and apply to the treatment of minorities a rule comparable to the 'minimum civilized standard' prescribed by international law for the treatment of foreign nationals. Thus, in closing its consideration in 1933 of petitions alleging brutality towards Ukrainian prisoners in Polish jails, a Minorities Committee (France, Norway and Spain) rejected any contention that it could only review the petitions "from the standpoint of equality of treatment between members of the minority and the majority", maintained that the applicable treaty provisions "confirm obligations under natural law", and reported to the Council that Poland and the committee agreed that the beating of prisoners was "an illegal and barbarous act", for which the guilty persons must be punished.[9]

Except in cases where it could be reasonably asserted that minority rights, as such, were not involved, attempts to obtain restrictive legal interpretations of the minorities treaties regularly failed. This was true of four advisory opinions provided to the Council (three regarding Poland and one regarding Albania), and of one judgement in a contested case (brought by Germany against Poland), by the Permanent Court of International Justice.[10] It was also true, without exception, with regard to the advice provided to the Council by ad hoc committees of jurists, to which legal questions regarding the interpretation of the treaties were referred on eight occasions between 1922 and 1934.

In short, the treaties provided strong protection for minority rights, if carried out in practice. What became critically important, then, was the willingness of the States concerned to carry them out, and the effectiveness of the international supervision provided by the Council of the League.

The main lines of the Council's procedure, as established in October 1920, continued throughout the twenty-year period that the minorities protection system was in effect. Petitions claiming an infraction, or danger of infraction, of one of the treaties, were accepted from any source, from within or without the state concerned, and not limited to persons or groups whose own rights had allegedly been violated. Receivability of a petition was initially determined by the Minorities Section of the League Secretariat. If the State concerned challenged a Secretariat decision that a petition was receivable, that decision was referred to the Council president, who usually named two additional Council members to assist him in the review. If the State was unwilling to accept the Council president's decision, it could take the question of receivability to the full Council for a public review and decision. This was done only once, by Lithuania in circumstances already described. The decision as to receivability involved, essentially, determining whether the petition contained allegations which, if true, would constitute a treaty violation. The only other grounds for finding a petition not receivable were the advocacy of political separation of the minority from its State, submission by an anonymous or unauthenticated source, the use of violent language, or duplication of complaints recently acted on.[11]

The criteria for receivability were not particularly difficult to meet, and in practice the League Secretariat and Council were not restrictive in their application of the criteria. Approximately 55 per cent of all petitions were found to be receivable,[12] an unusually high proportion for this type of procedure.[13]

When a petititon had been found receivable, it was sent to the Government complained against, for any observations the Government might wish to make. Observations were almost always provided, a period of two months being allowed to the Government concerned for that purpose. The petition and the Government's observations were then circulated to all members of the Council. Originally these documents were distributed to all League Members, but after receiving strong objections from Poland and Czechoslovakia, the Council decided in 1923 that distribution would be limited to Council members.[14] In urgent circumstances, as determined by the League Secretary-General, petitions could be distributed to Council members immediately, without waiting for the Government's observations.

The information thus obtained from petitioner and Government did not mark the beginning of a legal process to which they were parties. Instead, the petitioner officially disappeared from the scene at this point. There was normally no further official communication with a petitioner after the decision on receivability was made, and statements made in the petition were viewed as simply being for the information of Council members.

Under the various minorities treaties, each Council member had the right to bring to the Council's attention, i.e., to place on its agenda, any actual or threatened treaty violation. The Council then had full authority to take any necessary action. However, it could not consider alleged infractions until one or more members had placed the matter on its agenda. This was no doubt an unwelcome reponsibility, so far as most individual Council members were concerned, as it required some Council member to accept the role of accuser. A way out was found, from the very beginning through the procedure of referring each receivable petition, together with the Government's observations, to a three-member Minorities Committee, consisting of the Council chairman (a position rotated among all members) and two other members named by him. This 'Committee of Three' with the assistance of the Minorities Section of the Secretariat, reviewed the petition during the next regular Council session and decided what to do about it. If ultimately it decided to place the matter on the Council's agenda, there was a certain safety in numbers, and a strictly bilateral dispute could be avoided with the State whose actions were being criticized.

Even then, the placing of a minorities complaint on the Council's agenda, where it would be discussed and dealt with publicly, took place very infrequently. Altogether only fourteen minorities questions were referred to the Council by minorities committees, out of a total of about 325 taken up by the committees.[15]

Besides referral by minorities committees, there were two other ways whereby alleged violations of the minorities treaties could be placed on the Council agenda. One was the placing of the question on the agenda by an individual Council member, bypassing the review by a Committee of Three, a right which all Council members had under the minorities treaties. This was done on three occasions, each time by Germany, in the years 1929 to 1932, with regard to alleged violations by Poland of the rights of its German minority. A second possible procedure, available to all Members of the League, instead of to Council members only, was to place an alleged violation on the Council agenda under Article 11 of the League Covenant, which authorized such action with regard to "any circumstance whatever affecting international relations which threatens to disturb international peace or the good understanding between nations upon which peace depends". This was done several times between 1924 and 1928, notably by Lithuania, with regard to Poland's treatment of its Lithuanian minority, and by Albania, concerning Greece's actions toward its Albanian minority. Use of this tactic made it possible for any and all League Members to evade the normal procedure, and to present minorities problems in the form of a dispute between two States, which the normal procedure was specifically intended to avoid. The Council therefore, in 1928, on the occasion of a second Albanian complaint against Greece under Article 11, refused to accept that complaint, concluding that the minorities protection system was "intended not only to prevent that questions concerning the protection of minorities should acquire the character of a dispute between nations but to ensure that States with a minority within their borders should be protected from the danger of interference by other Powers in their internal affairs". Article 11, the Council said, should only be invoked in grave cases involving a menace to the maintenance of peace. All other minorities cases should follow the normal procedure.[16] From that time on, no minorities complaints reached the Council under Article 11.

When, through one means or another, the question of an actual or threatened infraction of a minorities treaty came before the full Council, the Council's powers were theoretically quite extensive, the treaties empowering the Council to "take such action and give such direction as it may deem proper and effective in the circumstances".[17] This power was modified, however, by the right of the State complained against to sit as a member of the Council, with the right to vote, when a complaint against it was being discussed, and by the requirement for unanimity in any vote taken.[18] In other words, there was no possibility of adopting, by vote of the Council, a decision which was unacceptable to the State complained against. The process before the Council was, instead, one of negotiation and pressure, aimed at finding some mutually satisfactory solution, just as it had been at the committee stage.

There remained one possibility of obtaining a legally binding decision regarding an alleged violation of a minorities treaty, without having to have the approval of the State complained against. This was through the exercise of the right of any Council member, provided for in the minorities treaties, to take to the Permanent Court of International Justice any dispute regarding the application of the treaties. Three such cases were filed with the Court, all by Germany against Poland, but only one was pursued to a conclusion, the other two being withdrawn by Germany at the time of its withdrawal from League membership in 1933.

The only major exception to the above procedures was with regard to minorities complaints from Polish or German Upper Silesia. Special treaty arrangements in effect from 1922 to 1937 provided two alternative procedures: a local procedure, whereby minorities petitions were submitted for an advisory opinion to the President of an Upper Silesian Mixed Commission (Felix Calonder, a former Swiss federal councillor), subject to appeal to the Council if the petitioner was not satisfied with the action then taken by the Government; and a right of direct petition to the Council, without using the local procedure. Altogether about seventy Upper Silesian minorities questions reached the Council's agenda through one or the other of these procedures, far more than it received from all other sources. Some were of major importance, but many were relatively trivial;

in either case, they went directly to the full Council, without any preliminary screening by a committee.

The main work in the League's review of minorities petitions was done, however, not by the Council itself but by its minorities committees, assisted by the Minorities Section of the Secretariat. The work of the committees was done in private. No official committee minutes were kept, and only after 1929 did the committees make formal reports to the Council on the conclusions which they reached, except in those rare cases when a petition was referred to the full Council. The absence of publicity regarding the work of the committees led to the widespread impression that nothing was being done. "The public knew nothing of the work of the Committees of Three and the belief was current that petitions sent to the League were simply shelved", according to Secretary-General Sir Eric Drummond.[19] In fact, that was far from being the case. Unofficial minutes of the Minorities Committee meetings, prepared by the Minorities Section for its own use, and available for the years 1923–1932, indicate that only about 35 per cent of the complaints referred to the Minorities Committees were disposed of by a decision of the Committee at its first meeting not to pursue the matter further.[20] In the great majority of cases, the Committee began instead a dialogue with the Government concerned, seeking additional information as to the merits of the complaint, and often seeking to obtain from the Government agreement to reverse policies adopted or actions taken, or to pay compensation for damages done.

As might be expected, there was the greatest possible variation in the degree of success achieved in these Committee endeavors, depending in part on the degree of cooperation extended by the Government concerned. There was also a great variation in the frequency and seriousness of complaints, from one State to another. In general, the States subject to the League's minorities protection system may be categorized as follows:

(a) *States whose actions produced virtually no complaints: Austria, Bulgaria, Estonia, Latvia.* Austria and Bulgaria, after their wartime defeat and territorial losses, contained little in the way of linguistic or religious minorities. Minorities Committees dealt with one petition each regarding Estonia and Latvia, protesting against the application of agrarian reform, but there appear to have been no other receivable complaints against those two States.

(b) *States whose actions produced complaints, but were almost entirely uncooperative in resolving them: Lithuania, Turkey.* Lithuania, because of its inability to get any effective League support in its dispute with Poland over Vilna, took a generally contemptuous attitude toward League activities, and made it clear that it considered the minorities protection system a sham. Turkey, having successfully defied the major Powers after its defeat in the war, and having forced a renegotiation of the Peace Treaty, felt little need to be conciliatory on minorities questions. Council members and the Secretariat had no effective means to exert pressure on these States, even if they wished to, and discussions with them of minorities complaints typically had no result.

(c) *States whose actions produced some major complaints, and tended to be cooperative in dealing with them: Albania, Czechoslovakia, Hungary, Yugos-*

lavia. Germany, which was subject to a minorities treaty only so far the province of Upper Silesia was concerned, would also be in this category. With these States, the normal range of minorities questions were encountered, especially disputes as to allegedly discriminatory application of agrarian reform, and as to the freedom of minorities to maintain their own schools, press, and cultural activities. Two questions which reappeared for consideration on various occasions were Czechoslovakia's obligation to give local autonomy to its Ruthene province – an obligation which it never carried out –; and quota limitations which Hungary placed on the admission of Jews to universities, – a practice which it agreed in 1928 to abandon, after repeated criticism by Minorities Committees and the Council.[21]

(d) *States whose actions produced a continuing flow of major complaints, and were willing to modify their actions when subjected to pressure: Greece, Poland, Romania.* Complaints were constant from the German minority in Poland and the Hungarian minority in Romania regarding questions of property and schools. Major accusations of acts of violence and brutality toward Germans and especially Ukrainians in Poland came before Minorities Committees and the Council in 1931, as did similar accusations from time to time with regard to Bulgarians in Romania. (An even more drastic episode of violence toward minorities was the massacre of Assyrian Christians by Iraqi military units in 1933, which led to the only minority petition to the League regarding Iraq.) Minority complaints regarding Greece were fewer in number but no less persistent, having to do with expropriation of property and attempted expulsions of Moslem Albanians, and property disputes with Russian and Bulgarian monasteries at Mount Athos. The Minorities Committees and the Secretariat were actively involved with these disputes, year in and year out.

The Minorities Section of the League Secretariat regularly played the key role in the review of minorities complaints. It was never a large organization, nine professional-level staff being the largest number it attained; the Section's responsibilities included Danzig and Saar matters, as well as minorities questions. Two of the Directors of the Section were especially influential: Erik Colban, a Norwegian, Director from 1919 to 1927, and Pablo de Azcárate, a Spaniard, a member of the Section from 1922 and Director, 1930–33.[22] When a petition was received, the staff of the Section first determined its receivability and, if it was found receivable, invited the Government's comments. A summary of the main allegations and the replies to them, in the context of the applicable minorities treaty, was then prepared, and served as the main working document when the Minorities Committee met, during the next Council session. Typically, at the Committee meetings, Colban or Azcárate (or sometimes Secretary-General Drummond, who also was a frequent participant in the Committee meetings) would recommed a specific course of action to the Committee; for example, that it close consideration of the case, request certain additional information from the Government, or suggest certain actions to the Government. If the Committee agreed with the recommendations made to it, as it usually did, it would then authorize the Minorities Section to write on the Committee's behalf to the Government concerned or to discuss the problem unofficially with the Government's

Geneva representative, to obtain additional information or statements of policy. As a result of these discussions, usually conducted entirely by the Section staff but on occasion with the participation of Minorities Committee members, some mutually acceptable solution to the problem would eventually evolve. Either the Government would accept the Committee's view of what actions were necessary, or the Committee, advised by the Minorities Section, would agree to settle for something less than initially seemed desirable, on the grounds that the Government would go no futher.

In addition, the Minorities Section was in regular informal contact with petitioners – at least those with representatives in Geneva – to hear whatever they wished to say. These constant contacts with representatives of Governments and minorities in Geneva were supplemented by trips made from time to time by Colban and Azcárate to the eastern European countries, and discussions there with both Government and minority spokesmen.

From these activities, and from the informal records of the Minorities Committee meetings, it is clear that the staff of the Minorities Section took its responsibilities seriously, and brought a high level of competence to its task. It is also clear that it strongly favored dealing with minorities complaints in this informal, unpublicized fashion, with freedom to compromise when that seemed politically necessary or desirable, and with its own central role in the review and negotiations maintained. There was clearly a conviction on the part of the Section, and on that of Secretary-General Drummond, that in this way maximum concessions could be obtained from the States concerned. The system also had the advantage, from the Secretariat's standpoint of enforcing the unusually strong role of the Minorities Section as a source of continuity and expertise in the review process, while also protecting it from outside scrutiny and pressure.

Proposals were frequently made, in the League Assembly and at the meetings of non-governmental international organizations, for establishment of a Permanent Minorities Commission by the League to act on minorities complaints, or for adoption of more formal and public procedures by the Council committees, similar to domestic adiministrative or judicial review procedures. These were regularly opposed by the Secretariat.

The most serious attempt at major procedural change was led by Raoul Dandurand, Canadian representative on the Council from 1927 to 1930. Dandurand, a French Canadian and a lawyer, was sympathetic to stronger minorities protection, which he thought could be obtained through greater publicity and more formal, judicial-type procedures. He submitted detailed procedural proposals to this effect to the Council in 1929; a thorough procedural review was supported at the same time by German Chancellor Gustav Stresemann. In June 1929 the Council adopted procedural revisions proposed by a Council committee, to which the Canadian proposals had been referred. The procedure revisions fell far short of the Canadian proposals but did abandon in some substantial respects the secrecy which had surrounded the work of the Minorities Committees.[23]

In particular, the procedural changes called for a written report from the Minorities Committee to the full Council whenever review of a petition was completed. Provided the Government consented, these reports were published in the League's *Official Journal*, and became public information. In fact, during the years 1929 to 1939, about 40 per cent of the reports (71 of 179) were published, a substantial increase in the information available of the petitioners and the public. In addition, since each Council member received a copy of the unpublished reports, it is safe to assume that the results of those reviews too were relatively widely known.

Other procedural changes were of less significance. Annual statistical reports were published giving such information as the number of petitions submitted, the number found receivable, the number of Minorities Committee meetings, and of cases closed. This information was useful primarily to defend the Council and the Secretariat against charges of inactivity. During discussion of the procedural changes by the Council in June 1929, Dandurand had obtained from Drummond a public statement that Minorities Committees could, if they wished, request additional information of petitioners, rather than of Governments only, and that that had, in fact, already been done on one occasion.[24] In spite of this recognition of the possibility of further official contact with petitioners, as late as March 1932 such contact had been made on only one additional occasion. That was in October 1930 when a Minorities Committee, at the suggestion of German Foreign Minister Curtius, one of its members, asked a petitioner for additional specific information regarding its claim that Romania was refusing to admit large numbers of Hungarian children to the Hungarian minority schools.[25] When the possibility of such requests to petitioners was raised by Committee members, the Minorities Section almost invariably recommended against such action, preferring not to antagonize States and to maintain its own unofficial contacts.

The other key role in the League's minorities protection system, besides that of the Minorities Section, was of course that of the Minorities Committees. Their greatest weakness was their lack of continuity and, to a large extent, of expertise, so that they had to rely on the staff of the Minorities Section for both. The Committees usually met only during Council sessions, which were held four times a year, as a rule. There was, in addition, the regular replacement of the non-permanent Council members, who served three-year terms. While in theory the individual, most frequently the foreign minister, who represented his Government on the Council itself, would also sit on the Minorities Committees, usually this task was delegated either to the foreign office legal adviser, or to the Government's permanent representative in Geneva. These individuals might in time develop some expertise in minorities questions, but such questions were inevitably only one of many things with which they were concerned during Council sessions. They did, however, have access to their foreign minister, or other delegation head, and top-level political attention could thus be obtained for minorities questions when warranted. The availability of such attention was vitally necessary to the success of the system, since ultimately the only real weapon in dealing with a recalcitrant Government was pressure from other Governments.

A few of the leading political figures of the day took a strong interest in minorities matters, instead of leaving them to their subordinates. Most noteworthy in this regard was Austen Chamberlain, British Foreign Secretary from 1924 to 1929, who during those years personally represented Great Britain at at least 24 meetings of Minorities Committees, where his approach could perhaps best be characterized as one of cautions support for the observation of minority rights. In contrast, his most prominent colleagues on the Council, French foreign minister Aristide Briand and German foreign minister Gustav Stresemann, appear to have personally represented their countries at only five meetings and one meeting of Minorities Committees, respectively, although both were active participants in debate on those minorities matters which reached the full Council.

On those occasions when a minorities question was referred to the full Council by a Minorities Commitee, responsibility for it within the Council passed from the Committee to the Council member who served as rapporteur, in much the same way as it did to the Minorities Committees.

During the years from 1922 to 1937, when minorities questions regularly came before the Council, the responsibility of rapporteur for minorities questions was exercised successively by Brazil, Colombia, Japan, Ireland and Spain, all States geographically and ethnically removed from the area to which the minorities treaties applied. The function carried out by the Council rapporteur was essentially the same as that of the Minorities Committee, that is, to attempt to find a solution mutually acceptable to Council members and to the State immediately concerned. An important difference was that the recommendations arrived at would be a matter of public knowledge, published in the Council minutes even if dealt with in a private session. This could generate pressure on States to cooperate, but could also harden positions in response to political pressures at home.

In addition, once a case had come before the Council and no longer needed to be dealt with in secret, techniques other than private discussions and correspondence could be used. On two occasions, field operations aimed at protecting minority rights were organized by the Council, with the consent of the State concerned. In 1924 Council appointees serving as neutral members of a Mixed Commission overseeing a compulsory population exchange which was being carried out by Greece and Turkey, were given the added responsibility, as the Council's mandatories, of assuring that Albanian Moslems were not expelled from Greece to Turkey. The mandatories, headquartered in Constantinople, were assisted by staff located at Salonika and in Epirus. Regular reports were submitted to the Council until the operation was completed in 1926.[26] In 1927 the Council instituted an inquiry into admissions to German minority schools in Polish Upper Silesia. Under the direction of the President of the Upper Silesian Mixed Commission, acting for the Council, Felix Calonder, a school inspector for the canton of Luzern, Switzerland, determined whether individual children's knowledge of German was sufficient for them profitably to attend the German-language schools and, if so, they were admitted without further challenge from the Polish Government. Questions which arose in carrying out this arrangement were referred to the Council rapporteur for settlement.[27]

In 1924 the Council had approved a still more far reaching plan, agreed to by Greece and Bulgaria, for League Resident Representatives to oversee, on a continuing basis, the carrying out by both States of their obligations with regard to their Bulgarian and Greek minorities, respectively. The arrangement, however, proved abortive, as the Greek Government withdrew its approval before implementation had begun.[28]

The League Assembly had no responsibility for actions on specific minority complaints. It did, however, on frequent occasions, both in Committee and in the full Assembly, discuss the minorities procedures followed by the Council, and on occasion adopted resolutions giving its views on those procedures, which it generally supported. The Assembly debates provided the opportunity for a full airing of the views of those who thought the system went too far, and those who thought it did not go far enough. By and large, the latter views tended to predominate. While the Assembly was in no position to bring about significant changes in the system, the periodic review there of how it was working no doubt generated some pressure both on individual States and on the Council to take their responsibilities seriously.

The degree of vitality of the minorities protection system directly reflected that of the League of Nations as a whole. The number of petitions received began to decrease sharply in 1932, and was relatively insignificant from 1935 on. In October 1933, when Germany announced her withdrawal from the League, she simultaneously ceased all involvement with the minorities protection system. Initially the Hitler Government had continued its predecessors' policy of demanding full compliance with the minorities treaties, especially by Poland in its treatment of its German minority. For example, a new case was filed against Poland with the Permanent Court of International Justice, regarding alleged discrimination in the application of agrarian reform; another, having to do with the taxation of mining properties, was actively pursued. Both these cases were withdrawn in October 1933.

One major controversy arose over a minorities question between the League and the Nazi Government, as a result of Germany's application of anti-Semitic measures in German Upper Silesia, restricting Jews in their various trades and professions. A petition objecting to these policies came before the Council in May 1933. The German spokesman insisted that Germany would observe its international obligations regarding minorities (applicable only to Upper Silesia, and due to expire in 1937), but objected to any Council action. Eventually, however, Germany abstained on a proposed Council resolution – thus permitting it to be adopted – stating that all German nationals in Upper Silesia were entitled to equality in law and in fact.[29] This situation was extensively discussed in the context of Germany's minorities obligations, in the Sixth Committee of the Assembly in October 1933, various States criticizing German policies and actions. (One of Germany's critics was the Swiss representative on the Committee, William Rappard, then Director of the Graduate Institute of International Studies in Geneva.)[30] On 11 October, 1933, Germany's intent was announced to vote against a French resolution reaffirming that the minorities treaties "must be applied without exception to all classes of nationals of a State that differ from the majority of the population in race, language or religion".[31] The resolution was therefore declared "not adopted" by the Assembly.[32] Three days later, with Germany's announcement of its withdrawal from League membership, all opportunity to exert pressure on Germany through the mechanism provided by the League came to an end.

The second major blow to the functioning of the minorities protection system came from Germany's perennial antagonist, Poland. In a statement to the Assembly on 13 September 1934, Polish Foreign Minister Joseph Beck announced – at a time when the usual large number of minorities complaints against Poland was pending – that Poland would refuse all further cooperation with the League's minority protection system, until such time as it was extended to all States.[33] In the ensuing debate, this unilateral repudiation of its treaty obligations by Poland was generally denounced, but the other States remained as unwilling as ever to consider a general minorities protection system, applicable to themselves. Poland adhered to its decision, refusing thereafter to send information or comments on minorities complaints.

No other State followed Poland's example in repudiating its treaty obligations. However, by 1935–36, the first full year following the withdrawal of German and Polish cooperation with the system, only 15 minorities petitions were received by the Secretariat, as compared with a high of 204 petitions in 1930–31. When what proved to be the last session of the Council adjourned in December 1939, there were only seven minorities petitions pending, all having to do with Romania.

The minorities protection system was the only important League of Nations activity not revived and continued by the United Nations. In the aftermath of the World War II the prevailing attitude was to let States deal with their minorities as they saw fit, which entailed, among other things, accepting the expulsion of the large German minorities from Poland and Czechoslovakia. (There had been one major precedent for this action during the League of Nations period, the compulsory population exchange between Greece and Turkey.) More recently there has been, of course, a strong revival of international interest and activity in the protection of human rights, including a right of petition to international authorities, as evidenced by the European Convention on Human Rights and the International Covenant on Civil and Political Rights. The emphasis, however, has been on the rights of all individuals, rather than on rights specifically related to membership in linguistic and religious minorities.

Was the League's minorities protection system, then, a failure? It is particularly difficult to find a firm basis for answering this question. Somewhat paradoxically, while in its origins the system was intended to serve primarily political goals, its successes would appear to have been essentially humanitarian rather than political. Certainly, in the comparatively few years available to it, it did not do away with the centuries old antagonisms between eastern European ethnic groups. Did it in fact intensify them? Operation of the system was characterized by challenge and controversy over alleged unfair treatment, and manipulation of minorities' discontents by Governments hoping to maintain cohesive and dissatisfied minorities, as a basis for eventually regaining lost territories. But these activities could have been expected in any case, and continued fully after the effective demise of the minorities protection system in the mid-1930's. What was added by the system itself was the possiblity of settlement by mediation and conciliation by third parties, where States were willing to accept such practices. In the longer run, had time been available, perhaps successes of this sort would have had important and benefical political effects. In the short run, in any case, humanitarian achievements were many: compensation, or more generous compensation, for expropriated property; withdrawal of restrictions on minority educational, cultural and religious activity; punishment of at least some lower-level officials responsible for acts of violence and brutality, and governmental pledges to prevent the recurrence of such acts, and so on. Humanitarian achievements of this sort were in themselves no small accomplishment in the eastern Europe of the 1920's and 1930's, and even in the absence of clear-cut and immediate political benefits, would appear more than enough to justify the minorities protection system as a useful and creative innovation in international organizational activity.

Notes

1 LoN, Verbatim Report of the Sixth Meeting of the Second Session of the Council of the League of Nations, 13 February 1920, p. 21.
2 LoN, Procès-Verbal of the Tenth Session of the Council, 22 and 25 October 1920, p. 13, 33, 143, 145.
3 *A History of the Peace Conference of Paris,* H. W. V. Temperley, editor, London, Oxford University Press, v. 5, 1924, p. 112–120.
4 Minorities provisions applicable to the Free City of Danzig and to Finland's Aaland Islands also were placed under League guarantee, but without a right of individual petition to the League.
5 *A History of the Peace Conference, op. cit.*, p. 435.
6 LoN, Minutes of the Fiftieth Session of the Council, *OJ,* 6 June 1928, p. 888–893.
7 See LoN Publication 1927. I.B.2, "Protection of Linguistic, Racial and Religious Minorities by the League of Nations", for the texts of the minorities treaties.
8 LoN, doc. C.315.1932.I, 19 February 1932.
9 LoN, *OJ,* October 1933, p. 1118–20.
10 Permanent Court of International Justice, Advisory Opinions of 10 September 1923, 15 September 1923, 15 May 1931, and 6 April 1935; Judgement of 26 April 1928.
11 LoN, Minutes of the Twenty-sixth Session of the Council, *OJ,* 5 September 1923, p. 1293–4. Except for the last-mentioned, these criteria were already in effect by December 1921; see *OJ,* January 1922, p. 51–2.
12 Approximately 150 of 300 in the years 1921–29, LoN, Report of the Committee Instituted by the Council Resolution of 7 March 1929, *OJ,* p. 1149; 338 or 583 in the years 1929–39 (compiled from annual statistical reports published in the *Official Journal*). This does not include petitions submitted under the special procedure for Upper Silesia.
13 Compare, for example, the slightly more than two per cent of all applications declared admissible in the years 1955–78, under the European Convention on Human Rights, "Stock-Taking on the European Convention on Human Rights", January 1979, p. 137).
14 LoN, Minutes of the Twenty-sixth Session of the Council, *OJ,* 5 September 1923, p. 1292–4 and p. 1428.
15 The total number of minorities questions dealt with by minorities committees of the

Council is substantially less than the total number of receivable petitions (approximately 488), because the latter includes a large number of supplementary and closely related petitions joined together as single questions for committee consideration.

16 LoN, Minutes of the Fiftieth Session of the Council, *OJ*, 9 June 1928, p. 942–4.

17 Article 12 of Polish minorities treaty (League of Nations Publication 1927. I.B. 2, p. 45).

18 League of Nations Covenant, Articles 4 (5) and 5 (1).

19 LoN, docs., Minutes of Directors' Meeting, 16 January 1929.

20 LNA, S. 340.

21 *Ibid.*, Minorities Committee Meeting of 7 March 1928.

22 Azcarate is the author of two informative books on the minorities protection system: *League of Nations and National Minorities*, Washington, Carnegie Endowment for International Peace, 1945; 216 p.; *La Société des Nations et la Protection des Minorités*, Genève, Centre européen de la Dotation Carnegie pour la paix internationale, 1969. – 103 p.

23 For a full discussion of the Dandurand proposals, and the action taken regarding them, see Richard Veatch, *Canada and the League of Nations*, Toronto, University of Toronto Press, p. 101–114.

24 Documents relating to the Protection of Minorities by the League of Nations, *OJSS*, no. 73, 1929. – p. 15.

25 LNA, S. 340, Minorities Committee Meeting of 2 October 1930.

26 LoN, Minutes of the Thirty-second Session of the Council, *OJ*, 11 December 1924, p. 145, 234–5; May 1925, p. 643, LoN, Minutes of the Forty-second Session of the Council, *OJ*, 19 September 1926, p. 1405.

27 LoN, Minutes of the Forty-fourth Session of the Council, *OJ*, 12 March 1927, p. 400–403, 593; May 1927, p. 621.

28 LoN, Minutes of the Thirtieth Session of the Council, *OJ*, 29. September 1924, p. 1349–52; LoN, Minutes of the Thirty-third Session of the Council, *OJ*, 14 March 1925, p. 478–82.

29 LoN, Minutes of the Seventy-third Session of the Council, *OJ*, 6 June 1933, p. 844–9.

30 LoN, Records of the Fourteenth Ordinary Session of the Assembly, Plenary Meetings, *OJSS*, no. 115, p. 88.

31 *Ibid.*, 10 October 1933, p. 71–2.

32 LoN, Records of the Fourteenth Ordinary Session of the Assembly, Plenary Meetings, *OJSS*,no. 115, p. 88.

33 Records of the Fifteenth Ordinary Session of the Assembly, Plenary Meetings, *OJSS*, no. 125, p. 43.

La Société des Nations et le colonialisme
Le Mandat international: Une vieille idée pour demain?

Yves Collart
Institut Universitaire de Hautes Etudes internationales
Genève

> "The system of mandates, which is to play so large a part in the settlement of the German colonies and the Ottoman Empire, is really a new policy for dealing with an old danger to international society – the existence in its midst of derelict countries . . ."
>
> Manchester Guardian,
> January 29, 1920

> . . . "As the Colonial Mandates will form a new phenomenon in International Law, and will probably be documents of lasting historical importance . . ."
>
> Letter from Dr. van Hamel to the Secretary General August 8, 1919[1]

> "The era of complete independence [. . .] is not as yet visible on the horizon of time . . ."[2]
>
> Lord Lugard, 1926

On peut envisager d'aborder le sujet qui nous occupe ici dans au moins trois perspectives historiques différentes. Il est évidemment hors de question de les retenir toutes – ou même, au reste, de traiter, en si peu de pages, convenablement d'aucune. Comme, de surcroît, celle qui va être choisie peut paraître assez paradoxale, il convient de préciser d'emblée, pour prévenir tout malentendu, les mobiles de ce choix et de définir le type de préoccupations auxquelles s'efforcent de répondre les réflexions qui vont suivre.

Dans une première perspective – la plus étroite du point du vue chronologique, mais sans doute la plus conforme à l'esprit de ce colloque – on concentrerait l'attention, dans un temps historique fini, sur l'expérience propre de la Société des Nations à l'égard de la question coloniale, dans la mesure – à la fois marginale et partielle – où elle s'est trouvée mêlée aux activités de la Société. C'est alors, bien sûr, tout le système des mandats qui serait principalement en point de mire, *wie es eigentlich gewesen ist,* en quelque sorte – son origine, son fonctionnement, ses effets – un chapitre en soi immense par ses prolongements ou par la problématique qu'il soulève, quoique la place qui lui revient dans la pondération générale de l'œuvre de la Société soit en vérité relativement modeste.[3]

Dans une deuxième perspective, celle-là de longue durée, on ne retiendrait l'activité de la Société des Nations en ce domaine que par rapport à l'évolution historique globale du phénomène colonial, avant comme après elle. Si le système des mandats demeure encore, en ce qui concerne la Société, l'élément prépondérant, ce sont alors, à l'égard du problème d'ensemble, des questions d'une toute autre nature qui surgissent, au centre desquelles se situe, dans ce long terme, la dialectique complexe entre la domination coloniale et l'essor, sinueux et subtil, des forces de décolonisation. La part historique de la Société – qui n'est plus elle-même, dans cette deuxième perspective, que relative – ne prendrait alors tout son sens qu'à travers les multiples prolongements qui se déroulent au-delà d'elle, notamment dans l'action de l'Organisation des Nations Unies, une action qui débouche, après les bouleversements que l'on connaît, sur »l'émancipation« du Tiers monde.

Quels que soient les mérites et les justifications de ces deux approches distinctes, qui permettent notamment, en dépit des immenses zones d'ombre, de se mouvoir en terrain relativement solide et correspondent au domaine propre de l'historien: l'exploration du passé, c'est pourtant dans une troisième perspective, assurément insolite, que l'on a choisi d'aborder ici le problème des mandats internationaux. Elle est insolite, d'abord, parce que du point de vue chronologique, elle est entièrement axée sur le temps présent, et bien davantage encore, sur l'avenir. Non qu'il soit interdit à l'historien de s'y aventurer: sous deux rapports au moins, il devient même impératif qu'il le fasse. Tout d'abord, en vertu d'un précepte fondamental, si bien formulé par Marrou, qui inspire tant de travaux de notre génération: »l'historien interroge le passé«, et surtout, »il lui pose les questions que le présent« – où il se situe lui-même comme témoin et comme acteur – »lui suggère«.[4] C'est donc à une relecture constante de l'histoire des temps révolus que cette démarche engage, une relecture qui, sous la pression du contemporain, révèle indéfiniment de nouveaux problèmes, de nouvelles sources, ou un éclairage différent des questions anciennes, qui ne sont jamais établies une fois pour toutes. Cette ouverture de l'historien sur le présent et sur l'avenir (quels que soient les problèmes méthodologiques qu'elle soulève) est rendue d'autre part impérative sous l'effet, plus pressant qu'il ne l'a jamais été auparavant, de la »crise de notre temps«, comme nous y invite notamment Pierre Chaunu (à propos d'une question, il est vrai, très particulière), lorsqu'il s'en prend à la démission des historiens devant les défis de leur époque, eux à qui appartient »l'exploration de la mémoire collective, sa mise au service des hommes angoissés de comprendre, pour mieux prévoir et agir«.[5]

En second lieu, le choix de cette troisième perspective, centrée sur le présent et sur l'avenir, est insolite en vertu de son *objet*, celui-là même qui nous a conduit à une interrogation sur l'histoire du mandat international à laquelle aucune recherche antérieure ni aucune compétence ou inclination particulières ne nous destinaient. Il s'agit d'un problème tout à fait spécifique de notre temps, un problème d'autant plus grave qu'il est plus négligé: *le sort des micro-territoires.*

Nous reviendrons tout à l'heure sur ce qui peut caractériser cette catégorie particulière d'»unités« politiques – comme on dit – sur tout ce qui rend leur situation actuelle intenable et leur avenir angoissant, sur la nécessité inéluctable d'imaginer des solutions neuves à ce problème. Qu'il suffise, pour l'instant, d'évoquer l'existence de cette espèce de frange résiduelle de la décolonisation, cette poussière d'îles et d'îlots (abusivement déguisée, si souvent, pour les besoins des juristes et des planificateurs de l'ordre mondial sous le nom irréaliste d'archipels), ces peuples épars dans l'immensité des océans, ces laissés-pour-compte du système international actuel qui n'a été conçu ni par eux, ni à plus forte raison pour eux, et où ils n'ont pas leur place. Il devient impératif d'attirer l'attention sur ces anomalies de la communauté internationale moderne, sur cette portion infime et dispersée de la communauté humaine qu'il faut bien appeler – avec toute la témérité qu'implique le recours à une expression en complet porte-à-faux par rapport à l'idéologie dominante des dernières décennies: »le Cinquième monde«, celui des indépendances impossibles. Pour lui (nous y reviendrons par la suite) pas de salut hors de trois solutions: le maintien d'une domination coloniale anachronique, la totale déréliction, ou alors l'application de certaines méthodes de gestion et de responsabilité internationales, dont les modalités restent à inventer. Elles impliquent pourtant, prioritairement, une enquête de type historique sur les solutions analogues, même totalement impertinentes aujourd'hui, qui ont pu être utilisées dans le passé, non pour en extraire des modèles utilisables plus tard mais pour en tirer les leçons qu'à de multiples égards, elles ont probablement à nous fournir.[6]

On comprend peut-être, maintenant, les raisons pour lesquelles nous avons donné la préférence à cette troisième perspective, et l'on perçoit sans doute en quoi elle nous ramène, par une espèce de cheminement à rebours, à l'expérience du mandat international sous le régime de la Société des Nations dont elle pouvait sembler, au contraire, nous éloigner complètement. C'est pourquoi, avant de revenir tout à l'heure sur le monde alarmant des îles condamnées, il convient de s'arrêter un moment sur cette période de l'entre-deux-guerres où le système international – puisque c'est de lui qu'il s'agit – s'articulait, incomplètement, autour de la SdN. Après ce qui a été dit jusqu'ici, on comprendra aussi qu'il est hors-de-propos – tâche qui serait d'ailleurs insurmontable – d'esquisser dans son ensemble le fonctionnement du système des mandats; il s'agit simplement d'exprimer certaines des réflexions qu'il nous suggère a posteriori et qui sont susceptibles d'éclairer, en enjambant le temps, les problèmes que soulève pour tous, aujourd'hui, le destin des archipels.

Il se pose d'abord, sur un plan très général, des questions de nature heuristique qui découlent aussi bien de la période que du domaine particuliers dont nous nous occupons ici. Comment ne pas mentionner, par exemple, le sentiment d'inconfort qu'éprouve parfois l'historien devant une certaine ambivalence de l'organisation internationale et de l'armature juridique qui la sous-tend, comme devant le type de littérature qui lui est souvent consacré. A la fois fait historique et secteur du droit, au carrefour du politique et de la norme, reflet des grands courants du temps et véhicule de leur application concrète, l'organisation internationale comporte une ambiguïté qui pèse incontestablement sur le travail de l'historien. Car s'il ne saurait négliger les vastes mouvements d'idées – essentiels dans le tissu de l'Histoire elle-même – ni la proclamation de grands principes – qui lui posent du reste toujours, comme homme ancré dans son temps, des questions personnelles – l'historien a toujours pour tâche principale, en fin de compte, l'étude du singulier. Aussi est-il parfois dérouté par l'espèce d'irréalisme qui, en certaines matières, se dégage inévitablement du processus propre à l'organisation internationale, vouée par la nature des choses à l'application universelle de ces principes, et peu sensible, par conséquent, à ce que Paul Veyne appelle »les différences«.[7] Or nulle part, plus que dans le domaine colonial, ce décalage entre la généralité de la règle, et la spécificité du cas, ne paraît aussi évident.

En ce qui concerne, d'autre part, l'époque de l'entre-deux-guerres, on est en droit de se demander si – par rapport à la longue durée – elle n'est pas exposée aux menaces de distorsion ou d'erreur de pondération que ferait peser sur elle une double illusion d'optique: soit qu'elle ait, pour ainsi dire, passé trop vite, étant une de ces périodes denses où, selon l'expression lumineuse de Maurice Bourquin, »l'histoire se précipite et prend des raccourcis«;[8] soit qu'écrasée entre le monde gigantesque qui s'achève en 1914 et celui, à tous égards révolutionnaire, qui s'ouvre en 1945, elle n'apparaisse trop volontiers sinon comme une parenthèse, du moins comme une phase de transition. C'est ainsi, par exemple, que le système international nouveau mis en place en 1919–1920, les avatars de son évolution par la suite ont été très tôt éclipsés par les bouleversements de la Deuxième Guerre mondiale, et surtout par le nouvel effort de reconstruction d'un ordre global, héritier sans doute du précédent mais qui n'en est que partiellement le continuateur. L'effet de ce phénomène sur l'historiographie est évident: l'ampleur comparativement énorme du système des Nations Unies, ajoutée à la gravité extrême des questions auxquelles il s'est trouvé rapidement confronté, a tout naturellement polarisé l'attention et tend à obscurcir, sinon à mettre de côté, la période antérieure, au risque de réduire la Société des Nations à une espèce de simple prélude, de surcroît stigmatisé par le long déclin de l'Institution. Il est donc important, il est même capital du point de vue de l'Histoire – soucieuse de dégager les accidents et les continuités – d'y revenir, et ce n'est pas le moindre mérite de ce colloque que de nous y ramener.

En troisième lieu, en dépit ou à cause de ce qui vient d'être dit, la tentation de dresser des bilans comparatifs comporte, du point de vue de la réflexion historique, des limites qu'il est essentiel de respecter.[9] La Société des Nations d'une part, l'Organisation des Nations Unies d'autre part appartiennent à des temps historiques différents. Qu'il s'agisse d'analyser leur fonctionnement, leurs structures, leur action, d'évaluer leur influence sur l'évolution du monde, ou inversement celle de l'environnement global sur leur dynamique respective, elles sont chacune partie d'un *moment* de l'histoire, d'un réseau infiniment complexe de forces innombrables dont les éléments ne sont comparables que jusqu'à un certain point. Aussi l'historien doit-il parfois s'avouer réfractaire devant beaucoup d'études »horizontales«, excessivement fondées, à son gré – et non sans quelque ironie, venant de sa part – sur l'analyse sempiternelle des textes constitutifs et des déclarations, ou sur la comparaison minutieuse des mécanismes institutionnels. Sans doute une évolution sensible s'est-elle dessinée, depuis l'entre-deux-guerres, dans la littérature spécialisée – une illustration, précisément, de l'influence que peuvent exercer des »temps« différents sur la vision des choses – et l'on doit saluer comme ils le méritent les efforts qui ne cessent de se manifester pour déployer, dans toutes les directions possibles, l'étude de l'organisation internationale, ou des institutions diverses qui la composent. Il demeure que le problème évoqué ici est certainement très sensible, et spécialement important, en ce qui concerne la question coloniale, à laquelle nous allons maintenant nous arrêter plus particulièrement.

Vu sous l'angle exclusif de l'organisation internationale, l'examen de ce problème est singulièrement périlleux: il est facile, voire tentant, de tomber dans l'un des pièges évoqués tout à l'heure. La place croissante que la question coloniale a prise parmi les préoccupations des Nations Unies, le rôle accélérateur à double effet qu'y a joué le processus de décolonisation – c'est-à-dire l'influence de l'Organisation sur ce mouvement, puis du mouvement sur elle – la prise de conscience universelle de l'émergence du Tiers monde et des problèmes qui l'affligent, ajoutés à bien d'autres causes plus profondes du déclin des empires, sont de nature à projeter, rétrospectivement, un éclairage déformant sur l'œuvre de la Société des Nations à cet égard, et induisent notamment à négliger le décalage qui sépare les deux organisations dans le temps. L'effet de ce phénomène peut d'ailleurs s'exercer dans des directions opposées. D'une part, en alimentant l'appréciation dite »cynique« de l'œuvre de la Société en la matière: loin d'avoir ouvert une brèche, même étroite, dans l'édifice colonial, elle l'aurait au contraire consolidé, ou du moins protégé par une espèce de légalisation supérieure de la situation coloniale. L'ordre chronologique dans lequel – au cours du règlement de la paix – le système des mandats a été mis en place (notamment la répartition et la succession des décisions qui s'y rapportent entre les Puissances alliées d'une part et les organes de la Société de l'autre),[10] l'aspect classique – derrière le compromis, politique plus que juridique, finalement adopté – du partage des dépouilles opimes, le processus de fait accompli résultant soit des accords du temps de guerre, soit de l'occupation effective par les futurs mandataires des territoires confiés par la suite à leur administration, le caractère géographiquement très partiel du système par rapport à l'ensemble du terrain colonisé, le manque d'audace de la Commission permanente des Mandats quant à l'extension, ou même à l'exercice de ses tâches, les revendications coloniales, dans le cadre même de la Société, de certaines puissances, notamment celles de l'Allemagne,[11] cherchant à récupérer – par le truchement du système des mandats lui-même – un espace d'expansion outre-mer: ce sont là, outre bien d'autres considérations encore, autant d'arguments sur lesquels repose cette interprétation.

Inversement, le risque existe aussi d'exagérer, à rebrousse-temps, le rôle de précurseur joué dans ce domaine par la Société des Nations, en soulignant avec excès l'idéologie – notamment l'objectif du *self-government* – présumée régir son action, l'application apparemment scrupuleuse des mécanismes de contrôle instaurés par elle (essentiellement la procédure des rapports fournis par les mandataires, et leur minutieux examen), enfin la continuité remarquable par laquelle s'opère, au-delà de la guerre, le raccord, dans ce domaine, avec l'Organisation des Nations Unies: n'est-ce pas par une filiation directe qu'en 1945 le système des Mandats vient aboutir, ou plutôt mourir, dans celui de la Tutelle, bientôt privé il est vrai – à part la Namibie – de tout objet, mais surtout dépassé sur sa gauche par la Résolution 1514, puis par l'activité effrénée et tonitruante du Comité des vingt-quatre, et plus encore peut-être sous l'effet terriblement efficace – mais parfois à double-tranchant – de sa philosophie directrice sur l'indépendance à n'importe quel prix?[12]

En vérité, c'est dans une perspective différente, et qui dépasse largement l'organisation internationale comme telle, qu'il faut aborder ce problème: celle qui historiquement embrasse toute l'évolution du phénomène colonial, dans sa globalité. Elle doit prendre en compte tous les facteurs, quelle que soit leur nature, qui, bien en-deça de la Première Guerre mondiale, composent et animent les relations complexes entre la domination coloniale et les forces contraires qui viennent, peu à peu, en saper les fondements, pour déboucher finalement sur l'émancipation juridique du Tiers monde. Sans doute l'organisation internationale – qu'il s'agisse de l'O.N.U. ou de la SdN – reflète-t-elle cette évolution; mais elle ne le fait qu'imparfaitement, et surtout incomplètement, parce qu'elle n'est elle-même, du même coup et parmi beaucoup d'autres, que l'un de ces facteurs. Dans cette perspective, l'éclatement de la décolonisation visible et formelle après 1945 est peut-être trompeur, dans la mesure où il n'est que l'aboutissement d'un cheminement de très longue haleine, dont les jalons successifs, pour être moins évidents, n'en sont pas moins marquants, ni par conséquent moins dignes de retenir l'attention.

Dans cette optique, à la fois globale et de longue durée, l'époque de l'entre-deux-guerres se révèle – en ce qui concerne l'évolution du problème colonial – comme une période d'une importance exceptionnelle: elle est même véritablement cruciale au sens étymologique du terme. C'est-à-dire qu'elle marque le carrefour entre un phénomène séculaire d'expansion coloniale qui déjà s'essouffle mais qui se poursuit encore, et les forces nombreuses qui, sur toutes sortes de plans, minent progressivement l'édifice établi: il est hors de doute, avec le recul du temps, qu'elles ont déjà un caractère décisif et irréversible, même si elles n'apparaissent que fort peu aux yeux des contemporains, et si la conséquence finale de ces lézardes allait devoir dépendre, pour que le monument s'écroule, de l'énorme secousse provoquée par la Deuxième Guerre mondiale. Période, donc, contradictoire et ambiguë: d'un côté – celui des métropoles – une foi persistante dans la justification morale et dans l'utilité des possessions coloniales (rendues évidentes, s'il le fallait, par leur contribution à la Grande Guerre); elle se manifeste, par exemple, dans les pressions qu'exercent de nouveaux candidats à l'acquisition de territoires outre-mer,[13] ou encore – sur un tout autre plan – par les grandes expositions coloniales, autour de 1930, qui célèbrent avec emphase l'excellente conscience d'une Europe convaincue de son bon droit (sinon encore de sa force), de la solidité de son oeuvre comme de l'accomplissement de sa mission civilisatrice à travers le monde. Il s'y mêle pourtant, en filigrane, bien des doutes: car c'est aussi l'époque des mises en question[14] et du réaménagement des empires, soit qu'il s'agisse, notamment sous l'effet de la Grande Crise, d'interrogations (qui à vrai dire ne sont guère nouvelles) sur le profit réel tiré du domaine impérial comme sur le coût qu'entraîne son maintien, soit qu'il s'agisse de réactions obligées, de type politique, aux divers courants qui, dans les métropoles, poussent au changement.[15]

De l'autre côté – principalement en terrain colonisé – c'est l'éclosion et l'essor de toutes sortes de forces contraires à la domination coloniale, dont les racines réelles plongent sans doute très profondément dans le temps et sont peut-être congénitales de la colonisation elle-même. Si toute cette fermentation ne se fait, à l'époque, que très partiellement sentir, la plupart de ces forces sont aujourd'hui parfaitement identifiées mais elles sont, en revanche, inégalement connues, et très improprement appréciées dans la mesure où celles qui se révéleront, en fin de compte, comme décisives se développent lentement dans la profondeur sociale, et mentale, des territoires colonisés. Or ce qui s'y est passé réellement demeure encore enfoui, aujourd'hui, sous une ombre opaque qu'explique sans doute l'indigence documentaire, mais bien davantage encore l'européocentrisme tenace sous l'influence duquel l'histoire du lien colonial n'a cessé de privilégier l'extrémité des métropoles. Ces forces de changement comprennent, par exemple, la naissance (parfois bien antérieure à la Première Guerre mondiale) et le mûrissement de tous les nationalismes, la lente formation – dans les métropoles et plus tard sur place – des militants et des futurs dirigeants du vaste mouvement de fond, sous des oscillations épidermiques, vers l'indépendance,[16] la contagion – d'un terrain colonisé à l'autre – du lest progressivement jeté, ici ou là, par le dominateur colonial, l'action du Komintern,[17] bien sûr, dans sa lutte contre l'Occident capitaliste par colonies et nationalisme interposés, et la création corrélative en territoire colonial des premiers partis communistes, l'émergence des syndicats, la spirale des révoltes et combien d'autres facteurs encore . . .; sans parler des forces agissant dans les métropoles elles-mêmes, ou celles qui découlent de l'évolution du système mondial, notamment le déclin relatif, dans l'équilibre général, des puissances coloniales.

Il s'agit donc là d'un réseau, extrêmement complexe, de forces et de courants antithétiques, divers, dispersés et agissant à des niveaux différents, mais qui constitue néanmoins la vraie trame, lentement élaborée, où apparaîtra soudain, après 1945, le dessin d'une nouvelle géographie dans la distribution des forces politiques du monde. Sans doute, dans beaucoup de cas, la Deuxième guerre rassemble-t-elle encore, plutôt qu'elle ne disperse, les empires; et les signes ne manquent pas qui font croire encore, lorsqu'elle est sur le point de se terminer, que ces empires tiennent bon, ou qu'en tout cas leurs détenteurs ne sont guère enclins à les abandonner.[18] D'où, probablement, la négligence de cette phase de l'entre-deux-guerres – pourtant à tous égards essentielle – dont témoignent tant d'ouvrages consacrés au Tiers monde contemporain et qui ne lui accordent qu'à peine des révérences de langage comme à un pâle, insignifiant et lointain prélude.

C'est donc à l'intérieur de ce vaste contexte, et par rapport à lui, qu'il faut essayer de situer maintenant brièvement le rôle de la Société des Nations. On se rappellera en effet qu'il n'est pas dans notre propos d'en esquisser la chronique, mais simplement de soulever quelques-unes des questions qui mériteraient, à son sujet, une investigation historique plus poussée, et qui sont par ailleurs choisies en fonction de deux préoccupations très précises: d'une part, l'approfondissement de notre connaissance du phénomène colonial *en général*, d'autre part et surtout, le caractère de *précédent* du Mandat – quelle que soit sa valeur – à l'égard des solutions de type international qu'il faudra bien imaginer si l'on veut sauver d'un dépérissement fatal certains territoires minuscules du monde contemporain. *Grosso modo*, ces questions s'articulent autour de trois thèmes principaux: la relation entre le système des mandats et les données générales de la situation coloniale, puis ce qu'on pourrait nommer »l'idéologie« du système, enfin certains problèmes relatifs à son fonctionnement. En fait, ces thèmes s'entrecroisent sans cesse, de sorte qu'il est malaisé de les isoler, et ceci d'autant plus qu'ils s'insèrent ici dans une perspective à long terme.

Il serait évidemment absurde de s'appesantir sur ce qui peut nous paraître, aujourd'hui, en contradiction flagrante avec les tendances profondes dont nous sommes les témoins. De tels contrastes résultent justement de ces »temps historiques« différents qui interdisent, comme on l'a souligné plus haut, les comparaisons »horizontales« et les jugements de valeur. Ainsi en va-t-il, par exemple, du principe – véritablement essentiel dans le système des mandats – de l'*open door*, héritier direct des arrangements coloniaux du XIXe siècle,[19] en opposition totale à celui de la souveraineté sur les ressources naturelles, une notion plus récente mais qui fait solidement partie, depuis 1952, de l'arsenal idéologique des Nations Unies. Non seulement l'application du principe de la porte ouverte a pour conséquence de maintenir, et même de légaliser, la division internationale du travail issue du Pacte colonial, dont l'héritage grève si lourdement, aujourd'hui, la situation du Tiers monde, mais elle multiplie ses effets en élargissant, si l'on peut dire, le système de l'exclusif et en étendant de fait à tous les Occidentaux un droit fondamental à l'accès aux matières premières et aux marchés outre-mer. Il ne fait guère de doute que, dans une perspective à long terme, la contradiction est réelle entre l'obligation de promouvoir »le bien-être et le développement de ces peuples« prévue par l'article 22 du Pacte, et l'application qui leur est faite de ce principe. C'est encore, dans un tout autre domaine, le fonctionnement de la Commission permanente des Mandats (C.P.M.), sa composition, le climat où baignent ses travaux qui se singularisent et qui n'annoncent en rien la formule paritaire future des organes de Tutelle, et moins encore celle, quasi unilatérale, du Comité des vingt-quatre – pour ne pas parler des objectifs poursuivis, des moyens mis en oeuvre ni du ton des débats. Il est enfin facile – trop facile, de relever toutes les oppositions qui séparent non seulement le temps des Mandats du nôtre, mais qui mettent la SdN, à cet égard, en contradiction avec elle-même: l'expédient politique contre les principes, l'application partielle et partiale contre l'universalité, le caractère théoriquement provisoire du système – impliquant donc une volonté d'y mettre fin un jour par des mesures préparatoires adéquates[20] – et son exécution plus soucieuse, en fait, de maintenir l'ordre établi que de provoquer des bouleversements.

En revanche, certaines continuités, ou certaines permanences méritent davantage de retenir l'attention, qu'il s'agisse de points particuliers soulevés dans le fonctionnement du système des mandats ou d'obstacles auxquels il s'est heurté. Il est par exemple frappant que la C.P.M. ait voué une attention particulière – peu importent sa vigueur ou son succès – à des questions telles que le problème foncier (capital aujourd'hui), la préservation des traditions locales et ancestrales, ou mis un accent répété sur la philosophie même de la »mission sacrée«, ou de »l'intérêt réciproque« (puissamment alimentée par la contribution personnelle de Lord Lugard à ses travaux)[21]: car on en retrouvera les traces plus tard, en dépit de contradictions apparentes, dans la patiente élaboration d'un droit international du développement, d'une responsabilité collective à cet égard, et même dans le concept d'un patrimoine commun de l'humanité. Du côté des obstacles ou des difficultés, ce sont par exemple les problèmes de relations entre ce qu'on appellerait aujourd'hui le centre (le siège de la Commission) et le terrain (qu'elle percevait, de toute évidence, fort mal),[22] le problème du contrôle et de ses modalités, la composition même des organes responsables et l'équilibre délicat entre experts prétendument choisis *ad personam* et représentants gouvernementaux; c'est aussi la dichotomie entre les objectifs fixés par des principes et tout ce qui entrave, sur place, leur application pratique, la dimension financière du système, enfin le dilemme permanent, du point du vue du mandataire, entre les pouvoirs étendus de décision, d'exécution, de changements qui sont nécessairement requis pour l'exercice de sa tâche, et le devoir – inhérent à cette tâche elle-même, de respecter les structures sociales, les inclinations, les habitudes de ceux à qui il a affaire, alors que la promotion de leur »bien-être« et de leur »développement« impliquerait précisément qu'elles soient – les unes comme les autres – profondément modifiées. Sur tous ces points – et sur beaucoup d'autres encore – la continuité jusqu'à nos jours est frappante: ils sont le lot de tous les organes, à quelque niveau qu'ils opèrent et jusqu'à celui de l'individu, qui sont confrontés, d'une manière ou de l'autre, aux problèmes du développement ou impliqués dans des missions de coopération technique.

Il fallait bien souligner d'abord, au prix d'une fastidieuse énumération, ces éléments de désuétude ou de permanence, parce qu'ils illustrent à leur façon combien l'expérience de la SdN s'inscrit en réalité dans des dimensions beaucoup plus vastes et ne peut être évaluée correctement que par rapport à elles. C'est donc sur d'autre plans, et surtout d'autres points que ceux ordinairement abordés, que le système des mandats dans le cadre de la Société des Nations pose de véritables questions à l'historien, ou plus exactement encore, qu'il a, lui, des questions à lui poser. Evoquons-en rapidement quelques-unes.

Il faut mentionner en premier lieu le besoin qu'il éprouve de dépasser la littérature contemporaine de la Société, excessivement marquée, à son goût, par le »juridisme« évoqué plus haut, et d'exploiter comme elles le méritent, et dans des directions différentes, les ressources documentaires d'une extrême richesse que la Société des Nations a laissées derrière elle. Elles semblent se prêter admirablement à cette »relecture« dont on parlait tout à l'heure, c'est-à-dire non pas pour retracer par le menu l'histoire même des mandats, déjà bien amorcée,[23] mais pour tenter de combler les trous qui, dans l'état actuel de nos connaissances, obscurcissent encore considérablement l'évolution du phénomène colonial entre les deux guerres, ou parce que le temps présent s'en vient nous suggérer des interrogations nouvelles.

Le trou le plus béant dans l'évolution de la dialectique coloniale à cette époque concerne – comme on l'a déjà suggéré – ce qui se passe *en terrain colonisé*, c'est-à-dire la germination des forces de décolonisation, le rôle des hommes et des groupes, leur vision du monde, de leur sort et de leur destin, du mécanisme colonial lui-même où ils sont enfermés. Il est frappant – mais guère surprenant – que la littérature spécialisée sur les Mandats, traitant, selon la formule reçue, des *»inter-*

ested parties« – qui sont en réalité au nombre de quatre – s'étende presque exclusivement sur les débats de Genève, sur les gouvernements concernés et sur les activités du mandataire sur place. Les *»natives«*, eux, n'apparaissent guère que comme »objet«, ou à travers le miroir – sans doute déformant – des rapports périodiques remis à la Commission; mais on ne les »voit« pas. Nous suggérons ici qu'un progrès de nos connaissances pourrait sans doute être réalisé dans le sens indiqué par un dépouillement systématique des *pétitions* reçues (et donc pas seulement celles qui ont été, plus ou moins, retenues): il sera peut-être décevant, mais il est aussi prometteur. Car il est frappant de constater la place extrêmement mince qui leur est généralement réservée dans les ouvrages spécialisés, pour la simple raison qu'ils s'attardent sur le *mécanisme* – d'ailleurs appliqué restrictivement – des pétitions,[24] et non sur leur *contenu*, qui n'est presque jamais mentionné. Le serait-il d'ailleurs, il est probable que l'historien, mû par son intuition propre, y puiserait autre chose que le juriste, soucieux d'analyser, avant tout, une procédure.

Sur ce plan documentaire, nous pensons encore – dans un tout autre ordre d'idée – à la valeur inestimable que peuvent revêtir aujourd'hui, dans une certaine perspective, les *rapports*, de plus en plus fouillés et étendus, soumis par les mandataires sur les territoires confiés à leur administration. Il y a là sans doute, pour chacun de ces territoires, des informations irremplaçables – si orientées qu'elles puissent être – sur une certaine tranche de leur passé. Or lorsqu'on songe qu'ils ont tous, sauf deux,[25] accédé depuis lors à la souveraineté, que la récupération de sa propre histoire est à la fois un passage obligé de la marche à l'indépendance et un facteur essentiel à la formation d'une identité nationale, qu'enfin il est naturel de pouvoir aller quérir, dans le passé, des éléments d'explication à une situation présente, il est permis de souligner l'attention que devraient porter les territoires qui ont jadis fait l'objet de ces rapports sur ce type de documentation. Alors que ces documents figurent, soigneusement reliés, sur les rayons des bibliothèques européennes, on peut se demander s'ils existent, par exemple, à Nauru – qui de surcroît ne fait pas partie de l'O.N.U. – et si par impossible ils s'y trouvaient s'ils y sont consultés et par qui?

Un autre genre de question, en vérité d'une immense ampleur, que l'historien est amené à se poser concerne non pas tant le *fonctionnement* de la Commission permanente des Mandats, que la *vision* qu'elle pouvait avoir de sa mission; c'est-à-dire non par rapport aux textes qui la lui dictaient, mais par rapport aux problèmes de son temps, à l'état et à l'évolution du monde, dans la durée, donc la question de savoir, en fin de compte, si l'on peut déceler, derrière le déroulement des travaux de la Commission une espèce de perception du phénomène colonial comme tel, de son origine, de ses effets, et de son évolution prévisible ou encore, plus précisément, de son propre rôle par rapport à lui? On pourrait s'étendre à perte de vue sur ce problème, qui demande en soi toute une recherche. Ce qui paraît certain, c'est que la C.P.M. ne s'est jamais considérée elle-même comme le rouage d'un processus de »dé-colonisation«, un terme d'ailleurs (même écrit d'une pièce) totalement anachronique à l'époque; mais plutôt comme un exemple de »bonne« gestion coloniale, animée par la justification plus théorique que réelle qu'elle déboucherait un jour, imprévisible et lointain, sur une hypothétique indépendance; un peu comme l'entendait en Angleterre, durant la même période, le

Labour (dans un esprit qui inspirait bien avant lui les socialistes de la IIème Internationale)[26] lorsqu'il réclamait qu'on étende à *toutes* les colonies le régime du mandat international.[27] Ce qui paraît également évident c'est la réticence de la Commission à élargir de quelque manière que ce soit la sphère de ses compétences. Guère gênée par le Conseil, qui lui faisait confiance, ni davantage par l'Assemblée, elle poursuivait sa tâche avec beaucoup de conscience dans un climat d'entente et de coopération, notamment avec les puissances mandataires qu'on cherchait visiblement à ne point heurter, un climat de bienséance qui n'est pas marqué de violents éclats et à peine par des tensions passagères. Nous sommes là entre gens de bonne compagnie, aux vues très largement similaires, pour qui la »mission sacrée de *civilisation*«[28] ne pouvait évidemment signifier – ainsi le voulait l'époque – qu'une civilisation *à l'européenne;* et ce n'est sans doute pas un hasard, dans cette perspective, si c'est généralement le Japon qui est désigné comme étant le véritable échec du système.[29] En outre, la règle selon laquelle les puissances mandataires devaient rester minoritaires au sein de la C.P.M.[30] est en réalité trompeuse dans la mesure où certains des membres de la majorité »représentaient« des Etats qui, sans être chargés d'un mandat, étaient néanmoins des puissances coloniales;[31] sans doute la Commission était-elle censée se composer d'experts, choisis *ad personam* pour cette haute fonction: mais il est aisé de démontrer par quels liens étroits ils demeuraient pourtant liés à leurs gouvernements respectifs.

Peut-être peut-on alléguer que la mission de la Commission lui était dictée par des textes précis, qui en fixaient du même coup les frontières, même s'il est vrai que plus tard – autre exemple de l'influence de temps différents sur la marche des institutions – l'O.N.U. n'allait pas s'embarrasser de pareilles limites. Mais ce qu'il faut pourtant relever, c'est que le Pacte lui-même offrait des possibilités qui sont demeurées inexploitées: c'est le cas, par exemple, de l'article 23 b), timide précurseur des dispositions futures sur les territoires non-autonomes, qui prévoyait que »les Membres de la Société [. . .] s'engagent à assurer le traitement équitable des populations indigènes dans les territoires soumis à leur administration«. On considère communément que cet article est demeuré lettre morte: cela ne signifie pas, cependant, qu'il soit resté complètement inaperçu mais bien plutôt qu'on s'est gardé de saisir les occasions d'agir qu'il pouvait cautionner. C'est ainsi, par exemple, qu'un *»Memorial«* du 28 mars 1922 est expédié par le *Synod of the Reformed Presbyterian Church of Scotland* au Secrétaire général de la Société mais à l'attention du Conseil, à propos des Nouvelles-Hébrides, un territoire qui n'était, il est vrai, pas placé sous mandat, pour y dénoncer maints excès dont souffrait la population autochtone – . . . »the abuses rampant under the Condominium between France and Great Britain« . . . »various injustices of the most glaring nature [. . .] perpetrated on the helpless natives« . . . »an interesting people [. . .] threatened with extinction« . . . Or cette pétition se heurte à une fin de non-recevoir de la part de la Société, après avoir passé par la Section juridique et la Section des mandats, et non sans que l'application éventuelle de l'article 23 b) ait été dûment considérée. Mais ce qu'il faut souligner, c'est que s'il se manifeste alors un certain regret d'avoir à opposer un refus à cette requête, il n'a rien à voir avec une interprétation, large ou étroite, de l'esprit des mandats pour la protection des *»natives«* ainsi malmenés: c'est ce que montre, de façon révélatrice, l'annotation de William E. Rappard sur une des pièces du dossier: »It always strikes me as very unfortunate when we are obliged to send negative and non committal answers to protests against real abuses emanating from serious and important organisations. I suppose the League of Nations has no stronger friends in the world than those circles from which the enclosed memorial comes«.[32] C'est donc bien le *Synod*, dans l'intérêt suprême de la Société, qu'il importait surtout de ménager. Peut-être peut-on donc conclure des considérations qui ont été exposées que l'action voulue par la Société des Nations dans ce domaine, et plus particulièrement en son nom par la Commission permanente des Mandats, a eu probablement pour effet d'accomoder, plutôt que de progressivement réduire, l'emprise du fait colonial sur le système mondial.[33]

Autant, et plus encore peut-être que la vision du phénomène colonial par la Société, c'est la perception inverse qui nous intéresse. Quelle image pouvait-on bien se faire, en terrain colonisé de la SdN en général, de sa mission particulière à l'égard de la domination coloniale ou de l'évolution de ses travaux dans ce domaine? Ici, nous rous mouvons dans un terrain difficile, semé d'embûches, et qui ne laisse guère de place, faute de pouvoir disposer d'une documentation adéquate, qu'à des conjectures. Cette question doit pourtant être soulevée avec fermeté, tant elle revêt d'importance si l'on veut parvenir à éclairer l'un des secteurs les plus obscurs de l'histoire coloniale en général, et de la décolonisation en particulier. Une telle entreprise commence avec les principes wilsoniens: non pas leur origine et leur mise en œuvre – qui sont bien connues – ni même l'interprétation du cinquième des Quatorze points, d'une rare ambiguïté, mais l'écho qu'ils ont pu avoir en terrain colonisé et, le cas échéant, l'itinéraire par lequel ils s'y sont frayé un chemin. Toute cette recherche reste à faire, comme à l'égard de la Société des Nations par la suite, dans une perspective similaire. Là encore, une étude minutieuse des pétitions s'impose, car elles figurent sans doute en bonne place parmi les témoignages utilisables. Mais il faudrait pouvoir ne pas s'arrêter à leur *contenu*, et chercher à en savoir davantage sur *leur origine*. Si, par exemple, Marcus Garvey adresse au Conseil de la SdN des pétitions, innombrablement contresignées, au nom et pour la défense de la race noire,[34] si des chefs tribaux du Cameroun, dans un document par ailleurs éloquent sur l'effet des trois dominations coloniales successives que ce territorie a subies, réclament leur souveraineté sous la haute et directe autorité de la Société,[35] n'est-on pas en mesure d'y trouver des éléments de réponse aux problèmes de perception qui viennent d'être évoqués? Quelle image ces hommes se faisaient-ils donc de la SdN, de ses pouvoirs, de ses objectifs, par quels moyens pouvait-on connaître, notamment dans les territoires sous mandat B et C, le déroulement de ses travaux à leur propre sujet? En d'autres termes, quelle est la *genèse* réelle de telles pétitions et, si nous parvenons à la connaître, ou du moins à la repérer, quels enseignements peut-on en tirer sur le monde colonial lui-même, sur l'image qu'il a de lui et de son environnement extérieur, en un mot sur tous les facteurs qui influencent l'évolution de sa mentalité collective? Là encore, tout ou presque reste à faire; mais il se peut que la documentation propre à la Société des Nations permette de fournir des réponses à ce type de question qui la dépassent en réalité largement.

Certes, il en est beaucoup d'autres qui mériteraient d'être soulevées, ne serait-ce parfois que pour leurs prolongements ultérieurs, mais qui ne peuvent être abordées ici: par exemple le rôle des personnes, la notion de régionalisme par rapport aux Mandats, la question délicate des frontières, celle des travailleurs indigènes et des migrations forcées, l'équilibre subtil entre la discrétion et la publicité ou certaines décisions curieuses comme celle consistant à ne reconnaître aucune nationalité aux habitants de certains des territoires inclus dans le système. Au reste, il ne s'agit point de le juger, de mesurer la part d'idéalisme ou d'expédient politique qu'il comporte, ni surtout d'apprécier la valeur de la formule par rapport à son application et à ses résultats dans un temps historique déterminé.

Car l'essentiel, c'est bien que la Société des Nations ait laissé derrière elle l'idée même de mandat international. Il est en effet permis d'imaginer que loin d'avoir fait son temps, cette idée puisse resurgir tout à coup et qu'à défaut de toute autre, elle contribue à résoudre l'un des problèmes les plus épineux – sinon les plus apparents – de notre propre temps.

*

Voilà qui nous ramène, pour terminer, sur ce qui constituait notre point de départ: cette espèce de »Cinquième monde«, composé exclusivement de territoires insulaires, de milliers d'îles plus ou moins minuscules, plus ou moins dépourvues, que le système mondial actuel, tendant à universaliser une société internationale formée d'Etats souverains, est incapable d'accomoder, et par conséquent condamne à l'abandon, au dépérissement et à l'oubli.

Le point essentiel, ici, c'est qu'en dépit de l'idéologie proclamée avec force depuis 1960 par les Nations Unies, le mouvement vers la décolonisation totale se heurte, dans sa phase ultime, à des limites qu'il ne peut pas franchir; c'est-à-dire qu'elle laissera inévitablement subsister un résidu géographique, une dentelle de tout petits territoires, dispersés sur les mers, pour qui l'indépendance – au sens juridique de la souveraineté – n'est tout simplement pas concevable. Sans doute, »dans les conditions difficiles du monde moderne« (une phrase qui figurait déjà dans l'article 22 du Pacte, mais sur le sens de laquelle on s'est fort peu interrogé à l'époque), l'indépendance n'est-elle qu'une notion relative, et tel qui paraissait hier incapable de se gouverner seul a bel et bien accédé depuis à la souveraineté.[36] On sait bien aussi – après deux décennies de débats sur le développement – qu'indépendance nationale et indépendance tout court sont des termes qui ne se recouvrent pas. Il reste que pour les territoires auxquels nous songeons ici, cette souveraineté demeure, ou demeurerait vide de sens, faute de pouvoir disposer des moyens les plus élémentaires pour en assurer l'exercice. On trouve là une illustration du fossé, voire de la contradiction qui peuvent séparer certains principes à vocation universelle – tel le droit à l'autodétermination – et les limites que leur opposent en fait les conditions propres à certains cas véritablement singuliers.

Il est étrange qu'on ait été si peu attentif aux dimensions de ce problème, et que notamment le Comité des vingt-quatre ne semble guère s'être préoccupé des sérieuses conséquences que l'affirmation massive du droit à l'indépendance pouvait entraîner pour certains micro-territoires, dont il a eu pourtant l'occasion d'examiner le cas.[37] C'est en réalité sous un autre angle que l'O.N.U. a abordé, passagèrement, la question: lorsqu'en pleine vague de décolonisation, le Secrétaire général U Thant, dans son rapport de 1967 puis de 1968, s'est soudain inquiété d'un éventuel envahissement de l'Organisation par une quantité d'Etats minuscules, »ces entités exceptionnellement petites par leur superficie, leur population et leurs ressources humaines et économiques«[38] qui seraient par conséquent incapables de remplir les obligations incombant à ses membres aux termes de l'article 4. Pourtant, aussitôt éclipsé par les problèmes gigantesques que posait à tous le Tiers monde déjà décolonisé, celui des micro-territoires a bien vite disparu dans les sables; c'est ce que concède, par un euphémisme remarquable, un rapport relativement récent de la C.N.U.C.E.D. sur le sujet, dont la conclusion recommande notamment qu'on entreprenne »une étude sur la viabilité des petits pays insulaires – question qui a été quelque peu négligée jusqu'à présent«.[39] Il est d'autre part évident que les termes mêmes de la confrontation Nord-Sud, les tentatives de négocier, globalement, un nouvel ordre mondial ont eu l'effet regrettable – dont on s'est bientôt rendu compte – d'»uniformiser« le concept de Tiers monde et de négliger *ipso facto* ses différences. Les petits pays minuscules, ainsi rejetés dans l'ombre ou implicitement inclus – ce qui est pire – dans des catégories qui ne les concernent pas, ont fait les frais de ce procédé et cela d'autant plus qu'ils n'avaient pas voix au chapitre.

Or, ce qui rend spécifique – et alarmante – la situation des petits territoires insulaires, c'est qu'aux deux grandes considérations qui sous-tendent le principe des Mandats et plus encore, par la suite, celui de la Tutelle – le droit des peuples à décider eux-mêmes de leur destin et la constatation qu'ils sont parvenus à des stades très différents de développement économique et social – il s'en ajoute, pour certains micro-territoires, une troisième: la certitude où l'on se trouve *d'avance* que par leurs propres forces, ils ne seront *jamais* en mesure de se développer au-delà d'un certain point. Ils sont donc condamnés à dépendre toujours d'un appui extérieur, ou voués – ce qui parfois revient au même – à n'être que la proie d'autrui. Et sous l'effet d'un amer paradoxe, ils sont même d'autant plus promis à cette dépendance que la nouvelle conception des problèmes du développement à l'échelle mondiale tend à rejeter sur les pays du Tiers monde la responsabilité d'un effort prioritaire et le soin de déterminer eux-mêmes leur propre »stratégie«, une tâche que la plupart des micro-territoires ne sont guère en état d'assumer.

C'est ainsi qu'on en vient à se demander s'il n'existe pas, entre deux solutions également aléatoires – une souveraineté impossible, ou le maintien perpétuel de la domination coloniale – l'hypothèse d'une situation de type tutélaire qui permette, par ses modalités pratiques et juridiques, d'assurer la survie de certaines communautés insulaires.

Il est bien sûr impossible d'aborder ici tout ce qui caractérise le monde des archipels, ou ce qui hypothèque si lourdement leur avenir. Le point central qu'il suffit peut-être de souligner, c'est que tout en souffrant de la plupart des maux qui affligent le Tiers monde en général, ils connaissent en sus des difficultés qui leur sont propres, ou qui mettent un coefficient aux problèmes communs. Il est par exemple permis de penser que l'héritage de la période coloniale pèse particulièrement lourd sur la situation présente des archipels, dans la mesure où souvent, les découpages ou les regroupements territoriaux opérés, au fil de l'histoire, par les puissances rivales ont été plus capricieux encore en ce qui les concerne, que dans les grands espaces continentaux. C'est ainsi que sans vouloir jouer les fées Carabosse sur le berceau du dernier-né de la communauté internationale, on peut se demander quel avenir attend les Nouvelles-Hébrides, issues de la monstruosité juridico-politique du condominium franco-anglais et livrées presque d'un coup, cette année, à tous les défis de l'indépendance.[41]

On peut aussi évoquer tout ce qu'implique, pour le fonctionnement politique d'un archipel, la dispersion territoriale, la fragmentation et les distances: des distances qui ne se mesurent ni en milles, ni en kilomètres,[42] mais en nombre de ports, de bateaux, de pistes d'atterrissage, et finalement en coût, ou plus subtilement encore en images réciproques, en connaissance ou en ignorance mutuelles, en volonté de domination comme en griefs d'abandon ou de partialité, et qui rendent monumentale la tâche d'édification d'une *communauté nationale*. La souveraineté effective, dans ce cas, c'est peut-être avant tout une question de communications. Et tandis que partout on prône l'intégration régionale de vastes ensembles géographiques, les archipels sont eux-mêmes menacés, en permanence, de désagrégation: ils portent véritablement en eux, par la nature des choses, le virus de la sécession. Sans doute suggère-t-on souvent des solutions de décentralisation, ou même de type fédéral, pour parer à leur éclatement: il se trouve malheureusement pour eux que les solutions de cette nature sont en général les plus coûteuses, les plus gourmandes en personnel qualifié, les plus exigeantes en matière d'expérience politique,[43] autant d'éléments qui font défaut aux petites communautés insulaires, incapables de maîtriser certaines notions que de telles solutions impliquent, comme par exemple la redistribution des revenus, ou le partage des responsabilités dans l'exercice d'une souveraineté divisée verticalement, en forme de poupées russes.

C'est encore le problème de la population qu'il faudrait mentionner, tant il peut paraître paradoxal qu'un petit territoire insulaire puisse souffrir *à la fois* d'être trop peuplé – atteint comme ailleurs par l'explosion démographique – et de ne pas l'être assez, dans la mesure où le »décollage« politique et économique suggère un palier minimum quant au nombre des membres de la communauté concernée.

Enfin, si une extrême vulnérabilité vis-à-vis des influences extérieures est un trait distinctif de tous les pays les moins développés, elle se double pour les micro-Etats d'une dimension supplémentaire: ils sont tout particulièrement exposés à l'action pernicieuse des *individus* eux-mêmes. On peut ne pas accorder de crédit aux rumeurs qui ont couru sur les ingérences personnelles qui auraient gouverné, de loin, la sécession manquée d'Espiritu Santo, juste avant l'accession à l'indépendance des Nouvelles-Hébrides.[44] Mais les exemples abondent qui montrent combien il est facile à des individus résolus à exploiter la naïveté, l'inexpérience, ou les possibilités de corruption inévitables dans une communauté humaine peu développée de quelques milliers de personnes, de faire modifier ses lois, transformer son régime foncier, ou de faire adopter le plus légalement du monde par un parlement-miniature, ignorant de la portée de son acte et trompé par des promesses fallacieuses de gains fabuleux, un décret introduisant, par exemple, une procédure de divorces-éclairs, comme cela s'est produit il n'y a pas longtemps dans une île minuscule des Caraïbes.[45] Comment donc protéger les petits Etats insulaires contre cette nouvelle espèce de conquistadors?

Il n'est guère aisé de conclure quand de par la nature du problème traité et des réflexions d'ordre spéculatif auquel il a donné lieu, il n'y a pas de véritables conclusions à proposer. Le problème des micro-territoires est réel, même s'il est largement ignoré aujourd'hui. Il appelle des solutions que le système international n'est actuellement pas en mesure de lui offrir. Sans doute, aucune recette ne peut-elle être extraite comme telle du passé, et l'expérience du Mandat sous la Société des Nations n'a, dans la conception la plus généreuse de son esprit, qu'une valeur limitée de précédent, dans un temps historique qui n'est pas le nôtre. Ce précédent n'est pourtant pas négligeable: il montre en effet que si l'administration internationale directe d'un territoire – que le Général Smuts considérait, selon une expression fameuse, comme *»paralysis tempered by intrigue«*[46] – n'est guère praticable, la délégation totale de compétence, sous un contrôle éloigné, ne l'est pas davantage. L'idée du Mandat comporte pourtant le mérite inestimable – en commun, par exemple, avec le système fédéral – d'être avant toute chose un *principe* qui se prête, tant que sa finalité est respectée, à des modalités d'application infiniment diverses. Il est donc certainement possible d'imaginer des voies similaires, comme est en train d'en explorer le *Commonwealth Secretariat* dans le domaine de l'assistance juridique[47] qui permettent d'assurer aux micro-territoires une protection, un encadrement et un soutien sans lesquels ils n'ont, littéralement, pas d'avenir.

Notes

1 ASdN 1919–1927/1/661/161 (R 1).

2 Sir Frederick J. D. Lugard, *The Dual Mandate in British Tropical Africa*, Edinburgh, William Blackwood & Sons, 1926. 3rd ed., p. 198.

3 La littérature consacrée aux Mandats est immense. Mais si l'on se fonde sur l'ouvrage de F. P. Walters, *A History of the League of Nations*. London, Oxford University Press, 2 v. 1952. – 833 p. qui demeure encore un ouvrage de base sur l'histoire de la SdN, on constate que le système des mandats n'y occupe qu'une place relativement insignifiante.

4 Henri-Irénée Marrou, *De la connaissance historique*, Paris, Seuil, 1954. – 304 p., et du même, »Comment comprendre le métier d'historien« dans Charles Samaran (sous la direction de), *L'Histoire et ses méthodes*, Paris, Gallimard, 1961. – p. 1465–1539 (Encyclopédie de la Pléiade), ». . . l'enquête historique est [. . .] orientée vers l'explication de la conjoncture présente, cherchant à nous faire comprendre ce qu'est l'homme – la societé, la civilisation – d'aujourd'hui«, *ibid.*, p. 1479; cf. également Marc Bloch, *Apologie pour l'histoire ou métier d'historien*, Paris, Armand Colin, 7 ème éd., 1974, 167 p.

5 Pierre Chaunu, *Le refus de la vie*, Paris, Calmann-Lévy, 1975. – p. 12.

6 Il est sans doute inutile de souligner combien des réflexions qui se situent dans la perspective indiquée sont, par la nature des choses, aléatoires et tout ce qu'elles comportent inévitablement de spéculatif, et par conséquent de provisoire.

7 Paul Veyne, *L'inventaire des différences*, Paris, Seuil, 1976. – 64 p.

8 Histoire de la Sainte-Alliance, Genève, Georg, 1954. – p. 15.

9 Un bon exemple, pourtant, d'une telle entreprise comparative, sur la question qui nous occupe ici, est l'ouvrage de R. N. Chowdhuri, *International Mandates and Trusteeship Systems – A comparative study,* The Hague, Martinus Nijhoff, 1955. – 328 p.

10 Dans quel ordre, et de quelle manière, s'est déroulée cette introduction du système – c'est-à-dire »qui a fait quoi et quand?« – c'est là une question d'une réelle importance: elle a été parfaitement mise en évidence par H. Duncan Hall, *Mandates, Dependencies and Trusteeship,* Washington, Carnegie Endowment for International Peace, 1948. – chap. X, p. 130 ff.; cf. notamment les tableaux synoptiques montrant l'imbrication des décisions prises par le Conseil suprême des Alliés d'une part et par la Société des Nations d'autre part, *ibid.*, p. 136 ss.

11 Cf. par exemple Wolfe W. Schmokel, *Dream of Empire: German Colonialism 1919–1945.* New Haven, Yale University Press, 1964. – 204 p.; G. Maroger, *L'Europe et la question coloniale; revendications coloniales allemandes, aspirations coloniales polonaises,* Paris, Sirey, 1938. – 464 p.; cf. aussi, à titre d'illustration de certaines réactions à la politique allemande dans ce domaine, ASdN, 1933–1946/6A/27984 (R 4137).

12 Cf. Maurice Barbier, *Le Comité de Décolonisation des Nations Unies.* Paris, Pichon et Durand-Auzias, 1974. – 757 p.

13 Cf. *supra,* note 11. A cet égard, il convient de mentionner l'affaire éthiopienne, sur quoi tant a été écrit, mais sous l'angle presque exclusif de l'application ou de l'échec du système de sécurité collective de la SdN, alors que son aspect colonial, notamment ses effets sur la mentalité collective des populations africaines, demeure singulièrement à l'arrière-plan: cf. à cet égard le témoignage rapporté par J. S. Coleman montrant combien la conquête de l'Ethiopie a pu attiser les nationalismes et durcir les confrontations raciales: "... the Italian conquest of Africa's historic kingdom made him [one of the most militant and uncompromising nationalists in Nigeria] aware for the first time that the struggle of the future was between white and black", *Nigeria, Background to Nationalism,* University of California Press, 1963. – p. 209; dans le même sens, mais du point de vue du gouvernement blanc de l'Afrique du Sud, voir par exemple l'intervention, le 13 septembre 1935, de M. C. te Water à l'Assemblée de la SdN, et les craintes qu'elle exprime: League of Nations, *OJSS.* no. 138, p. 66–67.

14 Aucun témoignage n'exprime sans doute plus éloquemment cette ambiguïté, mélange subtil de foi et de doute, que le fameux ouvrage d'Albert Sarrault, paru précisément à ce moment crucial de l'entre-deux-guerres: *Grandeur et servitude coloniale.* Paris, éd. du Sagittaire, 1931. – 285 p.

15 En ce qui concerne la Grande-Bretagne, voir par exemple l'excellente étude de Kenneth Robinson, *The Dilemmas of Trusteeship, Aspects of British Colonial Policy between the wars.* London, Oxford University Press, 1965. – 95 p.

16 Sur cette émergence des nationalismes, et sur les hésitations qui en marquent le cheminement, voir par exemple le récit autobiographique de Fehrat Abbas, *Guerre et révolution d'Algérie,* notamment le premier tome: *La nuit coloniale.* Paris, Julliard, 1962. – 233 p.

17 Voir notamment les thèses sur la question nationale et coloniale votées au deuxième Congrès du Comintern en 1920, Jane Degras, *The Communist International 1919–1943. Documents.* London, Oxford University Press, 1956. – v. 1, p. 142–144, et surtout celles du sixième congrès, en 1928, *ibid.*, v. 2, p. 521–2.

18 Un des meilleurs exemples de cet état d'esprit est sans doute fourni par la Conférence de Brazzaville, réunie du 30 janvier au 8 février 1944 dans le but d'examiner les formules de réaménagement du domaine colonial de la France, mais qui exprime clairement l'intention – par-delà les réformes envisagées – de resserrer, plutôt que de distendre, les liens impériaux; ainsi la fameuse déclaration qui ouvre les recommandations adoptées par la

conférence sur »l'Organisation politique de l'Empire Français – Organisation politique intérieure des Colonies« où il est affirmée que »les fins de l'œuvre de civilisation accomplie par la France dans les colonies écartent toute idée d'autonomie, toute possibilité d'évolution hors du bloc français de l'Empire: La constitution éventuelle, même lointaine, de self-governments dans les colonies est à écarter«, *La Conférence africaine française de Brazzaville 1944*, Paris, Ministère des colonies, 1945. – p. 32; le ton avait du reste été donné par le discours d'ouverture du général de Gaulle, tout à la gloire de l'oeuvre accomplie par la France dans ce domaine. *Mémoires de guerre*, tome 3, *l'Unité 1942–1944*. Paris, Plon, 1954. – p. 555–557.

19 Notamment l'Acte de la Conférence de Berlin du 26 février 1885 et la Déclaration de Bruxelles du 2 juillet 1890, sans aucun doute confirmés dans leur esprit, plus qu'amendés, par la Convention de St. Germain-en-Laye du 10 septembre 1919 sur la révision des documents précités, cf. Manley O. Hudson, *International Legislation*. Washington, Carnegie Endowment for International Peace, 1931. – v. 1, 1919–1921, p. 344–352.

20 L'article 22 du Pacte, paragraphe 1, se réfère clairement aux »colonies et territoires [. . .] habités par des peuples *non encore* capables de se diriger eux-mêmes . . .«, souligné par nous.

21 Auteur de la thèse qui fournit le titre de son fameux ouvrage, et sur laquelle il se clot: »Let it be admitted at the outset that European brains, capital, and energy have not been, and never will be, expended in developing the resources of Africa from motives of pure philanthropy; that Europe is in Africa for the mutual benefit of her own industrial classes, and of the native races in their progress to a higher plane; that the benefit can be made reciprocal, and that it is the aim and desire of civilised administration to fulfill this dual mandate«, Lugard, *op. cit.*, p. 619; sur Lord Lugard, voir notamment la remarquable biographie de Margery Freda Perham, *Lugard: The Years of Authority, 1898–1945. The Second Part of the Life of Frederick Dealtry Lugard, Later Lord Lugard of Abinger*. London, Collins, 1960 (la première partie, *Lugard: The Years of Adventure*, a été publié en 1956) 748 p.

22 Ce point concerne toute la question des »enquêtes sur place«, soulevée à plus d'une reprise par la Commission permanente des Mandats, notamment en octobre 1925, lors de sa septième session, cf. C.P.M. procès-verbaux VII (1925) p. 219, mais interprétée, en fin de compte très restrictivement, du fait »que la Commission ne s'est pas reconnu le droit de procéder à des enquêtes sur place dans les territoires sous mandat sans une autorisation expresse du Conseil et [. . .] qu'elle n'a pas pu se résoudre à suggérer au Conseil de lui conférer ce droit, les opinions des membres de la Commission étant partagées en ce qui concerne l'opportunité et l'utilité de telles enquêtes«, *Le Système des Mandats, Origine, principes et application* (SdN, doc. 1945. VI. A.1, p. 46).

23 Cf. *Manuel bibliographique sur la Societé des Nations*, version provisoire. Etabli par Victor-Yves Ghebali, Genève, Bibliothèque des Nations Unies, 1980. – (Publications, Série C, no. 3, v. 1) p. 177–259.

24 Cf. *Aperçu de la procédure en matière de pétitions concernant les territoires sous mandat*, doc. SdN C.545.M.194.1927.VI et CPM procès-verbaux XII (1927) p. 176–178.

25 C'est-à-dire la Namibie et la Micronésie, qui comprend notamment les anciens territoires sous mandat confiés à l'administration japonaise.

26 Voir en particulier les débats (Troisième Commission) et les résolutions du Congrès de Stuttgart, en 1907, *VIIème Congrès Socialiste International tenu à Stuttgart du 16 au 24 août 1907*. Compte rendu analytique publié par le Secrétariat du BSI, Bruxelles, 1908.

27 Cf. par exemple British Labour Party, *Labour and the Nation*, London, 1928 et *The Empire in Africa: Labour's Policy*, London, 1926.

28 Article 22, paragraphe l du Pacte; souligné par nous.

29 Même après avoir quitté la Société, le Japon est demeuré membre de la Commission permanente des Mandats, non sans y être exposé à de vives critiques pour être soupçonné de construire des fortifications militaires dans les territoires soumis à son administration, en contradiction flagrante avec les termes des mandats C, cf. CPM, procès-verbaux XXII (1932), p. 114–115. C'est pourtant à des raisons d'ordre politique interne, concernant notamment le système de gouvernement, qu'on attribue souvent l'échec japonais en matière de mandat, ainsi Hall: »in an autocratic system, where free publicity is not possible, no mandate or trusteeship system could operate«, *op. cit.*, p. 212.

30 Constitution de la CPM, lettre (a), *Journal Officiel*, I (1920), p. 90; composée à l'origine de 9 membres, puis de 10 avec l'admission d'un représentant allemand en 1927, *Journal Officiel* VIII (1927), p. 1120 (tandis que W. E. Rappard avait été nommé par le Conseil, en 1924, en qualité de membre extraordinaire), la Commission ne pouvait donc pas comprendre plus de quatre membres ressortissants d'une puissance mandataire, soit la Belgique, la France, le Japon et le Royaume-Uni – l'Italie, privée de mandat, se voyant octroyer, à titre de compensation, la présidence de la Commission. cf. Tableau général de la composition de la CPM pendant toute la durée de son existence *in* Hall, *op. cit.*, p. 181–2.

31 C'est le cas de l'Espagne, des Pays-Bas, du Portugal.

32 ASdN, 1919–27/11/19962/19962 (R 602).

33 Peut-être d'ailleurs la question se pose-t-elle de savoir si elle l'aurait même consolidé: c'est là tout le problème – dans lequel nous ne pouvons pas entrer ici – qui consiste à évaluer les influences réciproques qui ont pu s'exercer entre les territoires soumis à mandat et les territoires coloniaux qui ne l'étaient pas.

34 ASdN, 1919–1927/1/14410/13940 (R 39); 1928–1932/6A/7158/7158 (R 2344).

35 Pétition du 19 décembre 1929, CPM 1045.

36 Stewart Easton, dans *The Twilight of European Colonialism. A Political Analysis.* London, Methnen, 1961. – consacre un chapitre aux territoires qu'il considère sans hésiter, dans sa perspective d'alors, comme »too small for complete independence«, *op. cit.*, p. 239–271; or la plupart ont accédé depuis à l'indépendance et sont devenus membres des Nations Unies.

37 Dans son rapport annuel pour 1966–1967, le Secrétaire général des Nations Unies rapporte que »le Comité spécial [Comité des vingt-quatre] a porté une attention particulière aux petits territoires. Tout en reconnaissant qu'ils présentaient des problèmes particuliers [. . .] le Comité spécial était cependant convaincu que les dispositions de la Déclaration [Déclaration sur l'octroi de l'indépendance aux pays et aux peuples coloniaux, Résolution 1514 (XV) de l'Assemblée générale] leur étaient pleinement applicables«, Assemblée générale, Documents officiels: vingt-deuxième session, supplément no. 1 (A/6701), p. 72; tout récemment encore, le même Comité – avec toute la désinvolture de Ponce Pilate – se bornait à exprimer ses bons voeux aux Nouvelles-Hébrides, à l'occasion de leur indépendance, sans guère s'interroger sur les perspectives qui les attendent: "In a consensus on the New Hebrides, the Committee noted with satisfaction that the Territory had attained independence on 30 July, as the Republic of Vanuatu, in accordance with the Declaration on decolonization, and warmly congratulated the people and the Government of Vanuatu upon their accession to independence and wished them peace and prosperity in their newly acquired status", *U.N. Chronicle*, November 1980, v. XVII, no. 9, p. 23.

38 Assemblée générale, Documents officiels: vingt-deuxième session, supplément no. 1A (A/6701/Add. 1) p. 22–23; Assemblée générale, Documents officiels: Vingt-troisième session, supplément no. 1 (A/7201), p. 47, et supplément no. 1A (A/7201/Add. 1), p. 22. Le Secrétaire général suggérait d'établir une distinction entre le droit à l'indépen-

dance et le »statut intégral« de membre des Nations Unies, proposant qu'on envisage pour les »micro-Etats« des formes nouvelles d'association.

39 *Pays insulaires en voie de développement*, Publications des Nations Unies, New York, F.1974.II.D.6, p. 9.

40 Ce point a été souligné avec vigueur par M. McNamara, président de la Banque mondiale, dans son discours annuel de 1979, lorsqu'il examine les *approaches to a new international development strategy:* "Within the international framework of a development strategy for the Eighties, individual developing countries must develop their own plans of action [. . .] It is only such concrete programs on the national level that can translate international intent into actual improvements in the lives of individuals [. . .] Most of this effort will, of course, have to come from the developing countries themselves", *Address to the Board of Governors,* by Robert S. McNamara, Belgrade, Yugoslavia, 2 October 1979. – p. 27.

41 Voir René Chiroux, »Les Nouvelles-Hébrides sur le chemin de l'indépendance: nouvelles menaces dans l'océan Pacifique«, dans *Défense nationale,* janvier 1979, p. 35–47; Raymond Goy, »L'évolution institutionnelle des Nouvelles-Hébrides: du condominium à l'indépendance«, dans *Revue du droit public et de la science politique en France et à l'étranger,* sept.–oct. 1979, p. 1347–1381; »Die Neuen Hebriden vor der Unabhängigkeit«, dans *Neue Zürcher Zeitung,* 27 juillet 1980; »L'indépendance difficile« dans *Le Monde,* 6–7 juillet 1980.

42 Voir à ce propos les articles consacrés aux archipels dans le projet de nouvelle convention internationale sur le droit de la mer A/CONF. 62/WP.10/Rev. 2, Partie IV, Etats Archipels, articles 46 ff.

43 Voir par ex. K. C. Wheare, *Federal Government,* 4th edition, London, Oxford University Press, 1963. – 266 p.

44 Le mouvement sécessionniste de Jimmy Stevens aurait été provoqué et alimenté en sous-main par des hommes d'affaires américains, sous le couvert de la »Phoenix Foundation« dans le but d'établir à Espiritu Santo un »tax-free haven«, cf. *International Herald Tribune,* 3 June, 1980, p. 1.

45 Cf. K. W. Patchett and J. R. Young, Tourist Divorces and the Abuse of a Small State's Legal System: A Study of the Montserrat Matrimonial Causes for Foreigners Ordinance, 1978, MS, 1980. – à paraître dans *American Journal of Comparative Law.*

46 *The League of Nations. A Practical Suggestion.* London, Hodder and Stoughton, 1918. – p. 18.

47 Cf. K. W. Patchett, *Legal Resource Needs in Small States – Report on Bermuda and the Caribbean.* London, February 1980. – MS, à paraître.

Postface

Marlis M. Steinert et Victor-Yves Ghebali

Au terme de nos travaux, il serait justice de rendre son dû à César: il convient donc de souligner que l'idée du présent Symposium sur l'histoire de la Société des Nations, douze lustres après la naissance de celle-ci, revient aux gardiens naturels de son précieux héritage archivistique et documentaire – les hauts responsables ainsi que les fonctionnaires compétents de la Bibliothèque des Nations Unies à Genève. C'est à ces mêmes gardiens qu'il faut attribuer le mérite du projet de *Manuel bibliographique sur la Société des Nations*, projet mené à chef par Victor-Yves Ghebali et que l'auteur a présenté, à l'occasion du Symposium, sous la forme provisoire d'un ouvrage en trois forts volumes brochés.[1] Répertoriant quelque 10.000 titres publiés entre 1920 et 1980, ce guide méthodique et critique met désormais à la disposition du monde de la recherche un usuel bibliographique qui vient opportunément s'ajouter aux usuels déjà existants dans le domaine archivistique et dans le domaine documentaire. Par cette réalisation prestigieuse, la Bibliothèque des Nations Unies a apporté l'élément qui manquait encore au triptyque des instruments de travail indispensables à l'étude scientifique de l'histoire et des activités de la Société des Nations.

Les circonstances se trouvaient ainsi on ne peut plus favorables à la réunion d'un certain nombre de spécialistes et de chercheurs intéressés à la SdN en vue de dresser en quelque sorte l'état de la question – *the state of the cart.* Cela s'imposait d'autant plus qu'il n'existait toujours pas à ce jour de bilan tant soit peu serein sinon objectif de l'expérience sociétaire. Il allait en outre pratiquement de soi qu'une telle réunion tînt ses assises à l'Institut universitaire de hautes études internationales, institution établie en 1927 par deux anciens hauts fonctionnaires sociétaires – les professeurs William Rappard et Paul Mantoux – pour contribuer sur le plan universitaire à l'expérience de coopération internationale que représentait alors l'établissement à Genève de la SdN. Telle est l'origine de cette première rencontre entre historiens et autres spécialistes de la SdN qui, venus de partout dans le monde, ne se connaissaient pour la plupart jusque-là que par leurs écrits respectifs. La qualité des divers rapports et communications[2], l'extrême richesse des débats ainsi que le caractère fructueux des contacts personnels directs ont fait du présent colloque une telle réussite académique que l'ensemble des participants a exprimé le désir de voir l'expérience se renouveler, voire se poursuivre sur une base plus ou moins périodique.

Mais le Symposium n'a pas fait que révéler l'intérêt croissant suscité par les questions relatives à la SdN au sein des milieux universitaires: il a surtout eu le mérite particulier d'éclairer pour la première fois les lacunes, souvent importantes, qui existent dans la recherche relative à l'institution genevoise. Ces lacunes sont le produit de multiples facteurs, à commencer par un facteur d'ordre psychologique: la déception causée par les défauts flagrants, le déclin puis la faillite de la SdN – les désillusions de la génération de l'entre-deux-guerres étant sans conteste à la hauteur de ses espoirs. Ces lacunes doivent être considérées comme la conséquence de l'ouverture assez tardive de certaines archives nationales et, plus encore, comme l'expression d'une tendance spécifique dans l'étude des relations internationales – celle qui privilégie le rôle des acteurs purement étatiques (déterminant il est vrai, mais non exclusif) par rapport à celui des institutions internationales. En réalité, l'histoire diplomatique ne saurait être confondue avec l'histoire des relations internationales, domaine relativement récent et dont l'histoire des organisations internationales représente une province pratiquement inexplorée. De fait, les secteurs à défricher ici sont rien moins que négligeables. On peut en distinguer cinq principaux.

En premier lieu, l'histoire des relations entre la SdN et les divers acteurs étatiques du système international de l'entre-deux-guerres demeure encore des plus pauvres. Le poids, le rôle et la signification du facteur »Société des Nations« dans la politique étrangère des Etats membres ou non membres constitue ainsi un secteur où la recherche pourrait se développer avec un réel profit. Il existe d'ailleurs à cet égard une lacune particulièrement spectaculaire: le cas des rapports France-SdN, lacune qui s'explique essentiellement par le penchant (déjà relevé plus haut) des historiens en faveur de l'histoire diplomatique classique.

En deuxième lieu, on peut remarquer que l'on ne dispose guère d'études valables portant sur l'action de certains groupes d'Etats, comme ceux d'Amérique latine par exemple, ayant tenu une place importante ou originale au sein de la Société des Nations.

En troisième lieu, il y a un secteur qui reste vierge dans sa presque immensité: celui de l'opinion publique. Il ne serait pas inutile que l'on puisse disposer de monographies portant soit sur l'opinion publique de tel ou tel pays ou groupe de pays, soit sur l'attitude des groupes de pression, des parlements, des partis politiques, etc.

En quatrième lieu est particulièrement frappante l'absence des analyses concernant le rôle de personnalités de premier plan aussi bien que celles de moindre envergure – qu'il s'agisse d'hommes d'Etat, de hauts fonctionnaires, de délégués permanents . . . S'il existe bien quelques travaux valables entrepris dans une optique juridique ou politologique sur les institutions de la SdN, ils n'ont pas encore de contrepartie sur le plan historique.

En cinquième lieu, et *last but not least,* d'énormes territoires en rapport avec la coopération économique, sociale et humanitaire entreprise dans le cadre institutionnel de la SdN méritent d'être défrichés: presque tout reste à faire ici . . .

Parallèlement à ces cinq grands axes de recherche, il revient naturellement aux historiens de compléter et d'approfondir nos connaissances dans les divers domaines ayant déjà fait l'objet de travaux conçus dans une autre optique et sur lesquels le présent volume et le *Manuel bibliographique* précité fournissent un grand nombre d'informations.

Notes

1 ***Bibliographical Handbook on the League of Nations/Manuel bibliographique sur la Société des Nations.*** Provisional edition/Edition provisoire. Prepared by/établi par Victor-Yves GHEBALI. Genève, Bibliothèque des Nations Unies, 1980, 3 v. – 918 p.

2 Le présent volume ne reproduit pas l'intégralité des communications; certaines d'entre elles n'ont pu être insérées pour des raisons d'ordre technique.

Réminiscences

VLADIMIR SOCOLINE
Genève

Mesdames, Messieurs,
J'ai demandé la parole parce que je ne suis pas sûr d'assister au centenaire. Veuillez m'en excuser.

Bravo et merci à nos remarquables conférenciers. Qu'importe si tel personnage est moins sucré que nature. Merci à la recherche et à nos organisateurs de ne pas se confiner dans le témoignage indirect.

Je ne représente que moi-même, momie farcie de souvenirs. Briand disait: »Mon ami Chamberlain a le sens des affaires . . . internationales.« Je l'ai eu autrefois sous la forme effacée de perspicacité.

Je tiens ma modeste expérience d'un jeune homme de mon âge. Engagé volontaire de la Première Guerre mondiale, attaché, après cette boucherie, à tout ce qui, selon ses propres fluctuations, représentait la marche vers la paix, il voue à la paix les instants qui lui restent dans cette Suisse pacifique et bénie où il est né, sans oublier le pays pour lequel il a jadis combattu, qu'il a servi et pour lequel son affection demeure. Puissent les psychologues du dimanche en tirer leur horoscope. Voici en vrac quelques lignes pour la petite histoire.

1920, le Molard. Le cortège se dirige vers la Réformation, G. Motta en tête. Le public est celui que vous connaissez, pas délirant du tout mais saluant poliment le héros de l'entrée de la Suisse à la SdN.

En 1927, premier contact direct URSS-SdN. Mesures contraignantes motivées par le terrorisme. Malaise, mauvaise humeur. Délicates et efficaces interventions de Sir Eric Drummond, en tout point secourable. Les délégués de l'Est se sentent comme des Américains à la cour de Georges III d'Angleterre; mais quand on ne leur marche pas sur les bottes, les voilà anges en Suisse, *wie Gott in Frankreich*. Les moins rôdés ont de la peine à croire que parmi la fine fleur locale bien des messieurs vont en tram, voire à bicyclette, portent souvent des souliers à clous et ne fraient pas volontiers avec les excellences étrangères. De nombreux sympathisants de l'endroit semblent mal comprendre d'être tenus à l'écart par les délégués et regrettent visiblement que le style copain ne soit pas du tout dans les cordes de ces camarades venus du froid et dont le chef est un prince nerveux qui fait un peu peur aux notables de sa suite. Quelques-uns ne remarquent pas le lac mais tous veulent voir les rues où vécut Lénine, le célèbre disparu. Ces détails sont aussi des facteurs d'évolution.

A la limitation des armements, les experts se battent. Dans une commission, c'est tantôt le chlore qui est visé, tantôt les farfadets qui pensent s'en servir contre le prochain. Dans une autre commission, un super-expert déchaîné menace ses vis-à-vis de prendre les armes contre eux face aux mines joyeuses des amateurs de pacifisme original. Un cénacle restreint médite sur les noms d'honorables spécialistes: Réquin et Mouchard. Admiration pour le travail. Staline, à qui l'on fait l'éloge de l'habile secrétariat SdN, pique une rage froide, la plus dangereuse. Un délégué propose trois séances par jour, début à sept heures du matin. Un grand zélateur de nuits laborieuses (le Colonel Beck) s'exclame: »Sept heures du matin! Connais pas, jamais vu.«

N'oublions pas les femmes, non seulement les célébrités comme L. Weiss. Je pense à celles du secrétariat. Je pense à Mlle Boisseau notamment, et à Mlle Bavay. N'oublions pas les absents, souffrants, comme M. Pelt, et tous ceux qui sont morts après avoir servi la SdN: Rappard, Monnet, Comert, Walters, Bonnet, Hoden et tant d'autres. Réactionnaire civilisé, ancien inspecteur des finances, anglomane autant qu'anglophile, il est secondé par une Anglaise de parfaite distinction. Il ne fait pas grand cas des ministères saute-mouton de France, a horreur du moindre gauchisme, excuse facilement les abus de droite, jamais ceux de gauche. Est galant, serviable, grand liseur, n'aime pas la République, ne s'en cache pas, correspond avec le pouvoir en France mais préfère manifestement les Anglais, sans hypocrisie aucune. Il déteste et redoute l'URSS, se réjouit de l'expulsion de celle-ci et des mesures suicidaires entreprises contre elle pendant la guerre de Finlande. Considère comme un bien tout ce qui fait obstacle à Moscou, même si c'est dangereux pour la France. Il reçoit très bien mais les sybarites n'aiment pas dîner chez lui quand le grand patron y est, à cause des effluves, genre choux de Bruxelles, et malgré le quart Vichy pourtant très soigné. Mon prédécesseur a presque battu Avenol, car il voulait jouer un rôle dynamique parallèle. Il estimait que le pacifisme pleurard est idiot, qu'il faut faire peur aux bellicistes. Avenol le lui interdit. Pour ma part, stoïque, oh combien, je me plie élastiquement aux volontés sans éclat d'Avenol, porte-parole des patrons, en ayant soin, pour connaître la maison, de m'assurer le concours de volontaires des sections: politique, désarmement, information. Ils m'ont beaucoup appris, je les en remercie. Ils m'ont parfois diverti par leur dédain des statistiques et leurs pieuses façons d'aborder le fatal satanisme qu'à leurs yeux je représentais. Heures savoureuses avec de très nombreux visiteurs: ministres variés et divers, journalistes du sexe, quelques explorateurs de provenance parfois indéterminée, Assyriens, amis de la France et de la gloire.

Résidu de folklore proustien, cette grande dame, radicalement différente des patriciennes suisses, qui me demande d'une voix forte à une réception nombreuse, en parlant d'une autre belle dame: »Elle est cul, moi je trouve. Non?«

Une voix poivrée m'attaque avec violence à propos d'Alexandrette; je trouvais la façon de traiter l'affaire nuisible à la SdN, elle non. J'appris qu'Avenol lui avait suggéré de me faire taire. Quand la résistance française, vers la fin de la guerre, inquiéta Avenol, il revint en Suisse. Malade, il se traînait vers l'église St. Joseph, inspirant surtout la pitié: le prétendu esprit de conciliation remplaçait le consensus ou la véritable négociation.

Comme dans un ministère, il y avait un mouvement centripète autour du chef et en même temps un mouvement centrifuge de dispersion idéologique et professionnelle; le pôle d'attraction, si l'on peut dire, Avenol, n'était pas assez aimanté; sans puissant moteur central, l'amenuisement de la troupe par l'épuration, comme dans un couvent – ou un parti qui lui ressemble – n'a pas pour effet une concentration d'énergie; la perte de substance, Japon, Allemagne, Italie, URSS, ne pouvait signifier »la vie continue« ou »le bon débarras nous rend plus forts«, et l'on pouvait se demander si à l'extrême complexité des facteurs de désagrégation ne venait pas se superposer chez Avenol la défense du *job*, où il est facile à un chef de se prendre, en tout état de cause, pour ce qu'il devrait être, ou d'être un roi de théâtre se cramponnant au trône devenu imaginaire. Imaginez l'Assemblée nationale suisse sans Conseil national; la SdN était cela, d'où des maux incurables. Ce n'était pas parce que de puissants Etats s'en allaient ou étaient chassés qu'ils cessaient d'exister et de peser sur l'état du monde.

Il y avait au secrétariat des hommes remarquables. J'ai toujours gardé l'amical souvenir d'un bibliothécaire, homme de cœur et d'esprit raffiné, historien érudit; Monsieur l'ambassadeur Breycha-Vautier voudra bien me pardonner cette allusion maladroite. Marcel Hoden avait beau pratiquer les arrivées tardives, il était prompt à pressentir les convulsions de la conjoncture.

Dans un ordre tout différent, il y avait parmi les polyglottes de talent une espèce de génie, un Britannique pittoresque. Avec l'accent inimitable que vous devinez, agrémenté d'appogiatures amenées par des flots de substances altérantes de degré élevé, il pouvait dire: »Les Français nous en . . . quiquinent avec leur mauvaise tête cartésienne mais ils ont raison de dire qu'à la SdN on est mal payé, mais on rigole.«

Le décalage des longueurs d'onde Est-Ouest polluait l'atmosphère politique. Il créait aussi des aberrations. Ainsi, un érudit à l'esprit délié passait facilement pour un sombre abruti quand il était jugé par le point cardinal opposé. Le contrepoids de ces misères était, pour certains, le mal russe dont les mordus typiques étaient Madame Curie, Langevin, Joliot-Curie et R. Rolland, grand ami de Moscou, de Genève et de la paix.

Notre grand juriste au nom lacustre, Pilotti, doit répondre à des journalistes en quoi consiste la justice de Mussolini. Pilotti lève lentement les bras au ciel et les laisse bravement retomber. Grand succès auprès des journalistes.

Pendant une séance de la coopération intellectuelle, aïeule de l'UNESCO, Gonzague de Reynold, Paul Valéry et un modeste poète membre de la Commission font des HaïKïs japonais, prétexte pour imputer à la guerre russo-japonaise la tristesse des temps présents. Les ministres Politis, Benes, Titulescu représentaient des pays certes illustres mais sans ambitions planétaires; ils étaient de tous les débats. On les appelait les trois Grâces.

Si je me laissais aller, les petits faits divers dureraient jusqu'au lever du soleil.

Un illuminé de la galerie lance sur les excellences du Conseil SdN un paquet de tracts. Il est ceinturé par une ruée de messieurs en civil qu'on avait pris pour le public. Réflexions sur la difficulté d'assurer la sécurité tout en respectant la liberté.

Il y avait, bien sûr, les trois Suisses: le regretté Carl Burckhardt dépendait de la maison mais n'y était pas à demeure; feu de Montenach, bon Suisse lui aussi et grand admirateur de la Sérénissime République; puis Monsieur Edouard de Haller qui fut, depuis, plusieurs fois ambassadeur. Un homme d'Etat s'apprêtant à lui rendre visite dit une fois: »Je vais prendre l'air chez une neutralité gracieuse«. Fonctionnaires internationaux, nos trois patriciens suisses rappelaient bien la physionomie politique de leur pays, politique qui ressemble à la conduite d'un honnête homme.

On ne trouvait pratiquement plus de mannequins à monocle figurant pour eux-mêmes le nombril du monde entier. Les lois suisses assimilaient le Secrétaire général à un chef d'Etat; il avait un conseil de la couronne, composé d'hommes très compétents; lui, qu'on appelait »le pape« au temps de sa splendeur, fut baptisé, vers la fin, »général des secrétaires« ou »gardien des paons exterritoriaux de l'Ariana«. Le grand patron de l'institution s'appelait Londres (avec *s*). Paris aussi était un grand patron mais son numéro changeait aussi souvent que le gouvernement de la France, oscillant entre 0,9 et 0,1. Les patrons sous-estimaient l'URSS qui demeurait, à leurs yeux, l'empire sinistre, inquiétant et chancelant des premières années de la révolution; quelques satellites de Paris et Londres étaient obnubilés par le souvenir de la Paix de Riga, qui consacra la grande victoire polonaise sur l'Armée rouge en 1919. De son côte, l'URSS surestimait l'Occident et lui attribuait des malices géniales, probablement différentes de la réalité.

Autre tableau, au plan militaire. Le maréchal Jegorov disait: »Si la France préfère l'amour de la Pologne à l'alliance militaire avec nous, je lui donne trois semaines«. Ce genre de prophétie était alors à la mode: les lanciers polonais devaient être à Berlin en trois ou six semaines; après les premières difficultés allemandes en URSS, les Anglais donnaient à Moscou six mois avant de mourir. Le secrétariat emmagasinait les bruits et les portait au loin.

Après avoir été le premier et le plus vigoureux partisan des droits égaux de l'Allemagne, l'URSS, après 1933, ne s'attendait pas à la carence des patrons SdN devant les redoutables infractions au Pacte. Les soupçons de l'URSS en furent ravivés et la paix en fut directement menacée. Les journaux qui disaient que personne ne songeait à dresser Russes et Allemands les uns contre les autres offraient aux Soviétiques une pinte de bon sang. Puis ce fut Munich et son fatal corollaire, la guerre de Finlande, et le déchaînement des véhémences qui voulaient ignorer l'essentiel: que de grands empires avaient abdiqué et que l'inéluctable sacro-egoismo a horreur du vide.

SdN, société des espoirs, halte agitée sur la voie dangereuse où, depuis l'aube des temps, cheminèrent utopistes généreux, penseurs opiniâtres, et prophètes de la paix. Quelques apôtres estiment qu'il est inutile de s'en faire, que le hasard pourvoira. D'autres, avec Einstein, pensent que Dieu ne joue pas aux dés.

C'est un privilège d'avoir, pour finir, l'illusion de transmettre aux historiens d'aujourd'hui et de demain un faible reflet de cette étincelle qui, malgré tous les malheurs passés et à venir, ne s'éteindra jamais. Mes 85 ans vous saluent et vous bénissent.

Annex/Annexe

List of participants*
Liste des participants*

Mme SUSANNA ALESSI	Mission du Saint-Siège 24, chemin Colladon CH-1209 Genève
M. URS ALTERMATT Professeur ordinaire	Département d'histoire de l'Université de Fribourg 30, Staufferstrasse CH-3006 Berne
M. ETTORE ANCHIERI Professeur (emeritus)	Faculté de sciences politiques de l'Université de Padoue 5, Via San Pio X I-Padua Italie
* Mr. GEORGE BAER Professor of History Chairman, Board of Studies in History	Adlai E. Stevenson College University of California Santa Cruz, California 95064 U.S.A.
M. PETRE BARBULESCU Chef de section Editura Politica	Piata Scînteii 1 Bucarest Roumanie
* Mr. JAMES BARROS Professor Department of Political Economy	University of Toronto 100, St. George Street Toronto, Canada M5S 1A1
M. ROLAND BLÄTTLER Professeur Institut d'histoire	Université de Neuchâtel 41, Faubourg Hôpital CH-2000 Neuchâtel
Mme M. ROSA BOCETA Diplomate, Conseiller d'Ambassade	Mission permanente d'Espagne 72, rue de Lausanne CH-1202 Genève

* contributors; rapporteurs.

M. JEAN-JACQUES BOUQUET Maître au Gymnase, Lausanne Lecteur à l'Université de Berne	Coteau de Belmont 4 1815 Clarens CH-Vaud
M. ARTHUR BREYCHA-VAUTIER Ancien ambassadeur Ancien bibliothécaire en chef de la Bibliothèque de la Sociéte des Nations et de la Bibliothèque des Nations Unies, Ancien directeur de l'Académie diplomatique de Vienne	Langg A-9560 Feldkirch (Kärnten) Austria
M. PHILIPPE CAHIER Professeur de droit international	Institut universitaire de hautes études internationales 132, rue de Lausanne CH-1211 Genève 21
* M. YVES COLLART Professeur d'histoire et politique internationales	Institut universitaire de hautes études internationales 132, rue de Lausanne CH-1211 Genève 21
Mme MONIQUE CONSTANT Conservateur d'archives	Service des archives Ministère des Affaires étrangères 17, rue du Laos F-75015 Paris
Mme SOLIDAD DIEZ-PICAZO Attaché à la Mission permanente d'Espagne	Mission permanente d'Espagne 72, rue de Lausanne CH-1202 Genève
Mr. THEODORE DIMITROV Chief, Acquisitions and Cataloguing Section United Nations Library Geneva	Palais des Nations CH-1211 Geneva 10
* M. CHRISTIAN DOMINICÉ Professeur de droit international Directeur de l'Institut universitaire de hautes études internationales	Institut universitaire de hautes études internationales 132, rue de Lausanne CH-1211 Genève 21
* Mr. MARTIN D. DUBIN Associate Professor International Relations Programme	Northern Illinois University DeKalb, Illinois 60115 USA

* Mr. GEORGE EGERTON
Associate Professor
Department of History
The University of British Columbia
2075 Wesbrook Mall
Vancouver, B. C. Canada V6T 1W5

M. JEAN-CLAUDE FAVEZ
Professeur ordinaire, ancien doyen de la Faculté des Lettres de Genève
27, chemin de la Vendée
CH-1213 Petit-Lancy/Genève

* M. ANTOINE FLEURY
Chargé de cours à la Faculté de Lettres de Genève
22, chemin du Gué
CH-1213 Petit-Lancy/Genève

M. LIVIO FORNARA
Assistant conservateur
Musée du Vieux Genève
5, Promenade du Pin
1204 Genève

M. JEAN-CLAUDE FRACHEBOURG
Secrétaire général de l'Institut universitaire de hautes études internationales
Institut universitaire de hautes études internationales
132, rue de Lausanne
CH-1211 Genève 21

Mme JUDIT GARAMVÖLGYI
Privat-docent
Institut d'histoire de l'Université de Berne
4, Engehaldenstrasse
CH-3012 Berne

M. CURT GASTEYGER
Professeur d'histoire et politique internationales, Directeur du Programme d'études stratégiques et de sécurité internationale
Institut universitaire de hautes études internationales
132, rue de Lausanne
CH-1211 Genève 21

M. TITUS GEORGESCU
Professeur, Vice-Recteur de l'Université de Bucarest
64, Gheorghiu Dej Str.
Bucarest
Roumanie

M. PHILIPPE GERN
Professeur, Institut d'histoire de Neuchâtel
41, Faubourg de l'Hôpital
CH-2000 Neuchâtel

* M. VICTOR-YVES GHEBALI
Chargé de recherches et d'enseignement à l'Institut universitaire de hautes études internationales
Institut universitaire de hautes études internationales
132, rue de Lausanne
CH-1211 Genève 21

* M. ATLE GRAHL-MADSEN
Professor, Norwegian School of Economics and Business Administration
Department of Law
Uppsala University
9A, Svartedisksveien
N-5000 Bergen, Norway

M. ION GRECESCU
Juriste, Association de droit international et de relations internationales
47, Chaussée Kiseleff
Bucarest I
Roumanie

M. GEORGES GRLICA
Bibliothécaire
Institut Battelle
Centre de recherche de Genève
95, avenue de Bois-de-la-Chapelle
CH-1213 Onex/Genève

M. WOLF GRUNER
Privat-docent
Fachbereich Sozialwissenschaften
Hochschule der Bundeswehr, Munich
62 Wilhelmshöhenstr.
D-8130 Starnberg,
Federal Republic of Germany

* Mr. JEAN HALPERIN
Professor, former Chief of Languages Service
United Nations
55, route de Florissant
CH-1209 Geneva

M. LOTHAR HILBERT
Professor, Seminar für Zeitgeschichte
Université de Tübingen
36, Wilhelmstrasse
D-74 Tübingen 1
Federal Republic of Germany

M. PETER HURNI
Assistant, Institut d'histoire de l'Université de Berne
4, Engehaldenstrasse
CH-3012 Berne

Mr. MARKKU JÄRVINEN
Chief Archivist
UNESCO
UNESCO Place de Fontenoy
F-75700 Paris

M. LUBOR JILEK
Chercheur, Fonds national suisse de la recherche scientifique
1, chemin du Mont-Tendre
CH-1007 Lausanne

Mr. BADR KASME
Deputy Chief Librarian
UN Library, Geneva
Palais des Nations
CH-1211 Geneva 10

* Mr. CHRISTOPH KIMMICH
Professor, Department of History, Brooklyn College of the City University of New York
Brooklyn College
New York 11210

Mrs. MARIE-ELISABETH KLEE
President
Stresemann Gesellschaft
Deutschherrenstraße 137
D-5300 Bonn 2
Federal Republic of Germany

M. ANDRÉ LASSERRE
Professeur ordinaire de sciences sociales et politiques
Université de Lausanne
16, Clochette
CH-1018 Lausanne

Mr. ADRIAN MANNING
Professor of Modern History
University of Nijmegen
27, Bosweg
NL-6571 Cd Berg en Dal
The Netherlands

M. VLADISLAV MARJANOVIC
Assistant, Institut d'histoire contemporaine
Marksa i Engelsa 11
Belgrade
Yugoslavia

* M. NORBERT MEIENBERGER
Privat-docent
Ostasiatisches Seminar
Mühlegasse
CH-8001 Zürich

* Mr. ALEXANDER MENZIES
Canadian Department of Finance
Ottawa, Ontario
Canada KlA 0G5

M. FLAVIO MERONI
Secrétaire d'Ambassade
Mission permanente de la Suisse
près les organisations internationales
9–11, rue de Varembé
CH-1202 Genève

Mme BEATRIX MESMER
Professeur ordinaire
Institut d'histoire de l'Université de Berne
4, Engelhaldenstraße
CH-3012 Berne

Mme VIORICA MOISUC
Assistante de recherche
Institut d'études historiques et sociopolitiques
Boulevard de la République 60
Bucarest
Roumanie

M. MIKLOS MOLNAR
Professeur d'histoire et politique internationales
Institut universitaire de hautes études internationales
132, rue de Lausanne
CH-1211 Genève 21

Mme MARIE-RENÉE MOUTON
Maître-assistant d'histoire
Université des sciences sociales de Grenoble
2, Place Paul Mistral
F-38000 Grenoble
France

* Mr. GARY B. OSTROWER
Associate Professor
Division of Human Studies
Alfred University
Alfred, New York 14802
U.S.A

Mme GILBERTE PEROTIN
Archiviste, Chef du Service
Archives, Communications et Microfilms
Union Internationale des Télécommunications
Place des Nations
CH-1211 Genève 20

* Dr. ANIA PETER
58, Im Lohgraben
CH-4104 Oberwil

Mme MARTA PETRICIOLI
Professeur associé
Université de Gênes
Piazza B. Brunelleschi 19
I-Florence
Italie

S. E. M. FRANÇOIS PICTET
Ambassadeur
Mission permanente de la Suisse
près les organisations internationales
9-11, rue de Varembé
CH-1202 Genève

* Mme NICOLE PIETRI
Maître assistant d'histoire contemporaine, Faculté des sciences humaines de l'Université de Poitiers
8, rue René Descartes
F-86022 Poitiers
France

* Mrs. INGEBORG PLETTENBERG
2, Scheidter Str.
D-6600 Saarbrücken 3
Federal Republic of Germany

Mme JOHANNA RAHUSEN
Troisième secrétaire
Ambassade des Pays-Bas
11, Kollerweg
CH-3006 Berne

M. JEAN-PHILIPPE RAU
Lic. ès lettres
Enseignant secondaire
3, rue de l'Hôtel-de-Ville
CH-1204 Genève

M. LOUIS-EDOUARD ROULET
Professeur ordinaire d'histoire nationale et générale aux Universités de Berne et Neuchâtel
Institut d'histoire
41, Faubourg de l'Hôpital
CH-2000 Neuchâtel

* M. ROLAND RUFFIEUX
Professeur ordinaire d'histoire moderne et contemporaine aux Universités de Lausanne et de Fribourg
3, chemin des Kybourg
CH-1700 Fribourg

S. E. Dr. ULRICH SAHM
Ambassadeur
Mission permanente de la République fédérale d'Allemagne
28c, chemin du Petit-Saconnex
CH-1211 Genève 19

Mrs. RENATA SARACENO
United Nations, Geneva
Information Service
Palais des Nations
1211 Geneva 10

M. ERNEST SCHMIDT
Conseiller d'Ambassade
Mission permanente de la République fédérale d'Allemagne
Case postale 191
CH-1211 Genève 19

M. STANISLAW SIERPOWSKI
Professeur à l'Université de Poznan
Institut d'histoire
124/126, rue Marchlewskiego
PL-61-874 Poznan
Poland

Mr. WERNER SIMON
Archivist, League of Nations Archives
United Nations Library Geneva
Palais des Nations
CH-1211 Geneva 10

* M. JEAN SIOTIS
Professeur d'organisation internationale
Institut universitaire de hautes études internationales
132, rue de Lausanne
CH-1211 Genève 21

* M. VLADIMIR SOCOLINE
Ancien sous-secrétaire général de la Société des Nations
2, route de Malagnou
CH-1208 Genève

Mme CHRISTINE SOMERHAUSEN
Lic. en histoire
5, avenue Bois Dimanche
B-1150 Bruxelles
Belgique

* Mrs. ZARA STEINER
Fellow, New Hall
Cambridge
G. B. 30BF
United Kingdom

* Mme MARLIS STEINERT
Professeur d'histoire et politique internationales
Institut universitaire de hautes études internationales
132, rue de Lausanne
CH-1211 Genève 21

M. CONSTANTIN SVOLOPOULOS
Professeur agrégé d'histoire diplomatique, Faculté de droit et des sciences économiques de l'Université de Thessalonique
7, rue D. Gounaris
Salonigre
Grèce

* M. MARCEL VAÏSSE
Professeur, Institut d'histoire des relations internationales contemporaines, Université de Paris I (Panthéon-Sorbonne)
131, rue de la Convention
75015 Paris
France

* Mr. RICHARD VEATCH
Professor, Department of Political Sciences
The University of Winnipeg
The University of Winnipeg
515 Portage Avenue
Winnipeg, Manitoba
Canada R3B 2E9

M. GIUSEPPE VEDOVATO
Professore ordinario di Storia dei trattati e politica internazionale
Università di Roma
10, Via Lucio Afranio
I-00136 Roma
Italia

Mr. NEVILLE H. WAITES
Lecturer in Contemporary
French History
Faculty of Letters
University of Reading
University of Reading
Whiteknights, Reading, Berkshire
RG6 2AA
United Kingdom

* Mr. HEINZ WALDNER
Chief Librarian
UN Library, Geneva
Palais des Nations
CH-1211 Geneva 10

M. ERNEST WEIBEL
Professeur à l'Université de Neuchâtel
Président de l'Association suisse de science politique
18, Racherelles
2036 Cormondrèche
CH-Neuchâtel

Mr. SVEN WELANDER
Chief, League of Nations Archives and Historical Collections Unit
Palais des Nations
CH-1211 Geneva 10

M. WERNER G. ZIMMERMANN
Prof. Dr. Phil.
Université de Zürich
Archives d'Etat de la Ville de Zürich
Stadtarchiv Zürich
CH-8001 Zürich

Name Index

FSC
www.fsc.org
MIX
Papier | Fördert gute Waldnutzung
FSC® C083411

Kolibri 360 GmbH
Ferdinand-Jühlke-Straße 7
99095 Erfurt, Deutschland
produktsicherheit@kolibri360.de